South-Western

Introduction to Business

Authors

Robert A. Ristau
Emeritus Professor of Business Education
Eastern Michigan University

Steven A. Eggland
Professor of Vocational Education
Teachers College
University of Nebraska

Les R. Dlabay
Associate Professor of Business
Department of Economics and Business
Lake Forest College

James L. Burrow
Associate Professor
North Carolina State University

Anne Scott Daughtrey
Professor Emerita of Management
College of Business and Public Administration
Old Dominion University

3d Edition

Vice-President/Editor-in-Chief: Dennis M. Kokoruda
Managing Editor: Carol Volz
Developmental Editor II: Willis S. Vincent
Developmental Editor: Bob Sandman
Production Manager: Carol Sturzenberger
Production Editor: Mark Cheatham
Photo Editor: Linda Ellis
Photo Research: Meyers Photo Art, Alix Roughen
Internal Design: Ann Small
Cover Design: Envoi Design/Ann Small
Composition/Page Makeup: GTS Graphics
Copyeditor: Jeanne Busemeyer

Copyright © 1997

by SOUTH-WESTERN EDUCATIONAL PUBLISHING

Cincinnati, Ohio

ISBN: 0-538-65688-3

Library of Congress Catalog Card Number: 95-070481

1 2 3 4 5 6 7 8 9 0 Ki 99 98 97 96

Printed in the United States of America

International Thomson Publishing

South-Western Educational Publishing is a division of International Thomson Publishing Inc. The ITP trademark is used under license.

Preface

(This preface is primarily addressed to the student. A complete description of the course is found in the Teacher's Wraparound Edition.*)*

Introduction to Business, 3d edition, will introduce you to the world of business and help prepare you for the economic roles of consumer, worker, and citizen. This course will also serve as a background for other business courses you may take in high school and in college, assist you with consumer decision making, prepare you for future employment, and help you effectively perform your responsibilities as a citizen.

How to Use This Text

This text is carefully designed to function as a learning tool. It is organized into 11 units with three or more chapters in each unit for a total of 43 chapters (see the table of contents following this Preface).

Each unit begins with a Business Brief that offers a contemporary view of various business topics to enhance the unit. Each unit concludes with a Focus On Careers that will enrich your knowledge of the career opportunities that await you.

Each chapter begins with a list of Chapter Objectives and Key Terms. The objectives help you focus on the learning that will take place in the chapter. The Key Terms appear in a list at the beginning of each chapter and are bold within the text. These terms are also defined in the Glossary, which includes convenient page number references.

Each chapter has a number of headings that should be previewed to help you understand the chapter content. These headings can also function as a topical outline for a chapter if your studying method includes taking notes in outline format. The Key Ideas feature at the end of each chapter summarizes the major learning for that particular chapter and correlates with the Chapter Objectives.

Special Features

Many special features have been included in this text to enhance the content and broaden your knowledge of the world. Those enhancements include:

Business Brief: At the start of each unit, a Brief focuses your attention on issues and trends affecting businesses and consumers. Critical Thinking questions follow each Business Brief so that you may analyze the issues raised in each Brief.

Environmental Perspective: Ecology and environmental issues continue to be important topics of public concern. This feature will highlight issues that businesses and consumers are facing in preserving our natural resources.

Ethical Perspective: The news media are full of stories about unethical behavior in business and the effect of this unethical behavior on businesses and individuals. This perspective will present ethical dilemmas that consumers encounter in real life.

Global Perspective: Global business topics provide information and activities to enhance preparation for working in the global economy. These topics provide practical, real-life information about trading across national boundaries.

Legal Perspective: Many laws affect business workers and customers. This feature introduces you to some of these important laws that guarantee your rights as a consumer.

Technological Perspective: Technology touches almost every part of our life, especially our work life. Computers, electronic cash, and the Internet create new opportunities and challenges for businesspeople. This feature provides information about technological advances that are influencing the way we do business.

Cultural Perspective: A variety of cultures have made contributions to our business world as we know it today. Some of these features focus on historical contributions while others describe a present-day situation. This feature will help strengthen your awareness of the value of diversity in the work force and society.

Cultural Notes: Bite-size pieces of cultural information are presented in the margins. These notes will enhance your knowledge of cultural diversity.

FYI ("For Your Information"): These marginal notes emphasize important points from the chapter and sometimes present additional interesting information about business. FYIs add interest and background to the concepts you are studying.

Net Facts: These notations in the margin define Internet terminology and give useful background information about the Internet. You will be able to use this knowledge in your classes and career as the Internet becomes a bigger part of our lives.

Career Highlights: Various jobs are highlighted using the *Dictionary of Occupational Titles* as the source. This feature will increase your knowledge about various career choices.

Key Ideas: This summary of the chapter highlights the key concepts that have just been presented, and it will help you understand the important points raised in the text material.

Focus On Careers: At the end of each unit, this spotlight gives in-depth descriptions of various careers as they relate to the unit. This information will help broaden your understanding of different career paths.

End-of-Chapter Activities

The end of each chapter provides Increasing Your Business Vocabulary, Reviewing Your Reading, Using Your Business Knowledge, Calculating Business Problems, Applying Technology, and Making Decisions for practicing the new skills learned in the chapter. These questions and activities will allow you to demonstrate your grasp of the concepts.

Increasing Your Business Vocabulary gives you the opportunity to review the Key Terms that were presented in the chapter. Reviewing Your Reading allows you to review important concepts. Using Your Business Knowledge enables you to apply chapter material to real-world situations. Calculating Business Problems gives you an opportunity to demonstrate fundamental math skills (many chapters contain metric problems to familiarize you with the metric system). Applying Technology provides you with a problem to solve using commercial database, word processing, or spreadsheet software. Making Decisions gives you an opportunity to solve business and consumer problems using concepts learned in the chapter.

Template

Introduction to Business now enables you to actually complete the end-of-chapter Applying Technology problems using database, spreadsheet, or word processing software! A template file is provided for every Applying Technology problem so that you may use real-world software and get hands-on experience using the computer.

Reference Material

Reference material at the end of the text includes four appendices, a glossary of terms, and an index. Appendix A, Using a Calculator and Computer Keypad, includes information for proper use of the calculator and computer keypad. Appendix B, Math Review, provides a quick review of basic arithmetic procedures for solving problems. Appendix C, Determining Percentages and Interest in Business, gives practice calculating percentages. Information provided in Appendix D, Using the Metric Measurement System in Business, will help you become familiar with the metric system. This appendix will serve as a helpful reference when working end-of-chapter problems.

The glossary lists all the terms defined in the text with their definitions and page number location for easy reference. The index shows the location for each topic in the text which will be useful if you do not know where to find specific information.

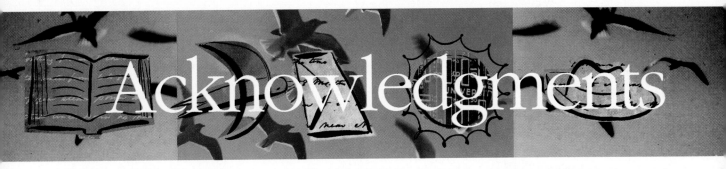

Acknowledgments

We would like to acknowledge and thank the following instructors who contributed to the review process for this edition.

E. Jane Alter
Business Education Teacher
Centerville High School
Dayton, OH

Celeste Arms
Business Teacher/
   Department Chair
James Bowie High School
Arlington, TX

Diana Blackshear
Business Teacher
Cy-Falls High School
Cypress, TX

Elaine R. Chapman
Business Education Teacher
Choctaw County High School
Butler, AL

Sharon Childers Collett
Teacher/Co-Op
   Director/Department Chair
Franklin County High School
Frankfort, KY

Ann M. Douglas, Ed.D.
Business Education Teacher-
   Coordinator
Grissom High School
Huntsville, AL

Tracy Forstall
Business Teacher
Northshore High School
Slidell, LA

Peter A. Fulcer
Director, Vocational and Adult
   Education
Loudoun County Public Schools
Leesburg, VA

Leola B. Highsmith
Business Education Teacher
Martin Luther King High School
Philadelphia, PA

Ann Ehret Hobler
Business Education Chairperson
Glen A. Wilson High School
Hacienda Heights, CA

Jean Holbrook
Supervisor of Business
Roanoke County Schools
Roanoke, VA

Nancy Hoppe
Business Education Teacher
Peet Junior High School
Cedar Falls, IA

Azalene Johnson
Business Department Chairperson
Louisville Male Traditional High
   School
Louisville, KY

Glenda Igo Maikell
Business Teacher
A.S. Johnston High School
Round Rock, TX

Jennifer McDonald
Business Education Teacher
Princeton High School
Cincinnati, OH

Patricia McSpadden
Vocational Business Education
   Instructor
McKenzie High School
McKenzie, AL

Joyce K. Rowe
Business Teacher/Department
   Chair
Monterey High School
Lubbock, TX

Holly Sagues
Accounting/Business Technology
   Teacher
Reviewer of Internet Activity
   Worksheets
Winter Park High School
Winter Park, FL

Jerome C. Strozzi
Marketing Education Coordinator
Orange High
Orange, NJ

Jim Willet
Business Education Instructor
Audubon Community School
Audubon, IA

We would like to acknowledge
the following instructor for
creating the Internet Activity
Worksheets found in the
Teacher's Activity Guide.

Armand Seguin
Associate Professor of Vocational
   Technical Education
Dakota State University
Madison, SD

We also appreciate the ongoing
feedback provided by the
classroom professionals who use
Introduction to Business every
day!

Table of Contents

South-Western

Introduction to Business

Unit One

Our Economic Environment

1 Economic Decisions
Explains the basic economic problem.

2 Economic Systems
Describes several features of our market economy.

3 Economic Roles
Cites examples to show how each of your three economic roles is important in our economic system.

chapter

4 Economic Measurements
Explains three ways to measure economic progress.

What do you think of when you hear the word "business?" Some of you may think of jobs, others may think of merchants who deal with consumers, and still others may think of the millions of firms that make up our global economy. Business provides the bulk of our employment as well as the products and services we enjoy. For the moment, let's focus on employment.

As a prospective employee, how might you be affected by "business" in the future? Employers will demand hard work from you. They will expect you to be flexible and responsive to change. Your key to successful employment will be lifelong or continuous learning. A lifelong passion for learning will provide you with the abilities and attributes you can transfer from one work environment to another.

Future workers must be creative thinkers and problem solvers. You will also need the foundation skills and attitudes on which employers can build. As an employee, you must be responsible, comfortable with technology, and able to work as a member of a team. The team approach to handling work is common in business today. Teams work on a particular project and then disband when the project is completed. Being able to work well with co-workers as a team member will determine your future success.

If you plan to seek employment in our economy, you probably have asked, "What kind of opportunities are available to me in business?" In reality, the size of many businesses will continue to decrease. Large companies will employ fewer people. Some leading companies will slow their growth in terms of the number of people employed. There will be many small businesses, including what has been described as a "world of networked one-person enterprises." Small businesses will have an increasingly important role in our economy. You may ask: "Who is affected by these changes in business?"

Three primary groups will be most affected by changes in "business":

- young adults without a high school diploma;
- semi-skilled workers in manufacturing;
- people over 40, often employed by large companies.

Many people in these groups do not have the basic skills and attributes that make them flexible and responsive to change.

What about you? There will be opportunities for you in both large and small businesses. A key to your job success will be your ability to transfer your skills from one work environment to another. Investing in your personal growth and self-development will help you remain responsive to change.

Critical Thinking

1 *Why do small businesses play such an important part in our economy?*

2 *What can you do now to help prepare yourself for a future in our economy?*

You and Our Economy

Chapter One

Key Terms

needs

wants

goods (products)

services

economic resources (factors of production)

natural resources

human resources (labor)

capital resources (capital)

basic economic problem (scarcity)

economic decision making

Economic Decisions

Objectives

After studying this chapter and completing the end-of-chapter activities, you will be able to:

1 Distinguish between needs and wants.

2 Explain the difference between goods and services.

3 Describe the economic resources used in the production of goods and services.

4 Explain why the basic economic problem forces you to make choices.

5 State the six steps in the decision-making process.

Sigdor and Duke were riding a bus to their jobs at a fast-food restaurant. Duke was looking at the businesses along the way. Duke nudged Sigdor and said, "Look at those ZXXY909's in that car dealer's window—I need one of them cars bad!"

"*Those* cars badly," corrected Sigdor. "But how can *you* afford to buy one?" he continued. "You don't even have enough money for the gas and insurance."

Duke went on. "Hey, look at that place. They're having a sale on professional sports jackets. I need a new jacket; maybe I could get that Red Wings jacket I need, too." Sigdor just shook his head.

"And listen to this," Duke said excitedly, "I know about a great sale on CD players and a new ultra-focus sound system. There are just so many things I need. I can't wait until I get a credit card; then my troubles will be over." "No," mused Sigdor, "then they'll just begin!"

NEEDS AND WANTS

Duke's desire to buy the things he sees and hears about is not unusual. We have many things that we want. The question is, "Do we *need* everything we see or hear about?"

Needs Are Basic to Survival

Things that are necessary for survival are called **needs.** Food, clothing, and housing are the basic needs that most people have. We often desire things beyond our basic needs. The car Duke wants is not necessary to his survival. He can get around without it, but he wants a car anyway.

Illus. 1-1
Basic items such as food, clothing, and housing meet our basic needs.

Wants Add to the Quality of Life

Things not necessary for survival but which add comfort and pleasure to our lives are called **wants.** You may want a new designer jacket, a stereo system, and a school ring. You could live without them, but having them would make life nicer and more fun for you. When we talk about needs and wants, we often lump them together and just call them wants.

Unlimited Wants

Wants never end. Our wants are limited only by our imagination. Your new jacket will satisfy you temporarily, but soon another "nicer" jacket appeals to you. One want fulfilled may lead to other wants. Sigdor bought a tennis racket that he wanted for a long time. That want was fulfilled; then he needed tennis balls. He also bought some tennis shorts and joined a tennis club. Our wants go on and on. For many reasons, our wants keep changing. We can never satisfy all of them. This is true for everyone—our wants are endless.

GOODS AND SERVICES

We satisfy most of our wants with goods and services. Goods and services are key words in the study of business, and you will use them often. **Goods** are things you can see and touch. Designer jackets, CD players, T-shirts, and soccer balls are examples of goods. All of the things that satisfy our material wants are goods. Food, a television set, gasoline, cement, books, a bicycle, and clothes are examples. Goods are also called **products.**

Not all of our wants can be met with things you can see and touch. Some wants are satisfied through the efforts of other people or by equipment. These efforts are called services. When you go to a movie, make a deposit at the bank, get a haircut, take a swimming lesson, use your telephone, or ride a bus, you are using **services.** When you pay the hairstylist to cut your hair, you are buying a service performed by a person. When you deposit a coin to play a video arcade game, you are buying a service performed by a piece of equipment. We need both goods and services to satisfy our wants. Supplying goods and services is what business is all about.

What do students want from life? In a recent survey of high school students, the largest group was more concerned with academic achievement than popularity or athletic glory.

Personal resources are things like time, money, or skills that we use to satisfy our wants.

Illus. 1-2
When a need is met by the efforts of other people or equipment it is called a *service*.

ECONOMIC RESOURCES

Goods and services do not just appear as if by magic. You cannot create goods from nothing or supply a service without some effort. The means through which goods and services are produced are called **economic resources** (also called **factors of production.**) There are three kinds of economic resources: natural, human, and capital resources. All three are needed to produce the goods and services that satisfy our wants.

Today more people work in jobs that provide services than in jobs that produce products.

Natural Resources

The raw materials supplied by nature are called **natural resources.** All of the materials that come from the earth, the water, or the air are natural resources. We take iron ore, gold, oil, and copper from the earth to use in making many products. We also grow vegetables in the soil and take fish from the water for food. We use oxygen from the air to help sick people in hospitals breathe and to make such products as carbonated water for colas. All of the goods we use today began with one or more natural resources.

Human Resources

Natural resources do not satisfy our wants by themselves. It takes people to turn them into goods and make the products and services available to us. **Human resources** are the people who

Illus. 1-3
Raw materials supplied by nature are called *natural resources.*

work to produce goods and services. **Labor** is another name for this factor of production. Human resources include people who run farms and factories, manage banks, design machines, process food, announce the news on television, check out our purchases at the supermarket, police the streets, or teach introduction to business courses. Human resources are very important in producing goods and services.

Capital Resources

The tools, equipment, and buildings that are used to produce goods and services are called **capital resources.** Office buildings, factories, tractors, carpenters' tools, computers, delivery trucks, and display cases are examples of capital resources. If you use a bicycle to deliver newspapers, your bicycle is a capital resource. It is the equipment you use to provide the newspaper delivery service. Likewise, a computer used by a bank to prepare a report of a customer's account is a capital resource. The grill used to cook the hamburger you buy for lunch as well as the restaurant building are capital resources.

The word **capital** is often used in place of capital resources, especially when referring to the fac-

Capital goods are important because they help us produce efficiently—that is, faster or cheaper.

tors of production. Capital includes money that is needed to run a business. A person may say she or he is trying to raise $40,000 in capital to expand a business or that she or he has a $10,000 capital investment in a store operated by friends.

All three economic resources—natural, human, and capital—are necessary to produce goods and services to satisfy our wants. Unfortunately, we do not have an endless supply of these resources.

LIMITED RESOURCES

If Duke had a lot of money, do you think he could buy all of the things he would want? In reality, money is a limited resource. Therefore, Duke cannot buy everything he wants. Have you had the experience of wanting many things without having the money to pay for them?

Newscasts often report shortages of certain items. In recent years, oil, lumber, and sugar have been reported as scarce. We do not have an endless supply of these economic resources. Because of pollution, we do not have an endless supply of clean air, water, and land. We also have shortages of certain kinds of human resources in some career areas. Since our natural and human resources are limited, we are limited in what we can build and produce.

Scarcity Affects Everyone

Just as meeting your unlimited wants with limited resources is a problem for you, so it is for everyone—your family, your neigh-

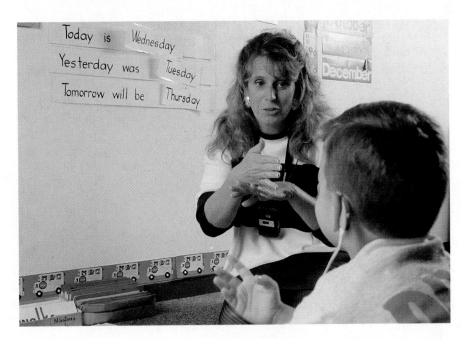

Illus. 1-4
A skilled human resource, such as this teacher of hearing-impaired students, provides a unique and valuable service.

An *economist's* job duties include:
- Studying ways in which society uses scarce resources
- Analyzing costs and benefits of distributing and consuming goods and services
- Conducting research, collecting and analyzing data, monitoring economic trends, and developing forecasts.

bors, and your school club. People all over the world are affected by scarcity. For this reason, we refer to the conflict between unlimited wants and limited resources as the **basic economic problem** (also called **scarcity.**)

The members of your family may not be able to afford many of the things they want because the wages of your father or mother are needed for food, clothing, the house payment, the electric bill, or your school expenses. Your neighbors and the families of your friends face the same economic problem. Your school club might want to hire a band for its annual dance; but, because its money is scarce, the club may have to use CDs instead.

Scarcity Affects Businesses and Governments

Just as individuals face the basic economic problem, so do businesses, governments, and all agencies that supply goods and services. A growing business might want to enlarge its plant and parking lot, but because the land it owns is limited and locating elsewhere would cost more than it can afford, it cannot do both.

All levels of government face the problem of supplying the almost unlimited wants of their citizens with limited resources. For example, your town may wish to give a large wage increase to police officers and firefighters. However, because taxes may not provide enough money, the increase might have to be smaller in order to provide other services, such as a new school building or additional employees to collect the garbage. Cities, states, the United States, and all other nations must cope with the problem of providing the many services citizens want from limited resources—the taxes collected to pay for the services. Someone must decide which services will be provided. How do you, other individuals, businesses, and governments decide which of the unlimited wants to supply?

ECONOMIC CHOICES

Since you cannot have everything you want, you must choose which of the things you want most and can afford. Suppose you earn $15 a week. If you spend it on movies and pizza with your friends on Friday night, you will not have enough left to go to the hockey game on Saturday. So you must make a

FYI

An orderly approach to decision making can help you organize your thinking about problems and can result in effective decisions.

choice. You must decide which of your wants—the movie and pizza with friends or the hockey game—is more important to you. You must determine which alternative will satisfy you the most.

One of the purposes of this book is to help you learn how to make wise economic decisions. Learning and following a logical process will help you make better decisions.

Making Economic Decisions

There is a way that you can make almost any kind of decision; it is a proven way for good economic decision making. **Economic decision making** is the process of choosing which wants, among several wants being considered, will be satisfied. Once you learn the process, your decision making will be easier and your decisions may be better.

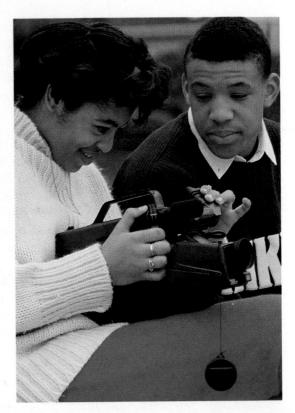

Illus. 1-5
Economic decision making involves satisfying your wants and needs.

The Decision-Making Process

There are six steps in the decision-making process. You will use the model shown in Figure 1-1 as you proceed through this book. This process is used by many businesses and individuals to make important decisions.

Figure 1-1
There are six steps in the decision-making process

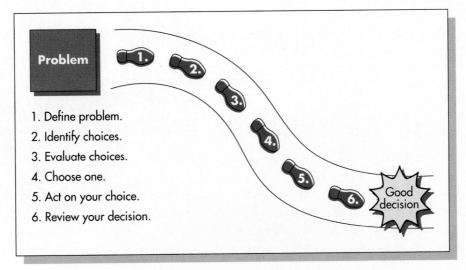

Problem

1. Define problem.
2. Identify choices.
3. Evaluate choices.
4. Choose one.
5. Act on your choice.
6. Review your decision.

Good decision

Every baby born in the United States today will use 1,500 pounds of copper in his or her lifetime.

1. *Define the problem.* If you have only $20 and want to buy several items, your problem is how to spend the money in a way that will give you the most satisfaction. In each situation, the problem must be defined in order to make a decision that will lead to its solution.

2. *Identify the choices.* There may be many choices or only two or three. In the movies, pizza, and hockey game decision, you had two wants or choices. There may be other choices, or alternatives, too. For example, you might decide to save your money instead of going to either place. It is important to consider all of the alternatives in making a decision.

3. *Evaluate the advantages and disadvantages of each choice.* If you go to the movie, you will enjoy seeing the show; but you will miss the excitement of the hockey game. You also might miss being with your family on a Saturday outing. If you save the money and

Environmental *Perspective*

Wetlands: A Quality of Life Factor

Marshes and bogs are commonly called "wetlands." Our land is spotted with marshes and bogs that filter water and purify it. Wetlands provide a habitat for many animals and birds. In some areas of the country, wetlands help prevent floods.

As we continue to build shopping centers, housing developments, condominiums, and other structures on vacant land, we sometimes destroy a critical natural resource—our wetlands. Wetlands are important for a healthy environment. Laws have been passed to help protect areas where wetlands are endangered. Business obviously is affected by these laws.

What have businesses done to expand and still protect wetlands? Some businesses, after completing new facilities, have restored part of the property to wetland status. Many businesses realize that the need to expand and create new jobs does not necessarily have to conflict with preserving our natural resources. Business decisions are often made with the well-being of the environment in mind.

Critical Thinking

1 *Why is it important to have wetlands where animals and birds can live and reproduce? What benefits do we as a society receive from the wetlands?*

2 *What are some things you can do to help preserve our environment, including wetlands?*

do neither, you will have the money for other things later. Some decision makers have found that it helps to write down the choices and to list the advantages and disadvantages of each. Being sure of your choices will help you with the next step.

4. *Choose.* This is really getting down to the "nitty gritty" of the problem. Even if you have done the first three steps as best you can, this is often a difficult step. You must learn to select from your choices the one that you believe will be the best for you and your interests at this particular time.

5. *Act on your choice.* This is the "take-action" step. If you have chosen to go to the movie, go and enjoy it. Try not to worry about the other choices that you decided against. Some people agonize so much over making the choice, they fail to enjoy the activity they decided upon. Life is full of choices. Everyone probably regrets a decision from time to time. Using the six-step decision-making process each time you face an important decision will help you improve your ability to make choices.

6. *Review your decision.* Was your decision a good one? On a scale of one to ten, what score would you give your decision for the satisfaction it provided? What was right about it? What was wrong with it? Did you define the real problem? Did you evaluate your choices thoroughly enough? If you had it to do over, would you make the same choice? Did you miss a choice that might have been a better alternative? This step gives you the opportunity to think about your decision and learn from it so that you can make better decisions in the future.

NET FACTS

The Internet is a telecommunications system that connects many different networks of computers. The Internet is often called a "network of networks."

The word "decide" means to cut off or to cut the knot. Choosing one thing involves cutting yourself off from something else.

Some decisions must be made quickly, and you will not have time to go through all of these steps. For example, if you are in a building when a fire alarm sounds, you will not have time to consider many choices before you decide to get out! For most decisions, however, following this six-step process will help you make better choices. The process has proven to be useful for businesses, governments, and individuals.

As you progress through this book, you will have an opportunity to practice the decision-making process with some situations presented at the end of each chapter—in "Making Decisions." You will apply the six-step decision-making model.

Key Ideas

1 We all have needs that are basic to life and wants that improve the quality of life.

2 Goods are things we can see and touch. Services are tasks performed by people and equipment to satisfy needs and wants.

3 Economic resources vital to the production of goods and services are natural, capital, and human.

4 The basic economic problem of scarcity causes economic choices to be made by businesses, governments, and individuals.

5 Use of the decision-making model results in informed decisions benefiting the economy.

End of Chapter Activities

Increasing Your Business Vocabulary

The following terms should become part of your business vocabulary. For each numbered item, find the term that has the same meaning.

basic economic *3*
problem (scarcity)

capital resources
(capital)

economic decision
making

economic resources
(factors of produc-
tion)

goods *5*

human resources
(labor)

natural resources *4*

needs *9*

services

wants *10*

1 The process of choosing which want, among several wants being considered, will be satisfied.

2 The means through which goods and services are produced.

3 The problem which faces individuals, businesses, and governments of satisfying unlimited wants with limited resources.

4 Raw materials supplied by nature.

5 Things you can see and touch.

6 Tools, equipment, and buildings used in producing goods and services.

7 Things that are necessary for survival, such as food, clothing, and shelter.

8 People who work to produce goods and services.

9 Things that are not necessary for survival but that add comfort and pleasure to our lives.

10 Things that satisfy our wants through the efforts of other people or equipment.

Reviewing Your Reading

1 Give two examples each of needs and wants.

2 Explain why wants are unlimited.

3 Explain the ways in which businesses provide goods and services to satisfy our needs and wants.

4 Give one example of a service provided by a person and one by a machine.

5 How are economic resources involved in satisfying our needs and wants?

6 Name the three kinds of economic resources and give an example of each.

7 How important are human resources in producing goods and services? In what ways are natural resources and capital important?

8 Give two examples to show that economic resources are limited.

9 Explain what is meant by the basic economic problem.

10 Do businesses and governments also deal with scarcity? Give some examples to support your answer.

11 Name the six steps in the decision-making process.

Using Your Business Knowledge

1 Review the examples of limited resources given in the chapter. For each of the three economic resources, give two examples not listed in the text.

2 Sheila's father told her that with the family's limited resources, she will have to choose between a pair of hiking boots and season tickets to the ball games during the school year. This means that Sheila is on Step 3 of the decision-making process. List the advantages and disadvantages of Sheila's two choices.

3 Everyone must cope with the basic economic problem. Give one example to show how scarcity was dealt with for each of the follow-

ing: your family, one of your school's sport teams, your community, and the federal or state government.

4 Think about the clothes you own. Name one piece of clothing that you own but no longer wear. Give two reasons why you do not wear the item and tell how this situation contributes to unlimited wants.

5 List two businesses in your community that sell goods, two that sell services, and two that sell both.

6 Name some of the natural resources that were used in making each of the following: denim jeans, a pizza, jogging shoes, and this textbook.

Calculating Business Problems

1 The Jenkins family has a monthly take-home pay of $1,560. Each month they pay for the needs listed at right.

Item	Amount
House payment	$410
Electric bill	105
Water bill	20
Food	375
Clothing	80

   a. What is the total monthly payment for the needs?

   b. How much is left for other needs and wants?

   c. What percentage of the Jenkins' take-home pay is being spent for needs?

---

2 Amelia Descartes entered an open 10-K (kilometer) Run sponsored by her church to raise money needed by the local children's hospital which was short of funds. The 10-K Run drew 110 runners from the school and the community. Each runner paid a $5 entrance fee, $1.50 of which was used to cover publicity, awards, and other expenses, with the remainder going to the hospital. (For help with problems involving metrics, see Appendix D.)

   a. How long is the 10-K run, expressed in miles?

   b. If all of the participants completed the run, how many kilometers did they cover in total?

   c. How many miles did they cover?

   d. How much could the class donate to the children's hospital to help meet their needs?

---

3 Forest fires take a heavy toll on land and timber resources, as shown recently in the Wildfire Report at right for protected areas (those which are under the control of state and federal agencies, such as the Department of Agriculture or the Department of the Interior). Study the table and answer the questions that follow.

Acres of Protected Land		
	Federal	State and Private
Total land area	685,552,000	840,163,000
Area burned by wildfires	946,000	3,235,000
Number of fires reported	15,400	173,800

   a. What is the total acreage of protected land?

   b. What was the total number of fires reported in protected areas for the year?

   c. How many acres were burned in the protected areas?

   d. What was the average number of acres (show in round numbers) of federally protected land burned per fire?

   e. How do these wildfires affect the problem of limited resources?

4 To protect natural resources, businesses and various levels of government recently spent the amounts shown in this table in one year for water and air quality control activities.

Quality Control Expenditures (In Millions of Dollars)		
Agency	**Water**	**Air**
Businesses	$18,857	$18,396
Federal government	110	639
State and local governments	10	403

a. How much did businesses spend on pollution control for air and water?
b. How much did each level of government spend during the year to protect the quality of air and water?
c. What was the total spent by all levels of government for air and water control?
d. What percent of the total amount was spent by all levels of government?
e. For which resource was the most money spent? What was the amount spent on the resource?
f. In what way might the action by business and government help to alleviate the problem of scarcity?

Applying Technology

Using the *Introduction to Business* template and your database program software, select problem CH01. After the problem appears on your screen, complete the following activities. Then, after you have completed each step, display or print a report for each activity. If you do not have a printer available, answer the questions before you leave the computer.

1 Sort the database in ascending order by title of videotape. Answer the following questions:

a. What is the eighth videotape listed?

b. What is the eleventh videotape listed?

2 Sort the videotapes in descending order by company name. Answer the following questions:

a. What is the first company listed?
b. What is the last company listed?

3 Select and list the videotapes that were released in the first six months of the year. How many videotapes are listed?

Making Decisions

Metrocity is a large, growing community. One of its problems has to do with land use. There is a big piece of land that borders a lake on the southeast side of the city. The land has been vacant for several years. Young people of the community occasionally use the area for unauthorized picnics and swimming.

The owners of the land have defaulted on their taxes. The city now has to decide what to do with the land. A group of citizens, who call themselves "Citizens for Better Living," want the city to develop the land as a recreational area complete with swimming and picnic areas. A local business group wants to buy the land for a luxury hotel and conference center—something the city does not have.

To develop the land for recreational purposes will cost $250,000. Funds also will be required to staff the area and to police and maintain it. The sale of the land for a hotel and conference center will provide $110,000 in revenue for the city. When the hotel and conference center are operational, there will be tax money coming into the city. But the community badly needs a recreational area, and the local citizens already pay high taxes for city services. The city manager has been asked to resolve this issue.

1 What are the advantages and disadvantages of the choices facing the city manager?

2 If you were the city manager, which choice would you favor? Why?

Chapter Two

Economic Systems

Key Terms

economic system

custom-based economy

directed or planned economy

market economy

marketplace

capitalism (free or private enterprise system)

voluntary exchange

business

private enterprise

private property

profit

profit motive

competition

Objectives

After studying this chapter and completing the end-of-chapter activities, you will be able to:

1 List the three economic questions that must be answered by every society.

2 Describe three types of economic systems.

3 Identify five features of our market economy.

4 Explain why economies are mixed systems.

5 Explain why market economies are becoming common around the world.

Laszlo was a shoemaker in a country in which the government made economic decisions. He was told how many shoes he could make and sell each year. Things are now different in Laszlo's country. His country no longer has a central committee that does all the planning. Today Laszlo does his own planning and determines the number and style of shoes he will sell. Department stores and shops in Laszlo's country display a variety of shoes available for sale to consumers. His country has a market economy. A market economy is one in which individuals are free to engage in business transactions. In such an economy, the questions of what, how, and for whom to produce are determined by the operation of markets. A market is an arrangement that allows buyers and sellers to come together to trade goods, services, and resources. Buyers and sellers participate freely in that market; it is open to all who want to participate and have the means to do so. The activity of buyers and sellers is not controlled—there is voluntary exchange.

Voluntary exchange allows buyers and sellers to come together in a market to trade goods, services, and resources. For example, consumers may exchange their resources (usually money) for what producers decide to make available to them (goods and services.) Voluntary exchange occurs only when the trading parties believe that they will be better off after the exchange.

KEY ECONOMIC QUESTIONS

Even in market economies, governments have some influence on how the nation's resources are used. Regardless of how a country lets it market operate, there are key economic questions which must be answered because of scarce economic resources. The three economic questions are:

1. What goods and services are to be produced?
2. How should the goods and services be produced?
3. For whom should the goods and services be produced?

What To Produce?

Nations differ in their wants just as individuals do. In one country, resources may be used to produce spaceships and to explore other planets. Another might use its resources to build the biggest and best military force. Some might use most of their resources to provide such consumer goods as cars, television sets, dishwashers, and recreational parks. Still other countries might have such limited resources that they must concentrate on providing only the basic needs of food, clothing, and shelter.

Meeting some or all of its people's wants is a challenge. A country must learn how to best use its resources. A nation that concentrates too heavily

The word *market* derives from the Latin word *mercari* which means "to trade."

e have accomplished much through technology to reduce human labor (muscle power)—today we use less than 1 percent of the muscle power used prior to the Industrial Revolution.

on military goods may not have enough resources left for consumer goods and services. On the other hand, if all of its resources are used to supply consumer goods and services, it may not be able to protect its people from outside forces. Decisions must be made on which kinds of goods and services are valued the most and best serve the nation.

How To Produce?

A country that has a great many people but limited capital resources might build roads by having many workers use equipment that requires much manual labor. In another country, road building may be accomplished with only a few workers using labor-saving equipment, such as bulldozers and power earthmovers. In the first case, the country uses its human resources to offset its lack of capital resources. In the second case, the country does the job with more capital resources and less labor. The second method is more efficient and enables the country to complete the road much sooner. As you can see, economic resources combine in different ways to produce the same goods and services. Each nation decides which combination of resources will best suit its circumstances.

For Whom To Produce?

A nation must decide which of its citizens should benefit from the production of goods and services. A country must also consider whose needs and wants are the most critical. Additional questions include: How will the goods and services be distributed? Should the goods and services be shared equally among the people? Should people who contribute more to producing the goods and services be able to get a larger share of them? If you have the money, shouldn't you be able to buy anything you want with your money?

In some economic systems, you can buy whatever you want and can afford. But in others, your ability to buy may be limited by the country's answer to the earlier question, "What to produce?" For example, a large share of a country's resources might be used to produce capi-

Illus. 2-1
Goods are produced through human and capital resources.

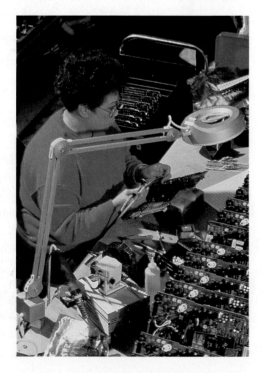

tal goods, such as tractors or industrial robots. That country might limit its production of consumer goods, such as high-fashion clothes and CD players. Consumer goods then become scarce. In the United States, with our plentiful supply of goods and services, what you buy is largely determined by the amount of money you have and are willing to spend. In addition, the amount of money that you receive in wages will be affected by many things, including your abilities and how you use them. Figure 2-1 illustrates a variety of responses to the three basic economic questions.

TYPES OF ECONOMIC SYSTEMS

A nation's plan for answering the key economic questions is called its **economic system.** There are several kinds of economic systems operating in the world today. Governments which are democratic, socialistic, or communistic take differing approaches to how they allow their economic systems to operate. There are no systems that operate in a pure form.

Figure 2-1

Basic economic questions face every society.

Three Basic Economic Questions

1. What goods and services are to be produced?

2. How should the goods and services be produced?

3. For whom should the goods and services be produced?

Custom-Based Economy

In some countries, mainly those which are developing and considered to be third-world countries, the answers to key economic questions are established by custom. In a **custom-based economy,** goods are produced the way they have always been produced. Children of each generation are taught to use the same method to make the same goods their parents and grandparents produced. The custom may be weaving cloth on a hand loom, making straw baskets, or planting rice by hand. Goods typically are produced by hand with simple tools using people or animals for energy. Change and growth occur slowly in countries whose economies follow customs and in which the people are poor in material goods.

Directed (Planned) Economy

In some countries, economic questions are answered by the owners of the resources. In a **directed** or **planned economy**, resources are owned and controlled by the government. The officials of the government, usually through central committees, decide what and how goods will be produced and how they will be shared. They decide how much of the nation's resources will be spent on military uses and how much will be used to produce consumer and capital goods. They decide how much grain will be grown and how many pairs of shoes will be produced. In some countries, government leaders assign people to careers based largely on the leaders' view of the needs for producing the goods and services. They plan all phases of the economy and command that the plans be carried out, using the military or a police force to do so if necessary. In directed economies, the average citizen has little to say about how the three economic questions are answered. The freedom of the people is always limited in this system.

Illus. 2-2

In a custom-based economy, production methods are based on tradition.

Market Economy

The third type of economic system is a **market economy.** Market economies are generally found in countries that have democratic forms of government. Here the three questions are answered by individuals through buying and selling activities in the marketplace. The **marketplace** is any place where buyers and sellers exchange goods, services, and some form of money. People who order goods from a mail-order catalog, go to a movie, buy food in a supermarket, subscribe to cable TV, buy shares of stock, or have a sweater cleaned are operating in the marketplace. When an airline orders a new jet, a business launches a satellite, or the government hires computer operators, each is operating in the marketplace. No one tells the consumers what to buy and no one tells businesses what to make and sell.

Consumers and businesses make economic decisions based on their own interests. For example, you may use your money to buy a leather jacket. One of your friends may spend his or her money to take tennis lessons and another may buy a compact disc player. When people in a market economy buy a product, they help to answer the question, "What to produce?" Resources are combined in such a way that the goods people want and buy will be produced. This answers the question, "How to produce?" Since people buy what they want and can afford in a market economy, they largely answer the question, "For whom to produce?"

OUR ECONOMIC SYSTEM

Were you able to identify our economy as you read the three types? If you selected "market economy," you were correct. As you know, the main differences among economic systems involve who owns the economic resources and who makes the decisions about production and distribution. Our system fits the definition of a market economy. But our economic system also has other names.

Another name for the economic system in the United States is capitalism. **Capitalism** means that economic resources are usually privately owned by individuals rather than by the government. Individual owners are free to decide what they will produce with the resources. This freedom of the individual to choose what to produce provides the rationale for another name: **free** or **private enterprise system.** The terms capitalism and free or private enterprise system mean the same thing. They refer to a system in which most economic resources are privately owned and decisions about production and distribution are largely made by **voluntary exchange** in the marketplace.

One of the problems with the term "free enterprise" is that some think too much about "free" and too little about "enterprise"—the work required to succeed.

There are many aspects of our economic system that make it different from other systems of the world. You are aware that the words "freedom" and "individual choice" are frequently used in discussing our economy. Let us examine five major features, or rights, of our market economy as shown in Figure 2-2.

Private Enterprise

A **business** is an establishment or enterprise that supplies us with goods and services in exchange for payment in some form. The right of the individual to choose whether to own a business, what business to enter, and what to produce with only limited government direction is referred to as **private enterprise**. This private enterprise right ensures your freedom to decide how you will earn a living. In a private enterprise system, you may start or invest in any business you wish as long as you obey the law in doing so. You are free to choose to be a bricklayer, teacher, karate instructor, business owner, astronaut, dancer, or anything you strive for.

As a businessperson, you are generally free to offer goods and services at times, prices, and places of your choice. You are free to succeed or to fail in a business you select. Of course, there are some regulations that prevent you from performing activities that would harm others. For example, you may not dispose of chemical wastes in a way that would pollute the environment. Nor can you practice surgery unless you have been granted a medical license by the appropriate agency in the state in which you plan to practice surgery. These regulations are not designed to limit freedom but to protect people from harmful practices.

Private Property

If your family owns the home in which you live or the television set you watch, the family is enjoying the right of private property. The right of **private property** means you can own, use, or dispose of things of value. You may dispose of things you own by selling them, giving them away, or even by throwing them away. In our country, you can own any item and do what you want with it, as long as you do not violate a law in doing so. You also have the right to own, use, and sell whatever you invent or create.

Businesses also have the right to own property. This property includes land, buildings, tools, and the goods the business produces. Businesses also have the right to use and dispose of their property in any lawful way.

Figure 2-2
Features of the United States market economy.

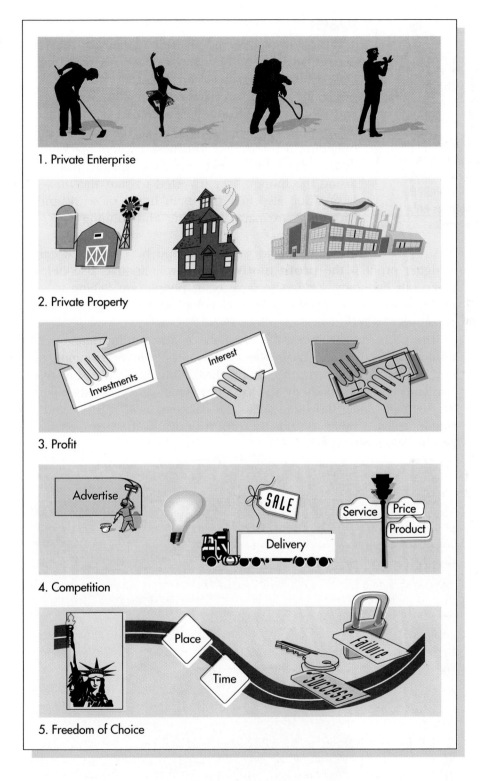

1. Private Enterprise

2. Private Property

3. Profit

4. Competition

5. Freedom of Choice

Sellers mark up the price of goods they purchase before selling them, but their profit is much less than the markup—sometimes only 1 percent on their sales.

Profit

Businesses supply goods and services to the marketplace for one main reason—to earn money. Unless business owners can expect to make a profit, they would not want to put time, energy, and money into an enterprise. **Profit** is the money left from sales after subtracting all the costs of operating the business. Business owners are entitled to make profits because they run the risk of losing the money they invested to start the business. They also face the extra hours of work and stress that are part of owning and running a business.

The desire to work hard and be creative to earn a higher profit is the **profit motive.** This profit motive also helps make our economy strong. Because of it, people are willing to invest money in a business and to develop new products to satisfy consumers' wants.

The profit motive is not the only reason for putting time, money, and effort into businesses. Some people enjoy bringing out new products or improving existing ones. Others get pleasure from knowing that the goods or services they produce make other people happier. Some individuals like the excitement of starting and running new a business. But the profit motive is the heart of the private enterprise system.

Illus. 2-3
The profit motive encourages a business owner to take the risk of operating a business.

Competition

You probably have seen television commercials that make you want to buy a "new" and "improved" product. A supermarket may claim in bold letters, "Ours are the lowest prices in town." An ad in a magazine urges you to buy the basketball shoes being modeled by a famous player. The rivalry among businesses to sell their goods and services to buyers is called **competition.**

This feature of a market economy gives you as a consumer the opportunity to make choices among countless goods and services that are available. You make these choices by comparing prices, quality, appearance, usefulness, and appeal of the goods and services you buy. And, if you are not satisfied with a purchase, you are free to buy from a competing business another time. Competition encourages business owners to improve products, offer better services, keep prices reasonable, and produce new things.

Freedom of Choice

You have learned that the private enterprise system gives you the right to enter a business or career of your choice, to own property, to make a profit, and to compete. You also have other rights that contribute to your economic freedom of choice.

NET FACTS

An Internet address is a set of numbers or words that identifies a unique user or computer. Every user and computer on the Internet must have a different address so that the system knows where to send electronic mail and other data.

Illus. 2-4
Our economic system is market based and provides a bountiful variety of products for consumers.

You have the right to buy where and what you please. The sale of some products and services that the government declares harmful to you, however, may be prohibited. Some products may have to carry a warning message.

There are a number of other rights that we have that you probably take for granted. You have the right as a worker to organize with other workers. Through such organization, you can strive to improve working conditions. You have the right to travel when and where you please in this country and to many other countries. You also have the right to express your opinions in newspapers, over radio and television, and in talking with others as long as you do not slander another person. The private enterprise system provides greater freedom of choice to the individual than any other economic system.

MIXED ECONOMIC SYSTEMS

An economic system usually gets its name from the way its economic resources are owned and controlled. But economies are complex and do not neatly fall under one category or another. In

GlobalPerspective

Guangdong Province, China

Would you expect to go shopping for blue jeans, CD players, and Barbie dolls in shops located in mainland China? Would you expect an Avon salesperson to call at your door? Would you expect to see businesses popping up almost overnight? Well, that is happening today. There is a sort of economic revolution under way on the southern coast of China. The region, called Guangdong, has less than 0.5 percent of China's land and houses 16 million people.

Many businesses have come in from neighboring Hong Kong. About three million Guangdong citizens work in 30,000 plants that are run by Hong Kong businesses or that contract with Hong Kong businesses. As a result, the average annual wage for Guangdong citizens is $600, twice that of the rest of China.

Capitalism in Guangdong is an exception in an otherwise communist China. But the prosperity of Guangdong brings good tax revenue to the central government of China, so the province is left alone.

Critical Thinking

1 What do you think will be the future of Guangdong province?

2 What effect do you think this "experiment" will have on the rest of China? on countries that trade with China?

general, we think of most countries as having mixed economic systems.

Some countries combine government ownership and control of basic industries with some private ownership of consumer-goods businesses. In some countries, a limited amount of private enterprise is tolerated. For example, after farmers in some directed economies meet the government's quota for crop production, they are allowed to sell the rest of their crop in a free market and keep the profit.

In the United States there is some government regulation of business. There are also some government-operated enterprises, such as the post office, schools, and city water agencies. Our economic system is not pure capitalism, so it is often referred to as modified or mixed capitalism.

EMERGING MARKET ECONOMIES

The economic success of market economies has caused many countries to reexamine their economic systems. Many directed or controlled economies have not prospered in comparison to market economies. Directed economies are not designed to meet the wants and needs of individuals. In most controlled economies, workers with different skills and responsibilities receive similar wages. Therefore, there is little incentive for people to work hard.

The weaknesses of controlled economies have caused many nations throughout the world to change to a market economy. The most notable example is the collapse of communism in the Soviet

Illus. 2-5

Government ownership and control of basic industries results in a scarcity of consumer goods, as shown in this Moscow dairy market.

ndoubtedly, the biggest disadvantage of being in business for oneself is the risk of losing one's investment.

Union. The Soviet Union was dominated by today's Russia. In the case of the Soviet Union, an entire generation was forced to do without many consumer goods such as cars, home appliances, and adequate housing. Emphasis was placed on industrial development. Today Russia is gradually moving toward a market economy. Other countries once within the Soviet bloc, such as Poland, Hungary, and the Czech Republic, have made great strides toward establishing new economies. All of these economies now experience voluntary exchange and benefit from it.

One of the new "rights" that Laszlo now has is the "right to fail." There was a measure of security in his former economy. Laszlo knew how many shoes he would make and sell. Laszlo now does not know exactly how many of his shoes will sell. However, Laszlo has the potential to profit if his shoes are as good or better than those of his competition. Free enterprise has given Laszlo an opportunity to succeed in the marketplace if he operates a dynamic business.

Key Ideas

1 Every society must answer the questions: what to produce, how to produce, and for whom to produce.

2 There are three types of economic systems: custom-based, directed or controlled, and market.

3 The five important features of our market economy are private enterprise, private property, profit, competition, and freedom of choice.

4 Economies are complex and do not fall easily and neatly into one category.

5 Market economies have replaced most controlled economies because of the successes of market economies around the world.

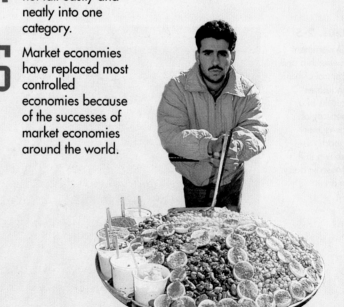

End of Chapter Activities

Increasing Your Business Vocabulary

The following terms should become part of your business vocabulary. For each numbered item, find the term that has the same meaning.

business

capitalism (free
or private enter-
prise system)

competition

custom-based
economy

directed or
planned economy

economic system

market economy

marketplace

private enterprise

private property

profit

profit motive

voluntary
exchange

1 A nation's plan for making decisions on what and how to produce and how to distribute goods and services.

2 An economic system in which goods are produced the way they have always been produced.

3 Buyers and sellers make their own economic decisions to determine what the price will be for goods and services produced and sold.

4 Any place where buyers and sellers exchange goods and services for some form of money.

5 The rivalry among businesses in selling to buyers.

6 The right of the individual to choose whether to own a business, what business to enter, and what to produce with only limited government direction.

7 The right to own, use, or dispose of things of value.

8 An economy in which individuals are free to engage in business transactions with buyers who are able and willing to buy and sellers who supply goods and services from which they earn a profit.

9 An economy in which resources are owned and controlled by the government.

10 The desire to work hard and be creative to earn a higher profit.

11 An economic system in which most economic resources are privately owned and decisions about production are largely made by free exchange in the marketplace.

12 Money left from sales after subtracting the cost of operating the business.

13 An establishment or enterprise that supplies goods and services in exchange for some form of payment.

Reviewing Your Reading

1 What are the three key economic questions that every society must answer to set up an economic system?

2 What are the major characteristics of the three types of economic systems?

3 Who owns and controls most economic resources in a system of capitalism?

4 What are the five features of our market economy?

5 What does the right to earn a profit influence a business owner to do?

6 What does the right of private property entitle the owner to do?

7 Give three ways in which consumers benefit from competition among businesses.

8 In addition to the profit motive, give two other reasons that might encourage people to invest their time, money, and energy in operating their own businesses.

9 In addition to private property and private enterprise, what are four other rights that are included in our economic freedom of choice?

10 Explain the nature of a mixed economy.

11 What are some reasons why market economies are becoming popular around the world?

Using Your Business Knowledge

1 How is the question of what goods and services will be produced determined under a custom-based system?

2 Who decides what will be produced in a directed, planned economic system?

3 Explain and give examples showing how enterprises stay in business when they sell at higher prices the same goods and services sold by other businesses.

4 If we can choose any kind of work we wish under the right of free enterprise, why can't individuals open a law office, practice dentistry, or pilot a plane when they feel they are ready to do so?

5 If the United States operated as pure capitalism, what are several changes that might occur?

6 It has been said that the term "market" in our market economy refers to an idea and not to a place. What do you think this means?

7 Explain how the decisions of buyers and sellers in the marketplace largely answer the question of what to produce in our private enterprise system.

8 Even though we have many free-doms under our economic system, there are many activities that we are not free to do. For example, we are not permitted to hunt and kill animals that are designated as endangered species. List several activities that we are not allowed to do in our society.

Calculating Business Problems

1 Countries that make efficient use of capital goods can produce more with fewer people in a shorter time than countries in which many workers perform the work by man-ual labor. Study the figures at right for farm workers and their yearly output in two different kinds of economic systems; then answer the questions that follow.

	Private Enterprise System	Directed, Planned System
Agricultural labor force	4,380,000	34,350,000
Number of people supplied with food from the output of each farm worker	49	7

a. How many more people were working in agricultural jobs in the directed, planned economy than in the private enterprise system?

b. In which system was each farm worker more productive?

c. In terms of people supplied from the output of each farm worker, how much more productive was the worker cited in item (b)?

2 Lani Oolan compares food prices in newspaper ads each week before doing her grocery shop-ping. One week she found these prices for Grade A eggs at three competing supermarkets: Food Mart, $1.09 per dozen; Farm-to-You, $1.17 per dozen and 20 cents off with a newspaper coupon; and Kitchen Pride, special, 2 dozen for $2.09.

a. At which store would Lani pay the lowest price per dozen?

b. Will the coupon be an advan-tage? Explain.

c. Do you think the fact that there were three stores from which Lani could buy eggs benefited her in any way?

3 The table shows the average number of working hours for a worker in three capital cities in different countries. Each worker lives under a different kind of economic system. The table shows how many hours an average plant worker would have to work to earn enough money to buy the items listed.

a. How much longer than workers in Capital No. 1 must workers in Capital No. 3 work to earn enough to buy food for four for a week?

b. How much longer than a worker in Capital No. 1 must a worker in Capital No. 2 work to earn enough to buy the weekly food needed?

c. How many eight-hour days would a worker in each capital city have to work to earn enough to buy the color television?

	Capital No. 1	Capital No. 2	Capital No. 3
Hamburger meat, 1 pound	17.0 min.	29.0 min.	56.0 min.
Color television, large screen	65.0 hrs.	132.0 hrs.	701.0 hrs.
Toothpaste	16.0 min.	13.0 min.	27.0 min.
Bus fare (2 miles)	7.0 min.	11.0 min.	3.0 min.
Men's shoes (1 pair)	8.0 hrs.	7.0 hrs.	25.0 hrs.
Week's food for family of four	18.6 hrs.	24.7 hrs.	53.5 hrs.

d. If the color television costs $650, what would workers' wages in Capital No. 1 be per hour?

Applying Technology

Using the *Introduction to Business* template and your database program software, select problem CH02. After the problem appears on your screen, complete the following activities. After you have completed each step, display or print a report for each activity. If you do not have a printer available, answer the questions before you leave the computer.

1 Select and list the ZIP Code areas in which the average household income was greater than or equal to $30,000. How many ZIP Codes are listed?

2 Sort the ZIP Code areas in descending order by population. Answer the following questions:

a. What is the fourth ZIP Code area listed?

b. What is the last ZIP Code area listed?

3 Sort the database in ascending order by average monthly housing expenses. Answer the following questions:

a. What is the first ZIP Code area listed?

b. What is the fifth ZIP Code area listed?

Making Decisions

Johakaim Jameson owns and operates a one-man deli. His regular and faithful customers love his "JJ Special." Recently he developed a new recipe and created his "Bountiful Muffin"—good tasting and nutritious. His new muffin is growing in popularity and is bringing in new customers. His problem: He can spend only four hours each day making "JJ Specials" and/or "Bountiful Muffins." He can make 50 specials in an hour and earns a 50-cent profit on each. He can make 60 muffins in an hour and can earn 60 cents on each.

1 How should Johakaim divide his production time between the "JJ Special" and the "Bountiful Muffin" to keep his profits up and to satisfy his customers?

2 If you were Johakaim, what are some things you could do to resolve this dilemma?

Chapter Three

Key Terms

demand

supply

standard of living

labor (or worker) productivity

public goods

Economic Roles

Objectives

After studying this chapter and completing the end-of-chapter activities, you will be able to:

1 Identify three economic roles each person performs.

2 Explain how consumers affect the supply and demand for goods and services.

3 Explain the impact of worker productivity on our standard of living.

4 Explain the role of citizens in our economy.

ianfranco left his college campus right after his ten o'clock accounting class. He hurried to catch the bus so he would arrive at his part-time job on time. He works as a bank teller to earn money for college. He is also gaining work experience to go along with his accounting major. After work, he bought a new shirt that he needed. That evening, he reviewed in the newspaper issues to be decided in the next day's election. In the morning before class, he went to the polling place to cast his vote for a school levy. He also voted for a city council woman who showed support for environmental issues that Gianfranco believes are important. He may not be aware of it, but he performed three economic roles. Can you identify the three roles?

ECONOMIC ROLES YOU PERFORM

You also have three economic roles to play. A look at Gianfranco's activities will help you to identify those roles. As a consumer, he purchased a good (shirt) and a service (bus transportation). As a worker, he helped provide a service as a bank teller. As a citizen, Gianfranco voted on an economic issue (school levy) and supported a candidate for city council.

You and everyone you know will play many different roles in life. You may become a famous recording star, a business executive, or even the president of the United States. A friend of yours may become a swimming coach, an electrician, a minister, or a computer programmer. While you and your friend may follow different career paths, some of the roles you play will be the same.

The three roles that all people share are those of consumer, worker, and citizen. It is true that some people do not work out-

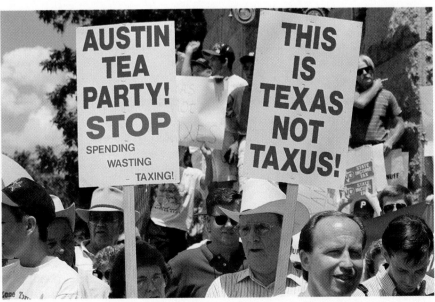

Illus. 3-1
Your citizen role may include being active in the political system.

side the home for wages, and some people may not exercise their right to vote. However, we all are affected in some way by these three economic roles. As you perform these roles, you will make decisions that affect not only you, but the entire economy as well. Understanding how the private enterprise system works will help you understand the importance of your decisions—and may even help you make better ones—in each of your economic roles. In the remainder of this chapter, you will look at how your roles fit into the United States economy.

YOUR CONSUMER ROLE

As you learned in Chapter 2, we have a market economy in which buyers and sellers freely make economic decisions in the marketplace. You also learned that these decisions basically answer the question of what will be produced. The buying decisions of all consumers—individuals, businesses, and governments—provide the answer to how we will use our scarce resources. The important role you and all other consumers play in making these decisions is one of the most interesting characteristics of our system. Individual buying decisions have a great influence on our market economy. Individual consumers buy more than two-thirds of all goods and services produced. It is easy to see that consumers play a central role in our economic system.

It may seem to you that the United States economy is a big, unorganized system in which everyone does just about as he or she pleases. You may wonder how the system can work when each business makes its own decision about what to produce and each buyer makes a decision about what and where to buy. But the system does work and it works well. Let's explore how your consumer decisions affect the system.

Dollar Votes Help Create Demand

As a consumer, you help businesses make their decisions. You do this by buying—or not buying—certain goods and services. When you buy something, you are casting a dollar vote for it. You are saying to a business, "I like this product or service, and I'm willing to pay for it." When a business receives your dollar votes and those of other consumers, it knows the demand for its products. **Demand** means the quantity of a product or service that consumers are willing and able to buy at a particular price.

You and other teenagers in the United States spent $99 billion on consumer goods and services in a recent year.

Demand Helps Determine Supply

Knowing the demand tells a business what type and what quantity of products and services to supply. **Supply** means the quantity of a product or service that businesses are willing and able to provide at a particular price. Suppliers usually will produce a product or service as long as it can be sold at a price that covers the costs of operating the business to make and sell it, plus a reasonable profit. This is why you can buy a hamburger for about $1.50, but you will not find any for 35 cents. Suppliers of hamburgers could not cover their costs and make a profit at the 35-cent price.

Together, supply and demand play an important part in our market economy. The buyers and sellers in the marketplace that you read about in Chapter 2 help to determine not only what will be produced, but also what the price will be. Let's see how that works.

Demand and Supply Affect Prices

Have you ever wondered how a business decides what price to charge for a product or service? Why does a sweater cost $60 and a new car $15,000? Why does the price of a swimsuit drop in the fall of the year or the cost of food go up after a long summer's drought? Shortages of a product affect supply and prices.

A business must decide what price to charge for a product or service. The price cannot be too high, or consumers won't buy; or if it's too low, there will be no profit. Generally speaking, prices are carefully determined after a good deal of study.

The demand for a product affects the price. If many people want (or demand) a particular product or service, its price will tend to go up. Christmas cards are priced higher in November and early December when many people want to buy them. Have you noticed, however, that the prices of the cards are often cut in half the day after Christmas? When demand is low, prices are usually lower.

Supply also affects the price of a product. Remember that a supplier needs to cover the costs of operating the business and make a reasonable profit. Prices are set to do these two things. If a supplier of jogging shoes, for example, sets a price too high, people will not buy the shoes. Therefore, the supplier will have to lower the price in order to sell the shoes. Of course, if the price is set too low, operating costs will not be covered; the supplier

NET FACTS

The Internet is not a single network but a super network made up of more than 50,000 smaller networks.

FYI

About two-thirds of the $99 billion teenagers spend is their own money earned from jobs or received as gifts and allowances.

will lose money and soon go out of business. All this means that the supplier must produce a good product and operate in an efficient way. Prices can then be set at reasonable levels so that consumers will be willing and able to buy the products.

Of course, other factors may be involved in the pricing process. The prices of some products tend to stay high, for example, because the materials from which they are made are limited by nature. Diamonds have been found in only a few countries of the world and in relatively small quantities. Therefore, the price of diamonds is high.

Competition Keeps Prices Reasonable

Competition helps keep prices at a reasonable level. Businesses must set prices to cover operating costs and to earn a reasonable profit. But what is to prevent a seller from charging an unreasonably high price in order to earn larger profits? The answer is competition. You will remember from Chapter 2 that competition is one of the main characteristics of the private enterprise system. If one

Cultural *Perspective*

The Legacy of Arabic Numerals

Did you know that the numbers we use today are of Arabic origin? Arabic numerals are 0, 1, 2, 3, 4, 5, 6, 7, 8, 9 and are based on a value of 10. Combining these various numbers creates other numbers with different values. Because these Arabic numbers are based on 10, we are able to write numbers in columns and perform mathematical operations.

Early civilizations did not always use Arabic numbers. Other numbering systems, such as Roman numerals, were used instead. Roman numerals are based on letters such as I, V, X, L, C, D, and M. These letters represent various values, and when several letters are combined, a number is represented. Roman numerals are not based on 10 as are Arabic numerals. Therefore, a column of Roman numerals is difficult to add.

Muslims added the symbol for zero to a system that they borrowed from Indian mathematicians. As the Muslims conquered other lands, they spread the idea of their new number system. The Arabic numbers we use today are based on that system. Thanks to the contributions of Muslims to the development of mathematics, we use a system of numbers that is easy to write and easy to use.

Critical Thinking

1 What is the importance of Arabic numerals in performing mathematical calculations?

2 Can you think of examples in our society where Roman numerals are still used?

store offers cassette tapes for $12.95 but another offers the same tapes for less, you probably would say to the merchant with the higher price, "Forget it. I can buy that same tape at a store down the street for $10.95." If the owners of the store keep the price at $12.95, and do not compete in other ways—such as delivery or other services—they will soon go out of business because not many people will buy tapes at the higher price.

YOUR WORKER ROLE

Competition affects prices in another way, too. When a product has a very high demand and is making money for one supplier, other business-people will begin to offer the product also. With several businesses offering the product, one of the suppliers could not afford to sell at extremely high prices. Consumers would go to the competitors to buy. This also tends to cause suppliers to produce goods and services efficiently. If a supplier cannot produce the product at a low cost so that it can be sold at competing prices, other suppliers who do so will get all of the business and the inefficient producer will be forced out of the market. In this way, competition tends to allow only efficient producers—those who can supply good products at competitive prices—to survive in the marketplace. Competition, then, aids the consumer by helping to keep prices and profits at reasonable levels.

No matter what price is set on products and services in the marketplace, you cannot enjoy the products and services unless you have the money to buy them. This is where your worker role comes into the picture.

Career Highlights

A statistical clerk compiles and computes data according to statistical formulas used in statistical tests, performs mathematical computations, and compiles charts and graphs used by economists and marketing research analysts.

Your Standard of Living

Your standard of living is affected by the money you earn as a worker. Most people work to earn money. You will earn money for a variety of reasons. The main reason will be to buy the things you need and want. Most of your needs are provided by others: parents, guardians, or relatives. Before long, you will be meeting your own needs with the money you earn. Your success as a worker will be the most important factor in determining your standard of living. The term **standard of living** refers to the way you live as measured by the kinds and quality of goods and services you can afford. We use our earnings to buy the things we need to maintain and improve

FYI

Price fixing is illegal—businesses with comparable products must charge prices based on their own costs of doing business.

our standard of living. Your worker role, then, supports your consumer role.

Your Productivity as a Worker

The main way we improve our standard of living is to produce more as workers. One of the reasons this country has progressed so far in such a short time is that it has had a varied and skilled work force. We have provided this work force with technological advancements that have increased our productivity (see Figure 3-1). **Labor (**or **worker) productivity** refers to the quantity of a good that an average worker can produce in an hour. High productivity has enabled us to achieve a standard of living that is among the highest in the world.

As a worker, you will want to improve your productivity so that you can increase your earnings and your standard of living. Pro-

Illus. 3-2
Your worker role provides you with the money to buy the things you want and need.

Figure 3-1
Labor productivity increases with training and use of technology.

ductive workers help increase the overall standard of living of our nation. You will learn more about productivity and about your worker role in other chapters in this text. Now, let us consider your third role in the private enterprise system.

YOUR CITIZEN ROLE

The "911" emergency system is an example of a public good.

So far, we have considered how you will satisfy your own wants and needs through your worker and consumer roles. But there are some needs and wants that you will not be able to satisfy for yourself.

As a citizen, you pay taxes. Your community uses the taxes collected to provide public goods, such as schools, parks, and civic centers where plays and concerts are performed. **Public goods** are something needed by a community and provided by its government. Public goods make a community a better place in which to live by improving the quality of life for everyone.

As a citizen, Gianfranco joined other citizens in making some economic decisions for the common good. He wanted to help assure quality schools for the children of his community. He wanted to help preserve the environment. His citizenship role allowed him to do that when he cast his vote.

Your citizen role will allow you to make these kinds of decisions in your community as well. This process is known as *collective decision making*. As citizens, we decide collectively how some of our scarce resources will be used and what will be provided for

Illus. 3-3
Public goods and services improve the quality of life.

our common use. As a citizen, you should remember that government cannot supply all that you and other people want. It, too, must make choices as to which services it can afford to provide. You will learn more in Unit 2 about services provided by local, state, and national governments.

Key Ideas

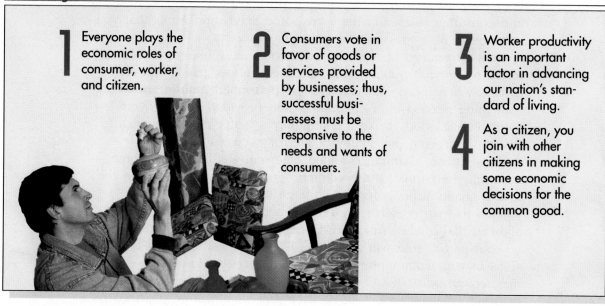

1 Everyone plays the economic roles of consumer, worker, and citizen.

2 Consumers vote in favor of goods or services provided by businesses; thus, successful businesses must be responsive to the needs and wants of consumers.

3 Worker productivity is an important factor in advancing our nation's standard of living.

4 As a citizen, you join with other citizens in making some economic decisions for the common good.

End of Chapter Activities

Increasing Your Business Vocabulary

The following terms should become part of your business vocabulary. For each numbered item, find the term that has the same meaning.

demand

labor (or worker) productivity

public goods

standard of living

supply

1 The quantity of a good an average worker produces in one hour.

2 The quantity of a product or service that businesses are willing and able to provide at a particular price.

3 A measure of how well people in a country live—the quantity and quality of wants and needs that are satisfied.

4 The quantity of a product or service that consumers are willing and able to buy at a particular price.

5 Things that are needed and provided by a community and are equally accessible to everyone.

Reviewing Your Reading

1 State the three economic roles that most people in the United States perform.

2 Explain the way your dollar votes help to create demand.

3 Give one example each to show how demand and supply affect prices.

4 Suppliers usually set their prices to cover what two factors?

5 If a business has overstocked a product, would it be likely to raise or lower the price of the product?

6 Would the price of a product made with scarce natural resources tend to be high or low?

7 What effect does competition have on prices?

8 Give an example to show how competition tends to make businesses more efficient.

9 In what way does your worker role support your consumer role?

10 In what way might your selection of a career affect your future standard of living?

11 Give one example to show the importance of productivity in your worker role.

12 Give two examples of activities you perform in your citizenship role.

Using Your Business Knowledge

1 When the demand for small cars increases, what might the suppliers of large models do to sell their cars?

2 Name two products other than those cited in the text that are usually high-priced because they are scarce.

3 Discuss the importance of the consumer in a market economy.

4 If workers produce fewer goods and services than they are expected to produce, what effect will their lowered productivity have on the nation's standard of living?

5 Since Americans have the freedom to make individual choices in the marketplace, why would they make some decisions collectively?

6 Choosing your career is one of the most important economic decisions you will make. Can you explain why?

7 In your citizenship role, you will be performing a variety of activities in addition to voting on economic issues. After discussing this with friends and members of your family, list several activities that a good citizen does for either his or her personal satisfaction or for the common good.

Calculating Business Problems

1 The Video Rental Center purchased 24 dozen video tapes of a blockbuster new movie, at a cost of $20 per tape, to sell during the Christmas season.

   a. How many individual tapes did Video Rental Center buy?
   b. What was the total cost of the tapes?
   c. In January, the shop had one-fourth of the tapes left. How many tapes were unsold?
   d. If demand had dropped after the holidays, would the shop be more likely to increase or decrease the price to sell the tapes?

2 At the top of the next page is a table showing information about the voting activity of young people in three national election years. Year Two was a presidential election year; Year One and Year Three were congressional election years. Study the data and answer the questions that follow.

   a. How many 18- to 20-year-olds voted in each year?
   b. How many 18- to 20-year-olds reported they registered but did not vote in Year Three?
   c. How many more 18- to 20-year-olds reported they voted in the presidential election year than in Year One?

d. Why do you think so many more voted in a presidential election year than in a congressional election year?

Year	Number of People Age 18 to 20 Years Old (In Millions)	Percent Reporting They Are Registered To Vote	Percent Reporting They Voted
One	12.1	35.0%	19.8%
Two	11.2	47.0	36.7
Three	10.7	35.4	18.6

3 Diamonds are called precious gems because they are so scarce. Diamonds are used not only in jewelry but also in industrial production for cutting and grinding other materials. They are found in only a few places in the world. The leading producers are South Africa, Zaire, Botswana, and Russia. The table shows the diamonds imported by the United States in two recent years.

a. What was the increase in value

Year	Volume (In Millions)	Value (In Millions)
One	6.3 carats	$2,275
Two	8.2 carats	$3,007

of the imported diamonds in Year Two over Year One?

b. What was the percent of increase in the carat weight of the imported diamonds in Year Two over Year One?

Applying Technology

Using the *Introduction to Business* template and your spreadsheet program software, select problem CH03. After the problem appears on your screen, complete the following activities. Then, after you have completed each step, display or print the completed spreadsheet or graph for each activity. If you do not have a printer available, answer the questions before you leave the computer.

1 You are planning to attend a concert. The Demand Table in problem CH03 shows how many tickets you would be willing to buy for yourself and your friends at different possible prices per ticket. For example, you would be willing to buy 11 tickets at a price of $15 each. Using the Demand Table, create a graph with Quantity of Concert Tickets Demanded on the x-axis. Looking at your graph from left to right, does the line slope downward or upward?

2 Another student at your school is selling concert tickets as part of a fund-raising drive. The student who is selling must choose a price at which to sell the tickets. The Supply

Table in problem CH03 shows how many tickets the seller would be willing to supply at different possible prices per ticket. For example, the seller would be willing to sell 11 tickets at a price of $45 each. Using both the Demand Table and the Supply Table, make a graph with the Quantity of Concert Tickets on the x-axis, Price of Tickets Demanded in one range, and Price of Tickets Supplied in another range. Answer the following questions:

a. What is the Quantity of Concert Tickets at the point at which the two graphs intersect?
b. What is the Price of Tickets at the point at which the two graphs intersect?

3 Go to the part of problem CH03 in which the following four columns appear: Price of Tickets, Quantity of Concert Tickets Supplied, Quantity of Concert Tickets Demanded, and Supply–Demand. Enter formulas in the column Supply–Demand. For each row, the formula should subtract the Quantity of Concert Tickets Demanded from the Quantity of Concert Tickets Supplied. Answer the following questions:

a. What is the value of Supply–Demand at a price of $30?
b. How does this result compare to your answers to Question 2?

Making Decisions

Comparable worth means that people should receive equal pay for jobs that require similar levels of education, training, and skills. Comparable worth can be difficult to assess. Take the following situation as an example.

Amelia has worked on her job only three years. However, she turns out six more "gizmos" every hour than her co-worker, Jothan, who has been on the job for five years. Yet Jothan's salary is the same as Amelia's. Amelia feels cheated. Jothan has more education and training than Amelia and, therefore, has been assigned to troubleshoot the production process when problems occur. Jothan feels that he deserves to be paid a higher salary.

1 Should Amelia and Jothan receive the same salary? Why or why not?

2 Can you think of a measurement system other than the number of "gizmos" produced per hour for evaluating job performance?

Chapter Four

Key Terms

gross domestic product (GDP)

base year

GDP per capita

business cycle

prosperity

recession

depression

recovery

inflation

deflation

Economic Measurements

Objectives

After studying this chapter and completing the end-of-chapter activities, you will be able to:

1 Explain how Gross Domestic Product (GDP), GDP per capita, and labor productivity are used as measurements of economic performance.

2 Describe the four phases of the business cycle.

3 Describe inflation and deflation.

4 Discuss some of the possible developments in the future growth of our economy.

An important part of life is measuring performance. In a recent basketball game, Rosa Rivera of Middletown High School scored 19 points, pulled down 8 rebounds, and had 7 assists. Later that day, Akira Eto, an aspiring amateur ice skater, scored 5.6 during his short program. By any standard, these were good performances.

How about you? How much have you grown in the past ten years? You can say, "I am ten years older." Or, "I am 50 pounds heavier." Or, "I now wear shoe size 10C." There are a lot of ways in which we can measure our own growth.

You grow in many other ways, too. As you mature, your abilities increase. You depend less on your parents and begin to plan for your future and look toward a career. You might be working part time and saving money for the future. Your grades may be improving so that you will have a better chance of getting into college.

You can measure your body growth by looking in a mirror, stepping on a scale, or trying on new shoes in a different size. Your interests, actions, and achievements measure your mental and psychological growth. Improvement in grades and the size of your savings account measure the extent to which you have goals and are meeting them.

These are just a few of the ways by which you can measure various growth factors in your life.

MEASURING ECONOMIC GROWTH

Economic growth refers to a steady increase in production of goods and services in an economic system. Just as you can use different ways to measure your own growth, we can use different methods to check on the growth of our economy. A high rate of employment and a low rate of business failures are two indications that our economy is doing well. However, the most important ways by which we can measure how well we are doing relate to how much we produce to help satisfy the needs and wants of our people.

Today more than 120 million Americans work in thousands of different jobs and produce thousands of different products and services: hamburgers, snowmobiles, amusement parks, nail polish, electronic games, fire engines, carry-out chicken dinners, garbage collection, medical services, concerts. The list is almost endless. The total of all the goods and services that Americans produce is the output or production of our nation. We have only about 7 percent of the world's land and 5 percent of the world's population, yet our output accounts for more than 25 percent of all goods and services produced in the world.

Gross Domestic Product (GDP)

One way to find out how well our economy is doing is to compare output from year to year. The federal government collects information from producers and estimates our national output. The most widely used estimate is the gross domestic product (formerly gross national product). The **gross domestic product,** or **GDP,** is the total dollar value of all final goods and services produced in our country during one year. It is one measure of how the economy is performing.

GDP includes three major categories of expenditures:

1. what consumers spend for food, clothing, and housing;

2. what businesses spend for buildings, equipment, and supplies; and

3. what government agencies spend to pay employees and to buy supplies.

A growing GDP means more jobs and greater consumer satisfaction.

There are some goods and services not included. For example, GDP does not include the value of the work we do for ourselves, such as cutting our own lawn or building a picnic table for our yard. However, if we buy the lawn service or the picnic table from businesses, they would be included. Only final goods, such as cars, are counted when we measure GDP. Intermediate goods used in manufacturing, such as steel and fabrics, are not included in GDP. If intermediate goods were counted as well, the value of the intermediate goods would be counted twice.

Illus. 4-1
GDP does not include the value of work we do for ourselves.

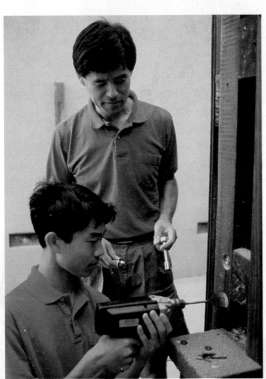

If the GDP increases from year to year, this is a good sign that our economy is growing and is healthy. Even though we have had some bad years, our economy has enjoyed a steady climb over its history. GDP was more than $7 trillion in a recent year. Writing down the figure 7 followed by 12 zeros will give you an idea of how big our economy really is when we measure it in dollars.

There is one big difficulty in comparing a country's GDP from year to year, however. Prices of what we produce do not stay the same from year to year. Prices go up and down—almost always up. In order to make comparisons that are fair and accurate, we need to take the current prices and adjust them each year so that they are equal in value over a period of years. Let's look at an

Our GDP is three times that of Germany, 10 times that of China, and 20 times that of Argentina.

example of an economy with less complicated figures than ours.

Suppose the fictitious nation of Robaland produces only megalamps. The output of Robaland is shown in Figure 4-1.

Note that under current prices the GDP for 1995 is $1,500. On this basis, you could say that the GDP (the total output) increased three times since 1985. However, this assumption is wrong. Actually, Robaland made no progress in producing megalamps. In each of the years, 1,000 units were produced. If prices were adjusted to account for price increases, the dollar value would have been $500 each year.

In this example, 1985 was the base year. **Base year** means the year chosen to compare an item, such as price, to any other year. We can choose any year as the base year, just as we chose 1985 to compare the GDP of Robaland.

Figure 4-1
GDP of Robaland: number of items produced remains the same; prices increase each year

Year	Number of Megalamps Produced	Current Price per Megalamp	GDP at Current Prices	Prices Adjusted to 1985	GDP at Constant Price
1985	1,000	$ .50	$500	$.50	$500
1990	1,000	$1.00	$1,000	$.50	$500
1995	1,000	$1.50	$1,500	$.50	$500

Figure 4-2 shows a different picture. In 1995, Robaland produced three times as many megalamps as in 1985. If GDPs at

Figure 4-2
GDP of Robaland: number of items produced increases; prices also increase each year

Year	Number of Megalamps Produced	Current Price per Megalamp	GDP at Current Prices	Prices Adjusted to 1985	GDP at Constant Price
1985	1,000	$ .50	$500	$.50	$500
1990	1,500	$1.00	$1,500	$.50	$750
1995	3,000	$1.50	$4,500	$.50	$1,500

current prices are compared, the GDP increase in 1995 was nine times that of 1985 ($4,500 ÷ $500 = 9). However, that figure can be misleading, too. Prices were higher in 1995. In constant prices, the GDP in 1995 was three times that of 1985—exactly the same as the actual increase in the total number of megalamps produced.

Constant dollar GDP is the value of gross domestic product after taking out the effect of price changes. When we convert any dollar measure to constant dollar terms, we take out the effect of price changes. Only actual, or real, changes remain. For this reason, we often use the term *real GDP* or GDP in real terms.

GDP Per Capita

The more goods and services we produce, the healthier our economy gets. Just referring to the dollar value of GDP as a measure of economic growth does not tell the whole story. Another way to measure economic growth is GDP per capita or output per person. **GDP per capita** is calculated by dividing GDP by the total population (see Figure 4-3). For example, suppose that there is no change in GDP this year over last year. Suppose, also, that the population increases. You can see that the same output would have to be divided among more people. An increase in GDP per capita means that our economy is growing. A decrease may mean that our economy is having trouble.

Labor Productivity

As you learned in Chapter 3, *productivity* is measured in terms of the number of items produced per worker. An important source of economic growth is an increase in output per worker. Improvements in the quality of capital resources (primarily equipment), worker training, and management techniques have resulted in more output from the same number of workers. This increase in goods

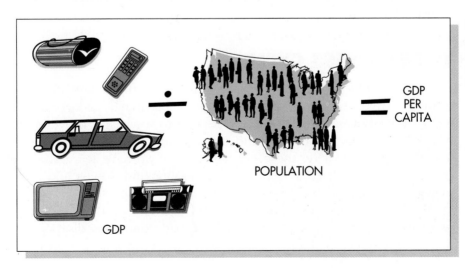

GDP

POPULATION

GDP PER CAPITA

Figure 4-3
Can you see how per capita output is measured?

NET FACTS

A host is a computer that is attached directly to the Internet and that provides services to users. Host computers are also called *servers*.

and services from the same amounts of labor is called a *productivity increase.*

During the past 25 years, the rate of growth in labor productivity has had some ups and downs. While there has been an increase in productivity in many of those years, the amount of the increase has become smaller than in the past. And in a few cases, productivity has actually decreased. At the same time, wages climbed steadily. In one recent ten-year period, wages increased five times more than did labor productivity.

If wages increase faster than gains in productivity, the cost of producing goods increases and prices rise accordingly. So even though workers earn more money, they are not able to improve their standard of living very much because of rising prices. For that reason, a great deal of attention has been given in recent years to ways of motivating workers to increase productivity. By doing so, the workers will be contributing to a higher standard of living in the nation as well as improving their own life-styles.

Our ability to produce more and more goods and services as our country developed has made it possible to reduce the number of hours in a workweek. In the early 1890s, the average worker put in about 60 hours a week. Our average workweek has decreased to generally less than 40 hours. Even though we work fewer hours and have more leisure time, we produce more and earn more than ever before. We can produce more in less time because we use modern technology and efficient work methods. We also have many highly skilled workers. Although productivity historically has increased nearly every year, increases have tended to become smaller. An improvement in productivity has been noted for the 1990s.

THE BUSINESS CYCLE

You probably have heard people talking about the many changes in the economy. They speak about bad times and good times, rising prices, a new business coming to town and providing new jobs, or a factory closing and causing hundreds of workers to lose their jobs. What do these changes mean? We have learned over the decades that our economy has its ups and downs and that good times and bad times seem to run in cycles.

All nations experience good times and bad times—that is a fact of life. Fortunately, over a period of time bad conditions disappear and good conditions return. If we look at the economic changes that have occurred during our country's history, we can see that they form a pattern of good times to bad times and back to good times. This movement of the economy from one condition to another and back again is called a **business cycle.**

Business cycles are the recurring ups and downs of GDP. Business cycles have four phases. Let's look at the good times first.

Prosperity

At the high point of the business cycle, we enjoy prosperity. **Prosperity** is a phase of the business cycle when most people who want to work are working and businesses produce goods and services in record numbers. In this phase, wages are good and the rate of GDP growth increases. The demand for goods and services is high. Shopping malls become very busy places. Marketplaces "hum" with business activity. People are optimistic about the economy and feel good about themselves. This *boom* period is usually the peak of the business cycle. Prosperity, however, does not go on forever. The economy eventually begins to cool off and activity begins to slow down.

Recession

When the economy slows down, we enter a phase of the business cycle known as recession. **Recession** is a period where demand begins to decrease, businesses lower production of goods and services, unemployment begins to rise, and GDP growth slows for two or more quarters of the calendar year. This phase may not be too serious nor last very long, but it often signals trouble for some groups of workers. Auto workers, for instance, are often one of the first groups to feel the pinch of a recession. Then other businesses that supply goods and services to the auto makers, such as steel and fabric manufacturers, find their business activity tapering off. Consequently, these firms cut back on production and some may go out of business. This drop in related businesses is called the *ripple effect.* Eventually, production weakens throughout the economy, and total output declines in the next quarter. Some recessions last for long periods of time as fewer factors of production are used, and total demand falls.

Depression

If a recession deepens and spreads throughout the entire economy, the nation may move into the third phase, depression. **Depression** is a phase marked by a prolonged period of high unemployment, weak sales of goods and services, and business

*J*apan has a "lifetime employment principle"; during a recent recession it maintained an unemployment rate of only 3%.

The difference between a recession and a depression can be illustrated by the following example: In a recession, people have to tighten their belts; but in a depression, they can't afford a belt to tighten.

failures. GDP falls rapidly during a depression. Fortunately, our economy has not had a depression for more than half a century. This period (1930-1940) is referred to as the Great Depression. Approximately 25 percent of the American labor force was then unemployed. Many people could not afford even the basic needs. Food and clothing were given out in the "bread lines" of churches and other charitable agencies. Depression was not only an appropriate name for the state of the economy, it fit the mood of the people also. They were emotionally as well as economically depressed.

Recovery

Depressions also do not go on forever. A welcome phase of the business cycle, known as recovery, begins to appear. **Recovery** is the phase in which unemployment begins to decrease, demand for goods and services increases, and GDP begins to rise again. People gain employment; consumers regain confidence about their futures and begin buying again. This new demand causes businesses to produce more and to employ more workers. Recovery may be slow or fast. As it continues, the nation moves into prosperity again.

Illus. 4-2

During the Great Depression, many people lined up for free food.

INFLATION AND DEFLATION

Another problem with which our nation has had to cope is inflation. **Inflation** is a sustained increase in the general level of prices. One type of inflation occurs when the demand for goods and services is greater than the supply. When a large supply of money, earned or borrowed, is spent for goods that are in short supply, prices increase. Inflation was a serious problem in the decades of the 1970s and early 1980s. Government, businesses, and individuals continued to increase their spending and prices continued to rise. Even though wages (the price paid for labor) tend to increase during inflation, prices of goods and services usually rise so fast that the wage earner never seems to catch up.

Global Perspective

Hyperinflation

In the United States, we enjoy a moderate rate of inflation, generally about 3 percent to 6 percent a year. But moderate rates of inflation are not reality throughout some parts of the world, especially Latin America. For instance, in some South American countries, the annual rate of inflation has been as high as 300 to 400 percent. This phenomenon is known as *hyperinflation*.

If left unchecked, it can run rampant, feed on itself, and create severe distortions in the economy. People learn to anticipate next month's price hikes, and everyone, from the largest companies to street vendors, includes the expected rate of inflation into prices asked.

"So what?" you ask. "Don't salaries go up when prices go up?" Too bad; it doesn't work that way and consumers usually feel the pinch. For instance, in one South American economy, you might buy from a grocer a package of cookies marked $1.69. By the end of the week, the price might have increased to $1.89.

So how do consumers survive? Many families buy all of their groceries for the month as soon as the wage earner gets paid. If they do not buy right away, their money will buy fewer groceries later in the month. The challenge for workers is not so much making money but keeping what they have made. From week to week, the same amount of money buys less and less.

Critical Thinking

1 *What effect would it have on your life, and that of your family and relatives, if the inflation rate in the United States were to increase to over 300 percent?*

2 *What wage increases would you expect to receive if our inflation rate more than doubled each year?*

Cultural Notes

According to the United States Census Bureau, the population of the United States will exceed 392 million by 2050. At that time, Hispanics will make up our nation's second-largest ethnic group behind white non-Hispanics. The fastest growing segment of our population is Asians and Pacific Islanders. The population of this group is rising at the rate of four percent a year. By 2050, Asians and Pacific Islanders will make up 10 percent of the population. The Arab-American population, composed of immigrants from Lebanon, Egypt, Jordan, Syria, and Iraq, is also starting to increase in numbers.

Most people think inflation is harmful. Consumers have to pay higher prices for the things they buy; therefore, as workers, they have to earn more money to maintain the same standard of living. Producers may receive higher prices for the goods and services they sell. However, if wages go up faster than prices, businesses tend to hire fewer workers and so unemployment worsens.

Mild inflation (perhaps 2 or 3 percent a year) can actually stimulate economic growth. During a mildly inflationary period, wages often rise more slowly than the prices of products. The prices of the products sold are high in relation to the cost of labor. The producer makes higher profits and tends to expand production and hire more people. The newly employed workers increase spending, and the total demand in an economy increases.

You will learn more about measuring inflation in Chapter 18 when you learn about one *price index*—the Consumer Price Index (CPI). A price index is a number that compares prices in one year with some earlier base year. There are different kinds of price indexes.

There is an opposite to inflation called deflation. **Deflation** means a decrease in the general level of prices. It usually occurs in periods of recession and depression. Prices of products are lower, but people have less money to buy them. The most notable deflationary period in the United States was during the Great Depression of the 1930s. Between 1929 and 1933, prices declined about 25 percent.

OUR ECONOMIC FUTURE

The ability of an economy to produce output determines its growth. We have come a long way under our private enterprise system. We know it works well. We also know that it can be made to

An upward movement of the general price level causes an increase or "rise in the cost of living."

work even better as we strive to develop new technologies and find solutions to our economic problems.

Serious economic problems exist within our economy that need to be solved. Many people do not have access to adequate health care. Some people do not have proper housing, especially in large cities. Our nation's traffic and crime problems are matters of concern to many citizens. Too many workers are unemployed or do not have appropriate employment. Having a "good" job is an important part of life for most people.

And what lies ahead on the technology front? Will computer-controlled robots perform most of the routine tasks in our factories? Will we see housekeeping chores done entirely by machines? Will we raise crops under water or on other planets? Will we work at home communicating with business associates using computers? These are some of the things occurring now or predicted for the 21st century.

No one knows for sure just how these changes will affect our future. We do know, however, that to maintain or increase our existing standard of living and to prevent unemployment from rising, we must increase our economic growth continuously. Economic growth is important because it provides jobs and enables people to better meet their needs and wants.

Illus. 4-3

Our economic future is shaped by many kinds of technological advances. Pictured here is an artist's impression of the Solar Satellite Power System that may one day collect energy from the sun for use as a power source.

Key Ideas

1 We measure our economic performance by calculating our gross domestic product, our per capita output, and labor productivity.

2 A business cycle has four important phases: prosperity, recession, depression, and recovery.

3 Inflation is a general rise in the level of prices; deflation is a decrease in the general price level.

4 There are some exciting possibilities for the future of our economy as we solve economic problems and use new technologies to increase output.

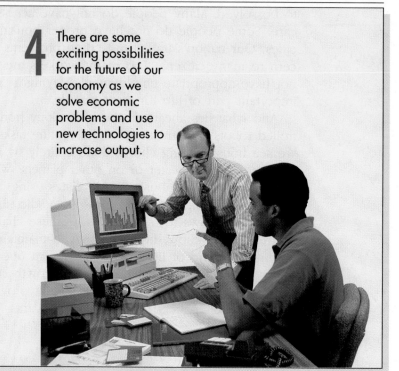

End of Chapter Activities

Increasing Your Business Vocabulary

The following terms should become a part of your business vocabulary. For each numbered item, find the term that has the same meaning.

base year

business cycle

deflation

depression

gross domestic product (GDP)

inflation

GDP per capita

prosperity

recession

recovery

1 The total value of all final goods and services produced in a country in one year.

2 The year chosen to compare an item, such as price, to the same item in another year.

3 The GDP divided by the total population of a country.

4 The movement of an economy from one condition to another and back again.

5 A phase of the business cycle when most people who want to work are working and businesses produce goods and services in record numbers.

6 A period where demand begins to decrease, businesses lower production of goods and services, unemployment begins to rise, and GDP growth slows for several quarters.

7 A phase marked by high unemployment, weak sales of goods and sevices, and business failures.

8 A phase of the business cycle in which unemployment begins to decrease, demand for goods and services increases, and GDP begins to rise again.

9 An increase in the general price level.

10 A decrease in the general price level.

Reviewing Your Reading

1 Compare the United States with the rest of the world in land size, population, and output of goods and services.

2 "One way to find out how our economy is doing is to compare output from year to year." What does this statement mean?

3 The spending of what three groups is included in GDP?

4 If prices of goods and services remain exactly the same over a long period of time, would it be fair and accurate to compare a country's GDP from year to year at current prices?

5 Explain the use of a base year in measuring output.

6 What is the difference between current prices and adjusted prices of goods and services?

7 How is per capita output determined and used?

8 Name three factors that have contributed to the high output of goods and services over the history of our economy. What changes have taken place in productivity in recent years?

9 Give an example to explain how productivity is related to the standard of living.

10 What is characteristic of each phase of the business cycle?

11 Why is a high level of inflation generally considered harmful to our economy?

12 What are some economic problems that need solving in our economic system?

Using Your Business Knowledge

1 The GDP of a developing country in Africa increased 3.6 percent in one year from $5.6 billion to $5.8 billion. Does this mean the country had a 3.6 percent increase in the amount of goods and services produced?

2 If you and your classmates have jobs for which you are paid wages, you are contributing to the GDP. Survey your classmates who work and determine how much your class has contributed to the GDP in one week. (To protect confidentiality, report earnings on slips of paper without names.)

3 The GDP of Country A is $400,000. The GDP of Country B is $800,000. Does this mean that the per capita output of Country B is about twice that of Country A? Explain.

4 As you have learned, the GDP of the United States in a recent year was more than $7 trillion in current dollars. Ten years before, it was less than half that amount. In the next few years, the GDP is expected to pass the $8 trillion mark. What difference does it make to you and to other people in your community whether the GDP is increasing or decreasing?

5 Explain how high wages and low productivity can increase the price you pay for goods and services.

6 Explain how productivity has helped to increase a U.S. worker's leisure time.

7 Suppose that many auto and steel plants close throughout a country and that thousands of workers lose their jobs in a relatively short time period. If the country has been enjoying prosperous times, it may now be headed into what phase of the business cycle? Describe other conditions that might begin to occur.

Calculating Business Problems

1 The 1995 production schedule of Robaland listed on page 54 shows its GDP at current prices of $4,500 and at constant 1985 prices of $1,500. If Robaland's population of 1995 was 500, what was its per capita output?

a. At current prices?
b. At constant prices?

2 Some very simple machines such as the wheelbarrow and the hand truck have increased productivity or output per worker hour. Seth Kisco, who works in a warehouse that imports many of its goods, can move from the loading pier to storage one 30-kilo box at a time by hand. Using a hand truck, he can move three 30-kilo boxes at once in the same amount of time.

a. Seth can move six boxes in one hour without using a hand truck. What is his productivity?

b. If he uses a hand truck, what is his productivity?

c. How many workers without hand trucks would it take to do the same work Seth does with a hand truck?

d. How many pounds can Seth move in an hour with a hand truck? (See Appendix D for information regarding metric conversions.)

---

3 A small Asian country produces teakwood carvings of water buffalo to sell to tourists. The country's production record is shown in the table.

a. What is the country's GDP at current prices for each year?

b. What is the amount of increase in the number of items produced in Year Two over Year One?

c. What is the rate of increase in the number of items produced in Year Three over Year Two?

Year	Number of Carvings Produced	Current Price per Carving
One	1,000	$ .50
Two	2,000	$1.00
Three	4,000	$2.00

d. If the country expects to maintain the same rate of increase for another year, how many water buffalo carvings will it need to produce?

---

4 Productivity for Novaville was 25 units per worker hour in 1985. Productivity increased 20 percent between 1985 and 1990. What was the productivity figure for 1990? If the rate of increase is maintained, what will the figure be in 1995? in 2000? Workers are paid a rate of $.30 per unit. How much did workers earn per hour in 1990? If their rate increases to $.35 in 1995 and $.40 in 2000, how much would they earn per hour in those years?

Applying Technology

Using the *Introduction to Business* template and your spreadsheet software, select problem CH04. After the problem appears on your screen, complete the following activities. Then, after you have completed each step, display or print the completed spreadsheet or graph for each activity. If you do not have a printer available, answer the questions before you leave the computer.

1 The first table in problem CH04 is similar to Figure 4-1 on page 54. Enter formulas to complete the columns for GDP at Current Prices, Prices Adjusted to 1997, and GDP at Constant Price. Answer the following questions:

a. What is the GDP at Current Prices for 2006?

b. What is the GDP at Constant Price for 2000?

2 The second table in problem CH04 is similar to Figure 4-2 on page 54. Enter formulas to complete the columns for GDP at Current Prices, Prices Adjusted to 1997, and GDP at Constant Price. Answer the following questions:

a. What is the GDP at Current Prices for 1999?

b. What is the GDP at Constant Price for 2005?

3 Create a single graph combining the results of both tables in problem CH04. Use the Year column as the *x*-axis. Use GDP at Constant Price from the first table for one range; use GDP at Constant Price from the second table for the other range. Answer the following questions:

a. Looking at the graphs from left to right, how would you describe the directions of the graphs?

b. Why does each graph look the way it does?

Making Decisions

In determining GDP, only *final goods and services* are included. This avoids having some items counted more than once. For example, a mining company sells iron ore to a steel-producing firm. That firm sells the steel to an auto manufacturer who uses it to produce a car. The iron ore, converted to steel, is counted once—in the price paid for the car, the final product. Read carefully the following list of goods and services produced in our economy and then answer the questions.

a. An electric toaster oven bought as a gift.

b. Telephone service installed in a government office.

c. Fiberglass sold to a company for use in making boats.

d. Grooming services for your pet.
e. Paper sold to a newspaper publishing company.
f. A computer paid for by the city government.
g. A computer bought for your family's use.
h. Broccoli bought by a food-processing firm.

1 Which of these items should be listed as a good and counted in GDP? Give reasons for your answer.

2 Which of these items should be listed as a service and counted in GDP? Give reasons for your answer.

A career in the American free enterprise system could be anything you want it to be. If you have enough interest to acquire the training for it, you could be a corporate executive, an opera singer, or a professional clown. The choice is yours.

Each unit in this text will help you prepare to make your choice by outlining career opportunities in the area discussed in the unit. Since this unit introduces you to our market economy, this career section will focus on the people who work in the economics profession. Broadly defined, *economics* is the social science that deals with how society allocates its scarce resources among its unlimited wants and needs.

Job Titles

Job titles commonly found in this career area include:

- Economist
- Marketing Research Analyst
- Financial Manager
- Operations Research Analyst
- Consultant
- Statistician
- Statistical Clerk
- Budget Analyst
- Economics Professor

Employment Outlook (through 2005)

- Job growth will be slow to average.
- Competition will be keen for most jobs.
- Teaching jobs will decline as college enrollments decline.
- Most new jobs will be in finan-

cial services, research, consulting, and government.

Education and Training

- Economists must have at least a bachelor's degree; most have master's degrees and many have doctorates.
- All jobs within this career area require at least a high school diploma for entry into the occupation.
- Special training in statistics, mathematics, and computer technology applications is common to all jobs.

Salary Levels (in recent years)

Salaries will vary widely, depending upon the educational background, experience of the worker, and place of employment. Average (median) salaries:

- Economists: entry level, $22,700; with advanced college degree, $65,000–$78,000
- Statisticians: with advanced college degree, $54,000
- Statistical clerks: $15,000
- Budget analysts: $39,700

Critical Thinking

1 Which job titles in this career area appeal to you most? Give some reasons for your choice.

2 What are some things you will have to do to achieve success in the career you selected?

Economics

Two Unit

Business and Government in Our Global Economy

70

If you walked down the streets of Taipei, Barcelona, Cairo, and Buenos Aires, you would likely see some "signs of home." Perhaps you would notice a Burger King, the golden arches of McDonald's, or the red-and-white logo of KFC. As you crossed streets in these cities, you might have to watch out for speeding American-made cars. As you passed young people on the sidewalks, you would recognize jackets emblazoned with the emblems of U.S. sports teams and jeans with the labels of U.S. designers.

What is taking place here? Why are consumers in these cities buying American-made products? The answer relates to global dependency. *Global dependency* exists when many items consumers need and want are created in other countries. People frequently need and want products from other countries.

Companies sell to consumers in other countries to expand business opportunities. However, U.S. companies that sell their products in other countries often learn the hard way about doing business abroad. For instance, after establishing operations in an Asian country, a U.S. doughnut company learned that the people of this country did not like cinnamon. But cinnamon was the main ingredient in the company's traditional doughnuts. So, the company reduced greatly the amount of cinnamon in the doughnuts sold there. Gradually the company increased the amount of cinnamon. Today, people in this country like the traditional doughnut.

Another example of learning the hard way involved a toothpaste manufacturer. The manufacturer advertised its toothpaste as leaving a "fresh" taste. However, the people in this country preferred what they considered a clean, medicinal taste.

Why do these differences in consumer preferences exist? The answer lies in the word culture. Culture is the sum of a country's way of life, and it influences buying decisions. Culture sets the boundaries of what can and cannot be done.

Some parts of culture are taught in homes, in schools, in religious institutions, and at work. Still other parts are learned through experiences. Not all cultural groups, however, share their experiences willingly with outsiders.

Understanding cultural differences is a challenge for all U.S. businesses. The United States trades freely with Canada and the United Kingdom in part because the business cultures are somewhat similar. These similarities allow business to be conducted in similar ways.

To a large extent the future success of U.S. businesses will depend on their ability to sell products in the international marketplace. Becoming aware of and adjusting to various cultural differences is the first step toward success in the global economy.

Critical Thinking

1 *What are some ways in which you are taught about our culture? How does our culture influence your buying decisions?*

2 *What are some examples of our global dependency on other countries?*

Cultural Differences and Business Opportunities

Chapter Five

Key Terms

extractor

manufacturer

marketer

channel of distribution

direct channel of distribution

indirect channel of distribution

retailer

wholesaler

service business

Business in Our Economy

Objectives

After studying this chapter and completing the end-of-chapter activities, you will be able to:

1 Give an example of the four basic kinds of businesses.

2 Describe seven kinds of activities performed by businesses.

3 Explain how jobs are created in our economy.

When you or your friends buy a pair of jeans, you very likely do not think much about the chain of businesses involved in making the jeans and getting them to the stores where you bought them. Most people don't. But there is an interesting sequence of events that occurs between the creation of your pair of jeans and your purchase of them.

First, the cotton is planted and harvested; then it is made into cloth and dyed different colors. The jeans are designed, made up in various sizes, labeled, boxed, and then stored until they are sold and transported to the store from which you and your friends buy them.

Several businesses are involved in this process. These businesses are different in many ways but are alike in that they help to put a product or service that you want on the market. That is what business is all about. There are more than 20 million business firms in the United States. While there are some differences among them, they all supply or help to supply goods and services to satisfy your wants and needs. Learning about them will help you understand what business does.

FOUR KINDS OF BUSINESSES

You and your family buy from many kinds of businesses. You buy food from a supermarket, shoes from a shoe store, furnace repairs from a plumbing and heating company, financial services from a bank, a car from an auto dealer, and electricity from a utilities company. In all of these cases, you are dealing with businesses that sell products and services to you and to other consumers.

Extractors

A business that grows products or takes raw materials from nature is called an **extractor.** The farmer who grows and sells cotton for your jeans is an extractor. Silver and coal miners are also extractors, as are those who dig copper in Montana, fish for salmon in Alaska, pump oil in Louisiana, grow fruit in California, and run lumber mills in Washington. Sometimes the extractor's products are ready to be sold just as they come from the earth or the sea, like the clams in New England, potatoes from Idaho, or pecans from Georgia. However, most food products and raw materials need some processing or change in form before the consumer can use them.

Manufacturers

A **manufacturer** takes the extractor's products or raw materials and changes them into a form that consumers can use. The manufacturer might make a product such as a snowmobile or process a product

The United States in a recent year had over 2 million farms and more than 33,000 mining operations.

Illus. 5-1

Cotton is an example of a raw material that needs some processing before it is useful to consumers.

such as frozen and packaged vegetables. Other manufacturers may construct sections of a building that, when put together, become a house for people to live in. Some manufacturers are only a part of the total activity of producing goods from the extractor's products.

Think about those jeans again. The entire process might require several steps, which may be performed in several different locations, before the jeans are ready for you to purchase. For example, a textile mill in North Carolina takes cotton grown on an Alabama farm, spins it into yarn, and makes the yarn into cloth. A plant in

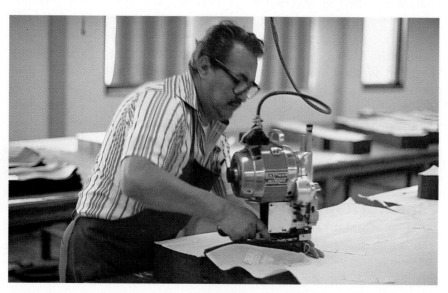

Illus. 5-2

A manufacturer (as in this jeans factory) changes raw materials into a product that consumers can use.

New England then dyes or prints the cloth, and a clothing manufacturer in New York buys the cloth and makes it into jeans. Together, extractors and manufacturers are industries that change the form of resources from their natural states into products for consumers.

Marketers

Our skilled labor force and our advanced technology enable producers to make thousands of different products at a reasonable cost. However, if these products are not available where and when you and other consumers want to buy them, their value diminishes.

If all of the goods you use had to be bought directly from their producers, it would be a problem. You would have to fly to Central or South America to get a banana. You might have to drive to Minnnesota or Michigan to buy your favorite cereal. Buying products in that way would be inefficient and expensive.

The services of many businesses are often needed before goods actually reach consumers. A business that is involved with moving goods from producers to consumers is called a **marketer.** The activities of marketers are called *marketing*.

Marketing includes more than just transporting and selling products. Marketers also help to identify, develop, and test new products to see whether consumers will like them and buy them. They package goods to protect products and to present them in attractive and convenient sizes. They also store the goods until they are needed by other marketers or consumers. They even design store windows and arrange displays in supermarkets to attract your attention. All of these marketing activities add value to products by bringing them to where the consumer is, at a time they are wanted, in the assortment wanted, and at prices the consumer is willing to pay.

Marketing bridges the gap between producers and consumers. Of course, you can buy certain products directly from some producers. For example, you may buy eggs and vegetables directly from a farmer or a handmade basket from a craftsperson. However, most products will be handled by several marketers before they reach the place where you buy them. The path that a product travels from producer to consumer is called the **channel of distribution.**

Illus. 5-3
Marketers arrange eye-catching displays to attract our attention.

The channel that brings products to the consumer directly from the producer is called the **direct channel of distribution.** Eggs and vegetables sold directly from a farm are examples of that channel in operation. Most consumer goods will travel through an **indirect channel of distribution,** a channel involving at least one and sometimes several middle firms before goods reach the consumer. Figure 5-1 shows how these two kinds of channels of distribution function.

Many farmers sell their vegetables to your local grocery store, a retailer, from which you buy them. A **retailer** is a business firm that sells products directly to the consumer. Farmers, however, may sell their entire crop of vegetables to a wholesaler, a large distribution firm. A **wholesaler** is a business firm that buys products in large quantities from producers, sorts and unitizes them, and then sells them in large quantities to retailers. The retailer in turn sells the products in smaller quantities to you. A product may travel through several middle firms in the process.

Service Businesses

A business firm that does things for you instead of making or marketing products is called a **service business.** Service businesses over the past several years are the fastest growing part of our business world. The number of people employed full time in service industries has reached over 13 million. By the year 2005, it is expected that four out of five jobs will be in businesses that provide services to others.

Some service businesses serve individual consumers, some serve other businesses, and some serve both. Today you can find service businesses to move you from New Jersey to Arizona, fly you to Singapore, style your hair, wash your car, figure your income tax, board your pet, or provide almost any service you need or do not want to perform yourself. Businesses also need services. A service business might help a company export its product to the Czech Republic for the first time, install a new computer system, or train a group of employees on how to access and use databases.

An increasing number of people who are retired, or who have leisure time and money to spend, look for businesses to provide opportunities for recreation, travel, and the like. Single parents and

Figure 5-1
Direct and indirect channels of distribution bring goods to consumers.

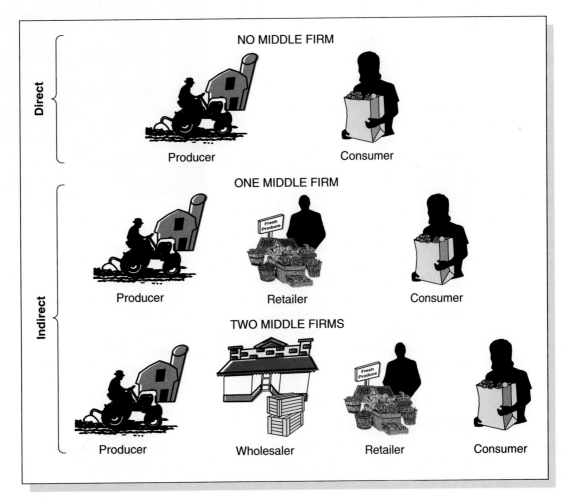

parents who both work have created a need for extensive child care services. Working parents tend to pay someone to perform many services that they once did for themselves. These are just two examples of service businesses that have increased greatly in size in recent years.

BUSINESS ACTIVITIES

Businesses may be large or small, simple or complex. A business might operate in just one community while another has worldwide operations. Although individual businesses differ in organization and operation, most perform seven basic activities. Let's examine these activities.

Generating Ideas

Someone must first think about a new product, a service, or an improved process or piece of equipment that can be put on the market. A business begins with someone's idea for a good or a service that will meet consumers' needs and wants. Examples include jogging shoes, lawn care businesses, and automatic load lifters for pickup trucks.

Illus. 5-4
Many businesses concentrate on providing services to other businesses.

Once a business is established to sell a good or service, it must continue to develop ideas in order to survive. In our market economy, businesses compete with other firms that sell the same or similar products. To compete successfully, they must look for new or improved products and services. Many firms have research and development personnel who work full time creating, researching, and developing ideas that might result in new products and services.

Raising Capital

As you learned in Chapter 1, businesses need capital resources to operate. Start-up money is critical and must be found to start the business. This may come from the owner's personal funds, from loans from banks or other financial institutions, or from others who wish to invest in the business. You will learn how one business obtained start-up money in Chapter 6.

Established businesses must continue to raise capital throughout the life of the firm. Companies may need to borrow money to buy equipment, to redesign a plant, build a new office building, or to buy another business. Most capital is obtained through loans from financial institutions, such as banks, or from people who wish to invest in the business.

Jim Reid, deep-sea diver turned "ball bandit," built a business retrieving golf balls from golf course water holes and restoring the balls for resale; in 1992 he sold his business for $5.1 million. He still has yet to play one round of golf.

Buying Goods and Services

Businesses buy goods and services both for resale and for their own use. The owner of a men's clothing store, for instance, must buy slacks, jackets, suits, coats, and other items to sell. The store owner also needs sales tickets, a cash register, display cases, and other supplies. Services offered by other businesses, such as advertising space in a newspaper or a window cleaner to wash the display windows, will be needed.

In addition, businesses that manufacture products need to buy raw materials to produce their products. Buying raw materials, such as wheat, oil, plastic, steel, or chemicals, is an important activity in operating some businesses.

The Mayo Clinic, in Scotsdale, Arizona, purchased $99 million worth of supplies and services from local merchants over an eight-year period; in that same period of time, patients and visitors spent over $150 million in the Scotsdale area.

Using Human Resources

Businesses cannot operate without people. Except for the one-person business, all firms need to have a system for carrying out activities that attract, employ, and develop human resources. These include recruiting, or finding, workers; interviewing and testing applicants; selecting employees; training and developing both new and experienced employees; and appraising job performances. You will learn more about this activity in Chapter 41.

Human resources management requires a knowledge of equal opportunity laws, health and safety regulations, and employee rights relating to issues such as promotions, transfers, layoffs, and firings. These activities are often carried out by a human resources, or personnel, department.

NET FACTS

A browser is a software program that gives access to most Internet services. A browser is required to connect to the multimedia documents on the World Wide Web.

Marketing Goods and Services

As you have learned earlier, marketing involves a variety of activities, all directed toward providing the kind of product or service desired by consumers. Many marketing activities occur before a product is produced and ready for distribution and sale. Marketing today includes product service planning. Marketers assist in the design and development of products and services that will meet the needs of prospective customers.

You might think of marketing and production as two sides of a coin. Businesses must produce and sell a needed product or service if they expect to succeed in the marketplace. Businesses use marketing to increase their effectiveness and the profits they make. Marketing is explained in detail in Chapter 42.

Producing Goods and Services

The heart of a successful business is the production of quality products and services. The good or service must be produced at the scheduled time, in the appropriate quantity and quality, and at competitive cost in order for the firm to stay in business. Assembling the people, raw materials, processes, and equipment to accomplish this task is essential to all businesses. Production also is explained in detail in Chapter 42.

Keeping Records

All businesses must have some kind of a record keeping system. Most of these systems today utilize computer technology. Many records must be completed and compiled in the report to enable the owner or manager to know how the business is doing. Business managers need to know how much they have sold, how much of what they sold was returned by customers, and how much they owe to others. They need to know the amount they are spending for building repairs, rent, salaries, and other expenses. These records are important for

1. determining whether a business is making or losing money,

2. providing information for management decisions, and

3. supplying data for a variety of government reports, including tax forms.

THE IMPACT OF NEW BUSINESSES ON A COMMUNITY

When a new business opens, it begins paying wages to its employees. This is money that has not been in the community before. Workers spend this money for goods and services. The money is then spent again by the businesses from which those goods and services were bought. For example, part of each worker's income is spent for food. The grocery store manager uses part of this money for products to sell in his or her store. The manager also pays part of it to employees, who in turn spend their money somewhere else for other goods and services. If new people come to the community to work, more houses will probably be needed. Local builders will hire more workers and buy more materials. As each dollar is spent, each business is likely to buy more goods and hire more people to meet its customers' demands. This endless spending chain starts with businesses hiring employees and paying wages.

Global Perspective

Joint Ventures

Sometimes a business firm wants to do business in an international market. One type of international partnership is the joint venture. This arrangement is especially popular when companies want to explore new markets while sharing the risk. Cooperation is the critical ingredient for success.

A *joint venture* is a special type of partnership. Two or more companies form an alliance to perform various business activities. Each business has a strength that is needed by the other. One company may provide most of the financing, another the channel of distribution, and another the production facilities.

Joint ventures can be created for just about any kind of business project. There are many examples of successful international joint ventures, especially in the automobile industry. The joint venture of Toyota and General Motors—called New United Motor Manufacturing, Inc.—is often cited as a success story. However, only about one-third of joint ventures meet their specific goals. A successful joint venture must be well managed, and good communication among the partners is a necessity.

Critical Thinking

1 What are some necessary ingredients of a joint venture?

2 If a U.S. firm were interested in forming a joint venture, what advice would you give to help this firm succeed?

New businesses also buy products and services, such as electricity, office furniture and supplies, equipment, and tools. Some of these items will be bought from local businesses. The additional sales provide local businesses with more income; in turn, these businesses may hire more employees to meet the demands of increased business.

Businesses also tend to attract other businesses. When one business settles in a community, other businesses often come to supply it. For example, small businesses may spring up to supply a large factory with such things as small parts, office supplies, cleaning services, and advertising services. Each of these smaller businesses hires people and buys goods and services. Thus, more jobs and more income are created in the community. You will learn more about how businesses benefit and contribute to a community in Chapter 7.

Key Ideas

1 Four basic kinds of businesses are extractors, manufacturers, marketers, and service businesses.

2 Businesses must perform the following activities: generating new ideas, raising capital, buying goods and services, using human resources, producing goods and services, marketing goods and services, and keeping records.

3 New jobs are created when new businesses locate within a community.

End of Chapter Activities

Increasing Your Business Vocabulary

The following terms should become part of your business vocabulary. For each numbered item, find the term that has the same meaning.

channel of distribution

direct channel of distribution

extractor

indirect channel of distribution

marketer

manufacturer

retailer

service business

wholesaler

1 A business involved with moving goods from producers to consumers.

2 The path that a product travels from producer to consumer.

3 The process through which goods are bought by the consumer directly from the producer.

4 A business that takes an extractor's products or raw materials and changes them into a form that consumers can use.

5 The process through which goods move through one or more middle firms between the producer and the consumer.

6 A business firm that sells directly to the consumer.

7 A business that grows products or takes raw materials from nature.

8 A business that does things for you instead of making or marketing products.

9 A middle firm that assists with distribution activities between businesses.

Reviewing Your Reading

1 Give an example of the four basic types of businesses.

2 What is meant by the statement that some extractors' products are ready to be sold to the consumer in their natural states?

3 Name several marketing activities other than transporting and selling goods.

4 What is the difference between a direct and an indirect channel of distribution?

5 To whom do wholesalers and retailers sell their products?

6 Cite seven activities that are performed by most businesses.

7 Explain ways in which new businesses benefit a community.

Using Your Business Knowledge

1 List three marketing activities that might be involved in getting a home computer from the manufacturer to the retail store that sells it.

2 Name two products that you might buy through a direct marketing channel.

3 Kim Sun operates the Sea Isle Treasures shop in the waterfront marketplace of her city. She sells fresh flower arrangements and leis as well as shell jewelry and ornaments. Give two examples of the following:

a. Goods which she would buy for resale.

b. Goods she would buy for use in her store.

c. Services she might offer to her customers.

d. Services she might buy from other businesses.

4 The Chamber of Commerce and the Economic Development Council of Central City have persuaded a fiberglass processing plant to open in the city's industrial park. The company expects to employ 200 people there. Name at least five ways in which the city would probably benefit from the new business.

Calculating Business Problems

1 The Juan Iglasias Company is considering building a cannery in Santa Rosa. The company's accountants estimate the monthly income and expenses for the new plant as shown in this table.

a. What is the total amount of the cannery's monthly expenses, including taxes?

b. What will be the cannery's profit after taxes if the estimates are accurate? (Calculate after-tax profit by subtracting the total estimated expenses and taxes from estimated income.)

Income from sales	$200,000
Expenses:	
Salaries	$100,000
Raw materials purchased	60,000
Rent on equipment	6,500
Miscellaneous expenses	5,000
Taxes	8,400

c. What is the percent of after-tax profit based on income from sales?

2 The fish catch and the value of the catch along the Atlantic coast for two years are shown in this table.

Areas	Catch (In Millions of Pounds)		Value (In Millions of Dollars)	
	Year One	Year Two	Year One	Year Two
New England	788	563	$327	$449
Mid-Atlantic	244	156	97	114
Chesapeake Bay	718	617	130	131
South Atlantic	473	249	148	155

a. What was the total weight of the catch for all the Atlantic areas, expressed in full (including the zeros) for Year One and Year Two?

b. Did the fish catch for any of the areas increase in Year Two?

c. What was the dollar value of the catch in Year One and Year Two?

d. Did the dollar value of the catch increase in any area in Year Two?

---

3 A new business, Katerina Enterprises, moved into Capital City. In 1997, the business paid $18,500 in property taxes. In that same year it paid a 5 percent tax on its year-end merchandise inventory of $26,200. Three new businesses started up to serve Katerina Enterprises and its employees. Those new businesses paid the following in property taxes in 1997: $2,300, $5,300, and $1,900 respectively.

a. How much did the community receive in 1997 from the taxes paid by Katerina Enterprises?

b. How much did the community receive in 1997 in property taxes from the three start-up companies?

c. What is the total community benefit, in terms of taxes paid in 1997, as a result of Katerina Enterprises locating in Capital City?

Applying Technology

Using the *Introduction to Business* template and your spreadsheet program software, select problem CH05. After the problem appears on your screen, complete the following activities. Then, after you have completed each step, display or print the completed spreadsheet for each activity. If you do not have a printer available, answer the questions before you leave the computer.

1 Make two copies of the spreadsheet so that you have a total of three income statements. Do not copy the table entitled Net Income Comparisons. On the first income statement, enter a quantity of 1,000 and a price of $10. Answer the following questions.

   a. What is the amount of gross profit on sales?

   b. What is the amount of net income?

2 On the second income statement, enter a quantity of 2,000 and a price of $10. In the table entitled Net Income Comparisons, enter formulas to display the net income from the second income statement and to calculate the percentage of increase in net income from the first income statement to the second. Answer the following questions.

   a. What is the amount of net income on the second income statement?

   b. What is the percentage of increase in net income from the first income statement to the second?

3 On the third income statement, enter a quantity of 1,000 and a price of $25. In the table entitled Net Income Comparisons, enter formulas to display the net income from the third income statement and to calculate the percentage of increase in net income from the first income statement to the third. Answer the following questions.

   a. What is the amount of gross profit on sales on the third income statement?

   b. What is the percentage of increase in net income from the first income statement to the third?

Making Decisions

Sonja Barthalomew started a lawn mowing service. However, she could not charge as much as she needed to make the profit she desired. Her competitors only charged $15 per lawn while she charged $20. But she did a superior job cutting lawns. Still, potential customers did not want to pay the extra $5.

A friend, Eduardo Guadalupe, suggested that they work together. He was good at trimming shrubs and had ideas for improving landscapes with flowers and lawn ornaments. They would offer a unique service when they combined their businesses. They could charge an amount that would result in a good profit for both of them. They would seek out homes in neighborhoods with above-average income levels.

1 What will be special about the services that Sonja and Eduardo can offer together? What additional services might they include?

2 Why would above-average income levels be targeted?

Chapter Six

Business Structures

Key Terms

sole proprietorship

partnership

corporation

certificate of incorporation

shareholders

board of directors

dividend

franchise

franchisee

franchisor

cooperative

municipal corporation

Objectives

After studying this chapter and completing the end-of-chapter activities, you will be able to:

1 Explain how ownership differs among sole proprietorships, partnerships, and corporations.

2 State the advantages and disadvantages of the three major types of business ownership.

3 Name the five functions of managers.

4 Give examples of three specialized forms of business organizations.

When your club decides to undertake a major project, such as sponsoring a big weekend car wash, what is the first thing that must be done? You must get organized! Questions must be answered: Where will the car wash be held? What are the best hours for a car wash? What supplies will be needed and who will get them? How much should be charged?

Committees may be formed, and someone may be appointed as the project chairperson. One committee might look into locations for the car wash, another might list and get supplies needed, and another might decide how much to charge and also keep the financial records. And, of course, people will be needed to do the car washing—club members (the human resources) must be willing to work. Organization is necessary if the car wash project is to be successful and earn a profit for the club.

In a similar way, a business also must organize to produce goods and services for the consumer. Many questions must be answered in the organizing process. Who will make the decisions? Who will buy the goods to sell? Who will keep the records of what is bought and sold? Who will get the profits? If there is a loss, who must bear it? How a business is structured determines these decisions.

TYPES OF BUSINESS OWNERSHIP

There are three major types of business ownership. They are the sole proprietorship, the partnership, and the corporation. Later in this chapter you will learn about other types of business ownership, including franchises, cooperatives, and non-profit corporations.

A **sole proprietorship** is a business owned by one person. Most are small firms such as jewelry stores, restaurants, gas stations, and hair-styling salons. As Figure 6-1 points out, more than two-thirds of U.S. businesses are operated as sole proprietorships. The sole proprietor has complete responsibility for all business decisions. In most cases, he or she also works in the firm.

A **partnership** is a business owned and managed by a small group, often not more than two or three people, who become partners. By written agreement, these partners share the profits or losses and have unlimited liability for the debts of their business.

A **corporation** is a business owned by a number of people and operated under written permission from the state in which it is located. The written permission is called a **certificate of incorporation.** The corporation acts as a single individual on behalf of its owners. By buying shares of stock, people become owners of corporations. They are then known as **shareholders,** also called stockholders. A corporation may have very few owners, but most corporations have many owners. Thus, the corporation is a *legal entity* with an existence and life separate from its owners. Large corporations, such as IBM, Texaco,

Many well-known accounting and law firms are organized as partnerships.

Figure 6-1

There are three major types of businesses in our economy.

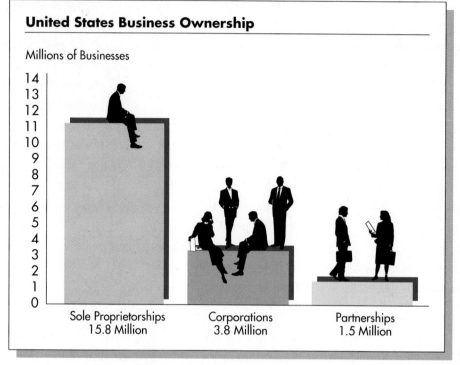

United States Business Ownership

Millions of Businesses

| Sole Proprietorships 15.8 Million | Corporations 3.8 Million | Partnerships 1.5 Million |

Source: Statistical Abstract of the United States, 1994, p. 539.

and General Motors, may have millions of owners. Even if you own just one share of a company, you are still one of its owners. Most mining, manufacturing, and transporting of goods are performed by corporations. In addition, many of our consumer goods are supplied by supermarkets, department stores, and other businesses organized as corporations.

The size and the nature of a business are key factors in choosing the best type of ownership for it. To help you understand each type of ownership, the next few pages tell a story of how a young person started a business and worked to make it grow.

GETTING STARTED IN BUSINESS

There are a number of ways of getting started in business. Let's consider the case of Julie Alcess. While in high school, Julie was a star player on her basketball team. She also worked part time at a number of different jobs after school and during summers. She thought about retailing as a career and took business courses in school. During her senior year, she became acquainted with the manager of the sporting goods store that supplied her school with equipment. The manager offered Julie a part-time sales job in his store.

After graduation, she accepted a full-time job in the store and continued to learn about small business operation. She took college night classes in business administration. Her selling techniques were excellent, and she quite often was put in charge of the store when the manager was gone for the day.

Julie earned a good salary and was able to save money as a sales clerk, but she dreamed about owning her own sporting goods store one day. She liked the idea of being her own boss.

Julie began planning for her own business. She located space that she liked in a new mall that was opening. A small store would get her started. She talked over her plans with her boss, and he encouraged her to pursue her dream.

Illus. 6-1
Sole proprietorships make up over two-thirds of U.S. businesses.

The easiest way to become a business owner is to buy a share of stock in a corporation.

She needed more money than she had in her savings account. Because she had a good work record and experience in the sporting goods business, the local bank gave her a start-up loan. She began by ordering merchandise, supplies, and equipment. Then she signed a one-year lease and paid the first month's rent. She resigned her job and opened Julie's Sports-4-All.

Julie was excited the day she greeted her first customers. She soon learned, though, that owning her own business required long hours and much decision making. She needed help. A good friend and schoolmate, Andy Davidson, was good in accounting and business law. In fact, he was studying to be an attorney. He agreed to help Julie keep the needed records and file the forms the government required.

Julie liked the feeling she got from running her own business. She was the sole owner of the business shown in Figure 6-2. All the profits—or losses—were hers. And Julie's new business responsibilities gave special meaning to functions of management learned about in her business courses.

A recent survey revealed that 8 out of 10 people had a "secret desire" to start a business of their own.

Figure 6-2
Julie is the sole proprietor of Sports-4-All.

MANAGING A SUCCESSFUL BUSINESS

Managers are the employees who are responsible for coordinating resources within a business—human, capital, and natural. Management activities are focused in five key areas: planning, organizing, staffing, leading, and controlling. In a small business such as Julie's, the owner usually performs these activities.

Planning

Julie remembered that this function included thinking, gathering and analyzing information, and then making decisions about all phases of the business. Goals must be set for the business and strategies devised for achieving them. Julie did a great deal of planning at the beginning. Later, however, she felt that she was spending too much time on day-to-day operations and did not have enough time for planning. She recalled that her instructor had warned about this pitfall in operating a small business.

Organizing

This function is the process of determining what work has to be done and who is to do each job. Jobs are assigned to workers and authority is given to certain people to see that the jobs are done. For example, Julie directs the work of two part-time sales clerks: Jason and Brianna. These workers report directly to her. The organizing process usually results in a diagram, called an *organization chart*, that shows work relationships. Although Julie's business is too small to require one, she sketched one out as shown in Figure 6-3. The chart shows that Julie has the authority to direct the work of her part-time employees. In turn,

illingness to take risk is an essential part of business ownership.

they are responsible to Julie to complete the work she assigns.

Staffing

Staffing includes all of the activities involved in finding, selecting, hiring, training, appraising, and rewarding the business's employees. Julie was able to perform these personnel activities for her two part-time workers.

Julie Alcess
Owner/Manager
Julie's Sports-4-All

Brianna Donavon
Sales Clerk

Jason Smythe
Sales Clerk

Figure 6-3
Julie's organization chart for her sole proprietorship.

Leading

The work of people must be directed so that their tasks will be performed correctly and on time. Influencing people to act according to company plans and procedures can be a difficult task. Effective leaders inspire workers to willingly perform their jobs and accept their share of responsibility for accomplishing the goals of the business. Leading requires good human relations and communications skills. Julie considers herself an effective leader.

Controlling

Owners must determine to what extent the business is accomplishing the goals it set out to reach in the planning stage. Controlling means comparing what actually happens with what was planned. If Julie had planned a 5 percent increase in sales for a three-month period, she would check the actual increase regularly to see whether she was moving toward her goal as planned. If, at the end of the second month she had already achieved a 4 percent increase, she could feel that her strategies were working well. If the increase were only 1 percent, she might consider a new strategy.

Controlling also means using the standards set up in the planning stage. For instance, if a business set a standard of production for workers to handle 12 customer inquiry calls per hour, the controlling activity would be to count the actual number of calls handled per hour for each employee. If the quality standard for each call was that the customer's questions would be answered and follow-up materials sent out, the controlling function would be to check each completed call and the follow-through. As you can see, controlling is directly related to planning.

The abbreviation "Inc." is used in our country to designate a corporation. In England and Canada, "Ltd.," and in Venezuela and Mexico, "S.A.," are used.

Julie wondered how she could handle all the management activities as her business grew. She also needed the help of someone who knew more about finance and law than she did. Julie believed that Andy Davidson would fit in well. He was willing to invest in the business, and he could take over accounting, personnel administration, and preparation of records and reports. They would make a good team. Bringing in a partner, she thought, would be a solution.

Julie talked with Andy about her idea of opening a larger store, adding more merchandise, and doing more promotions. She offered a partnership deal to Andy, and he accepted.

A Partnership Is Formed

Andy drew up a written agreement that provided the details of how their partnership would operate. It was called the *articles of partnership.* Included in the articles of partnership were the essential things they agreed upon:

1. The name of the new business will be Sports Abundant.

2. Julie Alcess will invest $80,000 in cash and property. Andy Davidson will invest $40,000 in cash.

3. Each partner will draw a salary of $2,000 a month.

4. Profits and losses after salaries are paid will be shared in proportion to each partner's investment: two-thirds to Julie Alcess and one-third to Andy Davidson.

5. Julie Alcess will have the main responsibility for sales, selection and purchase of merchandise, and customer and community relations. Andy Davidson will handle financial records, payroll, store maintenance, government reports, and other details of operating the business.

6. In the event of the death or the necessary withdrawal of one partner, the remaining partner will have the right to purchase the departing partner's share of the business.

Before they signed the articles of partnership, they discussed some of the legal responsibilities of becoming partners. For example, each partner could be held personally responsible for all of the debts of the business. This would even include debts incurred by the other partner without the first partner's consent. Each partner was also bound by the business agreements that the other partner made. To avoid problems, Julie and Andy agreed to discuss all

NET FACTS

Users of the Internet include schools, government agencies, businesses, libraries, colleges and universities, military bases, and more. In addition, every year more and more people can access the Internet from their homes.

important business matters, such as hiring people or signing a contract, before taking action.

The partnership, as shown in Figure 6-4, was very successful. At the end of the first year, there was a profit of $20,000 after the business expenses and the partners' salaries had been paid. Since they had agreed to share the profits in proportion to their investments in the business, Julie received two-thirds, or $13,333, and Andy received one-third, or $6,667.

A Corporation Is Created

Sports Abundant continued to grow. Julie and Andy were successful business partners. They saw a potential for a larger operation, one that would include large items such as boats and school gymnasium equipment. They wanted to enlarge their operation and open a branch in a major shopping mall being built in one of the suburbs. They spent much time coming up with new ideas for improving their business, an activity you read about in Chapter 5. To do these things, they needed more money. They thought about adding more partners but decided against it. They reasoned that they did not need partners to help them manage the business since they could hire qualified assistants and managers. Also, there would be personal risks in being responsible for the actions of other partners.

A corporation can sue or be sued; our courts consider a corporation to be a legal entity.

Andy suggested that they form a corporation. They would then not be personally responsible for the debts of the business. In case of a business failure, each member of the corporation could lose only the amount he or she had invested. They dissolved the partnership and drew up a plan for a new corporation, J & A Sports and Recreation, Incorporated. The corporation was to represent a

Figure 6-4
Sports Abundant was a successful partnership.

total investment of $240,000. Their financial records showed that the partnership was worth $180,000; therefore, they needed to raise another $60,000. Julie and Andy decided to divide the $240,000 into 24,000 shares, each with a value of $10. Based on the partnership agreement and the corporation plans, they divided the 24,000 shares this way:

1. Julie received 12,000 shares worth $120,000,
2. Andy received 6,000 shares worth $60,000, and
3. they offered for sale 6,000 shares valued at $60,000.

Information about the division of shares of stock and other information about the corporation was included in an application that was submitted to the state government. The application requested permission to operate as a corporation. After approving the application, the state issued a certificate of incorporation authorizing the formation of J & A Sports and Recreation, Inc.

Julie and Andy now were part owners of a corporation. They had received 18,000 shares of stock in proportion to their original investment in the former partnership. The 6,000 shares offered for sale were bought by 30 people who had confidence in the new corporation. The corporation now had a total of 32 individual shareholders, or owners. The owners received stock certificates like the one shown in Figure 6-5 as evidence of their part ownership of the corporation.

Julie and Andy, who were the controlling shareowners, called a meeting of the shareholders to elect officers, to make plans for operating a branch store, and to conduct other business. Each shareholder had one vote for each share of stock that she or he owned. Since Julie and Andy together owned 18,000 shares, they had enough votes to control the operation of the business.

At the meeting, seven people, including Julie and Andy, were elected as directors of the corporation. These seven people made up the board of directors. A **board of directors** is a group with responsibility to guide the operations of a corporation. The board's first act was to elect the executive officers of the corporation. The directors elected Julie Alcess as president, Jo Rabinski as vice president, Sue Chung as secretary, and Tom Lowe as treasurer. Andy decided to continue his law studies in pursuit of a career as a corporate attorney. He would eventually represent the new firm when legal matters arose. As full-time employees, Julie and the other officers receive regular salaries

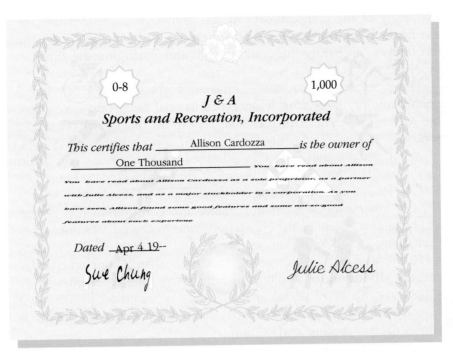

0-8   1,000

J & A
Sports and Recreation, Incorporated

This certifies that _____Allison Cardozza_____ is the owner of
__One Thousand__

You have read about Allison Cardozza as a sole proprietor, as a partner with Julie Alcess, and as a major stockholder in a corporation. As you have seen, Allison found some good features and some not-so-good features about each experience.

Dated _Apr 4 19--_

Sue Chung   *Julie Alcess*

Figure 6-5
A stock certificate shows ownership in a corporation. Allison Cardozza owns 1,000 shares of J & A Sports and Recreation, Inc.

for managing the business. An organization chart for J & A Sports and Recreation, Inc., might look like Figure 6-6.

The chart shows that the board of directors oversees the operations of the corporation. The directors are in the position of highest authority and will make policy decisions. When the board elected three of its members to hold corporate offices, it assigned authority and responsibility for the daily operation of the business to those officers.

The president, Julie Alcess, has the highest authority and is responsible to the board for her decisions. The other officers have specific functions. Sue Chung, the corporate secretary, has responsibility for managing the office function. She supervises office personnel employed to carry out the communication and clerical activities of the firm. As corporate secretary, she will also sign legal documents and reports of actions taken by the board of directors. The elected office of corporate secretary is an important executive position.

Jo Rabinski, vice president, is responsible for all of the sales and

Figure 6-6
J & A Sports and Recreation, Inc., has an expanded organization chart.

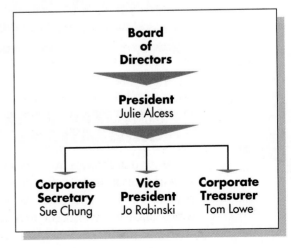

marketing of the company's products. Tom Lowe, the treasurer, is the financial officer of the business. His function includes preparing the budget, preparing financial reports, and managing the firm's investments.

The vice president, treasurer, and secretary have separate but equal authority over their assigned functions. Each one is responsible to the president. The president reports to the board of directors.

At the end of the year, after all taxes were paid, the corporation had a profit of $31,600. The board of directors voted to keep $10,000 of business profit for expansion and to divide the other $21,600 among the shareholders. Since the corporation had issued 24,000 shares, each of the 32 shareholders received 90 cents for each share of stock that he or she owned ($21,600.00 ÷ 24,000.00 = $0.90). The part of the profits that each shareholder receives is called a **dividend.** In addition to her salary, Julie received $10,800.00 ($0.90 × 12,000 shares). Andy received $5,400.00 ($0.90 × 6,000 shares) that helped to pay his college expenses. Figure 6-7 shows the prospering corporation.

Figure 6-7
Ownership of a corporation can change without affecting the organization and life of the business.

SPECIALIZED FORMS OF BUSINESS ORGANIZATIONS

As you now can see, choosing the right form of business ownership is central to a firm's success. And the first choice may not always be the right one. As shown in Figure 6-8, there are advantages and disadvantages to each of the major forms of business ownership.

Figure 6-8
Each form of business ownership has some advantages and disadvantages.

Type of Ownership	Advantages	Disadvantages
Sole Proprietorship	Easy to start business	Capital is limited to what the owner can supply or borrow
	Owner makes all the decisions and is own boss	Owner is liable (responsible) for all debts, even losing personal property if business fails
	Owner receives all profits	Long hours and hard work often necessary
		Life of the business depends upon owner; it ends if owner quits or dies
Partnership	Fairly easy to start the business	Each partner liable for business debts made by all partners, even to losing personal property if business fails
	More sources of capital available	Each partner can make decisions; more than one boss
	More business skills available	Partnership ends if a partner quits or dies
		Each partner shares the profit
Corporation	More sources of capital available	Difficult to start the corporation
	Specialized managerial skills available	Owners do not have control of decisions made each day, unless they are officers of the company
	Owners liable up to the amount of their investments	Business activities of the corporation limited to those stated in the certificate of incorporation
	Ownership can be easily transferred through sale of stock; business not affected by change of ownership	

In addition to the standard types of business ownership, there are some specialized forms of business organization with which you should be familiar. Each of these specialized types of business organizations plays an important role in our economy.

Franchises

If you have stayed in a national motel chain, eaten in a fast-food restaurant, or purchased a car from a dealership, you very likely bought services and goods from a franchised business. A **franchise** is a written contract granting permission to sell someone else's product or service in a prescribed manner, over a certain period of time, and in a specified territory. Franchises can be operated as a proprietorship, partnership, or corporation.

In a recent year, there were 499,000 franchised businesses. More than 81 percent were owned by one person or a group of people who received the franchise from a parent company to sell its products or services. This person or group is called the **franchisee.** Ownership of the remaining 19 percent was retained by the parent company granting the franchise, the **franchisor.**

The franchise agreement states the duties and rights of both parties. The franchisee agrees to run the business in a certain way. The name of the business, the products or services offered, the design and color of the building, the price of the product or service, and the uniforms of employees are determined by the franchisor. This standardizing of the franchised business means that customers can recognize a business and know what to expect when they buy a product or service from any one of them. You know approximately what kind of hamburger you will get when you buy at the "golden arches," whether you are in Miami, Kansas City, or Tokyo.

A franchise is a relatively easy business to start. The franchisor agrees to help the franchisee get started. National

Illus. 6-2

Most auto dealerships are part of a franchise system.

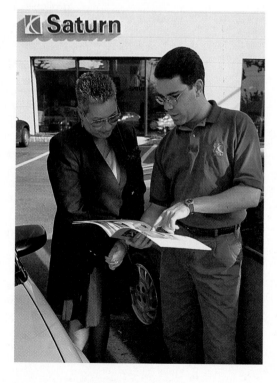

advertising of the product or service by the parent company is one of the advantages of a franchise. For its service, the franchisor collects a percentage of sales or an agreed-upon fee from the franchisee each year. Franchises usually require a large investment of capital to start. Not all franchises succeed. Some fail because the business is not competitive or because it is not in a good location. Nevertheless, franchises are a popular way of doing business.

Cooperatives

Sometimes people join together to operate a business known as a cooperative. A **cooperative** is owned by the members it serves and is managed in their interest. There are two main types of cooperatives. One type is a consumers' cooperative, an organization of consumers who buy goods and services more cheaply together

Environmental *Perspective*

Environmental Marketing Consultant

The public is concerned about our environment. So is corporate America. We are becoming increasingly aware that the earth's resources are not limitless. In fact, it is possible for us to run out of natural resources, or to pollute our water and air so badly that it will affect the way we live.

Corporations spend billions of dollars every year on protecting and preserving our environment. *Ecology*—the study of the relationships between living things and their environment—is a legal as well as societal issue of concern among today's managers and business owners. Many businesses are finding creative ways to make a profit without damaging the environment.

Many corporations now use the services of environmental marketing consultants in response to society's concerns about the environment. Clients range from large manufacturers to retail chains. These consultants help corporations achieve goals for the protection of the environment. They also help business firms in marketing and producing goods and services that are ecologically sound.

The environmental marketing consultant will be a key player in the efforts of businesses to protect and preserve our environment for many years in the future. Many companies find that strategies developed by a special consultant to conserve the environment help sell their products.

Critical Thinking

1 *What are some reasons why leading U.S. corporations are concerned about environmental problems?*

2 *Do you think that the role of the environmental marketing consultant will continue to be an important one?*

than each person could individually. Another is a producers' cooperative, usually a farmers' organization that markets products such as fruit, vegetables, milk, and grains. A producers' cooperative lets farmers work together for greater bargaining power in selling their products. They are often created by large numbers of small producers that want to be more competitive in the marketplace.

A cooperative is much like a regular corporation. Its formation must be approved by the state. It may sell one or more shares of stock to each of its members. A board of directors may be chosen by the members to guide the cooperative. However, a cooperative differs from a corporation in the way that it is controlled. In a regular corporation, a person usually has one vote for each share she or he owns. A cooperative may be controlled in two ways: each owner-member may have one vote, or each member's vote may be based on the amount of service he or she has bought from the cooperative. Most of the profits a cooperative earns may be refunded directly to members at the end of the business year. Part of the profit often is kept for expansion of the business.

Non-Profit Corporations

When driving into towns, you probably have seen signs like "Centreville–Incorporated." An incorporated town, called a **municipal corporation** or *municipality,* has its own officials, its own schools, its own police and fire department, and provides street repairs, street lighting, and other services for its citizens. A municipality levies taxes and passes rules and regulations to operate effectively. To function, a municipal corporation buys supplies, equipment, and services just as any business does and pays for them under the corporate name of the city. Unlike a business corporation, services are provided for its citizens with money from taxes levied rather than from making a profit. Stock representing ownership is not issued.

Other groups also organize as non-profit corporations. Like the municipal corporation, these organizations operate to provide a service, but not for profit. Among these are private colleges and universities, American Red Cross, Boy Scouts of America, Future Business Leaders of America, and Distributive Education Clubs of America. Both local governments and non-profit agencies find that the corporate form of organization provides the most effective way for them to deliver their services to the public.

Key Ideas

1 Sole proprietors and partners have unlimited liability for the debts of their businesses while the owners of corporations can only lose the amount they have invested.

2 Sole proprietorships and partnerships are easily formed while corporations must file reports with a state and obtain official approval.

3 Managers of all businesses must plan, organize, staff, lead, and control to be effective.

4 Specialized forms of business organizations include franchises, cooperatives, and nonprofit corporations.

End of Chapter Activities

Increasing Your Business Vocabulary

The following terms should become part of your business vocabulary. For each numbered item, find the term that has the same meaning.

board of directors

certificate of incorporation

cooperative

corporation

dividend

franchise

franchisee

franchisor

municipal corporation

partnership

sole proprietorship

shareholder

1 A group of people elected by shareholders to guide a corporation.

2 A business owned by one person.

3 An organization that provides services for citizens with revenue from their taxes and that does not have earning a profit as a goal.

4 An association of two or more people operating a business as co-owners and sharing profits or losses according to a written agreement.

5 A business made up of a number of owners but authorized by law to act as a single person.

6 A document, generally issued by a state government, giving permission to start a corporation.

7 The part of the profits of a corporation that each shareholder receives.

8 A person who owns stock in a corporation.

9 A business that is owned by the members it serves and is managed in their interest.

10 A written contract granting permission to sell someone else's product or service in a prescribed manner, over a certain period of time, and in a specified area.

11 The person or group of people who have received permission from a parent company to sell its products or services.

12 The parent company that grants permission to a person or group to sell its products or services.

Reviewing Your Reading

1 What advantages did Julie Alcess find in starting her own business?

2 What disadvantages did Julie find as the operator of a sole proprietorship?

3 Name the five activities that Julie performed as a manager.

4 What advantages over her original organization resulted when Julie Alcess entered into a partnership with Andy Davidson?

5 Name six items that should be agreed upon and recorded in the articles of partnership.

6 State two advantages that a corporation has over a partnership.

7 Name two disadvantages of a corporation.

8 What evidence of ownership did Julie and Andy receive when they changed from a partnership to a corporation?

9 Who actually manages a corporation?

10 Why does a corporation's board of directors keep part of the profit before dividing the remainder among the stockholders?

11 What are the three conditions of a franchise agreement?

12 Name one advantage and one disadvantage of operating a business as a franchise.

13 How does a cooperative differ from a regular corporation?

14 What is the difference between a municipal corporation and a business corporation?

Using Your Business Knowledge

1 Features of the five types of business organizations you studied in this chapter are given in the following statements. Name the type of organization to which each statement applies. Some statements may apply to two types of organizations.

   a. The owner is his or her own boss.

   b. If one of the owners makes a large, unwise purchase and the business cannot pay the bill, another owner might have to do so.

   c. The business can sell stock to raise more money.

   d. If a profit is made, the owner receives all of it.

   e. Owners agree on how they will divide profits and share losses.

f. Owners allow a board of directors to make decisions about the business.

g. Owners/operators agree to operate the business in a prescribed manner set forth by the parent company.

h. Owners must get written permission from the state in which the business is located before it can operate.

i. An owner may be added to help make business decisions.

j. The amount of control a person has in the business may depend upon the value of the products and services bought from the business during the year.

k. A percentage of sales or a set fee must be paid annually to a parent company.

2 Explain how the planning activity is related to the controlling activity.

3 Explain how the policies and management of a corporation with more than 10,000 shareholders could be controlled by just one shareholder.

4 The community of Grandview has petitioned its state government for a certificate of incorporation so that it can become a town. When Grandview becomes a corporation, can it sell stock and issue dividends to shareholders? Explain.

5 Sarah Gray and her partner, John Tolkin, fail in their business venture. The debts are about $8,000.00 greater than the value of the business. Gray has personal property worth more than $10,000.00, but Tolkin owns nothing. Could Gray's personal property be taken to settle the debts of the business? Explain.

Calculating Business Problems

1 Jake Simmons and Maury Gertz operate a small convenience store under a franchise agreement with a national company. The franchisor requires an annual payment of 5 percent of gross sales. At the close of the current year, the accountant who keeps the records for the Simmons–Gertz store reported gross sales of $523,250. How much will Simmons and Gertz pay to the franchisor for the year?

2 As an art major at a university, Lu-yin Chang specializes in creating inexpensive gemstone jewelry. To earn extra money, Lu-yin rents a stall and sells her art in the new festival marketplace in the revitalized downtown area. The table shows her income and expenses for the month of December.

a. What was the total of Lu-yin's expenses for December?

b. How much profit did Lu-yin make in December?

c. If Lu-yin puts 20 percent of her profit into a savings account before spending on personal needs, how much will she save in December?

Income from sales:	$850.00
Expenses:	
Rent for stall and utilities	$125.00
Polishing/mounting tools	45.00
Gemstones and supplies	110.00
Ad in the university paper	20.00

3 Scott and Kristie de la Garza own stock in four corporations. Here is a record of the stock they own and the dividend they received for each share at the end of the first quarter.

Company	Number of Shares Owned	Quarterly Dividend per Share
IBM	50	$1.10
Avon Products	20	.25
William Wrigley, Jr.	50	.18
PepsiCo	100	.21

a. How much dividend income did the de la Garzas receive from each of their four stocks for the quarter?

b. What was their total dividend income for the quarter?

c. If each corporation paid the same amount per share for the remaining three quarters, how much dividend income would the de la Garzas receive from each corporation for the year?

d. What total dividend income would the de la Garzas receive for the year?

4 After all expenses were paid, Grant Valley Consumer Cooperative had $13,000.00 of profit left over. Of this amount, $3,000.00 was set aside for expansion of the business. According to its policy, Grant Valley would refund to each member an amount in proportion to the amount he or she bought during the year. Since total sales for the year were $500,000.00, the refund would be 2 percent, or 2 cents for every dollar each member had spent at the cooperative during the year. The persons in the

Randy Likins	$1,000.00
Jill Peery	650.00
Sam Peery	750.00
B. E. Fonza	100.00
H. E. Reynolds	1,250.00

table were among the members; their total purchases are shown in even dollars.

a. How much refund did each of these members receive?

b. What was the total amount refunded to these five members?

Applying Technology

Using the *Introduction to Business* template and your word processing program software, select problem CH06. After the problem appears on your screen, complete the following activities. Then, print and sign your completed partnership agreement. If you do not have a printer available, save the partnership agreement on a data disk to give to your teacher.

1 You and your partner, Faith Ramirez, are starting a new business. Fill in the blanks with information about yourself. Where dates are required, use the last day of the current month.

2 Find all the words that appear in all capitals and change those words to boldface. Indent all the paragraphs.

Making Decisions

Jeremy Rindone is a successful furniture maker in a small shop that he built and designed. He earns a good living and gets great satisfaction from the high quality furniture he builds. His customers often praise his work.

A large, reputable corporation has approached Jeremy with a proposal to take over his manufacturing facility and incorporate it into their nationwide furniture manufacturing operation.

They offered Jeremy enough money so that his financial future would be secure. He also would be appointed to the board of directors of the nationwide firm and could also oversee production of his line of furniture.

Jeremy would like to continue his own business, but he recognizes that the offer he has received is a great opportunity to expand his line of furniture. He also is not sure how many more years he can continue to work for himself.

1 What are the advantages and disadvantages of Jeremy continuing to operate his own business?

2 What are the advantages and disadvantages of Jeremy selling his business to the corporation?

Chapter Seven

Social Responsibility and Business Ethics

Key Terms

social responsibility

non-renewable resource

ethics

business ethics

code of ethics

Objectives

After studying this chapter and completing the end-of-chapter activities, you will be able to:

1 Explain what is meant by the social responsibility of business.

2 Identify four social responsibility issues.

3 Give examples of socially responsible actions.

4 Describe the purpose of a code of ethics.

Jo Ann Homer is the successful owner-manager of J A Kitchen Crafts. This business supplies kitchenware to retail stores. She has great pride in her ability to provide fair employment for her employees. She also considers herself a socially responsible employer.

Jo Ann Homer, for example, is on the board of directors of the local United Way. Her business contributes generously to several community groups, particularly groups in the performing arts. She serves on the job-training committee of the local Economic Development Board, and her company participates in a school-to-work program for underprivileged youngsters.

Jo Ann also encourages her employees to be active in community affairs. Employees get time off with pay to fulfill volunteer commitments during working hours. In addition, she believes in supporting her community to help make it a better place in which to live. Her philosophy is: "Workers are likely to be more satisfied on the job if they believe their company actively contributes to community life."

SOCIAL RESPONSIBILITY ISSUES

Social responsibility refers to the obligation of a business to contribute to the well-being of a community. In considering its responsibility to society, a business must weigh the interests and concerns of many groups. A broadened social responsibility of business requires greater attention to social concerns, such as protection of the environment, minorities and women in the workplace, employment of the physically challenged and older workers, and a healthy and safe work environment.

Illus. 7-1

Businesses sponsor community activities and encourage their employees to participate.

Environmental Protection

Conservation—preserving our scarce natural resources—is a goal of many companies. For example, lumber companies that consume trees have reforestation programs. Some natural resources, however, cannot be replaced. A **non-renewable resource** is a natural resource that cannot be replaced when used up. Examples are gas, oil, and mined minerals such as copper and iron ore.

When the environment is contaminated with the by-products of human activity, the result is *pollution*. Some production operations cause pollution of our lakes, rivers, and air. A socially responsible business takes action to reduce or completely eliminate operations that cause pollution. Engineers design new equipment and facilities for minimizing the effect of pollution on our environment.

The federal government has set measurable standards for water and air quality. Those standards are monitored and enforced by an organization known as the EPA, or the Environmental Protection Agency. The EPA and businesses work closely together to reduce pollution and to make our environment healthier.

Our tropical rain forests, vital to the future of good air throughout our planet, are being destroyed at the rate of 50 million acres a day or the equivalent of 6,000 football fields per hour.

Workplace Diversity

Businesses are increasingly sensitive to the role of women, ethnic groups, the physically challenged, and older workers. The work force of a business should reflect the various groups that comprise the community. Members of these groups must have equal access to education, training, jobs, and career advancement. The major challenge facing businesses today involves learning how to manage a work force made up of the various cultures in our society.

Another issue involves the removal of employment barriers for women. Equal employment opportunity laws eliminated sex-based job descriptions and classified ads. Employers are not allowed to exclude women applicants unless the business can prove the job requires physical skills that women do not have.

Employers also have taken steps to accommodate individuals who are physically challenged. The Americans with Disabilities Act, along with other federal and state legislation, has caused significant improvements to be made toward accommodating workers who are physically challenged. Buildings

In certain browsers and other Internet programs, a bookmark or hotlist is a special file used to save addresses and locations. By saving and recalling addresses, it is easy for you to visit your favorite sites over and over.

Company safety programs often reward employees with cash bonuses, prizes, or additional vacation days for ideas that improve the safety of the workplace.

must have access for wheelchairs and people with sight or hearing problems must be accommodated on the job.

Other laws have been passed to eliminate discrimination against older workers. The passage of the Age Discrimination in Employment Act prohibits employers from using age as a basis for employment decisions (hiring, promotions, or termination from a job). The law protects all persons 40 and older.

Safety on the Job

Employees do not want to work in a place where accidents are common. Having a safe place in which to work is important to all employees. Workers should not have to worry about whether their equipment is safe. They should be able to work in an office or factory free from the hazards that could cause accidents. The work environment should provide maximum protection from fire and other hazards.

In addition to protection from physical harm, workers need to know how to avoid the unexpected. Therefore, safety also involves employee training in how to work safely, and what to do in the event of an emergency. Adequate training makes the workplace safer and helps employees feel more secure in their work environment.

To ensure the right to safety, most employers have implemented a variety of programs to protect workers. Our federal and state governments have also enacted legislation to make the workplace

Illus. 7-2
The Americans with Disabilities Act was designed to increase employment opportunities for those who are physically challenged.

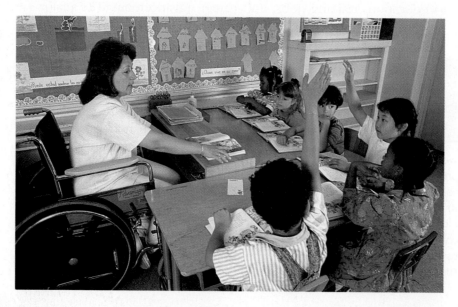

safer. Safety standards are regulated and enforced by agencies such as OSHA, the Occupational Safety and Health Administration.

Employee Wellness

A healthy work force is a productive work force. Businesses want employees to be healthy. Workers who have good physical health are valuable assets. Businesses today do a number of things to improve the health of their workforce. For instance, research has

Doing Business in the International Marketplace

International business offers many U.S. companies an opportunity for growth and expansion. But doing business in some countries may require a company to compromise its ethical principles.

Different values and standards cause ethical dilemmas for many U.S. companies. Here are three examples of ethical dilemmas:

1. In a developing European nation, a company must give money to certain government officials to sell its products. A U.S. company would view this behavior as a bribe. Bribes are considered unethical behavior in the United States.

2. To enter a new market in an Asian country, a U.S. company would have to give gifts and lavishly entertain key business and political leaders. Gift giving and lavish entertainment are practices contrary to the written policies of some U.S. companies. Establishing business in this Asian country could represent a 25 percent increase in the company's sales.

3. In a South American country, government officials will not license the operation of a U.S. manufacturer unless the company promises to buy all raw materials from certain South American manufacturers. The U.S. company considers this practice unfair and perhaps even unethical. The South American market presents tremendous potential for new customers. Company sales might increase by at least 10 percent.

Our society prefers that U.S. companies operate with high ethical and moral standards. Realistically it is very difficult—if not impossible—for businesses to operate in the international marketplace without experiencing some conflict in values. Each country has its own unique social and legal constraints. If a company in the international market observes both the spirit and letter of the laws of the other countries, then the activities of that company are usually considered to be socially responsible.

Critical Thinking

1 *Why do you think that some countries engage in practices such as those just described?*

2 *Would you take the steps necessary to get into these new markets? Why or why not?*

substantiated the bad affects of secondhand smoke and has led to smoke-free areas in most workplaces. Among programs offered are stop-smoking seminars, counseling for employees with drug problems, and weight-loss sessions.

Your general well-being as an employee needs to be protected, too. Clauses that relate to employee well-being are commonly included in labor contracts and company policy manuals. These clauses are *conditions of work* that pertain to the health and safety of employees while on the job.

In-company seminars on eating a balanced diet, getting proper exercise, and maintaining a healthy life style are some initiatives taken by companies to promote good health. Some businesses sponsor sports teams and encourage employees to participate. Larger companies may have physical fitness (or "wellness") centers in their buildings. Other businesses help pay for memberships in physical fitness clubs.

FYI

Workers who are healthy are absent less frequently, are more alert on the job, and make fewer errors.

Illus. 7-3
Some businesses encourage their employees to be healthy and to stay in good physical condition.

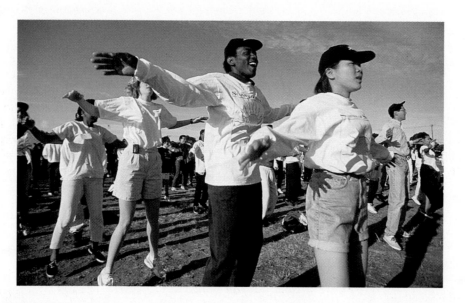

COSTS OF SOCIAL RESPONSIBILITY

In the long run, socially responsible actions by business may eliminate the need for government controls that regulate what a business can and cannot do. However, there are costs involved when a business takes socially responsible actions. Money must be spent for new non-polluting or safer equipment, for building renovations to remove hazards, for wellness and rehabilitation programs, and for social projects sponsored by a company.

As you learned in Chapter 2, a business must make a profit in order to stay in business. If a business does not earn a profit, the business will close and employees will be laid off. Spending on social programs must be restrained so a business can still earn a reasonable profit.

BUSINESS ETHICS

A socially responsible business also engages in ethical business practices. **Ethics** are principles of morality or rules of conduct. **Business ethics** are rules about how businesses and their employees ought to behave. Ethical behavior involves conformity with these rules; unethical behavior violates them. In dealing with business ethics, a code of ethics can help a business identify appropriate employee behavior.

A **code of ethics** is a statement of rules for guiding the behavior of employees or members of an organization. Codes of ethics address topics such as confidentiality of business information. Figure 7-1 shows a statement of values, called "Blue Box Values," that guide the ethical behavior of employees at the American Express Company, a large U.S. corporation.

A code must be worded in terms of acceptable behavior rather than forbidden action. Even with a code of ethics, the choice of appropriate behavior can cause dilemmas for decision makers within a business. Here are some examples of ethical dilemmas:

Cultural Notes

Julius Caesar first introduced "leap year" in 46 B.C. Caesar asked Egyptian astronomer Sosigenes to develop a calendar based on a 365¼ day year that was known as the Julian calendar. The Julian calendar allowed one extra day to be added every fourth year, giving us what we call leap year.

The solar year was calculated to be about 11 minutes longer than 365¼ days according to sixteenth-century astronomers. In 1582, the Gregorian calendar, which is what we use today, was adopted to correct this error. Therefore, we have a leap year every four years *except* century years that are not divisible by 400.

Many professional groups, such as lawyers, doctors, and teachers, publish codes of ethics.

- Should a company expand into a profitable market in another country where doing business requires giving expensive gifts to key government officials?

- Should a company take advantage of secret information accidentally obtained by an employee?

- Should a top-notch employee who has values contrary to what the company holds as important be held back from a promotion?

- Should a company continue to produce a popular product after it discovers a minor defect in it?

The ethical conduct of a business is greatly determined by its top management. Executives who exhibit strong moral character and make ethical business decisions set the ethical standards for a business. Companies concerned about ethical behavior in their employees have established educational programs on ethical con-

Figure 7-1

American Express has "Blue Box Values" to guide the behavior of its employees.

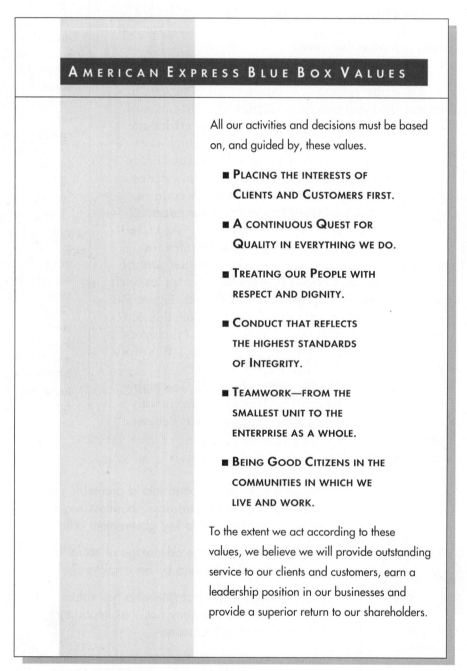

AMERICAN EXPRESS BLUE BOX VALUES

All our activities and decisions must be based on, and guided by, these values.

- PLACING THE INTERESTS OF CLIENTS AND CUSTOMERS FIRST.

- A CONTINUOUS QUEST FOR QUALITY IN EVERYTHING WE DO.

- TREATING OUR PEOPLE WITH RESPECT AND DIGNITY.

- CONDUCT THAT REFLECTS THE HIGHEST STANDARDS OF INTEGRITY.

- TEAMWORK—FROM THE SMALLEST UNIT TO THE ENTERPRISE AS A WHOLE.

- BEING GOOD CITIZENS IN THE COMMUNITIES IN WHICH WE LIVE AND WORK.

To the extent we act according to these values, we believe we will provide outstanding service to our clients and customers, earn a leadership position in our businesses and provide a superior return to our shareholders.

Source: Copyright © 1995 American Express Company

duct. These programs are designed to encourage employee honesty and integrity. Program topics range from making personal phone calls during work hours to taking supplies and materials for personal use (stealing). Employees are also instructed on how to make ethical decisions on the job.

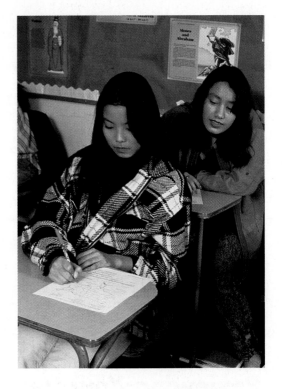

Illus. 7-4
Many employers are concerned that patterns of unethical behavior may transfer to the workplace.

Key Ideas

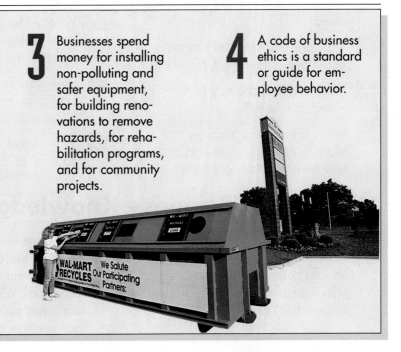

1 Socially responsible businesses care about their communities and help make them better places in which to live.

2 Social responsibility concerns relate to environmental protection, workplace diversity, safety on the job, and employee wellness.

3 Businesses spend money for installing non-polluting and safer equipment, for building renovations to remove hazards, for rehabilitation programs, and for community projects.

4 A code of business ethics is a standard or guide for employee behavior.

End of Chapter Activities

Increasing Your Business Vocabulary

The following terms should become part of your business vocabulary. For each numbered item, find the term that has the same meaning.

business ethics

code of ethics

ethics

non-renewable resource

social responsibility

1 Principles of morality or rules of conduct.

2 The obligation of a business to contribute to the well-being of a community.

3 Rules about how businesses and their employees ought to behave.

4 A natural resource, such as gas, coal, copper, and iron ore, that cannot be replaced once it is used up.

5 A statement of values and rules that guides the behavior of employees or members of an organization.

Reviewing Your Reading

1 In what ways was Jo Ann Homer socially responsible?

2 What are four social responsibility issues?

3 Why are businesses concerned about non-renewable resources?

4 What are four diversity in the workplace issues?

5 What are some protections that workers need in addition to protection from physical harm?

6 What are some programs of businesses that deal with the issue of worker health?

7 What is the advantage of a company taking socially responsible actions?

8 How does an ethical business decision differ from a social responsibility decision?

9 Why should a company have a code of ethics?

Using Your Business Knowledge

1 Name some ways in which businesses in your community are socially responsible; try to come up with examples different from those in our chapter.

2 What are some natural resources that you use every day? Which of those natural resources need to be protected? What can you as an individual do to avoid depleting our non-renewable resources?

3 Safety often is a matter of individuals being careful about where they place things and how they conduct their own business. Name several ways in which you and others can help make a workplace safe.

4 What does the term "discrimination" mean to you? What examples of discrimination in the workplace are you aware of?

5 Why do you think employers are willing to spend money to help employees improve their general health? Be specific about how a company might benefit.

Calculating Business Problems

1 Jo Ann Homer's business contributed 3½ acres of company property to the city for a park. Land in that area sells for $8,250 per acre. What is the value of the land that was donated? At first Jo Ann wanted the city to buy the land at one-half the selling price. If the city had done that, how much would it have cost the city?

2 J A Kitchen Craft's current building measures 60 meters by 90 meters. What is the square footage of that building? A new building with a more effective waste disposal system is being considered that measures 75 meters by 105 meters. What is the square footage of that building? (Round off to the nearest whole number when computing square footage.) How many additional square feet are in the new building?

3 The Johnson Manufacturing Co. has an annual operating budget of $750,000. Each year it budgets for the following expenses: pollution control equipment, $37,500; contributions to community projects, $22,500; employee fitness and sports programs, $7,500.

a. What percentage of the annual budget is allocated to each socially responsible action (pollution control, community projects, fitness/sports)? What is the total spent?

b. What will be the amount budgeted for each expense category next year if there is a 15 percent increase? What will be the total spent?

4 The National Corporation is housed in a building that was built 25 years ago. This building lacks suitable access for persons who are physically challenged. Modifications must be made to the building to meet current government regulations. The following will be done to comply with the law:

a. Ramps will be constructed leading up to the front and side doors of the building for $17,000.

b. Six doorways will be widened on the top floor to accommodate wheelchairs for $9,500.

c. Equipment will be purchased that can be operated by physically challenged persons for $19,700.

d. A company van that can be operated by the physically challenged will be purchased for $38,800.

What is the total cost incurred by the National Corporation? If the company's annual operating budget is $950,000, what percentage of that budget will be spent for these modifications?

Applying Technology

Using the *Introduction to Business* template and your word processing program software, select problem CH07. After the problem appears on your screen, complete the following activities. Then, print your completed Ethics Checklists. If you do not have a printer available, save the Ethics Checklists on a data disk to give to your teacher.

1 The paragraphs of the Ethics Checklist are in random order. Using the cut-and-paste or the move feature of your software, rearrange the checklist steps into a logical order.

2 Copy the Ethics Checklist into the space below Ethics Case 1. Below each step in the checklist, enter the results of applying that step to the situation in Case 1.

3 Copy the Ethics Checklist into the space below Ethics Case 2. Below each step in the checklist, enter the results of applying that step to the situation in Case 2.

Making Decisions

Mr. Rolfson, a prosperous property developer, thinks a mall should be built on a large piece of land that he owns. Mr. Rolfson is a respected business person in his community, and he has eagerly supported community programs for many years. He has been asked by some prominent community members to donate the land to the community for a city park. He knows that a neighborhood park will help resolve the shortage of recreational areas in his community.

Yet income from a mall located on his land could add to his profits each year. The extra income could then be used to support additonal social programs within his community.

1 What is the dilemma that Mr. Rolfson faces?

2 What advice would you give Mr. Rolfson? Back up your advice with sound reasoning.

Chapter Eight

International Business

Key Terms

international business

imports

exports

exchange rate

quota

tariff

embargo

balance of trade

balance of payments

multinational company or corporation (MNC)

Objectives

After studying this chapter and completing the end-of-chapter activities, you will be able to:

1 State the basic reason for nations doing business with each other.

2 Explain the concept of currency exchange rates.

3 List three barriers to international trade.

4 Explain the concepts of balance of trade and balance of payments.

5 Explain what is meant by a multinational corporation.

6 List several advantages and disadvantages of international business.

Just as we specialize and trade among our states and communities, other countries also take advantage of special factors of production that they have. They produce goods according to these advantages and trade with other countries to help provide for the wants of their citizens. This trading affects your daily life more than you realize.

What did your family have for breakfast this morning? Coffee, cereal, and sliced bananas, perhaps? If it were not for trading with Brazil for coffee and with Honduras for the bananas, you might have had only cereal. The sugar on your table may have come from the Philippines. Even your morning newspaper was printed on paper that may have come from Canada.

As you look around your house or apartment, you will find many products made in other countries. For instance, you may find a TV made in Japan or Korea; a stereo made in Taiwan or China; clothing made in Norway, Scotland, or Italy; kitchen appliances made in Hong Kong or Malaysia; and coffee from Brazil or Colombia. Also look around your classroom. Can you identify products made in other countries?

TRADING AMONG NATIONS

The majority of business activities still occur within a country's own borders. The making, buying, and selling of goods and services within a country is called *domestic business*. Your purchase of cereal produced in the United States is an example of domestic business. However, the United States today is part of a larger international business community.

International business includes all of the business activities necessary for creating, shipping, and selling goods and services across national borders. International business is frequently referred to as *foreign* or *world trade*. Evidence of foreign trade is everywhere.

While our country has many natural resources, a skilled labor force, and modern machines and methods of production, we cannot provide ourselves with all of the things we want. We go beyond our borders to get many things. We conduct trade with as many as 150 countries in one year.

Most nations of the world have special advantages. Brazil, for example, has an advantage over the United States in producing coffee. Saudi Arabia has an advantage over most other countries in crude oil. Australia has an advantage in wool. Korea and Taiwan have an advantage in the number of skilled laborers who can assemble electronic products. Compared with these and many other countries, the United States has advantages in the production of airplanes, tractors, computers, office equipment, and many varieties of food and other agricultural products.

One of every $7 of U.S. sales is to a foreign buyer.

Illus. 8-1
The United States enjoys an advantage in the production of several products.

Because of trade and modern means of transportation, nations everywhere can specialize in the kinds of production they can do best.

Importing

The things we buy from other countries are called **imports.** Did you know that imports account for our total supply of bananas, coffee, cocoa, spices, tea, silk, and crude rubber? About half of the crude oil and fish we buy comes from other countries. Imports also account for 20 to 50 percent of our supply of carpets, sugar, leather gloves, dishes, and sewing machines. In order to manufacture certain goods, we must import tin, chrome, manganese, nickel, copper, zinc, and several other metals. Figure 8-1 shows how dependent the United States is on imported raw materials.

Without foreign trade, many of the things we buy would cost more or not be available to our consumers. Other countries can produce some goods at a lower cost because they have the needed raw materials or have lower labor costs. Some consumers purchase foreign goods, even at higher prices, if they perceive the quality to be better than domestic goods. Or, they may simply enjoy owning products made in other countries. French perfumes, Norwegian sweaters, and Swiss watches are examples.

Customs officials are government employees who are authorized to collect the duties levied on imports.

Figure 8-1
Raw materials used in producing many products are imported by our country.

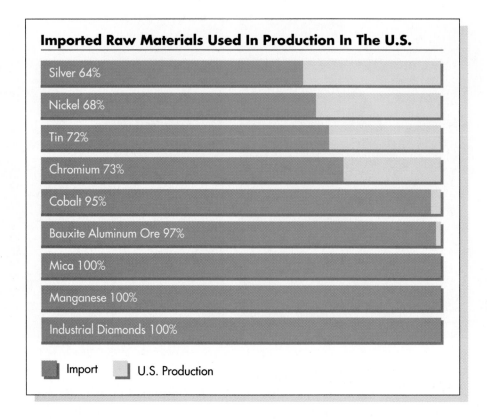

Imported Raw Materials Used In Production In The U.S.

- Silver 64%
- Nickel 68%
- Tin 72%
- Chromium 73%
- Cobalt 95%
- Bauxite Aluminum Ore 97%
- Mica 100%
- Manganese 100%
- Industrial Diamonds 100%

■ Import   □ U.S. Production

Exporting

The goods and services we sell to other countries are called **exports.** Just as our imports benefit you, our exports benefit consumers in other countries. Workers in countries throughout the world use factory and farm machinery made in the United States. They eat food made from many of our agricultural products and use our chemicals, fertilizers, medicines, and plastics. People in other countries like to view our movies; watch CNN and MTV; and read many of our books, magazines, and newspapers. Producing the goods and services we export employs many of our workers. One of every six jobs in the United States depends on international business. Figure 8-2 shows our trade of goods with seven nations and two regions.

Illus. 8-2
Many products are exported for sale in other countries.

Figure 8-2
We trade with many nations throughout the world.

U.S. Trade, 1994

Goods Exported (In Billions)		Goods Imported (In Billions)	U.S. Balance
$696	**All Countries**	**$805**	**—$109**
	Selected Nations and Regions		
114	Canada	129	−15
53	Japan	119	−66
51	Mexico	49	+ 2
27	United Kingdom	25	+ 2
19	Germany	32	−13
17	Taiwan	27	−10
9	China	39	−30
103	European Union	111	− 8
60	East Asia NIC's*	71	−11

*NIC= Newly Industrialized Countries
Source: Business America, March, 1995, p.21.

INTERNATIONAL CURRENCY

One of the challenges facing businesses involved in trading with other countries is the variety of currency in the world. Each nation has its own banking system and its own kind of money. For instance, Russia uses the ruble; the Netherlands, the guilder; Brazil, the real; India, the rupee; and Saudi Arabia, the riyal.

The process of exhanging one currency for another occurs in the foreign exchange market. The *foreign exchange market* consists of banks that buy and sell different currencies. Most large banks are part of the foreign exchange market and may provide currency services for businesses and consumers.

The value of a currency in one country compared with the value of a currency in another is called the **exchange rate.** The value of currency, like most things, is affected by supply and demand. The approximate values of the currencies of ten countries on a recent date in relation to the U.S. dollar (USD) are given in Figure 8-3.

When a U.S. company sells products to a Canadian firm, for example, the U.S. firm must convert

One of every six U.S. manufacturing jobs produces something for export.

Figure 8-3

Exchange rates fluctuate daily.

Exchange Rates Fluctuate Daily

Country	Currency	Units per USD*	Value in USD*
Britain	pound	.62 pounds	1.61
Canada	dollar	1.38 Canadian dollars	.725
Germany	deutsche mark	1.39 deutsche marks	.72
Greece	drachma	277.81 drachmas	.0036
Japan	yen	83.25 yen	.012
Saudi Arabia	riyal	3.745 riyals	.267
South Africa	rand	3.663 rands	.273
South Korea	won	770.20 won	.0013
Spain	peseta	124.9 pesetas	.0080
Venezuela	bolivar	170 bolivars	.00588

*United States Dollar

the Canadian dollars received in payment into U.S. dollars. On a given day in a recent year, each Canadian dollar was worth 72½ cents in the United States. What would the U.S. firm charge if goods worth approximately $10,000 in the United States were sold to a Canadian firm? The U.S. firm would have to charge $13,800 in U.S. dollars ($1.38 × 10,000 = $13,800). Canadian dollars when converted to U.S. dollars would then be worth $10,005 in U.S. dollars ($13,800 × .725 = $10,005).

Travelers and businesspeople must deal with currency exchanges as they go from one country to another. Exchanging currency is not as difficult as it may seem, however. Travelers in another country can simply go to a currency exchange window at the airport, train station, or local bank and buy whatever amount of local currency they want. How much of the local currency they will get depends on the value of the two currencies at that time. Rates are posted at exchange windows, and there is a charge made for exchanging currency.

Illus. 8-3

A currency's exchange rate is usually quoted in terms of other important currencies.

BARRIERS TO INTERNATIONAL TRADE

Our government establishes international policies that guide our activities, including trade, with other countries. Several devices may be used to control the importing and exporting of goods and services. Among these controls are three barriers: quotas, tariffs, and embargoes.

Quotas

One of the devices used by governments to regulate international trade sets a limit on the quantity of a product that may be imported or exported within a given period of time. This limit is a referred to as a **quota.**

Quotas may be set for many reasons. Countries that export oil may put quotas on crude oil so that the supply will remain low and prices will stay at a certain level. Quotas may also be imposed by one country on imports from another to express disapproval of the policies or social behavior of that country. Quotas can also be set by one country to protect one of its industries from too much competition from abroad. This often is done by a nation to shield its "infant industries," which need protection to get started. Our government in the past has imposed quotas on sugar, cattle, dairy products, and textiles.

Tariffs

Another device that governments use to regulate international trade is the tariff. A **tariff** is a tax that a government places on certain imported products. Suppose you want to buy an English bicycle. The producer charges $140, but our government collects a 20 percent tariff ($28) on the bicycle when it is imported. This means that you will have to pay $168 plus shipping charges for the bike. The increased price may cause you to decide to buy a U.S. manufactured bike at a lower price.

Some tariffs are a set amount per pound, gallon, or other unit; others are figured on the value of the good as in the example of the bicycle. By increasing the price for an imported product, a high tariff tends to lower the demand for the product and reduce the quantity of that import. On many occasions, it has been argued that tariffs should be used to protect U.S. jobs from foreign competition.

Embargoes

If a government wishes to do so, it can stop the export or import of a product completely. This

NET FACTS

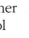

The Internet reaches schools in more than 140 countries around the world. Through E-mail and other connections, you learn about students in other countries and foreign students can learn about you.

Embargoes typically are used for political rather than economic purposes.

action is called an **embargo.** Governments may impose an embargo for many reasons. They may wish to protect their own industries from international competition to a greater degree than either the quota or the tariff will accomplish. The government may wish to prevent sensitive products, particularly those important to the nation's defense, from falling into the hands of unfriendly groups or nations. As with the quota, a government sometimes imposes an embargo to express its disapproval of the actions or policies of another country.

MEASURING TRADE BETWEEN NATIONS

As you learned in Unit 1, a major reason people work is to earn money to buy the things they need and want. That is, they sell their labor for wages and then spend the major part of those wages for goods and services. People usually try to keep their

Legal*Perspective*

Eliminating Trade Barriers

Since World War II, there has been a trend toward multinational integration. Multinational economic integration is the removal of barriers to the movement of goods, capital, and people. The simplest approach to integration is to establish a *free trade zone* in which participating nations trade freely among themselves without tariffs or other trade restrictions.

The North American free trade agreement (NAFTA) is just one of more than 14 multinational *trade agreements* in the world. The combination of the United States, Canada, and Mexico united over 370 million consumers into a $6.5 trillion market. The agreement eliminates over a period of time tariffs and other trade barriers between Canada, Mexico, and the United States.

Opponents of NAFTA worry that the United States will lose too many jobs to Mexico's lower-paid workers. Environmentalists point to the pollution generated by Mexican plants which do not usually meet the same ecological standards required of U.S. companies. Proponents of the free trade pact argue that the United States has everything to gain from a more prosperous southern neighbor. With fewer trade restrictions, U.S. and Canadian companies will increase Mexico's economic growth. As Mexico becomes more prosperous, its standard of living will rise. This, in turn, will spur greater demand for U.S. and Canadian exports to Mexico.

Critical Thinking

1 In what ways do you feel you will benefit from NAFTA?

2 Can you name other multinational agreements affecting trade within a region of the world?

income and spending in balance, knowing that if they spend more than they earn, they can experience financial problems. Nations are also concerned about balancing income with expenditures. When people buy more than their income allows, they go into debt. In the same way, when a country has an unfavorable balance of trade it owes money to others. *Foreign debt* is the amount a country owes to other countries.

Balance of Trade

Countries like to have a favorable balance of trade. That happens when they export more than they import.

The difference between a country's total exports and total imports is called the **balance of trade.** If a country exports (sells) more than it imports (buys), it has a *trade surplus* and its trade position is said to be favorable. But, if it imports more than it exports, it has a *trade deficit* and its trade position is unfavorable. Some countries continually buy more foreign goods than they sell.

A country can have a trade surplus with one country and a trade deficit with another. Overall, a country tries to keep its international trade in balance. Figure 8-4 shows the two possible international trade positions. After a long history of a favorable balance of trade, the United States has had a trade deficit every year for more than a decade. The trade deficit has been increasing. In a recent year, the U.S. trade deficit was over $155 billion.

Balance of Payments

In addition to exporting and importing of goods and services, other forms of exchange occur between nations that affect the

A retail manager is responsible for selling a wide range of merchandise and providing services directly to consumers. A person in this position hires and supervises employees, coordinates and directs all aspects of retail trade, monitors sales activities, develops merchandise plans, and monitors profits and losses. Retail managers also may coordinate displays and oversee special advertising and promotions.

Figure 8-4
A favorable balance of trade is desired by all nations.

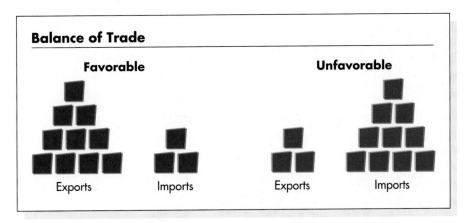

Balance of Trade

Favorable   Unfavorable

Exports   Imports   Exports   Imports

The United States, despite being the largest exporter in the world, has had a trade deficit for many years.

economy. Money goes from one country to another through investments and tourism. For example, a citizen of one country might invest in a corporation in another country. A business may invest in a factory or office complex in another country. Also, one government might give financial or military aid to another nation. Furthermore, banks may deposit funds in foreign banks. When tourists travel, they contribute to the flow of money from their country to the country they are visiting. Some countries limit the amount of money their citizens can take out of the country when they travel.

The difference between the amount of money that comes into a country and the amount that goes out of it is called the **balance of payments.** A country's balance of payments can either be positive or negative. A positive or favorable balance of payments occurs when a nation receives more money in a year than it pays out. A negative balance of payments is unfavorable. It is the result of a country sending more money out than it brings in.

GLOBAL BUSINESS ORGANIZATIONS

Today, as a result of widespread international business activities, thousands of multinational corporations exist. A **multinational company** or **corporation (MNC)** is an organization that conducts business in several countries and has management capable of doing business worldwide. MNCs usually consist of a parent company in a *home country* and divisions or separate companies in one or more host countries. The country in which the MNC locates is called the *host country*.

An MNC can become a major economic power in a host country. The workers of the host country may depend on the MNC for jobs. Consumers become dependent upon it for goods and services. The MNC may actually influence or control the political power of the country.

Multinational corporations can use either a global or multinational strategy. A *global strategy* uses a standardized product and marketing strategy worldwide. The same product is sold in essentially the same manner throughout the world. One example with which you are probably familiar is Coca-Cola. Under a *multinational strategy*, each national market is treated differently. Firms develop products and marketing strategies that appeal to the customs,

Many of America's largest multinationals are oil, auto, or chemical companies.

Illus. 8-4
Multinational corporations can use either a global or multinational strategy.

tastes, and buying habits of particular national markets. Many restaurant chains employ a multinational strategy when they tailor their menus to local tastes.

ADVANTAGES AND DISADVANTAGES OF INTERNATIONAL BUSINESS

You have already learned that there are many benefits to international business. We have an abundance of goods available, often at lower prices than if we produced the goods domestically. With international business, consumer choices increase.

For workers, career opportunities expand because of international business. International business creates jobs. Many businesses, large and small, increase sales and profits with foreign trade.

Many people view international business as a way to promote mutual understanding, communication, and respect among people of different nations. An old saying tells us that "countries that trade with one another do not have wars with one another." Nations that are business partners usually try to maintain friendly relations for economic reasons.

International business also creates some problems. The competition from foreign producers can also lower the demand for our own products. Workers in some industries have lost jobs as the result of this competition. In recent years, our textile, automobile, and electronics industries have felt the negative impact of international competition. International competition, on the other hand, has caused some industries to be more productive and to improve product quality. U.S. industries have shown that they can compete in the international marketplace.

Key Ideas

1 Nations do business with each other to increase the variety of goods and services available to their consumers.

2 An exchange rate is the amount of currency of one country that can be traded for one unit of the currency of another country.

3 Three barriers to international business are quotas, tariffs, and embargoes.

4 Balance of trade is the difference between a country's exports and imports. The difference between a country's total payments to other countries and its total receipts from other countries is the balance of payments.

5 Multinational companies conduct business activities in several countries and have management capable of doing business worldwide.

6 Advantages of international business include more goods available, lower prices, and an increased number of jobs; disadvantages include some loss of jobs and lowered demand for some U.S. products.

End of Chapter Activities

Increasing Your Business Vocabulary

The following terms should become part of your business vocabulary. For each numbered item, find the term that has the same meaning.

balance of payments

balance of trade

exchange rate

embargo

exports

imports

international business

multinational company or corporation (MNC)

quota

tariff

1 Goods and services sold to another country.

2 A limit on the quantity of a product that may be imported and exported within a given period of time.

3 An organization that conducts business in several countries.

4 The value of money of one country expressed in terms of the money of another country.

5 Goods and services bought from another country.

6 Stopping the importing or exporting of a certain product or service.

7 The difference between a country's total exports and total imports of goods.

8 A tax that a government places on certain imported products.

9 The difference between a country's total payments to other countries and its total receipts from other countries.

10 The business activities necessary for creating, shipping, and selling goods and services across national borders.

Reviewing Your Reading

1 Name several products that are typically found in U.S. households that are made in other countries.

2 Name a food, a raw material, and a manufactured good that we might not have without international trade.

3 What percentage of the following resources is imported: aluminum ore? silver? industrial diamonds?

4 State one reason why you might prefer to buy imported goods even at a higher price.

5 How are workers in some other countries affected by imports from the United States?

6 Why do we have exchange rates?

7 State three reasons for countries placing tariffs on imports.

8 How does a quota limit international trade?

9 What is the difference between balance of trade and balance of payments?

10 What strategies do multinational companies use to market products?

11 State two advantages and two disadvantages of international business.

Using Your Business Knowledge

1 It is said that no community or nation today can be completely independent. Do you agree or disagree? Explain.

2 How does international business contribute to a better standard of living for many people in various countries?

3 An American manufacturer of electric toasters wants to sell its products to the people of China. Can you think of some difficulties that this business might have in entering the Chinese market?

4 What is meant by "infant industries"? Give two examples of infant industries either in the United States or in other countries. Do you think that such industries should be protected by high tariffs? If so, how long should they be protected?

5 Some people believe that the United States should place stiff controls on imports of goods that compete with our businesses to prevent the "exporting of American jobs" to other countries. Give arguments for and against such a position.

Calculating Business Problems

1 The table shows the approximate value of some imported foods for two years. The values are listed in millions of dollars.

a. What is the total value in millions of dollars of the foods imported by the United States in Year One?

b. What is the total value in millions of dollars of the foods imported in Year Two?

c. Was there an increase from Year One to Year Two?

Food	Year One	Year Two
Meat and meat products	$2,339	$2,367
Fruits and nuts	2,717	2,781
Coffee	3,130	4,293
Sugar	936	670
Fish	3,985	4,691
Cocoa	564	418

d. What was the amount of increase or decrease?

2 Using the "recent date" information in Figure 8-3 on page 126, determine how many U.S. dollars someone could buy for these amounts of currencies from other countries:

a. In Japan, 120 yen
b. In Canada, 5 Canadian dollars
c. In Germany, 150 marks

3 To make their exports suitable for use in other countries, U.S. manufacturers must produce goods that are measured in the metric system. For example, if a manufacturer wanted to export paint, which is sold in gallons in this country, it would probably export the paint in 4-liter (about 1¼ gallons) cans. To what sizes would the items listed at right be converted for export to countries using the metric system? (See Appendix D.)

a. A quart bottle of liquid detergent
b. A 50-yard bolt of polyester fabric
c. An automobile engine measured in cubic inches
d. A 12-inch ruler
e. A bathroom scale that measures in pounds

4 The table shows approximate values of exports and imports going through nine ports in a recent year.

a. What is the total value in millions of dollars of the exports for the year? the imports?
b. Which port city reported the largest business in terms of value? What is the value?
c. Which port imported and exported the least amount? What is the value for each?

City	Exports (In Millions)	Imports (In Millions)
Boston	$18,300	$40,300
New York	33,400	67,000
Baltimore	12,100	31,300
Miami	18,600	31,500
New Orleans	14,400	17,100
Houston	21,700	27,700
Los Angeles	22,200	53,100
San Francisco	32,100	44,100
Chicago	33,700	54,800

Applying Technology

Using the *Introduction to Business* template and your database program software, select problem CH08. After the problem appears on your screen, complete the following activities. Then, after you have completed each step, display or print a report for each activity. If you do not have a printer available, answer the questions before you leave the computer.

1 Sort the database in descending order by amount of exports. Answer the following questions:

a. What country purchased the highest amount of exports from the United States?

b. What country purchased the second lowest amount of exports from the United States?

2 Select and list the countries that imported less than $10 million from the United States. How many countries are listed?

3 Sort the countries in ascending order by name of country. Answer the following questions:

a. What is the amount of exports from the United States to the third country listed?

b. What is the amount of imports into the United States from the last country listed?

Optional: Create a pie chart showing the exports to each country.

Making Decisions

Assume you have started a business that manufactures ceramic products. These products are *new and exclusive* on the U.S. market. Your market survey shows that consumers want them and will buy them for their homes. You already have invested in a small building, equipment, supplies, and materials. You have hired three people to work with you.

You soon discover that a trading partner of the United States has similar products to export. This country's labor costs are extremely low, and workers in this country receive few benefits. Your business, without foreign competition, could grow to employ hundreds of workers. You consider this foreign producer of ceramic products *unfair competition.*

1 What can our government do to help you get started and have a chance for success in your business?

2 What might the other country do if the U.S. government does not allow it to trade ceramic products freely?

Chapter Nine

Key Terms

interstate commerce

intrastate commerce

contract

patent

copyright

trademark

public utility

monopoly

antitrust laws

revenue

Government in Our Economy

Objectives

After studying this chapter and completing the end-of-chapter activities, you will be able to:

1 Explain protection provided by government.

2 Explain methods used by government to regulate our economy.

3 Describe how government assists business.

4 Explain the role of government in producing goods and services and hiring workers.

5 Explain two ways that government raises money.

In Chapter 2, you learned that government plays a role in every economic system. You also learned that your role as a citizen and voter affects decisions made and actions taken by government. In our private enterprise system, our government's role is much less extensive than in other economic systems but is nevertheless an important one.

The role of government changes as newly elected officials take office and as different political parties become dominant. As issues facing our society change, so must our government change. But there are some fundamental, basic roles of government. Government is primarily concerned with these roles:

- Providing services for members of our society.
- Protecting citizens, consumers, businesses, and workers.
- Regulating utilities and promoting competition.
- Providing information and assistance to businesses.
- Purchasing goods and services.
- Hiring public employees.
- Raising revenue.

Each of these roles has either a direct or indirect impact on business expansion, consumer affairs, and economic growth in our economy.

OUR GOVERNMENT—FEDERAL, STATE, AND LOCAL

The main goal of the federal government is to oversee the activities that involve two or more states or other countries. In general, the Constitution gives the federal government the power to regulate foreign and interstate commerce. Business transactions involving companies in more than one state are called **interstate commerce.** For example, a trucking company that ships products to several states would be regulated by the federal government.

Illus. 9-1
The federal government regulates interstate commerce.

State governments regulate business activities within their own boundaries. **Intrastate commerce** refers to business transactions involving companies that do business only in one state. For instance, a trucking company that hauls products only within a state's boundaries would be regulated by that state and not the federal government.

All states have delegated some of their legislative authority to local governments. Local governments include county boards and city or town councils. Local governments provide services needed for an orderly society, such as police and fire protection.

Government both encourages competition in the marketplace and controls it through legislation and government agency rules and regulations.

GOVERNMENT PROTECTS

Government protects our rights in obvious ways. Citizens are protected through government-provided police and fire-fighting services. We also have armed forces to provide for our national defense. National security is a major concern of our federal government.

Laws have been established to help provide a safe work environment. As a worker, you have a basic right to safe working conditions. For example, safety standards for building, machines, and chemicals are set by government agencies. Government inspection and regulation of work areas helps to reduce the number of job-related accidents.

Additional government regulations stem from the need to protect the basic human rights of workers. For example, you cannot be denied work because of your race, religion, sex, or age. Selection of someone for a job must be based on job requirements, training, and experience and not on prejudices and personal biases.

Several laws exist to prevent air, water, noise, and chemical pollution. Other laws forbid the burning of substances that make our air unsafe to breathe. The Environmental Protection Agency (EPA) was established by the federal government to ensure that businesses would comply with the laws.

Another example of government protection is through contracts and special property rights. An enforceable contract is one that meets certain requirements, which we will examine next. Patents, copyrights, and trademarks are important areas of federal law for many businesses. They protect the inventions and ideas that might generate profits for a company in the future.

Contracts

An agreement to exchange goods or services for something of value, usually money, is fundamental to doing business. That agreement is called a **contract.** A contract may be written or unwritten but certain elements must be included for the contract to be enforceable. Figure 9-1 highlights the main provisions of every enforceable contract. Examples of contracts include a lease to rent an apartment, a credit card agreement, and documents that state the terms of a purchase.

Both consumers and businesses benefit from government enforcement of contracts. If you agree to have repairs made on your car for $65, the business firm must perform the work as agreed upon and you must pay for the work when completed. If work is not done correctly or if you fail to make the payment, legal action through our court system can be taken to force the work to be corrected or for you to pay. Without enforcements, dishonest consumers or business owners could refuse to honor their agreements, and our daily business activities would be very unpleasant.

Valid, enforceable contracts must contain:

Agreement — An offer must be must be made, and an acceptance must occur.

Competent Parties — Those entering into the contract must be of legal age and must be mentally competent.

Consideration — Something of measurable value must be exchanged by the parties involved.

Legality — The contract must be for a product or service that may be legally sold; also no fraud or deception exists in the agreement.

Figure 9-1
Valid and enforceable contracts are important to consumers and businesses.

Intellectual Property Rights

Intellectual property is purely intangible; that is, a person cannot touch it. Intellectual property discussed in this section includes patents, copyrights, and trademarks.

When individuals or companies create new products, they may obtain a patent. A **patent** gives the inventor the exclusive right to make, use, or sell the item for 17 years. For example, a company that creates a new method to record programs from television could obtain a patent for this process to prevent other companies from making or selling recorders using this process.

In a similar manner, a **copyright** protects the creative work of authors, composers, and artists. Copyright protection continues for the life of the person receiving the copyright and for 50 years after the person's death. Examples of copyright statements can be found on the front pages of most books. Copyrights are identified with the symbol ©.

Another form of protection given to a business by government is a trademark. A **trademark** is a word, letter, or symbol associated with a specific company or product. Company names, team

Reading the "fine print" in a contract must be done *before* signing it—our courts do not protect us from our own "folly."

Illus. 9-2
Business conventions are often held to promote new inventions and product ideas.

emblems, and label designs may be registered with the government. A trademark can be very valuable since many are famous throughout the world and often identified with a symbol, called a *logo*. Can you think of some well-known logos that you see frequently?

GlobalPerspective

Yoruba of Southwestern Africa

If you take a journey to the southwestern part of Africa, you might visit the area of Yoruba in Nigeria. The 20 million Yorubans trace their history back to A.D. 1200. Their land is divided into numerous city-states and villages. City-states are ruled by a king (oba). The king, a ritual leader, is believed to have divine powers. Villages are governed by chiefs.

Yoruba has rich farmlands. Maize (corn), yams, peanuts, and beans are among crops raised for local consumption. Cacao, used in making chocolate, is one of this area's specialties. Cacao is exported and is the main cash crop.

Most of the men are farmers; women do no farm work. Yurobans are skilled in many crafts. Handwoven cloth, reed baskets, metal-work, and pottery are among the crafts sold in the lively open markets.

Women control much of the marketplace, and a woman's status is largely determined by her position in the market.

Critical Thinking

1 In what ways are the Yorubans different from or similar to us in the United States?

2 If you lived in Yoruba, what might be your role as a worker?

Illus. 9-3
Logos help consumers identify business products.

GOVERNMENT REGULATES

Business activity in the United States is organized as a private enterprise or free market system. Private organizations own the factors of production and choose efficient methods of production in order to earn a profit. Price and output decisions are made not by government decrees, but by the actions of thousands of businesses operating under varying economic conditions. Our government does get involved, however, in our private enterprise system by regulating utilities and preventing unfair business practices.

Regulating Utilities

Most goods and services you use are obtained from private businesses that are relatively free of government regulation. However, a **public utility** is an organization that supplies a service or product vital to all people. These include companies that provide local telephone service, water, and electricity. A public utility is selected to serve a community. If your city had six different electric companies, each with its own utility poles, lines, and expensive equipment, the service you would get would be more expensive and less efficient. Also, the extra poles and wires would create an unsightly environment.

Our federal government generally receives 85 percent of its revenues from taxes and 15 percent from borrowing.

While many utility companies are privately owned, they are closely regulated by government. Therefore, public utilities cannot set prices as they wish. The rates charged for items such as electricity, water, or natural gas must be approved by a government agency.

Preventing Unfair Business Practices

Most businesspeople are fair and honest, but a few may try to take advantage of their customers or competitors. Government attempts to promote fair competition. If a company charges different prices to different people for the same product, it is treating its customers unfairly. Likewise, if one business receives lower rates for the same quality and quantity of supplies than others, it has an advantage. Such action results in unfair competition.

A **monopoly** exists when a business has control of the market for a product or service. While a public utility monopoly may be beneficial by making sure people receive a needed service at a fair price, other monopolies may not be good for the economy. For example, if all food stores in your city were owned by the same company, consumers might not be treated fairly. This business could charge high prices and provide poor-quality products. When competition exists, consumers get the values at the fairest prices.

One government action designed to promote competition and fairness and to prevent monopolies was the passage of **antitrust laws.** Antitrust laws also prevent other unfair business practices such as false advertising, deceptive pricing, and misleading labeling. Each of these unfair practices hurts competition and reduces consumer choice.

The Sherman Act (1890), the first antitrust law, declared illegal "every contract, combination . . . or conspiracy in restraint of trade or commerce."

America is a nation of cultural diversity in which many languages are spoken. Some statistics show that one in seven people will grow up in the United States knowing a second language. Statistics also show that the most common first language, other than English, is Spanish.

GOVERNMENT ASSISTS BUSINESSES

Government helps businesses by collecting and reporting valuable information. Data collected by the government can assist in planning for the future. Information about incomes, prices, worker availability, and business failures can help a businessperson make wiser decisions. For example, census information can help a business decide where the most potential customers live. The Bureau

NET FACTS

The Internet can be found on all seven continents, including Antarctica. A host at the South Pole sends out scientific and weather information.

of Labor Statistics, the Department of Agriculture, and the Department of Commerce are a few of the government agencies that provide information.

Government loans can also be obtained to help new businesses get started. The federal government, through the Small Business Administration (SBA), is an important source of business loans. Farmers and others may receive financial help in times of extreme hardship such as during a drought, flooding, or other natural disasters. Destruction of home and property by a tornado may qualify a person for a low-interest government loan. These programs are designed to promote the economic well-being of our society.

GOVERNMENT PURCHASES PRODUCTS AND SERVICES

All levels of government buy and use a wide range of items. As you learned previously, some services are provided more efficiently by government. Roads, schools, national defense, police and fire protection are some examples.

Government spends a great deal of money each day to buy a variety of products and services. Total federal, state, and local government purchases of goods and services account for about 20 percent of all the goods and services produced in the United States. Governments buy everything from file cabinets to buildings to fleets of automobiles to military jet aircraft. In this role, government is an important economic force. Many businesses depend on government contracts for their survival. For instance, government pays businesses to construct highways and build schools.

GOVERNMENT HIRES WORKERS

Government is the single largest employer in our economy. About one of every nine workers is a public employee. Most people think only of police officers, fire fighters, and sanitation workers as government workers; but government employs the same types of workers as private businesses. Administrative assistants, lawyers, teachers, meat inspectors, and data analysts are examples. Although the number of government employees has grown slowly in recent years, good employment opportunities in government continue—in spite of efforts to

More than 15 million people in our country work full time for federal, state, and local governments.

eliminate or reduce the size of some agencies.

GOVERNMENT RAISES MONEY

Government must have a way to raise money to fund operations and pay wages to workers. Government income is called **revenue.** Governments can obtain revenue through taxes and borrowing. In addition, governments can raise revenue in other ways. Fines for traffic violations and other violations of the law provide revenue for government. Fees and licenses are also a source of income. Certain types of enterprises require a business license. For example, insurance and real estate agents pay a fee for the privilege of conducting business. Governments also charge fees for such things as drivers' licenses and fishing privileges.

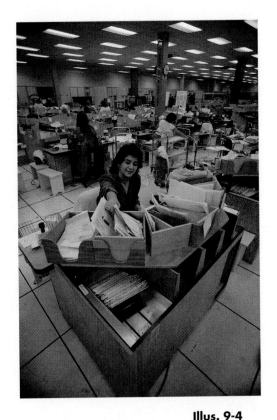

Illus. 9-4
Government at all levels continues to be a major employer, as shown by this IRS service center.

Taxes

A government establishes tax policies to pay for the services it provides. Taxes are levied on earnings, the value of property, and on the sale price of goods and services.

Your earnings as an individual are subject to an income tax. *Income taxes* are levied on the income of individuals. The individual income tax is the largest source of revenue for the federal government. Corporate income taxes also provide government revenue. The corporate income tax is based on business profits.

A major source of revenue for local governments is the real estate *property tax*. This tax is based on the value of the land and the buildings attached to the land. Most property tax revenue is used to pay for schools and other local government services, such as police protection and community parks. Businesses also pay a property tax.

The cost of buying things can be increased by a sales tax. A *sales tax* is a state or local tax on goods and services that is collected by the seller. If you buy a can of paint for $15.00 and the state sales tax is 6 percent, the seller collects $15.90 from you. The seller then will pay 90 cents to the state, but you were the one who provided the money for the tax.

Paying taxes is a responsibility of citizens and businesses. You should pay your fair tax but not more than your share. Tax laws and policies are established to help make the paying of taxes fair and equitable. Whether a particular tax or tax policy is fair and equitable is always subject to debate. Businesses, in spite of public misconceptions, pay a lot of taxes to all levels of government.

Borrowing

Government income from taxes and other sources may not always be enough to cover the costs of providing services. Borrowing is another activity of government. When a government wants to build a building, such as a new court house or convention center, the revenue needed is often raised through borrowing.

Government borrows money by selling bonds. When you buy a government bond, you are helping to finance the services provided by government. Banks, insurance companies, and other financial institutions help finance our governments by purchasing bonds in large quantities. (You will learn about bonds in Chapter 30.) By borrowing money, the government becomes a debtor and must pay interest on its debt. Bonds issued by the U.S. government are backed by the "full faith and credit" of the federal government. Bonds issued by our federal government are considered the least risky of all debt.

Key Ideas

1 Government protects our rights as citizens through police and fire services; as consumers and business owners through the enforcement of contracts and intellectual property rights; and as workers through laws that require safe working conditions.

2 Government regulates utilities and prevents unfair business practices.

3 Government collects and reports valuable information, and provides loans to help businesses get started or overcome natural disasters.

4 Government buys a variety of goods and services and employs workers.

5 Government raises revenue through taxes and borrowing.

End of Chapter Activities

Increasing Your Business Vocabulary

The following terms should become part of your business vocabulary. For each numbered item, find the term that has the same meaning.

antitrust laws

contract

copyright

interstate commerce

intrastate commerce

monopoly

patent

public utility

revenue

trademark

1 A business that supplies a service or product vital to all people; the price charged for the service (or product) is determined by government regulation rather than by competition.

2 Business transactions involving companies that do business only in one state.

3 Government income.

4 Laws designed to promote competition and fairness and to prevent monopolies.

5 Protection of the work of authors, composers, and artists.

6 An agreement to exchange goods or services for something of value.

7 The exclusive right given to a person to make, use, or sell an invention for a period of 17 years.

8 Business transactions involving companies in more than one state.

9 A word, letter, or symbol associated with a specific product or company.

10 A business that has complete control of the market for a product or service.

Reviewing Your Reading

1 What are the three levels of government?

2 How do interstate and intrastate commerce differ?

3 How does government protect society?

4 Explain how the enforcement of contracts helps consumers and businesses.

5 Why does the government grant special property rights such as copyrights and patents?

6 List ways in which government protects workers.

7 Why can one public utility serve a city better than several similar public utilities?

8 When is a monopoly not in the best public interest?

9 Name two ways in which government assists private businesses.

10 What types of products and services do governments buy?

11 What are two ways in which government raises revenue?

Using Your Business Knowledge

1 Below is a list of some of the public services provided by government. For each service, tell whether the federal, state, or local government would most likely have the responsibility for the service. (Some services may be provided by more than one level of government.)

   a. Fire protection
   b. Education
   c. Parks and recreation
   d. Water supply
   e. Highways between cities
   f. Assistance to low-income families
   g. Sewage and trash disposal
   h. Public buses
   i. Police protection
   j. Public libraries
   k. City street maintenance
   l. National defense

2 Make a list of public utilities that serve your community.

   a. What services do they provide?
   b. Do you think it would be better for these services to be offered by several competing businesses? Explain your answer.

3 Each day people enter into many contracts both written and unwritten.

   a. Give examples of contracts between a consumer and a business, between two businesses, and between a worker and a business.
   b. What services are provided by government to enforce contracts?

4 Two students are discussing the topic "Government is Our Biggest Business." Dan believes that some government activities are in direct competition with private businesses and that this is unfair. He believes that government should limit its activities to those that private businesses cannot or will not undertake. Brian thinks that government should undertake any business activities that it can perform better or less expensively than private business. What do you think? Give some examples of business activities undertaken by both private businesses and by government.

5 Why do you suppose government raises revenue through bonds which create debt and require interest payments when government could raise the revenue through an increase in taxes?

Calculating Business Problems

1 A city government spends $186,000 a month on public services. Of that amount, 46 percent is used for fire and police protection.

  a. How much is spent each month for fire and police protection?

  b. How much is spent each month for other services?

  c. How much is spent by the city in a year for fire and police protection?

---

2 In a city in which there are 90,000 employed workers, 18,000 are public employees. Of this number, 6,000 are employed by the federal government, 8,000 by the state, and 4,000 by the city.

  a. What percent of all workers are public employees?

  b. What percent of the public employees are employed by the federal government?

  c. What percent of all employees are employees of the state government?

---

3 The town of Clarksville wants to expand the main street from two to four lanes. To do so, 150 feet of land is needed. How many meters of land will be used for the road-widening project? (See Appendix D.)

---

4 Listed at right is the cash income and expenditures record of the Midland Public Library for one year.

  a. What was the total of the cash on hand and cash received during the year?

  b. How much was paid out during the year?

  c. What percent of the total cash received was accounted for by town and state appropriations? (Round your answer to the nearest whole percent.)

  d. What percent of total expenditures was accounted for by salaries? (Round your answer to the nearest whole percent.)

Income	
Cash on hand, beginning of year	$ 1,250
Town and state appropriations	52,000
Income from investments	1,795
Gifts	1,645
Fines on overdue books	550
Miscellaneous income	325

Expenditures	
Salaries	$23,500
Books and periodicals	6,775
Utilities	1,525
Insurance	780
Equipment and supplies	1,455
Cleaning and repairs	420
Library binding	675
General administrative expenses	715

Applying Technology

Using the *Introduction to Business* template and your word processing program software, select problem CH09. After the problem appears on your screen, complete the following activities. Then, print your completed contracts. Sign Contract 1 as the government official and Contract 2 as the building owner. If you do not have a printer available, save the contracts on a data disk to give to your teacher.

1 You are a county government official authorized to rent office buildings. You must complete a rental contract for an office building. Above Contract 1 is a list of items related to you and your county government office. Cut and paste the items into the appropriate blank spaces in the contract. When dates are required, use the first day of the current month.

2 You own an office building that your county government would like to rent. Above Contract 2 is a list of items related to you and your building. Cut and paste the items into the appropriate blank spaces in the contract. When dates are required, use the first day of the current month.

Making Decisions

Centerville badly needs a new All-Sports Complex—the ASC. The ASC will be located near the center of town and will have facilities that will appeal to just about every kind of individual who wants to exercise or play sports.

The complex will cost $250,000. There are two financing proposals:

No. 1: Issue $250,000 worth of bonds at an interest rate of 4 percent. The town will pay $10,000 per year in interest for 15 years. The total interest would be $150,000. The amount borrowed ($250,000) would have to be paid off in 15 years. Fees charged to users of the complex would pay the interest each year and the amount due bondholders ($250,000). Construction of the complex could begin immediately.

No. 2: Establish a ¼ percent city sales tax on all purchases. The revenue needed could be raised in about 5 years. There would be no user fee charged to residents of Centerville. Construction of the complex would be delayed a few years.

1 What are the advantages and disadvantages of the two proposals?

2 Which proposal do you favor, and why?

The people who operate businesses are called managers. A manager's job typically involves a number of planned and unplanned activities. Many of these activities involve solving problems by making decisions. Managers must be able to make decisions that improve operations, handle disagreements among workers, and allocate resources efficiently. Some of these decisions are made after quick analysis of a situation; others involve more study and investigation.

Job Titles

- Bank Managers and Officers
- Branch Store Managers
- City Managers
- Department Managers
- Education and Training Managers
- Export Managers
- Hospital/Health Service Managers
- Hotel Managers and Assistants
- Labor Relations Managers
- Management Analysts
- Human Resource Managers
- Public Relations Managers
- Retail Managers
- Sales Managers

Employment Outlook

- Managers, administrators, and proprietors make up one of the largest career categories, with more than 15 million employed.
- Career opportunities will increase slowly as large businesses tend to reduce the size of their work forces and eliminate some management positions.
- Opportunities as proprietors of small businesses will continue to be excellent.
- Faster than average growth is expected in health services and in the hotel/motel industry.

Education and Training

- Managerial positions generally require some education beyond high school plus a good work record in a responsible position.
- Courses in business administration with a degree from a two-year or four-year college are desirable.
- Training in the basic functions of management is desirable before moving into a manager's position. (Some firms offer management training programs.)

Salary Levels

Salary levels vary widely depending upon a manager's education, training, work experience, and the business in which she/he is employed. Average (median) salaries include:

- Financial managers in banks and other institutions, $39,700
- Hotel managers, $32,500 to $38,400
- Health services managers, $46,600 with some reaching the $100,000+ level
- Managers in our federal government, $42,100

Critical Thinking

1 Which job titles in this career area appeal to you most? Give reasons for your choice.

2 What are some things you will have to do to achieve success in the career selected?

Management

Unit Three

Technology for Business Decisions

"I received an E-mail today with the sales figures from our Asian office."

"Don't forget to check the Internet for the latest exchange rates for foreign currencies."

A few years ago, these statements would not have made any sense. Today statements like these are a common part of our daily conversations.

Global information networks and on-line computer services make it possible to access more information from your home or office than is available in any library. The foundation of computer network communications is the Internet, an "information highway" that connects schools, government agencies, businesses, and homes.

The Internet includes *E-mail* service for sending messages electronically from one computer to another anywhere in the world. An E-mail address has three parts. Reading from right to left, the first part is the domain, a three-letter code indicating the type of organization: *gov* is for government, *edu* is for an educational institution, *com* is for a commercial or business organization, and *mil* is for a military E-mail address. The second part—immediately following the "at" (@) sign—is the name of the computer receiving the message. The third part—immediately before the @ sign—is the name of the user receiving the message.

Another Internet service is the World Wide Web, referred to as the *Web*. This service allows you to browse through text, graphics, video clips, and sound bites from thousands of information sources. For example, you can view current weather maps, or art from a museum along with an audio commentary.

Internet information providers offer a wide variety of services, including homework hotlines, current reference materials for doing reports, and discussion forums on a wide range of financial, economic, and political topics. On-line users may also post their resumes and search for job opportunities on the computer network. A variety of business information can be accessed on the Internet, such as investment information.

Internet users may also copy computer programs available on the network. Software is available for video games, stories with graphics and sound, and learning activities. You can access software for budgeting, calculating net worth, determining loan payments, and graphing investment portfolios.

As more businesses use the Internet for marketing products and services, shopping from home will increase. In the future, and maybe as soon as tomorrow, you will be able to order everything you need while sitting at your computer.

Critical Thinking

1 *What types of technology make the Internet possible?*

2 *How can global computer networks benefit people throughout the world?*

The Information Superhighway

Chapter Ten

Key Terms

data

computer system

hardware

multimedia system

software

computer network

input device

central processing unit (CPU)

program

application software

operating system software

computer language

memory

disk drive

CD-ROM

output devices

Computers In Business

Objectives

After studying this chapter and completing the end-of-chapter activities, you will be able to:

1 Explain the elements of a computer system.

2 List devices used to enter data into a computer system.

3 Discuss the importance of a computer program.

4 Describe different types of storage devices.

5 Explain methods for reporting the results of a computer system.

6 Describe the effects of computer systems on our society.

"The French Club will meet today during sixth period," Ms. Jenkins announced to her class. "The topic for discussion will be computers in international business."

Fran looked at her friend Brenda and said, "That doesn't make sense! What do computers have to do with the French Club?"

"Recently our club decided to use a database program to keep track of our membership records," said Brenda. "In addition," she went on, "the club is using E-mail to talk to students in France. Then, we are planning a video conference with other French clubs around the United States. And we will also use our computer network to..."

"Wait a minute!" Fran exclaimed. "Database! E-mail! Video conference! Computer network! I don't understand any of this!"

"Well it's really pretty easy," responded Brenda, "and you can start by coming to the meeting today after school."

COMPUTER SYSTEMS IN YOUR LIFE

A few years ago people would have thought it unusual to shop from home by computer or to pay an electric bill using only a telephone. Today, however, these activities, and many others, have become common as a result of computers.

Nearly every business uses some type of computer. Quick, efficient processing is necessary for a company to control its operating costs, to manage its resources, and to stay competitive. Employment in today's workplace requires the use of computers for various business activities.

Uses of Computers

Computers are everywhere. These electronic devices process sales records, test scores, and sports statistics. Computers in business are used mainly to store, process, and report information. However, computers are also used to design factories, control traffic patterns, and measure the health of medical patients.

Computers enable people to handle data quickly and efficiently. **Data** consist of facts in the form of numbers, letters, words, or special symbols. Data with which you are probably familiar include addresses, school grades, and earnings from a part-time job. Data are usually combined into groups called *files* that are used to process and store information.

American engineer Herman Hollerith designed a computer for the 1890 census, making census data available in two and a half years, five years faster than the 1880 census! Today, preliminary census results are available almost immediately.

Illus. 10-1
Computers are commonly used in business situations to store and retrieve data.

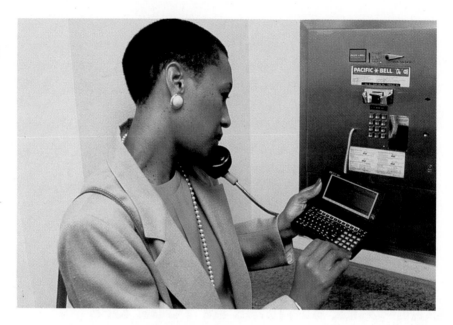

The amount of information used each day in our society is extensive. When you consider the billions of business transactions, checks, and school records that are processed each day, you can see that computers make life easier.

Elements of a Computer System

A home video game, a notebook computer, and an automated highway toll collection system all have four basic components:

One of the first input devices used by computers were punch cards. Each punched hole represented a unit of data—such as a letter or number. Computers read the holes in the cards to process and store data.

1. an input device, such as a keyboard,

2. a processing unit that manages data,

3. memory and storage facilities, and

4. an output device, most likely a printer.

These components, shown in Figure 10-1, combine to create what is called a **computer system.** The physical elements of a computer system are called the **hardware.** Examples of hardware include keyboards, monitors (or screens), chips, and printers.

New hardware for computer systems becomes available almost daily. For example, a **multimedia system** presents information using a combination of

Figure10-1

Every computer system has four main elements.

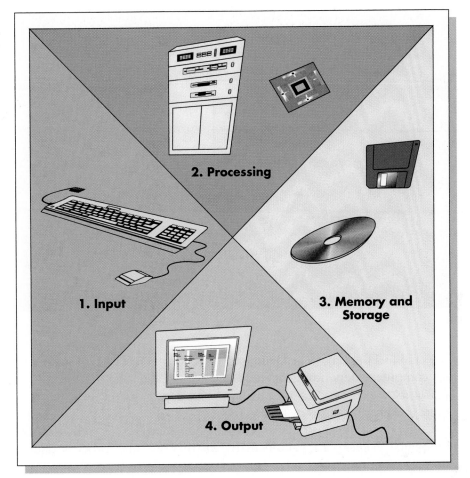

2. **Processing**

1. **Input**

3. **Memory and Storage**

4. **Output**

sound, graphics, animation, and video. In the past, this type of system was only available in large companies. Now, multimedia computer systems are becoming common in small businesses and homes.

In contrast to hardware, **software** refers to the instructions that run the computer system. Types of software commonly used in business organizations are word processing, spreadsheets, database, and communications programs.

You are probably most familiar with a *microcomputer,* also called a *personal computer (PC)*. These computers fall into two categories—desktop and portable models. Companies commonly link many desktop personal computers to create a **computer network.** Global computer networks also exist, such as the one the French Club will use to communicate with students in other countries.

Illus. 10-2

Visible parts of this desktop computer system include a keyboard, central processing unit, and a monitor for data, graphics, or video.

Portable PCs may be called *notebooks, sub-notebooks,* or *palm-top* computers depending on their size. Small, handheld *personal digital assistants* process information with a pen stylus used to write on the pressure-sensitive screen.

Large computer systems used in business are called *mainframe* computers. These can handle many instructions and process data faster. Very large mainframe computers are referred to as *super computers*.

INPUT: GETTING STARTED

The first major component of a computer system is known as input. While people are mostly concerned with the end results of computer operations, there also has to be a starting point. Data are entered into a computer system with an **input device.** A commonly used input device is the keyboard, which allows you to input letters, words, numbers, and other symbols or commands.

A keyboard combined with a visual display screen may be referred to as a *computer terminal.* A terminal is usually part of a communications network connecting several computers. These communi-

Programmers use computer languages to write the instructions for telling a computer what functions to perform. The most common computer languages are ALGOL, APL, ASCII, C, COBOL, FORTRAN, Pascal, and PL/I.

cations networks may be created to handle banking transactions or to send information from one library to another.

Another input device is the mouse, which is a handheld device used to point to a certain command (or image) on the computer screen. For example, if you want to save a file, move the mouse pointer to the drawing of a filing cabinet on the screen. Then click the mouse on the symbol. The data will then be stored for future use.

The following are other types of input devices:

- A controller for a video game system allows you to instruct the movement and actions of game characters.

- Touch-sensitive screens allow you to touch or point at the correct command to enter data.

- Scanning devices—such as the Optical Character Reader (OCR)—read numbers, letters of the alphabet, and symbols directly from a printed or handwritten page and translate them into a format that can be recognized by the computer.

- Voice-activated systems allow you to enter data through voice commands. Instead of entering a complex series of computer instructions, you will be able to say, "Subtract the amount of this payment and determine how much money I have left in my account." The computer will be able to translate your words into instructions it can understand and will be able to perform the necessary processing.

PROCESSING: MAKING THINGS HAPPEN

The second major component of a computer system is known as processing. How do data become meaningful information to be used by organizations and individuals? This activity occurs in the **central processing unit (CPU),** which is the control center of the computer. The CPU is the "brain" of a computer system. In a PC, the CPU consists of tiny wafers or chips, no bigger than your thumbnail. These chips are tiny pieces of silicon imprinted with circuits that carry instructions and data by electronic pulses.

Despite the automated process by which a computer operates, your efforts are still needed. Someone must tell the system what to do. The most common way to give instructions to a computer is with a program. A **program** is a series of detailed, step-by-step instructions that tell the computer what functions to complete.

Illus. 10-3

Computer chips in the central processing unit of a personal computer are imprinted with circuits that carry instructions and data.

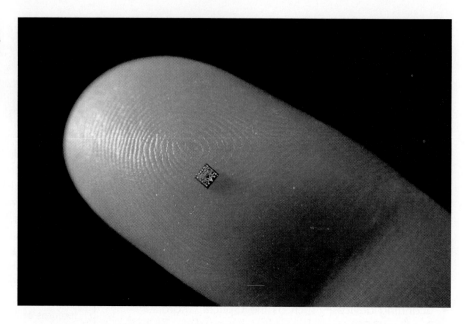

The two main types of computer programs are application software and operating system software. **Application software** refers to programs that perform specific tasks such as word processing, database management, or accounting.

Operating system software translates a computer user's commands and allows application programs to interact with the computer's hardware. Two commonly used operating systems are MS-DOS (Microsoft's Disk Operating System) and Windows, a graphical user interface (GUI) system. With a GUI, commands are displayed with small graphics (called *icons*).

Most complex and powerful computer programs are in formats that are difficult to understand. The format of a computer program is a **computer language,** a system of letters, words, numbers, and symbols used to communicate with a computer. Since a wide variety of ready-to-use programs are available, most people do not have to create their own programs.

MEMORY AND STORAGE: SAVING THINGS FOR LATER

The third major component of a computer system is known as memory. When in use, a program is stored in a location called **memory.** This memory within the computer is also called *internal* (or *primary*) *storage*. During processing, both the program and any data entered with an input device are stored in memory.

Memory capacity is measured using terms such as *bit, nibble, byte,* and *kilobyte (K)*. Figure 10-2 shows these measures. To give you an idea of a computer's internal storage capacity, it would take at least a 1K computer to store the information on an average page in this book.

Primary storage cannot store all of the programs and all of the data needed by computer users. Therefore, *auxiliary* (or *external*) *storage* that is not part of memory is available for storing both programs and data. Disks and tapes are examples of auxiliary storage devices.

A **disk drive** is used to store information on a magnetic medium so that the information can be recalled and used again. Disks on which programs or data are stored come in two basic forms. A floppy disk is a small, pliable, oxide-coated plastic disk in protective covers. A hard disk is built into the computer and is made from rigid material that does not bend. It allows storage of tens of millions of characters. Both types of disk systems use coded magnetic spots to represent information.

A **CD-ROM** (compact disk, read-only memory) is a data storage device that uses laser optics for reading data. One CD-ROM makes it possible to store over 250,000 pages of text.

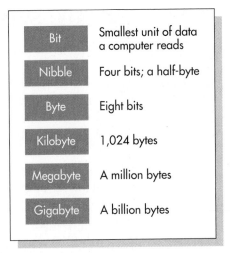

Bit	Smallest unit of data a computer reads
Nibble	Four bits; a half-byte
Byte	Eight bits
Kilobyte	1,024 bytes
Megabyte	A million bytes
Gigabyte	A billion bytes

Figure 10-2
These are measurements used to store information.

One CD-ROM can store as much information as 600, 3½-inch floppy disks.

Illus. 10-4
CD-ROMs and floppy disks store information for future use.

OUTPUT: SEEING THE RESULTS

The fourth major component of a computer system is known as output, the phase of computer operations of greatest interest to most people. Your score on a video game, the results of a test, or the sales for a new product are important outcomes of data-processing activities. **Output devices** present data in a form that can be retrieved later or may be communicated immediately.

Most often output is displayed on a computer screen or monitor. For example, you can view sales reports sorted by salesperson, by geographic area, or by product. With a video game, the screen shows scores for each player.

As of the mid-1990s, most home computer users still had dot-matrix printers. However, this is expected to change as ink-jet and laser printers become available at lower costs.

Global Perspective

Computer Systems for Foreign Language Translation

While on the job at an exporting company, you receive a phone call from a customer in Kenya. Unable to understand the caller's language, you switch on the language translator service. This software allows you to understand, in your language, the comments and questions of your customer.

Computerized translators recognize speech in one language and convert the spoken words into another language. In a language translation system three capabilities work together—speech recognition, machine translation, and speech synthesis. The computer recognizes words spoken in the first language and converts the words into a computer file. Then, the words are translated into the second language, also in a computer file. Finally, a voice synthesizer "speaks" the translated version. A typical one-page letter can be translated in less than one hour.

The earliest language translator programs only had a vocabulary of about 500 words. However with advanced technology, today's systems can process all the words in typical dictionaries for commonly used international business languages, such as Arabic, Chinese, English, French, German, Italian, Japanese, Korean, Portuguese, Russian, Spanish, and Vietnamese.

In the future, an English-speaking businessperson might say, "I would like to register for the conference." Using a computerized translator, a German businessperson will hear, "Ich wuerde mich gerne zur Konferenz anmelden."

Critical Thinking

1 How does a language translation computer system work?

2 How do computerized language translators improve global business activities?

Illus. 10-5
Large color laser printers can print a colorful art poster.

NET FACTS

Cyberspace is the electronic world of the Internet that exists only on computers. Cyberspace is sometimes called *virtual reality.*

Viewing on a screen allows you to see quickly the results of your data processing efforts. However, the screen only allows you to see a limited number of lines at one time. Quite often, the computer may be instructed to produce a copy of the processed data on a printer, an output device that produces results on paper.

Three main types of printers are commonly available. First is the dot-matrix printer, which prints 40 to 80 characters per second. This type of printer uses a movable printhead with pins, or wires, that shoot out and strike a ribbon. Second, an ink-jet printer uses a printhead with a series of little holes. These little holes, called *nozzles,* spray ink onto the paper to create the appropriate letters and images. Third, laser printers use an electrophotographic method of printing, similar to a photocopy machine. These printers produce high-quality documents at rates of as high as several thousand lines per minute.

COMPUTER SYSTEMS IN ACTION

Each day in banks, stores, offices, factories, homes, and not-for-profit organizations, the use of computer systems is expanding. As managers plan and implement computerized activities, they must omputers make it possible for people who are disabled to work and run their own businesses. For example, special scanners read documents and present them in an audio format so that workers who are blind can use printed materials.

decide how best to use technology to serve the production and distribution needs of the organization. They must also balance the costs of efficient data entry with the benefits of fast, accurate information.

New technology will continue to expand the potential uses of computers in business. New software will eliminate some occupations while increasing job growth in others. It will also continue to change the way our work is done. Remember, however, that computers do not make decisions. The information obtained from computer software is just a tool to help in the decision-making process.

Key Ideas

1 Computer systems consist of data, hardware, and software. The four main components of a computer system are the input device, the processing unit, the memory and storage facilities, and an output device.

2 Commonly used input devices are the keyboard, mouse, video game controllers, touch-sensitive screens, scanners, and voice-activated mechanisms.

3 A computer program makes it possible to accept, process, and store data.

4 The main types of storage devices are the internal memory in a computer and disks (such as floppy disks, hard disks, and CD-ROMs).

5 Data processing results are most commonly reported on a computer screen or in a printed report.

6 Computer systems provide the information needed by managers to make business decisions.

End of Chapter Activities

Increasing Your Business Vocabulary

The following terms should become part of your business vocabulary. For each numbered item, find the term that has the same meaning.

application software

CD-ROM

central processing unit (CPU)

computer language

computer network

computer system

data

disk drive

hardware

input device

memory

multimedia system

operating system software

output devices

program

software

1 Computer programs that perform specific tasks such as word processing, database management, or accounting.

2 Mechanisms used to present data in a form that can be used or retrieved later or may be communicated immediately.

3 A data storage device that uses laser optics for reading data.

4 Several computers linked into a single system.

5 The control center of the computer.

6 The combination of an input device, a processing unit, memory and storage facilities, and an output device.

7 A series of detailed step-by-step instructions that tell the computer what functions to complete and when to complete them.

8 Software that translates a computer user's commands and allows application programs to interact with the computer's hardware.

9 A mechanism used to enter data into a computer system.

10 Facts in the form of numbers, alphabetic characters, words, or special symbols.

11 A computer system that presents information using a combination of sound, graphics, animation, and video.

12 A device that is used to store information onto a magnetic disk so that the information can be recalled and used again.

13 Storage locations for the instructions and data that the computer will use.

(Vocabulary continued on the following page.)

14 A system of letters, words, numbers, and symbols used to communicate with a computer.

15 The components or equipment of a computer system.

16 Instructions that run a computer system.

Reviewing Your Reading

1 What are the main uses of computers in businesses and other organizations?

2 What are the four components of a computer system?

3 What devices can be used to input data into a computer system?

4 What is the purpose of the central processing unit?

5 What is the purpose of operating system software?

6 How does the process of storing data on a floppy disk differ from storing data on a CD-ROM?

7 What are the common types of output of a computer system?

8 How will new technology affect the uses of computers in business?

Using Your Business Knowledge

1 Which of the following items are hardware and which are software?

  a. monitor (screen)
  b. a word processing program
  c. chips
  d. keyboard
  e. an operating system program
  f. disk drive
  g. mouse
  h. printer

2 What are the advantages of a mouse as an input device as compared to a keyboard?

3 Is a visual display screen an input device or an output device? Explain.

4 What types of business activities can be performed more efficiently by using a computer system than by doing the tasks manually?

Calculating Business Problems

1 Using the measurements in Figure 10-2 on page 161, how many bytes of information could be stored in a 640K computer?

2 Marvin Trotsky requested sales information from the computer about the Lightning pickup trucks from each of five sales districts in the United States. The computer-generated report is shown as follows. Calculate the data that are missing in the report.

U.S. Region	Trucks Allocated	Percentage Sold	Number of Trucks Sold	Current Inventory*
East	4,200	16%	—	—
Southern	7,075	29%	—	—
North Central	9,500	—	—	5,700
Southwest	—	20%	600	—
Northwest	100	—	—	86

Trucks Allocated − Trucks Sold = Current Inventory

3 A notebook computer sells for $2,800. The printer costs $450 and the yearly maintenance fee is $70.

a. How much will the buyer pay for all three items if it is a cash purchase?
b. If all items are purchased, how much will the monthly payments be if there is a 10 percent interest charge and there will be 12 payments?
c. How much will the buyer save if there is a 2 percent discount on the computer and printer for paying cash within ten days of purchase?

Hint: Refer to Appendix C: Determining Percentage and Interest in Business.

4 The Bank of El Paso installed an automated teller machine (ATM). The ATM costs $19,000 plus $2,500 maintenance per year. If the machine replaced 2½ tellers whose salaries were $26,000 a year, how much was saved per year by installing the computer?

Applying Technology

Using the *Introduction to Business* template and your database program software, select problem CH10. After the problem appears on your screen, complete the following activities. Then, after you have completed each step, display or print a report for each activity. If you do not have a printer available, answer the questions before you leave the computer.

1 Select and list all computer systems costing less than $2,400. Answer the following questions:

a. What is the second computer system listed?
b. What is the last computer system listed?

2 Select and list the computer systems that can be purchased from companies with ZIP Codes of 09203 and 09204. How many computer systems are listed?

3 Select and list the computer systems that have a memory size greater than 400 megabytes. Answer the following questions:

a. What is the first computer system listed?
b. What is the third computer system listed?

Making Decisions

Before a computer system can do business activities, the process or procedure that the hardware will execute must be defined. A flowchart is a visual presentation of the steps in a process or procedure. Computer programmers use this device to break down a process so that it can be understood by the computer.

1 What steps would need to be taken by a computer to total and compare the sales of three different products for the past three years?

2 What problems could occur when a programmer tries to write software to instruct a computer to perform this task?

Chapter Eleven

Key Terms

management information system (MIS)

electronic mail (E-mail)

word processing software

menu

desktop publishing

graphics software

database

database software

spreadsheet software

integrated software

computer-assisted instruction (CAI)

telecommuting

modem

fax

Computer Applications

Objectives

After studying this chapter and completing the end-of-chapter activities, you will be able to:

1 Describe the purpose of a management information system.

2 Explain the benefits of word processing software and desktop publishing.

3 Identify uses of database software.

4 Discuss situations when spreadsheet software could be used.

5 Identify uses of technology in retailing, public service, and education.

6 Describe how technology allows people to work at home.

169

Josh Aki arrived on the first day of his new part-time job at NBI Distributors. This retailing company sells a variety of products by mail, telephone orders, and computer.

"Josh, please outline a report with the sales results of the new products we have introduced over the past six months," was the request of his supervisor. Based on comments from other employees, Josh knew that some of the products were doing well and others were just sitting in the warehouse. However, Josh wasn't sure how to approach this task.

Alicia saw that Josh looked confused, so she helped him by saying, "Check the database for sales results, summarize the data on the spreadsheet program, and prepare your report with our word processing software."

"Thanks for your help," Josh responded. "However, now I think I have even more questions to ask!"

MANAGEMENT INFORMATION STSTEMS

Managers need information to make business decisions. A **management information system (MIS)** is an organized system of processing and reporting information in an organization. Computer systems and software are essential components of management information systems. A company may need a departmental budget with expected income and expenses for the next three months. Using a special program, past company data and future projections can be combined to create this budget. The resulting document helps managers plan future business decisions.

Components of an MIS

As shown in Figure 11-1, the four main phases of an MIS are gathering data, analyzing data, storing data, and reporting results. These activities allow an organization to obtain needed information in four main categories:

1. financial information, including budgets, sales reports, and financial statements

2. production and inventory information, including production summaries, lists of tools and supplies, and finished goods reports

3. marketing information, including data on customer needs, current economic conditions, and actions of competitors

4. human resources information, including salaries, employee benefit data, and employee evaluations.

Data Sources

The information for an MIS comes from several sources. *External* data sources are outside an orga-

A vailable on the Internet, a newsgroup is an external data source consisting of collected articles about a specific topic. If your company is planning a new factory in Africa, accessing a newsgroup can provide current information about economic, social, and political trends in that geographic region.

Figure 11-1
A management
information
system provides
information for
business deci-
sions.

nization. Financial institutions, government agencies,
and customers are examples of external data
sources. In contrast, *internal* data sources provide
input from within the organization. Internal data
includes accounting records, inventory information,
and company sales figures. While gathering raw data
may be an easy task, changing these facts and figures into meaningful information is the major goal
of an MIS.

The MIS in Action

What activities are involved in a management
information system? How is needed information for
business decisions communicated to managers? The
operation of the MIS involves the following steps:

A form of electronic
messages has been around
since the early 1800s, when
Samuel F. B. Morse invented
the telegraph. That system
required a knowledge of
codes for each letter of the
alphabet, and the receiver
of the message had to be
present to record it.

NET FACTS

On the Internet, you can visit libraries from around the world, take a class from a teacher on the other side of the country, order merchandise, and transfer money from your checking account to your savings account. More and more information and services appear on the Net every day.

1. identify the information needs of the organization

2. obtain facts, figures, and other data

3. process, analyze, and organize data in a useful manner

4. distribute information reports to those who make decisions

5. update data files as needed.

Computer networks are commonly used in an MIS to distribute information to managers, employees, and others. These networks connect computers, printers, and other equipment within a company or around the world. Worldwide networks are created through telephone lines, satellites, and other communication technology.

Also important for communicating information is **electronic mail,** also called *E-mail*. E-mail gives users the ability to send data quickly through a computer system. After an employee prepares a letter or report, the document is sent electronically to another computer on the local or world-wide network. Electronic mail allows information to be exchanged without preparing a hard copy of the document, saving time and money.

Illus. 11-1

Most personal computers within an organization are connected by a network.

WORD PROCESSING SOFTWARE

Every organization has a constant flow of reports, correspondence, and other information. **Word processing software** is used to create and revise written documents. Word processing allows the user to enter, store, revise, and print text for letters, memos, reports, or standard business forms.

Benefits of Word Processing

Using computerized word processing, you can create, store, retrieve, and print frequently used letters, memos, and reports. Ease of editing, revising, and updating text allows you to quickly move a paragraph or add and delete words, sentences, or paragraphs. Word processing software allows you to check spelling and grammar by pushing one or two keys or pointing and clicking your mouse. Also possible is writing a letter or memo once and then personalizing copies with the names and addresses of different people.

These activities are easy since most software allows you to select a task from a **menu,** which is a list of computer functions that appear on the screen (see Figure 11-2). For example, you may be asked if you want to save, edit, or create a new document. After making your menu selection, you are able to perform that task.

Figure 11-2

A menu makes it easy to select commands for operating the software.

File Writer 4.1

1—Create new file
2—Revise existing file
3—Add to existing file
4—Print existing file
5—Help screens
6—Exit program

Desktop Publishing

Word processing activities are commonly expanded to produce newsletters, brochures, and other publications. **Desktop publishing** is the process of writing and designing high quality publications with the use of personal computers. A desktop publishing system includes the hardware and software needed to create professional formats with artistic designs. Many organizations use this method to publish high quality materials at a low cost.

In the chapter opening, Josh's supervisor wanted him to present data in a report format. However, instead of just listing numbers, Josh could have communicated the data clearly and quickly with the use of a graph or diagram. **Graphics software** is a computer program that prepares charts, graphs, and other visual elements. This software can create bar charts, line graphs, and pie charts as well as specialized graphics in the form of maps and other drawings. The use of graphics makes communication much clearer than the use of words alone. Computer graphics are commonly used in television commercials, movies, training materials for employees, and business documents.

MAINTAINING RECORDS WITH DATABASE SOFTWARE

"Create a list of employees who have perfect attendance on the job during the past six months." These types of requests are quite common in organizations. A **database** is an organized collection of information with the pieces of information related to one another in some way. For example, an inventory clerk may require a list of products sold, while the sales manager may need similar information sorted by the customers who purchased the products or the salespersons who sold the products. Each of these reports would come from the same database, but would require different sorting and rearranging.

Creating a Database

Database software processes a database. As shown in Figure 11-3, a database program can arrange and sort information in different ways. An organization might use database software to handle records for employee information, sales and inventory, and accounting. Business owners and managers depend upon different databases for making decisions about day-to-day operations and for meeting long-term organizational goals.

Database Use in Business

The data stored in a database are commonly used and shared in several ways. Data may be stored in one personal computer, and only the user of that computer can access the data. Or, data may be stored in a central location and may be accessed by several people on the computer network.

In recent years, *database marketing* has become popular. Software is used to maintain, analyze, and combine customer information files. The information about customers is then used to increase sales by better serving customer needs. For example, a household with young children might receive advertising about educational software. Using a database increases the chance of reaching potential customers who are likely to buy the product.

BUSINESS DECISION MAKING WITH SPREADSHEET SOFTWARE

In the past, accountants used worksheets on paper with many rows and columns of information. Such a worksheet is an example of a manually prepared *spreadsheet*, which involves columns and rows of data. **Spreadsheet software** is a computer program that formats data in columns and rows in order to do calculations.

Figure 11-3
Database software is used to arrange information into needed reports.

Sales Database

Date	Customer	Amount	Salesperson
Nov. 3	L. Collins	$ 58	Ellis
Nov. 9	V. Owen	$ 12	Ellis
Nov. 14	A. Browing	$178	Jones
Nov. 15	F. Brock	$ 45	Lowery
Nov. 16	L. Collins	$317	Ellis
Nov. 21	F. Brock	$216	Lowery
Nov. 24	L. Collins	$ 84	Ellis
Nov. 25	A. Browing	$193	Jones
Nov. 28	F. Brock	$ 61	Jones
Nov. 30	V. Owen	$111	Lowery

Database Selection—Sales Report

Salesperson	Total Sales
Ellis	$ 471
Jones	$ 432
Lowery	$ 372
Total Sales	$1,275

Database Selection—Customer Accounts

Customer	Amount Due
F. Brock	$ 322
A. Browing	$ 371
L. Collins	$ 459
V. Owen	$ 123
Total Amount Due	$1,275

The Basics of Spreadsheets

Spreadsheet software makes data entry easier and more accurate. Also, spreadsheets make computations—such as totals, percentages, and averages—quickly and accurately with the use of built-in formulas.

The location where a column and row intersect is called a *cell*. As a spreadsheet is created with specific information, words, numbers, or formulas are entered into the cells. Other built-in features of spreadsheet software include formatting (for dollars or percentages), changing column widths, and copying of cells.

A *data-entry clerk* has an important role in the computer systems of business organizations; accurately keys numbers, words, and other data for future use by the company; and must have keyboarding skills.

Computations with spreadsheets are more accurate because the computer will not make errors as a person might. As always, however, if the user instructs the computer to use the wrong formula, the results will be inaccurate.

Using Spreadsheet Software

Spreadsheets are used to prepare payroll records, financial statements, budgets, and other financial documents (see Figure 11-4). This software may also be used to do a *what-if* analysis of a situation. For example, a manager may want to see the effect of different prices on profit. The spreadsheet automatically calculates each situation as the data are entered.

Cultural *Perspective*

Calculators in Europe

"**M**ay I borrow your pebble?" This is a question one business math student might have asked another—in ancient Rome! The word *calculator* comes from a Latin term that means calculus or pebble.

This early Roman calculator used a system of tiny stones that were inserted in the grooves of a counting board. The board was divided into columns for ones, tens, hundreds, thousands, and so on. This system allowed merchants to keep track of their business transactions.

Over a thousand years later in 1642, Blaise Pascal, a French mathematician, developed the first adding calculating machine. This device was called the Pascaline and was the basis for adding machines invented in the 1800s and early 1900s.

Today, electronic calculators make it possible to perform mathematical operations that previously took several minutes or longer. Built-in functions on calculators quickly allow you to compute averages, square roots, and interest payments. This is quite different from ancient Roman times or the times of Pascal and his students in

the 1600s. But without the contributions of calculating pioneers, we would not have the electronic calculators we have today.

Remember, the next time you have trouble with your calculator, at least you don't have to count stones!

Critical Thinking

1 How do the needs of a society influence the creation of new inventions?

2 What effect might the invention of the adding calculating machine have had on early business activities?

Figure 11-4
A spreadsheet may be used to prepare the financial reports and documents of a business organization.

```
       A        B        C        D        E        F        G        H
 1                   19-- PROJECTED INCOME STATEMENT
 2
 3 ESTIMATED SALES    1000000
 4
 5 COST OF GOODS SOLD  722000
 6
 7 GROSS PROFIT        278000
 8
 9 LESS EXPENSES:
10   SALARIES          150000
11   ADVERTISING        50000
12   UTILITIES          30000
13   INSURANCE          30000
14
15 TOTAL EXPENSES      260000
16
17 PROFIT BEFORE TAX    18000
18
19
20 ESTIMATED SALES     950000
21
22 COST OF GOODS SOLD  685900
23
24 GROSS PROFIT        264100
25
26 LESS EXPENSES:
27   SALARIES          142500
28   ADVERTISING        47500
29   UTILITIES          30000
30   INSURANCE          29000
31
32 TOTAL EXPENSES      249000
33
34 PROFIT BEFORE TAX    15100
35
36
37      19-- PROJECTED INCOME STATEMENT WITH VARIABLE RESULTS
38
39                         PERCENT OVER/UNDER FORECAST
40                   %0      -5%      -10%      +5%      +10%
41
42 ESTIMATED SALES    1000000  950000   900000  1050000  1100000
43
44 COST OF GOODS SOLD  722000  685900   649800   759100   794200
45
46 GROSS PROFIT        278000  264100   250200   291900   305800
47
48 LESS EXPENSES:
49   SALARIES          150000  142500   135000   157500   165000
50   ADVERTISING        50000   47500    45000    52500    55000
51   UTILITIES          30000   30000    30000    30000    30000
52   INSURANCE          30000   29000    28000    31000    32000
53
54 TOTAL EXPENSES      260000  249000   238000   271000   282000
55
56 PROFIT BEFORE TAXES  18000   15100    12200    20900    23800
57
```

Integrated Software Packages

Word processing, database, and spreadsheet software are called single-function software packages. These programs each have one purpose. In contrast, **integrated software** is a computer program capable of doing more than one basic function. Common integrated software packages combine word processing, database, spreadsheet, and graphics applications along with a communications module for E-mail.

A major advantage of integrated software is the convenience of moving data from one portion of a program to another. For example, a spreadsheet or graph could be combined with text in a word processing document.

COMPUTER APPLICATIONS IN ORGANIZATIONS

Technology is changing the way we do business by allowing new services such as shopping at home or banking in supermarkets. The use of computers is increasing in almost every type of organization.

Sales and Retailing

Other than in the office, computers probably have the greatest impact in stores. Salespeople enter sales information as a purchase takes place. A computer automatically updates the inventory record when an item is bought, sold, or returned. The amount of the sale and other transaction information is recorded in the company's database. In addition, a receipt or invoice is prepared for the customer.

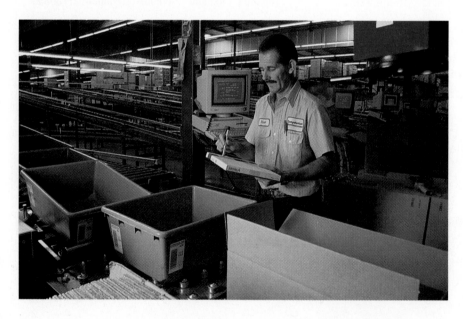

Illus. 11-2

In addition to their use in retail stores, bar code scanners are used in warehouses to maintain inventory.

Public Service

Government agencies use computers to maintain records. For example, the federal government keeps Social Security records for all past and present workers in the United States and military records for people who have served in a branch of the military. Agencies continually expand their use of computers. Medical information can be found within seconds to save lives. Police records can be sent from state to state minutes after a crime has occurred, helping to solve the crime. Schools and other agencies can transfer records easily when someone moves to another area of the country.

Education

Computers have become very important teaching devices. Computers make it possible to train and test workers in a variety of professions. Office workers learn to use word processing software, while also receiving instruction on the proper use of grammar, spelling, punctuation, capitalization, and document forms. Airline pilots use computerized simulators to learn and improve skills needed for flying new types of aircraft.

Computer-assisted instruction (CAI) is the use of computers to help people learn or improve skills at their own pace. With CAI, students work at a speed that best serves their needs. The student does not have to go to a school building for instruction. The

Spelling and grammar checking features have not replaced your need for good writing skills. For example, a spell checker will not be able to detect an error such as *previous friend* when in fact you intended to enter the phrase *precious friend*.

Illus. 11-3

With computer-assisted instruction, students can work at their own pace at home or in the classroom.

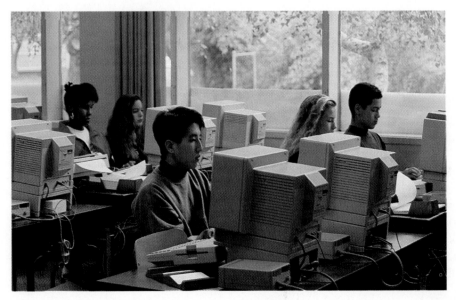

student can learn at home on a computer network system connected to a central training location.

TELECOMMUTING AND THE HOME OFFICE

Each morning, Brad Collins gets ready for work, eats breakfast, and travels to his office . . . in the next room! Brad is one of over 40 million Americans doing all or part of their work at home. **Telecommuting** is a term used to describe the activities of a worker using a computer at home to do a job. Telecommuting saves travel time and costs and results in less traffic along with reduced noise and air pollution.

Each year more and more people become telecommuters. This working arrangement is especially attractive to people who have difficulty leaving their home to go to work, such as workers who are disabled or parents who desire to be near their children. A work-at-home arrangement is most common among workers such as

- writers
- editors
- researchers
- accounting clerks
- sales representatives
- computer programmers.

The Internet, a worldwide computer network, makes it possible to send an E-mail message anywhere in the world. For example, a message sent to *president@whitehouse.gov* will go to the President of the United States.

Database programs not only search, sort, and select records by various *fields* (items of data), but this software can also calculate totals for customer accounts and other information.

They can easily send their reports, documents, and ideas to their employers' offices by computer.

Telecommuting is made possible with computers and other technology. A **modem** is a device that allows a person to communicate with other computer users through telephone lines. A modem allows an at-home computer to communicate with the computer system at the company's main office.

Working at home is more practical since the development of a device that transmits a copy of a document from one location to another. A **fax,** or *facsimile,* machine allows the rapid sending or receiving of copies through telephone lines. Telecommuters can easily submit completed work and obtain new assignments with the use of a fax machine.

Key Ideas

1 The major goal of a management information system is to change raw data (facts and figures) into information that can be used by managers.

2 Word processing software allows efficient creation, revision, and storage of letters, memos, and reports.

3 Database software arranges and sorts information in different ways to provide lists about customers, products, or other business data.

4 Spreadsheet software can be used to prepare payroll records, financial statements, budgets, and what-if reports.

5 Technology has expanded the use of computers in retailing, public service organizations, and education.

6 Computers, modems, fax machines, and other technology have made it possible for an increasing number of people to work at home.

End of Chapter Activities

Increasing Your Business Vocabulary

The following terms should become part of your business vocabulary. For each numbered item, find the term that has the same meaning.

computer-assisted instruction (CAI)

database

database software

desktop publishing

electronic mail (E-mail)

fax

graphics software

integrated software

management information system (MIS)

menu

modem

spreadsheet software

telecommuting

word processing software

1 A computer program that uses a row-and-column arrangement of data to perform calculations.

2 The use of computers to help people learn or improve skills at their own pace.

3 A list of computer functions that appears on the screen.

4 A computer program that processes an organized collection of information.

5 A term used to describe the activities of a worker using a computer at home to perform a job.

6 A computer program used to create and revise written documents.

7 A process of writing and designing high quality publications with the use of microcomputers.

8 The delivery of correspondence through a computer system.

9 An organized system of processing and reporting information in an organization.

10 A computer program that prepares charts, graphs, and other visual elements.

11 A device that allows you to communicate with other computers through the use of telephone lines.

12 A system in which a copy of a document is transmitted from one location to another through an electronic device connected to telephone lines.

13 A collection of organized data whose elements are in some way related to one another.

14 A computer program capable of performing more than one basic function.

Reviewing Your Reading

1 What are the four phases of a management information system?

2 What are the four main categories of information used by most organizations?

3 How do external data differ from internal data?

4 What are the benefits of computerized word processing?

5 What function does database software serve?

6 What types of reports can be prepared using spreadsheet software?

7 What are the main advantages of integrated software?

8 In what ways have computers helped businesses involved in sales and retailing?

9 What aspects of public service have been made more efficient by computers?

10 What are the benefits of computer-assisted instruction (CAI)?

11 What types of careers are best suited to telecommuting?

Using Your Business Knowledge

1 List examples of (a) external data and (b) internal data used by most companies

2 List three on-the-job tasks that a person might perform more efficiently with the help of a computer.

3 Identify which of the following computer applications would be performed using word processing software, database software, spreadsheet software, and graphics software.

   a. Preparing a report of new equipment purchased for each office of a company.
   b. Preparing a list of employees that is sorted by ZIP Code.
   c. Creating a form letter to go to new customers of a mail-order business.
   d. Creating a pie chart showing the portion of sales of each product.
   e. Preparing a document listing the total sales for each geographic area of the country.
   f. Listing the employees who have not missed a day of work in five years.
   g. Sending a letter to each employee who has not missed a day of work in five years.
   h. Creating a budget for the new office that will be opened in another city.

4 Who would benefit from schools that would allow students to take classes at home by computer?

5 Describe the benefits to workers, employers, and society when an organization allows some of its employees to do all or part of their work at home.

Calculating Business Problems

1 Rico Sanchez bought a personal computer for $2,100. He also bought a disk-drive unit for $1,300 and a printer for $3,150. If he bought five floppy disks at $1 each, how much did he pay for everything?

2 After Rico Sanchez (Question 1) had his computer, disk-drive unit, and printer for a year, he decided to sell them. If he sold them for 75 percent of what he paid for them, how much did he receive for the three items?

3 Lonnette Franco paid the following monthly fees for her modem service during the year.

  a. How much was Lonnette's yearly expense for the modem service?

  b. How much was Lonnette's average monthly cost for this service?

January	$35.84	July	$36.74
February	18.48	August	22.00
March	31.79	September	31.05
April	61.75	October	33.32
May	51.58	November	85.37
June	33.15	December	50.57

Applying Technology

Using the *Introduction to Business* template and your spreadsheet program software, select problem CH11. After the problem appears on your screen, complete the following activities. Then, after you have completed each step, display or print the completed spreadsheet for each activity. If you do not have a printer available, answer the questions before you leave the computer.

1 Determine student preferences for each type of software used in the business classes at Hamilton High School. What is the total number of students who prefer using word processing software?

2 What is the total number of students who prefer using database software?

3 What is the total number of students who prefer using spreadsheet software?

Optional: Create a pie chart showing the preferences for each type of software.

Making Decisions

Johnny Tom and Billie Chan are planning to start a small shop selling imported products. Johnny believes they need to purchase an integrated software package for preparing documents and maintaining records. Billie believes that individual word processing, database, and spreadsheet programs would better serve their needs.

1 What are possible advantages of single-function programs over an integrated software package?

2 What factors should Johnny and Billie consider when selecting software for their business?

Chapter Twelve

Key Terms

robots

artificial intelligence (AI)

expert systems

computer-aided design (CAD)

on-line computer service

SMART card

white-collar crime

piracy

computer virus

Your Future with Technology

Objectives

After studying this chapter and completing the end-of-chapter activities, you will be able to:

1 Explain how technology is affecting employment.

2 List the benefits of using robots and other technology in business operations.

3 Discuss how computers help expand global business activities.

4 Identify the services that technology can bring to your home.

5 Explain transportation improvements resulting from technology.

6 Discuss social concerns associated with computers and technology.

Herb Cunningham had just lost his sixth job in seven years. Although he is a talented worker, demand for his skills as an inventory clerk are declining. Computerized scanning systems keep track of inventory in most companies.

"I guess it's time to upgrade my skills," Herb commented to his son, Joe. "I'm going to enroll in that computer training program. Then next time I'll be able to move easily into another job."

"That might not be enough, dad," responded Joe. "You better also learn how to operate a robot, access artificial intelligence, and download a file from a computer network."

"I'm not sure I'll be able to learn all of those, son," was Herb's reply.

"But, dad, I'll be here to help you," said Joe, "and you can start by letting me show you how this video game works!"

TECHNOLOGY AND OUR ECONOMY

The times in which we live are both exciting and frustrating. New uses for computers and other technology are discovered almost daily. Medical researchers have developed computerized body parts that respond when the brain gives the command for action. Data clerks are able to store billions of bits of data in a small area that cannot be seen with the human eye. And of course, computers are used to create special effects for motion pictures and at amusement parks. As you read this, thousands of people are developing new uses for computers that will be ready in the near future.

Many people think computers are taking away their jobs. What is actually occurring, though, is a shift in the job duties and skills needed to work in business and industry. When workers are replaced by computers, companies need to retrain the workers with skills in programming, operating, or repairing computer systems. *Displaced workers,* or workers who are unemployed because of changing job conditions, must adapt to the changing job market in order to have continued employment. What actions can companies and workers take to be ready for the new jobs of the future?

As computers and other technology become more important in our lives, the ability to use this technology is vital to each person's economic survival. *Computer literacy* is the ability

Illus. 12-1

Computers are being used to improve productivity and efficiency in every area of business.

to use computers to process information or solve problems. While you do not have to understand how to program a computer to use it, you do need to know how to enter, store, process, and retrieve information.

Computers are present in almost every business situation to help improve efficiency and productivity. Computers can be found in oil fields, warehouses, retail stores, hospitals, offices, and factories.

Robots

"Only Bel-comp can save us now!" the crew captain in the movie said as the spaceship raced out of control toward the uncharted planet. Most of us have seen robots and other computer systems in science fiction movies set in outer space and in the future. However, real-life **robots,** mechanical devices programmed to do routine tasks, are used in many factories. An example of where robots are used is assembly line work that requires repeated tasks. Early robots did only simple tasks such as tightening a bolt on an automobile.

Today, robots exist that can see, hear, smell, and feel. Robots are able to work 24 hours a day. These computerized workers can work in dangerous situations such as outer space, underwater, or underground.

Expert Systems

Have you ever wanted a quick answer to a question without having to find a book or person who knew the answer? **Artificial intelligence (AI)** is software that enables computers to reason, learn, and make decisions using logical methods similar to the methods humans use. An example of artificial intelligence are computer programs that make decisions about complex topics. For example, software exists that asks people questions about their health in order to determine solutions to potential problems. This software allows people in areas without doctors to receive better medical care.

Computer programs that help people solve technical problems are called **expert systems** and are now available for medical services, financial planning, and legal matters. Expert systems are based on the knowledge of human experts in many specialized areas. Therefore, these systems provide intelligent answers as effectively as human experts in those subject matters. For example, employees of the Internal Revenue Service use an expert system to quickly answer questions from taxpayers.

As technology changes career opportunities, workers will need to update skills three or four times in their lifetimes to remain employable.

Computer-Aided Design

Many of the products you use each day were created with the use of computers. **Computer-aided design (CAD)** refers to the use of technology to create product styles and designs. CAD allows you to try different sizes, shapes, and materials for a new machine, automobile, or food package. This process can be used to experiment with many variations before spending time and money building a model or actually going into production.

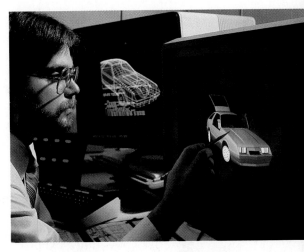

Illus. 12-2
With computer-aided design (CAD), a designer may experiment with many different variations before spending time and money on an actual production model.

TECHNOLOGY AND GLOBAL BUSINESS

Multinational computer systems, along with software that translates information from one language to another, make it possible to conduct business around the world without leaving your computer. Instant transmission of data with the use of satellites makes even the farthest point on earth as close as a button on your computer. Increased global business can have an important impact on world trade and international relations.

Import and export trades can take place using a computer system, with the goods then being shipped from the closest location to save time and money. For example, you may order an item from a company in Italy by using a computer. When the Italian marketers receive your order on their computer, they check a database and discover there are five such items in stock in Canada. They instruct the Canadian importers by E-mail to ship the items to you; you receive them the next day. You pay the Italian company, and the Italian and Canadian companies settle their accounts later—through the computerized banking system.

Another way of bringing people together to do business is *video conferencing*. This system allows people in different geographic locations to meet "face-to-face" by satellite for sales presentations, training sessions, and other types of meetings. A sales staff in Peru can make a presentation to potential customers in Spain, South Africa, Pakistan, and the United States without leaving Peru.

Someday you are likely to start the day with the following greeting: "It's 6 a.m." By saying, "I'm up!" you can stop the message from your voice-activated clock radio.

YOUR WINDOW TO THE WORLD

At home, your computer system provides shopping assistance, financial and other information, and entertainment.

On-Line Computer Services

While sitting at a computer, you can now have access to every book, magazine, and newspaper ever published. Or, you can shop at home by video for food, clothing, and other products. An **on-line computer service** is a computer network connection with information, shopping, and entertainment services. Each day more and more people are banking at home, making travel arrangements, checking the community event calendar, and comparing prices at several stores without leaving home. Each of these is possible as homes are connected to major databases.

You can also use on-line services to obtain software for doing household activities on a personal computer. Programs can keep a list of names and addresses of people to whom you send greeting cards, or you may store your favorite recipes by categories. A family's medical history can be kept on file, or you can have an inventory of household items for insurance records in case of theft or damage. In addition, computer programs may be used for personal financial record keeping, budgeting, writing checks, and preparing your income tax return.

SMART Cards

While most people are familiar with credit cards and electronic banking cards, few may be aware of the existence of a **SMART card,** a plastic card with a silicon chip for storing information. The chip within the card stores such data as your current account balance, credit history, and even medical information for emergencies.

In the future, SMART cards will be used to allow quick check-in at hotels and auto rental companies.

A SMART card has the potential to take the place of money and checks because each transaction is recorded on the chip as it occurs. Every time a purchase is made, the amount of the transaction would be deducted from the balance in your SMART card account. The card would also serve as a personal record keeper for travel and other expenses. In addition, a SMART card can be used to prove you paid for merchandise you want to exchange, to gain admittance to your place of work, or to unlock and start your car without keys.

Cultural Notes

America is a nation of cultural diversity in which many languages are spoken. These various languages have particular words that reflect their particular cultures. In all cultures, there is typically a term by which people describe themselves as being human. For example, the Alaska Natives, or Eskimos, use the term Inuit, or "the people", to describe themselves.

Interactive Television

While many people have talked back to the television over the years, it is now possible for your TV to "hear" you. *Interactive television* combines cable television with computer software to create two-way communications systems. Consumers may obtain movies on demand, make travel reservations, shop from home, play video games, and send and receive E-mail.

Virtual Reality

"I just visited the mountains of Switzerland, but didn't leave my living room!" This statement is possible with *virtual reality* (VR) technology that provides three-dimensional computer

Advanced technology is expected to add smell and touch sensations to virtual reality experiences. Can the *taste* of VR be far behind?

Ethical *Perspective*

Are Computers a Threat to Personal Privacy?

Would you want your friends, relatives, neighbors, or employer to know every detail of your personal and financial life? Today, the average person has her or his name in many databases. When you are born, a record of your birthday, address, and parents' names is created. In addition, when you apply for a driver's license, buy a home, apply for credit, or open a checking account, you are creating a trail of data. Starting with just your name and Social Security number, computer database experts may be able to identify your place of employment, salary, credit record, children's names and ages, and magazine subscriptions.

Companies can benefit from using computerized databases in several ways. Marketing campaigns are more efficient if commercials and ads are targeted only to consumers who are most likely to buy the products. Increased sales can mean increased salaries and job opportunities. Nevertheless, computerized databases can be misused. Easy access to computer data may allow dishonest people to invade privacy or make illegal credit card purchases and unauthorized withdrawals from bank accounts.

Companies and government agencies have taken some actions to safeguard the information in their databases. Restrictions on data, however, must be balanced against the fact that freedom of information is an important liberty in our society.

Critical Thinking

1 What are the benefits and dangers if *all* databases become easily accessible to anyone?

2 What actions should companies and government take to protect the privacy of information? What actions should not be taken?

Illus. 12-3

Virtual reality technology includes special viewing goggles which create three-dimensional images with sound.

images with visuals and sound. VR makes use of special viewing goggles allowing the user to "walk" through situations. Besides travel and entertainment, this technology could be used for educational and business activities. Teachers can take students to visit ancient Egypt or view a manufacturing plant in operation. Motor vehicle and real estate salespeople will be able to show customers their products without the buyer ever leaving home.

TECHNOLOGY AND TRANSPORTATION

Almost every type of transportation involves computers. Each new model of motor vehicle makes increased use of computerization. Many aircraft fly to their destinations under the control of computers. Rapid transit trains are scheduled and operated by computer systems.

Our daily transportation is greatly influenced by the computer. Computers were first used in automobiles to regulate speed, climate, and audio systems. The use of technology in your car has been expanded to include computer-voice safety systems that warn drivers and passengers about unfastened seat belts, open doors, and engine problems.

Future expectations for automobiles include radar systems to alert drivers about potential collisions, video screens with maps to plot your route, and sensing devices that will allow you to travel with the use of an *automatic pilot*.

Motor vehicles with crash-avoidance radar systems are already in production. Drivers will be warned with lights and buzzers of potential collision situations.

Illus. 12-4
This electronic traffic navigation system guides the driver to his destination.

SOCIAL CONCERNS ABOUT COMPUTERS

Every new development has advantages, accompanied by potential problems. Expanded computer use has resulted in concerns about health and safety, criminal activities, and privacy. While computers are beneficial to our society, the wise person will not place complete faith in the reliability or safety of computer systems.

Potential Health Dangers

During our lifetimes, we have learned that various products and substances can be dangerous. While little danger exists from using computers and other technology, some people have encountered discomfort from on-the-job activities. For example, eyestrain and vision problems have been associated with prolonged work with computer screens. Muscle tension and nerve damage can occur from too many hours at a keyboard. These and other concerns have resulted in guidelines from labor organizations and government agencies for safe computer operation.

Computer Crime

Wide use of computers has led to an increase in **white-collar crime,** illegal acts performed by office or professional workers while at work. Workers may steal money, information, or computer time through improper use of databases or illegal access

nteractive television will make videograms possible. You will be able to send personalized video messages to family and friends.

NET FACTS

A branch or section of the Internet is called a *domain*. Domains can be assigned according to country, region, or state, or according to type of organization, such as education, commercial, government, or military.

to computer systems. While the typical bank robbery results in a loss of $10,000, computer crimes involving bank records average hundreds of thousands of dollars. Theft of a physical item is obvious; however, theft of computer time or information from a database is usually more difficult to detect.

Piracy, which is stealing or illegally copying software packages or information, is also a growing problem. Companies that develop software may lose more than half of their profits to information pirates who violate the law. Copyright laws, which are discussed in Chapter 9, apply to software as well as books and music.

Destructive efforts are also a concern to computer users. A **computer virus** is a program code hidden in a system that can later do damage to software or stored data. The virus may be programmed to become active on a certain date or when certain data are accessed. While some computer viruses are harmless, only showing up as a funny message, others have been known to destroy critical government records.

Privacy Concerns

One of the greatest challenges facing computer users is the need to guarantee privacy. Some dishonest people have learned how to illegally access computer databases. While some laws exist to protect your privacy, many concerned people believe these regulations are not strong enough. Some businesses are becoming stricter about who can access and use company information. Also, tighter security systems are being developed. Some organizations change the password needed to access information several times a day to protect their databases.

A rrested computer criminals sometimes agree to help law enforcement agencies stop other computer thieves. These reformed criminals may also be hired to help companies create security methods for their computer systems.

Key Ideas

1 Workers who lose their jobs because of technology need to be retrained with new skills related to programming, operating, or repairing computer systems.

2 Robots, expert systems, and computer-aided design (CAD) are present in almost every business situation to help improve efficiency and productivity.

3 Technology expands global business activities through fast, efficient communication and distribution systems.

4 On-line computer services, SMART cards, interactive television, and virtual reality allow people to purchase merchandise, financial and other services, and entertainment in more convenient ways.

5 Technology has increased the efficiency and safety of motor vehicles, airplanes, and other modes of transportation.

6 Expanded computer use can result in concerns about health and safety, criminal activities, and privacy.

End of Chapter Activities

Increasing Your Business Vocabulary

The following terms should become part of your business vocabulary. For each numbered item, find the term that has the same meaning.

artificial intelligence (AI)

computer-aided design (CAD)

computer virus

expert systems

on-line computer service

piracy

robots

SMART card

white-collar crime

1 Mechanical devices programmed to do routine tasks.

2 Technological assistance used to create product styles and designs.

3 A plastic card with a silicon chip for storing information.

4 A computer network connection with information, shopping, and entertainment services.

5 Stealing or illegally copying software packages or information.

6 Programs that assist people in solving technical problems.

7 An illegal act performed by office or professional workers while at work.

8 A program code hidden in a system that can later do damage to software or stored data.

9 Programs that enable computers to reason, learn, and make decisions using logical methods similar to the methods humans use.

Reviewing Your Reading

1 How have computers affected employment?

2 What are the advantages of using robots for various job tasks?

3 How can computer-aided design (CAD) save time and money for business?

4 What effect might computers have on global business activities?

5 What benefits are provided by on-line computer services?

6 What types of information might be stored on a SMART card?

7 How is technology making automobile driving safer?

8 What types of health concerns are associated with computer use?

9 What types of crimes are committed by computer users?

Using Your Business Knowledge

1 How is it possible for the increased use of computers to create more jobs than are lost?

2 How can expert systems be used to help people solve medical, legal, financial, and other technical problems?

3 What would be the potential benefits from the use of SMART cards in handling everyday transactions?

4 What actions could be taken by organizations to prevent computer crime?

Calculating Business Problems

1 The Barkley Corporation usually sends about 3,800 pieces of mail per month at $0.42 each. If the firm switches to electronic mail service at a cost of $1,250.00 per month, how much money would it save or lose?

2 A scientist working eight hours a day can analyze 15 medical reports per hour using a computer. Before using the computer, the scientist could analyze 2 reports per day. How many more medical reports per five-day workweek can the scientist analyze by using the computer?

3 Rose Bokungu operates a language translation service. Her computer program can translate Swahili to English at a rate of 50 words per minute. Rose charges $25 per hour for translations. If Rose receives the following three documents in Swahili, what will her fee be to translate all three documents: letter, 680 words; report, 2,500 words; magazine article, 1,320 words?

4 The Coulter family travels by car to visit a relative every month. They recently bought a new car equipped with a computer that can plan travel routes and improve engine performance and gas mileage. The family's usual route is 57.5 miles long and their old car used to get 25 miles per gallon. The computer in the new car planned a route that is 54 miles long and improved gas mileage to 30 miles per gallon. If the average price of gasoline is $1.20 per gallon, how much money per trip will the new car save? (Solve the problem using two decimal places.)

Applying Technology

Using the *Introduction to Business* template and your word processing program software, select problem CH12. After the problem appears on your screen, complete the following activities. Then, print your completed letter and sign your name as purchasing agent. If you do not have a printer available, save the purchase order on a data disk to give to your teacher.

1 As an employee of Rose Bokungu's Translation Service, you are responsible for sending a purchase order for software and hardware to a computer supply company. Enter the information in the spaces provided. Also enter the grand total for the purchase order.

To: Edgar Wu Company
6745 Michigan Avenue
Clinton, IA 51503

Order No.: P4331
Date: November 1 of the current year
Ship Via: Truck
Date Wanted: November 15 of the current year

Quantity	Description	Unit Price	Total
3	Easy Translate Software	100.00	
1	Super Fast Desktop System	4,000.00	

2 Make a copy of the entire purchase order and place it in a different part of your document.

3 For the second purchase order, replace the given information with the following data. Also enter the grand total for the purchase order.

To: McIntire Computers, Inc.
405 Lewis Street
Big Sur, CA 93920

Order No.: P4332
Date: November 2 of the current year
Ship Via: Truck
Date Wanted: December 1 of the current year

Quantity	Description	Unit Price	Total
2	Billing Manager Software	900.00	
2	Big Power Workstations	8,700.00	

Making Decisions

The Kendall Manufacturing Company assembles electronic devices used in offices and homes. They employ about 600 people in various office, factory, and warehouse positions. Currently, all factory and warehouse jobs are done manually. Managers at Kendall are considering replacing 150 assembly line workers with a computerized system. The company can save $135,000.00 a year in operating costs by using this new technology.

1 What factors should the company consider before using the computerized assembly line system?

2 If the company uses this new system, what should the company do to help workers who are displaced by this technology?

Thousands of new jobs have been created because of the increased use of computers. Computer and technology workers must meet the demands for information within their organizations. People with a variety of skills and educational backgrounds can find career opportunities working with computers and technology.

Job Titles

Job titles commonly found in this career area include:

- Computer-Aided Design (CAD) Technician
- Computer-Laboratory Technician
- Computer Operator
- Computer Programmer
- Computer Systems Analyst
- Computer Teacher (in schools and for industry)
- Data Processing Machine Mechanic
- Database Design Analyst
- Industrial Robot Operator
- Information Processing Engineer
- Instrumentation Technician
- Sales Representative for Computer Systems and Software
- Software Engineer
- Technical Support Specialist
- User Support Analyst
- Word Processing Operator
- Word Processing Supervisor

Employment Outlook (through the year 2005)

- The Bureau of Labor Statistics expects growth in computer and technology-related jobs.
- Since nearly 80 percent of the labor force will be working in service industries, most computer-related jobs will be in service organizations.

Education and Training

- Most computer-related jobs require education beyond high school.
- This training may be achieved through a specialized vocational program or a college degree program.

Salary Levels (in recent years)

- Computer operators receive salaries ranging from $22,000 to $40,000.
- Computer programmers earn from $25,000 to $70,000.
- Systems analysts have salaries that range from $30,000 to more than $80,000.

Critical Thinking

1 How might changing economic conditions affect the demand for computer-related employment positions?

2 Why is a basic understanding of computers important in every career field?

Computers and Technology

Unit Four

Careers in Our Global Economy

chapter

202

In their search for ways to improve morale, a growing number of businesses are focusing on the motivational aspects of the job itself. Companies realize truly high morale results from a work environment in which employees obtain satisfaction from their work. Several strategies used by businesses to improve the work environment and employee morale include job enrichment, job enlargement, and flexible work schedules. The purpose of these strategies is to help workers excel in their work as well as improve morale.

Job enrichment involves redesigning the work to give workers more authority to plan their activities and to decide how the work should be accomplished. Workers are allowed to trade jobs with others or to learn related skills. Enrichment means that employees have an opportunity to be more creative and to set their own pace within the limits of the overall work schedule. *Job enlargement* is a simple expansion of a worker's assignments to include additional, but similar, tasks. Rather than performing three tasks, a worker might be given an opportunity to complete six similar tasks. Enlarging a job might lead to job enrichment, but not necessarily. Job enrichment could occur when employees are given greater authority and responsibility for achieving work goals.

Many companies have found flexible work schedules to be a good way to attract and motivate talented employees. *Flextime* allows employees to set arrival and departure times within constraints specified by an organization. Several alternative work-scheduling practices are also used to offer workers flexibility.

A *compressed workweek* is one in which employees work the same number of hours in fewer days than the typical five-day workweek. For example, some companies let employees work their 40-hour weeks in four-day shifts of 10 hours each. Still relatively rare in American business, *job sharing* involves the division of one full-time position among two or more people. Rather than sharing their jobs with another employee, some workers opt for *part-time work* in which they work less than the standard (40-hour) workweek. Another alternative, which has become very popular, is *home-based work*. Employees work their same jobs, but do the work at home instead of in the office. These workers are called telecommuters.

The strategies just described are only a small part of what employers can do to improve employee morale. Obviously, the key to good morale lies in such factors as the work itself and the potential for achievement, recognition, responsibility, and advancement.

Critical Thinking

1 *Can you think of situations where the strategies just described would be effective? Ineffective? List them and explain your reasoning.*

2 *Investigate the meaning of the term "family friendly." What are examples of strategies used by businesses in your area to promote a "family friendly" work environment?*

What Contributes to High Employee Morale?

Chapter Thirteen

Human Resources in Our Economy

Key Terms

work force

service-producing industry

goods-producing industry

derived demand

downsizing

immigrants

Objectives

After studying this chapter and completing the end-of-chapter activities, you will be able to:

1 Explain why human resources are a vital economic force.

2 Identify types of industries and occupational groups in our work force.

3 Discuss five factors that affect job opportunities.

4 Explain how the workplace is changing.

The contributions of labor, a factor of production, are vital to the economic growth of our nation. Labor includes all of the men and women involved in obtaining products from nature, converting raw materials into useful products, selling products, providing services, or supervising or managing others. The term refers to anyone who works, from the chief executive officer of a huge corporation to a self-employed gardener.

As you learned in Chapter 1, there are three factors of production: natural, capital, and human. Many people recognize labor (the human factor) as the most important. Without people working on jobs, tools and equipment could not be operated, and buildings and roads could not be built. Labor is our work force—a vital ingredient in the production of goods and services for consumers. You will learn more about human resources in Chapter 41.

THE U.S. WORK FORCE

Our **work force** is made up of all the people 16 years and older who are employed or who are looking for a job. There are more than 120 million people who have full-time or part-time jobs in our work force. Most jobs require at least a high school education and often some special training. Some jobs require only basic skills and a willingness to work hard and learn on the job—but those jobs are disappearing rapidly. Some jobs are high paying and some are low paying; some involve working mainly with machines and technology, while others involve working mainly with people and information.

Types of Industries

Our business world consists of hundreds of thousands of companies that provide a variety of jobs. The jobs in our business

Illus. 13-1
Most well-paying jobs in our economy require some level of technical training or higher education.

NET FACTS

The World Wide Web is a sub-network of computers that displays multimedia information, including text, graphics, sound, and video clips. Web documents also contain special connections that allow users to switch to other documents that could be on computers anywhere in the world.

world may be organized in a variety of ways. The Bureau of Labor Statistics (BLS), which is part of the U.S. Department of Labor, researches thousands of different jobs. The BLS publishes many useful materials about current and projected employment opportunities. Two BLS publications, *The Occupational Outlook Handbook and Occupational Outlook Quarterly*, offer up-to-date information that you can use to find out about many types of jobs.

There are two major types of industries analyzed in the *Occupational Outlook Handbook*. (See Figure 13-1.) The **service-producing industry** includes businesses that perform services that satisfy the needs of other businesses and consumers. For example, service companies include health care facilities, insurance companies, retail stores, and transportation organizations. The **goods-producing industry** includes businesses that manufacture many kinds of products. These companies are involved in construction, manufacturing, mining, and agriculture.

Our economy has experienced a change over the years from an emphasis on goods-producing businesses to service-producing businesses. The BLS estimates that virtually all job growth will occur in these businesses with four out of five, or more than 104 million people, employed in service businesses by the year 2005.

Occupational Groups

Another way of looking at our work force is to consider groups of occupations. Occupations are affected by industry trends and current developments in certain types of businesses. Occupations in groups are affected differently. Twelve occupational groups used

---

Industry Categories

Service-Producing Industries	**Goods-Producing Industries**
• Personal and business services	• Construction
• Retail and wholesale trade	• Manufacturing
• Finance, insurance, and real estate	• Mining
• Government	• Agriculture
• Transportation, communications, and public utilities	

Figure 13-1

The *Occupational Outlook Handbook* divides jobs into two major industry categories—service-producing and goods-producing.

by the BLS, along with future employment prospects for each group, are shown in Figure 13-2.

Occupations also are referred to in terms of two very broad groups: white-collar and blue-collar. A *white-collar worker* is one whose work involves a great deal of contact with other people and the handling and processing of information. Most white-collar workers are employed in offices and stores and include professional, managerial, and clerical workers.

A *blue-collar worker* is one whose work primarily involves the operation of machinery and equipment. Blue-collar workers are employed in factories, in machine shops, and on construction sites. Increased use of computers and information technology in factories

Figure 13-2

Some occupational groups have good growth potential.

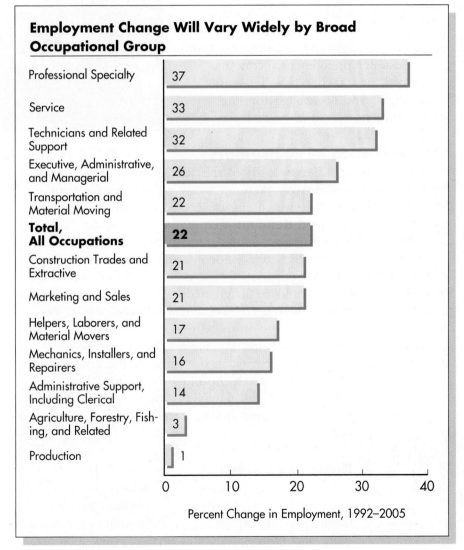

Employment Change Will Vary Widely by Broad Occupational Group

Occupational Group	Percent
Professional Specialty	37
Service	33
Technicians and Related Support	32
Executive, Administrative, and Managerial	26
Transportation and Material Moving	22
Total, All Occupations	**22**
Construction Trades and Extractive	21
Marketing and Sales	21
Helpers, Laborers, and Material Movers	17
Mechanics, Installers, and Repairers	16
Administrative Support, Including Clerical	14
Agriculture, Forestry, Fishing, and Related	3
Production	1

Percent Change in Employment, 1992–2005

Source: Bureau of Labor Statistics

and construction is changing the role of blue-collar workers and is causing a need for higher levels of education and training.

White-collar and blue-collar workers are equally important in our work force. Both types of workers are needed if we are to satisfy our economic needs and wants.

CHANGING JOB OPPORTUNITIES

The jobs held by people in our work force are subject to a variety of factors that can cause the need for these jobs to change. Some of these influences may cause jobs to be eliminated, while others will cause the work to be modified. Changes may require employees to develop new skills and get different training. Consumer preferences, economic conditions, new technology, business competition, and societal factors are strong influences on the work force.

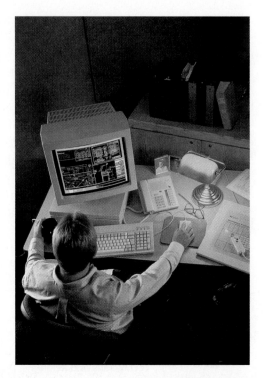

Illus. 13-2
The job of a white-collar worker often involves communication with others and the handling and processing of information.

The Influence of Consumers

You learned in Chapter 2 about the "dollar votes" cast by consumers in the marketplace. Preferences by consumers have an important effect on the availability of jobs in our work force. Jobs are affected by **derived demand;** that is, the demand for factors of production, such as human resources, are dependent on consumer demand for a product or service. For instance, if most consumers decided to wear clothing made of blue denim, workers who make blue denim clothing would be in great demand. If consumer choice shifted away from blue denim, fewer workers would be needed by companies producing those goods.

Sometimes new products entering the market make those already available obsolete, at least in the mind of the consumer. Workers producing the old product may find that their jobs will be eliminated. New jobs, however, would be created by the demand for the new products.

You cannot tell the importance of a worker by the "color of his or her collar."

Business Cycles

Stages of the business cycle, which you learned about in Chapter 4, affect job opportunities. When businesses are expanding and consumers are buying more and more goods and services, new jobs are created to meet the growing demand. As workers earn more money, they spend more on goods and services that they need and want; the growing demand continues.

High prices cause consumers to decrease their buying. When interest rates increase and both businesses and consumers find it difficult to borrow money, demand for goods and services decreases. As a result, jobs may be eliminated or the number of workers reduced. The workers in turn have less money to spend for their needs and wants. They also are hesitant to spend what money they do have because they are not sure of their future earnings. This tendency to spend less further decreases the demand for goods and services.

New Technologies

As you will recall from Unit 3, *technology* refers to the use of automated machinery, electronic equipment, and integrated systems to help increase the efficiency of producing goods and services.

Seventy-five percent of the jobs in the near future will not require a college degree but will require specialized education and training.

Cultural *Perspective*

The Maori People and Fishing Charts

Did you know that the Maoris of New Zealand perfected a way of predicting the best times to fish? Fishing was a means of sustaining life for the Maori people. By studying the moon and developing correlations with feeding activity of fish, they perfected charts that predicted the best times to fish. The Maoris also devised ecological "sea laws" to protect fishing grounds and shellfish beds.

Today those charts, which have been confirmed over the centuries, are computerized. Projections can be made for use throughout the world. Anyone in the United States can determine the best days and the best time of day to fish. *Outdoor Life* magazine has published those charts for seven consecutive years.

Maoris were the first people to settle on the islands of New Zealand. This group of people came from other Polynesian islands in the eighth century. According to one legend, the Maoris left their homes "across the great sea" in a fleet of canoes. Over the years, they intermarried with Europeans who settled in New Zealand, and some moved from their villages to the cities of New Zealand. However, today's Maoris still continue to harvest the riches of the sea and preserve many traditions of their ancestors.

Critical Thinking

1 What are some of the cultural traditions of the Maoris?

2 What are other skills for which the Maori people are noted?

A *word processing supervisor's* job duties include:

- Supervising and coordinating activities of workers who operate word processing equipment
- Advising department personnel in techniques of letter writing
- Recommending changes in procedures to effect savings in time, labor, and other costs
- Assigning workers to training programs.

Computers and robots are examples of technology. Integrated systems link computers with each other to make communication and data sharing easier. Robots continue to change the types of jobs and worker functions in manufacturing companies. Technology continues to influence how office workers perform their jobs.

Business Competition

Businesses must be competitive to stay in business, and costs are a major factor. The cost of running a business affects jobs and workers. When profits begin to decrease, the business must look for ways to improve its profits. Installing new equipment and systems that allow workers to produce more goods and services in less time often is a solution. Businesses may also decide to downsize. **Downsizing** is a planned reduction in the number of employees needed in a firm in order to reduce costs and make the business more efficient.

Societal Trends

Social trends, such as the age makeup of our population, also influence employment opportunities. The 16- to 24-year-old category in our population will be a smaller proportion of the work force by the year 2005. Greater employment opportunities will exist for young people and immigrants.

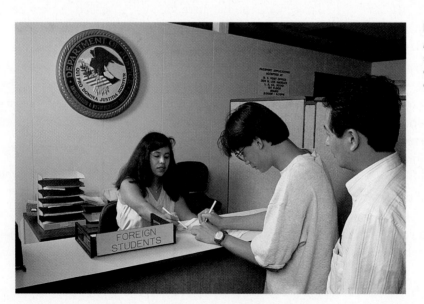

Illus. 13-3
Many foreign students become U.S. citizens.

Immigrants are people from other countries who come to live in our country for a variety of reasons. Many immigrants become U.S. citizens. Immigrants have made important contributions to our economy throughout the history of our country. They often fill jobs that otherwise would go unfilled. Immigrants often start businesses that provide services that otherwise would not be provided.

The importance of *people* to the success of an organization is stressed in the very definition of management: The use of people and other resources to accomplish organizational goals.

THE CHANGING WORKPLACE

The American workplace has changed considerably in the past decade. Much of this change is due to the role of the federal government, the makeup of the work force, and the increased use of technology.

Government has reached into the day-to-day management of employees through congressional legislation, agency guidelines, and Supreme Court decisions. Three areas of government regulation have affected the management of human resources: equal employment opportunity, especially for people with disabilities; pensions and retirement issues related to an aging work force; and job safety and employee health.

The makeup of the work force is becoming more varied. Employees may have different heritages from all around the globe. Employees may also be younger or older than average, be physically challenged, or speak English as a second language. Today's companies treat each employee fairly so that all employees can contribute to their companies' success.

In the past several years, more than one million immigrants have come into the United States each year. A large number were admitted because of their special job skills.

Technology is important in the workplace for improving efficiency in order to stay competitive in international markets. Computerized systems and robots have greatly reduced the need for production workers in certain manufacturing industries—steel, autos, tires, and farm equipment. Sophisticated computer and communications systems have also reduced the need for certain types of office employees such as typists, bookkeepers, and clerks.

Key Ideas

1 Tools and equipment could not be operated nor could roads and buildings be built without human resources.

2 Both goods-producing industries and service-producing industries employ people in a variety of occupational groups.

3 Consumer influence, business cycles, new technologies, business competition, and societal factors affect job opportunities.

4 Factors affecting the workplace of the future include the role of government, the changing work force, and technological improvements.

End of Chapter Activities

Increasing Your Business Vocabulary

The following terms should become part of your business vocabulary. For each numbered item, find the term that has the same meaning.

derived demand

downsizing

goods-producing industry

immigrants

service-producing industry

work force

1 All people 16 years and over who are employed or are looking for a job.

2 Businesses that perform services to satisfy the needs of other businesses and consumers.

3 Businesses that manufacture many kinds of products.

4 A demand for factors of production affected by consumer demand for a product or service.

5 Planned reduction in the number of employees needed in a firm.

6 People from other countries who come to live in our country for a variety of reasons and often become citizens.

Reviewing Your Reading

1 How does labor influence our economy?

2 How many workers are employed in our work force?

3 Name two publications of the Bureau of Labor Statistics that offer information about the job market.

4 What types of businesses are expected to provide the most jobs in the year 2005?

5 What occupational groups are expected to have the largest growth by the year 2005?

6 How do business cycles influence job opportunities?

7 In what ways does competition among businesses affect job opportunities?

8 What are two societal factors that affect job opportunities?

9 What are three workplace changes that have affected employment opportunities?

Using Your Business Knowledge

1 What type of businesses would require the majority of their operating expenses be spent for labor expenses? Name some organizations that have extensive costs for buildings, equipment, and machinery.

2 Prepare a list of service-producing and goods-producing industries that are represented in your community. List some of the job titles found in each business on your list.

3 Give examples of how immigrants have affected our work force and our economy.

4 How could each of the following changes in our economy affect the job market?

a. Lower interest rates
b. New technology used by a business
c. Decreased consumer spending on travel
d. Downsizing by several businesses
e. Higher prices for food products
f. A downturn in the business cycle

5 Give examples of technology and telecommunications you have observed in banks, retail stores, and offices.

Calculating Business Problems

1 In a recent decade, mining employment declined from 1,027,000 workers to 709,000.

a. How many jobs were lost in the mining industry?

b. What was the percentage of decrease? (Round off your answer.)

2 One of the large stores in a shopping center employs 48 salespeople, 6 department managers, 2 credit clerks, 2 secretaries, 1 accountant, and 1 store manager.

a. How many employees, including the store manager, are there in this store?

b. If the credit clerks, secretaries, and accountant make up the office staff, the office staff is what percentage of all employees?
c. If two-thirds of the salespeople work part time, how many part-time salespeople are there? How many salespeople are full-time workers?

3 In the year 2005, 17 percent of the work force is expected to be 55 years old and over, 63 percent will be between 25 and 54 years old, and 20 percent will be between 16 and 24 years old. If there are 133 million people in the work force in the year 2005, how many will be in each age category?

4 For the following occupational categories, the number of workers and the expected growth rate are given.

Category	Current Employment (In Millions)	Expected Growth Rate (Percent)
Government employees	8.6	9
Construction	4.9	18
Finance, insurance and real estate	6.3	26
Wholesale trade	5.7	27

a. For each job group, how many new employment positions are expected?

b. For each group, what will be the total number of jobs based on the projected growth rate?

c. What will be the total employment for these four job categories?

d. What is the average expected growth rate for these four occupational categories?

5 A business firm has 29,800 employees. Over the next 10 years, the firm anticipates that 22 percent of its employees will retire. In addition, there are approximately 900 who leave each year for other employment and are replaced. Because of research and development resulting in many new products, the firm will likely add 250 new employees each year to handle customer orders.

a. How many employees will retire in the ten-year period?

b. What percentage of the employees leave each year for other employment?

c. What will be the total number of employees at the end of the ten years?

Applying Technology

Using the *Introduction to Business* template and your spreadsheet program software, select problem CH13. After the problem appears on your screen, complete the following activities. Then, after you have completed each step, display or print the completed spreadsheet for each activity. If you do not have a printer available, answer the questions before you leave the computer.

1 In the Difference column, enter a formula to calculate the increase or decrease from the Baseline Employment to the Projected Employment.

Copy the formula to calculate the increase or decrease for each occupational category. Format the Difference column for commas and no decimal places. Sort the spreadsheet in descending order by Difference. Answer the following questions.

a. Which occupational category has the largest increase?

b. How many occupational categories show projected decreases?

2 In the Percentage Change column, enter a formula to calculate what percentage of Baseline Employment is represented by the Difference. Copy the formula for each occupational category. Format the Percentage Change column for percentage with 1 decimal place. Answer the following questions.

a. What is the third largest projected percentage increase?

b. How many occupational categories have a projected Percentage Change of less than +1 percent and greater than −1 percent?

3 At the bottom of the spreadsheet, enter labels and functions to show the sums of the Baseline Employment, Projected Employment, and Difference columns. Enter a formula to calculate the total Percentage Change. Format the totals with commas and no decimal places. Answer the following questions.

a. What is the total of the Difference column?

b. What is the projected Percentage Change of total employment?

Optional: Create a bar chart of the Percentage Change for each occupational category.

Making Decisions

The A-1 Textile Company has come upon hard times. The firm's profits have shrunk to a point where the company must reduce costs or eventually go out of business. A-1 has been a major employer in the community of Cottonburg for many years. The firm employs 300 workers who average $22,000 a year in wages. To remain in business, A-1 must cut $2 million from its payroll and cut other operating expenses. The owners plan to lay off approximately one-third of the workers to avoid closing the business.

1 Do you agree with the owners in their decision? Why or why not?

2 What other course of action might the owners take to remain profitable and stay in business?

Chapter Fourteen

Planning a Career

Key Terms

occupation

career

career planning

government employment office

career information interview

mobility

values

talent

ability

tentative career decision

Objectives

After studying this chapter and completing the end-of-chapter activities, you will be able to:

1 Explain what is meant by career planning.

2 List important sources of career information.

3 State approaches that can be taken to learn about values and abilities.

4 Describe five steps to follow when making career decisions.

5 List at least three sources for financing additional education.

Dan Capparus was reading the local newspaper. He was impressed by the number of help wanted ads placed by businesses in his community. The ads said that certain kinds of training were needed or that applicants needed experience in certain business operations. He wondered where businesses got those kinds of workers. He could not help but observe that the ability to use computers and certain computer programs was mentioned quite often.

Dan thought about his own situation. He still had a few years of school left, and he wondered if he were taking the right courses to get the career that he wanted in the future. Then he realized that he really did not know for sure what kind of career he really wanted. For some reason or other, he had not given this important subject a lot of thought. Then he wondered what strategies he might use to improve his awareness of careers. He decided to consult with his school counselor. Her insight proved to be invaluable. Dan quickly learned about three approaches to career awareness: studying careers, developing self-awareness, and making an initial career decision.

STUDYING CAREERS

An **occupation** is a task or series of tasks that is performed to provide a good or service. People are hired to fill occupations, and they are paid for the work they perform. A *goal* is something specific you want to achieve. A **career** is a goal in life that is fulfilled through an occupation or series of occupations.

You actually have a kind of career goal now: to complete your schooling and prepare for your future. Your occupation right now is to take the right courses and earn good grades. When you enter a career in the world of work, your career goal may be to become a department store manager or an office administrator. Your first occupation then could be as a salesperson in a department store or as an office receptionist. With a good work record and additional training, you could be promoted to those higher positions.

Career planning is the process of studying careers, assessing yourself in terms of careers, and making decisions about a future career. This process begins by making some decisions about your interests and the occupation you want to have someday. Career planning requires an investigation of several occupations within a career area. You must find out about duties performed, education and training required, and the wages paid. You should learn about what it takes to succeed and about the advantages and disadvantages of certain occupations.

The study of careers is a continuous process. New career opportunities occur all the time. You do not just decide to study careers for one day or one

FYI

Not setting a goal is like trying to find an object when you don't know what is lost.

Illus. 14-1
Career planning requires much forethought and investigation.

week. It is important to view learning about careers as a lifelong activity, something that continues even after you begin your career.

FINDING INFORMATION

We all need help in career planning. There are several sources of help for you right in your own school and community. Some information covers careers in general. Other information is more specific about occupations and careers in your local area. You should look into as many sources of information as possible.

Your own school is a good place to start. Many school libraries have career resource materials. You may find the *Occupational Outlook Quarterly* or other publications of the Department of Labor's Bureau of Labor Statistics to be quite helpful. For example, *The Occupational Outlook Handbook* gives detailed information on hundreds of occupations. Included are job duties, working conditions, education and training requirements, advancement possibilities, employment outlook, and earnings.

Career World is magazine that publishes information about a variety of careers, often looking at careers of the future. *The Encyclopedia of Careers and Vocational Guidance* can give you basic information about many occupations and career areas. Organizations, such as the Insurance Information Institute, publish materials dealing with their particular career areas. There are database programs and on-line computer programs that can be used to access up-to-date information on occupations and sources of education and training.

A recent survey found that 47 percent of women workers and 57 percent of men workers felt they had a career—the others said they "just had a job."

Your school may have a career resource center. Some schools locate them in the library, some in the counseling office, and others in departments such as business education and vocational education. These resource centers normally have a wide variety of materials available. You may find magazines, brochures, pamphlets, films, videotapes, and CDs on careers. You may also have computers in your school that are connected to centralized computer files of career and education information.

Newspaper help wanted ads are also useful in career planning. Reading the help wanted ads in your local newspaper or a large metropolitan paper can give you a good idea of what jobs are in demand. Reading those ads can help you discover what employers are looking for in the people they hire. Sometimes ranges of beginning salaries are shown.

Another good source of information for career planning in many communities is the **government employment office.** These are tax-supported offices that help people find jobs and that provide information about careers. Employers who need workers often contact government employment offices for help. They may also contact private employment agencies for the assistance needed. Employment offices can provide up-to-date information about the job market in your local area. They also can help you look for part-time, summer, or full-time work.

Illus. 14-2

Part-time or summer jobs can prove to be an excellent source of job information.

GETTING INSIGHT INTO WORK

One of your best sources of information about work is other people. Most workers are happy to explain what they do. This process of talking to other people about their jobs is called *networking*. The advantage of networking is that your contacts are not limited to the people you know personally. You probably can find a person who works at almost any job in which you are interested.

Part-time or summer jobs can also give you insight into work. Useful information can be learned by being alert to what is going on around you as you work. You may have already had experiences with part-time or summer jobs.

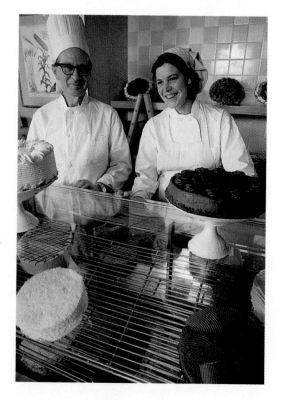

A formal way to gain insight into a career is through a career information interview. A **career information interview** is a planned discussion with a worker to find out about the work that person does, the preparation necessary for that career, and the person's feelings about his or her career. Career information interviews are an excellent way to get valuable information. Interviews will help you gain insight into what actually happens in a particular career area. They also might show you how important it is to plan ahead and prepare for the right career.

You will find that most workers like to talk about their career experiences. However, before you begin a career information interview, you should think about the questions you want to ask. Here are some questions that are often asked:

- How did you get your present occupation? Did other occupations lead you to this one? If so, what were those occupations?

- In what ways do you find your occupation to be satisfying? In what ways is it dissatisfying?

- What are some tasks you perform in your occupation?

- In what ways do you think your occupation is better than others? In what ways is it not as good?

- What do you believe are some of the most important qualifications for the work you do? What training and education are needed?

- What advice would you give a young person who is considering this line of work?

You should keep notes on what you learn through career information interviews. The experiences of others will provide important career planning information that you will continue to find valuable.

If a particular career interests you, ask your teacher or guidance counselor about the possibility of becoming a *job shadow* at a particular company employing workers that reflect your career interest. Job shadowing allows you to spend time with a worker for a day or a week to learn about a certain occupation.

Illus. 14-3
A career information interview while job shadowing can provide important insights into a career area.

GETTING INSIGHT INTO YOURSELF

Each person has individual needs and wants that influence their lives. For instance, you may have to decide whether you want to work in the geographic area in which you now live or whether you are willing to move to where the job you really want is located. There may be reasons why you would prefer to live and work near your home. However, people who successfully pursue the careers of their choice often have mobility. **Mobility** is the willingness and ability of a person to move to where jobs are located. The lack of mobility of our work force leads to locational unemployment. *Locational unemployment* occurs when jobs are available in one place but go unfilled because those who are qualified to fill those jobs live elsewhere and are not willing to relocate.

As you look into careers and learn about jobs and the work involved, you will get a feeling for certain occupations and career areas. You may like or dislike certain occupations without knowing why. There are personal aspects of career planning that are important. Becoming aware of these personal aspects and your values are important in career planning.

Your Values

Your **values** are the things that are important to you in life. They must be considered along with

FYI

Values can influence your educational plans as well as your career choices. Consider your goals in life when choosing schools, majors, and courses.

NET FACTS

Netiquette is an Internet phrase that refers to the rules of conduct and behavior on the Net. For example, don't send unwanted advertising, do keep your messages brief and to the point, and don't use ALL CAPS unless you mean to shout.

facts about occupations and careers. There are a number of ways you can learn about your values. Your counselors or business teachers may have exercises or activities that can help you learn about your values. These exercises show how you rank items such as prestige, money, power, achievement, independence, leadership, security, or belonging. Each of these may influence you, directly or indirectly, when you select your occupation.

You can begin to examine some of your values by answering certain questions. Your answers will help you to understand what things you consider important. Each answer should be thought through and analyzed. Here are some examples of those kinds of questions:

- Is it important to me to earn a lot of money?

- Am I mainly interested in work that provides a service for others?

- Is it important for me to have an occupation that others think is important even if I do not really care for it?

- Do I want an occupation that is especially challenging and may require additional schooling?

- Would I be willing to start in a job that pays a lower salary than another if that job were more challenging and offered better opportunities for future advancement?

- Do I consider investing in education or occupational training to be as important as spending for other things?

There may be other questions you can think of, but these will give you a good start.

Another activity is to consider what you would do if someone gave you a large sum of money to be used in any way you desire. Would you start your own business? Would you hire a jet and travel throughout the world? Would you develop a foundation to support athletics for underprivileged children? Would you help build up a run-down neighborhood? Would you buy the biggest wardrobe someone your age ever had? Would you use the money to finance an expensive education? Your answers will tell you something about your personal values.

Determining your own value system can be a painful and slow process. Assuming responsibility for your own actions and decisions will strengthen the values that you hold.

Your Talents and Abilities

Each of us has certain talents and abilities. A **talent** is a natural, inborn aptitude to do certain things. We often say someone has a "natural talent." An **ability** is the quality of being able to perform a mental or physical task. Your talents and abilities, along with your career goals and interests, are important in career planning.

There are a number of ways you can learn about your abilities. Think about the courses you have taken and the grades you have received in school. What kinds of courses have you taken? In which ones have you done your best work? Which courses have been easiest for you? Which have been the most difficult? Which do you like the best? Answers to questions such as these will identify your talents and abilities.

GlobalPerspective

International Business Careers

As trade among nations expands, the number and types of global careers will increase. Experts predict that by the turn of the century, over 70 percent of our business will be with international clients. How can you go about acquiring information about overseas job opportunities?

Finding information about international career opportunities may seem difficult. However, the following sources may be consulted when planning an international career:

- *U.S. employers with international offices:* Contact the company's human resources department or public relations office. Request information about the company's business activities and career opportunities in other countries.

- *Embassies of foreign countries:* Contact embassy officials for information about the culture, employment opportunities, and any needed documents, such as work permits or work visas.

- *U.S. federal government agencies:* Contact the Department of State or the Department of Commerce, which have business representatives in most countries of the world.

- *World Trade Centers Association (WTCA):* Contact one of the World Trade Centers located in major U.S. cities.

These centers promote global business relationships and international trade.

Do not forget, however, people who are recognized for their success in international careers. Individuals with international business experience are excellent resources for learning about career opportunities overseas and often have useful knowledge about prospective employers.

Critical Thinking

1 *What do you think would be the most interesting and challenging aspect of an international career?*

2 *What might you do to prepare yourself for an international career?*

Illus. 14-4

You'll need a variety of learning experiences to determine your talents and abilities.

Abilities can be developed, and that is important to keep in mind. If you are weak in a certain area, you may want to take courses that will improve that area. For instance, employers continue to tell us that basic skills in writing, reading, and computing are very important to them. If you are not strong in composing letters and reports, you should take additional courses in English, preferably business English. If reading is a problem for you, get help in that area, too. If computations, including working with fractions and decimals, are difficult for you, additional courses in math, including business math, would be desirable. The idea is to strengthen your weak areas *before* you go into full-time work. You can plan your courses and future activities to help you grow toward your chosen career.

MAKING CAREER DECISIONS

Each person must eventually make his or her own career decision. Too often the decision is made when full-time work begins. But that is too late, especially if certain training and education are required.

Making initial career decisions while you are in school has many advantages. One advantage is that in school you have a lot of good information readily available. But more important, early career planning will help you select the right courses. An early career decision can also encourage you to become involved with organizations such as Future Business Leaders of America, Distribu-

Successful people have become "career entrepreneurs"—they continue to do career planning and information searching throughout their work lives.

tive Education Clubs of America, and Junior Achievement that teach you about business and help you prepare for a career.

Your decision may be a **tentative career decision,** that is, a decision that is subject to change or modification as new information is received. A tentative decision is much better than no decision at all. Your career decision will give you a direction that is needed, and you will find a new kind of interest in what you do.

How can you be sure that you are making the best career decision possible? There is no way to guarantee a perfect decision. But good decisions generally are made by those who follow the right steps. Here are some steps to follow in making your career decision:

1. Gather as much information as you can.

2. Analyze what you have learned about careers and about yourself.

3. Think about different plans of action and what might happen if you follow each one.

4. Select what seems to be the best plan of action and follow it.

5. Evaluate your career decision from time to time.

Your search for the right career could continue for a long time. In the years ahead, some of your values and goals will change. You will develop new interests and abilities. New jobs and careers will come along for you to learn about. You should be ready to make career-decision changes when they are called for in your situation.

GETTING ADDITIONAL EDUCATION

As you know, some occupations require education and training beyond high school. Two-year schools—usually called community colleges or junior colleges—offer a wide variety of training in many career areas. Four-year colleges and universities, both public and private, provide education and training for many career areas and professions. Private business schools that specialize in certain job training, such as radio and television or computer technology, are other sources for career preparation.

You should consider the cost for additional schooling as an investment in your future—an investment that will help you earn higher wages in the future. There are a number of ways in which you can get help financing additional schooling. Most schools have financial aid programs that you should investigate. These programs include scholarships, student loans, and work-study opportunities. Some financial aid programs are based on your record as a student while others are based on financial need. Part-time work also is a common way in which young people finance the additional education needed to pursue the career of their choice. You should evaluate these methods of financing an education as you continue your career planning and decision making.

AN EXAMPLE OF A GOOD APPROACH

Brianna Bunton learned about career planning in a number of ways. Brianna prepared a career report on becoming a corporate lawyer as a requirement for her Introduction to Business class. She also interviewed the legal counsel for a local corporation. Her report gave her doubts about whether she really wanted to pursue a career in law and whether she could afford the additional schooling.

A course in accounting that Brianna completed in her junior year led her to believe that the accounting field was one that she would like to enter. She did some reading about accounting careers. With her computer skills, she was able to get a part-time job in an accounting office the following summer. While on the job, she learned about how an accounting office operates. Her job gave her an opportunity to talk to several accountants and auditors about their careers. When school began again in the fall, she took the second-year accounting course. She also enrolled in additional courses in math and English. The accountants had recommended that she get more course work in both of those areas. She also took the office laboratory course to become more familiar with office procedures. Brianna worked hard to get good grades; she knew that those grades would be important later if she were to achieve her future goal. With her good grades and attendance, she was confident that she could receive some financial aid when she entered college.

The accountants suggested that Brianna should "reach for the top"—and that meant more schooling along with accounting work experience. Brianna wants to eventually take the state accounting examination. If she passes it, she will become a certified public accountant (CPA).

Brianna continues to work part-time for the accounting firm. She also is enrolled in her local college, where she is majoring in accounting. She has a career plan and is following it. Very likely someday it will be "Brianna Bunton CPA."

Key Ideas

1 Career planning is a process of looking into careers and into oneself to determine what preparation should be made for a future career.

2 Important sources of career information include school libraries, career resource centers, government publications, government employment offices, and career information interviews.

3 Personal values can be determined through answering a series of questions. Talents and abilities can be learned through analyzing courses taken and liked or disliked.

4 When making a career decision, including a tentative one, there are five decision-making steps that should be followed: (a) gather information; (b) analyze what has been learned; (c) think about different plans of action; (d) select a plan of action; and (e) evaluate the career decision.

5 Scholarships, student loans, and part-time work can help students gain the needed additional education beyond high school.

End of Chapter Activities

Increasing Your Business Vocabulary

The following terms should become part of your business vocabulary. For each numbered item, find the term that has the same meaning.

ability

career

career information
interview

career planning

government employ-
ment office

mobility

occupation

talent

tentative career
decision

values

1 The process of studying careers, assessing yourself in terms of careers, and making decisions about a future career.

2 A tax-supported agency that helps people find jobs and provides information about careers.

3 A planned discussion with a worker to find out about the work that person does, the preparation necessary for the career, and the person's feelings about the career.

4 The willingness and ability of a person to move to where jobs are located.

5 A task or series of tasks that are performed to provide a good or service.

6 The things that are important to you in life.

7 A career decision that is subject to change or modification as new information is received.

8 A natural, inborn aptitude to do certain things.

9 A goal in life that is fulfilled through a job or a series of jobs.

10 The quality of being able to perform mental or physical tasks.

Reviewing Your Reading

1 Why should you study careers?

2 What are several sources of information about careers?

3 Explain how a career resource center can be helpful.

4 What information can be gained from reading newspaper want ads?

5 For what purposes have government employment offices been established?

6 How can career information interviews help you in career planning?

7 Why is mobility important in looking ahead to future careers?

8 What are some of the things you should learn about your values?

9 How can courses and grades tell you something about your talents, abilities, and interests?

10 What steps are involved in career decision making?

11 What help is available to assist you in financing additional schooling?

Using Your Business Knowledge

1 There is a great deal of information that can be learned about business operations, interpersonal and customer relationships, and other experiences from working a part-time or summer job. Give some examples of what might be learned through these kinds of experiences.

2 Describe how you would conduct a career information interview. What would you do to prepare for it in advance?

3 What are some good sources of information about jobs in your local community? Comment on how you might use each one.

4 Make a list of your talents and abilities, and then note the ones in which you feel you are strong or weak. Indicate how you might use your strengths in career planning. Also indicate what action you might take to strengthen your weaker abilities.

5 When you discover what your values are in relation to such things as prestige, power, and recognition, how will your values affect your thinking about future careers?

6 Why should your career decisions be considered tentative rather than once-and-for-all decisions?

7 Why is investing in additional education something that should be considered in career planning?

Calculating Business Problems

1 Carrie Ainge works as a clerk in a law office. She works 40 hours per week and is paid $11.25 per hour. She saves one-third of what she earns to create a fund so that she can go to law school.

a. How much does Carrie earn in one week? How much is she able to save each week?

b. Without considering interest she would earn on savings, how much would she save in 10 weeks? in 15 weeks? in 25 weeks?

c. If Carrie needs to save at least $8,000 before she can consider going to law school, for how many weeks will she have to save in order to reach or exceed the $8,000 goal?

2 Shana Dansweif works as a manager for a trucking firm. Shana has to keep records of the number of trucks going out and coming in each day, and she must keep a record of the number of miles driven by each driver. Last Monday there were 17 trucks on the road, 3 on the lot being loaded, and 2 in the shop being repaired.

a. On Monday, the trucks on the road averaged 175 miles each. How many total miles were driven that day? If all of the trucks were on the road the following day and averaged the same number of miles, how many total miles would be driven?

b. If all of the trucks were driven for 5 days, and the average miles per truck increased to 190 miles, what would be the total number of miles driven?

c. If the cost of operating a truck is $3.75 per mile, how much did it cost the company to operate their trucks in each of the three previous situations?

---

3 Bobby Stevenson works in an office that is 12 feet wide and 14 feet long. The ceiling is 10 feet high. (See Appendix D for information regarding metric conversions.)

a. What are the dimensions of his office in meters?

b. His desk is 30 inches high, 54 inches long, and 36 inches wide. What are the dimensions of his desk in centimeters?

c. A cleaning fluid that is used to keep his furniture looking nice comes in 1-liter, 2-liter, and 5-liter containers. How many quarts of cleaning fluid are there in each container? If the firm uses 50 gallons of cleaning fluid per year, how many 2-liter containers do they use in one year?

---

4 Nancy Subarb-Sisterrse attends a college where the tuition and fees amount to $9,500 per year. The books and supplies she buys total $1,200 per year. In addition, she has general living expenses of $11,600 per year. She has three sources of income: financial aid of $3,500 per year, a scholarship that pays one-half of her tuition, and a work-study job from which she earns $5,300 per year.

a. How much income does Nancy receive each year from her three sources of income?

b. How much does it cost Nancy to go to this college each year?

c. What percentage of her annual college costs are covered by her three sources of income? (Round off your answer.)

d. If her Uncle David said that he would lend her the money she needs beyond her three sources of income, how much money would Nancy have to borrow each year?

Applying Technology

Using the *Introduction to Business* template and your database program software, select problem CH14. After the problem appears on your screen, complete the following activities. Then, after you have completed each step, display or print a report for each activity. If you do not have a printer available, answer the questions before you leave the computer.

1 Sort the database in ascending order by job title. Answer the following questions:

   a. What is one of the duties of the tenth job title listed?

   b. What is the last job title listed?

2 Select and list the jobs that are in the Sales Clerks group. How many jobs are listed?

3 Select and list the jobs that have *DOT (Dictionary of Occupational Titles)* numbers greater than 080.000-000 and less than 100.000-000. Answer the following questions:

   a. How many jobs are listed?
   b. What are the duties of the first job listed?

Making Decisions

Jeff Barbson is looking to his future and wondering what kind of career he should prepare for. His father is the city's civil engineer. His mother is a buyer in a major department store. Both of his parents are successful and enjoy their careers. Both of them have talked with Jeff about their work. He has visited his father's office and has worked as a sales clerk in his mother's store.

Jeff's favorite subjects are computers, economics, and art. His least favorites are history, English, business law, and math. He earns his best grades in computers and art.

Jeff's father wants him to be an engineer because there is a need for engineers in their state. His mother wants him to go into retailing. Jeff would like to go to medical school and become a heart specialist.

1 Based on his school record, which of the three career areas do you think he should choose?

2 What advice would you give Jeff regarding career planning?

Chapter Fifteen

Key Terms

letter of application

personal data sheet

personal references

position application form

ability test

position interview

personnel interviewer

exit interview

Succeeding in the World of Work

Objectives

After studying this chapter and completing the end-of-chapter activities, you will be able to:

1 Write a successful letter of application and personal data sheet.

2 Identify sources to use in getting job leads.

3 Fill out an application form acceptable to an employer.

4 Explain how pre-employment tests are used by employers.

5 List eight things to do to prepare for a good interview.

6 State eight things that help lead to success on the job.

7 Describe several ways to get along with co-workers, and explain how to properly exit a job.

Francisca Negalo has just graduated from high school. Her summer job is working in the records office of the city assessor's office. She also worked part-time for the Tempest Tea Pot Company as part of her school work experience program.

Francisca is now ready for full-time employment. The assessor's office has no openings, so she has registered with the government employment office in hopes of finding employment in accounting. Her high school business education program included computer applications and two years of accounting. She has learned to use spreadsheets, databases, and a computer-based accounting system. With her good grades, she feels confident that she can get an accounting job in some local business firm.

Francisca is watching the help wanted ads, too. She also has let her teachers and her school counselor know about her desire to get a full-time job. Francisca plans on continuing her accounting studies in a night school program at a local two year college. She plans to earn an associate's degree in accounting. Eventually she will transfer to a university and work toward a bachelor's degree in business administration. For now, though, she needs to get a job and earn some money.

Someone from the government employment agency called Francisca and told her about an opening for an accounting clerk at a local technical college. The position sounded good to her, so she decided to apply. Interested applicants were requested to send a letter of application to the office of the vice president of finance.

"Someday," Francisca mused, "I am going to be a Certified Public Accountant and have my own business. But for now, this job will get me started on my career. I just have to get it."

APPLYING FOR A JOB

Francisca had learned about letters of application in her high school introduction to business class. She remembered that a **letter of application** is a sales letter about an applicant written for the purpose of getting a personal interview. She recalled that it needed to be a courteous, businesslike letter that focused on her interest in and qualifications for the job.

When you write your letter of application, keep in mind that it basically is a sales letter. Like any good sales letter, a letter of application should attract the employer's attention and interest. It should create a desire to meet you, the applicant. Your letter should urge the reader to invite you to come for an interview. Figure 15-1 shows Francisca's well prepared letter of application. Note that the letter is neat, courteous, and to the point. A carelessly written letter may cause the employer to think that you will be a careless worker. Your letter represents you, and it must compete with other letters of application for the reader's attention.

Francisca's letter mentions that a personal data sheet is enclosed with her letter. A **personal data sheet**, also called a *résumé*, is a summary of important job-related information about yourself. It

Figure 15-1
Your letter of application represents you. It should cause the reader to want to meet you in person.

1602 Collegewood Drive
Madison, WI 53711-2821
June 25, 19--

Dr. David Haugen
Vice President of Finance
Lakeview Technical College
Madison, WI 53706-3692

Dear Dr. Haugen:

The advertisement in the *Daily Chronicle* for an accounting clerk describes just the job I want. Please consider me as an applicant for that position.

The ad said that you are looking for a bright and alert person who is conscientious and interested in long-term employment. My record at Four Lakes High School and part-time employment record will show that I have the qualities you desire. My career goal is to someday become a Certified Public Accountant. An accounting clerk's position in your office will allow me to get an important start on my career.

My business education program at Four Lakes High School included courses in introduction to business, computers, office procedures, and accounting. I also completed four years of English and three years of math. For each of my last semesters, I was on the honor roll. In our work experience program, I worked ten hours a week during my senior year for the Tempest Tea Pot Company, where I learned a great deal about office work and human relations. My summer job in the city assessor's office is helping me to work accurately with figures.

Enclosed is a personal data sheet giving my qualifications in more detail. I would appreciate an opportunity to interview with you. I may be reached by telephone at (608) 555-0308 anytime during the day.

Sincerely yours,

Francisca Negalo

Francisca Negalo

Enclosure

describes your education and work experience and lists the names of people who have agreed to be your personal references. **Personal references** are people who can give a report about your character, your education, and your work habits. The people you might select as references could include teachers, religious leaders, adult friends, former employers, and others. Look at Francisca's data sheet in Figure 15-2.

Figure 15-2
Francisca's personal data sheet has important information that is relevant to the job.

PERSONAL DATA SHEET

NAME:	Francisca Negalo
TELEPHONE:	(608) 555-0308
ADDRESS:	1602 Collegewood Drive Madison, WI 53711-2821
EDUCATION:	Four Lakes High School Graduated June 10, 19-- Emphasis: Business Education

Business Subjects Studied: Activities:
   Introduction to Business   Member of Pep Club
   Computer Applications   Treasurer, Future
   Accounting I and II   Business Leaders
                       of America

WORK EXPERIENCE: Records Clerk, Tempest Tea Pot Company; one year, part-time, cooperative education. General Clerk, City Assessor's Office, summer

OTHER ACTIVITIES: Member of Alph Chi youth group at First Christian Church. Member of East Side YMCA swim team

REFERENCES:

Mr. Tim Schilling
Business Teacher
Four Lakes High School
1234 Monona Drive
Madison, WI 53722-1619

Mrs. Phyllis Lipton
Office Manager
Tempest Tea Pot Company
707 Coffee Lane
Middleton, WI 53611-4912

Mr. Dan Verwith
Records Department
Administrator
City Assessor's Office
16 Capitol Avenue
Madison, WI 53702-1101

USING SOURCES OF JOB LEADS

Francisca's approach to finding a job was a good one. She knew what kind of job she wanted. Several sources were used to obtain job leads. Francisca also was willing to wait for the right job opportunity if necessary.

Finding job openings is an important part of getting that first job. No one source is necessarily better than others. You need to let as many people as possible know that you are looking for a job. Your relatives, friends, neighbors, and others will be good potential sources of job leads.

The sources you use for information about career planning can help you get job leads, too. Your school counselors and business teachers can be very helpful. If your school has a placement office, be sure to register with that office. You should also contact employment agencies. Newspaper want ads are also helpful. You should visit businesses and inquire about their openings. Some businesses post help-wanted signs in their windows. Getting a job means going out and looking around. Finding a job can be hard work, but it is worth the effort.

There is an increasing level of skill demanded in the workplace. Most employers report that skill requirements have increased over the past three years.

COMPLETING AN EMPLOYER'S APPLICATION FORM

A few weeks after mailing her letter of application and personal data sheet, Francisca received a phone call from the administrative assistant to the financial vice president of the technical college. They wanted Francisca to come in for an interview. "That's it!" Francisca shouted, "I'm going to get the job."

Francisca did not realize that there were a few more steps to be taken. She made an appointment for the job interview and arrived at the vice president's office on time. The secretary in the vice president's office made Francisca feel welcome when she arrived. Francisca was asked to fill out an application form that was required of all job applicants at the college. She was taken to a desk where she could complete it.

A Census Bureau's "Reality Check" on the workplace revealed that employers believe that only 80 percent of U.S. workers are proficient in their jobs—schools failed to provide preparation for work for the other 20 percent.

An employer frequently has each job applicant complete a position application form even after a letter of application and a personal data sheet have been provided. A **position application form** is a document used by an employer that asks for information related to employment. The form gives the employer standard information about each job applicant and becomes part of a permanent file. These forms typically ask for your name, address, Social Security number, education, work experience, the job for which you are applying, references, and other qualifications. They usually are filled out in longhand; this gives your potential employer a look at your penmanship.

The information on your personal data sheet will help you complete the application form and should be taken along to the interview. Completing the position application form should be seen as the *first job task* your employer asks you to perform. Supply each item requested; do not leave questions unanswered. Take the assignment seriously. A poorly prepared application form may give the wrong impression about you. Observe the application form filled out by Francisca in Figure 15-3.

Figure 15-3
Francisca filled out the position application form neatly, completely, and accurately.

LAKEVIEW TECHNICAL COLLEGE
APPLICATION FOR EMPLOYMENT

Name _Francisca Negalo_
(First) (Middle) (Last)
Social Security No. _399-48-6951_
Date _July 15, 19--_

U.S. Citizen _X_ yes
___ no, if not, type of visa _____
Do you have any physical condition that may prevent you from performing certain kinds of work? _No_
Have you ever been convicted of a felony or misdemeanor or are there any felony charges against you pending disposition? _No_
If yes, give date(s) and nature of the act(s) and disposition _____
Have you ever been compensated for an on-the-job accedent? _No_ If yes, explain _____
Have you served in the U.S. Armed Forces? _No_ What branch _____ Type of discharge _____ Rank _____
Dates of service _____ If you were deferred—why? _____
In case of emergency, notify _Maryanne Negalo_   _520 Nancy Blvd., Sun Prairie, WI_   _(608) 555-1710_
(Name)   (Address)   (Phone)

List all employment within the past ten years **EMPLOYMENT HISTORY**

NAME OF EMPLOYER and Immediate Supervisor	ADDRESS and Telephone Number	POSITION HELD Occupation and Duties	Monthly Rate	Dates Employed From	To	Reason for leaving
Tempest Tea Pot Company Mrs. Phyllis Lipton	707 Coffee Lane Middleton, WI 555-1010	General office work including some recordkeeping	$5/hr.	9/94	6/95	Temporary-Coop.
City Assessor's Office Mr. Dan Verwith	16 Capitol Avenue Madison, WI 555-1122	Records Clerk Recorded data using computer	$6/hr.	6/95	--present	

EDUCATION

Level	Name	Address	Years Attended From	To	Date Graduated	What did you specialize in? Degree(s) Received
Elementary	Hillside Elementary	16 N. 45th St.	1983	1991		
High School	Four Lakes	1234 Monona Drive	1991	1995	June 10	
Trade School						
Business College						
College						
Graduate						
Other						

PERSONAL REFERENCES
Other Than Immediate Relatives

Name	Address	Telephone Number	Occupation	Years Known
Mr. Tim Schilling	1234 Monona Drive, Madison	555-1099	Teacher	3
Rev. David Crane	937 Culpepper Ct., Madison	555-4661	Pastor	12
Mrs. Susan Collins	1602 Woodrale, Madison	555-0065	Secretary	5

Type of work you would consider _Accounting_   Full, or part time? _Full time_
Minimum salary you would consider _$14,000_ Would you consider temporary work? _No_ Date available for employment _Immediately_

The information contained here is true to the best of my knowledge and belief. I realize that any falsification in this application constitutes grounds for dismissal. In this connection, I authorize all previous employers to provide Lakeview Technical College with any information concerning my employment. I further authorize Lakeview Technical College to verify any other information I have provided in this application. I FURTHER UNDERSTAND THAT THIS APPLICATION BECOMES INACTIVE AFTER THREE MONTHS.

Signature _Francisca Negalo_   Date _July 15, 19--_

TESTING POTENTIAL EMPLOYEES

In addition to the information provided on application forms, some employers also use preemployment tests to screen applicants for skills and abilities that are needed to perform certain jobs. Examples of preemployment tests include keyboarding tests, word processing tests, calculating tests, and number and word arranging (filing) tests. These are frequently called ability tests. An **ability test** is one that measures how well a job applicant can perform certain job tasks.

Testing makes it possible to compare each job applicant on the same basis. Two applicants, for example, may have completed a high school course in computer applications and received "B"

Technological*Perspective*

Working at Home

A unique grouping of small businesses are those operating from individual homes known as *cottage businesses.* Telephones, computers, modems, and fax machines have made it possible for some people to work anywhere. In a recent year, our Department of Labor reports that more than 3.6 million people worked for wages in their homes, including 122,100 who were ages 16 to 24.

The cottage business concept is not new, however. In fact, this approach to work was popular among manufacturers in the 1700s and 1800s. The most important goods produced by early cottage businesses included clothing, shoes, cigars, and hand-decorated items. The onset of the Industrial Revolution after the Civil War brought about far-reaching changes in business organizations—including complex machinery, huge factories, large numbers of workers, and more capable managers. The Industrial Revolution brought about a gradual increase in the size and scope of manufacturing operations.

Today the trend is away from large business operations and toward businesses that provide services. The use of computers along with related technology, such as teleconferencing and E-mail, has allowed highly specialized work to be done at home. Word process-

ing and accounting are examples of work commonly done in homes throughout our country.

Opportunities will increase for those who prefer to work at home rather than commute to a workplace. Human skill and initiative along with new technologies will serve as the basis for many new and continuing kinds of cottage businesses, particularly in service-producing industries.

Critical Thinking

1 What are the basic elements that have allowed working at home to become popular in our country?

2 What are some work-at-home opportunities that you can see for yourself and others in the future?

NET FACTS

The Internet's Online Career Center is an employment database to which job hunters can submit personal data via E-mail **(occ-info@occ.com).** There are more than 30,000 résumés stored there.

grades. One applicant, however, might have excelled in spreadsheet applications while the other was outstanding in word processing. High school teachers do not all grade using the same standards, either. So by testing each applicant, the employer can use the test results to compare the skills of each person being considered for the job and be more objective in the selection process.

You should view a test as just another instrument used by employers to evaluate the abilities of job candidates. If you do the best you can on a test under whatever circumstances the test may be given, you need not worry about the results. Employers realize that taking a test in an office, often using unfamiliar equipment, can affect test results.

HAVING A SUCCESSFUL INTERVIEW

The next step in securing employment, and the most important one, is the position interview. A **position interview** is a two-way conversation in which the interviewer learns about you and you learn about the position and the company. These interviews frequently are conducted by personnel interviewers in large companies. A **personnel interviewer** is someone who has special training in talking with job applicants and hiring new employees. Whoever does the interviewing wants to find out about such things as your appearance, manners, use of language, and general suit-

Illus. 15-1
During a position interview, the interviewer learns about you and you learn about the position and the company.

ability for the work in that business. You need to prepare for your interview as carefully as you prepared your letter of application and personal data sheet. The following tips will help you have a good interview:

- Be on time for the appointment.

- Go alone to the interview. Do not take friends or relatives with you.

- Dress properly. Do not be too formal or too informal. Wear the type of clothing that is appropriate for the company and the job for which you are applying.

- Try to be calm during the interview. Avoid talking too much, but answer each question completely using good eye contact. Ask questions intelligently. Let the interviewer guide the discussion.

- Leave when the interviewer indicates that the interview is over.

- Thank the interviewer for the opportunity to discuss the job and your qualifications.

- After the interview, send a brief thank-you letter to the person with whom you interviewed.

- Be patient after the interview. It may take several weeks for the company to complete all of its interviews and make its selection.

Most employees who are fired are let go because they cannot get along with others—an employment success factor that tests cannot measure.

There are a number of different approaches that an interviewer may take. Most interviewers will try to put you at ease when your interview begins. As the interview progresses, there are a number of questions that could be asked by the interviewer. Questions asked by interviewers generally fall into three categories: general information questions, character questions, and stress questions. Here are some examples:

- Why should we hire you for this particular job?

- What are some of the activities you like to do in your spare time?

- What courses have you taken that will help you on this job?

- What are your career goals?

- Do you plan to continue your education now or in the future?

- Do you have any friends or relatives who work here?

- What are your major strengths? What are your major weaknesses?

The interviewer may also review your test results and discuss specific job requirements with you.

Francisca had two interviews. Her first was with the administrative assistant, Admir Coppalois, and then she was interviewed by the head of the accounting unit. The interviews turned out to be a pleasant experience, and Francisca felt good about her interviews when she left the technical college. She had come prepared, and what she learned made her eager to work there if the position were offered to her.

Francisca was offered the job of Accounting Clerk II. Her school record and work experience qualified her for that position. She was very pleased. She began her first day with enthusiasm and high expectations. The job she was offered was just what she had planned for.

In preparing for her first day on the job, Francisca recalled what she had been taught about behavior that helps lead to success on a job:

- *Ask questions.* If you do not understand directions, have them repeated and listen carefully. You need to understand what is expected of you.

- *Avoid complaining about a heavy workload.* If you seem to have more work to do than you can handle, talk with your supervisor about it. Don't try to do more work than you can reasonably handle in an attempt to impress your employer.

- *Honor the time provided for breaks.* Abuse of rest periods and lunch breaks by extending the time limits is a bad business practice. Even if others do it and seem to get by with it, respect your company's policy.

- *Be attentive to your appearance.* Dressing neatly and being well groomed lets others know that you believe your job to be important. Employers often find that sloppy dress and appearance reflect sloppy work habits.

- *Be on time.* Arriving late or leaving early is a poor practice for any employee, especially a new one. On occasion, tardiness or having to leave early might be necessary—but tardiness should be explained, and early departures should be approved in advance.

- *Be friendly with everyone.* Success on the job involves human relations. Respect your co-workers and learn to get along with them. However, do not let friendliness interfere with either your work or theirs.

- *Do work that is well done and on time.* Work that is sloppily done or turned in late can affect others in the office. You are part of a team; take pride in what you do as part of that team. Paying attention to detail lets your co-workers know that you can do your job well.

SUCCEEDING ON YOUR FIRST JOB

- *Follow the rules.* Rules are developed for the good of everyone in your work unit. Not paying attention to company policy can bring trouble to you and others. If a rule seems unfair or unreasonable, discuss it with others and find out why it has been established. You may eventually be able to influence changes.

When you begin a new job, remember that your employer is just as eager as you are for you to succeed. Generally you will find the other employees willing to help you through the first few days. You probably will make a few mistakes in the process of learning your job. The important thing is to learn from each mistake and to avoid repeating it. You will need to be a good listener, too. Your job will test your ability to follow directions and to produce good work. It should be a challenging experience for you.

The word "attitude" can make a *big* difference. It could be the difference between having just another job or being happy and successful in your work. A positive attitude causes you to learn and grow in your job and cooperate with other workers. As a result, you will probably find your job more satisfying and your work more enjoyable. If you project a tentative, unsure attitude through your speech, appearance, and actions, you will be perceived as a tentative, unsure worker even if your work is excellent. Always think, speak, dress, and act positively to project an image that will help you build a successful career.

Francisca has demonstrated readiness for her full-time employment. She has progressed from her work as a student into a career as a full-time worker. The record she built as a student—her good attendance record, the courses she took, the activities in which she participated, and the grades she earned—was important when she was considered for employment. Her school record showed that she was conscientious and capable of good work. Career planning plus a good school record adds up to a successful start in the world of work.

Illus. 15-2

This trainer's positive attitude projects an image of career success.

GETTING ALONG WITH CO-WORKERS

Building good relationships with other employees will improve your own efficiency and influence your future. The following are a few fundamental rules that can help you get along with others.

1. Learn from the others with whom you work, even if they do things differently from the way you were taught in school. Avoid assuming you are right and they are wrong. If you have an idea for improving work procedures, find the right time to suggest improvements.

2. Be on friendly terms with as many people as you can. The person who delivers the mail, the person who cleans the office, the secretary to the president, and others are important people in many ways. Any of your co-workers may be able to help you someday in ways unknown to you now.

3. Learn to accept and give praise when it is due. When you have done something well and you are given credit for it, accept it graciously and appreciatively. When others do something nice, say a good word to them. Learn not to overdo praise, however. False praise will get you nowhere and will raise suspicions about your motives.

4. Show others that you are dependable. Little things, such as returning phone calls promptly and responding to messages without unnecessary delay, tell others that you care about what you do and can be trusted to do your work. When others have a positive impression of you, they will want to work with you and will want to help you succeed.

Illus. 15-3
It is essential to build good relationships with other employees.

5. Look ahead to future opportunities. People with whom you develop good relationships may be promoted to higher positions in a business. Having "friends in high places," as the saying goes, may help you get ahead. The people who respect you for what you can do may have an influence on your future career.

EXITING A JOB

Francisca now must tell her present employer that she will be leaving. Even though it was not a permanent position, leaving on good terms is important. Here are a few tips on how to leave a job gracefully.

- Give a proper notice. Do not just walk into your supervisor's office one day and announce that you are leaving. Give at least a two week notice. Write a short, polite letter of resignation; include the date of the last day you will be working.

- Try to finish all of the special projects that have been assigned to you. If they are not completed, leave a note showing the next person where to begin.

- If there is an **exit interview,** an interview in which your employer asks questions about how you liked your work and what improvements might be made, be constructive and cooperative.

- Let your co-workers know that you appreciated the opportunity to work with them and wish them well. Leaving on a positive note is good for you and for the work unit you are leaving.

A *bookkeeper's* job duties include:
- verifying, allocating, and posting details of business transactions to general and special ledgers
- completing reports to show cash receipts and expenditures, profit and loss, etc.
- preparing payroll withholding and tax reports.

Key Ideas

1 Letters of application and personal data sheets are important and must be prepared carefully.

2 Sources of job leads include friends, relatives, neighbors; school counselors and teachers; school placement office; employment agencies; newspaper ads; help wanted signs; career publications.

3 Completing an employer's application form is an important "first job task" and should be done carefully, neatly, and completely.

4 Preemployment tests are used by employers to screen applicants for skills and abilities that are needed to perform certain jobs.

5 To have a successful position interview, you should be on time, go alone, dress properly, be calm, leave when it is over, thank the interviewer, send a brief thank-you letter, and be patient in waiting for a response.

6 The following behaviors help lead to success on a job: asking questions, avoiding complaining, honoring break time, having a good appearance, getting to work on time, being friendly, doing work well, and following rules.

7 Getting along with co-workers includes learning from them, being friendly with everyone, accepting and giving praise, and being dependable. In leaving a job, give proper notice, complete existing projects, have a constructive exit interview, and show appreciation to co-workers.

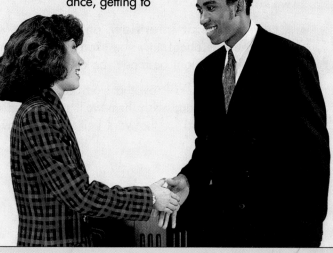

End of Chapter Activities

Increasing Your Business Vocabulary

The following terms should become part of your business vocabulary. For each numbered item, find the term that has the same meaning.

ability test 7

exit interview 8

letter of application 1

personal data sheet 2

personal references 6

personnel interviewer 5

position application 3
form

position interview 4

1 A sales letter about an applicant written for the purpose of getting a personal interview.

2 A summary of job-related information about yourself.

3 A document used by employers that asks for information related to employment.

4 A two-way conversation in which the interviewer learns about you and you learn about the job and the company.

5 Someone who has special training for talking with job applicants and hiring new employees.

6 People who can give a report about your character, education, and work habits.

7 A test that measures how well a job applicant can perform certain job tasks.

8 An interview in which an employer asks questions about how an employee liked his/her work and inquires about job improvements that might be made.

Reviewing Your Reading

1 What is the purpose of a letter of application and a personal data sheet?

2 Who are some people who can be asked to be personal references?

3 Identify several sources of information for job leads.

4 List six categories of information that should be included on a personal data sheet.

5 What is the first job task that you will perform for an employer? Why is it important to perform this task correctly?

6 Why are preemployment tests used by employers?

7 What are some tips that will help you have a good position interview?

8 What questions are commonly asked during a position interview?

9 What are some things you can do

to help you succeed on your first job?

10 What are some things you should do to get along with co-workers?

11 What are some things you can do to exit a job on good terms?

Using Your Business Knowledge

1 Name at least six people you know whom you could ask for help in finding a full-time job. Also identify several local organizations or agencies you could contact for help in finding a job.

2 If you were in charge of hiring people for jobs, what information would you want to get about applicants? How would you go about getting this information? What are some specific questions you would ask if you were to interview the applicants?

3 Your personal data sheet should list several references. Application forms also ask for references to be listed. Make a list of three or more references you could use right now. Then note the type of information each reference could give that would be of help to a potential employer.

4 Write a personal data sheet that you could use right now if you were to apply for a part-time or full-time job. After it is completed, think about whether or not you need to consider being more involved in school, church, or community activities. Think about whether or not your personal data sheet would impress an employer and what you could do that could be included in future personal data sheets to better present yourself.

5 Information has been received about three job openings in your community. Each is quite different and requires a different kind of background and preparation. Assume that you are qualified for only one position. Make up whatever qualifications you think you would like to present to a prospective employer. Then write a letter of application for the position.

a. Reliable person is needed to handle a variety of responsibilities in a small business office. Must be able to work without supervision and communicate effectively with people who call in for information. Word processing and filing skills are desirable. Salary is better than average in this community.

b. Salespeople are needed for an auto parts department and for a cosmetics department of a major retail establishment. Applicants should have some familiarity and/or experience with selling. Hours are flexible, although some evening and weekend work will be required. Benefits are especially attractive; incentive bonus policy can provide a good income for the right person.

c. Ours is a leading bank in this region. We are in need of capable people who want to begin a career in banking. Our training program starts at the bottom, but provides a great opportunity to learn the ins and outs of the banking industry. Business majors are preferred, but liberal arts majors may apply. We are an equal opportunity employer. Salary is competitive.

6 Design an application form similar to the one in Figure 15-3 on page 238 and supply whatever information you think necessary to apply for one of the jobs mentioned in Question 5.

7 Give several examples of what you might do and not do as a new employee in order to develop positive relationships with your co-workers.

8 What kinds of questions would you ask in an exit interview if you were the supervisor interviewing a word processing specialist who is leaving?

Calculating Business Problems

1 Emilie Antoine is a personnel interviewer. On Monday, she interviewed 7 job applicants; on Tuesday, 6 applicants; on Wednesday, 9 applicants; on Thursday, 5 applicants; and on Friday, 8 applicants.

a. How many job applicants did Emilie interview that week? What was the average number per day?

b. On Wednesday, the first interview took 50 minutes; the next 2 each took 40 minutes; the next 4 took 35 minutes each; and the last 2 took 45 minutes each. How many total hours did Emilie spend in these interviews? What was the average length of the interviews?

2 The Human Resources Department of the Tempest Tea Pot Company has 1 personnel manager, 1 administrative assistant, 2 word processing specialists, 2 personnel interviewers, 1 affirmative action/union affairs specialist, and 1 clerk-receptionist. The manager and administrative assistant each have worked for Tempest for 17 years; each of the word processing specialists has worked there for 5 years; and the others have worked there just 1 year.

a. How many total years of employment do the 8 Human Resources Department employees have? What is the average number of years of employment per worker?

b. The administrative support staff consists of the 2 word processing specialists and the clerk-receptionist. The word processing specialists are paid $8.00 per hour, and the clerk-receptionist is paid $7.50 per hour. They each work 35 hours per week. What total wages do these three workers earn in a week? in a month? in a year?

c. If the word processing specialists

receive a 6 percent increase in wages each year, what will be their hourly wages next year?

3 Two data sheets were received by the Human Resources Department. The data sheets listed the height and weight of the applicants and contained the following data. (See Appendix D.)

Mr. Barnfeld: height: 175 cm
weight: 79 kg

Figure the same for the clerk-receptionists. How much will each earn in a 40-hour week that year?

Mr. Oatsown: height: 185 cm
weight: 72 kg

a. Which of the applicants is the tallest? by how many inches?
b. Which of the applicants weighs the most? by how many pounds?

Applying Technology

Using the *Introduction to Business* template and your word processing program software, select problem CH15. After the problem appears on your screen, complete the following activities. Then, print your completed résumé (or personal data sheet) and application. If you do not have a printer available, save the résumé and application on a data disk to give to your teacher.

1 Fill in the résumé with information

about yourself. Delete any sections that you do not use.

2 Use desktop publishing features to give a professional appearance to the résumé you completed in Activity 1.

3 Fill in the job application with information about yourself. Enter Not Applicable in any sections that do not apply to you.

Making Decisions

Rhonda Allison is the plant manager for the All-In-All Manufacturing Company. Over the past several months, a number of valuable workers have quit their jobs. From reports on exit interviews, Rhonda has learned the following: (1) experienced workers believe that their salaries are below average for the business community; (2) equipment that is being used is old, does not perform efficiently, and in some cases is dangerous; and (3) workers are not getting along well primarily because the supervisor is not good at handling people.

Rhonda does not know what to do about these problems. The board of directors is encouraging the company to cut costs to remain competitive. Any request for salary increases or equipment purchases would not be received favorably. The supervisor is a long-time, faithful employee with an excellent previous work record.

1 What is Rhonda's basic problem?

2 What actions would you take if you were Rhonda?

Chapter Sixteen

Key Terms

small business

venture business

bankruptcy

creditor

closing

Small Business Administration (SBA)

Small Business Institutes (SBIs)

Service Corps of Retired Executives (SCORE)

venture capital

entrepreneur

entrepreneurship

Opportunities in Small Business

Objectives

After studying this chapter and completing the end-of-chapter activities, you will be able to:

1 Give a definition of a small business.

2 State at least five reasons why small businesses fail.

3 Describe several sources of help for small-business owners.

4 List at least seven characteristics of successful small-business owners.

Wan-Hoo Lin has been working for the Wedoit Rite Computer Company for the past three years. Wan-Hoo enjoys his work and has learned a great deal about the computer business. He has always been good at troubleshooting and debugging computer programs. In fact, in his spare time he has helped several friends and business acquaintances with problems they encountered with their computers.

Wan-Hoo feels ready to venture out on his own. He has been told that with his experience, skills, and knowledge of computers he would do well in a business of his own. He already has a number of contacts to help him get under way. Wan-Hoo likes the idea of being his own boss although he also is aware of the risks of being in business for oneself.

Wan-Hoo has no family expenses and no major debts. His car is paid for and he saves as much of his wages as possible—he has more than $7,000 in his bank account. He has a simple life style and no bad habits that drain his income. The small house he rents could serve very nicely as his business office.

Wan-Hoo "bit the bullet" by starting his own company, W-H-L Computer Services. He became one of several million small-business owners in the United States. Wan-Hoo and others like him are willing to contribute a great deal of time and energy as well as personal economic resources in return for a reasonable profit.

SMALL BUSINESS OPPORTUNITIES

When we use the term **small business,** we are referring to a business that:

- Usually has the owner as the manager.
- Is not dominant in its field of operation.
- Employs fewer than 500 people.
- Usually is local, serving the nearby community.

You may be surprised that a small business may employ up to 500 people. However, many are smaller. Businesses with only one to four employees are a major factor in our work force.

When you begin your career, you very likely may be working in one of our nation's small businesses. During the past decade, the majority of new job openings were in small businesses. Small businesses provide excellent career opportunities.

You may also consider going into business for yourself. There are many small-business opportunities for people who, like Wan-Hoo, are ready to

A recent survey revealed that one-third of small-business owners started with less than $5,000—only 21 percent started with more than $50,000.

take that step. More than 230,000 businesses were started in recent years, and it is expected that new business growth will continue to be high. Starting your own business can be an exciting, although risky, beginning to a career.

Most small businesses begin as sole proprietorships. It is not unusual, however, for a person to begin his or her own business through a franchise agreement (franchises were discussed in Chapter 6). Many small businesses eventually become incorporated. The advantages of a corporation, as pointed out in Chapter 6, are reasons why some small-business owners decide to incorporate their businesses. The most common form of ownership for small businesses, however, continues to be the sole proprietorship.

Small businesses are found in all of the industries you learned about in Chapter 13. A recent analysis showed that the largest percentage of small businesses are found in retailing—27.5 percent, and in services—23.8 percent (see Figure 16-1). Wan-Hoo's new business venture would place him in the computer services industry.

Some small businesses are classified as venture businesses. A **venture business** is one that has been in operation for less than three years and has no employees other than the owner. Wan-Hoo's business would be a venture business.

Cultural Notes

Companies today are very interested in achieving a balance in the work force. They recognize that there are advantages in a work force that has the same ethnic and cultural composition as their customers.

Illus. 16-1

Wan-Hoo's computer consulting business is just one example of thousands of small business start-ups that occur every year.

Figure 16-1
All of these industries have small businesses, but retailing and services have the greatest percentage.

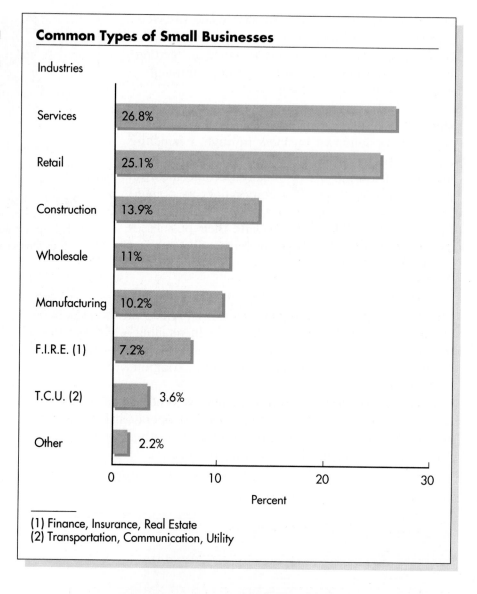

Common Types of Small Businesses

Industries

Industry	Percent
Services	26.8%
Retail	25.1%
Construction	13.9%
Wholesale	11%
Manufacturing	10.2%
F.I.R.E. (1)	7.2%
T.C.U. (2)	3.6%
Other	2.2%

Percent

(1) Finance, Insurance, Real Estate
(2) Transportation, Communication, Utility

SMALL BUSINESS PROBLEMS

Small businesses make many contributions to our economy as innovators of new products and developers of new production processes. Small businesses adjust more quickly to changing market demands than do large businesses. They also can experiment with new products and new methods of production without waiting for approval from management committees or boards of directors.

Not all small businesses succeed; in fact, their failure rate tends to be quite high. In a recent annual report by the President to the

U.S. Congress on the "State of Small Business," 63,912 bankruptcies were reported among small businesses and 830,000 closings. A **bankruptcy** is a situation in which a business does not have enough money to pay its creditors even after selling its equipment and other capital resources. A **creditor** is a person or business that is owed money. A **closing** is a situation in which the business is discontinued with a loss to at least one creditor. Although these figures represent a small percentage of small businesses, the number of failures is of some concern. In addition to these official figures, some small enterprises just quietly go out of business when the owner believes that he or she is not doing well enough to continue.

Illus. 16-2
Small businesses such as this street vendor can adapt more quickly to market demand.

In a typical year, more than half of the businesses that fail have been in operation less than five years and are classified as small businesses. The reasons for failure are quite varied. The following are the most common reasons for failure:

- Not keeping adequate records.

- Not having enough start-up money.

- Lack of sales and management experience.

- Lack of experience with the type of business.

- Not controlling operating expenses.

- Poor location for the business.

- Failure to manage payments due from customers for purchases made.

ankruptcy is not an easy way out—it is an "action of last resort."

Each of the above causes of failure can be overcome with the right kind of assistance. As a prospective small-business owner, you may need special help in the areas of management, accounting, personnel, and finance.

HELP AVAILABLE FOR SMALL BUSINESSES

Small-business owners can get assistance from a number of sources. Universities and colleges have individuals on their faculties who can give advice and assistance to people who are starting or have started their own businesses. Local organizations of business-people, such as Junior Chambers of Commerce, have members who can help others with business problems.

Our government has an agency set up to help small businesses; it is called the **Small Business Administration (SBA).** The SBA is a government-funded organization that helps small-business owners borrow money as well as manage their businesses more efficiently. Information about the SBA and its services can be obtained by contacting an office in your city or state or by writing to the SBA, 1441 L Street, Washington, DC 20416.

The SBA fulfills its mission through a variety of means. The SBA has a large number of publications designed to assist small-business owners. The SBA provides assistance with financing and offers special programs on how to operate small businesses. **Small Business Institutes (SBIs)** are programs offered in cooperation with colleges and universities to provide management counseling.

The SBA is also responsible for the formation and operation of organizations known as SCORE. **SCORE** stands for the **Service Corps of Retired Executives** whose members can provide assistance in special areas of operation, such as finance, accounting, and marketing. Members of SCORE are retired local businesspeople who volunteer their services and are paid only a basic amount to cover their travel expenses.

Other special services provided by the SBA include the Small Business Investment Companies (SBICs) and a specialized Section 301(d) SBIC, commonly called a Minority Enterprise SBIC (MESBIC). SBICs are set up to provide venture capital and management services. The providing of **venture capital**—money used to start up a new small business or help a business expand during a growth period—is an important service.

A large number of small-business owners are women. The SBA operates an Office of Women Business Owners. It also has special publications dealing

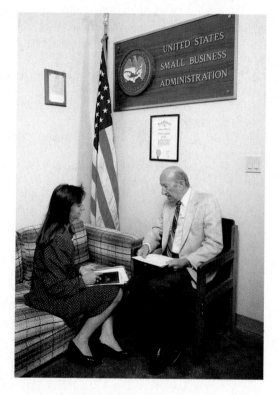

Illus. 16-3
The Small Business Administration provides a variety of services to owners of small businesses.

with women who are small-business owners, such as *Women Business Owners: Selling to the Federal Government.*

CHARACTERISTICS OF BUSINESS OWNERS

You probably already have concluded that small-business owners must know a lot of facts and perform many business functions in order to be successful. In addition to a knowledge of business operations and management skills, small-business owners must have certain personal characteristics. Some characteristics of successful small-business owners are that they

- Can do things on their own; they are self-starters.

- Have leadership abilities; they can get others to do what has to be done.

NET FACTS

FAQs stands for Frequently Asked Questions. Many Internet hosts provide files containing answers to FAQs about their services.

Legal *Perspective*

What Is Bankruptcy?

Bankruptcy, the legal non-payment of financial obligations, is a common occurrence among small-business owners. Bankruptcy occurs when a business owes substantially more than the value of all the things it owns (assets). Declaring bankruptcy is one solution to the problem of having too much debt. The bankruptcy procedures allow the business to make a fresh start.

Our bankruptcy laws provide two plans. In one plan, the business retains some basic assets. Other assets are sold to pay creditors; some who are owed money receive just a portion of what is owed. With the other plan, creditors cannot collect what is owed for a period of time. The business tries to resolve the financial crisis under a court-approved plan.

Bankruptcy releases a company from the burden of debt. This release is called a *discharge.* Discharges through bankruptcy are available to a particular debtor once every six years. A record that debts were discharged in a bankruptcy proceeding stays on a debtor's record for ten years. A bankruptcy record usually reduces a debtor's ability to get credit during that period. And credit is basic to our way of doing business today.

Critical Thinking

1 *What is the basis on which bankruptcy is declared?*

2 *Who gets helped and who gets hurt in a bankruptcy situation?*

A recent survey revealed that 62 percent of Harvard Business School's 1974 graduates were working for small business firms 18 years later.

- Can take charge of things; they assume responsibility.

- Like to plan what must be done; they are good organizers.

- Are hard workers; they work long hours on the job.

- Are decision makers; they can make decisions quickly when necessary.

- Can be trusted; they mean what they say.

- Are achievers; they will work on a task until it is finished.

- Have good health; they exhibit energy.

Illus. 16-4

Owning a small business can be rewarding for those who have the right personal characteristics.

The above characteristics are based on an SBA publication called *A Checklist for Going into Business.* In addition, some researchers also have discovered the following characteristics to be important for small-business owners:

- They would rather work for themselves, even if they made considerably less money than working for someone else.

- They are at least 24 years old (fewer than 10 percent are under age 24).

- They have had a variety of business experiences, often with someone who is a successful small-business owner.

- They desire to use their skills and abilities and have control over their lives.

YOUNG ENTREPRENEURS

An **entrepreneur** is someone who takes a risk in starting a business to earn a profit. Having a real desire to be your own boss, developing a good initial plan for a business, having special skills and abilities, and coming up with some innovative ideas are important factors in starting your own business.

Can you think of some service or product that is not being offered that could be in demand? Is there some service or product that you personally could offer more efficiently or with better results than others are doing now? Is there some special talent that you have that could become the foundation for a business of your own? If so, you have the basis for a new business enterprise.

There are still good opportunities for entrepreneurship through small business ownership. **Entrepreneurship** is the process of starting, organizing, managing, and assuming the responsibility for a business. Here are some real-life examples of young entrepreneurs.

Larry Villella was only 11 years old when he got an idea that developed into a business. He did not like moving the family lawn sprinkler around when his chore was to water the lawn. So he went into the basement and cut a sprinkler into a c-shape that fit around trees and shrubs. Four years later, his little company, Villella's ConServ Products, had sold about $70,000 worth of products.

Ban Narasin of Manhattan showed some business ability at the age of 12 when he talked his father into giving him $65 so that he could get into a comic book convention as a dealer. He bought and sold comic books at that convention and came home with a $2,500 profit. Seven years later he started a business called Boston Prepatory, a men's sportswear manufacturer. In 1993, his sales totaled $8 million.

Geoff Allen of McLean, Virginia, was a whiz at a computer. He learned to write his own programs when he was too young to begin selling them. At the age of 19, he started Source Digital Systems. His company did video editing, produced animations, and created video kiosks for point-of-sale purchases. Within a few years, his business sales were about $5 million with projections for sales to grow to over $8 million.

Key Ideas

1 A small business is one that has the owner as a manager, is not dominant in its field of operation, employs fewer than 500 people, and usually serves a local community.

2 Small businesses fail because owners do not keep adequate records, do not have enough start-up money, lack sales and management experience, lack experience in the type of business owned, do not control operating expenses, have a poor business location, and fail to manage payments due from customers.

3 Small-business owners can get help from the Small Business Administration, from Small Business Institutes, and from organizations such as SCORE.

4 Successful small-business owners tend to be self-starters, leaders, planners, hard workers, decision makers, and achievers; they are responsible, trustworthy, and healthy individuals.

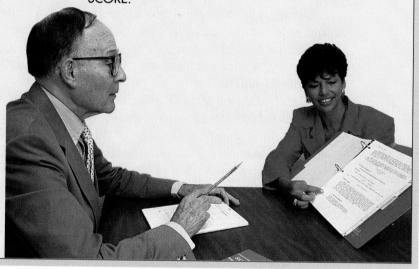

End of Chapter Activities

Increasing Your Business Vocabulary

The following terms should become part of your business vocabulary. For each numbered item, find the term that has the same meaning.

bankruptcy

closing

creditor

entrepreneur

entrepreneurship

Service Corps of
Retired Executives
(SCORE)

small business

Small Business
Administration (SBA)

Small Business Institutes (SBIs)

venture business

venture capital

1 A business that has been in operation for less than three years and has no employees other than the owner.

2 A group of retired executives who can provide assistance to small-business owners.

3 Someone who takes a risk in starting a business to earn a profit.

4 A situation in which a business does not have enough money to pay its creditors even after selling its equipment and other capital resources.

5 A person or business that is owed money.

6 A situation in which a business is discontinued with a loss occurring to at least one creditor.

7 Money used to start up a new small business or help a business expand during a growth period.

8 Programs offered in cooperation with colleges and universities to provide management counseling.

9 A business that usually has the owner as manager, is not dominant in its field of operation, employs fewer than 500 people, and usually serves its nearby community.

10 A government-funded organization that helps small-business owners borrow money as well as manage their businesses more efficiently.

11 The process of starting, organizing, managing, and assuming the responsibility for a business.

Reviewing Your Reading

1. In which industries are the greatest percentages of small businesses found?

2. State seven common reasons for business failures.

3. What are three specific things that the SBA does to help small businesses?

4. Name several publications of the SBA.

5. What is SCORE, who are its members, and what assistance does it provide for small businesses?

6. What are some characteristics of successful small-business owners?

7. Name three important factors to be considered before starting your own small business.

Using Your Business Knowledge

1. Why is your career likely to begin in a small business?

2. In what ways are small businesses major contributors to our economy?

3. Why are most of the small businesses found in the retailing and service industries?

4. How could each of the reasons why small businesses fail be overcome?

5. Why are retired executives willing to work with small-business owners in solving their problems?

6. Why do you think the government established the SBA?

7. Which of the 12 characteristics of successful small-business owners do you presently have? Which ones do you believe you could develop while in school?

8. What are some future small-business opportunities in which you might be interested?

Calculating Business Problems

1. Chuck Polley wants to open a sporting goods store. He has been told that he should have at least $35,000 to invest in his new business. He has $3,000 in his bank account, a friend will lend him $4,000, and he can get a bank loan for $10,000.

   a. How much money does Chuck have available for investing now?
   b. How much will he have to borrow to come up with the $35,000?
   c. If he can get an additional $5,000 loan on his credit card account, how much will he still need?

d. If the local bank is willing to lend him $10,000, will he have enough then to start his busi- ness? If not, how much will the shortage be?

---

2 Sandy Noble owns and operates a beauty salon. On Monday, he worked 12 hours; on Tuesday, 8 hours; on Wednesday, 9 hours; on Thursday, 8 hours; on Friday, 11 hours; on Saturday, 6 hours. He earned $1,595 that week, and his expenses were $785.

a. How many total hours did Sandy work that week? What was the average number of hours per day?

b. How much did he have as profit after subtracting expenses from the money he took in? How much profit did he make per hour worked?

c. If Sandy worked for the Shear Delight Beauty Parlor, he would be paid $12.50 per hour. How much more does Sandy earn a week in his own business compared to working for another beautician if he works the same number of hours?

---

3 Tracy Gardner operates a fleet of five trucks. Three trucks cost her $18,000 each, and two trucks cost her $31,000 each. Last week each of the five trucks averaged 250 kilometers of driving. Tracy's business makes $17.25 for each mile driven by the trucks. (See Appendix D)

a. How much does Tracy have invested in her five trucks? If Tracy's goal is to earn 10 percent per year on her investment, how much should she earn on those trucks?

b. How much does Tracy earn on the total miles driven by her trucks in the situation described above?

c. If four of the trucks each carried an average load of 1,125 kilograms of materials, how many pounds did each truck carry? How many pounds did the four trucks carry? If one truck hauled liquids and averaged 1,900 liters per haul, how many gallons were there per haul?

d. Does Tracy's business earn enough to meet her goal? How much short or over the goal are the actual earnings? What is the percentage that was actually earned?

---

4 Assume that a state employs a total of 550,000 workers and that the state has the same percentage of workers in each of the eight industries as shown in Figure 16-1 on page 254. Use the following percentages: Construction, 13.9 percent; Finance, Insurance, Real Estate, 7.2 percent; Manufacturing, 10.2 percent; Retailing, 25.1 percent; Services, 26.8 percent; Transportation, Communication, Utility, 3.6 percent; Wholesale, 11.0 percent; Other, 2.2 percent. How many workers would there be in each industry in that state?

Applying Technology

Using the *Introduction to Business* template and your database program software, select problem CH16. After the problem appears on your screen, complete the following activities. Then, after you have completed each step, display or print a report for each activity. If you do not have a printer available, answer the questions before you leave the computer.

1 Sort the database in descending order by owner's years of experience. Answer the following questions:

   a. Which owner has the most years of experience?

   b. Which owner has the third fewest years of experience?

2 Select and list the companies that are less than five years old. How many companies are listed?

3 Sort the companies in ascending order by product name. Answer the following questions:

   a. Which product is listed most often?

   b. What is the last product listed?

Making Decisions

Wan-Hoo has worked hard to build up a good business. He has many customers, and they are pleased with his services. His new business is a source of satisfaction—he likes being his own boss and feeling good about what he accomplishes.

But finances are a problem. Wan-Hoo had to borrow $20,000 to get the supplies and equipment he needed to get started. His day-to-day business expenses are more than he had expected.

A number of his customers are slow in making payments. Wan-Hoo does not have time to pursue customers who are slow in paying their bills. Late-paying customers make it difficult for him to pay his bills on time. His creditors are quite unhappy with him. He has more debt than he considers desirable. He wonders: Should I declare bankruptcy? Should I just go out of business? Should I try to get someone to help me get these financial problems under control?

1 What is the basic problem that Wan-Hoo faces?

2 What would you suggest that he do?

A dministrative support functions consist of a variety of tasks and responsibilities performed by support personnel to assist managerial, technical, and professional employees. Rewarding and challenging careers can be found in these occupations. The increased use of computers and integrated office systems are factors influencing opportunities in these occupations.

Job Titles

Job titles commonly found in this career area include:

- Accounting Clerk
- Bookkeeper
- Benefits Clerk
- Clerk Typist
- Customs-Entry Clerk
- Data Entry Clerk
- Export Clerk
- File Clerk
- Foreign-Exchange Position Clerk
- Letter-of-Credit Clerk
- Secretary
- Statistical Clerk
- Word Processing Machine Operator

Employment Outlook (through the year 2005)

- Job growth will decline through the year 2005.
- In several occupations, including secretaries and file clerks, job opportunities will increase because of the need to replace retiring workers.
- Employment in health industry businesses is expected to be better than average.

- Many of the job opportunities will be in small businesses.

Education and Training

- A high school diploma is a requirement for employment.
- Employers state a preference for applicants who have completed business courses.
- Some employers look for some education beyond high school, especially in two-year business administration programs.
- Skill in operating computers, good keyboarding skill, and a knowledge of business procedures are desired by employers.

Salary Levels (in recent years)

- Administrative support occupations generally pay in the range of $13,000 to $24,000 a year for beginning workers. The salary paid depends upon the company, the geographic area, and the skills of the worker.
- Average (median) salaries: secretaries, $24,100; file clerks, $9,000 to $13,000; statistical clerks, $15,000; and data entry clerks, $13,000 to $15,000. Experienced workers earn an average of $32,900 (secretaries), $14,700 (file clerks), and $18,000 (data entry clerks).

Critical Thinking

1 Which job titles in this career area appeal to you most? Give some reasons for your choices.

2 What are some things you will have to do to achieve success in the career you selected?

Administrative Support Careers

Unit Five

Consumers in the Economy

The Marketing Concept

Businesses have learned that responding to customer wants and needs must be their first priority. Successful companies have adopted a strategy that is known as the marketing concept. The term *marketing concept* is using the needs of customers as the primary focus in producing goods and services. The main objective is the satisfaction of customers' wants and needs.

Marketing was not always an important part of business. Indeed, marketing was not even a term used in business until the last half of the twentieth century. American business folklore attributes the following statement to Henry Ford: "The public can have any color [automobile] it wants, as long as it's black." Even if this statement was not actually made by Ford, it was expressed in his attitude toward customers during the years that the Model T Ford dominated the auto market. During that time, the Ford Motor Company, and many other businesses, were guided by what manufacturing wanted to make, not by what customers wanted to buy. Eventually, however, the Ford Motor Company reacted to customer wants and began to manufacture cars in a variety of colors.

Today the Ford Motor Company marketing executives are very interested in their customers. They are constantly at work trying to learn more about auto customers' wants and needs. The Ford Motor Company now, for example, uses a method to gauge the thought processes that precede the decision to buy a new car. They carefully study target groups of car buyers through the use of focus group interviews to learn about their needs and wants. Information gained from these interviews is used by Ford executives to make decisions about colors, styles, prices, options, engines, and other factors that would influence consumer decisions.

Another business segment that has successfully employed the marketing concept is the mail-order industry. Most mail-order companies have learned the obvious, that consumers want to be assured of a no hassle return process in the event that problems arise with their order. Well known and rapidly growing mail-order companies like L.L. Bean, Eddie Bauer, and Lands' End treat customers well. One of them has stated in its catalog, "Every item we sell is covered by our unconditional guarantee. No time limits, no exceptions, no fine print, no questions asked. We stand behind every piece of merchandise we sell. And we always will—it's a tangible expression of our commitment to putting our customer's needs first."

These are only two examples of successfully identifying and responding to the needs of customers. The most successful businesses are ones who consider the needs of customers and work hard to satisfy their needs.

Critical Thinking

1 *How do you think businesses find out about the needs and wants of customers?*

2 *Why do you think today's consumers feel more empowered to express their wants and needs to American businesses?*

Chapter Seventeen

Key Terms

consumer

grade

label

opportunity cost

The Informed Consumer

Objectives

After studying this chapter and completing the end-of-chapter activities, you will be able to:

1 Describe the informed consumer in our economic system.

2 Identify three types of consumer organizations.

3 Name two government agencies that provide consumer information.

4 List three ways in which businesses provide consumer information.

5 List the seven questions which informed consumers should ask when selecting the best product or service.

"I have spent three weeks going all over town trying to decide on a sleeping bag to buy for our camping trip," complained Kirsten. "I didn't realize how many choices of styles, quality, and prices that are available. It is too difficult for me to make a decision without some help!"

"Have you read any consumer magazines to get information on how to buy a sleeping bag?" asked Joshua. "If you go to the library, you can read through several publications for rating information that might make your decision a lot easier. I will go to the library with you and show you how to find this information."

"I knew there had to be a better way than spending time and gasoline running all over town! Thanks for the offer!"

A consumer is a person who buys and uses goods or services. All of us consume products and buy services every day. We buy food, clothing, school supplies, and appliances. We also pay for services each time we go to a movie, the dentist, or a car wash. All of these activities make us consumers. American businesses provide us with goods and services. But it is our job to be wise consumers and make appropriate decisions as to which products or services to buy.

A wise consumer is an informed consumer. However, in order for us to be informed consumers in our economic system, we must acquire information about products and services before we buy them.

THE CONSUMER

Consumers have the power to decide to buy or not to buy goods and services. Businesses go to great lengths to be responsive to the needs of consumers. Without satisfied consumers, businesses would not make sales, earn profits, or remain in business.

People usually seek the highest standard of living that their incomes will allow. You can get more for your money and raise your standard of living by becoming an informed consumer. In fact, your standard of living is probably determined more by how wisely you spend than by how much money you earn.

Your consumer behavior reflects and determines your life-style. You may choose to be thrifty and buy only the products and services you need to live or you may buy products and services that you could easily do without.

We have an obligation to society to be wise and efficient consumers. Our world has only a limited supply of natural resources, such as petroleum, metals, clean air, and clean water. Sometimes uninformed consumers unnecessarily waste these irreplaceable resources and/or contribute to damaging our environment.

The words consumer and customer mean the same and may be used interchangeably.

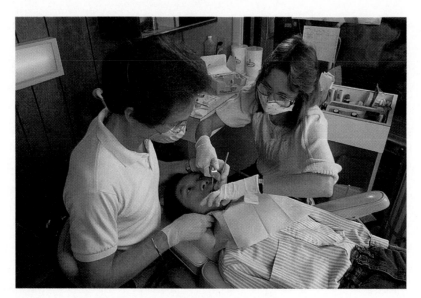

Illus. 17-1
Whether purchasing a product or a service, consumer decisions drive the economy.

CONSUMER INFORMATION ORGANIZATIONS

In order to help inform consumers, several organizations or branches of organizations have been developed. The testing these organizations do and the advice they give is usually objective. These organizations may publish magazines, award seals, and in some cases endorse products for quality and safety. Three basic types of organizations exist: product-testing organizations, print publishers, and broadcast organizations.

Product-Testing Organizations

Product-testing organizations have as their main purpose the testing of products and services. Manufacturers pay these private firms to perform safety tests on products.

Perhaps the best known of these organizations is the Underwriters Laboratories, Inc. Underwriters Laboratories tests electrical components of products from all over the world for fire and electrical safety. The symbol of the Underwriters Laboratories is an indication that the product has been tested and judged safe for normal use.

Another organization is the Association of Home Appliance Manufacturers (AHAM). This group develops and updates the performance standards of such appliances as refrigerators, air conditioners, and freezers. The AHAM seal signifies that a product has met the association's performance standards. Other seals include the Factory Mutual Approved Mark and the seal of the American Gas Association.

Illus. 17-2

The symbol of the Underwriters Laboratories indicates that the product has been judged safe for normal use.

Print Publishers

Some organizations have as one of their goals the reporting of scientific, technical, and educational information about products and services. Some are nonprofit organizations, such as Consumers Union, Inc., which perform independent tests on consumer goods and publish articles on the quality of the goods. Consumers Union publishes its findings in a monthly magazine called *Consumer Reports*. Consumers' Research, Inc., is an independent, nonprofit organization that presents articles on a wide range of topics of consumer interest. The magazine, *Consumers' Research*, analyzes products, services, and consumer issues.

Some magazines that are published for a profit endorse products but only after those products have been tested. *Good Housekeeping* and *Parents* are examples. Any product advertised in these magazines can display the magazine's seal. The Good Housekeeping Seal promises the product will be replaced or your money refunded if the product is found to be defective within one year of purchase. *Consumers Digest* and *Bottom Line* are two other publications designed specifically for the purpose of providing objective consumer information.

In the financial world, there are many periodicals that cover topics of interest to consumers. *Money, Kiplinger's Personal Finance Magazine, Fortune,* and *The Wall Street Journal,* for example, evaluate and report on the performance of investments such as

n order to remain unbiased, the *Consumer's Research* magazine accepts no advertising.

stocks, bonds, mutual funds, real estate, precious metals, art, and coins.

There are also specialty magazines or newspapers that provide information about specific kinds of products or services. These publications cover topics such as cars, computers, boats, sound equipment, travel, and education. They help consumers understand technical or complex products and services. Often comparative ratings are given for products or services.

Broadcast Organizations

Like magazines and newspapers, radio and television also are sources of consumer information. Many stations carry regular programs that inform the public about product safety, care and use of products, and shopping tips, such as the best food buys of the week. In addition, many broadcast talk shows are designed to help listeners with their consumer problems.

CONSUMER INFORMATION FROM GOVERNMENT

Federal, state, and local governments also help people become informed consumers. The federal government, for example, formed the Consumer Information Center to serve as headquarters for consumer information. This agency issues catalogs four times a year. Each catalog lists numerous publications of special interest to consumers. In addition to making government publications available, the Center publishes the results of government research and product tests. The agency has distribution centers in several major cities.

The United States Department of Agriculture (USDA) is another source of consumer information. USDA publications specialize in information about food—judging quality, buying wisely, improving buying practices, planning meals, improving nutrition, and other farm- and home-related topics.

The USDA also inspects and grades foods and makes that information available to consumers in the form of a grade. A **grade** indicates the quality or size of a product. For example, beef may be stamped "prime," "choice," or "select." The USDA shield means that the product has been inspected and approved by that government agency.

Other government agencies that provide information to consumers include the Office of Consumer

Affairs, Federal Trade Commission, Food and Drug Administration, Consumer Product Safety Commission, National Highway Traffic Safety Administration, Department of Health and Human Services, and Environmental Protection Agency. In each case, the name of the agency suggests its area of concern and responsibility. States, cities, and counties have consumer agencies which provide consumer information.

CONSUMER INFORMATION FROM BUSINESSES

Businesses provide information to consumers. As a public service and in an effort to sell goods and services, businesses make information available through advertising, product labels, customer service departments, business specialists, and Better Business Bureaus.

Advertising

Advertising is probably the most popular source of consumer information. Since the main purpose of an advertisement is to convince you to buy a product or service, you should use it with care as a source of consumer information. Advertising can be useful if you know which product or service you want and if you can overlook strong appeals to buy a particular product or service.

Useful advertisements often tell you what the product is, how it is made, and what it will do. Advertisements give facts that you can use to compare the product with other competing products. Beware of advertising claims that really tell you nothing about the product. If an advertisement states that a product is better, ask, "Better than what?"

Another type of advertising that originates with consumers is called word-of-mouth advertising. Information from a consumer who has already purchased the product or service you are interested in buying is one of the most effective sources of consumer information. Most of us, when planning a purchase, go to someone who already owns the product and ask, "How do you like it?" This word-of-mouth source of consumer information should not be underestimated by consumers or businesses.

Labels list ingredients with the main ingredient first and remaining ingredients in descending order of quantity.

The BBB cannot force a business to do what a consumer wants or help either party break a legal contract

Product Labels

A **label** provides useful written information about the nature or content of a product. The label may tell you what the product is made of, its size, how to care for it, and when and where it was made. The label on a shirt should tell you what it is made of and provide laundering instructions.

Customer Service Departments

Many businesses have special departments devoted to customer service. Some firms provide customers with booklets on a variety of consumer topics. For example, banks and insurance companies publish booklets to help consumers manage their money. Some large retail firms provide printed materials to help consumers with their buying problems. JCPenney and Sears, for example, publish pamphlets to help customers improve their buying skills.

Business Specialists

Sometimes it is wise to get advice from an expert before purchasing a product. This is especially true if you have never bought such an item, if the item is very complicated, or if it is very expensive. Houses, business machines, and used cars are examples of products that should not be purchased without an expert's advice. For example, most of us could not judge whether the furnace in a house is safe or the central air conditioning is adequate

Illus. 17-3
A label provides information about the nature or content of a product.

for the size of the house. A certified house inspector could give reliable advice about these items.

Better Business Bureaus

In an effort to improve credibility, businesses all across the country have joined together in a self-regulation effort and created Better Business Bureaus (BBB). Many communities have a Better Business Bureau. Better Business Bureaus are supported by dues paid by member businesses. The bureaus work to maintain ethical practices in the advertising and selling of products and services and to combat consumer fraud. BBBs are concerned with developing more informed and satisfied consumers.

Better Business Bureaus can provide helpful information. For example, suppose you were planning to buy a used car from a particular dealer. You could call the Better Business Bureau to find out what experiences others have had with that dealer. If consumers have reported problems with the firm, you could find out about these complaints. Better Business Bureaus give facts only; they do

Environmental *Perspective*

Marketing Green Products to Consumers

Green products are goods manufactured or packaged in an environmentally safe way. Many companies have found that protecting the environment helps sell their products. From this concern have emerged green products which are products that have been manufactured or packaged in a way to be environmentally safe.

Green products have been developed by businesses to satisfy consumer demand. Consumers recognize that some products, or the packages the products come in, may have a negative effect on our environment. For example, aerosol cans release fluorocarbons into the air which may reduce the thickness of our ozone layer. Therefore, businesses have responded by creating pump spray bottles for products such as hair spray and window cleaners. Other companies have begun packaging their products in recycled paper and cardboard containers. This special packaging may increase the cost of some products. However, some consumers are willing to spend more money for environmentally sound products. This situation highlights two crucial questions that society faces: Are the benefits of preserving the environment worth the costs? And, are we willing to pay now for a better environment in the future?

Critical Thinking

1 Identify three products or product packages that are environmentally sound. Describe their packages.

2 How much more would you be willing to pay as a consumer for an environmentally safe product? Explain your answer.

not recommend products or firms. They give you the information they have, but you are free to interpret it and to make your own decision. The services and programs offered by a Better Business Bureau can help you be a more informed, knowledgeable, and satisfied consumer.

EFFECTIVE CONSUMER PRACTICES

You may not always use good consumer skills in the purchase of every product or service. Sometimes there will not be time to do so, and at other times it may not be worth the effort when making a minor purchase. You can, however, develop the habit of using good judgment in making the most of your purchases.

Whenever you plan to buy anything, you must make a number of important decisions. Your answers to the following questions will help you choose the best product or service for you:

1. Would you rather buy this item instead of another desired item that costs the same amount of money?

2. Which business or businesses should you visit?

3. What quality of goods or services do you want to buy?

4. What price are you willing to pay?

5. Should you pay cash or buy now and pay later?

6. Do you really need this item now or can you wait awhile?

7. If you make this purchase, what other important item may you have to do without?

NET FACTS

The communications structure of the Internet is the global telephone system, which is a network of networks working together. By using the phone system, the Internet has worldwide coverage and significant potential for growth.

FYI

When you give up something in order to have something else that is more important to you, you are making a trade-off.

Use reliable consumer information to judge each purchase according to whether it will meet your needs better than something else you could buy. Not buying one article so that you can buy another article can be viewed as an opportunity cost. An **opportunity cost** is the value of any alternative that you give up when you buy something else or make another choice. For example, suppose you want both a new sweater and a seat for your bicycle, but have only enough money for one or the other. If you choose the seat, you must give up the sweater. Part of the "cost" of the seat, then, is the opportunity to have a new sweater.

Key Ideas

1 An informed consumer acquires information about products and services before buying.

2 Three basic consumer information organizations are product-testing organizations, print publishers, and broadcast organizations.

3 Government agencies such as the Office of Consumer Affairs, the Federal Trade Commission, and the Consumer Product Safety Commission develop useful information for consumers.

4 Businesses supply consumers with information through advertising, product labels, customer service departments, specialists, and the Better Business Bureau.

5 An informed consumer will ask questions before purchasing a product.

End of Chapter Activities

Increasing Your Business Vocabulary

The following terms should become part of your business vocabulary. For each numbered item, find the term that has the same meaning.

consumer

grade

label

opportunity cost

1 A person who buys and uses goods or services.

2 The value of any alternative that you give up when you buy something else or make another choice.

3 An indication of the quality or size of a product.

4 A written statement attached to a product giving useful information about its nature or contents.

Reviewing Your Reading

1 What power does the consumer have?

2 What are two examples of product-testing organizations?

3 What are two nonprofit organizations that publish consumer magazines?

4 What are two financial periodicals that cover topics of interest to consumers?

5 Which government organization specializes in information about food—judging quality, buying wisely, improving buying practices, planning meals, improving nutrition, and other farm- and home-related topics?

6 Why do businesses provide information to consumers?

7 How can advertising help you become a better consumer?

8 What is the concern of the Better Business Bureau?

9 What are the seven important questions you should ask before purchasing a product or service?

Using Your Business Knowledge

1 Why do you think a good businessperson with good products or services to sell would like to have customers who are well informed?

2 List three sources of consumer information about a bicycle.

3 Why do you think specialty newspapers and magazines are published and sold?

4 What kinds of advertisements are most valuable to consumers? Give an example.

5 One autumn day a woman and a man came to Carrie Franklin's door. They said they were chimney sweeps and would like to clean her chimney before she began using her fireplace. The man said it would be inexpensive and make her home safer because it would reduce the chances of a chimney fire. Mrs. Franklin looked out her window and saw the name "Chim Chim Chimney Sweeps" on the truck they were driving. How can she find out if the firm is reliable?

Calculating Business Problems

1 While studying an automobile buyer's guide, Teresa learned that the value of three new cars she was considering would decrease over the next four years. The figures are shown in the table.

Car Brand	Original Price	Total 4-Year Reduction in Value
Sunglow Convertible	$17,300	47%
Grocery-Getter	$ 9,850	23%
Muscle Car	$14,800	33%

a. At the end of four years, what will be the value of the Sunglow Convertible?

b. At the end of four years, what will be the value of the Grocery-Getter?

c. At the end of four years, what will be the value of the Muscle Car?

2 The advertisement shown at right appeared in a newspaper during the month of March.

a. By how much money were the finer coats reduced?

b. By how much money were the wool winter coats reduced?

c. By how much money were the raincoats reduced?

Save
Clearance Sale

Buy NOW! Buy for NEXT YEAR!
A small deposit will hold your selection.
Don't miss these values!

	Regular	Sale
Finer Winter Coats	$259.95	$174.95
Wool Winter Coats	199.95	149.95
Raincoats	74.95	59.95

3 Near the end of the summer, Wheeler's Garden Store marked down a number of items for quick sale. The regular selling price, reduced price, and cost of each item to the store are shown in this table. Each item was sold at the reduced price.

Item	Regular Price	Reduced Price	Cost
21-inch power mower	$194.99	$179.25	$151.50
Riding lawn mower	675.00	599.95	562.50
Electric hedge trimmer	54.00	49.32	40.50
Deluxe barbecue grill	97.45	74.52	81.75
Lawn furniture set	224.99	169.32	135.00
Total			$971.25

a. By what amount was each item reduced?

b. How much was realized on the sale of each item?

c. What was the total amount received from the sale of the five items?

d. By what percentage of the regular price was each item reduced?

4 Carlos needed to buy a small bookshelf for his bedroom. The space available for the bookshelf was 4.5 feet wide and 1 foot deep. At a local discount store, he found a boxed, ready-to-assemble bookshelf with dimensions 125 cm (centimeters) wide and 30 cm deep. At another store, he saw a bookshelf that measured 150 cm wide and 25 cm deep.

a. Determine if each bookshelf will fit into Carlos' bedroom. (Metric hint: One inch equals 2.5 centimeters.)

b. What suggestion would you make to Carlos about purchasing a bookshelf?

Applying Technology

Using the *Introduction to Business* template and your database program software, select problem CH17. After the problem appears on your screen, complete the following activities. Then, after you have completed each step, display or print a report for each activity. If you do not have a printer available, answer the questions before you leave the computer.

1 Sort the database in ascending order by name of the consumer agencies. Answer the following questions:

a. What is the first agency listed?

b. What is the third agency listed?

2 Select and list the agencies that provide legal services. How many agencies are listed?

3 Sort the agencies in descending order by ZIP Code. Answer the following questions:

a. What is the second agency listed?

b. What is the last agency listed?

Making Decisions

Pierre needs a new camera to take with him on his trip to Mexico as an exchange student. He is not a photography expert but has taken some pictures for the school newspaper. He intends to use the camera to take indoor and outdoor pictures of new friends he will meet as well as scenery he will encounter.

Pierre has about $150 to spend on the camera and wants the camera to be sturdy, to be easy to use, and to take good quality pictures.

1 What sources of information could Pierre use to find out what cameras are in his price range?

2 What two sources of information do you feel are best? Why?

Chapter Eighteen

Consumer Buying Decisions

Key Terms

comparison shopping

unit price

promotional sales

clearance sales

brand name

full-service stores

discount stores

specialty stores

factory outlet stores

supermarket

warehouse market

convenience stores

impulse buying

price index

Consumer Price Index

Objectives

After studying this chapter and completing the end-of-chapter activities, you will be able to:

1 List the five steps you should follow when you make a buying decision.

2 Name the four items that a comparison shopper will evaluate when making a purchase.

3 Explain the importance of a business's reputation, value of brand names, and the choices of stores when deciding where to buy items.

4 Describe how a good consumer decides when to buy.

5 List the steps a consumer can take to become an efficient shopper.

6 Describe the Consumer Price Index (CPI).

J uan met Michelle after school. "Hi Michelle. Have you finished your research on computers? Which one are you going to buy?"

"I don't know," replied Michelle. "I looked at the computers at Bright's Computer Store and they have the lowest price. I spent three hours checking out different computers. But I got the impression they didn't take me seriously because of my age."

Young people often voice the complaint that they aren't respected. Teens say that others don't treat them like the adults they aspire to be.

But nothing could be further from the truth when it comes to businesses' treatment of youth. Businesses recognize that youths have a lot of money to spend on goods and services that satisfy their wants or needs. When the time comes for youths to make buying decisions, businesses want young people to choose their products and services. With the change to a consumer-oriented business environment, you can be sure businesses respect young consumers.

Illus. 18-1
The needs and wants of young people are of great importance to many businesses, as shown by these consumer goods.

DECISION-MAKING STEPS

In Chapter 1, you were introduced to the steps in making a decision. As a consumer, you should follow similar decision-making steps when you make a buying decision. These steps are:

1. Identify your needs or wants. Be able to clearly state why you intend to buy something.

2. Know the choices that are available to you. These choices include price, quality, location, variety, reputation, and the like.

3. Determine the measure of satisfaction of your needs and wants. You will develop answers to questions such as "How much am I

Caveat emptor is a Latin term for "let the buyer beware."

willing to pay," "What quality level will be adequate?" and "How long am I willing to wait for the product?"

4. Consider the alternatives. At this stage, you will shop for the products and services that might satisfy your needs. You will compare them in terms of the criteria you have identified.

5. Finally, you will make the decision to buy.

DEVELOPING BUYING SKILLS

Good buying skills will make you a better consumer so that you can get greater value for your money each time you make a purchase. By acquiring these buying skills, you can learn how to compare prices, services, and value. These skills will also help you learn about sales and how to examine what you buy. Using these skills will help you to be happier with your purchases and more efficient in your buying activities.

Smart consumers, of course, are comparison shoppers. **Comparison shopping** means comparing the price, quality, and services associated with one product with those of another product. It also means studying advertisements to determine if what is being offered for sale is a real value. Except for utilities, such as water and electricity, or for very specialized goods, there are few things

Illus. 18-2
Smart consumers compare the price, quality, and service associated with similar products.

that are produced or sold by only one business. Therefore, you can choose where to buy and you can compare prices, quality, services, and sales.

Comparing Unit Prices

A **unit price** is a price per unit of measure. To calculate a unit price, you must divide the price of the item by the number of units per measure. For instance, suppose you want to buy a bag of frozen corn. In the supermarket, you see that a 16-ounce bag of Golden Frozen Corn costs $1.26. However, an 8-ounce box of Yellow Perfection Corn sells for $.69 per box. Which is the better buy for the dollar? Comparing the total prices only, it is not easy to decide. However, if each container also showed the cost per ounce, the unit price, you could quickly compare prices. In this case, the 16-ounce bag would show a unit price of 7.9 cents an ounce ($1.26/16). The 8-ounce box would be 8.6 cents per ounce ($.69/8). Unit pricing would quickly tell you that the 16-ounce bag is a better buy per ounce for the dollar.

Many stores help consumers compare value among various brands and sizes of the same product by showing the total price and the price of one standard measure, or unit, of the product. In the case of corn, a standard unit would be one ounce. If the store showed how much one ounce of each brand of corn costs, you could easily tell whether Golden Frozen or Yellow Perfection was a better buy regardless of the size of the containers.

Beware of advertisements that use "bait and switch" tactics. It is illegal for stores to advertise low-priced products that they do not have in order to get customers in their store and sell them other higher priced items.

Illus. 18-3

Often the unit price of a product is displayed so shoppers can easily compare prices of competing brands.

NET FACTS

Flames are angry messages sent to people who break the rules of netiquette, or the expected behavior of Internet users.

Comparing Quality

As a wise consumer, you should always try to examine a product before you buy it and make sure it will satisfy your needs. Even if you are not an expert, you can often tell whether it is exactly what you want. With experience, you will learn to recognize differences in quality.

Everyone wants his or her money's worth. High quality merchandise and services normally cost more. However, buying lower quality items can sometimes turn out to be more expensive than buying the higher quality items. For example, if you buy a low quality pair of tennis shoes and they wear out in a shorter period of time than the higher quality shoes, you will have to replace the low quality shoes sooner. Therefore, you may end up buying two pairs of low quality shoes in a short span of time. It may have been less expensive in the long run to buy the higher quality shoes that would not have to be replaced so soon for more money.

Comparing Services

A wise buyer compares services offered by businesses. Most businesses try to give good service, but types of services may differ. Some businesses sell for cash only; others extend credit as a service. Some businesses deliver goods; others do not. Some serve customers by keeping a very large stock from which selections may be made; others may have fewer items in stock.

Service is important, but you should not pay for more service than you actually need. You should know what you want, seek out what you want, and buy what you want at the best prices. In short, develop your skills as a comparison shopper.

Comparing Sales

The word "sale" is perhaps the most overused, and least trusted, word in marketing. You have probably seen "sale" signs a thousand times. Sales are used so often to try to sell goods that they are sometimes ineffective. When an item is really on sale, it is offered at a price lower than its normal selling price. Many "sales" are not really sales at all. Sometimes the sale involves regular goods at regular prices being heavily advertised with the word "sale." Retailers generally run three types of sales—promotional, clearance, and special-purchase.

About 115 million people in the United States use credit cards to buy goods and services.

Promotional sales are sales in which businesses promote the sale of regular merchandise by making temporary price reductions. Retailers typically do this when opening a new store or when publicizing the new location of an established store. Promotional sales are also used to build acceptance for new products or services by offering them at low introductory prices. Retailers hope that customers will buy the products at the reduced prices, like them, and then buy them at the regular prices in the future. Retailers also use promotional sales to attract customers in hopes that they will buy the sale merchandise plus other products that are not on sale.

Clearance sales are used to clear merchandise that stores no longer wish to carry in stock. This may be an end of season item, odd sizes and models, or a line of merchandise that the store no longer carries. Clearance sales usually offer some bargains, but it is important to be certain that you can use a sale item before you buy it.

Special-purchase merchandise is merchandise bought for a special sale rather than regular merchandise that has been reduced in price. Special-purchase merchandise may include goods purchased from a manufacturer who is overstocked, goods that are no longer made, or stock from a company that is going out of business.

FYI

Market research firms studying consumer buying habits have found that in supermarkets, people without shopping lists tend to buy more items (many of them luxury items) than do people with shopping lists.

Illus. 18-4
Retailers, such as those in this mall, generally run three types of sales—promotional, clearance, and special-purpose.

DECIDING HOW TO BUY

In today's competitive business environment, you have a wide variety of choices of where to buy a product or service. When selecting a place to make a purchase, you should consider the business's reputation, learn brand names of products, and then plan where to buy.

Business's Reputation

Most business owners readily acknowledge that the most valuable business asset is a good reputation. The wise business owner knows that a satisfied customer is likely to return. Businesses with good reputations have salespeople who know the uses and the quality of the goods and are concerned about matching the appropriate goods with customers' needs. If you buy from a business with a good reputation, you can usually rely on its salespeople to help you make wise selections.

Brand Names

A **brand name** is a name given to a product or service that is intended to distinguish it from other similar and/or competitive products or services. A brand name is created by the business that is selling the product or service. Brand names are designed to help build customer loyalty to a product or service.

Many brand-name goods and services are advertised nationally and are sold in almost every community. Among these goods are items such as clothing, shoes, tools, and cosmetics. Manufacturers of such goods often place brand names on the items they make. Timex, for example, is the brand name of a world-famous line of watches. These are called *national brands*.

Recognizing national brand names can help you as a consumer in two ways. First, you can usually expect uniform quality, even when brand-name goods are bought from different businesses. Buying brand-name goods is especially helpful when it is difficult to inspect for quality, such as canned goods. Second, brand names make comparison shopping possible.

Some stores have their own brand names called *store brands* or *house brands*. For example, Craftsman has been one of the brand names on tools sold by Sears. Store brands are usually sold at a lower cost than national brands. Buying store brands, therefore, may often save you money and offer good quality at the same time.

Take a pocket calculator with you when you go shopping. Unit prices are then easily calculated, and you can determine the best buy.

The National Advertising Review Board was created by the advertising industry to investigate complaints against national advertisers.

Some supermarkets carry unbranded items at reduced prices, called *generic products*. Generic products are less expensive because they do not require advertising and fancy packaging, thus saving the manufacturer money. These savings are passed on to consumers. The labels on generic products are often written with large bold print identifying the contents. There are sometimes only minor differences in quality and uniformity between generic and branded products.

Types of Merchants

When deciding where to buy, the consumer has a wide variety of choices available. The stores that sell goods are organized with unique characteristics. The choice of which type of store will depend upon the consumer's wants and needs.

Full-service stores offer a wide variety of goods and emphasize customer service. For example, they are likely to have a personal shopper, make deliveries, and wrap gifts. These stores, which are often called department stores, will usually have higher prices.

Global Perspective

Foreign Currency

As our world becomes smaller and global trade increases, more and more United States businesses will get involved in business transactions with companies in foreign countries. Transactions with foreign businesses may be stated in terms of U.S. dollars or the currency of the other country. If the transaction involves foreign currency, the U.S. business must convert the foreign currency into U.S. dollars before the transaction can be recorded.

The value of foreign currency can change daily. The exchange rate is the value of foreign currency in relation to the U.S. dollar. Current exchange rates can be found in many daily newspapers, by contacting a bank, or using an online service like the Internet or America Online. Because the rates change daily, the current exchange rates could be quite different from day to day.

The exchange rate is stated in terms of one unit of foreign currency. Using Germany as an example, the rate means that one German mark is worth .6757 U.S. dollars (or 68 U.S. cents). This rate would be used when exchanging German marks for U.S. dollars.

It is important for businesses to watch the value of the dollar when making purchases in overseas markets in order to get the most for their money.

Critical Thinking

1 Why would the value of foreign currency change daily?

2 How can businesses get the most for their money overseas by watching the exchange rate?

Discount stores, on the other hand, emphasize lower prices on their products. Most discount stores base their success on a high volume of sales and low prices. If service is not important to you, this may be where you should shop. Stores that have a special line of products for sale are known as **specialty stores.** They carry a wide variety of products in a narrow line such as sporting goods, jewelry, and women's shoes. Some specialty stores may also be discount stores. **Factory outlet stores** are becoming more and more popular and often have a reputation for selling high quality merchandise at low prices. Products are direct from the factory and sometimes have minor flaws. These stores offer goods at bargain prices.

In food retailing, there are three types of stores. The first is the **supermarket,** a large, full-service store that carries a wide variety of national, store, and generic brands at moderate prices. The **warehouse market** is a no-frills food outlet emphasizing the sale of large quantities of items at reasonable prices. **Convenience stores** are small stores that emphasize the sale of food items, an accessible location, and long operating hours. These stores usually stock popular items at higher prices.

For some products, you may wish to consider the convenience of mail-order or computer shopping. Several businesses offer you the opportunity to select merchandise from catalogs, cable shopping channels, or on-line computer services.

Cultural Notes

Cultural diversity in the workplace means there is a variety of workers from various racial, ethnic, and religion backgrounds.

Timing is the key to making wise purchases. The smart consumer takes time to plan purchases and buys at the right time. Also, the smart consumer avoids buying on impulse and is efficient when making purchases.

Take Your Time

"I just don't have the time" is the complaint of many people. It is often tempting to spend only a little time shopping. This is usually not a good practice. Spending more time planning purchases usually results in savings that reward you for the time spent. Taking your time usually means slowing down, visiting more stores, and giving yourself a chance to look for the best values. If you learn to pace yourself, you will probably find that your money goes farther toward buying the goods and services you need and want. As a good shopper, you should refuse to be hurried into buying anything. In this way, you avoid buying things that you really do not want or need.

DECIDING TO BUY

Time Your Purchases

For some goods and services, prices are lowest at predictable times. Good consumers know about those times and take advantage of them. Certain seasons and conditions favor goods and services being sold at reduced prices. Here are just a few examples:

- When fresh fruits and vegetables are at their peak, they are usually lower in price.

- Automobiles are usually less expensive at the end of the model year (September) before the new models are displayed.

- Winter clothing is often on sale in January.

- Firewood often costs less in the summer.

You can probably add to the list of products and services that are less expensive on a seasonal basis. Consumer magazines and newspaper articles, as well as radio and television programs for consumers, can help you add to this list.

Avoid Being Impulsive

The opposite of spending time and thought in shopping is buying too rapidly without much thought. This type of buying is called **impulse buying** and should be avoided to keep from making costly mistakes. Impulse buying often happens when an item is attractively displayed and a consumer suddenly decides to buy it. Sometimes impulse buying is harmless. Purchasing a small item like a bag of popcorn, a small gift for a friend, or a magazine is a pleasant part of life. The cost is small and the item is usually worth the price. However, buying more expensive items such as clothing, radios, or especially automobiles or homes on impulse can be costly. You may not really need the item, or it might not be the best value for the price. Best values are discovered by collecting information about an item and then carefully shopping for it.

One of the best ways to avoid impulse buying is to make a shopping list and stick to it. Many people use lists when shopping in grocery stores and supermarkets. Since most consumers are open to suggestion, an attractive display of products can tempt them to buy something that they had not planned to buy. You can save money if you make and stick to a shopping list whether it is for groceries, hardware, or clothing.

EFFICIENT SHOPPING

Skillful consumers are efficient in their shopping activities. They save time, energy, and money by planning. You can become a skillful shopper, too, by following these steps.

1. Plan your purchases carefully and make a shopping list. As you already know, a consumer with a list makes better decisions in the store and avoids impulse buying.

2. Use the telephone to help you. Using the Yellow Pages of the telephone book and calling businesses to find out if they have what you need is a very efficient practice. Often you can order goods and services by telephone.

3. You can save fuel by carefully planning the route of your trip. Unnecessary travel can add to the cost of a shopping trip.

EFFECT OF ECONOMIC CONDITIONS ON BUYING DECISIONS

Prices of goods and services are changing all the time. These changes in the value of a dollar have been a source of confusion and frustration to consumers for many years.

A **price index** can help consumers better understand what is happening to prices in our economy. A price index is a series of figures showing how prices have changed over a period of years. The federal government's Bureau of Labor Statistics (BLS) publishes several price indexes. These indexes are published in an effort to establish an objective measure of the economy and to help guide the consumer.

The **Consumer Price Index (CPI)** shows the changes in the average prices of goods and services bought by consumers over a period of time. Actually, the BLS compiles and publishes two CPIs. The CPI-W (wage earners and clerical workers) represents the buying experience of urban wage earners and clerical workers. It includes approximately 32 percent of the population. The CPI-U is a broader index. It covers about 80 percent of the population. The CPI-U (all urban consumers) includes such diverse groups as salaried workers, the unemployed, the retired, and the self-employed. The CPI-U is the more frequently quoted of the two.

The BLS checks prices throughout the country on a collection of goods and services often referred to as a "market basket." Categories of items included in the "market basket" are purchases you or your family might make of such things as clothing, food, fuel, and housing. As the average level of prices for a number of typical items changes, the CPI either goes up or down. The trend of the CPI has been upward.

Figure 18-1 shows the percentage increase in the Consumer Price Index (CPI-U) during the years 1988-1994. Changes in prices may not seem important from day to day, but over a number of years the changes may be very important.

Figure 18-1

Consumer Price Index Average Annual Increases, 1988-1994

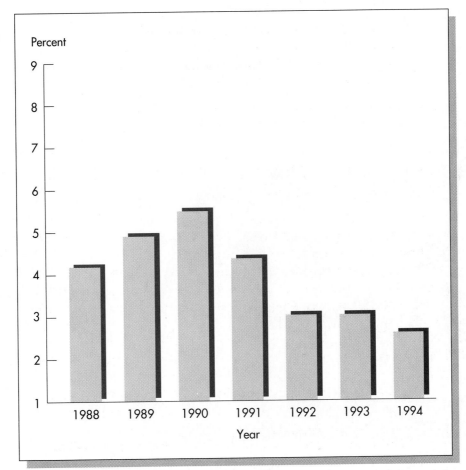

Source: U.S. Department of Labor, Bureau of Labor Statistics, CPI Detailed Report (Washington D.C.: U.S. Government Printing Office, November 1994)

Key Ideas

1 Deciding to buy should involve identifying your needs or wants, knowing the choices that are available to you, determining the measure of satisfaction of your needs and wants, considering the alternatives, and making the decision to buy.

2 Comparison shoppers will evaluate price, quality, service, and sales when making a purchase.

3 When deciding where to purchase items, a consumer should consider a business's reputation, value of brand names, and the choices of stores available.

4 As a good shopper, the consumer takes time when making purchases, buys when prices are lowest, and avoids impulse buying through the use of shopping lists.

5 To become an efficient shopper, make a shopping list, use the Yellow Pages of the telephone book to call businesses to find out if they have what you are looking for, and plan the route of trips to avoid wasting fuel.

6 The Consumer Price Index (CPI) shows the changes in the average prices of goods and services bought by consumers over a period of time.

End of Chapter Activities

Increasing Your Business Vocabulary

For each numbered item, find the term that has the same meaning.

brand name

clearance sales

comparison shop-
ping

Consumer Price
Index

convenience stores

discount stores

factory outlet stores

full-service stores

impulse buying

price index

promotional sales

specialty stores

supermarket

unit price

warehouse market

1 Stores that offer a wide variety of goods and emphasize customer service.

2 Buying too rapidly without much thought.

3 Large stores that sell large quantities of goods at low prices.

4 Comparing the price, quality, and services of one product with those of another product.

5 Stores that carry a wide variety of products in a narrow line.

6 A name given to a product or service to distinguish it from other similar products or services.

7 Stores selling products at low prices that sometimes have minor flaws.

8 A large, full-service food store with a wide variety of national, store, and generic brands at moderate prices.

9 The price per unit of measure of a product.

10 A no-frills food outlet emphasizing the sale of large quantities of items at reasonable prices.

11 A sale in which a price reduction is used to sell items that a store no longer wishes to carry in stock.

12 A small store that emphasizes the sale of food items, an accessible location, and long operating hours.

13 A sale in which items are sold below their regular prices to publicize the opening of a new store or location and to build acceptance for new products.

14 Shows changes in the average prices of goods and services bought by consumers over a period of time.

15 Series of figures showing how prices have changed over a period of years.

Reviewing Your Reading

1 What is the first step in the buying process?

2 How does unit pricing help consumers?

3 What is the difference between promotional sales and clearance sales?

4 What is the difference between a national brand and a store brand?

5 How can learning to recognize a national brand help you as a consumer?

6 What are generic products?

7 How should you avoid impulse buying?

8 Name three steps you can take to become an efficient shopper.

9 What is the difference between CPI-W and CPI-U?

Using Your Business Knowledge

1 Explain how values influence purchases.

2 What are some factors you might consider when deciding where to shop?

3 When would you consider an impulse purchase a harmless activity?

4 What are some "market basket" items that you and your family might purchase?

Calculating Business Problems

1 Following her arrival in the United States from Shanghai, China, Ms. Deng Hui wanted to shop for a new coat. She chose a coat that cost $235. Since it was during the month of December when she was ready to make this purchase, new acquaintances in the United States told her she could buy a similar coat on sale for $150 if she could only wait until January.

a. If Deng Hui waited until January to buy a coat, how much would she save?

b. If the clothing store purchased the coat at $120 and sold it to Deng Hui for $150, what is the difference between the store's cost and selling price of the coat?

2 Popper's peanut butter comes in an 18-ounce jar and is priced at $2.38. Georgia Pride peanut butter comes in a 24-ounce jar and is priced at $2.92.

a. What is the unit price of each brand?

b. Assuming the quality of each is equal, which is the better buy?

3 A consumer has two choices regarding where to buy a microwave oven. One option is an appliance specialty store. This store is located 10 kilometers round-trip from the consumer's home. A microwave oven can be purchased there for $154. A second option is a discount store located 100 kilometers round-trip from the consumer's home. The identical microwave oven can be purchased there for $135. Assume that the consumer's car costs 40 cents per mile to drive and that either purchase would require one round-trip to the store. Based on the price of the microwave oven and transportation costs alone (not service, reputation, etc.), which is the better buy?

4 Western Furniture and Appliance is moving to a new store. To avoid having to move a lot of merchandise, it is having a pre-moving clearance sale. Western has advertised that it will reduce the price of all merchandise in the store by 20 percent for one day.

a. What would be the sale price of a $979 sofa?

b. A customer paid $304 for a television set. What was the original price of the television set?

Applying Technology

Using the *Introduction to Business* template and your spreadsheet program software, select problem CH18. After the problem appears on your screen, complete the following activities. Then, after you have completed each step, display or print the completed spreadsheet for each activity. If you do not have a printer available, answer the questions before you leave the computer.

1 For each size box of detergent, enter a formula to calculate the price per ounce. Answer the following questions:

a. Which size box has the lowest price per ounce?

b. Which size box has the highest price per ounce?

2 Enter formulas to sum the prices of all the boxes and the sizes of all the boxes. Answer the following questions:

a. What is the sum of the prices?

b. What is the sum of the sizes?

3 Enter two formulas to find the average price per ounce for all the boxes. One formula should use the sums of the prices and the sizes; the other formula should use the unit prices of the boxes found in question 1.

a. What is the average price per ounce using the sum of the prices and the sizes?

b. What is the average price per ounce using the unit prices of the boxes?

Making Decisions

Consuela needed and wanted a new bicycle. She was aware that she had three basic choices—a mountain bike, a cross-training bike, and a road bike. The prices varied significantly among her choices. They were all available in varying degrees of quality from several reputable dealers.

1 Develop a list of questions Consuela might ask herself in response to step 3 of the buying-decision steps presented in the chapter.

2 Suggest an efficient shopping strategy that will help her get what she wants.

Chapter Nineteen

Key Terms

consumer movement

fraud

trade associations

guarantee

express warranties

implied warranties

Consumer Rights and Responsibilities

Objectives

After studying this chapter and completing the end-of-chapter activities, you will be able to:

1 Describe the consumer movement.

2 List the seven consumer rights.

3 Name and define five consumer responsibilities.

Monica Robinson finally bought the expensive leather purse for which she had been saving her money. But, unfortunately, after she used the purse for several weeks, the zipper broke. She took the purse back to the store from which it was purchased. Monica very politely and calmly described to the salesperson how the zipper broke. She also had her receipt from the purchase to show that the purse was only two months old. After the salesperson talked to the department manager, it was decided that the store would pay for the repair of the zipper. It took one week to repair the zipper, at which time Monica got her purse back as good as new.

This consumer problem had a pleasant ending; most of them do. It is usually not necessary to get upset or angry in order to get satisfactory results from businesses. In fact, most businesses are eager to solve problems that consumers have. They want happy, satisfied customers who will return to their businesses again and again.

Solving consumer problems is usually a matter of practicing good two-way communication. It is up to you to let the business know what you want. The job of the business is to tell you what you can expect to get.

YOUR CONSUMER RIGHTS

A pleasant relationship between the consumer and business has not always existed in the marketplace. In past years some businesses were viewed as often trying to take advantage of consumers. False claims were sometimes made about products, prices were often too high, and some products were unsafe. If a consumer was cheated, there was nowhere to turn except away from the offending business. To fight against unfair business practices, consumers joined together to demand fair treatment from businesses. This banding together gave rise to what is known as the **consumer movement**. As a result of this movement, public and private agencies, policies, laws, and regulations were developed to protect consumer interests.

A highlight of the consumer movement came in 1962 when President John F. Kennedy presented his Consumer Bill of Rights in a message to Congress. He declared that every consumer has the following rights:

1. The right to be informed—to be given the correct information needed to make an informed choice.

2. The right to safety—to be protected from goods and services that are hazardous to health or life.

3. The right to choose—to be assured of the availability of a variety of goods and services at competitive prices.

4. The right to be heard—to be assured that consumer interests will be fully considered by government when laws are being developed and enforced.

Illus. 19-1

As a consumer, you have specific rights.

In 1969, President Richard M. Nixon added a fifth right to the list; in 1975, President Gerald R. Ford added the sixth; and in 1994, during National Consumers Week, President William Clinton added the seventh.

5. The right to a remedy—the assurance of the right to legal correction of wrongs committed against consumers.

6. The right to consumer education—to learn about consumer rights and responsibilities as economic citizens.

7. The right to service—to be entitled to convenience, courtesy, and responsiveness to problems and needs.

EXERCISING YOUR CONSUMER RIGHTS

As a consumer you have the right to expect honesty and fair treatment from businesses. Few businesses are ever intentionally dishonest. However, being a skillful consumer means that you know the Consumer Bill of Rights and how to exercise them.

The Right to Be Informed

Most products and services are usually described in advertisements, on labels, or by a salesperson. You have a right to know what the product or service is and what it will do for you.

FYI

As an informed consumer, do not sign any agreements that you have not read or do not understand.

NET FACTS

Gopher is a program that uses a series of menus to lead users to files of information. Gopher is named for the Golden Gophers of University of Minnesota, where the program was developed.

There are situations in which false information is given to a customer in an effort to make a sale. This type of dishonesty is known as **fraud.** For example, if a salesperson knowingly sells you a car on which the odometer has been turned back 30,000 miles, a fraud has occurred.

However, all product information you receive cannot be expected to be perfectly accurate. Suppose, for example, you were looking for a used car for transportation to and from school. If a salesperson told you she thought the car would get about 20 miles to the gallon but it only got 18, you were not deceived. The salesperson may not have been accurate in judging gas mileage, but no guarantee was made.

When a salesperson exaggerates the good qualities of a product and says "It's the best," or "It's a great buy" there is no fraud. If, however, the salesperson tells you a car has new brakes and it does not, this is fraud.

The Right to Safety

Consumers have a right to be safe from harm associated with using products or services. No consumer should be injured from a properly used product. Several agencies work to assure the safety of consumers. The Consumer Product Safety Commission (CPSC)

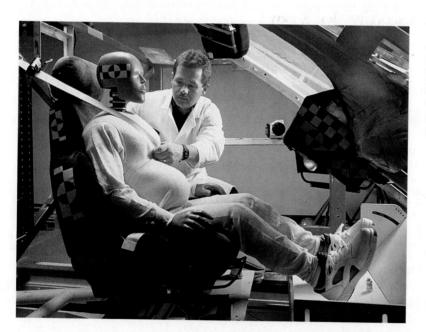

Illus. 19-2
Consumers have a right to be safe from harm associated with the products they purchase.

has the authority to set safety standards, to ban hazardous products, and to recall dangerous products from the market.

The Food and Drug Administration (FDA) makes certain that food, drug, and cosmetic products are not harmful to consumers. This federal government agency enforces laws and regulations that prevent the distribution of unsafe or misbranded foods, drugs, and cosmetics. The FDA also works to assure that product labels do not mislead consumers.

It is a federal offense to turn back the odometer on a vehicle without disclosing it before selling the vehicle.

The United States Department of Agriculture (USDA) also helps ensure consumer safety by setting standards for the grading of farm products that are sold from one state to another. The USDA also controls the processing, inspection, and labeling of meat products with grades according to their quality.

The Right to Choose

The right of consumers to choose from a variety of goods and services has become well established. In fact, one of the main activities of the Federal Trade Commission (FTC) is to prevent one firm from using unfair practices to force competing firms out of business. When a business has no competitors and controls the market for a product or service, it is said to have a *monopoly*. Competing firms encourage customers to buy from them by offering a variety of products and services at various prices. By driving away this competition, monopolies limit the right to choose.

The Right to be Heard

Most businesses have a customer service department to hear the concerns or complaints of customers. Some smaller businesses have a specific person assigned to that responsibility. Businesses are usually happy to take care of problems you have with their products or services.

There are several federal government agencies to assure your right to be heard. The Office of Consumer Affairs (OCA) coordinates and advises other federal agencies on issues of interest to consumers. Its primary concerns are to represent the interests of consumers, to develop consumer information materials, and to assist other agencies in responding to complaints. The OCA normally refers consumer problems to other appropriate agencies and uses complaints from consumers to promote legislation.

Buyer's remorse occurs when a consumer buys something and later regrets the purchase.

The Federal Trade Commission (FTC) also protects your right to be heard. As a consumer, you can complain directly to the FTC if you believe that any of your rights which come under its protection have been violated. The FTC regulates advertising and encourages informative and truthful advertising. It also requires textile companies to label wool and other fabrics with information telling what the material is made of and how to care for it.

State governments also support public agencies that are interested in hearing consumers' concerns. Usually the Office of the Attorney General and the Department of Consumer Affairs have some responsibility for protecting the rights of consumers. They can prosecute businesses for violation of state consumer-protection laws. These offices also inspect advertising practices. The State Office of the Attorney General and the State Department of Consumer Affairs can also handle other types of consumer matters such as automobile-repair problems, credit problems, and door-to-door sales practices.

In addition to publicly supported consumer protection agencies, there are some privately funded groups that help to make certain

Legal*Perspective*

Your TV Shopping Rights

With the increasing popularity of home shopping networks on cable TV comes the concern for accompanying consumer rights. What rights does a purchaser have after ordering goods advertised on one of these channels?

The Federal laws that protect TV shoppers are the same as those that govern purchases made by telephone. The TV-shopping company must send you the goods within 30 days or within another time period specifically stated by the company. The 30-day delivery clock starts ticking as soon as the company has received your credit card number or a valid check. If there is going to be a delay, the seller must notify you, either by phone or by mail. You then have the right to cancel your order.

If an unreceived or returned item is billed to your credit card, you have 60 days to dispute it. The credit card company then has 30 days to respond. Within 90 days of your letter, the card company must investigate the matter and explain to you why it believes the bill is correct or incorrect.

You don't have to pay the part of your credit card bill under dispute until the matter is resolved. But to avoid finance charges, you must pay the rest of your bill on time.

Critical Thinking

1 Do you think a consumer has any rights beyond those explicitly stated in this feature?

2 Do you know of any unethical practices associated with TV shopping either on the part of businesses or consumers?

you are heard. Perhaps the best known of these is the Better Business Bureau. As discussed in Chapter 17, the Better Business Bureau is chiefly concerned with problems arising from false advertising or misrepresented products and services. If you believe that your consumer rights have been violated by such practices, you can get help from the Better Business Bureau in your community. The bureau will usually ask you to report your problem in writing so that it can get all of the details correct. The Better Business Bureau will then try to persuade the business to remedy the problem or fulfill its promises for the product or service in question. Most businesses willingly carry out the bureau's requests.

All 50 states have passed "lemon" laws to protect car buyers from being stuck with malfunctioning, problem-ridden vehicles.

There are a number of other private organizations that help protect your right to be heard. Groups of similar businesses frequently form trade associations. These associations are made up of businesses engaged in the same type of business. Many **trade associations** establish standards of quality for the products that their members manufacture. These standards help customers receive the quality they expect when purchasing a product. Some trade associations also publish codes of ethics that members are urged to follow.

The Right to a Remedy

As a result of the consumer movement, many new laws were passed. These included the Fair Packaging and Labeling Act, National Traffic and Motor Vehicle Safety Act, Truth in Food Labeling Act, and Fair Debt Collection Practices Act. All of these laws were designed in part to provide assurances that consumers could seek a legal remedy if they were wronged.

Another form of remedy that consumers have is the protection provided through a guarantee. With some purchases, a consumer can expect a guarantee, or a warranty. A **guarantee** is a promise by the manufacturer or dealer, usually in writing, that a product is of a certain quality. A guarantee may apply to the entire item or only to some parts of it. It may promise that defective parts will be replaced only if a problem occurs during a specified period of time. No guarantee, however, covers damages caused by misuse.

When making a purchase, a skillful consumer asks about a guarantee. A guarantee is frequently in the form of statements like these: "The working parts of this watch are guaranteed for one year." "This sweater will not shrink more than 3 percent." "This lightbulb is guaranteed to burn for at least 5,000 hours." These kinds of guarantees are sometimes called **express warranties.**

They are made orally or in writing and promise a specific quality of performance.

You should insist on receiving a copy of the guarantee when you buy an item. You can also require the business to put in writing any other guarantees that have been offered. Written guarantees are useful if you need to return a faulty product. Guarantees are sometimes included in ads for the product. Keep a copy of the ad as evidence of the guarantee. Read the guarantee carefully to find out just what is covered and for what period of time.

Some guarantees are not written. They are called **implied warranties.** They are imposed by law and are understood to apply even though they have not been stated either orally or in writing. In general, the law requires certain standards to be met. For example, it is implied that health care products purchased over-the-counter at a pharmacy will not harm you when used according to the directions.

The Right to Consumer Education

In proclaiming this right, President Ford made a commitment on the part of the federal government to support consumer education. Traditionally, the focus of consumer education programs has been on individual decision making related to the purchase of goods and services. Although consumer buying decisions are important, educated consumers need to understand how their decisions affect our economy as well. Today consumer education focuses on consumer decisions that relate to the interaction between consumers and producers in our economic system. Educated consumers are aware that their decisions not only affect their lifestyles, but also have economic implications.

The Right to Service

The most recent addition to the list of consumer rights focuses on service to consumers. In the words of President Clinton, ". . . the technological complexity of much of what we buy and frequently the distance between buyer and maker or seller have expanded the importance of service." Less legalistic in its nature than the preceding rights, the right to service suggests consumers can expect convenience, courtesy, and responsiveness to consumer problems and needs. This right to service is as much a reminder to business as it is a right of consumers. The right to service encourages businesses to take steps necessary to ensure that products and services meet the quality and performance levels claimed for those products and services.

YOUR CONSUMER RESPONSIBILITIES

Consumers in our country are protected through hundreds of laws, yet every day examples of consumer difficulties are reported. Why? The answer probably lies with consumers themselves. They sometimes do not carefully meet their responsibilities as consumers. Those responsibilities are to be honest, be reasonable, report unethical practices, be informed, and be involved.

Be Honest

Most people are honest, but those who are not cause others to pay higher prices. Shoplifting losses have been estimated to be in the billions of dollars each year. Businesses usually make up losses that result from shoplifting by charging higher prices to everyone.

Some people who would not think of shoplifting may be dishonest in other ways. Businesses report many dishonest acts by customers. For example, a customer might buy a book, read it, and then return it for a refund. Customers have been seen taking lower priced tags from articles and putting them on the more expensive items they buy. There have also been many complaints about grocery store customers who try to use discount coupons for merchandise they have not purchased.

Illus. 19-3
Much of the cost of dishonest and criminal behavior must be charged back to customers through higher prices.

As a responsible consumer, you must be as honest with a business as you want it to be with you. You should be as quick to tell the cashier that you received too much change at the checkout counter as you are to say that you received too little. Remember that dishonesty, in addition to being illegal and unethical, usually results in higher prices for all consumers.

Be Reasonable

As a buyer, you are usually responsible for what you buy if the business has been honest with you. If you are dissatisfied, however, and wish to complain, you should complain in a reasonable way.

You should first be sure that you have a cause for complaint. Be sure that you have followed the directions for using the product. After you have confirmed the details of your complaint, calmly explain the problem to an employee of the business from which

The National Bureau of Standards sets regulations to ensure uniformity of weights and measures throughout the country.

you bought the item. In most cases, the business will be glad to correct the problem because it does not want to lose you as a customer. If you become angry or threatening, you risk getting an angry response that will only delay the solution to your problem.

If you believe that your complaint is not handled fairly by the salesperson or the customer service department, take the matter up with the owner or an official of the firm. If that fails and the firm is a part of a national company, a letter or telephone call to the customer service department at the headquarters often gets results. If you do not get a response within a reasonable time, a second effort including a letter sent to several consumer agencies will often bring a quick reply. If you fail to receive what you think is a fair adjustment, you may contact one of the following organizations:

- The Better Business Bureau.

- The local or state consumer affairs agency or the attorney general's office in your state.

- A lawyer or the Legal Aid Society if the problem is quite serious.

- In larger cities, the small claims court, which is operated for filing small claims only.

- A consumer help department.

Report Unethical Practices   *ON GUARD BUNCO:*

As a responsible consumer, you should report unethical business practices to prevent other consumers from becoming victims. For example, the hand brake on your two-week-old bicycle fails to work. The shop from which you bought the bike refuses to honor its guarantee to replace all parts that break under normal use within 90 days. After several unsuccessful attempts to get the bicycle fixed, you might be tempted to give up, pay someone else to fix your bicycle, and mark it off as a bad experience. However, that action will not prevent other people from losing money as you did. By reporting the matter to an agency discussed in this chapter, you might be able to get the shop to keep its word both to you and to future customers.

Be Informed

The most important responsibility you have as a consumer is to be informed. However, just having the right to be informed will not make you an informed consumer. You must find and use the information available to you. A producer might put a complete label on a product, but it is up to you to read and use the information on the label. To be an informed consumer, you should continually learn about the many goods and services available. You should also keep informed about your rights as a consumer. Learn about the laws and agencies that protect your rights and how to report a violation of your rights. Being an informed consumer is hard work, but the extra effort spent in making your dollars go as far as possible will be worth it.

Be Involved

In our democratic government, involvement is an important consumer activity. As a citizen, you have a responsibility to participate in government even if only to be an informed voter. As a consumer, you also have responsibilities. When the opportunity arises, make your concerns known to government officials or consumer agencies. Only when you become involved as a consumer can agencies do their jobs and legislative bodies pass appropriate laws.

Key Ideas

1 The consumer movement was created to fight unfair business practices. As a result of this movement, public and private agencies, policies, laws, and regulations were developed to protect consumer interests.

2 The Consumer Bill of Rights declares every consumer has: the right to be informed, the right to safety, the right to choose, the right to be heard, the right to a remedy, the right to consumer education, and the right to service.

3 Consumers have five basic responsibilities: be honest, be reasonable, report unethical practices, be informed, and be involved.

End of Chapter Activities

Increasing Your Business Vocabulary

The following terms should become part of your business vocabulary. For each numbered item, find the term that has the same meaning.

consumer movement

express warranties

fraud

guarantee

trade associations

implied warranties

1 When false information is given to a customer in an effort to make a sale.

2 Guarantees made orally or in writing that promise a specific quality of performance.

3 A promise by the manufacturer or dealer, usually in writing, that a product is of a certain quality.

4 Guarantees imposed by law that are not stated orally or in writing and which require certain standards to be met.

5 Organizations of businesses engaged in the same type of business.

6 The fight against unfair business practices by consumers joining together to demand fair treatment from businesses.

Reviewing Your Reading

1 What are the seven consumer rights?

2 What is the difference between fraud and exaggerating the good qualities of a product?

3 What are three governmental agencies that are devoted to consumer safety?

4 How does the Federal Trade Commission help consumers?

5 What are the responsibilities of the Office of Consumer Affairs?

6 What is the difference between an expressed warranty and an implied warranty?

7 What are five responsibilities of every consumer?

8 Give an example of consumer dishonesty.

9 How can a consumer complain in a reasonable manner?

10 Why should you report businesses that are following unethical practices?

Using Your Business Knowledge

1 Why, with all of the laws and organizations to protect consumers, do we continue to hear of examples of consumer fraud?

2 Give a real or imaginary example of a business monopoly. Tell why it is a monopoly.

3 Why do you suppose the government supports agencies that protect consumers?

4 Which of the consumer rights are you exercising right now?

5 Which of the following would be considered fraud? Explain your answers.

a. A salesperson says the sound system you are looking at is the best on the market. After you buy it, you find it rated in a consumer magazine as second best.

b. An advertisement for a bookcase cabinet claims it is made of solid walnut. Upon close inspection after buying the bookcase, you find out that it is only walnut veneer glued over less expensive plywood.

c. The person who sells an electric corn popper says it is completely washable. Before using it, you put it into a sink filled with water to wash it. The first time you try to make popcorn, there is a flash and the popper's electrical unit catches fire. When you return the popper to the store, the salesperson tells you that she did not mean the popper could be put under water. She says you should have known that electrical appliances should not be put in water. She refuses to give you either a refund or an exchange.

Calculating Business Problems

1 The Art Mart Gallery, a shop dealing mainly in prints and drawings, guarantees satisfaction with every purchase for a month. That means a customer can return a print or a drawing anytime within 30 days of purchase for a full refund. Last year's sales are given as follows:

Total sales $320,000; products returned for refund $6,400.

a. What percent of total sales was returned for refund?

b. What was the total amount of net sales, deducting the cost of refunds?

2 The Jones family ordered a new car from Germany. The express warranty said the average driver would get 48.3 kilometers for every 3.85 liters of gasoline used.

a. How many miles per gallon is this?

b. If they traveled 90 miles and used 10.5 liters of gasoline, did the car perform better or worse than the warranty claimed?

---

3 If you purchased a pair of jeans that had a waist size of 33 inches and were guaranteed not to shrink more than 3 percent, approximately how many inches would you expect the waist size to shrink?

---

4 Jane Franklin is thinking about subscribing to a weekly consumer magazine so that she can be better informed. The magazine is offering a special trial subscription of 26 weeks for $19.50. The normal subscription rate for 26 weeks is $32.50.

a. What is the normal cost per issue?

b. What is the cost per issue under the special subscription rate?

c. How much would Jane save per issue by taking advantage of the special subscription rate?

---

5 Jason Obliger purchased merchandise in several stores at the mall. When he got home and looked at his sales receipts, he was amazed at how much money he paid in sales tax. Sales tax is 5 percent in the city where Jason lives. His purchases were as follows: coat, $59; jeans, $29.95; CD, $12.99; and sunglasses, $15.59.

a. How much sales tax did he pay on the coat?

b. How much sales tax did he pay on the jeans?

c. How much sales tax did he pay on the CD?

d. How much sales tax did he pay on the sunglasses?

e. What was the total amount of his purchases before sales tax?

f. What was the total amount of sales tax that he paid on these items?

g. What was the total amount of his purchases plus sales tax?

Applying Technology

Using the *Introduction to Business* template and your word processing program software, select problem CH19. After the problem appears on your screen, complete the following activities. Then, print your completed letter. If you do not have a printer available, save the letter on a data disk to give to your teacher.

1 You just purchased a pair of in-line skates from a mail-order catalog. After using them for several weeks, the bolts that hold the wheels in place become loose and the wheels fall off. Before sending the skates back to the vendor, you should write a letter stating the problem and asking for assistance in correcting the situation.

a. Enter your address in the appropriate section at the beginning of the letter. Use the strikeover feature of your word processing program to replace or delete information that does not apply to you.

b. Complete each paragraph with the specific details of the situation. The paragraphs have been designed so you need only to insert the appropriate information.

2 You have now received an acknowledgement from the vendor of the defective skates. The vendor has requested that you return the skates for repair.

a. Using the same form letter that you used for your original letter, you will now create a letter that will accompany the skates. Enter your address in the appropriate section at the beginning of the letter. Use the strikeover feature of your word processing program to replace or delete information that does not apply.

b. Complete each paragraph with the specific details of the return. The paragraphs have been designed so you need only insert the appropriate information.

Making Decisions

Pill Soon Song recently bought a stereo system using an on-line computer service. When the stereo arrived, Pill discovered that it wasn't exactly the stereo he wanted. The advertisement had described the system as having two large speakers. But what he got instead were two small speakers. He is happy with the other components, but is quite upset with the speakers.

Pill E-mailed the on-line computer service from which he purchased the stereo and explained the situation. However, the service said that in their opinion the speakers were "large" even though specific sizes were not given. Therefore, they felt the speakers met the advertisement.

1 Did the merchant commit fraud by describing the speakers as large?

2 If Pill is not satisfied with the speakers, what actions can he take to get the speakers he wants?

Our economy has often been called a service economy. Partly as a result of our busy life styles, consumers are buying more and more services every year. People have their clothes washed and pressed, houses cleaned, and meals prepared. Many businesses have sprung up to meet these and other service needs.

The United States Bureau of Labor Statistics estimates that within ten years, the number of service-providing jobs will reach almost 110 million, more than four times the number of goods-producing jobs that are predicted to exist.

Job Titles

- Clerk
- Flight Attendant
- Fast-Food Worker
- Cook
- Sales Manager
- Home Health Aid
- Service Representative
- Merchandise Distributor
- Retail Manager
- Real Estate Agent
- Personnel Recruiter
- Hotel Manager

Employment Outlook through 2005

- Health services is one of the fastest growing service industries. A growing and aging population will continue to increase demand.
- Business services will generate many new jobs.
- Personnel supply services (temporary help agencies) is the largest sector in service occupations.
- Employment in wholesale and retail trade (apparel and accessory stores, appliance stores, restaurants), is expected to have significant growth.

Education and Training

Like the job duties, education and training requirements will vary. A business or marketing education program in your high school would provide a good start. Further education at a community college or four-year college may prepare you for management or ownership of a service business.

Salary Levels (in recent years)

Salaries vary widely but are competitive with salaries paid to similar employees in other career areas. Beginning salaries often hover around the minimum wage while management and ownership pay very well.

Approximate compensation:

- Beginning cooks and bakers: $6 to $8 per hour
- Executive chefs: over $40,000 per year
- Home health aids: $9 per hour
- Beginning hotel employees: minimum wage
- Hotel managers: up to $86,700 per year.

Critical Thinking

1 *Which job title in this career area appeals to you most? Give some reasons for your choice.*

2 *What are some things you will have to do to achieve success in the career selected?*

Service Occupations

Six Unit

Financial Institutions and Banking Services

chapter

"**S**ixteen dollars for cash machine fees!" exclaimed Hans George as he opened his bank statement. "I guess the cost of those cash withdrawals adds up fast!"

Hans George has a routine of using his cash card at an automatic teller machine several times a week. He really likes the convenience of obtaining cash. However, Hans also finds that when getting cash is easy, he easily overspends.

While automatic teller machines are easy to use, you must also consider fees and the potential for impulse buying. In recent years cash machine fees have risen from nothing to $1 or $2 per withdrawal.

How much can cash machine transaction fees cost? If you have two $1 transaction fees a week, you will pay $104 in fees over one year. Instead of paying this money out in fees, you could invest the money and earn interest (payments made to you when you invest). For example, you might be able to invest at an interest rate of 5 percent per year. Over five years, the money you pay in fees could have been saved and increased to more than $570. You have to ask yourself if such an amount of money is worth the convenience of a cash machine.

Another area where bank fees can add up quickly is overdrafts and stop-payment orders. You must carefully keep track of your account. Writing checks when you do not have enough money in your account to cover the checks can result in charges of as much as $20 or more every time you overdraw. Regularly having to issue stop-payment orders because of errors in writing or sending checks can also cause fees to accumulate.

Other sources of fees are printed checks and bank-at-home services. The cost of purchasing checks is expensive. You may be able to purchase checks at a lower cost by shopping around. Banking at home has become very popular, with the use of telephones or home computers to complete transactions. However, always be sure to weigh the appeal of fancy technology and convenience against equipment costs and monthly fees.

Banking fees involve trade-offs. Using cash machines, maintaining low balances, and banking at home may be beneficial to you. As businesses, however, banks need to recover their expenses by charging you fees. And you may decide that the benefits from using such services are greater than the costs.

You may decide, however, to lower the fees you pay. Banking fees and other charges can be reduced by comparison shopping at different financial institutions. Or, you may be able to reduce or eliminate these fees by negotiating with your bank manager.

Critical Thinking

1 What factors have caused banking fees to increase in recent years?

2 What actions can consumers take to reduce the cost of banking?

Beware of High Banking Fees

Chapter Twenty

The Banking System and Financial Services

Key Terms

commercial bank

Federal Deposit Insurance Corporation (FDIC)

savings and loan association (S&L)

mutual savings bank

credit union

consumer finance company

interest

electronic funds transfer (EFT)

safe-deposit boxes

investments

trust companies

Federal Reserve System (Fed)

Objectives

After studying this chapter and completing the end-of-chapter activities, you will be able to:

1 Explain how banks earn revenues.

2 Describe the major types of deposit-type institutions.

3 Name nondeposit financial institutions that serve consumers.

4 List six services provided by financial institutions.

5 Explain the activities of the Federal Reserve System.

6 Discuss how banks help communities and create economic growth.

"I finally got a job for the summer," Gerri told Mike. "I can save money and go on that trip."

"Where are you going to save your money?" asked Mike.

"At home, of course," responded Gerri.

"Are you kidding?" Mike went on to say. "That's danger-ous! Your money can get lost, or you might spend it before summer comes."

"Well what should I do with my money?" asked Gerri.

"Deposit it in a bank," answered Mike.

"Will it be safer?" asked Gerri.

"For sure," said Mike. "Banks and other financial institutions provide safety and growth for your money. Plus they help their customers in many ways with other financial matters."

"You're kidding! I guess it's time I learn about banking," Gerri responded.

THE BUSINESS OF BANKING

Have you ever thought of a bank as a business and you as a customer? Many people do not think of banks in this way. Yet, a bank is a business just like stores and factories. As a business, a bank sells services such as checking accounts, savings accounts, and loans. For their services, banks expect to earn revenues and make a profit. Banks earn most of their revenues by charging for loans to individuals, businesses, and government and by investing part of the money that customers deposit in the banks. Some examples of investments made by banks are given in the last section of the chapter.

Because banks are businesses, does that mean that anybody can start one? Well, not exactly. People who wish to start a bank must meet the requirements set by federal and state governments. Since the bank owners will handle other people's money, they are expected to be responsible citizens with high moral character. They must also have enough capital to start the business operations.

People who want to start a bank must apply for a charter from their state or from the federal government. If they apply to their state and a charter is granted, the bank will operate as a state bank. If the charter is from the federal government, the bank will operate as a national bank. In bank titles, N.A. stands for National Association and is used today in place of the word "national."

A bank's operations are regulated more strictly than the operations of most businesses. If a business other than a bank fails, only

Illus. 20-1

A bank is a profit-making business just like a retail store or a factory.

a few people lose money. If a bank fails, thousands of people are affected. Government regulation is necessary to assure the safety of customers' money. State banks operate under the banking laws of the state in which the banks are located. National banks operate under federal laws as well as those of the state in which they are located.

BANKS AND OTHER DEPOSIT-TYPE INSTITUTIONS

When someone says, "I'm going to the bank," the person might actually mean a credit union or a cash machine at the mall. As shown in Figure 20-1, financial institutions are usually classified by the types of services they offer. *Deposit-type institutions,* also called *depository institutions,* accept deposits for people and businesses to use in the future. The main types of deposit-type institutions are commercial banks, savings and loan associations, mutual savings banks, and credit unions.

Figure 20-1

The two main categories of financial institutions are deposit-type institutions and nondeposit institutions.

Nondeposit Institutions:

Life insurance companies

Investment companies

Consumer finance companies

Mortgage companies

Check-cashing outlets

Pawnshops

Deposit-Type Institutions:

Commercial banks

Savings and loan associations

Mutual savings banks

Credit unions

Commercial Banks

Most commonly, a bank is organized as a **commercial bank.** Commercial banks are often called *full-service banks* because they offer a wide range of financial services. Commercial banks offer checking accounts, provide savings accounts, make loans to individuals and to businesses, and offer other services. In large banks, these services may be handled in different departments, such as a savings department, a trust department, a real estate department, or an investment department.

In recent years, banks have opened full-service branch offices in shopping centers and grocery stores. These *financial supermarkets* offer everything from automated teller machines and loans to safe-deposit boxes.

The federal agency that helps to regulate banks and other financial institutions is the **Federal Deposit Insurance Corporation (FDIC).** It protects depositors' money in case of the failure of a bank or financial institution that is regulated by the FDIC. At present, the FDIC insures all accounts in the same name at each bank up to an amount of $100,000. Although the FDIC is a government agency, money for its operation is provided by banks. Almost 99 percent of all banks are FDIC members.

Savings and Loan Associations

Traditionally, a **savings and loan association (S&L)** specialized in savings accounts and making loans for home mortgages. In recent years, however, these financial institutions have expanded to offer a greater variety of financial services.

Recently, many S&Ls have changed to savings banks and now include the words *savings bank* in their titles. For example, Lifetime Savings and Loan Association has become Lifetime Savings Bank.

Mutual Savings Banks

A **mutual savings bank** provides a variety of services. However, it is organized mainly for savings accounts and to make loans to home buyers. This type of financial institution is owned by the depositors; the profits of the mutual savings bank go to the depositors. Mutual savings banks are located mainly in the northeastern United States.

Cultural Notes

Through a Hopi ceremonial dance, ultimate respect is shown for the environment and its preservation. As part of the dance, the Hopi impersonate kachinas, or spirits, who they believe control the natural world. Offerings are made in hopes that the kachinas will return favors by sending rain for the crops.

FYI

As of the mid-1990s, over 2,000 branches of commercial banks were operating in grocery stores and supermarkets.

Credit Unions

A **credit union** is a user-owned, not-for-profit, cooperative financial institution. Credit unions are commonly formed by people in the same company, government agency, labor union, profession, church, or community. Serving members only, credit unions accept savings deposits and make loans for a variety of purposes. Today, credit unions also offer other services such as

- special checking accounts
- credit cards
- mortgages
- home equity loans
- safe-deposit boxes
- investment services
- electronic banking services
- loans to small firms.

In recent years, there were more than 15,000 credit unions in operation. They are regulated by the National Credit Union Administration (NCUA), a federal agency similar to the FDIC. NCUA also insures a depositor's funds, up to $100,000, through its National Credit Union Share Insurance Fund. Some state-chartered credit unions have opted for a private insurance program.

The services offered at automatic teller machines are expanding to include the sale of bus passes, postage stamps, and gift certificates. Some ATM users can buy and sell mutual funds.

NONDEPOSIT FINANCIAL INSTITUTIONS

The other major category of financial institutions is nondeposit institutions. This description is used to refer to life insurance companies, investment companies, consumer finance companies, mortgage companies, check-cashing outlets, and pawnshops.

Life Insurance Companies

People commonly buy life insurance to provide financial security for dependents. Besides protection, many life insurance companies also offer financial services such as investments. Through careful investing in new and existing companies, life insurance companies can help to expand business in our economy. Life insurance is discussed in Chapter 35.

Investment Companies

Investment companies allow people to choose investment opportunities for long-term growth of their money. Many investors in our society own shares of one of the more than 1,600 mutual funds made available by investment companies. Investment companies and mutual funds are discussed in Chapter 30.

Consumer Finance Companies

A **consumer finance company** specializes in making loans for long-lasting or durable goods, such as cars and refrigerators, and for financial emergencies. Because consumer finance companies make loans, they are a part of the financial services industry. However, consumer finance companies do not accept savings as do banks and other financial institutions.

Mortgage Companies

Buying a home is an important activity in our society. Mortgage companies, along with other financial institutions, provide loans for purchasing a home or other real estate.

Check-Cashing Outlets

People who do not have bank accounts may use check-cashing outlets (CCOs) to cash paychecks and to obtain other financial services. CCOs offer a wide variety of services such as electronic tax filing, money orders, private postal boxes, utility bill payment, and the sale of bus and subway tokens.

Pawnshops

Pawnshops make loans based on the value of some tangible possession, such as jewelry or other valuable items. Pawnshops charge higher fees than other financial institutions.

Safe-deposit boxes require two keys to be opened. One is kept by the owner of the box; the other key is in the possession of the bank.

TYPES OF FINANCIAL SERVICES

Whatever your needs, a financial institution is available to serve you. As shown in Figure 20-2, the most common services of financial institutions are accepting deposits, transferring funds, lending money, storing valuables, providing financial advice and investment services, and managing trusts.

Accepting Deposits

Safe storage of funds for future use is an almost universal need. One of the main services that financial institutions offer is accepting money from their customers for safekeeping.

Figure 20-2

Banks and other financial institutions offer six main types of services.

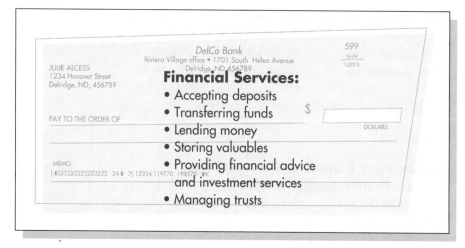

DelCo Bank
Riviera Village office • 1701 South Helea Avenue
Delridge, ND 456789

599
16-24
1220(7)

JULIE ALCESS
1234 Honover Street
Delridge, ND, 456789

Financial Services:

PAY TO THE ORDER OF

$

DOLLARS

- Accepting deposits
- Transferring funds
- Lending money
- Storing valuables
- Providing financial advice and investment services
- Managing trusts

MEMO

⑆222222222222222 24⑈ 7⑈ 12334 119770 198575 ⑆X

Sachi Kinoshita, a student who works part-time and summers, is an example of a customer who uses this service. Sachi earns a take-home salary of $210 a week from her summer job on a road construction crew. She wants to save part of her earnings for a down payment on a car. Sachi knows that if she carries the money with her or keeps it at home, she may be tempted to spend it or it may be lost or stolen.

To protect her money over the period of time it will take to save for the down payment, Sachi deposits some of her weekly pay in a savings account at the bank. By putting her money in a savings account, Sachi is saying to the bank, "I'm going to leave this money in my account for a fairly long period of time—maybe six months to a year or longer—and you can use it until I need it."

With Sachi's money, along with the funds of other depositors, the bank can make loans to other customers. Sachi will be paid by the bank for the use of her money. The amount paid for the use of money is called **interest.**

Let's say that Sachi deposits $500 of her summer wages in a savings account and leaves it there for a year. If the bank pays 4 percent interest on savings, Sachi's savings will have earned $20 in interest at the end of the year, and her car fund will have grown to $520. More complete discussions of interest appear in Chapter 28 and in Appendix C.

Transferring Funds

The ability to transfer money to others is necessary for daily business activities. Money deposited into a checking account can be used at any time by writing a check, which can then be deposited in the account of the person who receives the check.

Suppose that Eduardo Cruz has a checking account that he uses to pay bills. He can pay his bills by instructing the bank to pay out, or transfer, a certain amount from his account to someone to whom he owes money. The bank provides different ways through which Eduardo can do this. One of the most common transfer methods is by check. When Eduardo writes a check to his rental agent to pay his rent, for example, the bank subtracts the amount of the check from Eduardo's account.

Every year, however, more and more banking is done through electronic funds transfer. **Electronic funds transfer (EFT)** is a system through which funds are moved electronically from one account to another and from one bank to another. You can instruct your bank to transfer funds automatically, for example, from your savings to your checking account without writing a check. Or you can pay monthly bills, such as your phone bill or your rent, by instructing your bank to transfer the amount automatically each month from your account to the phone company or the rental agent.

Ethical*Perspective*

Check-Cashing Outlets and Pawnshops

About 17 percent of U.S. households do not have bank accounts. People who do not have bank accounts either do not choose, or feel that they are not qualified, to open a checking account. Typically a financial institution will not cash a check for you unless you have an account at that institution. For this reason, many people who do not have bank accounts use check-cashing outlets (CCOs). There are over 6,000 CCOs in the United States. CCOs may provide a useful service when banks are not an option.

As a fee for cashing a check, a CCO will charge anywhere from 1 to 20 percent of the face value of the check. The average cost is between 2 and 3 percent. This means a person could be charged $15 to cash a $500 paycheck. For some people, such charges could add up to significant portions of their total household budgets.

Another type of nondeposit financial institution is the pawnshop. Pawnshops make loans based on the value of some tangible possession, such as jewelry or other valuable items. Many people who may not qualify for loans at other types of financial institutions use pawnshops to obtain quick cash loans that may not be available from any other source. Pawnshops, however, charge higher borrowing fees than other financial institutions.

Critical Thinking

1 Are the fees charged by check-cashing outlets and pawnshops appropriate?

2 What actions might be taken to help people reduce the fees paid for financial services?

An ATM card is also commonly referred as a *cash card* or *debit card*. Using a debit card for a purchase is similar to writing a check, with the amount of the purchase deducted from your checking account.

You can go to your bank in person or write a letter instructing the bank to make electronic transfers for you. You can also give the instructions to the bank at an automatic teller machine (ATM). ATMs provide automatic teller service quickly and easily and are available 24 hours a day. Their popularity has brought about considerable growth in the EFT system, which is changing the way people do their banking. A fee may be charged by some banks for certain types of EFT transactions.

Other EFT services include:

- point-of-sale transactions in which ATM cards are accepted at gas stations, supermarkets, retail stores, and fast-food restaurants to pay for purchases.

- direct deposit in which your paycheck is automatically deposited in your checking or savings account.

- home banking in which payments are made and loans are obtained by customers using telephones and computers.

Lending Money

Many people, businesses, and governments borrow money at some time. For example, a business may want to borrow money to build a new warehouse or to buy more merchandise for resale. Individuals may borrow to buy a car or to pay college tuition. Banks will lend money to those who need to borrow if it seems likely that the loans will be repaid when due. In fact, banks want to make loans because banks receive most of their revenues from the interest they charge borrowers.

One way that banks can increase their loans is through offering credit cards. When you buy items such as clothing or sports equipment and pay for them with a bank credit card, such as MasterCard or Visa, you are borrowing money from the bank. Another way that banks can increase loans is by sending a limited number of checks with a customer's credit card statement, allowing the customer to use one of the checks to obtain cash or to pay a bill. If the customer uses the checks, the amount of each check is charged to the customer's credit card account. In effect, the amount of the check is a loan. Credit is discussed more fully in Unit Seven.

Cash machines have become very convenient with over 90,000 ATMs handling more than 8 billion transactions a years. ATMs can be found at workplaces, sporting and community events, amusement parks, and so on.

Storing Valuables

Besides offering a place to deposit money, banks offer **safe-deposit boxes** where you can store valuables. Because these safe-deposit boxes are in well-guarded vaults, they are the safest places to keep such things as jewelry, bond and stock certificates, birth records, a list of insurance policies, and a will. The box can be opened only by you or by someone who has been given the right to open it for you. Not even a bank has the right to open your safe-deposit box unless it is ordered to do so by a court. Safe-deposit boxes are rented by the year and come in a variety of sizes.

Illus. 20-2
Safe-deposit boxes are used for important papers and for valuables such as jewelry.

Providing Financial Advice and Investment Services

Many financial institutions help their customers by offering financial advice and investment services. Bank officials can advise customers about such things as whether it is wise to buy a certain house, how to manage money better, or how to exchange U.S. currency for foreign currency.

According to surveys, credit union customers report lower fees for checking accounts, lower loan interest rates, and higher levels of user satisfaction compared to other financial institutions.

Most banks offer advice on investments. **Investments** are savings that are put to work to earn more money. For example, money in a savings account is a type of investment because the savings account earns interest. Federal government bonds are another kind of investment that can be bought through a bank. For their customers, banks also buy bonds issued by businesses, by state and local governments, and by school districts. Investing is discussed in Unit 8.

Managing Trusts

Many banks manage investments on behalf of their customers. When they do this, the money or other property that is turned over to the banks for investment is said to be held in *trust*. This service can be offered through a trust company or through trust departments in banks. **Trust companies** are businesses that manage people's money and property for them.

Trusts are used by people of all ages, but they are especially useful for very young people and for some elderly people. A young person who inherits money may not have the skill and experience to manage it wisely. Elderly people who are ill may ask the trust department of a bank to manage their money. The bank makes investments and keeps the customers informed about what is happening to their money.

NET FACTS

The most efficient form of Internet connection is a direct connection. With communications hardware physically connecting you to the Net, data are transferred between hosts and your computer at the highest possible speeds and with the highest reliability.

THE FEDERAL RESERVE SYSTEM

One type of bank exists that will not allow you to make deposits. As an individual, you cannot open a savings account in a Federal Reserve Bank or borrow money from it. A Federal Reserve Bank is a bank for banks. Its relationship to member banks is similar to the relationship of your bank to you.

Structure of the Federal Reserve System

The federal government set up the **Federal Reserve System (Fed)** to supervise and regulate member banks in order to help the banks serve the public efficiently. All national banks are required to join the Federal Reserve System, and state banks may join. Banks that join the system are known as *member banks*. The United States is divided into 12 Federal Reserve districts, with a central Federal Reserve Bank in each district, as shown in Figure 20-3.

Federal Reserve Activities

You may go to your local bank to deposit money or to get a loan. The Federal Reserve Bank serves its member banks in the same way. It accepts their deposits, lends them money, and provides them with other banking services.

One service provided by the Fed is the holding of reserves. Banks cannot lend all of the money they receive from their

Figure 20-3

Locate the Federal Reserve district in which you live. Is there a Federal Reserve Bank or branch in a city near you?

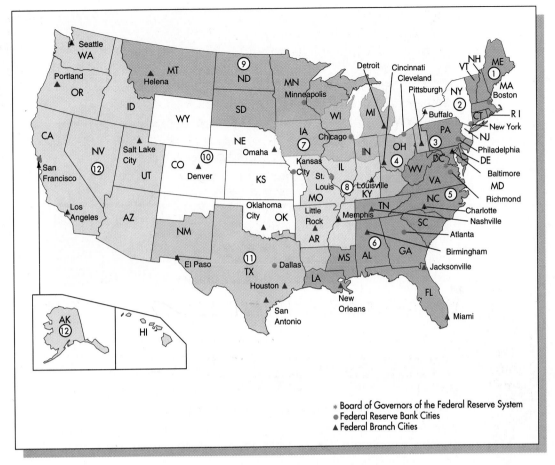

* Board of Governors of the Federal Reserve System
● Federal Reserve Bank Cities
▲ Federal Branch Cities

customers. The government requires banks to keep a certain amount of customers' money on deposit with the Federal Reserve System in case additional funds are needed to meet the daily needs of their customers. Therefore, a bank will lend only a certain percentage of its customers' deposits and keep the rest in reserve. For example, if a customer deposits $1,000 and the bank is required by the Federal Reserve System to hold 15 percent of all deposits in reserve, the bank can lend 85 percent of the new deposit, or $850 (100% − 15% = 85%). This regulation is designed to help the banking system and the economy operate efficiently and to protect depositors' money.

The Federal Reserve System buys and sells federal government bonds as part of its efforts to increase or decrease the money supply in our economy. The Fed's actions to affect the economy are called *monetary policy.*

Illus. 20-3
Bank deposits are put to work to finance new businesses and to build community projects.

FINANCIAL INSTITUTIONS AND ECONOMIC GROWTH

The activities of financial institutions affect each of us in many ways. Several million people work in the offices of America's banks, savings and loan associations, credit unions, and other financial institutions. Banking services are commonly used to

- build homes
- start new businesses
- plant crops
- finance educations
- buy goods
- pave streets
- build hospitals
- buy new business equipment

Banking services are made possible through the savings you and others deposit. Deposits do not remain idle in bank vaults. They are put to work. When you and others deposit money in a bank, you are helping to create jobs and economic growth that benefit your community and our society.

Key Ideas

1 Banks earn most of their revenues by charging for loans they make and by investing part of the money deposited by customers.

2 The main types of deposit-type institutions are commercial banks, savings and loan associations, mutual savings banks, and credit unions.

3 Nondeposit financial institutions include life insurance companies, investment companies, consumer finance companies, mortgage companies, check-cashing outlets, and pawnshops.

4 The most common services offered by financial institutions are accepting deposits, transferring funds, lending money, storing valuables, providing financial advice and investment services, and managing trusts.

5 The Federal Reserve System serves member banks by accepting their deposits, lending them money, and providing other services.

6 Banks and other financial institutions serve communities by employing people and lending money to build homes, start new businesses, plant crops, finance educations, buy goods, pave streets, build hospitals, and buy new business equipment.

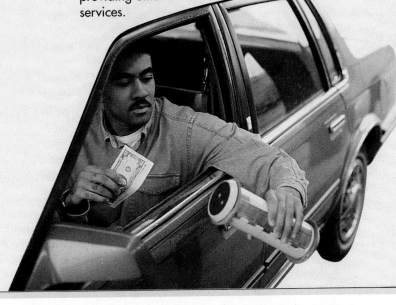

End of Chapter Activities

Increasing Your Business Vocabulary

The following terms should become part of your business vocabulary. For each numbered item, find the term that has the same meaning.

commercial bank

consumer finance company

credit union

electronic funds transfer (EFT)

Federal Deposit Insurance Corporation (FDIC)

Federal Reserve System (Fed)

interest

investments

mutual savings bank

safe-deposit boxes

savings and loan association (S&L)

trust companies

1 A bank owned by depositors that mainly handles savings accounts and makes loans to home buyers.

2 A bank that offers a full range of financial services.

3 A nationwide banking plan set up by our federal government to supervise and regulate member banks.

4 An amount paid for the use of money.

5 Financial institutions that specialize in managing the money and property of others.

6 A financial institution that specializes in savings accounts and loans for mortgages.

7 A not-for-profit financial institution formed by people who have like occupations or live in the same community.

8 A financial institution that specializes in making loans for long-lasting or durable goods and financial emergencies.

9 A federal agency that protects depositors' money in case of the failure of a bank or financial institution that it regulates.

10 A secured area in a bank vault for storing valuables.

11 A system through which funds are moved electronically from one account to another and from one bank to another.

12 Savings that are put to work to earn more money.

Reviewing Your Reading

1 How do banks earn most of their revenue? Name two other ways in which banks earn revenue.

2 What is a full-service bank?

3 What is the purpose of the Federal Deposit Insurance Corporation?

4 What are the main nondeposit financial institutions?

5 List six services provided by banks.

6 Give an example of an electronic funds transfer.

7 What is the purpose of a safe-deposit box?

8 What two age groups find trust departments of banks especially helpful? Why?

9 Name three services the Federal Reserve System provides for its member banks.

10 Give three examples to show the importance of banks to your community.

Using Your Business Knowledge

1 "In a private enterprise system, anybody who wants to open a bank should be allowed to do so." Do you agree with this statement? Give reasons for your answer.

2 Alicia Perez and Miguel Morales operate a video rental store. Each day they deposit all of the cash they receive except a small amount of change and a few bills they keep in their safe. Explain why they are wise to follow this method of handling money.

3 List the type of banking service that you think each following group or individual would be most likely to use. Explain your answer.

a. A person planning to open a fitness center
b. A musical group
c. A wealthy senior citizen
d. A buyer of a van
e. A high school recycling club

4 Jake Olsen's "Great Jake's Great Brownies" won $1,000 in an original recipe bake-off contest sponsored by a local television station. He has decided to put all of his winnings in the bank. List several questions Jake might want to ask before choosing whether to put the money in a checking or a savings account.

Calculating Business Problems

1 The FDIC insures deposits in banks up to $100,000. The insurance is paid for by the banks just as individuals buy insurance for their homes or cars. Based on the amount of deposits in the financial institution, the regulating agency sets the amount charged. The data at right show the rate charged in a recent year and a proposed rate change.

a. What is the percentage of increase in the rate?

Fidelity National Bank
Deposits: $6,590,000
Current insurance rate per $100 of deposits: 23.7 cents
Proposed rate per $100 of deposits: 27 cents

b. What is the cost of Fidelity's insurance at the current rate?

c. What will Fidelity's cost of insurance be at the proposed rate?

d. What is the amount of the increase?

---

2 Sachi Kinoshita is saving money for a car. She worked 12 weeks during the summer on a road construction crew. Her take-home pay was $210 a week.

a. If she deposited each paycheck in the bank, what was the total amount she deposited during the summer?

b. If she put $90 each week in her savings account, how much did she save during the summer?

c. If she leaves her accumulated summer savings in the bank for a year at 3.5 percent interest, how much will she have available for a down payment on a car at the end of the year?

Hint: Refer to Appendix C: Determining Percentage and Interest in Business.

---

3 On June 1, Susan Pohlnik had a checking account balance of $140. She has her paychecks automatically deposited into her account. Her earnings for June were $1,080. During the month, she wrote checks for $87, $146, $29, and $292. She had $120 auto- matically transferred from her checking account to her savings account. In addition, she used her ATM card to withdraw $60 in cash. The bank charges 75 cents for each EFT transfer or withdrawal. Find Susan's bank balance after these transactions.

4 To raise money for a party for patients at a local children's hospital, the business club at Martin Luther King High School sold cans of trail mix. The 0.5 kilogram cans sold for $3 each. The students deposited the total amount of their sales each week in the school's accounting office. The records of the three students with the highest November sales appear in the table at right.

Date	Jose Santos	Darlana Jones	Carl Perlman
Nov. 5	14 cans	3 cans	6 cans
12	8	6	5
19	6	10	5
26	15	12	7

a. How many cans did each of these students sell?

b. How much money did each student deposit during November?

c. How many kilograms of trail mix did each student sell?

d. If the trail mix cost the students $1.46 per can, what was the amount of their profit on sales for November?

Applying Technology

Using the *Introduction to Business* template and your database program software, select problem CH20. After the problem appears on your screen, complete the following activities. Then, after you have completed each step, display or print a report for each activity. If you do not have a printer available, answer the questions before you leave the computer.

1 Select and list the Federal Reserve branches (not the banks) in Districts 7 through 12. How many branches are listed?

2 Sort the database in ascending order by state. Answer the following questions:

a. What is the seventh bank or branch listed?

b. What is the twelfth bank or branch listed?

3 Sort the database in ascending order by type as the primary field and by city as the secondary field. Answer the following questions:

a. What is the first bank (not branch) listed?

b. What is the last bank (not branch) listed?

Making Decisions

Fran and Bill Hamilton recently moved to a new community. They are having trouble deciding whether to use a financial institution near their workplaces or near their home. The Hamiltons have the opportunity to do business with a credit union, a national bank with many branches, a local bank with strong personal service, or a savings and loan association.

1 What factors should the Hamiltons consider when selecting a financial institution?

2 How could Fran and Bill obtain information about the financial institution that would best serve their needs?

Chapter Twenty-One

Opening a Checking Account

Key Terms

service charge

money market rate

sharedrafts

signature card

joint account

deposit slip

endorsement

blank endorsement

special endorsement

restrictive endorsement

check stub

check register

Objectives

After studying this chapter and completing the end-of-chapter activities, you will be able to:

1 Describe four advantages of having a checking account.

2 Explain the difference between the two major types of checking accounts.

3 Explain the process of opening a checking account.

4 Discuss the purpose of an endorsement.

5 Demonstrate three types of endorsements and explain when each is used.

6 Describe the purpose of a check stub and check register.

"I do not believe in checking accounts," Bob said. "Cash is much easier for all my daily business activities. You'll never catch me holding up a line at a cash register while I write out a check."

"Aren't you worried that you might lose your money?" was Georgette's reaction. "Or, what if you have to prove that you made a payment?"

"I can get a receipt," Bob responded. "I still say that using cash only is better than sometimes using checks and sometimes cash."

"Yes, but a bank will have a record of your check even if you lose your receipt," Georgette replied. "Won't you just consider using a checking account? There are many good reasons. I think that you and I need to have a talk about the advantages of having a checking account."

ADVANTAGES OF A CHECKING ACCOUNT

Having a checking account provides a person with several benefits. These advantages include convenience, safety, proof of payment, and a record of finances.

Convenience

When you open a checking account, you will find that it will be a convenient way to handle your business affairs. With a checking account, you can write checks at home and pay bills by mail. Or, you can make payments automatically through the EFT system. Both methods save time and money.

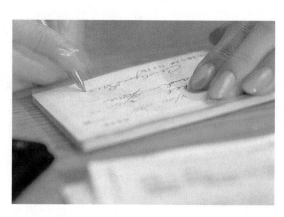

Illus. 21-1
A checking account is a convenient way to handle your business affairs.

Safety

A checking account also has many safety advantages. People who keep a great deal of money on hand risk losing it by fire, theft, or carelessness. When money is at home, a greater temptation also exists to spend it needlessly. With a checking account, you will need to keep only a little cash on hand for small purchases.

Another safety feature is that you can safely send a check through the mail because it can be cashed only by the person or business to whom it is made payable. Sending cash through the mail is not safe, because if it is lost, there is no way to recover it. However, if a check is lost, it can be replaced.

As you learned in Chapter 20, the money you deposit in the bank is protected in another way. If your bank is a member of the Federal Deposit

ach year in the United States over 60 billion checks are written.

Insurance Corporation, your deposit will be insured up to $100,000.00. Always check to see if the financial institution in which you deposit your money is insured.

Proof of Payment

An important advantage of paying by check is that, once cashed, a check is legal proof of payment. For example, suppose you write a check each month for $30 to pay for piano lessons at the Mallard Music Studio. The studio will deposit your check at its bank. The studio's bank will then send the check to your bank where it will be subtracted from your account. If the studio makes an error in its records and later tells you that a past month's fee was not paid, your canceled check will prove that you made the payment.

Record of Finances

Another advantage of checking accounts is that they provide a record of your finances. With a checking account, you must record every deposit you make and every check you write. You can tell from these records how much you are spending, where your money is going, and how much you have remaining in your account. The organized records you keep can help you manage your money.

An *accounts payable clerk's* job duties include:
- Verifying that invoices from suppliers have been approved for payment.
- Keeping track of due dates of invoices.
- Preparing checks to pay approved invoices on or before their due dates.

Illus. 21-2

A checking account is an easy method of recording your finances.

TYPES OF CHECKING ACCOUNTS

Checking accounts differ from one bank to another and from one part of the country to another. They differ in the features they offer customers. Checking accounts also differ in costs. A **service charge** is a fee a bank charges for handling a checking account. When you are ready to open a checking account, you should visit several banks to find out what services each offers and what fees it charges. Comparison shopping for your checking account will enable you to choose one that best suits your needs.

While there are many types of checking accounts in use, they can be viewed in two basic categories: regular checking accounts and interest checking accounts.

Regular Checking Accounts

If you write a large number of checks each month, you probably should use a regular checking account. With most banks, there is no service charge for a regular checking account as long as the account balance does not fall below a certain amount during a month. This minimum monthly balance varies, but it is likely to be $300 or higher. A *minimum monthly balance* is a stated amount that an account must not fall below.

Sometimes the service charges are figured on the average monthly balance of the account during the month. An *average monthly balance* is the sum of the daily balances divided by the number of days in the month. The account may fall below a certain minimum on some days, but must average at or above the minimum at the end of the month to avoid a service charge. Some banks do not charge service fees on checking accounts if the depositor also keeps a certain balance, often $1,000, in a savings account at the same bank. At some financial institutions, service charges are waived for students or customers 65 years old or older.

Interest Checking Accounts

Many financial institutions offer checking accounts that earn interest. However, these accounts usually require a minimum monthly balance or an average monthly balance of $500 or more. As long as the account meets the balance requirement, the bank will pay interest on the checking account. If the account falls below the required amount, the bank usually pays no interest and will usually also add a service charge to the account. The charges may include a monthly charge, a fee for each check written, or both of these service charges.

The rates of interest that banks pay their customers also vary. In recent years, typical rates have

Until a few years ago, only banks offered checking accounts. Today, checking accounts are also available at credit unions and savings and loan associations.

ranged from 2 to 4 percent depending on economic conditions. Usually, a bank will offer a higher rate of interest when a higher balance is maintained. The interest rate may be tied to the current cost of money in the marketplace, known as the **money market rate.** The money market rate is the interest rate that big users of money, such as governments and large corporations, pay when they borrow money. The money market rate varies from day to day.

Banks offer interest checking accounts with varying rates tied to the money market rate. As the money market rate changes, so does the rate the banks pay holders of certain types of accounts. To avoid changing rates daily or weekly, however, the bank determines the average of the daily money market rates for the month and pays the depositor that average rate for the month. For very large accounts, rates higher than money market rates are sometimes available.

ooking at the front of a check, the right side of the check is called the *leading edge* and is processed first through a sorting machine. The left side of a check is referred to as the *trailing edge*. The endorsement is made on the back of the trailing edge.

Other Types of Checking Accounts

In addition to the two basic kinds of checking accounts, several other types are available. You may need to write only a few checks each month and wish to keep a small balance in your checking account. For depositors with such needs, many banks offer special checking accounts. Charges on the accounts vary, but the basic charge is about 10 to 20 cents for each check written. There may also be a small monthly service charge for the account.

Savings and loan associations and other financial institutions commonly offer checking services. Credit unions may provide checking accounts for members. Members of credit unions are called *shareholders* when they have money on deposit, and their checks are called **sharedrafts.** This means a draft (withdrawal) is made on the member's shares of ownership (deposits) in the credit union. Interest rates may vary and the number of sharedrafts per month may be limited.

OPENING A CHECKING ACCOUNT

Opening a checking account is fairly easy no matter what type of account you choose. You can simply take your paycheck or cash to the new-accounts desk in a financial institution. The representative will help you sign a signature card, make your deposit, and select your checks. Some banks, however, may require you to be at least 18 years old to open a checking account.

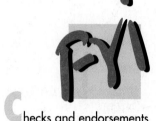

Checks and endorsements should be written in ink so they cannot be altered.

The Signature Card

A bank will deduct money from a checking account to cover checks only when authorized to do so by the depositor. Therefore, the bank must keep the depositor's signature on record to compare with the signature that appears on his or her checks. For this reason, you will be asked to sign your name on a card when you open your account. This card is called a **signature card** and is the bank's official record of your signature. You must use the same signature on each check you write. Figure 21-1 shows a signature card for Alicia Garcia.

Sometimes two or more people have an account together. This is known as a **joint account.** Each person who will write checks on the account must sign the signature card. Any signer of the card in a joint account can write checks on the account as if he or she were the only owner. A signature card for a business would show the name of the business and the signatures of those authorized to sign checks for the business.

Making the First Deposit

When you deposit money in a checking account, you fill out a deposit slip or a deposit ticket. A **deposit slip** is a form on which you list all items you are depositing—currency, coins, or checks.

Figure 21-1

The signature on your checks must match the one on your signature card that is on file at your bank.

Second National Bank
PERSONAL CHECKING ACCOUNT

○ JOINT AND SEVERAL (Payable to the order of either or the survivor)
● INDIVIDUAL (If payable on death to named survivors, fill in section below)
___ Indicate number of signatures required

Alicia Garcia
SIGNATURE

_____
SIGNATURE

Alicia Garcia   or _____
PRINT OR TYPE NAME(S)

19684 Absaroka Dr., Houston, TX 77083-5549   *2 years*
ADDRESS   CITY AND STATE   ZIP CODE   HOW LONG? MO. YRS.

555-6403   *720J64-TX*
HOME PHONE   DRIVERS LICENSE NO./STATE

PAYABLE ON DEATH OF DEPOSITOR TO SUCH OF THE FOLLOWING NAMED AS SURVIVE DEPOSITOR:

_____

(PRINT OR TYPE NAME − DESIGNATION BY OTHER MEANS IS NOT SUFFICIENT.)
Office: _____   Date: *April 10, 19--*

	201-24-1590	*1648-7214*
OFFICER APPROVAL	SOCIAL SECURITY NUMBER	ACCOUNT NUMBER

The deposit slip shows your name, your account number, the date, the items deposited, and the total amount of the deposit. Most banks print the depositor's name, address, and account number on deposit slips and checks. Since these will not be ready when you open your new account, you will use a blank deposit slip. Figure 21-2 shows a deposit slip made out by Alicia Garcia. Her deposit consisted of $60.00 in currency, $1.75 in coin, and her paycheck for $270.10, for a total of $331.85.

Each check is identified by the number of the bank on which it was drawn. This number is assigned to each commercial bank by the American Bankers Association. You can see the three parts of this number in Figure 21-3. The first part of the number above the line indicates the city or state in which the bank is located. The second part is the number assigned to the individual bank. The number below the line is a Federal Reserve number that banks use in sorting checks. The two top numbers of each check deposited should be listed on the deposit slip, as shown in Figure 21-2.

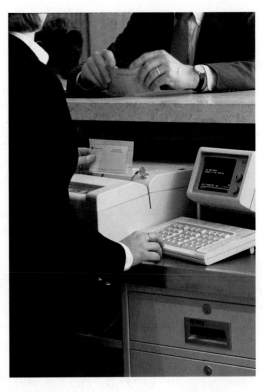

Illus. 21-3

To deposit money in a checking account, first complete a deposit slip.

Figure 21-2

Alicia Garcia has completed a deposit slip for a total deposit of $331.85.

CHECKING ACCOUNT DEPOSIT SLIP		DOLLARS	CENTS
	CURRENCY	60	00
	COIN	1	75
NAME _Alicia Garcia_	1 CHECKS 68-36	270	10
	2		
	3		
DATE _April 10_ 19--	4		
	TOTAL FROM OTHER SIDE		
	TOTAL	331	85
This deposit is accepted subject to verification and to the rules and regulations of the Bank.	LESS CASH RECEIVED		
	TOTAL DEPOSIT	331	85

IF MORE THAN 4 CHECKS, LIST ON REVERSE SIDE. ENTER TOTAL HERE

Second National Bank
HOUSTON, TX 77083-9073

ACCOUNT NUMBER _1648-7214_

Figure 21-3
Each commercial bank in the United States is assigned a number by the American Bankers Association.

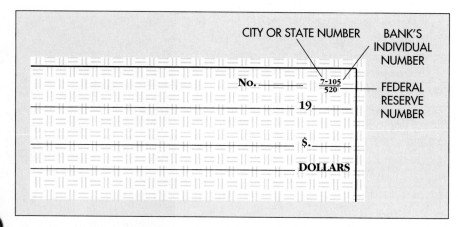

CITY OR STATE NUMBER — BANK'S INDIVIDUAL NUMBER

No.

$\frac{7\text{-}105}{520}$ — FEDERAL RESERVE NUMBER

19

$.

DOLLARS

ENDORSING CHECKS FOR MAKING DEPOSITS

Before Alicia can deposit her paycheck, she must endorse it by writing her name on the back of the left end of the check. An **endorsement** is written evidence that you received payment or that you transferred your right of receiving payment to someone else.

The Purpose of Endorsements

Before you cash, deposit, or transfer a check to another person or business, you must first endorse the check. When you endorse a check, your responsibilities are almost as great as if you had written the check yourself. As an endorser, you are actually making this promise: "If this check is not paid by the bank, I will pay it." The three main purposes of endorsements are as follows:

1. Endorsements allow the recipient of the check to cash, deposit, or transfer it to someone else.

2. Endorsements serve as legal evidence that the receiver cashed or transferred the check to someone else.

3. Endorsements mean that the endorser will pay the check in case the next owner of the check cannot collect the money.

Placement of Endorsements

The federal government has guidelines for financial institutions that require money deposited to

Checks may be purchased from your bank or other sources. Ads for mail-order companies that sell low-cost checks may be found in magazines or the Sunday newspaper.

customers' accounts be available to them in a certain period of time. The time between the receipt of the deposit by the bank and its availability to the depositor is called the *float*. Evidence that the bank followed the time regulations is its stamped endorsement on the check. Because these stamps are usually large, the guidelines also limit the space on the check for the payee's endorsement. Your endorsement must be made in the 1½-inch space on the left side of the check. Figure 21-4 shows a diagram for the payee's endorsement.

These space regulations are very specific. If you write anything outside the 1½-inch limit, it may cause the check to be returned. Further, you may be liable for fees for returned checks and other penalties as a result of endorsements that are unreadable, misplaced, or incomplete.

When making a deposit by mail never send cash because it may be lost or stolen.

Cultural *Perspective*

Babylonian Banks and the Incan Record Keeping System

As a society becomes larger and more complex, the need for financial systems becomes greater. One example is the Babylonian civilization in Asia Minor. Over 7,000 years ago, the Babylonians had banks and a method for transferring funds. An early form of checks was used to draw money in one place and to pay in another. The Babylonians required that most business transactions be put in writing and signed by the parties involved. This is believed to be one of the first verified uses of business documents.

Another example is the Incan civilization in South America. Have your ever been "at the end of your rope" when trying to keep track of financial matters? Perhaps that phrase relates to the Incan record keeping system. Incan record keepers used small ropes of different colors and sizes, and knotted and joined them in different ways to help keep track of data. These ropes, called *quipu*, were used to keep track of census data, gold mine output, inventory in a storehouse, and important historic dates.

Both the Babylonians and Incas developed practices that served as foundations for the financial systems and record keeping methods in operation today.

Critical Thinking

1 Why are documents important for efficient business activities?

2 If we didn't have computers today, what types of financial record keeping systems might be used in our society?

Figure 21-4

The payee's endorsement is limited to 1½ inches on the back of the check at the trailing edge.

TYPES OF ENDORSEMENTS

Different endorsements serve different purposes. As you handle the checks you receive, you will probably use each of the four types of endorsements discussed in the following sections. Let's start with the endorsement that Alicia Garcia used for her paycheck.

Blank Endorsement

An endorsement that consists of only the endorser's name is called a **blank endorsement.** To endorse a check, sign your name in ink exactly as it is written on the face of the check. The endorsement should match your signature on the signature card. If the name on the check is different from your official signature, you will need to endorse the check twice. In Figure 21-5, Alicia first endorsed her paycheck "A. C. Garcia" as her name

ome checks have carbonless paper attached. The copies made when you write checks may also be used to maintain a record of deposits and checks written.

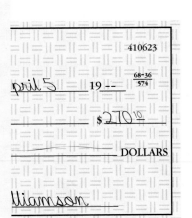

Figure 21-5
Why did Alicia
have to endorse
this check
twice?

appeared on the check. Then she signed the check "Alicia Garcia"
as she had written her name on the signature card.

A blank endorsement makes a check payable to anyone who has
the check. This endorsement may be used at any time a check is to
be transferred, but sometimes another type of endorsement is better.

Special Endorsement

Suppose Nancy R. Brooks receives from her part-time job a paycheck made payable to her. She then wants to make that check
payable to Kunio Shinoda, who operates a service station where
she buys gas. The check is a payment on the bill she owes Mr.
Shinoda. If she uses a blank endorsement and sends the check to
Mr. Shinoda, he can cash it when he receives it. However, if the
check is lost before it reaches him, anyone who finds it can cash it.

To make sure that no one except Kunio Shinoda will be able to
cash the check, Nancy may use a **special endorsement,** which
includes the name of the person to whom the check has been
transferred. Special endorsements are also called *full endorsements*.
With this endorsement, she places the words "Pay to the order of
Kunio Shinoda" before her signature as shown in Figure 21-6. Mr.
Shinoda must sign the check before it can be cashed.

Restrictive Endorsement

A **restrictive endorsement** limits the use of the check to the
purpose given in the endorsement. For example, you may have
several checks that you want to mail to the bank. You could write
"For deposit only" above your signature, followed by your account

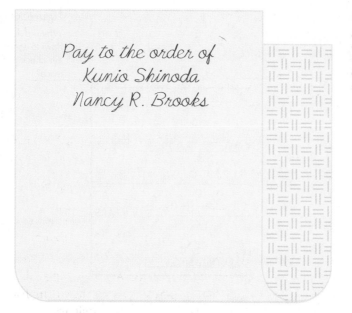

Figure 21-6
A special endorsement is used to transfer a check to someone else.

*Pay to the order of
Kunio Shinoda
Nancy R. Brooks*

number, as in Figure 21-7. This endorsement restricts use of the check so it can only be deposited to your account. If a check with such an endorsement is lost, it cannot be cashed by the finder.

*For deposit only
Nancy R. Brooks*

Figure 21-7
With a restrictive endorsement, if this check is lost, it cannot be cashed by the finder.

Businesses often use rubber stamps to imprint restrictive endorsements that require checks to be deposited to their accounts. A business thus has no risk of loss if an unauthorized person uses the stamp to endorse a check.

RECORDING THE DEPOSIT

When you make a deposit to your checking account, the bank teller will give you a receipt. The receipt may be printed by a computer at the same time that it registers the deposit in the bank's records. A deposit may also be made at an automatic teller machine located away from the bank building. Or, a deposit may be sent through the mail. The bank records your deposit and mails a receipt back to you.

When you become a depositor, your bank will supply you with blank checks bound in a check-book. Checkbooks may be supplied without charge on some kinds of accounts, but usually banks charge a fee when the depositor's name and address are printed on each check and deposit slip. Today checks may also be personalized with initials or background pictures of the depositor's choosing.

Besides the checks, a checkbook also contains forms on which a depositor writes a record of deposits made and checks written. In some check-books, this record is kept on the **check stub** that is attached to each check, as shown in Figure 21-8. Another type of checkbook provides a **check register,** which is a separate form for recording deposits and checks. When you make a deposit to your checking account, you should *immediately* enter the amount on the check stub or in the check register.

NET FACTS

SLIP and PPP connections use modems and telephone lines to connect to the Inter-net. SLIP stands for Serial Line Internet Protocol; PPP stands for Point to Point Protocol.

Figure 21-8
The check stub attached to a check provides one way to keep checking account records. The stub is completed when the check is written.

Key Ideas

1 A checking account provides convenience, safety, proof of payment, and a record of finances.

2 The main types of checking accounts are regular checking accounts, which may or may not charge fees, and interest checking accounts, which pay interest so long as the balance meets the requirements.

3 When opening a checking account, you must sign your name on a signature card, which becomes the bank's official record of your signature, make your deposit, and select your checks.

4 The purpose of an endorsement is to allow the recipient of the check to cash, deposit, or transfer it to someone else.

5 The three main types of endorsements are the blank, special, and restrictive endorsements.

6 The purpose of a check stub and check register is to record deposits and to maintain a record of checks written.

End of Chapter Activities

Increasing Your Business Vocabulary

The following terms should become part of your business vocabulary. For each numbered item, find the term that has the same meaning.

blank endorsement

check register

check stub

deposit slip

endorsement

joint account

money market rate

restrictive endorsement

service charge

sharedrafts

signature card

special endorsement

1 A form that accompanies a deposit and lists the items deposited—currency, coins, or checks.

2 A form attached to a check on which a depositor keeps a record of the checks written and any current deposit.

3 Written evidence that you received payment or that you transferred your right of receiving payment to someone else.

4 A separate form on which the depositor keeps a record of deposits and checks.

5 A card, kept by a bank, that shows the signatures of all individuals authorized to draw checks against the account.

6 A bank account that is used by two or more people.

7 An endorsement that limits the use of a check to the purpose given in the endorsement.

8 A fee a bank charges for handling a checking account.

9 An endorsement including the name of the person to whom the check has been transferred.

10 The current cost of money in the marketplace.

11 Withdrawals made on a member's shares of ownership (deposits) in a credit union.

12 An endorsement consisting of only the endorser's name.

Reviewing Your Reading

1 What are the advantages of a checking account?

2 Explain the difference between the two major kinds of checking accounts.

3 What is a sharedraft account?

4 Why does a bank require you to sign a signature card when you open a checking account?

5 What are the three purposes of endorsements?

6 Describe the placement of an endorsement. For what is the remaining space used?

7 If you wish to transfer ownership of a check from yourself to another person, would you use a blank, a special, or a restrictive endorsement? Explain.

8 Which endorsement would you use to limit the use of your payroll check to being deposited in your bank account?

9 What is the purpose of check stubs or a check register?

Using Your Business Knowledge

1 "You should shop for the best place to open a checking account as carefully as you shop for the best buy in any product or service." Give two reasons to support this statement.

2 Akeo Mori attends a technical school in the morning and works afternoons and weekends at a skating rink. He believes that if he deposits his earnings in a checking account and writes checks to pay the few monthly bills he has, he could better manage his money. What kind of checking account would you recommend for Akeo? Why?

3 If you sign your full name on the signature card when you open your checking account and then sign your nickname when you write your checks, do you think the bank should pay the checks? Give a reason for your answer.

4 Ann and Walter Neal have a joint checking account and both have signed the signature card. Must they both sign each check? Why?

Calculating Business Problems

1 Shana Brown wrote a check to make a deposit to her savings account and three checks to pay her monthly bills. The checks were written for the following amounts: savings, $110.00; rent, $350.00; electric bill, $100.82; gasoline bill, $78.75. This left a new checkbook balance of $290.25.

a. What is the total amount of Shana's monthly bills?
b. What is the total amount of Shana's four checks?
c. What was Shana's checkbook balance before she wrote the four checks?

2 Service charges for Tom Harding's regular checking account at Second National Bank are based on the bank's rate schedule, as shown at right.

During a recent six-month period, Tom's balances were April, $148.00; May, $201.97; June, $101.61; July, $418.53; August, $248.29; and September, $154.36.

Minimum Balance	Charge
0—$199.00	$6.00
$200.00—$399.00	$4.00
$400.00 and over	no charge

a. How much was Tom's service charge for each month?
b. What was the total service charge for the six-month period?

3 The Gulfstream Bank requires an average monthly balance of $1,500 on its interest checking account. Wanda Settle had an average monthly balance for June of $1,620.

a. Is Wanda eligible to earn interest on her account for June?

b. If the bank paid 4 percent annual interest on the average monthly balance, how much interest would she earn for June?

Hint: Refer to Appendix C: Determining Percentage and Interest in Business.

Applying Technology

Using the *Introduction to Business* template and your database program software, select problem CH21. After the problem appears on your screen, complete the following activities. Then, after you have completed each step, display or print a report for each activity. If you do not have a printer available, answer the questions before you leave the computer.

1 Select and list the financial institutions that provide interest checking accounts. How many financial institutions are listed?

2 Select and list the financial institutions that have minimum balances less than or equal to $300. How many financial institutions are listed?

3 Based on the list selected in Activity 2, select and list the financial institutions that have minimum balances less than or equal to $300 and service charges less than $5.

Making Decisions

Boni and Kara Hondre are college roommates. The sisters are considering getting a checking account together. They could get a joint account, or they might decide to get individual accounts.

1 How should Boni and Kara decide whether to get a joint checking account or an individual account?

2 What type of account do you recommend for the sisters?

Chapter Twenty-Two

Using Checks and Other Payment Methods

Key Terms

drawer

payee

drawee

forgery

overdrawing

postdated check

stop-payment order

certified check

cashier's check

traveler's check

money order

Objectives

After studying this chapter and completing the end-of-chapter activities, you will be able to:

1 Demonstrate proper check-writing procedures.

2 List tips for good check writing.

3 Explain the purpose of a stop-payment order.

4 Describe procedures for accepting and cashing checks.

5 Name three special types of checks.

6 List four sources of money orders.

7 Explain how payments are made through electronic funds transfer.

A licia Garcia had made her first deposit in her new checking account, and her friends knew about her account.

Her friend Joni asked her, "If I write you a check, could you pay me in cash? You can just deposit my check in your account later."

"How do I know your check is good?" Alicia asked.

"What! We've been friends for over ten years," Joni responded. "Don't you trust me?"

"Of course I trust you," said Alicia. "Just remember that if a check isn't good it can result in some expensive service fees."

The next day, Laura came up to Alicia and said, "I can't wait to mail away for this sweater.

However, the ad says 'no personal checks.' How can I pay for it?"

"Haven't you ever heard of a money order?" asked Alicia.

"A money 'what'?" asked Laura.

"Let me tell you about money orders," responded Alicia.

CHECK-WRITING PROCEDURES

Some checks are light blue or green in color. Other checks have a picture of a forest. Still others have an inspirational quote. All checks, however, contain basically the same information.

Elements of a Check

As you study Figure 22-1, you will find some terms that are used to identify the parts of a check. Three parties, as you see, are shown on each check: the drawer, the payee, and the drawee. The

Figure 22-1
A check has
many parts.

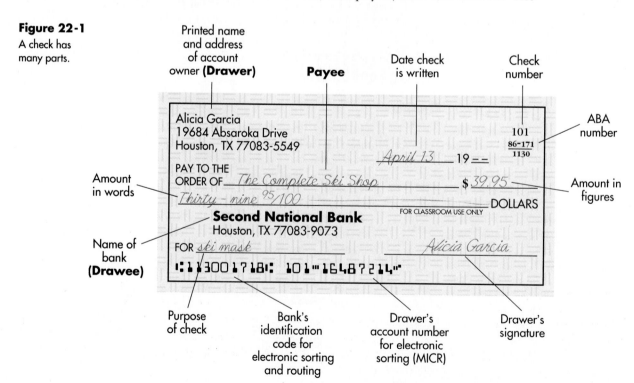

Printed name and address of account owner **(Drawer)**

Payee

Date check is written

Check number

ABA number

Amount in words

Amount in figures

Name of bank **(Drawee)**

Purpose of check

Bank's identification code for electronic sorting and routing

Drawer's account number for electronic sorting (MICR)

Drawer's signature

Alicia Garcia
19684 Absaroka Drive
Houston, TX 77083-5549

101
86-171
1130

April 13 19 --

PAY TO THE ORDER OF *The Complete Ski Shop* $ *39.95*

Thirty - nine 95/100 DOLLARS

FOR CLASSROOM USE ONLY

Second National Bank
Houston, TX 77083-9073

FOR *ski mask*

Alicia Garcia

⑈⑈300⑈7⑈8⑈ 101 ⑈16487214⑈

drawer is the owner of the account and the person who signs the check. The **payee** is the person to whom the check is written. The payee's name always appears after the words *Pay to the order of.* The **drawee** is the bank or other financial institution that pays the check.

Filling Out the Check Stub or Register

As you learned in Chapter 21, your checkbook will have a place for recording account activities. Two types of forms are commonly available—a check stub and a check register. The check stub is a form attached to the check by a perforated line. After the check is written, the check is torn off at the line and the stub remains in the checkbook.

A check register is a separate book, usually the same size as the checkbook. Compare the two forms shown in Figure 22-2. Note that both forms provide blanks to fill in the same type of information about the check. *Always fill out the stub or register first.* If you write the check first, you may forget to record the information before you transfer the check.

Figure 22-2 shows how Alicia Garcia would record her check for $39.95 to The Complete Ski Shop, using both a check stub and a register. Of course, she would use only one type, but you can see that she would record the same information on either form. Also note that there are other entries in the check register for checks written and deposits made.

Writing a Check

After completing the entry in the check register, you are ready to fill out the check. Remember that a check is an order to the bank to pay out your money, so be sure to fill out the check completely and carefully.

Seven steps are usually involved when writing a check:

Step 1 Write checks in order by number. Check numbers are usually printed on both the checks and the check stubs. Check registers have a space for you to write the check numbers. These numbers help you to compare your records with the checks that have been paid. If the numbers are not already printed on the checks, write them in the space provided.

To prove to her students that a check can be written on anything, a teacher in Woodstock, Illinois, once had a check cashed that was written on the side of a live pig!

Figure 22-2

A check stub is left in the checkbook when a check is removed. A check register is a separate form.

101	$	*39.95*
April 13		19 - -
TO	*Complete Ski Shop*	
FOR	*Ski mask*	

	DOLLAR	CENTS
BAL FOR'D		
DEPOSITS	331	85
4/10		
TOTAL	331	85
THIS CHECK	39	95
OTHER DEDUCTIONS		
BAL FOR'D	291	90

PLEASE BE SURE TO **DEDUCT** CHARGES THAT AFFECT YOUR ACCOUNT

ITEM NO. OR TRANSACTION CODE	DATE	DESCRIPTION OF TRANSACTION	AMOUNT OF PAYMENT OR WITHDRAWAL(−)	✓	TAX OR OTHER	AMOUNT OF DEPOSIT OR INTEREST(+)	BALANCE FORWARD
	19 --	TO *Opening deposit*				331 85	+ 331 85
D	4/10	FOR *Paycheck 271.10; cash 60.75*					BAL 331 85
		TO *Complete Ski Shop*	39 95				− 39 95
101	4/13	FOR *ski mask*					BAL 291 90
		TO *Second National Bank*	50 —				− 50 00
102	4/15	FOR *cash-current expenses*					BAL 241 90
		TO *Deposit*				50 —	+ 50 00
D	4/16	FOR *Birthday-Dad*					BAL 291 90
		TO *Skiing Update*	32 97				− 32 97
103	4/21	FOR *one yr. subscription*					BAL 258 93
		TO *J. T. Gore Sports*	— 87				− 87
104	4/22	FOR *postage due on 4/20 order*					BAL 258 06
VOID 105	4/22	TO *Johnson Masters* VOID FOR					BAL —
AT	4/23	TO *Cash from ATM* FOR *game tickets and dinner*	50 —				− 50 00 / BAL 208 06

Step 2 Write the date in the proper space on the check.

Step 3 Write the payee's name on the line following *Pay to the Order of*. The payee for Alicia's first check is The Complete Ski Shop, as shown in Figure 22-1 on page 356.

Step 4 Write the amount of the check in figures after the printed dollar sign. Write the amount close to the dollar sign so that a dishonest person cannot insert another number between it and the amount. Write cents figures close to the dollar figures so that additional numbers cannot be inserted.

Step 5 Write the amount of dollars in words on the line below the payee's name. Write the cents in figures as a fraction of a dollar. Begin writing at the far left end of the line. Draw a line from the fraction to the printed word *Dollars* to fill all unused space. Filling all unused space prevents a dishonest person from adding words to change the amount.

If the amount written in figures does not agree with the amount written in words, the bank may pay the amount written in words. If there is a considerable difference between the two amounts, the bank may call you for instructions concerning payment. The bank may also return the check to you and ask you to replace it. There is usually a charge, often as much as $20, when a check is returned for any reason.

Step 6   Write the purpose of the payment on the line at the bottom of the check. Later, after you receive your canceled check, this note about the purpose can serve as a reminder of why you wrote the check. Canceled checks are discussed in Chapter 23.

Step 7   Sign your checks with the same signature that you wrote on your signature card. Alicia Garcia is the drawer of the check in Figure 22-1 on page 356 and has signed her name on the proper line.

On checks issued by a business or other organization, the firm's name may be printed on the check and is often followed by the word *By*. The person who signs the check writes his or her name after *By*. This shows that the firm is the drawer. An example of a business signature is shown in Figure 22-3.

The bank may subtract from the depositor's account only the amounts of checks and electronic funds transfer (EFT) transactions that the depositor has authorized. If a bank cashes a check signed by someone who had no right to use the depositor's signature, the bank may be held responsible. Writing another person's signature on a check without his or her authority is a crime called **forgery.** A check with such a signature is a *forged check*.

Figure 22-3

Who is the drawer of a business check? Should Sarah Adams' account be charged for this check?

AY BANK & TRUST COMPANY		$\dfrac{86\text{-}42}{1031}$
	April 2,	19--
& Company		$ 330.69
thirty 69/100 ·		DOLLARS
	ORION MANUFACTURING, INC.	
	BY *Sarah Adams*	

TIPS FOR GOOD CHECK WRITING

Anyone who writes checks has a great deal of responsibility. However, following these tips can help you avoid problems caused by poorly written checks.

1. *Write checks only on the forms provided by your bank.* Checks can be written on just about anything—even a paper bag. Sorting and exchanging the millions of checks that are written every day is done using the Magnetic Ink Character Recognition (MICR) num-

Check-writing software is available for home computers. These programs prepare your checks and maintain a record of payments by type of expense.

bers printed on the check (see Figure 22-1 on page 356). If the check does not have these numbers, the sorting will be interrupted. The check may be delayed and a charge for handling the check may be made.

2. *Write checks in ink.* Using ink prevents someone from increasing the amount of the check. Many businesses use computers or machines called check writers to guard against possible changes in the check amount.

3. *Only write checks if you have money in your account to cover them.* Writing a check for more than you have in your account is called **overdrawing.** When an account is overdrawn, the bank may not pay the check. In addition, most banks charge the depositor for checks they have to return marked *insufficient funds.*

4. *Use the current date.* A **postdated check** is one that is dated later than the date on which it is written. For example, a check written on December 1 but dated December 5 is postdated. You might postdate a check because you do not have enough money in your account on December 1 to cover the check but you are planning to deposit money on December 3. This is an unwise business practice because the deposit on December 3 may not be made as planned.

5. *Avoid making checks payable to Cash or to Bearer.* If such a check is lost, it can be cashed by anyone. For this reason, you should never make a check payable to Cash unless you are going to cash it immediately. Even then, it is usually preferable to make the check out to yourself or to the bank as payee. That is what Alicia did with Check No. 102 in the check register in Figure 22-2 on page 358.

6. *Always fill in the amount.* If you leave it blank, you may be held responsible for amounts filled in by others.

7. *Void checks on which you make errors.* Do not try to erase or retrace your writing. No one who handles your check can be sure whether the

A cashier's check is called that because such checks were originally written by a bank employee known as a *cashier.* Some banks refer to cashier's checks as officer's checks, treasurer's checks, or manager's checks, depending upon who is authorized to sign them.

changes were made by you or by someone who had no right to make them. Individuals usually destroy voided checks; businesses usually file voided checks in case questions are ever asked about the use of a checking account. If you are going to file a check with an error, write *Void* across its face. Whether using a personal or a business checking account, note the check number and write the word *Void* on the stub or in the register to show that the check was not used. For example, Alicia voided Check No. 105.

8. *Record every payment from your checking account, whether the payment is by check or EFT.* Some people carry a few blank checks in their wallets instead of carrying their checkbooks. When one of these checks is used, the drawer should make a note of it and record it in the register as soon as possible. Also promptly record all transactions made at an ATM. Since no check is written, it is easy to forget to record cash machine withdrawals. However, a receipt is given for each transaction. Note the last entry in the register in Figure 22-2 on page 358.

Technological *Perspective*

Your Electronic Wallet in the 21st Century

Remember when most people's wallets bulged with cash, credit cards, blank checks, an ATM card, a driver's license, a medical insurance card, a company identification card, a phone card, and receipts? Technology now makes it possible for you to have all of these items in a single device.

A programmed access card, somewhat like the SMART card discussed in Chapter 12, would make it possible to activate business transactions and store data about financial and personal matters. You would be able to make "cash" purchases as well as buy on credit. You will have with you at all times an account of your driving record, medical insurance coverage, and employment documentation. When you return to your home computer, your card will allow you to display or print a record of your spending during the day.

Your programmed access card would eliminate the need for coins. Newspapers, soft drinks, and other inexpensive items could be bought with a swipe of your card through a computer terminal. Several fast-food restaurants and bus companies already offer this service.

In the future, when you think your wallet might be empty, you won't know for sure until you check your balance at the nearest computer terminal!

Critical Thinking

1 What are the benefits of an electronic wallet?

2 What potential problems are associated with increased use of technology for financial services?

STOPPING PAYMENT ON A CHECK

In certain situations, you may want to instruct your bank not to pay a check that you have written. Suppose Alicia Garcia's Check No. 118 for $52.67 to Joseph Fields was lost. Before she writes a new check, Alicia should ask the bank not to pay the first one. The bank will ask Alicia to fill out a **stop-payment order,** which is a written notice from the drawer telling the bank not to pay a certain check. The stop-payment order requests the following information: date, check number, amount, payee, and the drawer's signature.

Because banks charge a substantial fee for stopping payment on a check, payment of a check should be stopped only for good reason. You may learn, for example, that a check you have written to pay a bill was lost in the mail. Or, a check you have written may be stolen. Before you write a new check, you should stop payment on the one that was lost or stolen. To prevent the wrong person from cashing the check, you should notify the bank immediately.

ACCEPTING AND CASHING CHECKS

Your responsibility as a signer and as an endorser of checks is very important. According to law, a check is payable on demand, that is, at the time the holder of the check presents it for payment at the bank on which it is drawn. However, a bank may refuse to accept a check if it is presented for payment long after the date on which it was written. Some checks carry a printed notation, *Please cash within 60 days.* Therefore, you should present a check for payment within a reasonable time.

A check is valuable only when it is drawn on a bank in which the drawer has money on deposit. For this reason, you should accept checks only when they are written or endorsed by people whom you know and trust or those who provide valid identification. A check received from a stranger who cannot provide acceptable identification may be worthless.

Just as you should be cautious in accepting checks, you should not expect strangers to cash checks for you. If you ask someone who does not know you to cash your check, you will probably have to provide a form of identification. Some banks furnish identification cards that can be used on a business's credit-check terminal to verify electronically that a customer presenting a check has

Electronic traveler's checks are prepaid cash cards that allow a person to obtain a set amount of foreign currency when traveling in another country.

funds on deposit to cover the amount of the check. Checks are so commonly used in place of cash that you will usually have no trouble cashing them where you are known. However, legally, no one has to accept your checks.

Sometimes you may have to make a payment to an organization or person who will not accept a personal check. There is a way to have a bank guarantee that the check will be good. This guarantee makes the check acceptable when it otherwise would not be. Financial institutions provide several types of checks that they guarantee, including certified checks, cashier's checks, and traveler's checks.

Certified Checks

A **certified check** is a personal check for which a bank has guaranteed payment. The certification is stamped on the face of the check and is signed or initialed by a bank officer. Suppose Hazel Canton wants to make a payment to someone who does not know her and who does not want to accept her personal check. Ms. Canton could have her bank certify her check. If she has an account at the bank, she may pay a small fee. If she does not have an account there, the fee may be higher.

When the bank certifies Ms. Canton's check, the amount of the check is immediately subtracted from her account. This makes it impossible for her to withdraw the money for other purposes. If the check is not used, it may be returned to the bank and credited to her account.

Cashier's Checks

A bank usually keeps funds in an account of its own on which it writes its own checks. A **cashier's check** is a check that a bank draws on its own in-house funds. A cashier's check costs the amount of the check plus a service fee. These banker's checks are more acceptable than the personal checks of an individual whom the payee may not know.

Traveler's Checks

Carrying a large sum of money when you travel is risky since it can be lost or stolen easily. In addition, paying traveling expenses with personal checks may be difficult. You will be dealing mostly with strangers, and, as you have learned, strangers may not accept personal checks.

OTHER TYPES OF CHECKS

Most money orders can be written only for amounts up to certain limits. When the amount needed to be sent exceeds this limit, however, a person can buy several money orders.

NET FACTS

Many Internet connections from schools and homes are dial-in connections. With a dial-in connection, the Internet tools and programs are located on a host computer; your desktop computer can only display what the host processes.

Special forms designed for the traveler to use in making payments are called **traveler's checks.** You can buy them at banks, express companies, credit unions, and travel bureaus. They are sold in several denominations, such as $10, $20, $50, and $100. In addition to the value of the checks, there is sometimes a charge of one percent of the value. This means that $100 worth of traveler's checks will cost $101.

Traveler's checks have two places for your signature. When you buy the checks, you sign each one in the presence of the selling agent. When you cash a check or pay for a purchase with it, you sign it again in the presence of the person accepting it. That person checks to see that the two signatures are alike. When you cash the check, you also fill in the date and the name of the payee.

Traveler's checks, especially those widely advertised, are commonly accepted throughout the world. Almost any business is willing to accept a traveler's check because there is little chance of its not being signed by the right person.

When you buy traveler's checks, you should immediately record the serial number of each check on a form that is generally given to you by the issuing agency. When you cash each check, record the place and date you cashed the check on the same form. Keep this record separate from your checks so that you can refer to it if your checks are lost or stolen. Report lost or stolen traveler's

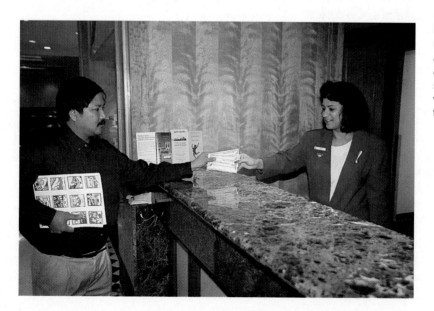

Illus. 22-1

Use traveler's checks to avoid carrying large sums of money when you travel.

checks immediately to the nearest bank or office where such checks are sold. The company that issued them will replace them.

SOURCES OF MONEY ORDERS

A person who does not have a checking account and who wants to send a payment through the mail may purchase a money order. A **money order** is a form of payment that orders the issuing agency to pay the amount printed on the form to another party. When you buy a money order, you pay the issuing agency the amount of the payment you want to make and a service fee.

Money orders are convenient because they can be purchased in many places. They are sold by banks, post offices, express companies, and telegraph offices. Many retail stores, such as supermarkets and drugstores, also sell them.

Illus. 22-2

For a fee, some companies other than banks will issue money orders and cash checks.

Bank Money Orders

Brad George wants to order a word processing computer program. One way he could pay for this purchase is to buy a money order from a bank. A *bank money order* is a form sold by a bank stating that money is to be paid to the person or business named on the form.

In the bank money order shown in Figure 22-4, Brad George is sending $72.50 to the Precision Software Company. He pays the bank $72.50 plus a service charge for the money order.

Figure 22-4

After payment is made, a bank money order is returned to the issuing bank.

Bank checks and money orders can be used for sending payments to other countries. Information about the methods of making payments to businesses or individuals in foreign countries may be obtained from the bank or from the place where the money order is purchased.

Postal Money Orders

Brad may also purchase a money order from the post office. When you buy a *postal money order,* the postal clerk registers by machine the amount in figures and words. You then complete the form by filling in the payee's name, your name and address, and the purpose of the money order.

You can send a postal money order safely through the mail because it can be cashed only after it is signed by the payee. If a money order is lost or stolen, the receipt copy that you receive may be used in making a claim with the post office. The payee may cash the postal money order at a post office or a bank or may transfer it to another person by filling in the information requested on the back of the money order.

Express Money Orders

An *express money order* is another payment method for Brad to use to pay for his software. Express money orders are sold by offices of the American Express Company, Traveler's Express Company, Federal Express Services Corporation, some travel agencies, and many retail stores, such as supermarkets, pharmacies, and convenience stores.

Telegraphic Money Orders

A television commercial told the story about a young bride and groom who were on a limited budget and driving an old car that had broken down. The couple called the bride's parents for help. "Please send the money soon, Mom," the bride pleaded tearfully, "or there won't be a honeymoon." In the next scene, the happy couple was pictured a short time later reaching across the counter at the telegraph office where the cash from home was counted out to them.

When buying a *telegraphic money order,* you buy a message directing a telegraph office to pay a sum of money to a certain person or business. Although his purchase of software is not urgent, Brad George could use a telegraphic money order. Telegraphic money orders are used mainly in an emergency when money must be delivered quickly.

EFT transactions at an automatic teller machine require using a private code number. This code number is commonly called a personal identification number (PIN).

ELECTRONIC FUNDS TRANSFER

As you learned in Chapter 20, electronic funds transfer (EFT) makes it possible to move funds by computer, for example at an ATM. EFT provides fast and inexpensive service.

Individuals can instruct their banks to pay automatically such monthly bills as utility and telephone charges. For example, some depositors have instructed their bank to make monthly utility payments automatically for them. Each month the utility company sends to the bank the bills for those depositors. The bank subtracts the amounts due from the accounts of the appropriate depositors. The amounts from the customers' accounts are added to the utility company's account.

Your employer can also pay your salary through EFT. *Direct deposit* has eliminated payroll checks for many companies. The bank subtracts the total amount of the payroll from the business's account and adds the amount earned to each employee's account, even if the employees' accounts are in several different banks. The computer is programmed to transfer electronically the amount of the salary to the appropriate bank for each employee.

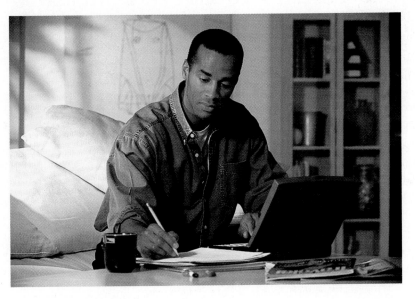

Illus. 22-3

From your home computer, you can transfer funds electronically and check your account balances.

Key Ideas

1 Proper check writing includes filling in the check register or check stub; writing checks in numerical order; and writing the date, payee, amounts, purpose, and proper signature on the check.

2 Good check writing tips include using check forms provided by the bank, writing in ink, not overdrawing, using the current date, not making checks payable to Cash or to Bearer, always filling in the amount, voiding checks with errors, and recording every payment.

3 A stop-payment order is a written notice from the drawer telling the bank not to pay a certain check.

4 Only accept checks written or endorsed by people whom you know and trust or those who provide valid identification.

5 Three special types of checks that may be used for payments are certified checks, cashier's checks, and traveler's checks.

6 The four main sources of money orders are banks, post offices, express companies, and telegraph offices.

7 Electronic funds transfer (EFT) makes it possible to move funds by computer through an ATM, automatic bill payment, and direct deposit.

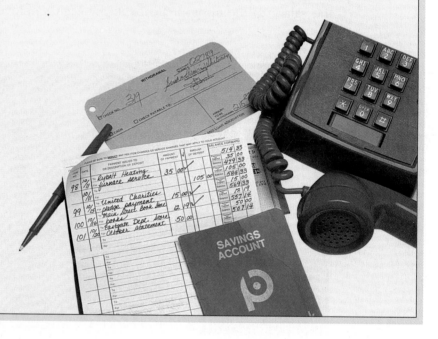

End of Chapter Activities

Increasing Your Business Vocabulary

The following terms should become part of your business vocabulary. For each numbered item, find the term that has the same meaning.

cashier's check 8

certified check 10

drawee 6

drawer 1

forgery 2

money order 11

overdrawing 9

payee 5

postdated check 4

stop-payment order 7

traveler's check 3

1 The owner of the account and the person who signs the check.

2 The crime of writing another person's signature on a check without his or her authority.

3 A form designed for the traveler to use in making payments.

4 A check dated later than the date on which it is written.

5 The person to whom the check is written.

6 The bank or other financial institution in which the account is held.

7 The form instructing a bank not to pay a certain check.

8 A check that a bank draws on its own in-house funds.

9 Writing a check for more money than is in one's account.

10 A personal check for which a bank has guaranteed payment.

11 A form of payment that orders the issuing agency to pay the amount printed on the form to another party.

Reviewing Your Reading

1 Who are the three parties involved with a check? Where are their names shown on the face of a check?

2 Why should the check stub or register be filled in before the check is written?

3 Name the seven steps in writing a check and tell how each part of the check should be written.

4 What risk is involved in making a check payable to cash or to bearer? What can you do to avoid the risk?

5 Under what conditions might you stop payment on a check?

6 Why should you present a check for payment within a reasonable time?

7 What is the difference between a certified check and a cashier's check?

8 Why are traveler's checks better for the traveler to carry than personal checks or cash?

9 What are the four sources of money orders?

10 Give an example of an electronic funds transfer.

Using Your Business Knowledge

1 Matt Huffman believes that it is a waste of time to record information on check stubs. "The bank sends me a statement each month; that's all I need," he says. How could you convince Matt that he should keep records?

2 Cher Alonso often makes deposits and withdrawals at the ATM that she passes on her way to work. However, she frequently forgets to record these banking activities in her check register and never seems to know how much money she has in the bank. Also, she has overdrawn her account twice and has had to pay a fee each time. Can you suggest a plan for Cher to follow that would allow her to use the automatic teller services and still be sure of having an accurate record?

3 Harvey Graham owed Leonard Saunders $58. He wrote a check to Mr. Saunders and mailed it to him. Later, Mr. Graham decided that he did not want to pay all of the debt at once. Therefore, he asked his bank to stop payment on the check. Do you think it was wise for Mr. Graham to make this request? Why?

4 The NaturFresh Supermarket requires its checkers to follow four rules when accepting checks: (1) Get two forms of identification (ID) from the customer. (2) Hand the check and the IDs to the manager for approval. (3) Stamp the check with the store's rubber endorsement stamp. (4) Place the check under the cash tray in the register drawer.

a. Why do you think the store requires two IDs?

b. Why do you think the check must be approved by the manager?

c. What kind of endorsement would most likely be on the rubber stamp?

d. What are the advantages of stamping the check immediately after accepting it?

e. Why do you think checks are placed under the cash tray instead of with the cash?

5 While on a vacation trip, the Mendoza family found in an antique shop an old jukebox made in the 1930s and in good working order. The family decided that it would be a good addition to the family recreation room. The jukebox cost $500 and the dealer would not accept a personal check or credit cards. What method could be used to pay for the jukebox?

Calculating Business Problems

1 Kathy Whiteside opened a checking account on June 1 and deposited $122.47, the amount of her first paycheck from her summer job as a day-camp counselor. During the month, she deposited three more paychecks of the same amount.

a. What was the total of Kathy's deposits?

b. During June, Kathy wrote four checks for the following amounts: $37.50, $25.00, $7.35, and $4.20. What was the total amount paid out in checks?

c. What was Kathy's balance at the end of June?

---

2 Michaela Jarrett bought traveler's checks from her credit union to pay for her family's vacation. She must pay a fee of 1 percent of the value of the checks. The denominations she chose were $400 in $50 checks and $200 in $20 checks.

a. How many $50 checks did she receive? How many $20 checks did she receive?

b. How much was the credit union's charge for the checks?

c. What was the total cost of Mrs. Jarrett's checks?

---

3 Julio Costa's ability to repair bicycles has developed into an after-school business. He can get parts more cheaply by ordering them from wholesale houses in several cities. He pays for his parts by postal money order. During the last three months, he made payments as shown in the table at right.

a. What was the cost of each postal money order? List the payments in a column and write the fee beside each.

b. What were the total fees for Julio's postal money orders for the three months?

Honda Cycle House	Harley Wheels, Inc.
$12.72	$81.04
$17.96	$ 9.16
$29.80	$47.08
	$20.00

The post office fee schedule is as follows:

Amount of Order	Fee
$0.01 to $ 35.00	$0.75
$35.01 to $700.00	$1.00

c. What was the total cost of the bicycle parts Julio ordered, including the cost of the money orders?

4 On August 10, Grace Whiteside of Seattle suddenly remembered that it was the twenty-first birthday of her twin grandsons, Tom and Terry of Athens, Georgia. She had forgotten to send to each grandson her usual gift of $1 per year of age. To get her gift to them on time, she decided to send a telegraphic money order for the total amount, addressed to both young men, and have it delivered to their home. She included this message: "Happy Birthday, Tom and Terry. My love and a dollar per year." The fee schedule is shown in the table at right.

a. How much money was sent as a combined gift?

Base Fee for Office Delivery:

Amount	Fee
$0—$50	$12
$50—$100	$14

Additional Fee for Home Delivery: $10.00

Message:
$2 minimum for 10 words
20 cents per word over minimum

b. What was the fee for the delivered money order, not including the message?

c. What was the charge for the message?

d. What was the total cost of Mrs. Whiteside's gift to Tom and Terry?

Applying Technology

Using the *Introduction to Business* template and your spreadsheet program software, select problem CH22. After the problem appears on your screen, complete the following activities. Then, after you have completed each step, display or print the completed spreadsheet for each activity. If you do not have a printer available, answer the questions before you leave the computer.

1 Format the date column to show the month and the date. Format the Withdrawal, Deposit, and Balance columns to show two decimal places with no dollar signs. Go to the cell beneath the Beginning Balance in the Balance column. Enter a formula to calculate the new balance no matter whether a withdrawal or a deposit is entered in the row. What is the formula you used to calculate the balance?

2 Enter the transactions shown in the table at right. Use the current year for dates. What is the balance as of November 27?

Date	Transaction
11/03	Check No. 456 to Farley's Auto Service for $56.90
11/05	Check No. 457 to Brown Community College Bookstore for $78.00
11/11	Check No. 458 to the Uptown Department Store for $45.30
11/13	Deposit of $340.60
11/16	Check No. 459 to Round Lake Community Charities for $30.00
11/22	ATM cash withdrawal of $100.00
11/24	Deposit of $150.00
11/27	Check No. 460 to Georgetown Credit Union for $250.00 deposit to savings account

3 Your bank pays interest on checking accounts on the last day of each month. On the row below the last transaction, enter November 30 in the Date column and Interest in the For column. In the Deposit column enter a formula to calculate 3 percent interest on the average of the beginning balance and the ending balance before interest. Update the balance and format as necessary. What is the balance as of November 30?

Hint: Refer to Appendix C: Determining Percentage and Interest in Business.

Making Decisions

Over the past few months, the Edfield family needed to make a variety of payments. These included:

a. the phone bill

b. monthly mortgage payments

c. rush items ordered from an out-of-state mail-order house that demands payment with each order

d. $300 sent by the fastest method when Mr. Edfield had an automobile accident 300 miles from home

e. monthly deposit into a savings account

1 What factors should the Edfields consider when selecting a method of payment?

2 For each of the situations, what payment method would you recommend for the Edfields?

Chapter Twenty-Three

Managing Your Checking Account and Other Financial Services

Key Terms

clearing

clearinghouse

bank statement

canceled checks

bank reconciliation

outstanding checks

Objectives

After studying this chapter and completing the end-of-chapter activities, you will be able to:

1 Explain how checks clear the banking system.

2 Describe the information on a bank statement.

3 Reconcile a checking account.

4 Discuss factors to consider when selecting a financial institution.

"**W**ow! According to the balance shown on this ATM receipt, I still have $456 in my checking account!" exclaimed Betsy. "How is that possible?"

"Has every check you have written cleared?" asked Jerry.

"What do you mean *cleared*?" questioned Betsy. "That's a term I'm not familiar with."

Jerry responded, "Every time you write a check, it takes a few days before it is presented to your bank for payment. Your balance won't be updated until all your checks have been returned to your bank."

"You mean someone has to walk into my bank with the check to obtain cash?" asked Betsy.

"Well, not exactly," responded Jerry. "Banks have an electronic transfer system that allows the amounts of checks to be added to and subtracted from the appropriate checking accounts."

"That sounds complicated," sighed Betsy.

"It's not that bad," Jerry commented. "It's better than having every person going to every bank from which she or he has a check."

PROCESSING YOUR CHECKS

Checks travel around the country and around the world in wallets, handbags, envelopes, mail pouches, planes, trucks, and on trains. They go in and out of houses, businesses, government offices, and banks of all shapes and sizes. They are written on, typed on, stamped on, and imprinted with oddly shaped characters in magnetic ink. Eventually, they find their way, still in good shape, back to the bank of the drawer. At this point, the checks are available to the depositor as proof of payment.

Returning checks to their original drawers may seem an impossible task. However, it happens through a carefully planned system. Eventually every check is returned to the drawer's bank to be paid and charged to his or her checking account. This process is called **clearing.** Clearing may be done within one bank, through a clearinghouse, or through the Federal Reserve System.

Local Check Clearing

Check clearing may involve one, two, or several banks and drawers within the same city. If both the drawer and the payee have accounts in the same bank, clearing is simple. The bank subtracts the amount from the drawer's account and adds that amount to the payee's account. A simple accounting transaction occurs.

When two different banks are involved, clearing is somewhat different. However, it is still fairly simple if the two banks are in the same area. Suppose Jon Gable's music group believes its new song will be a big hit. The group wants to get more practice time and get the song recorded. Jon persuades his father to rent a garage on the outskirts of town for

Millions of checks clear through the banking system every business day.

rehearsals. The rent for one month is $50. Mr. Gable sends the rental check, written on his account with the North River National Bank, to Arlene-Bayne Realty. Look at Figure 23-1 and follow the check as it travels to the two banks in the town where the Gables live and back to Mr. Gable.

Arlene-Bayne Realty endorses the check and deposits it in its account in the First Federal Trust Company. When First Federal receives the check, it adds $50 to the account of Arlene-Bayne Realty, endorses the check, and sends it to North River National for payment. After North River National receives the check, it pays First Federal $50 and subtracts that amount from Mr. Gable's account. The check is then marked paid by North River National and returned to Mr. Gable as his record of payment.

The Clearinghouse

In large cities with many banks, it would not be practical for each bank to send checks for payment to all banks on which the

Figure 23-1

Follow Mr. Gable's check through the clearing process.

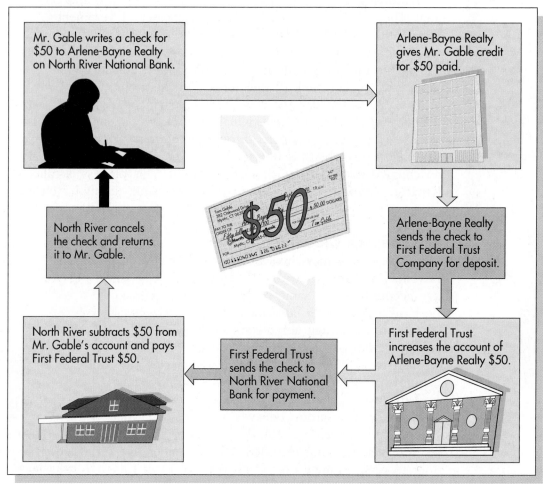

checks were written. Banks in the same area may be members of an association that operates a place to clear their checks every day. This place is called a **clearinghouse.**

The method for clearing checks through a clearinghouse is similar to the method discussed in the previous section. However, clearinghouses handle thousands of checks for many banks. In Figure 23-2, you see a simplified accounting entry showing the net

Figure 23-2

An accounting record of a net settlement may look like this.

Source: Federal Reserve Bank of New York.

balance settlement for three banks through the clearinghouse fund. Note that the function of the clearinghouse is simply to redistribute the amounts. The $2,200 received by the clearinghouse was balanced by the $2,200 paid out, with no net change in the clearinghouse fund.

An *automated clearinghouse (ACH)* transfers funds among banks using electronic payment entries. Through the ACH connection, funds can be easily transferred between accounts in different banks.

Federal Reserve Check Clearing

One of the services of the Federal Reserve System is clearing checks between banks in different cities. This process is more complex than clearing through a clearinghouse because of the volume of checks that must be cleared.

Illus. 23-1

The transfer of funds between financial institutions is highly automated.

Just as banks use a clearinghouse and their district Federal Reserve Bank for settlement of net balances, the Federal Reserve uses the Interdistrict Settlement Fund in Washington, D.C., to settle net amounts due among banks in the 12 districts. The Interdistrict Settlement Fund can be viewed as the Federal Reserve clearinghouse. Settlements are made through ACHs and electronic funds transfers.

Other financial institutions—such as credit unions, savings and loan associations, and brokerage firms—also handle checks. These firms usually have an account with a large bank, which they use in the same way as any other customer uses an account.

Your bank subtracts all of your cleared checks from your account balance. The cleared checks will either be filed at the bank or sent back to you with a report of your account.

YOUR BANK STATEMENT

As a depositor, you will need to review the record of your account that the bank keeps. At regular intervals, usually monthly, the bank will send you a report on the status of your account known as a **bank statement.**

Bank Statement Information

While bank statement formats vary, most present the following information:

- The balance at the beginning of the month

- The deposits made during the month

- The checks paid by the bank during the month

- Any automated teller transactions made during the month

- Any electronic fund transfers (EFT) or special payments the bank has made

- Service charges for the month, including charges for such special services as stopping payment on a check

- Any interest earned on the account

- The balance at the end of the month

See if you can locate examples of these items on the bank statement shown in Figure 23-3 on the next page.

Examining Returned Checks

For some checking accounts, banks return paid checks to depositors. For other checking accounts, banks do not return paid checks. When a bank does return paid checks, it will return with the bank statement any checks that have been paid during the month. Before the bank sends you your checks, it cancels each one, usually using a machine that stamps a cancellation number on the front or back of the check. The paid checks are called **canceled checks.**

Be sure to save your canceled checks; they are valuable records. Your check stub or register is your own record, but the canceled check is evidence that payment was actually received. Since the payee must endorse a check before it can be cashed, the endorsement proves that the payee received the check.

Suppose your bank does not return checks to depositors, and you need a certain check to prove that a payment was made. Banks that do not return checks often send a more detailed statement than banks that return checks. In most cases, information

Cultural Notes

The Chinese do not use the Gregorian calendar, but instead have their own calendar. In the Chinese calendar, years are in cycles of 60 and mini-cycles of 12 years. Each 12-year mini-cycle is named for an animal. The list starts with the rat, ox, tiger, hare, dragon, snake, horse, sheep, monkey, rooster, dog, and pig.

FYI

The Federal Reserve Bank of San Francisco created the first automated clearing-house (ACH) in 1972.

Figure 23-3

Alicia Garcia's bank statement showing transactions completed during April.

Second National Bank

Checking Account Statement

ACCT. 1648-7214
DATE 5/1/- -
PAGE 1

Alicia Garcia
19684 Absaroka Drive
Houston, TX 77083-5549

Please examine at once. If no errors are reported within 10 days, account will be considered correct.

BALANCE FORWARD	NO. OF WITH- DRAWALS	TOTAL AMOUNT	NO. OF DEP.	TOTAL DEPOSIT AMOUNT	SERVICE CHARGE	BALANCE THIS STATEMENT
0 : 00	14	433 : 89	4	826 : 95	3 : 00	390 : 06

CHECKS AND OTHER DEBITS			DEPOSITS AND OTHER CREDITS	DATE	BALANCE
			331.85	4/10	331.85
101	39.95			4/13	291.90
102	50.00			4/15	241.90
			50.00	4/16	291.90
103	32.97			4/22	258.93
104	.87			4/22	258.06
	50.00	ATW		4/23	208.06
106*	16.30			4/24	191.76
107	25.78			4/24	165.98
			175.00	4/24	340.98
109*	65.33			4/26	275.65
110	33.46			4/27	242.19
111	24.33			4/27	217.86
112	5.80			4/27	212.06
113	12.85			4/27	199.21
			270.10 AD	4/29	469.31
114	4.25			4/30	465.06
	72.00	AP TexPower		4/30	393.06
	3.00	SC		4/30	390.06

KEY TO SYMBOLS

AD-	AUTOMATIC DEPOSIT	PC-	PAID OVERDRAFT CHARGE
AP-	AUTOMATIC PAYMENT	PR-	PAYROLL DEPOSIT
ATD-	AUTOMATIC TELLER DEPOSIT	RC-	RETURN CHECK CHARGE
ATW-	AUTOMATIC TELLER WITHDRAWAL	RT-	RETURN ITEM
CC-	CERTIFIED CHECK	SC-	SERVICE CHARGE
EC-	ERROR CORRECTED	ST-	SAVINGS TRANSFER
OD-	OVERDRAFT	TC-	TRANSFER CHARGE

*Where this asterisk is shown, a preceding check is still outstanding or has been included on a previous statement.

on the statement will be sufficient to prove payment. However, if the check showing the endorsement is needed, a copy of it can be obtained. Banks keep a photographic record of all checks paid. Your check will be located in this record and a copy will be sent to you. There will probably be a small charge for this service.

THE RECONCILIATION PROCESS

You have learned about keeping a record of your account on check stubs or in a check register. The bank statement gives you a copy of the bank's record of your account. The balances on the two records may differ. Bringing the balances into agreement is known as reconciling the bank balance. The statement showing how the two balances were brought into agreement is called the **bank reconciliation.** Forms for reconciling are often printed on the backs of bank statements.

Finding Differences

The balances shown on your records and the bank statement may be different for several reasons. Here are the most common reasons:

- Some of the checks that you wrote and subtracted from the balance in your record may not have been presented to the bank for payment before the bank statement was made. These checks, therefore, have not been deducted from the bank-statement balance. Such checks are known as **outstanding checks.**

- You may have forgotten to record a transaction in your register. This is especially true if you use an ATM or have other EFT transactions. Failure to record these is a frequent cause of errors.

- A service charge that you have not recorded may be shown on the bank statement.

- You may have mailed a deposit to the bank that had not been received and recorded when the statement was made.

- If you have an interest-bearing account, you may not have added the interest shown on your statement to your record of your balance.

- You may have recorded the amount of a check incorrectly on your check stub or in the check register. Or, you may have added or subtracted incorrectly.

Calculating the Adjusted Balance

Let's see how a bank reconciliation is made. On May 4, Alicia Garcia received the bank statement shown in Figure 23-3 on page 380. The statement balance is $390.06. Alicia's checkbook balance is $416.56. She examined her canceled checks and found that checks numbered 108, 115, and 116 were missing. Check No. 105 had been voided. The others are outstanding. She listed these on the reconciliation form with the amounts for each and recorded the total. Her bank reconciliation is shown in Figure 23-4.

A *credit* transaction to your checking account refers to deposits and other increases in the balance such as interest earned. A *debit* transaction occurs when a check clears or a fee, such as for printing checks, is charged to your account.

Figure 23-4

A bank reconciliation helps you bring your records and the bank's records of your account into agreement.

YOU CAN EASILY
BALANCE YOUR CHECKBOOK
BY FOLLOWING THIS PROCEDURE

FILL IN BELOW AMOUNTS FROM YOUR CHECKBOOK AND BANK STATEMENT

BALANCE SHOWN ON
BANK STATEMENT $ 390.06

BALANCE SHOWN ON
YOUR CHECKBOOK $ 416.56

ADD DEPOSITS
NOT ON STATEMENT $ _____

TOTAL $ 390.06

ADD ANY DEPOSITS NOT
ALREADY ENTERED IN
CHECKBOOK $ _____

SUBTRACT CHECKS ISSUED
BUT NOT ON STATEMENT

108	$ 10.00
115	21.00
116	17.50

TOTAL $ 416.56

SUBTRACT SERVICE
CHARGES AND OTHER
BANK CHARGES NOT IN
CHECKBOOK
$ 3.00
Tex Power 72.00

| TOTAL | $ 48.50 | | TOTAL | $ 75.00 |
| BALANCE | $ 341.56 | | BALANCE | $ 341.56 |

THESE TOTALS REPRESENT THE CORRECT AMOUNT OF MONEY YOU HAVE IN THE
BANK AND SHOULD AGREE. DIFFERENCES, IF ANY, SHOULD BE REPORTED TO THE BANK
WITHIN TEN DAYS AFTER THE RECEIPT OF YOUR STATEMENT.

By using the reconciliation form, Alicia proved the accuracy of the bank statement and her record by

1. subtracting the total of the outstanding checks she had listed on the form from the bank statement balance; and

2. subtracting the service charge and the automatic payment of her electric bill from her checkbook balance.

In some cases, other additions or subtractions might have to be made in the reconciliation. For example, a charge made for stopping payment on a check should be subtracted from the checkbook balance. A deposit made late in the month might not appear on the bank statement and should be added to the balance on the bank statement. Interest earned should be added to the checkbook balance.

If the balances do not agree, either you or your bank has made an error. In that case, you should compare your canceled checks with those listed on the bank statement and with those recorded in your check register. Be sure that you have recorded all EFT transactions. Then carefully go over the calculations on your check stubs or in your check register. If you do not find an error in your calculations, contact your bank right away.

After you have reconciled your bank statement, correct any errors that you made on your register. The new balance now agrees with the bank statement. With your account updated, you can write checks on the new balance.

NET FACTS

Hypertext is an information retrieval system in which certain key words or pictures are linked to information in the same or a different document. Clicking on a hypertext word or picture instructs your Browser to find and load the information selected.

Legal *Perspective*

Who's at Risk for a Lost or Stolen Check?

Roberto Hernandez lost his checkbook while shopping. When he notified his bank, an official advised that Roberto stop payment on all outstanding checks and close the account. A stop-payment order for each of Roberto's ten outstanding checks would cost $20. The total cost of ten stop-payment orders would be $200. Roberto decided, therefore, to keep the account open.

While this action sounds risky, it may be appropriate.

The ten legitimate outstanding checks would clear as usual. If any checks were forged by someone who found the checkbook, the bank should not accept them as valid. The bank has the legal responsibility to spot a phony signature; a depositor is not liable to pay for checks with unauthorized signatures. Of course, banks don't check every check processed for forged signatures. But if you receive a canceled check with a forged signature, you should notify the bank. The bank must accept responsibility for accepting a forged check, which is also true of any business or individual who accepts checks.

A stop-payment order makes more sense when the goods or services purchased with the check are unsatisfactory. By stopping payment, a customer can negotiate to exchange the product or have the job done right.

Critical Thinking

1 *What actions should a person take when a checkbook is lost?*

2 *What are examples of situations when a stop-payment order is appropriate?*

SELECTING A FINANCIAL INSTITUTION

Using a checking account and other financial services is a consumer purchase decision. To obtain the best value for your financial services dollar, comparison shop based on services offered, safety, convenience, fees and charges, and restrictions.

Services Offered

As financial institutions offer more and more financial services, decisions become very confusing. To work through this marketplace maze, select the checking account with the lowest costs. Locate the best interest rate on your savings. Find the lowest interest rate for loans. Do not be attracted just by fancy financial product names or flashy services that you might never need or use.

Safety

As previously mentioned, most banks and financial institutions have federal deposit insurance. However, do not assume that this is the case at every financial institution. Make sure that the institution where you keep your savings is insured.

Convenience

Do you want 24-hour banking services? Do you want branch offices near your home or work? These are some of the factors you will need to consider as you decide about convenience. However, there is always a trade-off. More convenience will usually mean higher costs.

When the difference between the bank statement balance and your checkbook is divisible by 9, this error may be caused by a transposition of numbers. You might have entered $45.00 instead of $54.00, or you may have added $678.00 when you should have added $687.00.

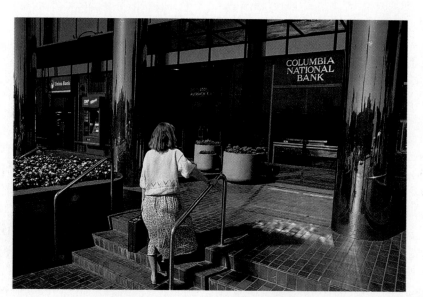

Illus. 23-2

Comparison shop among financial institutions to get the best value.

Fees and Charges

Financial services have costs. Compare your needs with the price you pay. Remember, seemingly low fees for using an ATM or having a checking account can possibly add up to hundreds of dollars within a few years.

Restrictions

Your costs are not always measured in money amounts. If you must keep $500 on deposit for a "free" checking account, you may be losing the opportunity to earn interest on those funds at another institution. Or if you must keep money on deposit for two years to earn a higher rate, you are restricted from using those funds for some unplanned purpose. Always balance your needs with the conditions imposed upon you. When you are not satisfied, shop around!

Key Ideas

1 Checks clear the banking system when financial institutions exchange funds based on the amounts of checks written and deposited by customers.

2 Information on a bank statement includes the beginning balance, deposits made during the month, checks paid by the bank during the month, ATM transactions, EFTs or special payments, service charges, any interest earned, and the balance at the end of the month.

3 Reconciling a checking account involves finding the differences between the balance on the bank statement and the balance in your checkbook.

4 To obtain the best value for your financial services dollar, investigate and compare services offered, safety, convenience, fees and charges, and restrictions.

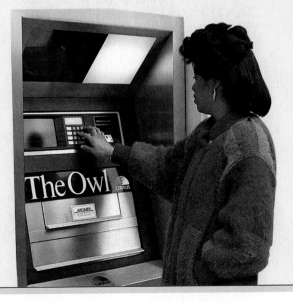

End of Chapter Activities

Increasing Your Business Vocabulary

The following terms should become part of your business vocabulary. For each numbered item, find the term that has the same meaning.

bank reconciliation 5

bank statement 6

canceled checks 2

clearing 4

clearinghouse 1

outstanding checks 3

1 A place where member banks exchange checks to clear them.

2 Checks that have been paid by the bank.

3 Checks that have not been deducted from the bank-statement balance.

4 Returning a check to the drawer's bank to be paid and charged to his or her checking account.

5 A statement showing how the checkbook balance and the bank statement were brought into agreement.

6 A report sent by the bank to a depositor showing the status of his or her account.

Reviewing Your Reading

1 How are checks cleared in the same bank?

2 What is a clearinghouse?

3 Explain the role of the Federal Reserve System in clearing checks.

4 What information is commonly included on a bank statement?

5 How does a depositor know that his or her checks have been paid?

6 Explain how you can prove that a certain payment was made if your bank keeps and files your checks instead of returning them to you.

7 For what six reasons might your bank statement and your checkbook balance differ?

8 What are the main steps taken when you reconcile a bank statement?

9 How would you record a service charge on your check stub or in your check register?

10 When comparing financial institutions, what factors should be considered?

Using Your Business Knowledge

1 Helen and Jim Hogan were talking about whether or not to save their canceled checks from their joint account. Jim says, "Throw them out; I hate a cluttered house." Helen reminds him, "Remember what happened last year when you tried to use your check register to prove you paid the furniture bill? I think we should save the canceled checks." Do you agree with Helen or Jim? Why?

2 What are the benefits and drawbacks of a bank not returning a depositor's canceled checks?

3 Isaac Ahlred has received his bank statement for the month of May. The bank statement shows a balance of $401.19, but his check register shows a balance of only $364.52.

a. What is the most likely reason that the bank balance is larger than Isaac's?

b. What steps should Isaac take to bring his balances into agreement?

4 Many people use the same bank for all of their financial services. Is this a wise consumer practice? Why or why not?

Calculating Business Problems

1 When the four banks in the town of Butler prepared to clear checks one day, they found that they had paid checks drawn on the other banks as shown in the following table.

Assuming that each bank makes an individual settlement with every other bank, calculate the amount that each bank will either pay or receive from every other bank. For example, First National holds $938.57 worth of checks drawn on Farmers' Trust. Farmers' Trust holds $443.74 worth of checks drawn on First National. Therefore, First National will receive from Farmers' Trust a settlement of $938.57 − $443.74 = $494.83.

| | Drawn On | | | |
Checks Held By	First National	Farmers' Trust	Merchants' Mutual	Butler Bank
First National	——	$938.57	$644.63	$1,158.64
Farmers' Trust	$443.74	——	$711.44	$ 208.45
Merchants' Mutual	$304.36	$522.82	——	$ 639.28
Butler Bank	$988.95	$326.31	$783.30	——

2 Olivia Cardona operates Spectacular Candles, a gift shop at the TriCity Mall. Her bank balance on June 1 was $471.04. During the Area Festival Week of June 1, she made the following deposits: $57.10, $101.96, $231.00, $198.04, $172.00, $298.30. During that week, Olivia wrote the following checks: to herself for salary, $225.00; to TriCity Mall for stall rental, $390.00; to Wrapping Classics, Inc., for wrapping supplies and bags, $154.80; and to TriCity Herald for an ad, $75.00. If her account falls below $500.00 on any day of the month, she pays a $10.00 service charge to her bank.

a. What balance should her check register show at the end of the week?

b. Should Olivia's June bank statement show a service charge based on her checking account activities for the first week? If so, how much?

3 When Gizella Ott began to reconcile her bank statement, she discovered that four checks she had written had not been paid by the bank. The amounts of the checks were $24.50, $7.28, $20.00, and $46.72.

a. What is the total amount of unpaid checks?

b. In order to reconcile the statement, should Gizella subtract the total outstanding checks from the bank statement balance or from her checking account balance?

4 In October, Tom Jones received his bank statement that showed a balance of $378.65. The service charge was $3.00. In examining his statement, he found that the following checks were outstanding:

No. 31, $7.16; No. 34, $15.10; and No. 35, $9.95. His checkbook balance at the end of the month was $349.44. Reconcile his bank statement.

Applying Technology

Using the *Introduction to Business* template and your spreadsheet program software, select problem CH23. After the problem appears on your screen, complete the following activities. Then, after you have completed each step, display or print the completed spreadsheet for each activity. If you do not have a printer available, answer the questions before you leave the computer.

1 Enter formulas to complete the Bank Statement Balance section of the bank reconciliation. What is the total of outstanding checks?

2 Enter formulas to complete the Checkbook Balance section of the bank reconciliation. What is the Adjusted Checkbook Balance?

3 What formula did you enter to calculate the Adjusted Checkbook Balance?

Making Decisions

Jess Thomas cannot get his bank statement and checkbook balanced this month. He keeps ending up with 10 cents more in his adjusted checkbook balance than in his adjusted bank statement balance. Jess called Dave Rogers, a customer service representative in the accounting department of Jess's bank. In his frustration, Jess told Dave that the bank must have made an error and demanded that Dave double-check Jess's bank statement. Dave answered that because the bank uses computers, it is impossible for the bank statements to contain errors. Dave said that Jess must have made the mistake and should do the double-checking himself. Jess decided that he had do something about the situation.

1 What options does Jess have to reconcile his checking account?

2 How can Jess get better service from his bank?

The financial industry offers a variety of career opportunities. Most financial workers are employed in commercial banks. Others work in specialized banks, savings and loan associations, credit unions, and finance companies.

Job Titles

Job titles commonly found in this career area include:

- Bank Branch Manager
- Cashier
- Commercial Teller
- Computer Operator
- Credit Union Manager
- Data-entry Clerk
- Economist
- Financial Manager
- Investment Analyst
- Loan Officer
- New Accounts Clerk
- Systems Analyst
- Trust Officer
- Word Processing Specialist

Employment Outlook (through 2005)

- The number of bank tellers, which in the past made up a large portion of bank employees, is expected to increase more slowly than the average for all occupations because of the increased use of automatic teller machines (ATMs) and other electronic equipment.
- As banks and other financial institutions expand into new services, new career opportunities will be created in fields such as investment counseling, estate planning, real estate, and insurance.

Education and Training

- Most beginning jobs in banking require at least a high-school education.
- Many entry-level employees also have had additional business preparation in community or technical colleges.
- Officers, professional personnel, and executives usually have college degrees.
- Bank workers who meet the public must be able to communicate well, be accurate, and have a professional-looking appearance.
- Most bank workers must be able to handle details and to work well under stress.
- A knowledge of computers is vital.

Salary Levels (in recent years)

- The salary of a banking chief financial officer in recent years ranged from $48,000 to $76,000.
- Average earnings of head bank tellers ranged from $14,000 to $20,000.

Critical Thinking

1 What factors have affected the changing career opportunities in the banking industry?

2 What employment skills are important for success in banking and financial services jobs?

FocusOnCareers

Banking and Financial Services

Unit Seven

Credit in Our Economy

Would you be surprised if someone told you that she or he could easily check a database to find out where you live, where you work, where you bank, and what problems you have experienced with credit (including bankruptcy)? How is this information about you so readily available to so many people? The answer lies with computer databases and electronic networks. Businesses and governments are constantly collecting, storing, sharing, and distributing data.

Can you think of the many ways that information about you becomes part of a record in some database? Most of the information in databases comes from information given voluntarily. For instance, you offer information when you fill out a credit application, apply for a telephone, register for a college class, apply for a driver's license, answer questions in a telephone survey, apply for insurance, go to court, and answer U.S. Census Bureau questions.

Privacy is a basic right to have information about you kept confidential. If you are concerned about your right to privacy, you have the same concern as four out of five consumers who responded to a recent public opinion poll. There are certain kinds of information about each of us that we may want to share only with family members and/or with close friends.

Among the databases of significance are the more than 400 million credit files in our country. Another large database is the Medical Information Bureau (MIB) that is used by over 800 insurance companies in the United States. More than 15 million U.S. consumers have medical conditions and their health records are recorded by the MIB.

While there is some reason to be concerned about these databases and personal privacy, there is no need for panic. Decisions about the granting of credit or the issuance of insurance policies are usually made based on accurate, up-to-date information. The information gathered is used for legitimate business reasons.

Nevertheless, some effort is being made to review federal privacy laws, such as the Privacy Act of 1974. Issues being considered include deciding what is private information and whether consumers should be asked to give permission before any credit or medical reports are released to others.

Critical Thinking

1 What dangers do you see in having private information so easily accessible to others?

2 What do you think should be done to help protect your privacy?

Databases and Personal Privacy

Chapter Twenty-Four

Key Terms

credit

debtor

creditor

trust

loan credit

sales credit

trade credit

credit references

character

capacity

capital

credit rating

The Fundamentals of Credit

Objectives

After studying this chapter and completing the end-of-chapter activities, you will be able to:

1 Explain what credit is.

2 Give examples of how credit is used by consumers, businesses, and governments.

3 State the difference between loan credit, sales credit, and trade credit.

4 Explain the basis on which credit is granted, including the three Cs of credit.

5 Give several advantages of using credit.

6 State at least four ways in which credit can be misused.

Although Polonius in Shakespeare's *Hamlet* cautioned, "Neither a borrower nor a lender be," using and providing credit have become a way of life in our economy. Credit is used extensively by consumers, businesses, and governments. For example:

- Adrianna buys gas for her car and uses her oil company credit card.
- Chi-luan applies for and receives a government loan to help with his college expenses.
- New Treads, Inc., receives a $2 million loan to build a new tire store in a downtown area.
- The state of Louisiana borrows $35 million through a bond issue to construct new college buildings.
- Hiawatha County borrows $250,000 to make emergency road repairs.
- Hedgpeth Industries borrows $50,000 to finance the purchase of additional inventory.

What do these people, businesses, and governmental institutions have in common? They all have wants, but lack the money to satisfy those wants. All of them borrow money to satisfy those wants. If they borrow, they will be receiving credit. Credit includes all borrowing other than financing to purchase a home.

Without credit, retail stores could not have a vast array of merchandise for sale if the merchandise had to be paid for before it was sold. Governments could not finance the building of roads and highways without borrowing money to get the projects underway. Many consumers could not purchase new cars, furniture, or appliances without receiving a loan. The amount involved may be large or small, but being able to borrow money or buy on credit at a time of need is an important aspect of our economic system.

WHAT CREDIT IS

Credit is the privilege of using someone else's money for a period of time. That privilege is based on the belief that the person receiving credit will honor a promise to repay the amount owed at a future date. The credit transaction creates a debtor and a creditor. Anyone who buys on credit or receives a loan is known as a **debtor.** The one who sells on credit or makes a loan is called the **creditor.**

Although the credit system uses forms and legal documents, it also depends on trust between the debtor and creditor. **Trust** means that the creditor believes that the debtor will honor the promise to pay later for goods and services that have been received and used. Without that trust, our credit system could not operate.

When you borrow a large amount of money or buy on credit from a business, you usually will be asked to sign a written agreement. The agreement states that you will pay your debt within a certain period of time. For example, Chi-luan had to agree

any consumers plan to use credit as a substitute for cash and pay the balance in full at the end of the month—but only 20 percent do so consistently.

to pay his tuition loan in full within two years after graduation. When Adrianna used her credit card to buy gas and signed the receipt, she agreed to pay for her purchase when the bill came at the end of the month. A credit agreement means that the debtor promises to pay and the creditor trusts that the debtor will pay the amount that is owed.

TYPES OF CREDIT

If you borrow money to be used for some special purpose, you are using **loan credit.** Loans are available from several kinds of financial institutions. Banks, credit unions, savings and loan associations, and consumer finance companies are the primary businesses that make consumer loans. Loan credit usually involves a written contract. The debtor often agrees to repay the loan in specified amounts, called installments, over a period of time. You will learn more about installment and other types of loans in Chapter 25.

If you charge a purchase at the time you buy the good or service, you are using **sales credit.** Sales credit is offered by most retail and wholesale businesses. Sales credit involves the use of charge accounts and credit cards by consumers.

Trade credit is used by a business when it receives goods from a wholesaler and pays for them at a later specified date. Trade credit terms often are stated "2/10, n/30." This means that the business can take a 2 percent discount if the bill is paid within 10 days from the billing date; the full or net amount must be paid within 30 days.

USERS OF CREDIT

If you are a typical American consumer, you will use credit for many purposes. You may use credit to buy fairly expensive products that will last for a long time, such as a car, house, or major appliance. Or you may use credit for convenience in making smaller purchases, such as meals and CDs. Paying for medical care, vacations, taxes, and even paying off other debts are other common uses of credit.

Businesses may secure long-term loans to buy land and equipment and to construct buildings. They may also borrow money for shorter time periods, sometimes for only one or two days but usually for 30 to 90 days, to meet temporary needs for cash. For example, merchants buy goods on credit, and manufacturers buy raw materials and supplies on credit. Businesses borrow on a short-term basis to get the cash they need while waiting for goods to be sold or for customers to pay for their purchases.

Local, state, and federal governments often use credit in providing goods and services for the benefit of the public. Governments may use credit to buy items such as cars, aircraft, and police uniforms. They may also borrow the money that is needed to build hospitals, highways, parks, and airports.

GRANTING OF CREDIT

You have already read that trust between the debtor and the creditor is essential if credit is to be granted. To become a debtor, you must be able to prove that you are a good credit risk. Not everyone who desires credit will receive it.

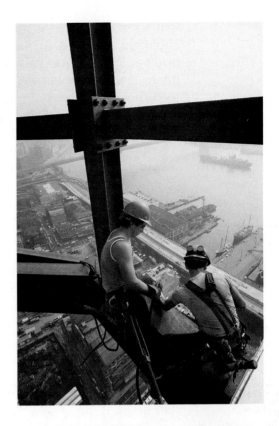

Illus. 24-1
Through credit, businesses secure long-term loans for construction of new office buildings.

Credit Information

The business that is considering you as a credit risk will generally ask you about your financial situation and request credit references. **Credit references** are businesses or individuals from whom you have received credit in the past and/or who can help verify your credit record. The answers to the financial questions and the information received from your credit references will help the business decide whether loan or sales credit should be extended to you.

You should be willing to give all required information readily and honestly. The following questions can be asked: How much do you earn? How long have you worked for your present employer? What property do you own? Do you have any other debts? Important decisions cannot be made without reliable answers to these questions.

The Three Cs of Credit

In deciding whether or not to grant you credit, businesses consider three factors, known as the three Cs—character, capacity, and capital.

Character refers to your honesty and willingness to pay a debt when it is due. If you have a reputa-

uying on credit is viewed by people in Germany and the Netherlands as living beyond one's means. *Schuld,* the German word for debt, means guilt.

tion for paying bills on time, you will meet an important condition for being considered a good credit risk. How you will pay your bills in the future usually can be predicted by how you have paid them in the past.

Capacity refers to your ability to pay a debt when it is due. The lender or seller must consider whether your income is large enough to permit you to pay your bills. If your income is too small or unsteady, granting you additional credit may not be wise even though you have had a good credit record in the past. On the other hand, your income may be very high; but if you already have many debts, you may not be able to handle additional debt.

Capital is the value of the borrower's possessions. Capital includes the money you possess and the property you own. For example, you may have a car that is paid for and a house on

In a recent year, it was reported that Wisconsin consumers led the nation in paying their bills on time—they also received the greatest number of unsolicited offers per capita for credit cards.

Ethical *Perspective*

Credit Repair Companies

Unfair and deceitful credit practices have been used by borrowers and lenders alike. Some borrowers are untruthful about their ability to repay. They borrow recklessly, and then sometimes search desperately for a solution to a credit problem. Others have no intention of ever paying back the money.

For example, Jamie kept falling farther behind on her credit card payments. Creditors kept asking for money. Jamie hated to open her mail. Some of her creditors said they would have to take her to court. She needed help. Her credit record was being ruined. She even thought about leaving town to avoid paying her debts.

One day she noticed an advertisement: "Credit Repair—Are you in trouble with past-due payments? Is your credit record being ruined? We can fix all problems quickly—come in today." That was what she needed—help, quick!

After paying the credit repair company some up-front money, Jamie soon discovered that her problem was not corrected. She, along with many others, was being misled. The company did nothing to help Jamie repair her credit record. Instead, the company used the money paid by Jamie and others to set up a similar fraudulent operation in another state.

Critical Thinking

1 *Why did the credit repair advertisement appeal to Jamie?*

2 *What are some things that you think Jamie should do to resolve her credit problem?*

which a large amount has been paid. You may also have a checking account and some savings that add to your capital, or you may have nothing except your present income. The value of your capital helps give the lender some assurance that you will be able to meet your credit obligations.

BENEFITS OF CREDIT

Both businesses and consumers benefit from the use of credit. Businesses benefit in several ways. By being allowed to buy on credit, customers will tend to purchase more, and the business will increase its profits. If the business buys its merchandise using trade credit, the merchandise can be paid for after it has been sold to customers.

As a consumer, you also can benefit from the wise use of credit. Here are some ways in which consumers benefit from their use of credit.

- *Convenience.* Credit can make it convenient for you to buy. You can shop without carrying much cash with you. There may be times when you do not have enough cash and have an urgent need for something. For example, if your car needs emergency repairs, you may have to wait until payday unless you can have the work done on credit.

- *Immediate possession.* Credit allows you to have immediate possession of the item that you want. A family can buy a dishwasher on credit and begin using it immediately rather than waiting until enough money has been saved to pay cash for it.

Illus. 24-2

Credit is a convenient way to make purchases.

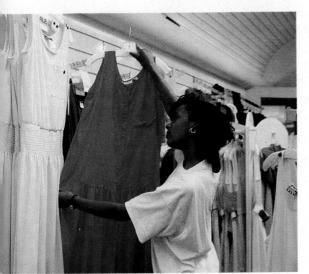

- *Savings.* Credit allows you to buy an item when it goes on sale, possibly at a much lower price. Some stores, especially department and furniture stores, often send notices of special sales to their credit customers several days before they are advertised to the general public. Therefore, credit customers have first choice of the merchandise and may obtain good bargains.

- *Credit rating.* If you buy on credit and pay your bills when they are due, you gain a reputation for being dependable. In that way, you establish a favorable **credit rating.** A credit rating is valuable during an emergency when you must borrow money or when you want to make a major purchase. It is also valuable in obtaining credit if you move to another community.

- *Useful in an emergency.* Access to credit can help you in an emergency. Having an oil company credit card, for example, can come in handy if you run out of gas and cash at the same time. Or, in a more serious situation, suppose you are working your way through college and suddenly lose your job. You may be able to get a loan to tide you over until you find another job.

PRECAUTIONS FOR USE OF CREDIT

Buying on credit is convenient and can be beneficial. However, there are some disadvantages if you are not careful in your use of credit. Some problems you as a consumer can encounter with unwise use of credit include the following:

- *Overbuying.* Overbuying is one of the most common hazards of using credit. There are several ways in which this happens. You may purchase something that is more expensive than you can afford. It is easy to say, "Charge it," for a suit that costs $390 when you would purchase a less expensive one if you had paid cash. Attractive store displays and advertisements attract us and invite us to make purchases. As a credit customer, you may be tempted to buy items that you do not really need.

- *Careless buying.* Careless buying may result if you become lazy in your shopping. You may stop checking advertisements carefully. You may fail to make comparisons, causing you to buy at the wrong time or the wrong place. Smart buyers know that at certain times of the year, the prices of some goods decrease. Credit can tempt you not to wait for a better price on an item you want.

- *Higher prices.* Higher prices may be paid. Stores that sell only for cash are able to sell at lower prices than stores that offer credit. Extending credit is expensive. It requires good accounting to keep accurate records

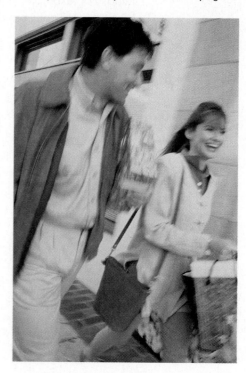

Illus. 24-3

Be cautious in your use of credit to avoid overbuying.

of each charge sale and each payment. When customers do not pay as agreed, there are collection expenses. Increased costs are passed on to customers in the form of higher prices. The cost of credit will be discussed in greater detail in Chapter 26.

- *Overuse of credit.* Overuse of credit can result in too much being owed. Buying now and paying later may sound like a good idea; but if too many payments are to be made later, the total amount that must be paid can become a problem. Consumers must keep records of the total amount owed to creditors so that they do not have monthly payments that exceed their ability to pay.

Credit card issuers lure consumers with more than 25,000 different kinds of special offers, including varying interest rates, fees, frequent-flyer miles, and merchandise discounts.

Businesses and governments, too, can get into trouble with the overuse of credit. Too much borrowing can lead to bankruptcy if the organization is not managed properly. Too many debts place a damaging strain on the finances of businesses and governments. Using credit wisely is important for consumers, businesses, and governments.

QUESTIONS TO ASK

Before making a final decision whether to buy on credit, there are some questions you as a consumer should answer: How am I benefiting from this use of credit? Is this the best buy I can make or should I shop around some more? What will be the total cost of my purchase, including the cost of charging the item? What would I save if I paid cash? Will the payments be too high considering my income? Answers to these questions will help you make wise credit decisions.

Key Ideas

1 Credit is the privilege of using someone else's money with the obligation to repay it at a future time.

2 Consumers use credit to buy cars, clothing, and furniture; businesses use credit to finance new equipment, expand facilities, and to take care of temporary cash needs; governments borrow money to build roads and schools.

3 You can borrow money from a financial institution—loan credit; you can charge a good or service at the time of purchase—sales credit; and a business can receive goods now and pay for them later—trade credit.

4 A business considers a person's character (honesty and willingness to pay debts), capacity (the ability to pay debts), and capital (the value of the person's possessions) in reviewing an applicant for credit.

5 Credit used wisely makes some buying more convenient, gives the purchaser immediate possession rather than waiting until later, allows buyers to take advantage of special sales, and establishes a person's credit rating.

6 Credit is misused if it results in overbuying, careless buying, paying higher prices in stores that grant credit, or incurring excessive debt.

End of Chapter Activities

Increasing Your Business Vocabulary

The following terms should become part of your business vocabulary. For each numbered item, find the term that has the same meaning.

capacity

capital

character

credit

creditor

credit rating

credit reference

debtor

loan credit

sales credit

trade credit

trust

1 A customer's honesty and willingness to pay a debt when it is due.

2 Credit offered at the time of sale.

3 A customer's ability to pay a debt when it is due.

4 A person's reputation for paying debts on time.

5 One who buys on credit or receives a loan.

6 Borrowing money to be used later for some special purpose.

7 The privilege of using someone else's money for a period of time.

8 A business receives goods from a wholesaler and pays for them later at a specified date.

9 Businesses or individuals from whom you have received credit in the past and/or who can help verify your credit record.

10 The value of the borrower's possessions.

11 The creditor's belief that the debtor will honor the promise to pay later for goods and services that have already been received and used.

12 One who sells on credit or makes a loan.

Reviewing Your Reading

1 Our credit system is based in part on trust. Who does the trusting, the debtor or the creditor? What does this party trust?

2 As a debtor, what are you promising to do?

3 Name several sources of loans.

4 What are some typical uses of credit by consumers? by businesses? by governments?

5 What does the term "2/10, n/30" mean? With what kind of credit is it used?

6 What kinds of information do creditors need before extending credit?

7 What are the three Cs of credit? Why is each one important?

8 What are some ways in which the use of credit is important to a business?

9 What are four advantages of buying on credit for consumers?

10 Name four problems that can be caused by the unwise use of credit.

11 What are some questions you should ask yourself when considering whether to use credit?

Using Your Business Knowledge

1 Why is trust so important in a credit transaction? Why is it necessary to have a written agreement to repay a loan?

2 Some people think it is a good idea to buy a few things on credit, even when they can pay cash. Why might this be a good idea?

3 Edward Adiska buys everything he possibly can on credit. If he does not have enough money to cover his monthly payments when they are due, he borrows money to pay them. His sister, Debbie, likes to buy things only after she has saved enough money to pay cash for them.

a. Whose plan do you think is better? Why?

b. What suggestions about the use of credit might you make to Edward and Debbie?

4 Gerry Shadle owns and operates a flower shop. She is considering expanding her shop to include home decorating items. At present, Gerry sells for cash only. How might extending credit help or hurt this business?

5 Here are some statements that people have made about credit. Read each statement and tell whether you agree or disagree and why.

a. "I should buy as many things as I can on credit because credit increases sales and helps business."

b. "If things were sold for cash only,

in the long run, prices would be lower and everyone would be better off."

c. "Buy on credit at least occasionally; make your payments on time; and keep a good credit rating, which will be valuable in an emergency."

d. "Credit should be used only in making expensive purchases, such as houses and cars, and never for everyday purchases, such as food and clothing."

Calculating Business Problems

1 The table at right shows the amounts of consumer credit reported in the United States for the years 1988-1994.

Year	Consumer Credit (In Billions of Dollars)
1988	$663
1990	738
1992	741
1994	790

a. What was the increase in consumer credit, in billions of dollars, from 1988 to 1990? from 1990 to 1992? from 1992 to 1994?

b. What was the average increase per year, in billions of dollars, for the six-year period from 1988 to 1994?

c. If consumer credit continues to increase at the 1988-1992 annual rate of increase, what will be the total amount of consumer credit (in billions of dollars) in the year 2002?

2 Last year O'Leary's Cycle Shop sold 2,200 ten-speed bicycles. The average sale price was $145, including tax. Seven out of every ten customers bought their bikes using O'Leary's credit plan.

a. What was the amount of the total sales of ten-speed bicycles?

b. What was the amount of total credit sales of ten-speed bicycles?

3 The Capital Area Transit System borrowed $1,800,000 to buy six new buses to expand its service to the suburbs. It is estimated that each bus will earn about $6,500 per month. It will cost approximately $1,500 per month for fuel, operating costs, and repairs on each bus. How many months will it take to pay for the six buses?

4 Amy Markson would like to be an airline pilot someday. Right now, she wants to learn to fly and get a private license. Her parents have agreed to pay half the cost of the lessons if Amy pays the other half. Amy checked with Superior Air Service and came up with the estimated costs shown in the table.

a. How much will it cost Amy to learn to fly and to get her license?

b. If Amy borrows her share of the cost from her grandparents, how

Fees and materials for ground instruction:	$480
24 hours of in-flight instruction:	$50 per hour
20 hours of solo flight time:	$32 per hour
Third-class student's license:	$80

much will she borrow?

c. If Amy repays her non-interest-bearing loan in 50 equal weekly payments, how much will each weekly payment be? If she repays $75 each month, how many months will it take to repay the amount she borrowed?

Applying Technology

Using the *Introduction to Business* template and your spreadsheet program software, select problem CH24. After the problem appears on your screen, complete the following activities. Then, after you have completed each step, display or print the completed spreadsheet. If you do not have a printer available, answer the questions before you leave the computer.

One decision-making tool used by some creditors is a credit-scoring spreadsheet. Information about an applicant for credit is entered into the spreadsheet. The spreadsheet assigns a point value to each piece of information. In this example, an applicant must have a point total of 65 or above to qualify as an acceptable credit risk. Enter information about the following credit applicants. Use a lowercase x in the column beneath the name to answer each question. The first line has been completed as an example. If you make a mistake, enter a blank space in place of the x you want to delete.

1 Enter a function to calculate the total credit score for each applicant. Enter an @IF function to answer the Application Acceptable question with a yes or no. Place the @IF function below each total.

2 Tony Kintampo has a telephone in his own name; rents a small room in a boarding house; has a checking but no savings account; has a store credit card; has a small finance company loan outstanding; is 19 years old; and has been on his present job for 14 months. Answer the following questions.

a. What is Tony's total credit score?
b. Is Tony's application acceptable?

3 Estela Sanchez does not have a telephone in her own name; shares rental of an apartment with three friends; has checking and savings accounts; has a bank credit card; has no finance company loans outstanding; is 27 years old; and has been on her present job for four years. Answer the following questions.

a. What is Estela's total credit score?
b. Is Estela's application acceptable?

Making Decisions

Ichiro Komuro is a fairly successful shop owner. He sells his merchandise at a fair price on a cash basis, provides good service, and does some newspaper advertising. For the past five years, he has made a small profit that has provided a decent living for him and his family.

Lately his business has fallen off. Other shop owners have begun to accept credit purchases. He does not want to extend credit to his customers. His small profit on sales will not permit the additional cost of handling credit transactions. However, he also knows that he must remain competitive to remain in business.

1 What is Ichiro's basic problem?

2 What would you advise Ichiro to do, and why?

Chapter Twenty-Five

The Uses of Credit

Objectives

After studying this chapter and completing the end-of-chapter activities, you will be able to:

1 Describe three types of charge accounts: regular, budget, and revolving.

2 Explain how a teenager may obtain his or her own charge account.

3 Describe the process by which bank credit card transactions are handled.

4 List common types of credit cards.

5 Explain how installment credit sales differ from credit card sales.

6 Describe two kinds of loans available to consumers.

7 List questions that should be answered before signing an installment sales contract.

redit can be helpful and harmful for consumers. Consumer credit provides the funds for the purchase of cars, furniture, travel, and many other goods and services that mark a high standard of living. However, at times, otherwise responsible individuals get into financial trouble by using too much credit.

When a salesperson asks: "Will this be cash or credit?" the customer frequently has several options. The customer might use a credit card that the store accepts; or if the purchase is expensive, he or she might sign an installment sales contract.

There are other ways to get credit. One consumer talked with a loan officer at a bank to get a loan for a new car. Another consumer applied for a loan to remodel his home. A common source of credit for consumers is through a bank or other financial institution.

You can see that there are a number of ways to obtain and use credit. When it is your turn to decide, you will make a better decision in terms of using credit when you have an understanding of the different kinds of credit available to you. Let's begin by first considering charge accounts.

TYPES OF CHARGE ACCOUNTS

Charging purchases and services is usually accomplished with a charge account. A charge account represents a contract between the firm offering it and the customer. Three types of charge accounts generally are available for your use. You may have a regular, budget, or revolving account.

Regular Accounts

A **regular account** is one in which the seller or provider expects payment in full within a specified period of time—usually 25 to 30 days after the billing date. The seller may set a limit on the total amount that may be charged during that time. Customers can purchase goods or services up to a fixed dollar limit at any time.

Regular accounts generally are used for everyday needs and small purchases. Regular account credit is commonly granted by those engaged in providing a service—doctors, dentists, plumbers, etc.

Budget Accounts

Some merchants and public utilities offer budget charge accounts. A **budget account** requires that payments of a certain fixed amount be made over several months. One budget plan offered by businesses is the 90-day, three-payment plan. Under this plan, you pay for your purchase in 90 days, usually in three equal monthly payments.

In a budget plan offered by many utility companies, an estimate is made of how much you will be

n a recent year, there were over 1 billion credit cards held by U.S. consumers; it is estimated that the number will be over 1.3 billion by 2005.

Cultural Notes

Cultural diversity in the United States has played an important role in the development of business enterprises. For example, in recent years soccer, which has long been popular in other parts of the world, has become a popular sport in the United States. The popularity of soccer here has created business opportunities. Soccer has created a need for producers and sellers of soccer equipment.

charged for gas or electricity during a certain period of time, such as a year. You then agree to pay a certain amount each month to cover those purchases. For example, you may be permitted to pay a certain amount of money each month to cover the cost of energy used for heating. This plan avoids large payments during winter months. However, you pay the same amount during warm months when heating is not required.

Revolving Accounts

The revolving account is the most popular form of credit. With a **revolving account,** purchases can be charged at any time but only part of the debt must be paid each month. It is similar to a regular account but has some added features. There is usually a maximum amount that may be owed at one time. A payment is required once a month, but the total amount owed need not be paid at one time. A finance charge is added, however, if the total amount owed is not paid. The **finance charge** is the additional amount you must pay for using credit, including interest and other costs such as credit insurance. Finance charges will be discussed in detail in Chapter 26.

Revolving charge accounts are convenient, but they can tempt you to overspend. The finance charges on unpaid balances are usually quite high, often 1½ percent per month (18 percent per year) or higher. However, there is generally no finance charge if

Illus. 25-1
A revolving charge account is the most popular form of credit.

payments are made within a specified period of time, such as within 25 days.

Some consumers prefer the revolving charge account because it permits the customer to buy products or services when the price is right, yet pay for it over a period of time. There is no pressure to pay the full amount at one time. In addition, further purchases can be made without adding unduly to the amount that must be repaid each month.

The average U.S. consumer has nine credit cards, including retail, oil company, travel and entertainment (T & E), and bank cards.

TEENAGE CHARGE ACCOUNTS

Under contract law, minors cannot be held liable for their personal debts. Therefore, businesses are not willing to open charge accounts in a teenager's name if he or she is a minor. There are special circumstances, however, under which a special charge account may be opened in a teenager's name.

Charge accounts for teenagers have a limit on the amount that can be charged, and the limit is usually lower than the amount set on charge accounts for adults. Generally a parent or guardian must agree to pay any balance due if the teenager does not. Sometimes the parent or guardian also must have a charge account with the business granting the credit.

Charge accounts for teenagers are usually regular or revolving. The accounts give teenagers a privilege and a freedom in buying that they otherwise would not have. If a teenager has an income of his or her own, the charge account can be the first step toward proving an ability to manage money wisely. It also is an opportunity to show that he or she is a good credit risk and can use credit wisely.

CREDIT CARD USAGE

Charging purchases and services is usually accomplished with credit cards. Credit cards are seemingly magical pieces of plastic that entitle owners to credit at stores, gas stations, and other businesses far and near. They have become very popular, and their use continues to increase. Most credit cards issued today are multipurpose cards—such as VISA, American Express, Discover, Bravo, Carte Blanche, and MasterCard—that can be used at thousands of stores, hotels, airlines, and other businesses.

In a recent year, it was reported that 62 percent of the families in the United States used one or more credit cards. Fifty-four percent used retail store credit cards and 40 percent used bank credit

Credit transaction slips for one day from around the world, if gathered in a central processing place, would make a pile higher than the tallest building in New York City.

cards. Most financial institutions issuing credit cards are affiliated with VISA International or the Interbank Card Association, which issues MasterCard.

Travelers especially like credit cards because they do not have to carry much cash with them. Many of the cards are accepted at businesses in all parts of the world. Businesses that accept credit cards often find that their sales increase because more customers are attracted if credit cards can be used.

Bank Cards

Bank credit cards have become very popular throughout the world. MasterCard and VISA are two of the best known. There usually is an annual fee that must be paid for the privilege of using these cards. Users of bank cards frequently end up paying a monthly finance charge.

Bank charge cards are issued to people whose credit ratings meet the bank's standards. A bank charge card, in effect, indicates that the credit rating of the cardholder is good. Agreements are made between banks and various merchants to accept the charge cards.

When you use your bank charge card, a credit sales slip that requires your signature is made out. The merchant collects all credit sales slips prepared during the day and sends them to the bank. The bank totals all of the sales slips received from a business.

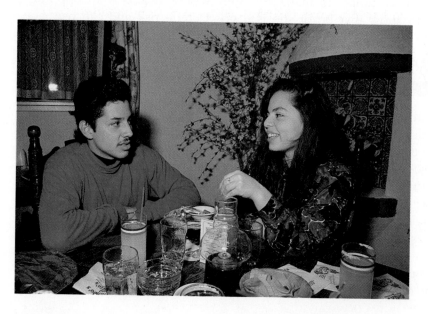

Illus. 25-2
Credit cards are commonly used in restaurants and hotels all over the world.

The businesses are paid for the sales amount minus a service fee. This fee is usually about 4 to 6 percent. At the 4 percent rate, a retail store would receive $960 from sales totaling $1,000 ($1,000 × .04 = $40). This fee covers the bank's expenses of processing the sales slips and collecting amounts owed from customers. The bank is doing the work that the businesses' own credit departments would have to do otherwise.

Business owners like bank credit cards for several reasons. For one thing, the bank decides if a customer is a good credit risk. The bank also assumes most of the trouble and expense of granting credit. Businesses receive their money, minus the service fee, immediately.

Customers like bank charge cards because they are accepted by so many businesses throughout the country. Bank charge-card users also like the fact that they receive only one monthly bill rather than many bills from the various businesses where they charge purchases.

In a recent year, there were 83 million oil company credit card holders who owed $3.4 billion on those cards.

Travel and Entertainment Cards

Carte Blanche, Diners Club, and American Express are widely used travel and entertainment (T & E) cards. Subscribers pay a yearly membership fee that is higher than the annual fee charged for bank cards. Cardholders are not given a spending limit and, for the most part, are expected to pay the balances due in full each month. T & E cards are used mainly to buy services such as lodging in hotels and motels, meals, airline tickets, and tickets for entertainment. Business travelers like to use them because the detailed records they receive from the card issuers are useful for business and tax record-keeping purposes. They offer proof of expenses incurred when traveling and entertaining customers.

In a recent year, U.S. consumers owed over $790 billion in installment credit; revolving charge accounts totaled over $281 billion.

Oil Company Cards

Major oil companies, such as Texaco, Chevron, and Shell, issue their own credit cards. However, many oil companies have found that it costs them too much to offer credit. Therefore, some have issued cards affiliated with VISA or MasterCard which are referred to as *co-branded* revolving charge accounts.

Retail Store Cards

Many retail stores offer their own credit cards to customers. These cards carry the names of the stores that issue them. These cards can be used only at the stores that issued them and are often referred to as single-purpose cards.

Having a retail store credit card is a convenience for the consumer. The store also knows that the consumer is more likely to shop there if he or she has one of its credit cards. Some stores have special sales that are advertised just to their credit card holders.

INSTALLMENT SALES CREDIT

For some types of purchases, especially those that are quite expensive and will last for long periods of time, installment sales credit often is used. **Installment sales credit** is a contract issued by the seller that requires periodic payments to be made at times specified in the agreement. Finance charges are added to the cost of the items purchased, and the total amount to be paid is shown in the agreement. Furniture and household appliances often are purchased using installment sales credit.

Using installment sales credit differs from using credit cards. Instead of just handing your credit card to a salesperson, you must fill out a credit application at the time of the purchase and receive

Cultural Perspective

Israelites and Usury Laws

The ancient tribes of Israel, which occupied the Land of Canaan as early as 1300 B.C., had many laws. Some of the laws dealt with money and credit.

The Israelites could lend money to members of their tribes who were in need, but they were not allowed to charge any interest on those loans. Every seven years all debts owed by Israelite tribesmen were cancelled so that there would be no credit hardship cases.

The Israelites could charge interest on loans to foreigners, but the interest rates had to be reasonable and not usurious—that is, excessive. One of their sacred songs reminded them that "he who lends money without usury" will do well.

In our economy today, most states have usury laws. Consumers need to know about usury laws of the various states. The amounts that may be charged as interest on loans or finance charges on credit sales transactions vary from 10 to 24 percent per year. Some states have removed previously established ceilings, allowing rates to be influenced by economic conditions.

Critical Thinking

1 Do you think that not charging interest on money loaned to family members is practical and fair?

2 Why is it necessary for states to pass usury laws?

credit approval. There are some special features of installment sales credit with which you should be familiar. Under an installment credit plan you will:

- Sign a written agreement (a sales contract) that shows the terms of the purchase, such as payment periods and finance charges.

- Receive and own the goods at the time of purchase. However, the seller has the right to repossess them (take them back) if payments are not made according to the agreement.

- Make a **down payment,** which is a payment of part of the purchase price; it is usually made at the time of the purchase.

- Pay a finance charge on the amount owed, because this amount is actually loaned to you by the seller.

- Make regular payments at stated times, usually weekly or monthly. For example, if a total of $120 is to be repaid in 12 monthly installments, $10 is paid each month. In some cases, a penalty is charged if a payment is received after the due date. In others, all remaining payments may become due at once if only one payment is missed.

CONSUMER LOANS

A loan is an alternative to charge-account buying or installment sales credit. There are several kinds of consumer loans available. The terms of the loans and the requirements for securing the loans differ.

One type of loan is called an installment loan. An **installment loan** is one in which you agree to make monthly payments in specific amounts over a period of time. The payments are called installments. The total amount you repay includes the amount you borrowed plus the finance charge on your loan.

Another kind of loan is called a single-payment loan. With a **single-payment loan,** you do not pay anything until the end of the loan period, possibly 60 or 90 days. At that time, you repay the full amount you borrowed plus the finance charge.

A lender needs some assurance that each loan will be repaid. If you are a good credit risk, you may be able to sign a promissory note. A **promissory note** is a written promise to repay based on a debtor's excellent credit rating. The amount borrowed, usually with some interest, is due on a certain date. The names given to the different parts of a promissory note are shown in Figure 25-1.

PRINCIPAL – the amount that is promised to be paid; the face of the note.

TIME – the days or months from the date of the note until it should be paid.

DATE OF MATURITY – the date on which the note is due.

DATE – the date on which a note is issued.

PAYEE – the one to whom the note is payable.

INTEREST RATE – the rate paid for the use of the money.

$ _950 00_   *Miami, Florida July 8* 19 _ _

Four months   AFTER DATE *I* PROMISE TO PAY TO

THE ORDER OF _Ann Biederman_

Nine hundred fifty   00/100   DOLLARS

PAYABLE AT _Community Bank, N.A._

VALUE RECEIVED WITH INTEREST AT _10_ %

NO. _147_ DUE _November 8, 19--_   *Melissa O'Neil*

MAKER – the one who promises to make payment.

Figure 25-1
A promissory note is one type of loan.

In some cases, you may be asked to offer some kind of property you own, such as a car, a house, or jewelry, as security. Property that is used as security is called **collateral.** You give the lender the right to sell this property to get back the amount of the loan in the event you do not repay it. This is called a **secured loan.**

If you do not have a credit rating established or property to offer as security, you may be able to get a relative or friend who has property or a good credit rating to also sign your note and become the legal cosigner. The **cosigner** of a note is responsible for payment of the note if you do not pay as promised.

CREDIT CONTRACTS

Credit is important in many ways. It is a privilege that millions of consumers and businesses enjoy. No matter what kind of credit is involved, legal responsibilities are created for both parties.

"KWYS" are four letters to keep in mind when signing any legal form; the letters stand for "know what you're signing." This applies to all credit contracts.

The installment sales contract is one of the most important forms you may sign. Before signing one, answer the following questions:

- How much are the finance charges? The total financing cost must be clearly shown in your contract.

Illus. 25-3
Make sure to read and understand an agreement before you sign it.

- Does the contract include the cost of services you may need, such as repairs to a television or a washing machine? If there is a separate repair contract, is its cost included in your contract? Will you be billed for anything separately?

- Does the contract have an add-on feature so that you can later buy other items and have them added to the balance that you owe?

- If you pay the contract in full before its ending date, how much of the finance charge will you get back?

- If you pay the contract within 60 or 90 days, will there be any finance charge or will it be as if you had paid cash?

- Is the contract you are asked to sign completely filled in? (Do not sign if there are any blanks. It is proper and businesslike to draw a line through any blank space before you sign the contract.)

- Under what conditions can the seller repossess the merchandise if you do not pay on time? *Repossess* refers to the right of the seller to take back merchandise in partial or full settlement of the debt.

Key Ideas

1 A regular charge account has the payment due at the end of each specified period of time; a budget charge account spreads payments over a period of time; a revolving charge account has a minimum amount that must be paid each month.

2 Teenagers may get a charge account in their own names if their parents or guardians sign for them or if the account has a low limit on the amount that can be charged.

3 When you use a bank charge card, a credit sales slip that requires your signature is issued. The merchant collects all credit slips prepared during the day and sends them to the bank. The bank charges your account for your purchases and bills you once a month for all the purchases you make.

4 Charge cards are issued primarily by banks and retail stores. Cards are also issued by companies that specialize in the credit card business.

5 An installment credit sale has a fixed amount of money that must be paid each month on the item purchased. Credit cards are issued by companies that bill you for the amount of purchases made during a billing period, such as a month.

6 Consumers can get installment loans or single-payment loans. An installment loan involves monthly payments over a period of time. With a single-payment loan, the amount borrowed is not repaid until the end of the loan period.

7 Before signing an installment contract there are important questions to be asked, such as what are the finance charges, is there an add-on feature, and will there be a refund of part of the finance charge if the loan is paid off early?

End of Chapter Activities

Increasing Your Business Vocabulary

The following terms should become part of your business vocabulary. For each numbered item, find the term that has the same meaning.

budget account

collateral

cosigner

down payment

finance charge

installment loan

installment sales credit

promissory note

regular account

revolving account

secured loan

single-payment loan

1 A credit contract issued by the seller that requires periodic payments to be made at times specified in the agreement with finance charges added to the cost of the purchase.

2 A type of loan in which you do not pay anything until the end of the loan period, possibly 60 or 90 days.

3 A type of loan in which the lender has the right to sell property used as collateral to get back the amount of the loan in the event the loan is not repaid.

4 A credit plan in which the seller expects payment in full at the end of a specified period, usually a month.

5 A credit plan that allows purchases to be charged at any time but requires that at least part of the debt be paid each month.

6 A type of loan in which you agree to make monthly payments in specific amounts over a period of time.

7 A credit plan requiring that payments of a certain fixed amount be made over several months.

8 Someone who becomes responsible for payment of a note if you do not pay as promised.

9 A payment of part of the purchase price that is made as part of a credit agreement.

10 A written promise to repay based on the debtor's excellent credit rating.

11 Property that is offered as security for some loan agreements.

12 The additional amount you must pay for using credit.

Reviewing Your Reading

1 What are three common forms of consumer credit?

2 What does it mean to have a regular charge account?

3 How does a budget charge account help a consumer with his or her budgeting? Give an example.

4 List two dangers of using revolving charge accounts.

5 What is the advantage of having a teenage charge account?

6 What percentage of families in the United States use one or more credit cards?

7 Describe briefly how bank credit cards work.

8 What is the difference between a bank credit card, a retail store credit card, and a T & E card?

9 What special features do installment sales credit contracts normally contain?

10 How do installment loans and single-payment loans differ?

11 What kind of person can get a loan based on a promissory note?

12 What is the difference between a promissory note and a secured loan?

13 What does a cosigner agree to when signing a loan agreement?

14 What questions should be answered before signing a loan agreement?

Using Your Business Knowledge

1 Not everyone believes in using credit. The following are statements that people who are for and against using credit might make. Read each one and then explain why you agree or disagree with each statement.

  a. "A bank card is nice to have. If I'm out of cash, I can still buy what I want."

  b. "I don't believe in using credit for most purchases. I pay cash for everyday items and use credit only for expensive items such as a new refrigerator, new carpeting, or a new car."

  c. "If I can't pay cash, I know that I can't afford it. I won't buy anything unless I can pay cash."

  d. "I often don't pay the full amount of my charge account when it is due; the finance charges are quite reasonable."

2 Many businesses would rather take credit cards than accept personal checks. Why do you think businesspeople feel this way?

3 Sue Ellen Ripley owns a sporting goods store and is considering joining a bank charge-card plan. Answer the following questions for her.

  a. What advantages would there be for her business if she did join?

  b. What will it cost her for the services the bank will provide?

  c. In what ways are the services the bank provides important?

4 Mark and Donna were discussing charge accounts. Mark said, "I don't like our utility company's budget plan—I have to pay more than I should during the warm months so they have my money to use and they don't pay me any interest." Donna gave several arguments in favor of the budget payment plan. If you were Donna, how would you describe the features of a budget payment plan that might convince Mark the plan is a good one for most customers?

5 Jamie has a good part-time job and is a responsible person who takes good care of her possessions. Jamie wants to buy a VCR, but has not saved enough money to cover the cost. When she asked the salesperson if the store would extend credit, Jamie was told, "No, you are too young." Jamie is 16 years old. What are some ways in which Jamie could get credit to purchase this VCR?

Calculating Business Problems

1 Alex Ramirez bought three gallons of paint on credit. The paint cost $8.40 a gallon. A finance charge of $0.25 was added to the purchase price of the paint. What was the total cost of Alex's purchase?

2 Charlene Presley owns a pet store and hobby shop. She thinks she should join a bank charge-card plan so that she can better compete with some large department stores. Her credit sales each month on a bank-card plan will be about $10,000.

  a. If the bank plan she joins charges Charlene 3 percent of her billings, how much would she pay for the bank's services in one month?

  b. How much would the bank owe her for that month?

  c. If her annual credit sales amount to $120,000, what would she pay for the bank's services for the year?

3 Eduardo Gomez bought 150 liters of gasoline for his motor home. He also needed 1.89 liters of oil. The gasoline cost $1.19 per gallon and the oil $2.29 per quart. What was the total amount of Eduardo's purchase? If he charged this purchase and paid 1½ percent in finance charges per month on the amount purchased, how much would he have to pay?

4 Li-ming Sun has a charge account with a department store. Her account is billed to her on the first of each month, and she is expected to pay in full by the last day of the month. If she does not, the store charges her a 1½ percent finance charge per month on the balance of the account. This past month Li-ming made the following purchases: two skirts at $15.55 each; one pair of children's shoes at $16.95; costume jewelry at $11.15; and a lamp at $22.10.

a. What is the total amount for which Li-ming will be billed on the first of the month?

b. If she pays only $20 on her account this month, what will be the amount of the finance charge when her bill comes next month?

Applying Technology

Using the *Introduction to Business* template and your database program software, select problem CH25. After the problem appears on your screen, complete the following activities. Then, after you have completed each step, display or print a report for each activity. If you do not have a printer available, answer the questions before you leave the computer.

1 Sort the database in descending order by annual fee. Answer the following questions:

a. Which lender charges the highest annual fee?

b. Which lender charges the fourth highest annual fee?

2 Select and list the lenders that offer credit insurance. How many lenders are listed?

3 Sort the database in ascending order by interest rate. Answer the following questions:

a. What is the third lowest interest rate available?

b. What is the second highest interest rate available?

Making Decisions

Pedro got himself into credit difficulty. He tended to spend foolishly and use his credit cards too often. Then he missed payments when they were due. He had five accounts with overdue payments.

Pedro needed a loan to pay off his charge accounts. The Go-Along Finance Company agreed to give him a loan if he could get a cosigner. When he asked his good friend, Susan Bekkee, to be a cosigner, she said "no problem." She had an excellent credit record and Pedro got a $4,000 loan at 15 percent interest.

Months went by. Susan did not even think about the loan nor did she see Pedro. Then the letter came: Pedro had failed to make his last five payments, and he had left town with no forwarding address. The letter demanded that Susan make up the back payments immediately and pay the balance due.

She knew that as a cosigner she was responsible for this debt; she did not want a negative report to be part of her credit record.

1 What mistake did Susan make in cosigning this loan?

2 What might she have done originally to help her friend Pedro?

Chapter Twenty-Six

Key Terms

interest rate

principal

time factor

simple interest

maturity date

annual percentage rate (APR)

credit insurance

The Cost of Credit

Objectives

After reading this chapter and completing the end-of-chapter activities, you will be able to:

1 Explain how simple interest is computed.

2 Distinguish between decreasing payment and level payment installment loans.

3 Explain the costs of credit in addition to interest.

4 Explain why it is important to shop for credit.

Using credit to purchase goods and services may allow you to be more efficient or more productive or to lead a more satisfying life. There are many valid reasons for using credit. A medical emergency may cause you to be strapped for money. You may be offered a new job and need a car to get to work. Or you may have the opportunity to buy something you need now for less money than you would pay for it later.

As more and more types of financial institutions offer financial services, your choices of what and where to borrow grow wider. Wise shopping for credit involves careful determination of the cost of credit. If you are thinking of borrowing money or opening a charge account, your first step should be to figure out how much it will cost you and whether you can afford it. After deciding to use credit, you must then shop for the best terms.

Consumer credit enables you to have and enjoy goods and services now and to pay for them through payment plans based on future income. Always remember, however, that credit is not free. There are a number of costs associated with credit that must be paid by those who use it.

INTEREST CALCULATIONS

The amount of interest you must pay on a loan or charge account should be clearly understood. To determine the amount you have to pay, it is necessary to know three things:

1. **Interest rate,** the percentage that is applied to your debt expressed as a fraction or decimal.

2. **Principal,** the amount of debt to which the interest rate is applied.

3. **Time factor,** the length of time for which interest will be charged. Let's look at the way interest is computed on loans.

Simple Interest

On single-payment loans, interest often is expressed in terms of simple interest. **Simple interest** is an expression of interest based on a one-year period of time. The formula for computing simple interest is:

$$I \text{ (interest)} = P \text{ (principal)} \times R \text{ (rate)} \times T \text{ (time)}$$

If \$1,000 (P) is borrowed at 9 percent (R) for one year (T), the amount of interest would be calculated as follows:

$$I = \$1,000 \times \tfrac{9}{100} \times 1 = \$90$$

Illus. 26-1

Make sure to calculate the interest you will pay in order to understand the true cost of a loan or charge account.

In calculating the interest, there are three basic things to remember: (1) the interest rate must be expressed in the form of a fraction or decimal; (2) interest is charged for each dollar or part of a dollar borrowed; and (3) the interest rate is based upon one year of time. Here is how it works:

1. Interest is expressed as part of a dollar. This part of a dollar, or percentage, is called the interest rate. Before using a percentage rate in a problem, you must change it to either a common fraction or a decimal. For example, an interest rate of 12 percent would be changed to a common fraction of $^{12}/_{100}$ or a decimal of .12.

2. When an interest rate is expressed as 12 percent per year, you must pay 12 cents for each dollar you borrow for a year. At this rate, if you borrow $1, you pay 12 cents in interest. If you borrow $2, you pay 24 cents. If you borrow $10, you pay $1.20, and so on. The amount of interest charged is calculated by multiplying the principal by the interest rate and then multiplying that result by the time period. Suppose that you borrow $100 for one year at 12 percent per year. Here is how the amount of interest is calculated:

$$I = P \times R \times T$$
$$I = \$100 \times {}^{12}/_{100} \times 1 = \$12$$

3. If you borrow $100 at 12 percent for one year, you must repay the $100 plus $12 interest, as you have just seen. If you borrow the same amount of money at the same rate of interest for two years, you pay twice as much interest, or $24. If the money is borrowed for three years, you pay $36, and so on. The amount of interest on $100 borrowed at 12 percent for two years is computed as follows:

$$I = P \times R \times T$$
$$I = \$100 \times {}^{12}/_{100} \times 2 = \$24$$

How is interest calculated if you borrow money for less than a year? The amount of interest is based on the fractional part of the year. The fraction may be expressed either in months or in days. A month is considered to be one-twelfth of a year, regardless of the number of days in the particular month. If you were to borrow $100 at 12 percent for one month, the interest would be:

$$I = P \times R \times T$$
$$I = \$100 \times {}^{12}/_{100} \times {}^{1}/_{12} = \$1$$

When a loan is made for a certain number of days, such as 30, 60, or 90 days, the interest is determined by days. To make the computation easy, a year is often considered 360 days. The interest on a loan for $100 at 12 percent for 60 days would be $2, as shown below.

$$I = P \times R \times T$$
$$I = \$100 \times {}^{12}\!/_{100} \times {}^{60}\!/_{360} = \$2$$

NET FACTS

The federal government has plans to link schools, government agencies, colleges, and universities to a network that will be much faster than the current Internet. This new network is called the National Research and Education Network (NREN).

Maturity Dates

The date on which a loan must be repaid is known as the **maturity date.** How is the maturity date determined? When the time of the loan is stated in months, the date of maturity is the same day of the month as the date on which the loan was made. If a loan is made on January 15 and is to run one month, it will be due February 15. If it is to run two months, it will be due March 15, and so on.

When the time of a loan is given in days, the exact number of days must be counted to find the date of maturity. First you would determine the number of days remaining in the month when the loan was made. For instance, if the loan were made on January 10, there would be 21 days to be counted in January. Then you would add the days in the following months until the total equals the required number of days. Suppose you wanted to find the date of maturity of a 90-day loan made on March 3. Here is how it would be done:

> March—28 days (31−3)
> April—30 days
> May—31 days
> June—1 day
> Total: 90 days
> Due Date—June 1

Installment Interest

When you borrow money, you may want to repay the loan in several partial payments instead of one large single payment. A loan that is repaid in partial payments is called an installment loan (or consumer loan). Each payment is called an installment. You can obtain installment loans from many banks, savings and loan associations, credit unions, and consumer finance companies. On an installment loan, the borrower is usually given a schedule of payments, or a payment book, that shows how much is to be paid each month.

With some loans, the amount of the interest is added to the amount you borrow, and you sign a promissory note for the total amount. The note may then be repaid in equal monthly installments. For instance, you may have borrowed $100, signed a note for $110, and agreed to repay the loan in 12 monthly installments of $9.16 each.

If you had borrowed $100 for one year and paid $110 at maturity, the interest rate would have been 10 percent ($10 ÷ $100 = .10 or 10%). But you paid off just part of the loan each month. You had the use of the entire $100 for one month and a smaller amount each succeeding month as you repaid the loan. In this case, the interest rate amounts to 18.5 percent.

On some installment loans, interest is calculated on the amount that is unpaid at the end of each month. Suppose that Armando Rivera borrowed $120 and agreed to repay the loan at $20 a month plus 1½ percent interest each month on the unpaid balance. His schedule of decreasing payments is shown in the first part of Figure 26-1. His father, Jason Rivera, obtained a loan of

Figure 26-1

There are two kinds of loan payment schedules: decreasing and level.

A Decreasing Loan Payment Schedule ($120 loan; 18 percent interest: monthly payments are $20 plus interest).

Months	Unpaid Balance	Interest Paid	Loan Repayment	Total Payment
1	$120	$1.80	$ 20	$ 21.80
2	100	1.50	20	21.50
3	80	1.20	20	21.20
4	60	.90	20	20.90
5	40	.60	20	20.60
6	20	.30	20	20.30
Totals	——	$6.30	$120	$126.30

A Level Loan Payment Schedule ($1,000 loan; 12 percent annual interest: $100 monthly payments).

Payment	Interest	Applied to Principal	Balance of Loan
			$1,000.00
$100.00	$10.00	$90.00	910.00
100.00	9.10	90.90	819.10
100.00	8.19	91.81	727.29
100.00	7.28	92.72	634.57
100.00	6.35	93.65	540.92
100.00	5.41	94.59	446.33
100.00	4.46	95.54	350.79
100.00	3.51	96.49	254.30
100.00	2.54	97.46	156.84
100.00	1.57	98.43	58.41
58.99	.58	58.41	——

$1,000. He agreed to repay $100 per month. The payment is applied to principal and interest. Mr. Rivera's repayment schedule is shown in the second part of Figure 26-1. He makes payments each month on a level payment schedule. Both kinds of payment schedules are used in loan transactions.

FINANCE CHARGES

Before you borrow money or charge a purchase, you should know exactly the cost of using credit. The **annual percentage rate (APR)** is a disclosure required by law, and it states the percentage cost of credit on a yearly basis. All credit agreements, whether for sales credit or loan credit, require disclosure of the APR.

redit experts consider credit insurance to be over-priced, but without it lenders would not approve loans.

Ethical*Perspective*

Credit Card Fraud

Protecting your credit card number is important! You don't have to lose your card to get cheated out of money—all a credit-card thief needs is the number of your account to use it.

Credit-card fraud is big business, but you can take some basic precautions to protect yourself. For example:

- Avoid giving card numbers or expiration dates over the telephone unless you initiate the call. Giving your card number to someone who calls you about winning a prize can turn into a *real surprise*. (The person calling often pretends to need your card number to verify your identity so you can win the prize.)

- Try not to give out your birth date or your social security number more often than is absolutely necessary. Both can be used to apply for a card in your name; you may not know about it until you are pressed for payment by the card issuer.

- Do not put a credit-card number on a check at a merchant's request. Almost half the states prohibit this practice, and VISA and MasterCard will not let merchants bill your credit card to cover a bounced check.

Even the latest technology has been used to commit credit card fraud. An on-line computer program, known as Credit Master, allows credit card criminals to generate fake credit card numbers that work. However, few consumers have reported losses from these fake numbers.

Critical Thinking

1 *What are some precautions you should use to help avoid having your credit card number used fraudulently by someone else?*

2 *Who is the real loser when credit cards are used fraudulently?*

A credit clerk's job duties include:

- contacting applicants and credit bureaus for information
- verifying loan documents
- securing, updating, and verifying information in credit reports
- performing basic clerical duties involving the use of computers and telephones.

In addition to interest, the APR includes other charges that may be made. *Service fees* involve the time and money it takes a creditor to investigate your credit history, process your loan or charge account application, and keep records of your payments and balances. Costs of collecting from those who do not pay their accounts may be costs that are passed on to borrowers. Uncollectible accounts are frequently referred to as bad debts or doubtful accounts. Lenders also commonly add an amount to cover the cost of credit insurance. **Credit insurance** is special insurance that repays the balance of the amount owed if the borrower dies or becomes disabled prior to the full settlement of the loan. Without your acceptance of credit insurance coverage, some lenders will not be willing to make a loan.

To make you aware of the total cost of credit, a federal law requires that you be told of the finance charge. As you learned in Chapter 25, the finance charge is the total cost of credit including interest and all other charges. This finance charge must be stated in writing in your contract or on your charge account statement. Figure 26-2 shows how the annual percentage rate and finance charges are shown on a credit card bill and on an installment sales contract. The APR is the key to comparing costs of credit, regardless of the amount of credit or how much time you have to repay it.

Illus. 26-2

Make sure to understand the complete costs of a credit agreement, including finance charges and service fees.

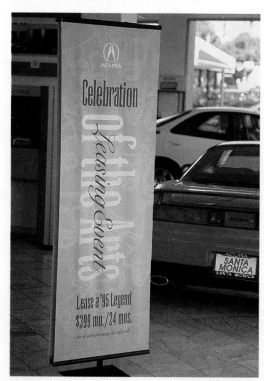

CREDIT ALTERNATIVES

If you have to borrow money or make a purchase on credit, you should consider not only the total cost of credit but also the available alternative sources of credit. Check with several lenders and compare the APRs.

If you make a purchase with a credit card, for instance, know which card has the lowest APR. If an installment sales contract is

DESCRIPTION		AMOUNT
PREVIOUS BALANCE		182.57
NEW PURCHASES	+	275.70
NEW CASH ADVANCES	+	.00
NEW TEXAS BANKARD PLUS™ PURCHASES	+	.00
CREDITS	−	.00
PAYMENTS	−	30.00
FINANCE CHARGE	+	4.70
NEW BALANCE	=	432.97
PAYMENT DUE DATE*		9/23/--

20989 7 28792

ACCOUNT INFORMATION	
DESCRIPTION	AMOUNT
TEXAS BANKARD PLUS BALANCE	.00
AVERAGE DAILY BALANCE	312.81

ANNUAL PERCENTAGE RATE 18%

*DATE NEW BALANCE MUST BE PAID IN FULL TO AVOID FINANCE CHARGE ON TRANSACTIONS BEING BILLED FOR THE FIRST TIME ON THIS STATEMENT (EXCEPT CASH ADVANCES AND TEXAS BANKARD PLUS PURCHASES).

NOTICE—SEE REVERSE SIDE FOR IMPORTANT INFORMATION

INSTALLMENT SALES CONTRACT AND SECURITY AGREEMENT

Sergio Sound Systems, Inc.
The South Mall • Amarillo, TX 79199

I (we) the undersigned buyer(s) buy from, and grant a security interest, to SERGIO SOUND SYSTEMS, INC. in this property:

Quantity	Description	Amount	
1	Model XV-466 Turntable	400	00
Description of Trade-in:			
	Sales Tax	16	00
	Total	416	00

Buyer's Name _Maria Benitez_
Buyer's Address _805 Elberon Ave_
City _Amarillo_ State _TX_ Zip _79199_

1	Cash Price	$	400.00
2	Less: Down Payment $ 40.00		
3	Trade-in $		
4	Total Down	$	40.00
5	Unpaid Balance of Cash Price	$	360.00
6	Other Charges _Sales Tax_	$	16.00
7	AMOUNT FINANCED	$	376.00
8	FINANCE CHARGE	$	37.68
9	Total of Payments	$	413.68
10	Deferred Payment Price (1 + 6 + 8)	$	453.68
11	ANNUAL PERCENTAGE RATE		18.5 %

Insurance Agreement

Credit life insurance is available at a cost of $ _3.00_ for the term of the credit. The purchase of insurance is voluntary and not required for credit.

I want insurance.

Signed: _____ Date: _____

I do not want insurance.

Signed: _Maria Benitez_ Date: _1/15/19--_

Signed: _____ Date: _____

The Buyer(s) agrees to pay to SERGIO SOUND SYSTEMS, INC. at their store the "Total of Payments" shown above in _12_ monthly installments of _34.47_ and a final installment of _34.51_. The first installment is due _February 15, 19--_ and all other payments are due on the same day of the month, until paid in full. The finance charge applies from _1/15/19--_

Signed: _Maria Benitez_ Date: _1/15/19--_

Notice to Buyer: You should get a copy of this contract when you sign. You can pay in advance the unpaid balance of this contract and get a partial refund of the finance charge based on the "Actuarial Method."

Figure 26-2

Lenders must show you the cost of your credit purchase and provide an agreement in writing.

required, consider whether an installment loan from a financial institution may be cheaper for you. When acquiring a loan, shop around just as carefully as you would for a new stereo, car, microcomputer, or any other major purchase. Borrowing money is costly, so make sure that you get the best loan. Some of the things you should check include the annual percentage rate, the

A college student recently reported having acquired 23 credit cards (totaling almost $34,000 in available credit) without needing any cosigners.

amount of the monthly payments, and the finance charge.

Always remember that when you use credit, you not only use someone else's money, but you also spend your own future income. If you decide to use credit, the benefits of making the purchase now (a more satisfying life, for example) should outweigh the costs of using credit. Effectively used, credit can help you have more and enjoy more. Misused, credit can result in excessive debt, loss of reputation, and even bankruptcy.

Key Ideas

1 The amount of interest is calculated by multiplying the interest rate times the principal times the number of days or months.

2 On decreasing payment loans, equal parts of the loan must be repaid each month plus interest on the unpaid balance. With a level payment loan, the borrower pays the same amount each month.

3 Costs of credit in addition to interest include service fees, the cost of collecting bad debts, and credit insurance.

4 The cost of credit varies among lenders; you can save money by shopping around to compare the APR, amount of monthly payments, and the total finance charge.

End of Chapter Activities

Increasing Your Business Vocabulary

The following terms should become part of your business vocabulary. For each numbered item, find the term that has the same meaning.

annual percentage rate (APR)

credit insurance

interest rate

maturity date

principal

simple interest

time factor

1 An expression of interest based on a one-year period of time.

2 The amount of debt to which the interest is applied.

3 The date on which a loan must be repaid.

4 The length of time for which interest will be charged.

5 Special insurance that repays the balance of the amount owed if the borrower dies or becomes disabled prior to the full settlement of the loan.

6 The percentage cost of credit on a yearly basis.

7 The percentage that is applied to a debt, expressed as a fraction or decimal.

Reviewing Your Reading

1 What three things must you know to be able to calculate interest? What is the simple interest formula?

2 In calculating interest, how many days are normally considered to be in one year?

3 How is the maturity date of a loan determined?

4 What is the difference between a decreasing payment and a level payment installment loan?

5 What are some costs that can be included in a finance charge?

6 By law, what information must be disclosed by creditors to make it easier for a consumer to compare finance charges?

7 List some things you need to consider when making a decision about obtaining a loan or using an installment sales contract.

Using Your Business Knowledge

1 Steve Beyer has charge accounts at three different stores. He also has a bank charge card and an oil company credit card that he uses quite frequently. Last month he took out a personal loan that requires him to pay $60 a month for the next 18 months. The total of the payments he makes on his three charge accounts is $222 per month. His monthly income, after taxes and other deductions, is $1,000. His normal expenses for an apartment, utilities, food, clothing and other necessities amount to more than $650 per month. Should Steve continue to make more credit purchases? What problems does Steve face at this time? What cost of credit is he experiencing?

2 Find the date of maturity for each of the loans in the table.

Date of Loan	Time to Run
March 15	4 months
May 26	3 months
July 31	5 months
April 30	30 days
October 5	45 days

3 Les Heddle checked into several loan possibilities. He needed $15,000 to do some remodeling in his upholstery shop. The Thrifty Loan Company offered him an APR of 16 percent for a three-year loan. Monthly payments, including finance charges, would be $555. The Greenback Bank offered him a five-year loan at 15 percent APR with a total monthly payment of $375. The Silk Purse Finance Lending Shop did not quote an APR figure but said, "We have a 'no frills' loan policy, and you can have a four-year loan with monthly payments at the amazingly low figure of $496 per month." Construct a loan comparison chart showing the lender, APR, loan length, monthly payment, total payment, and cost of credit. Then decide which loan would be the best for Les Heddle. Give reasons for your decision.

Calculating Business Problems

1 Using the formula for simple interest, find the interest charge for each of the following amounts for one year.

   a. $100 at 10 percent interest rate

   b. $500 at 12 percent interest rate

   c. $1,000 at 18 percent interest rate

   d. $25,000 at 10 percent interest rate

2 Jennifer Ward owns a large ranch and has a chance to buy additional land next to her ranch. She would need to put in a road so that she could move equipment onto the new land. The gravel road would be 3.3 kilometers long and would cost $800 per kilometer.

   a. How much would the road cost?

   b. If Jennifer had to pay 14 percent interest on a two-year loan to pay for the road, how much interest would she pay over that period? (See Appendix D.)

3 Before borrowing $200, Laura Demetry visited a small loan company and the loan department of a bank. At the loan company, she found that she could borrow the $200 if she signed a note agreeing to repay the balance in six equal monthly installments of $36.50. At the bank, she could borrow the money by signing a promissory note for $215 and repaying the balance in six equal monthly payments.

   a. What would be the cost of the loan at the small loan company?

   b. What annual interest rate would Laura be paying if she borrowed at the small loan company?

   c. What would be the cost of the loan at the bank?

   d. What annual interest rate would she pay if she borrowed at the bank?

Applying Technology

Using the *Introduction to Business* template and your spreadsheet program software, select problem CH26. After the problem appears on your screen, complete the following activities. Then, after you have completed each step, display or print the completed spreadsheet for each activity. If you do not have a printer available, answer the questions before you leave the computer.

1 For each of the problems shown, enter a formula to calculate the simple interest. Format your answers as currency with two decimal places. Answer the following questions:

   a. What is the amount of interest for Problem 1?

   b. What is the amount of interest for Problem 2?

2 Including the Number of Days per Year, copy all the data to an open part of the spreadsheet below the first set of data. In the second set of data, enter 360 as the Number of Days per Year. Answer the following questions.

   a. What is the amount of interest for Problem 3?

   b. What is the amount of interest for Problem 4?

3 Below the second set of data, enter formulas to calculate the difference between the interest amounts in the second set of data and the first set of data. Enter a formula to calculate the average of the differences. Label your answers and format the answers as currency with two decimal places. What is the average of the differences?

Optional: Create a bar chart comparing the differences in interest for each problem.

Making Decisions

Midori Yamaguchi plans to buy a new refrigerator that now costs $875. Since the current inflation rate is 4 percent, she expects the refrigerator to cost $910 if she postpones the purchase for a year. If she buys it now, she estimates that it would save her $150 in food costs during the next year. This purchase would enable her to buy food at special sales and in large quantities. The new refrigerator would also be more energy efficient than her current one; therefore, she would save on the cost of electricity. Midori can use one of the following options to purchase the new refrigerator.

Alternative A. Purchase the refrigerator now, withdrawing the $875 from her 5 percent savings account at a local bank.

Alternative B. Buy the refrigerator now with $75 down, and sign an installment sales contract. The payments are $76 a month for 12 months. The APR is 12.8 percent.

Alternative C. Postpone the purchase until she saves an additional $875. Her savings account earns interest at the annual rate of 5 percent.

1 What trade-offs should Midori consider in deciding whether to buy the refrigerator now or later? (A *trade-off* refers to what a person gives up by making a choice.)

2 If Midori wants to buy the refrigerator now, what trade-offs should she consider in deciding whether to use credit or pay cash from her savings?

Chapter Twenty-Seven

Credit Records and Regulations

Key Terms

creditworthy

credit record

credit application

credit bureau

statement or statement of account

credit memorandum

receipt

Truth-in-Lending Law

Equal Credit Opportunity Act

Fair Credit Billing Act

Fair Credit Reporting Act

debt-repayment plan

Objectives

After studying this chapter and completing the end-of-chapter activities, you will be able to:

1 Discuss credit applications, credit bureaus, and credit reports.

2 Explain what should be done in checking credit records.

3 Cite several credit laws and explain the protection they give.

4 Explain what can be done to build and keep a good credit history.

Assume that you have been issued a bank credit card. One day you mistakingly leave your credit card lying on a counter. When you return 15 minutes later, your credit card is gone. The sales clerk says that he has not seen it. You wait a few weeks to see whether it will be returned. It is not returned, so you write to the credit card company and explain what happened. Your next statement shows that more than $200 worth of merchandise was charged to your card before you reported it lost. What mistakes have you made, and what can you do now?

Several months later you are checking your charge account statement and find several errors on it. There is one charge for a purchase you did not make, and this is the third month in a row that this charge has shown up on your statement. One of your purchases was returned several weeks ago, but the credit does not show on your statement. Your last month's payment, which you made on time, also is not listed. What can you do about these errors?

Your friends, Monique and Gary Buckeye, had their loan application turned down. The loan officer explained that the credit bureau report on their credit record was not good. Monique and Gary were shocked; they always pay their bills on time, with only a few minor exceptions. They need this loan for home improvements. You wonder what they can do to correct this problem.

These credit problems can happen to anyone. If consumers know about credit laws and regulations, there are steps to take to avoid and correct problems. It also is important to know what information creditors need to have to make decisions regarding those who apply for credit.

CREDITWORTHINESS

You should understand what lenders need to know in order to make a decision about whether to grant credit. Generally, they want to be assured of two things: your ability to repay a debt and your willingness to do so. You may say that you can handle the debt, and you may assure them you will repay the debt according to the terms of the agreement. However, they need to have some evidence. They want to lend money, but lenders must minimize their bad debts. Lenders need proof that you are creditworthy.

Being **creditworthy** means that you have established a credit record that shows you are a good credit risk. Potential lenders will want to examine your credit record. Your **credit record** is a report that shows the debts you owe, how often you use credit, and whether you pay your debts on time.

There is other information that lenders will want to know. Lenders want to find out about your finances, such as how much you earn, what kinds of savings and investments you have, and whether you have any other sources of income. They may also want to know about your reliability; that is,

The three major companies that store data on consumers and provide information to lenders are TRW, Equifax, and Trans Union. Equifax maintains over 190 million credit files on U.S. consumers.

your occupation, how long you have been with your present employer, how long you have lived at the same address, and whether you own or rent your home.

Completing Credit Applications

When you apply for credit or a loan, you will be asked to fill out a credit application. A **credit application** is a form on which you provide information needed by a lender to make a decision about granting credit or approving a loan. Figure 27-1 is an example of a credit application. Read this application carefully and note the information that is requested. What information could you provide on an application of this kind?

One of the most important parts of the credit application is the listing of your credit references—businesses or individuals who are able and willing to provide information about your creditworthiness. Your signature on the credit application gives a lender permission to contact your credit references and inquire about your credit record. Your signature also indicates that you understand the terms of the type of credit for which you are applying and that the information you have provided is true. The credit application needs to be filled out completely, accurately, and honestly. You should sign it when you understand it and have provided the requested information.

Documenting Credit Data

Information provided on credit applications must be verified to assure its accuracy. Present and former employers can verify the dates of employment and salary figures. Banks and other financial institutions can report whether the applicants have the accounts listed on the applications. Landlords can indicate the length of time tenants have been renting and whether they pay their rent on time. Other creditors can report how credit applicants make payments to their accounts and how they repay their loans.

If you list a personal reference because you do not have sufficient business credit references, the person you list can indicate how he or she feels you conduct your personal business affairs. School personnel can indicate how reliable and trustworthy you were in school. In each case, the reference checked merely helps the credit manager to get a better picture of you as a credit risk so that an accurate appraisal of your creditworthiness can be made.

NET FACTS

HyperText Transfer Protocol, or HTTP, are computer instructions for displaying and sending hypertext documents from computer to computer. Most World Wide Web addresses begin with the letters *http*.

Figure 27-1

It is important to fill in all of the blanks on a credit application.

CREDIT CARD APPLICATION

Second National BankCorp

Important: Fill in all information requested below.

1. Information About Yourself *(Name of person in whose name card will be issued)*

☐ Mr.   ☐ Mrs.   ☐ Miss   ☐ Ms.   First Name   Middle   Last Name

(Courtesy titles are optional)

Home Address	Apt.	City		State	ZIP Code	How Long? Years ____ Mos. ____

Previous Address (if less than 2 years at present address)	Apt.	City		State	ZIP Code

Home Telephone ( )	Business Telephone ( )	Social Security Number	Date of Birth / /	No. of Dependents (Exclude Yourself)

Are You a U.S. Citizen? ☐ Yes ☐ No	If No, Explain Immigration Status	Are You a Permanent Resident? ☐ Yes ☐ No	Do You: ☐ Own ☐ Rent ☐ Other	Monthly Rent or Mortgage $

2. Employment Information *(Your total yearly income from all sources)*

Employer	Address	City	State	ZIP Code

How Long? Years ____ Mos. ____	Occupation	Yearly Gross Salary $	Other Income*	Source

Former Employer (if less than 1 year with present employer)	How Long? Years ____ Mos. ____	*Note: Alimony, child support or separate maintenance income need not be disclosed if you do not wish to have it considered as a basis for paying this obligation.

Nearest Relative Not Living with You	Address	City	State	Relation	Telephone

3. Other Credit

Major Credit Cards (Visa, MasterCard, etc....)	Account Number
Other Credit Cards (Dept. Stores, etc....)	Account Number
Other Credit	Account Number

4. Banking Information

☐ Checking	Name of Bank	City	Account Number
☐ Savings	Name of Bank (if different from above)	City	Account Number

☐ Other (Check here if you have any of the following:)   IRA   Money Market Account   Investments
CD   Stocks/Bonds   Cash Maanagement Account

5. Joint Account Information *(Complete for joint account or if you are relying on the income of another person to qualify for an account)*

First Name	Middle	Last Name		Relation

Home Address	Apt.	City		State	ZIP Code

Home Telephone ( )	Business Telephone ( )	Social Security Number	Date of Birth / /

Employer	Address	City	State	ZIP Code

How Long? Years ____ Mos. ____	Occupation	Yearly Gross Salary $	Other Income*	Source

Former Employer	How Long? Years ____ Mos. ____	*Note: Alimony, child support or separate maintenance income need not be disclosed if you do not wish to have it considered as a basis for paying this obligation.

6. Additional Cards *(Complete this section if you want cards issued to additional buyers on your account.)*

1. Spouse First Name	Middle	Last Name
2. Other First Name	Middle	Last Name

7. Signatures

I authorize the Second National BankCorp to check my credit record and to verify my credit, employment and income references. I have read the important information on the reverse side.

X _____   X _____

Applicant's Signature   Joint Applicant's Signature

I understand that Second National BankCorp may amend the account terms and charges specified in the Cardmember Agreement in the future.

Reporting Credit Information

In addition to checking with your employers, your landlord (if you rent a house or an apartment), and your credit references, usually a lender will check with a credit bureau. A **credit bureau,** or a credit reporting agency, is a company that gathers information on credit users and sells that information in the form of credit reports to credit grantors. Banks, finance companies, and retail stores are among the customers of credit bureaus.

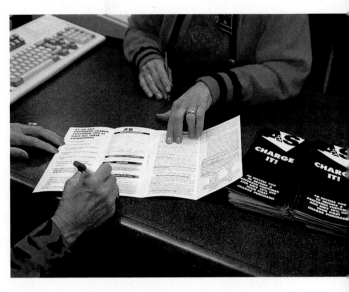

Illus. 27-1
Information you put on your credit application will be verified by the lender.

Credit bureaus keep records of consumers' debts but can record only information that is officially reported to them. Creditors often send computer tapes or other payment data to credit bureaus, usually on a monthly basis. The information shows if payments are up-to-date or overdue and if any action has been taken to collect overdue bills. Other information may be added to create a month-by-month credit history for the consumer accounts. Credit bureaus cooperate with each other and provide information to other credit bureaus. If you are new to a community and request credit, the local credit bureau can obtain information from the bureau in the community where you formerly lived. There are several credit bureau associations; one of the largest has about 1,500 credit bureaus among its membership.

Your credit record with a bureau is used to grade you as a credit risk. Credit bureaus do not make value judgments about any

The Consumer Credit Counseling Service, a reputable nonprofit organization with offices nationwide, provides help to people who have credit problems.

individual; they simply gather facts as reported to them. Your credit record is confidential. That is, it can be obtained only by you or those who have a legitimate reason for examining it.

Figure 27-2 is an example of a credit report that may be issued by a credit bureau. You will note that the top half contains background information about the individual, while the bottom half lists information about the individual's accounts and payment history. Note that at the bottom there is a reference to a public record showing a dispute between the consumer and a creditor that was settled in a small claims court. All of this information is of interest to credit grantors.

		Date Received 4/11/96	CONFIDENTIAL

FOR

FIRST NATIONAL BANK
Arborville, MT 83206

Date Received	4/11/96
Date Mailed	4/11/96
In File Since	APRIL 1990

CONFIDENTIAL
-FIRST AVENUE-
CREDIT BUREAU
Member Accociated Credit Bureaus, Inc.

Inquired As:
JOINT ACCOUNT

REPORT ON:	LAST NAME SOCOL	FIRST NAME ROBERTA	INITIAL G.	SOCIAL SECURITY NUMBER 123-45-6789	SPOUSE'S NAME HENRY R.

ADDRESS: 5421 MAPLE AVENUE	CITY: ARBORVILLE	STATE: MT	ZIP CODE: 83206	SINCE: 1988	SPOUSE'S SOCIAL SECURITY NO. 987-65-4321

COMPLETE TO HERE FOR TRADE REPORT AND SKIP TO CREDIT HISTORY

PRESENT EMPLOYER: THE ARTIST'S LOFT, INC.	POSITION HELD: DEPT. MGR.	SINCE: 10/90	DATE EMPLOY VERIFIED 12/90	EST. MONTHLY INCOME $5,000

COMPLETE TO HERE FOR EMPLOYMENT AND TRADE REPORT AND SKIP TO CREDIT HISTORY

DATE OF BIRTH 5/25/65	NUMBER OF DEPENDENTS INCLUDING SELF: 3	☒ OWNS OR BUYING HOME	☐ RENTS HOME	☐ OTHER: (EXPLAIN)

FORMER ADDRESS: 321 FIRST AVE.	CITY: ARBORVILLE	STATE: MT		FROM: 1980	TO: 1988

FORMER EMPLOYER: O'NEILL & ASSOCIATES	POSITION HELD: SALESPERSON	FROM: 2/86	TO: 9/88	EST. MONTHLY INCOME $1,960

SPOUSE'S EMPLOYER: TRI-CITY DEPT. STORE	POSITION HELD: ASSIST. MGR.	SINCE: 4/89	DATE EMPLOY VERIFIED 12/89	EST. MONTHLY INCOME $2,900

CREDIT HISTORY *(Complete this section for all reports)*

WHOSE	KIND OF BUSINESS AND ID CODE	DATE REPORTED AND METHOD OF REPORTING	DATE OPENED	DATE OF LAST PAYMENT	HIGHEST CREDIT OR LAST PAYMENT	BALANCE OWING	PAST DUE AMOUNT	PAST DUE NO. OF PAYMENTS	NO. MONTHS HISTORY REVIEWED	30-59 DAYS ONLY	60-89 DAYS ONLY	90 DAYS AND OVER	TYPE & TERMS (MANNER OF PAYMENT)	REMARKS
2	FIRST MONTANA BANK B 12-345	2/6/95 AUTOMTD. 12/89		1/90	2000	1100	-0-	-0-	2	-0-	-0-	-0-	INSTALLMENT	$100/MO.
3	SMITHSON'S DEPT. STORE D 54-321	2/10/95 MANUAL	4/85	1/90	650	100	-0-	-0-	12	-0-	-0-	-0-	REVOLVING	$ 25/MO.
2	MULTIBANK CREDIT CARD N 01-234	12/12/94 AUTOMTD. 7/91		11/94	790	100	100	1	12	1	-0-	-0-	OPEN	30-DAY

PUBLIC RECORD: SMALL CLAIMS CT. CASE #SC1001 PLAINTIFF: APPLIANCES UNLIMITED, INC.
    AMOUNT $225 PAID 4/4/90
ADDITIONAL INFORMATION: REF. SMALL CLAIMS CT. CASE #SC1001-5/30/90 SUBJECT SAYS CLAIM PAID
    UNDER PROTEST. APPLIANCE DID NOT OPERATE PROPERLY.

Figure 27-2
An example of
a credit report.

CREDIT RECORDS

You can help maintain a good credit record by keeping track of your purchases and payments. When you buy on credit, you should keep your copy of the sales slip or credit card receipt for your own records in the event a problem with billing arises. The businessperson will retain the other copies for billing purposes.

Your Statement of Account

You will receive a statement of account on a regular basis, usually monthly. The **statement of account,** or simply the **statement,** is a record of the transactions that you have completed with a business during a billing period. For credit card accounts, the statement lists all of your purchases from various businesses. Most statements show:

- The balance that was due when the last statement was mailed

- The amounts charged during the month for the merchandise or services you bought

- The amounts credited to your account for payments made during the month or for merchandise returned

- The current balance, which is the balance from the last statement, plus finance charges and the amounts of any new purchases, minus the amounts credited to you (old balance + finance charges + purchases − payments = current balance)

- The minimum amount of your next payment and when it is due.

Most statements are prepared by computers. A statement serves two basic purposes: it shows you how much you owe, and it gives you a record of your business transactions. A statement is shown in Figure 27-3.

Technological *Perspective*

Credit Databases

Databases are in common use throughout the business world. The United States is the biggest user of credit information contained in databases. Of the 6,200 databases worldwide, the United States produces and uses more than 50 percent of them.

The information you write on your credit or loan application may be verified through a database. Information stored in credit databases contain some of the following information about you:

1. your income level

2. how many credit cards you have been issued

3. what the balances are on your credit card accounts

4. where you are employed and for how long

5. where you live and whether you are a renter or owner

6. whether you have ever been in bankruptcy

7. whether you pay your utility and other bills on time.

Credit databases containing files on millions of consumers are maintained by three primary sources—Equifax, TRW, and Trans Union. These files are a powerful source of credit information. If you apply for a charge account, a personal loan, or a mortgage, your credit experience—or lack of it—will be a major factor considered by the creditor. A good credit rating is a valuable asset that should be nurtured and protected.

Critical Thinking

1 *What are some reasons you can think of why the United States is the biggest user of worldwide databases?*

2 *Are you concerned about personal data about you in a credit file? Why or why not?*

Purchases made during this billing period

The account balance last month

Account number

The amount of purchases

The amount that must be paid

Figure 27-3
Monthly statements give you important information that should be checked carefully.

You should check the accuracy of the statement by comparing it with your copies of sales slips and with your record of payments and credit memorandums. A **credit memorandum** is a written record of the amount subtracted from your account when you return merchandise. If you discover an error on a statement, you should notify the seller at once.

Credit card fraud is a major problem reported by the Federal Trade Commission. To avoid being defrauded, your credit card account statements need to be checked very carefully for errors.

One system used by consumers is to keep a file of sales slips when a credit card is used—each form normally has "sales draft, cardholder copy" printed on it. It is yours; keep it. When the statement arrives, check the items on the statement against the sales slips on file. If a charge is shown on the statement for which you do not have a sales draft, check that charge and report any error to the bank or credit card company immediately. Staple to the statement the sales slips for the items listed on the statement and file them for future reference. Also compare payments and previous balances with your records.

Cultural Notes

Cultural baggage describes the notion that individuals carry their cultural values, beliefs, and assumptions with them at all times. Our cultural baggage influences how we respond to situations.

The Importance of Accurate Records

Another thing that you can do to help avoid credit record problems is to keep your own records. This is a good personal business practice that too often is not followed.

Many errors are simply honest mistakes, and businesses are as eager to correct them as you are. Your creditworthiness may be at stake, and the reputation of the business may be hurt by bad publicity if errors are not corrected. When you receive a sales slip, a credit memorandum, or a monthly statement, you should examine it to make sure that it is correct.

When making a payment by check, write the date and the check number on the statement. Keep your statements and sales slips. They will be valuable in the future if any questions arise as to whether they have been paid. You should be able to prove that payment was made. You learned that a canceled check is valuable as evidence that payment has been made because it has the endorsement of the payee on the back.

There is no such thing as a "quick fix" for credit problems. Credit repair companies and credit clinics that charge huge fees and offer dubious guarantees are often fraudulent and need to be avoided.

When you do not pay by check, you need some other method of showing that you have made payment. A written form that acknowledges that payment was made is called a **receipt.** The receipt form has spaces for entering the number of the receipt, the date, the name of the person making payment, the amount of the payment in words, the reason for the payment, the amount in figures, and the signature of the person receiving the payment. A stub is filled out to show the same information. Figure 27-4 shows a receipt properly filled out. Each stub and receipt is numbered so that the customer's receipt can be compared with the creditor's stub if a dispute arises.

Figure 27-4

Tracy has given Tami a receipt for her $50 deposit on a school ring.

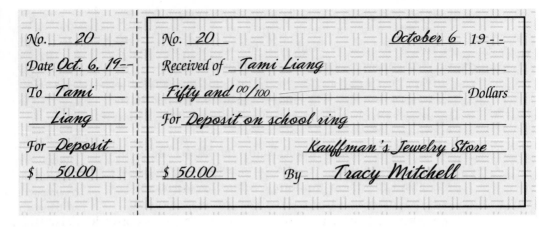

No. ___20___
Date _Oct. 6, 19--_
To _Tami_
   Liang
For _Deposit_
$ ___50.00___

No. ___20___   _October 6_ 19 _ _
Received of _Tami Liang_
Fifty and ⁰⁰/100 _____ Dollars
For _Deposit on school ring_
                    Kauffman's Jewelry Store
$ _50.00_   By ___Tracy Mitchell___

Sometimes a receipt is not given. Instead, the word "paid" is written or stamped on the bill or statement. The date and the initials or signature of the one who received your money should be included.

YOU HAVE RIGHTS

Most businesses are honest and forthright in their business dealings. Nevertheless, it has been necessary for our federal and state governments to pass laws to protect consumers who engage in credit transactions. The Truth-in-Lending Law of 1968 launched a series of laws that deal with various aspects of credit and lending practices. It was followed in 1980 by the Truth-in-Lending Simplification Act.

The **Truth-in-Lending Law** requires that you be told the cost of a credit purchase in writing before you sign a credit agreement. It requires, for instance, that the APR and total finance charge be clearly stated. The Truth-in-Lending Law also protects consumers against unauthorized use of credit cards. The law limits your liability to $50 for unauthorized credit card purchases made prior to notification of the issuer. You are not liable for any fraudulent charges made after you have notified the credit card company—even if someone charges several hundred dollars before you report your card missing. You can notify the company by telephone, but you should also put your notification in writing, citing the date of the phone call. In the example at the opening of this chapter, you would have a problem since you waited too long to report the loss of your credit card. You could be liable for more than the $200 charged before you reported your lost card.

The **Equal Credit Opportunity Act** prohibits creditors from denying credit because of age, race, sex, or marital status. Young people who may have just entered the labor market cannot be denied credit based only on their ages. Older, possibly retired, people also have special protection under this act. Married women who previously found it difficult to establish credit in their own names now have a legal right to do so. Under this law, a woman has a right to her own credit if she proves to be creditworthy.

Unless your state still requires age 21 as the legal age to enter into a contract, you cannot be denied credit based on your age alone. Your creditworthiness would have to be investigated. Any person who is denied credit must, upon request, be given a written statement of the reasons for rejection.

Another important piece of legislation is the Fair Credit Billing Act. The **Fair Credit Billing Act** is a law that requires prompt correction of billing mistakes when they are brought to the attention of a business in a prescribed manner. To get a correction of an error, you must notify the creditor in writing within 60 days after your statement was mailed. A good rule is to report errors as soon as you discover them. After you report the errors, the following four points are important:

- While waiting for an answer, you are not required to pay any amount in question.

- Your complaint must be acknowledged by the creditor within 30 days unless your statement is corrected before that time.

- You do not pay finance charges on any amount in error.

- If no error is found, the creditor must bill you again and may include finance charges that have accumulated plus any minimum payments that were missed while the statement was being questioned.

The Fair Credit Billing Act also provides that you may withhold payment of any balance due on defective merchandise or services purchased with a credit card. Your first step should be to contact the business and try to resolve the problem. Many situations can be corrected if the complaint is made in a courteous but firm manner. The law does protect you if you have made this "good faith" effort.

The **Fair Credit Reporting Act** is the law that gives consumers the right to know what specific information credit bureaus are providing to potential creditors, employers, and insurers. It provides that if credit is denied on the basis of information in a credit report, the applicant must be given the name, address, and phone number of the credit bureau that provided the information. In addition, credit records for both a husband and wife are kept if both are responsible for the debt. This allows a credit history to be developed for each spouse.

Prior to the passage of this law, many consumers were unaware that reports on their bill-paying habits were available to potential lenders. This act makes those reports available to the consumer and provides ways in which information can be accessed and corrected. It also requires that any information dealing with personal bankruptcy that is more than ten years old must be automatically deleted. Any other adverse information must be deleted if it is more than seven years old.

Monique and Gary Buckeye have a right to see their credit bureau report. They requested it and did not have to pay to see it since they had been denied credit. They discovered two errors. In their former community, there was a couple with a name similar to theirs. That couple's credit record was bad, and some of their unpaid debts showed up on Monique and Gary's report. Also, one bill that was disputed with a local retailer was recorded as not being paid.

Monique and Gary had a right to demand that the error of recording someone else's bad credit habits be removed from their record. They also were permitted to write a brief statement giving their side of the disputed bill with the local retailer. After taking these two actions, their good credit record was reestablished and they received the loan they needed.

YOUR OWN CREDIT HISTORY

It is important for consumers to know their rights under the law. However, building your own good record of creditworthiness is even more important.

Things You Can Do Now

To some extent you can begin building a credit record while you are still in school. Since trust and reliability are important when it comes to matters of credit, you can help to establish yourself by having a good record of grades and school attendance. Both employers and creditors know that behavior patterns developed in school tend to carry on after graduation.

In addition, it is good to have both a checking and a savings account. If you have a balance in each account and do not overdraw your checking account, a lender can see that you can handle money. Making regular deposits to your savings account also suggests that you will be a good credit risk.

Some people establish credit records by charging small purchases. For instance, if you buy a sweater on credit and make the payments according to the agreement, you have taken an important step toward proving you are a good credit risk. Or you may want to pay off your account within 30 days and avoid an interest charge. Either way you will be building a good credit record.

Having a good part-time or full-time employment record also helps to establish a good credit record. Changing jobs often does not look good to a creditor. Being on a job for two or more years is a positive part of a good credit record.

Sources of Help

If you find that you just cannot pay your bills when they are due, you should follow these four steps: First, contact your creditors and explain your situation. Second, make a realistic proposal for when and what you can pay; don't just say "I can't pay." Third, keep any promises you make. Fourth, make a written copy of your agreement to avoid disagreements later.

You may be able to work out a debt-repayment plan. A **debt-repayment plan** is an agreement developed cooperatively by a creditor and a debtor to reduce payments to a more manageable level and still pay off the debt. This plan is good for both the creditor and the debtor.

One thing to avoid is being misled by advertisements that tell you: "Erase bad credit! 100 percent guaranteed." Claims such as these are fraudulent. No one can unconditionally correct a bad credit record—it does not work that way. If you need help with a credit problem, contact a reputable organization such as the Consumer Credit Counseling Service.

Illus. 27-2

You can establish a good credit history by charging small purchases and making payments on time.

Key Ideas

1 A credit application is a document on which you provide information needed by a lender. A credit bureau gathers information on credit users. A credit record documents your credit history.

2 Credit statements should be checked carefully and errors reported as soon as they are discovered.

3 Laws and regulations protect you if your credit card is lost; they prohibit denial of credit because of age, race, sex, or marital status; and they provide ways of correcting errors in your credit history.

4 You can maintain a good credit history by paying your bills on time and working out a plan for repayment if you find it difficult to make payments to your creditors.

End of Chapter Activities

Increasing Your Business Vocabulary

The following terms should become part of your business vocabulary. For each numbered item, find the term that has the same meaning.

credit application

credit bureau

credit memorandum

credit record

creditworthy

debt-repayment plan

Equal Credit Opportunity Act

Fair Credit Billing Act

Fair Credit Reporting Act

receipt

statement or statement of account

Truth-in-Lending Law

1 A form on which you provide information needed by a lender to make a decision about granting credit or approving a loan.

2 A company that gathers information on credit users and sells that information in the form of credit reports to credit grantors.

3 An act that prohibits creditors from denying credit because of age, race, sex, or marital status.

4 A written form that acknowledges payment was made.

5 A written record of the amount subtracted from an account when merchandise has been returned.

6 A record of the transactions that you have completed with a business during a billing period.

7 A law that requires that you be told the cost of a credit purchase in writing before you sign a credit agreement.

8 An agreement developed cooperatively by a creditor and debtor to reduce payments to a more manageable level and still pay off the debt.

9 A law that gives consumers the right to know what specific information credit bureaus are providing to potential creditors, employers, and insurers.

10 A law that requires prompt correction of billing mistakes when they are brought to the attention of a business in a prescribed manner.

11 Having established a credit record that shows you are a good credit risk.

12 A report that shows the debts you owe, how often you use credit, and whether you pay your debts on time.

Reviewing Your Reading

1 What two things do lenders want to know before making a decision about granting credit?

2 Name three things lenders want to know about your finances and five things about reliability.

3 What is the purpose of a credit application? Why do credit references have to be listed?

4 What does your signature on a credit application signify?

5 What is the purpose of a credit bureau? Who uses its services?

6 What are some examples of the information contained in a credit bureau report?

7 In what ways is a receipt important? What information does it contain?

8 In what ways is a credit memorandum important?

9 What use might a debtor have for canceled checks?

10 What information is shown on a statement of account?

11 What is the procedure for checking a credit card account statement?

12 What are examples of laws that help protect consumers in credit transactions? What kinds of protection do they provide?

13 What should be done when errors are found in credit statements?

14 What are some things that can be done to build a credit record?

15 What kinds of help are available to debtors who have credit problems?

Using Your Business Knowledge

1 Sergio Torres operates a multimedia store. One day Bill Cross, a total stranger, asked if he could buy a CD-ROM encyclopedia on credit. Mr. Cross explained that he had just moved into town two weeks ago. The moving expenses took most of his cash, but he has a good job and will be able to pay $30 a month beginning next month.

a. What other information should Sergio get from Mr. Cross?

b. What sources of information could Sergio use before making a final decision?

c. Would you extend credit to Mr. Cross? Why or why not?

2 Cheryl Oakwood wants to open an account at the Hewitt Department Store. She objects, however, to giving the credit manager information about such things as where she has other charge accounts, whether she owns real estate, where she works, and in which bank she maintains an account.

a. Why did the credit manager want this information?

b. In what ways could a credit bureau report help this manager?

c. Does Cheryl have a right to refuse to give this information? If so, can credit be denied her?

3 Donna Stratford has been working on her first job for seven months. Her checking account has a balance of $159. She has also put aside $50 in cash for an emergency. She wants to buy a clock radio which sells for $69.95 at a store that offers credit. Donna has never used credit and would like to establish a credit rating. What can she do to get a credit record started? What advice would you give her if she decided to buy this clock radio on credit?

4 Following is a list of consumer transactions. For each, explain whether there would be a cash receipt, a credit memorandum, a canceled check, or a credit card sales slip. Also explain how and why each record should be saved, if you believe it should be saved.

a. Paid cash for flowers that had been ordered in advance

b. Bought a pair of shoes using a credit card

c. Returned a pair of slacks, purchased a week ago on a charge account, because they did not fit

d. Paid $35 in cash toward a $170 balance owed on a charge account with a local store

e. Wrote a check for $125 to pay off a credit card account balance

5 Suzanne Winters does not believe in buying anything on credit. She says that too many people get into trouble using credit cards and that there are too many errors made in credit transactions. She also believes that there is no protection for consumers using credit and no help if they get into credit difficulties. Explain to Suzanne ways in which laws protect consumers who engage in credit transactions and tell her about some of the kinds of help that are available for consumers who have credit problems.

Calculating Business Problems

1 The Country Boutique grants regular credit to people who have been steady customers. Today the boutique received checks in the mail from several customers as shown in the table:

Name	Amount Owed	Amount Paid
Enrique Navarro	$44.22	$44.22
Lynne Goldberg	10.00	5.00
Eloise Little	102.67	50.00
Sam Nader	54.89	25.00
Ruth Smith	19.35	19.35

   a. What was the balance in each account?

   b. What was the total amount received from charge customers?

2 Linda Spencer made the following credit purchases: gloves, $18; 2 purses at $23 each; necklace, $55; 3 pairs of shoes at $42 each. Later she returned the gloves and one purse and received a credit memorandum.

   a. What was the total of Linda's purchases before she returned the gloves and the purse?

   b. What was the amount of the credit memorandum?

   c. How much did she owe after she received the credit memorandum?

3 Saburo Nozaki bought some materials needed for the boat he was building. He purchased the following: 250 meters of board, $3.80 per foot; 90 meters of fabric, $8.15 per yard; and 50 liters of marine varnish, $26.95 per gallon.

(Refer to Appendix D.)

   a. What was the total amount of his purchase?

   b. If he were offered a 4 percent discount for paying cash, how much would he save on this purchase?

4 Dixie Kauffman used her bank charge card for the following purchases: Earl's Clothing Store, 2 shirts at $14 each; Wingo's Hardware Company, 2 gallons of paint at $10.75 each; PaDelford Family Restaurant, $24.75. She returned a gallon of paint and received a credit slip for $10.75 from Wingo's Hardware. Dixie's statement showed a balance of $152 from the previous month plus a finance charge of $2.28.

   a. If Dixie pays her account in full, how much will she pay?

   b. If she decides to make a minimum payment of $30, how much will she still owe?

   c. If the finance charge is 1½ percent per month on the unpaid balance, what will be the finance charge next month if she only pays the $30 this month?

Applying Technology

Using the *Introduction to Business* template and your word processing program software, select problem CH27. After the problem appears on your screen, complete the following activities. Then, print and sign your completed forms. If you do not have a printer available, save the forms on a data disk to give to your teacher.

1 You are applying for a credit card. Complete the application with information about yourself plus the following information. You have lived at your current address for 1½ years and your rent is $450 per month. You have been employed for two years. You make $7 per hour and work 8 hours per day, 21 days per month. Do not complete the sections for Other Credit, Joint Account Information, or Additional Cards. For the information that you enter, use a different font of type from the one used on the rest of the application.

2 You are preparing a retail installment contract. Complete the contract with information about yourself plus the following information: cash price, $437.50; down payment, $87.50; amount financed, $350.00; installment price, $507.02; finance charge, $69.52; annual percentage rate, 18 percent; number of months to pay, 24; monthly payment, $17.48. For the date of the first payment, enter the first day of the month following the current month. For the information that you enter, use italics and a different font of type from the one used on the rest of the application.

Making Decisions

Semantha Mae has been out of school for three years and has held four different jobs with different employers. She has been on her present job for two months.

Her monthly take-home pay is $1,362. She shares an apartment with two friends to keep expenses down, but she is always in debt. Each month she is short of what she needs to pay all of her charge accounts. Her checking account balance is low and the account is frequently overdrawn. She opened a savings account two years ago but has only $25 left in it after paying her dentist bill.

Semantha has decided it would be better to live by herself; she blames her roommates for her credit spending sprees. She has come to you for a loan of $2,000. Her new apartment will cost $400 a month, and she wants to pay off some of her bills that are past due. She assures you that she will pay you at least $50 each month.

1. What are some criteria you would use to determine whether a personal loan for Semantha would be a good idea? What additional information might you want?

2. Would you loan the money to Semantha? Why or why not?

You have learned about the important role credit plays in our economy. Most individuals and businesses find it necessary to use credit for some purchases. As a result, many workers are involved in the processing of credit.

Job Titles

Job titles commonly found in this career area include:

- Collection Clerk
- Credit Account Clerk
- Credit Authorizer
- Credit Card Clerk
- Credit Clerk
- Credit Manager
- Credit Reference Clerk
- Credit Reporting Clerk
- Loan Interviewer
- Mortgage Loan Processor
- Loan Officer
- Repossessor

Employment Outlook (through the year 2005)

- In most of these credit occupations growth will be average for all occupations through 2005.
- Computer technology will not have a negative impact on these jobs due to the interpersonal nature of much of the work.
- The need for replacements due to transfers and retirements will result in a good number of job openings for qualified applicants.

Education and Training

- A high school diploma is a requirement for all of these occupations.
- Employers prefer applicants who have completed business courses and have computer skills, especially database applications.
- Some employers look for education beyond high school, especially in two-year business administration programs.
- Credit managers generally have four-year college degrees and financial experience.

Salary Levels (in Recent Years)

- Credit clerical positions range from $15,000 to $23,000 for beginning workers with an average salary of $20,800.
- Credit managers range from $20,200 to $77,800; median salary, $39,700.
- The actual salary paid depends in part upon the company; the geographic area; and the education, skills, and experience of the worker.

Critical Thinking

1 Which job titles in this career area appeal to you most? Give some reasons for your choices.

2 What are some things you will have to do to achieve success in the career you selected?

Credit Occupations

Unit Eight

Savings and Investment Strategies

458

The headline could have read, "Final Score: Boston Celtics 104, Houston Rockets 98, stock price up ⅛!"

In the mid-1980s, the owners of the Boston Celtics, a team in the National Basketball Association (NBA), decided to take the team *public*. Taking the team public meant that ownership of the team was expanded to include other people. A limited partnership was created with shares sold on the New York Stock Exchange. Buyers of the shares were known as limited partners. The original owners became general partners.

A stock exchange, or stock market, is a place that brings sellers and buyers of stocks together. Sellers are hoping to find buyers who will pay higher prices for shares than what the sellers originally paid. In this way, sellers make a return on their investments. Buyers are looking for shares that are expected to increase in price so that the shares can later be sold at a profit. By negotiating with each other about prices, sellers and buyers determine whether the price of shares goes up or down.

Several million shares of Celtics stock were made available. This public offering, however, accounted for less than 50 percent of the value of the team. The general partners still controlled the team's overall operations.

Why did all the shares offered sell out within a couple of days? This investment opportunity had a unique appeal to sports fans. Recent championships and star players—such as Larry Bird, Robert Parrish, and Kevin McHale—made the Celtics popular.

Buyers of the shares believed that the price would go up over time.

Like most stocks, the price of the Celtics shares did change over time. When the team was winning, people wanted to be part of the action—not only as fans but also as owners. In addition, people wanted to own shares of the team in order to share in its profits. Profits resulted from ticket sales, television revenue, and money earned from the sale of shirts, hats, and other items with the team's name. When profits were high, share prices increased and investors earned about an 8 percent return. Investors also had the satisfaction of being part of a tradition that included 16 NBA championships.

As years passed, however, the Celtics started to lose star players. The team was not as popular or profitable. This decrease in performance resulted in lower profits, lower dividends, and lower share prices as demand declined.

All investments are risky. Questions you need to ask when putting money away for the future are: "Will this investment be the winner I need? Or will it be a loser in overtime?"

Critical Thinking

1 *Even though the first sentence mentions a loss by the Houston Rockets, they later won back-to-back world championships. If the Rockets had created a limited partnership, what effect would their championships have had on their share price?*

2 *How should a person select investments that serve long-term financial needs?*

A Slam Dunk Investment or a Missed Free Throw?

Chapter Twenty-Eight

Starting a Savings Program

Objectives

After studying this chapter and completing the end-of-chapter activities, you will be able to:

1 Explain why it is important to have a savings plan.

2 Compute interest on your savings.

3 Discuss the factors to consider when comparing savings plans.

4 Describe how savings help our economy.

"I'd sure like to buy that CD player," said Mel. "It has all the features I want and would be a great improvement over the one I have now. But it costs over $100! I can't afford it."

"Try saving your money," Hank said in an encouraging voice. "Maybe if you cut back on some of your other spending, you could save enough money to buy that CD player on your own."

"That would take forever," sighed Mel.

"It's easier than you think," responded Hank. "If you put aside just 35 cents a day, within a year you'd have over $125. If you save even more each day, you could buy the CD player and several new CDs."

"You're kidding!" exclaimed Mel.

"Really," said Hank. "Most people don't realize that saving small amounts of money on a regular basis can result in large amounts in the future, and that doesn't even include the interest you can earn."

"What's *interest*?" asked Mel.

"That's a story for later," said Hank. "I guess we need to sit down sometime and talk about planning your savings and investments."

WHY HAVE A SAVINGS PLAN?

Developing a savings plan should be part of everyone's personal financial activities. Savings are used to buy the goods and services we need and want as well as to prepare for future expenses and emergencies. When savings are invested and used by businesses and governments, savings help to keep our economy healthy.

Putting money aside in a systematic way to help reach a financial goal is a **savings plan**. How much you save, where you put your savings, and what you save for are important decisions. People save different amounts of money for different reasons and in different ways.

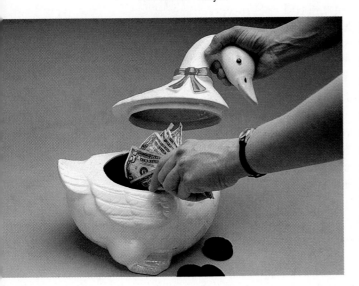

Josie Coramoto's parents have had a savings plan for years. Today they are using their savings for a down payment to buy real estate. They bought their home and make monthly payments on their mortgage. In addition, they make payments on ten acres of land they bought in a newly developed lake area. Mr. and Mrs. Coramoto also believe it is important to have money in the bank for emergencies. Every month, they deposit 10 percent of their income into a savings account.

Compared to people in most other nations, U.S. consumers save a very low percentage of their incomes.

Josie's older brother buys stocks and bonds with part of his wages. He is planning for his retirement years. Josie takes a certain amount of the money she earns baby-sitting and puts it in an envelope, which she keeps in a drawer in her room. As soon as she saves enough, she plans to buy a CD player.

A common trait is present in Josie's family: all family members save. Each member, however, has a different savings plan. All except Josie invest their savings. **Investing** means using your savings to earn more money. Josie is saving but not investing. She has a savings plan, but it offers no opportunity to earn money. Will you save and invest *your* money to make it grow?

HOW DO SAVINGS GROW?

A savings plan is important for your financial future. In addition to putting money aside as savings, you should have those savings working for you—that is, earning interest. Interest, as you learned in Chapter 20, is money you receive for letting others use your money. Financial institutions make loans and other investments with money they hold from savers. Savings put to work to earn interest is a form of investment.

Earning Interest

When savings and the simple interest earned on savings are invested, the increase over a number of years is larger than many people realize. **Simple interest** is interest that is computed only on the amount saved. For example, David Skinner is able to save $50 a month. In a year, his savings will amount to $600. In ten years, he will have saved $6,000. If he deposits his money in a savings program that earns 6 percent interest, paid every three months, his savings will increase rapidly as interest is added to his account. At the end of ten years, he will have more than $8,200 in his account rather than $6,000. Because of interest earned, his savings will have grown by more than $2,200.

David realizes the importance of this increase in his savings. He looks at a chart (see Figure 28-1) to see how much his savings will grow if he saves for a longer period. At 6 percent, his $50-a-month savings will grow to $14,500 in 15 years. Because interest rates change, David's account may grow even more. However, at certain times, David may earn less than 6 percent.

At the 6 percent rate, the interest David receives by the fifteenth year is more than the $50 he is putting in each month. He could actually start tak-

At 5 percent interest, compounded daily, saving just $1 a day for ten years will give you over $4,700.

Figure 28-1
Interest helps
savings grow.

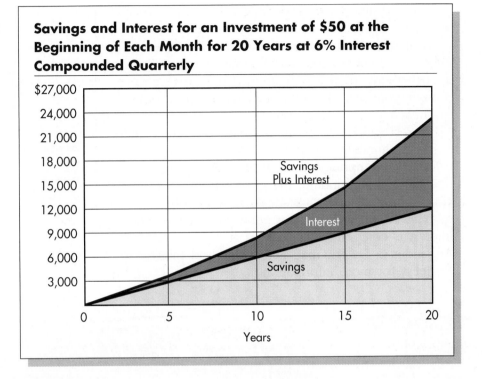

Savings and Interest for an Investment of $50 at the Beginning of Each Month for 20 Years at 6% Interest Compounded Quarterly

ing out $50 each month without decreasing the amount he has on deposit. He would have a permanent income of $50 a month. Often people fail to do this kind of planning for the future.

Compound Interest

People sometimes refer to a result called the *magic of compounding*. While no real magic exists, compounding of interest seems magical.

Compound interest is interest that is computed on the amount saved plus the interest previously earned. Compounding makes your savings grow faster than simple interest. After a number of years, the difference is quite significant.

In David's case, he is earning compound interest; that is, he is earning interest on the interest that is accumulating in his account. For example, simple interest of 10 percent on $1,000 is $100. However, if the interest is compounded, then the interest computed at the end of the next year will be based on $1,100 ($1,000 + $100 first-year interest). The 10 percent interest earned in the second

A *financial planner's* job duties include:
- Developing savings and investing plans for individuals and businesses
- Analyzing financial status of clients
- Discussing financial options with clients
- Preparing and submitting documents to implement savings and investing plans.

year would amount to $110. Interest the third year would be figured on $1,210 ($1,100 + $110 second-year interest) and would amount to $121. When interest is compounded, the amount of interest paid increases each time it is figured. If the interest were not compounded, the interest paid would be only $100 each year.

Interest can be compounded daily, monthly, quarterly, semiannually, or annually. Computers make calculating compound interest easy. The more frequent the compounding, the greater the growth in your savings. Figure 28-2 shows how rapidly monthly savings of different amounts increase when interest is compounded quarterly at 6 percent. (See Appendix C: Determining Percentage and Interest in Business for more information.)

Federal income tax must be paid on interest earned from most savings accounts. If you earn $100 in interest and are in a 28 percent tax bracket, you keep only $72.

Legal *Perspective*

The Truth in Savings Law

Which is better, $4.65 interest on $100.00 for a 360-day year or $4.73 on $100.00 for a 365-day year?

Situations like this used to make comparing savings accounts difficult. However, since 1993 when the Truth in Savings (TIS) law went into effect, consumers are presented with information to compare savings accounts. Truth in Savings requires that financial institutions provide the following information:

• fees on deposit accounts

• the interest rate

• the annual percentage yield (APY)

• other terms and conditions of the savings plan

TIS defines the *annual percentage yield (APY)* as the percentage rate equal to the total amount of interest that would be earned based on

• a $100 deposit

• the annual interest rate

• the frequency of compounding for a 365-day period

Using APY helps to eliminate confusion caused by the over 8 million variations of interest calculation methods. Before Truth in Savings, some financial institutions used 360-day years to calculate interest. Others used 365 or 366. APY, however, reflects the true amount of interest a saver should expect to earn.

TIS also requires that fees and the APY be provided on the customer's savings statement. The law also regulates advertising of deposit accounts to prevent deceptive promotions.

Critical Thinking

1 *How does the Truth in Savings law help consumers?*

2 *For financial institutions, what costs are associated with the Truth in Savings law?*

Figure 28-2

Even small amounts grow when interest is compounded.

Compound Interest

Monthly Savings	End of First Year	End of Second Year	End of Third Year	End of Fourth Year	End of Fifth Year	End of Tenth Year
$ 5.00	$ 61.98	$ 127.76	$ 197.76	$ 271.68	$ 350.32	$ 822.16
10.00	123.95	255.52	395.15	543.35	700.47	1,644.32
25.00	309.89	638.79	987.87	1,358.38	1,751.62	4,110.79
30.00	371.86	766.55	1,185.45	1,630.05	2,101.94	4,932.95
35.00	433.84	894.30	1,383.02	1,901.73	2,452.26	5,755.11
50.00	619.77	1,277.58	1,975.74	2,716.75	3,503.24	8,221.59

SELECTING A SAVINGS PLAN

Banks, credit unions, and savings and loan associations usually welcome small as well as large savings deposits. When deciding how to invest your savings, three main factors should be considered: safety, yield, and liquidity.

Safety

Today, most financial institutions have their savings accounts insured up to very large amounts. This insurance is a promise that your money will be available when you need it. Safety is assurance that the money you have invested will be returned to you.

Suppose you lend $100 to someone who promises to pay it back with 15 percent interest at the end of one year, a rate higher than banks pay. If the loan is paid back, you will receive $115 ($100 + $15 interest). However, if the borrower has no money at the end of the year, you may get nothing back. You may lose both the $100 you loaned and the $15 interest you should have earned. Investments are satisfactory when the safety of the amount invested and the interest to be paid can be depended upon.

Not all investors require the same degree of safety. Someone may have enough money to make 20 different investments. If one of them is lost, the investor still has the other 19. On the other hand, another person may only have a small amount of money and can make only one investment. One loss would be serious. Most people want to make investments that are as safe as possible.

The annual yield for an investment is computed by dividing the annual income from the investment by its cost. If you paid $50 for a share of stock that earned a $3 dividend, you would have a 6 percent yield ($3/$50).

NET FACTS

In the 1960s, the first version of the Internet was called the Advanced Research Projects Agency Network (ARPANET). ARPANET was designed so that scientists and military experts could keep communicating even if part of the network was damaged by a natural disaster or nuclear attack. Today's Internet is just as durable and flexible.

Yield

A good savings plan should earn a reasonable amount of interest. That is, your savings should have a satisfactory yield. The **yield**, also called the *rate of return,* is the percentage of interest that will be added to your savings over a period of time. Figure 28-3 shows the value of an original investment of $100 after 20 years at several different yields.

Usually higher yields and greater risks of loss go together. Investments with the federal government are the safest. When money is invested with individuals or businesses, it usually earns higher interest rates than those paid by the government because there is less safety. For example, while the government is paying 6 percent interest, one business may pay 8 percent and a business with a greater risk may have to pay 12 percent. Investors will not accept higher risks unless the yields are greater.

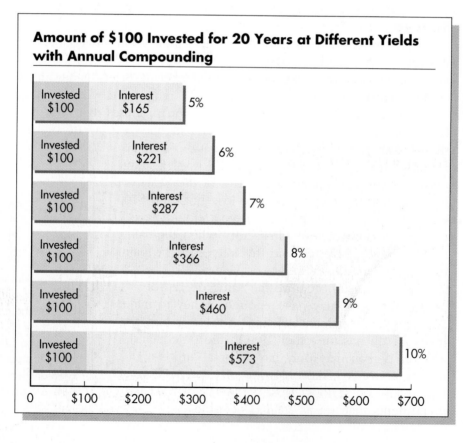

Amount of $100 Invested for 20 Years at Different Yields with Annual Compounding

Invested $100	Interest $165	5%
Invested $100	Interest $221	6%
Invested $100	Interest $287	7%
Invested $100	Interest $366	8%
Invested $100	Interest $460	9%
Invested $100	Interest $573	10%

0    $100 $200 $300 $400 $500 $600 $700

Figure 28-3
While a higher yield means greater growth, it may also mean greater risk.

The offer of a low rate of interest, however, does not guarantee safety. Similarly, high rates of interest do not mean that a loss will surely occur. The higher yields mean that investors generally believe that the situation involves a higher risk.

Liquidity

Sometimes you might need cash right away to pay unexpected bills or to take an unplanned trip. When an investment can be turned into money quickly, it is said to be a *liquid investment*. **Liquidity** is the ease with which an investment can be changed into cash without losing any of its value. This feature of an investment is important if you should need money for an emergency.

Suppose you have $5,000 on deposit in a bank. If you need money right away, you usually can go to your bank and withdraw it. On the other hand, suppose you own a piece of land that you bought for $5,000. The land may be a safe investment. If you need money immediately, however, you may find it difficult to sell the piece of land right away. You might even have to sell it for less than you paid for it if you cannot wait for a buyer who is willing to pay your price.

When you make a number of investments, you do not need all of them to have high liquidity. The amount of liquid investments you need will depend upon your personal situation and expected financial needs.

Inflation reduces the real rate of return on savings. For example, if you are earning 6 percent on your savings during a time when inflation is 5 percent, your inflation-adjusted rate of return is only 1 percent (6 – 5).

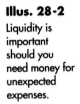

Illus. 28-2
Liquidity is important should you need money for unexpected expenses.

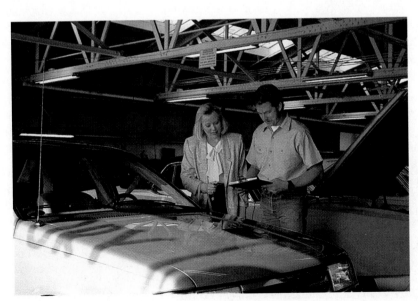

SAVINGS AND THE ECONOMY

Your savings serve a very useful economic purpose. Money borrowed from a financial institution may include your invested savings. These funds help individuals, businesses, and governments in different ways. People commonly borrow to pay for homes, motor vehicles, and college. When this money is spent, demand for goods and services is created. This, in turn, results in more jobs that allow even more spending by workers.

Businesses often borrow money to operate or expand their operations. Building a new factory, replacing old equipment, or selling a new product are common reasons for business borrowing. Each of these actions creates jobs and expands economic activity.

Governments may borrow to build highways, schools, or to provide other public services. Our economic system would be significantly weakened without savings and investments. Your invested savings contribute to our economic stability.

Illus. 28-3
Government and business often borrow to finance new construction projects.

Key Ideas

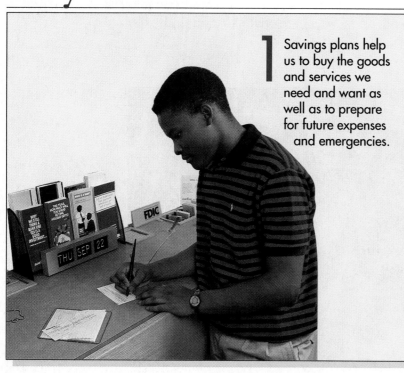

1 Savings plans help us to buy the goods and services we need and want as well as to prepare for future expenses and emergencies.

2 Interest earned on savings increases the value of the amount you have available to use in the future.

3 When comparing savings plans, a consumer should consider safety, yield, and liquidity.

4 Savings help the economy by making funds available to individuals, businesses, and governments for borrowing.

End of Chapter Activities

Increasing Your Business Vocabulary

The following terms should become part of your business vocabulary. For each numbered item, find the term that has the same meaning.

1 compound interest

6 investing

5 liquidity

3 savings plan

4 simple interest

2 yield

1 Interest computed on the amount saved plus the interest previously earned.

2 The percentage of interest that will be added to your savings over a period of time.

3 Putting money aside in a systematic way to help reach a financial goal.

4 Interest that is computed only on the amount saved.

5 The ease with which an investment can be changed into cash without losing any of its value.

6 Using your savings to earn more money for you.

Reviewing Your Reading

1 What are reasons why individuals should have a savings plan?

2 What are four different ways of saving?

3 When does money saved become an investment?

4 Why is interest that is compounded better than interest that is not compounded?

5 What will be the total savings if $10 is deposited monthly at 6 percent interest compounded quarterly for a period of ten years? (Use Figure 28-2 on page 465.)

6 Suppose you save $20 a month. If your savings plan compounds interest monthly, should you wait six months and invest $120 at that time, or should you make deposits each month? Why?

7 How is the safety of a savings plan measured?

8 Which of the following investments is liquid?
a. land
b. bank savings account

9 How do savings benefit the economy?

Using Your Business Knowledge

1 Yolanda Miller operates a pizza business, and she makes a nice profit. She keeps all of her business cash in a small fireproof safe in her basement. She has accumulated more than $2,000, more than she needs to buy supplies and meet unexpected business expenses. She wants to be sure that her money is safe and that she can get it when she needs it. What advice can you give Yolanda so that she can make better use of her money?

2 What factors affect the risk of an investment?

3 Donald Gorski has been saving money for the past year since he started working part-time. He keeps the money in a metal box in his bedroom. Donald's mother gives him $10 for every $100 saved to help him pay for a new car when he graduates from high school in two years. Donald has saved almost $1,000. Someone told him about a new business that pays 20 percent on money it borrows. Should Donald consider lending his money to this business? Why or why not?

4 Ella Chapman, a wealthy businessperson, invests $5,000 in a newly organized manufacturing company. Frank Brokaw earns a moderate salary, owns a small house, and has $5,000 in a savings account. He knows of Ella's investment. Because she has a reputation for being a good investor, Frank decides to invest in that company, too. Does the fact that the investment may be a good one for Ella Chapman mean that it is also a good investment for Frank? Explain your answer.

5 Jennie Wolfe has inherited $25,000. She graduated from high school three years ago, has a job in an accounting firm, is renting a small apartment with a friend, and has established a savings plan that she follows regularly. She does not want to take a chance on losing any of this inheritance, and yet she wants to get a good yield from investing it. She also believes that she will not need any large amounts of cash for the next several years. What advice would you give Jennie regarding how she should invest her inheritance?

6 What actions could employers and government take to encourage saving in our society?

Calculating Business Problems

1 Even small amounts add up to large sums in a short time. How much will each person below save in one year (365 days) if he or she saves the following amounts without interest being added?

a. Charles Jason: 20 cents a day
b. Carla Spivak: 95 cents a week
c. Alice Farney: $10 every two weeks
d. Nolan Robinson: $20 a month

2 Ramon Valdez wants a savings plan that will permit him to buy a CD player/tape deck that costs $450.

a. How much will he have to save each month to be able to make his purchase at the end of 6 months? at the end of 12 months? If he saves at the 12-month rate, how much longer would he have to save to buy a CD player/tape deck that costs $825?

b. Ramon learned that interest can double the amount of money you deposit if you leave it on deposit long enough. To find the number of years required to double the amount deposited, divide 72 by the interest rate. If Ramon deposited $360, how long would it take for his deposit to double if his account paid 4 percent interest? 6 percent interest? 8 percent interest?

3 Ceile Hamon deposited $50 in her bank account each month for 15 years.

a. What is the total amount that she has invested?

b. How much money is in her account if her deposits earn 6 percent interest compounded quarterly? (See Figure 28-1 on page 463.)

Applying Technology

Using the *Introduction to Business* template and your spreadsheet program software, select problem CH28. After the problem appears on your screen, complete the following activities. Then, after you have completed each step, display or print the completed spreadsheet for each activity. If you do not have a printer available, answer the questions before you leave the computer.

1 The table shown is similar to Figure 28-2 on page 465. The interest rate shown is an annual rate, and interest is compounded at the end of each month. Use the @FV function to complete the table. Watch absolute and relative cell references. The function for the first cell has been completed as an example.

Answer the following questions:

a. If you save $5 per month, how much will you have accumulated at the end of the fifth year?

b. If you save $35 per month, how much will you have accumulated at the end of the second year?

2 At the top of the table, enter 0.05 to change the interest rate to 5 percent. Answer the following questions.

a. If you save $5 per month, how much will you have accumulated at the end of the fifth year?

b. If you save $30 per month, how much will you have accumulated at the end of the first year?

3 At the top of the table, enter 0.07 to change the interest rate to 7 percent. Answer the following questions.

a. If you save $5 per month, how much will you have accumulated at the end of the fifth year?

b. If you save $10 per month, how much will you have accumulated at the end of the third year?

Optional: Create bar charts showing the accumulated savings over time at 7 percent annual interest for each amount of monthly savings.

Making Decisions

Cindy Redmond has $500 in a savings account that is paying her 4 percent interest. This money is being saved for a computer camp she plans to attend next summer. Cindy's friend, Rosalind Tate, knows of a local business project where the $500 could be invested at a 10 percent rate of return. This company has developed many successful business activities in the community.

1 What might be the advantages and disadvantages for Cindy of taking her money out of her savings and putting it into this other investment?

2 What advice would you give Cindy about this investment opportunity?

Chapter Twenty-Nine

Key Terms

regular savings account

savings account register

withdrawal slip

money market account

certificate of deposit (CD)

individual retirement account (IRA)

Using Your Savings Plan

Objectives

After studying this chapter and completing the end-of-chapter activities, you will be able to:

1 Explain how to open and use a regular savings account.

2 Discuss the features of a money market account.

3 Identify the advantages and disadvantages of a certificate of deposit (CD).

4 State at least four questions to consider when selecting a financial institution for your savings.

5 Explain why an individual retirement account (IRA) should be considered.

Ed sat down with his friends in the restaurant booth. Arthur looked at Ed and called out, "You're looking awfully proud today. You must have received a great birthday present."

"My parents gave me a CD," Ed said to his friends.

"What group is it?" asked Kendra. Kendra had one of the biggest collection of audio CDs

in town.

"No, it's not that kind of CD," responded Ed.

"Well, then it has to be a CD-ROM for your computer," Jock said. "Does it have super graphics?" Jock was never happier than when he was talking about computers.

"It's not that kind of CD either," Ed sighed. "This CD grows."

"You mean it's alive!" exclaimed Arthur.

"Don't you geniuses know anything?" Ed said in a disgusted voice. "This is a certificate of deposit that will grow in value for my college education."

"Oh! A savings account!" Ed's friends responded.

"This is a kind of CD that I want to learn more about," added Kendra.

REGULAR SAVINGS ACCOUNTS

In recent years, the types of savings programs available to consumers have expanded. Special savings accounts such as money market accounts, savings certificates, and individual retirement accounts have become widespread. However, regular savings accounts continue to be a popular part of most consumers' savings and investment plans. In recent years, more than 70 percent of U.S. consumers had a savings account in a financial institution.

A **regular savings account** is a savings plan with a low or zero minimum balance. Savers usually are allowed to withdraw money as needed, which means that a regular savings account has high liquidity. A regular savings account is an easy and convenient way to make systematic deposits. These accounts pay interest while keeping money safe. Savings accounts may be opened at a commercial bank, a mutual savings bank, a savings and loan association, or a credit union.

Opening a Savings Account

Opening a regular savings account is similar to opening a checking account, which you learned about in Chapter 21. You have to fill out a signature card, make a deposit to your account, and receive a savings account register.

Making Savings Deposits

A **savings account register** is shown in Figure 29-1. In this book, you must record each deposit or withdrawal as it is made. You must also add the interest when the bank reports it to you.

Club accounts are designed for a specific savings goal such as a vacation or holiday. These savings plans may have early withdrawal penalties and may pay lower rates than other types of accounts.

The bank periodically sends a statement to customers showing deposits, withdrawals, and any interest added to the account. As shown in Figure 29-2, a savings statement shows the balance of your account as of the date of the statement. It is important for

Figure 29-1

It is your responsibility to record each account transaction in the savings account register.

Date	Memo	(−) Amount of Withdrawal	(+) Amount of Deposit	(+) Interest Credited	Balance
					0|00
July 2	opened account		35|00		+35|00 / 35|00
July 25	part of summer earnings		50|00		+50|00 / 85|00
Aug. 5	birthday gift from parents		25|00		+25|00 / 110|00
Aug. 28	supplies for school	19|00			−19|00 / 91|00
Sept. 19	automatic teller	25|00			−25|00 / 66|00
Sept. 30	interest received			67	+|67 / 66|67

Figure 29-2

A savings account statement shows deposits, withdrawals, and any interest added to the account.

Second National Bank
Savings Account Statement

Tas-fan Sun
303 Lewis Manor
Houston, TX   77083-2170

Account Number 7666-0052

BALANCE FORWARD	NO. OF WITH-DRAWALS	TOTAL WITH-DRAWALS	NO. OF DEPOSITS	TOTAL DEPOSITS	INTEREST	BALANCE THIS STAEMENT
0 |00|	2	44 |00	3	110 |00	0 |67	66 |67

DATE	AMOUNT	TRANSACTION DESCRIPTION	BALANCE
07/02	+ 35.00	initial deposit	35.00
07/25	+ 50.00	deposit	85.00
08/05	+ 25.00	deposit	110.00
08/28	− 19.00	withdrawal	91.00
09/19	− 25.00	ATM withdrawal	66.00
09/30	+ 0.67	interest	66.67

NET FACTS

Hypermedia means using hypertext links to connect different types of media. Examples of different media are animation, graphics, pictures, sound, text, and video.

you to update your record and reconcile your savings account register with the bank statement. Errors you discover should be reported to the bank immediately.

When making a deposit, you fill out a deposit slip much like the ones used in making a checking account deposit. You present this slip and the money or checks you are depositing to the bank teller. You will be given a receipt for your deposit. You must then enter the deposit on your register. You may also mail in your deposits and make deposits through ATMs or electronic funds transfer (EFT).

Withdrawing Money

Normally, checks cannot be written against a savings account. If you need money from your savings account, you must fill out a withdrawal slip. A **withdrawal slip** is a written request to take money out of your account. You give the withdrawal slip and proper identification to the bank teller.

Before any withdrawal can be made, a teller must check the bank's record to be sure that you have enough money in your account to cover the withdrawal. If you are withdrawing money using electronic funds transfer, the bank computer will automatically check the balance in your account. The bank's record is official. However, if there is a difference between the balance in your register and the bank's record, the cause of the error must be determined and corrected. After the withdrawal is recorded on the bank's record, you will receive your money and a record documenting the withdrawal.

Whether you make your withdrawal at the bank or are withdrawing money using electronic funds transfer, the withdrawal should be recorded in your register. Keeping your record of the account balance is important.

Illus. 29-1
Carefully record each withdrawal and update your account balance.

MONEY MARKET ACCOUNTS

One of the special savings accounts available to consumers that allows them to earn higher yields is the money market account. A **money market account** is one that pays a variable interest rate based on rates paid to holders of short-term government debt, such as U.S. Treasury bills. (For more information about government debt, see Chapter 30.) Interest paid on money market accounts reflects interest being paid in the money markets.

Money market accounts generally do not require long-term deposits but usually have relatively large minimum balance requirements. With these accounts, the interest paid will vary daily or weekly. Be sure to know the current rate being paid in the money markets when opening one of these accounts. The yield from money market accounts will be higher than regular savings but somewhat less than long-term certificates of deposit.

The minimum deposit on a money market account is large and the funds are kept on deposit for a longer period of time. For these reasons, the financial institution can invest your deposit in higher yielding investments. Because the financial institution can earn higher yields, it can afford to pay you higher interest rates on your account. This relationship between size of the deposit and length of time on deposit means that money market accounts generally have higher yields than regular savings accounts.

In recent years, the yield for money market accounts has ranged from as low as 2 percent to as high as 12 percent, depending on the current level of interest rates.

CERTIFICATES OF DEPOSIT

To earn a rate of interest higher than on a regular savings account, three conditions are usually present:

1. A minimum deposit ($100, $250, $500, $1,000, or more) is required.

2. Your money must be left on deposit for a certain period of time, from a few days to several years.

3. If your money is withdrawn before the stated time, some of your interest may be lost and other penalties may be assessed.

A long-term time deposit that commonly meets these conditions and pays higher interest rates than regular savings accounts is referred to as a **certificate of deposit (CD).**

When you purchase a CD, you usually receive a numbered certificate (see Figure 29-3). The certificate indicates how much you deposited, what the interest rate will be, and when you may withdraw your deposit plus interest. It lists the rules and regulations

The Midvale Savings Bank
Midvale, Michigan 48196

40-030000-7-26

DATE June 4   19 --   6793-4

* * * * *   SOC. SEC. NO.
287-43-6841

TIME CERTIFICATE OF DEPOSIT NOT NEGOTIABLE · NOT SUBJECT TO CHECK

DEPOSITOR(S) ___Andrea Clippinger___
MIDVALE
DEPOSIT ___SAVINGS BANK___ 2,500dol's00cts ___ DOLLARS, $ 2,500.00

"We" means the financial institution. "You" means the depositor(s) named above. We will pay this certificate to you when you present and deliver it to us, properly endorsed (signed by you), on a maturity date. If more than one of you are named above, you will own this certificate as joint tenants with right of survivorship (and not as tenants in common). (You may change this ownership by written instructions.) We will treat any one of you as owner for purposes of endorsement, payment of principal and interest, presentation (demanding payment of amount due), transfer, and any notice to or from you. Each of you appoints the other as your agent for the purposes described above. We will use the address on our records for mailing notices to you. You cannot transfer or assign this certificate or any rights under it without our written consent.

This ___31 Day___   Time Certificate of Deposit matures on ___July 5___ , 19 --

☐ PRESENT THIS CERTIFICATE PROMPTLY AT MATURITY FOR PAYMENT. IT IS NOT AUTOMATICALLY RENEWABLE AND NO INTEREST WILL ACCRUE AFTER THE MATURITY DATE SHOWN.
☒ THIS CERTIFICATE MATURES ON THE MATURITY DATE STATED ABOVE. IT WILL BE AUTOMATICALLY RENEWABLE FOR SUCCESSIVE TERMS, EACH EQUAL TO THE ORIGINAL TERM, UNTIL ONE OF THE FOLLOWING THINGS HAPPENS: 1) THIS CERTIFICATE IS PERSONALLY PRESENTED FOR PAYMENT ON A MATURITY DATE OR WITHIN TEN DAYS AFTER THE MATURITY DATE; 2) WE RECEIVE WRITTEN NOTICE FROM YOU BEFORE A MATURITY DATE OF YOUR INTENTIONS TO CASH IN THIS CERTIFICATE; 3) NOT LESS THAN 14 DAYS BEFORE A MATURITY DATE WE MAIL TO YOU A WRITTEN NOTICE OF OUR INTENTION TO CASH IN THIS CERTIFICATE ON A MATURITY DATE.

INTEREST TO FIRST MATURITY DATE WILL ACCRUE AT THE YEARLY RATE OF

___7.00___ % USING A ___365___ DAY/YEAR ACCRUED INTEREST WILL BE

COMPOUNDED _____

PAID ___at Maturity___

___127 Stone Spring Way___

___Midvale, MI 48196___
Notify this institution immediately of any change in the above address.

AUTOMATIC RENEWALS: Each renewal term will be the same as the orginal term, beginning on the maturity date. The interest rate will be the same we offer on new certificates on the maturity date which have the same term, minimum balance (if any) and other features as this original term. You may call us on or shortly before the maturity date and we will tell you what the interest rate will be for the next renewal term. We will not pay interest after the last maturity date if this certificate is not automatically renewed.

Thomas Meyer _____ AUTHORIZED SIGNATURE
NOTICE: See Other Side for Penalty on Payment of Time Deposit Before Maturity

Figure 29-3
CDs are attractive to many investors.

that must be followed for the certificate to be honored and the higher interest rate to be paid. The certificate also states the penalties for withdrawing your deposit before the maturity date. To cash your CD, you must present and endorse the certificate at the financial institution.

EVALUATING WHERE TO PUT YOUR SAVINGS

Many types of financial institutions offer savings plans to consumers. Commercial banks, savings and loan associations, savings banks, and credit unions all provide regular and special savings accounts. Other organizations such as credit card companies and retail stores also offer financial services. These other organizations are sometimes referred to as *nonbanks*.

Questions to Ask

In choosing a financial institution for your savings, consider needs and goals. Answers to the following questions can help you choose the institution that is best for you:

- How safe is your money with that institution?

- How much interest do you want to earn?

- How frequently is interest compounded and added to your account?

- What services are offered that are important to you?

- Does the financial institution offer help in selecting the best savings plan from among its options?

- What are the institution's business hours? Is electronic banking available for after-hours transactions?

- Is the institution conveniently located?

The institution you select should offer a variety of savings and investment opportunities as well as friendly, efficient service.

Considering Safety

An important consideration is feeling sure that you will get back the money you deposit into a savings account. The safety of your

The International Credit Union Movement

What do entrepreneurs in Ghana, Indonesia, and many other countries have in common? Many small business owners around the world make use of credit union services.

The Techiman Women's Market Credit Union in Ghana has over 200 members. Loans are made to women who sell multicolored fabrics, produce, dried cassava (a starchy root), soup, furniture, and clothing. The vendors in this market need money for stall fees, supplies, school fees, and day care. Before the creation of the credit union, "moneylenders" were the main source of funds. The moneylenders charged as much as 50 to 60 percent for loans. Now, members can borrow at 18 percent interest.

Sri Mujiati belongs to Satu Bambu Credit Union in Indonesia. Until 1985, she made meatballs to sell at the local market in her village. Then the market became saturated with meatball vendors. Mujiati changed her product to cookies, and three years later, changed it again to noodles. Most recently she switched to selling banana chips. Loans from the credit union made it possible for Mujiati to fund her business, to be able to pay for her children's education, and to remodel her two-room home.

The World Council of Credit Unions reports that over 80 million people around the world are credit union members. Credit unions operate in more than 60 countries including Australia, Bolivia, Botswana, Bulgaria, the Czech Republic, Ecuador, El Salvador, Fiji, India, Mexico, New Zealand, Nigeria, and Singapore.

Critical Thinking

1 How do credit unions serve the personal and business needs of members?

2 Why are credit unions successful in areas that other financial institutions may avoid?

investment is something you need to examine before depositing your money into one of the savings plans. As you learned in Chapter 20, deposit insurance protects savings in most financial institutions.

If one of your investment goals is *safety*, it is wise to check on deposit insurance before you invest. Asking the question, "Is my deposit *federally insured?*" is appropriate when selecting a savings plan.

Sometimes it is possible to earn a higher rate of return on CDs from financial institutions in other states. Many banks have toll-free numbers for purchasing out-of-state CDs.

SAVING FOR RETIREMENT

Federal tax laws permit you to plan ahead for your retirement in a unique way. This can be done by placing a portion of your wages or salary in an account that you designate as an individual retirement account. An **individual retirement account (IRA)** is a tax-sheltered retirement plan that allows certain workers to invest up to $2,000 annually and pay no tax either on that sum or on its earnings until the money is withdrawn.

In recent years, for instance, a single worker who earned less than $25,000 per year in salary or wages could deposit up to $2,000 in an IRA and then deduct that amount from the adjusted gross income when filing a federal income tax form. Also, any interest earned on that IRA would be tax deferred. Individuals earning between $25,000 and $35,000 could deduct a reduced portion of earned annual income.

Single workers earning $35,000 or more could not deduct any wages or salary from the adjusted gross income. The interest earned on a nondeductible IRA, however, would still not be taxable until withdrawn. When you consider the impact of earnings accumulating tax deferred, the IRA can be an attractive investment.

Because an IRA is a retirement plan, penalties are assessed if withdrawals are made prior to age 59½. The penalty is a percentage of the amount withdrawn, and income tax also must be paid. An exception is made, however, if you incur a permanent disability and need to withdraw funds from an IRA.

Illus. 29-2

Tax-deferred earnings on an Individual Retirement Account can help to provide a comfortable retirement.

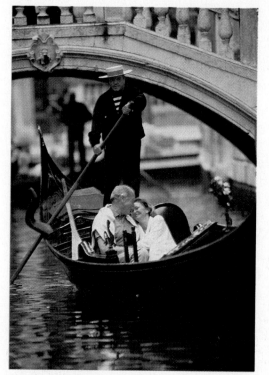

When you are ready to set up an IRA, you should consult a financial institution representative on current laws and procedures for establishing an IRA. Most financial institutions offer a variety of IRA plans. Money market accounts and CDs are commonly used for IRAs. Annuities (which you will learn about in Chapter 39) as well as mutual funds and common or preferred stocks (which you will learn about in Chapter 30) are among the investments that can be considered when setting up an IRA.

A regular savings account at a credit union is called a *share account*.

Key Ideas

1 When opening a regular savings account a signature card is signed, a deposit is made, and a savings account register is received.

2 A money market account pays a variable interest rate based on rates paid to holders of short-term government debt, such as U.S. Treasury bills.

3 A certificate of deposit (CD) provides a higher rate of return than other savings plans; however the funds must remain on deposit for a set time period.

4 When selecting a financial institution for your savings consider the safety, interest rate, compounding frequency, services offered, the business hours, and location.

5 An individual retirement account (IRA) allows a person to avoid taxes on deposits and interest earned until the money is withdrawn after age 59½.

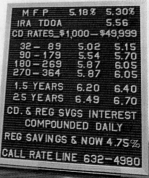

End of Chapter Activities

Increasing Your Business Vocabulary

The following terms should become part of your business vocabulary. For each numbered item, find the term that has the same meaning.

certificate of deposit
(CD)

individual retirement
account (IRA)

money market
account

regular savings
account

savings account register

withdrawal slip

1 A written request to take money out of your account.

2 A long-term deposit that has certain restrictions and pays higher interest rates than a regular savings account.

3 A special account that pays a variable interest rate based on rates paid to holders of short-term government debt.

4 A tax-sheltered retirement plan that allows certain workers to invest up to $2,000 annually and pay no tax either on that sum or on its earnings until the money is withdrawn.

5 A savings plan with a low or no minimum balance and the ability to make withdrawals at almost any time.

6 A record in which you record deposits, withdrawals, interest earned, and the balance of your savings account.

Reviewing Your Reading

1 Why are regular savings accounts a popular part of the savings and investment plans of most consumers?

2 What types of businesses offer savings accounts?

3 What steps would you follow in opening a savings account?

4 How does a depositor withdraw money from a savings account?

5 What affects the rate paid to savers who have a money market account?

6 Name three conditions that a depositor must accept to earn a higher rate of interest with a certificate of deposit.

7 What are some questions you should ask when choosing a financial institution where you might put your savings?

8 What are two restrictions placed on IRAs?

9 Why is it important to have a long-range goal when putting money into an IRA?

Using Your Business Knowledge

1 What characteristics of savings accounts make them especially good for students?

2 What are some procedures that you should follow when using a savings account register for your savings account? When should withdrawals and deposits be recorded in your register? How should the monthly or quarterly statements be used?

3 Financial institutions commonly pay a higher interest rate on special savings accounts than they do on regular accounts. Explain how they can afford to pay a higher interest rate on special accounts.

4 What is wrong with each of the following statements made by students who are discussing investing their savings?

a. Most savings accounts are alike, so why bother to shop around?

b. All young people should have IRAs.

c. Keeping your savings register up-to-date isn't important because the bank has the official record.

d. Always put your money in the savings plan that pays the highest interest regardless of your investment goal.

Calculating Business Problems

1 Joanne Olson plans to deposit $8 a month in a savings account.

a. How much will she deposit in the first 6 months?

b. If she increases her monthly deposit to $11 for the next 6 months, how much will have been deposited in 12 months?

c. How much will she have deposited in the first 18 months of her savings plan?

2 Three people have the following amounts deposited in regular savings accounts at different places: Dan Schweizer, $10,000 in a commercial bank; Margaret Zimmerman, $20,000 in a credit union; and Sumiyo Nagai, $45,000 in a savings and loan association. Each financial institution has insurance on account balances up to $100,000.

a. What is the total amount of money invested by all three depositors?

b. How much money would be lost, if any, by each depositor if all of these savings institutions went bankrupt?

3 Bernard Stahl can earn 5 percent on a regular savings account, 8 percent on a CD, and 11 percent on a money market account.

   a. If he invests $5,000, how much interest would he earn in one year in each of these plans? (Compute simple interest.)

   b. How much more would he earn on the money market account than he would with the regular savings account?

   c. If he decided to invest $2,000 in each plan, how much total interest would he earn in one year? In five years? (Compute simple interest.)

Hint: Refer to Appendix C: Determining Percentage and Interest in Business.

4 In a recent year, U.S. financial institutions had the record of accounts and deposits shown in the table at right.

   a. What percentage of the total of those deposits was in each of the different savings plans? (Round to the nearest tenth of a percentage point.)

	Savings Deposits
Regular savings accounts	$396 billion
Certificates of deposit	232 billion
Money market accounts	571 billion

   b. If the total saved in each plan increases 10 percent each year, what would be the total of those deposits the following year?

Applying Technology

Using the *Introduction to Business* template and your word processing program software, select problem CH29. After the problem appears on your screen, complete the following activities. Then, print and sign your completed forms. If you do not have a printer available, save the forms on a data disk to give to your teacher.

1 Complete the signature card for a new regular savings account. Fill in the blanks with information about yourself. For the information that you enter, use italics and a different font of type from the one used on the rest of the signature card.

2 You have purchased a $2,500 certificate of deposit. Complete the certificate with information about yourself. The following are other necessary data: use the current date at the top of the certificate, the term is 90 days, the maturity date is 90 days from the current date, the interest rate is 5 percent. For the information that you enter, use boldface and a different font of type from the one used on the rest of the certificate.

Making Decisions

Cesar Garcia received $5,000 from an aunt to use for college in three years. He is considering a regular savings account, a money market account, and a certificate of deposit. Over the next couple of years Cesar expects that his family may face financial difficulties due to the health of his parents.

1 What factors should Cesar consider when choosing a type of savings account?

2 What type of account would you recommend for Cesar?

Chapter Thirty

Investing in Bonds and Stocks

Key Terms

securities

bonds

corporate bonds

face value

municipal bonds

market value

preferred stock

common stock

price-earnings ratio (P/E)

stockbroker

commission

stock exchanges

investment club

mutual funds

Objectives

After studying this chapter and completing the end-of-chapter activities, you will be able to:

1 Explain how investing in bonds is different from investing in stocks.

2 Give reasons why organizations sell bonds.

3 Discuss the types of bonds sold by governments.

4 Describe differences between preferred and common stock.

5 Explain factors to consider when selecting stock investments.

6 Discuss the benefits of investment clubs and mutual funds.

7 Evaluate security investments based on financial needs, goals, safety, liquidity, and rate of return.

"We need to consider investments to supplement our savings account so we will earn higher returns for the future," Terress Mendoza said to her husband.

"What do you mean?" asked Alejandro. "Our jobs pay very well. We shouldn't have any financial difficulties."

"We might want to consider investments that could get us a better return, although there will be a bit more risk," responded Terress.

"What about safety?" wondered Alejandro. "We have to be careful."

"We have over $20,000 in our savings account," answered Terress. "That is money we will keep for emergencies. But with some of the other money we invest, we can take a little more risk and have the chance of increased returns."

"Are you sure that's what we should do?" Alejandro asked next.

"We have a good insurance plan," Terress explained. "So we can get into some other investments."

"Well, we better learn a little more about bonds and stocks before deciding whether or not to invest in securities," cautioned Alejandro.

TYPES OF SECURITIES

As you have learned, depositing money in a savings account is an easy way to invest money. However, there are other ways to invest, such as buying bonds and stocks. Some people do not consider investing in bonds and stocks because they are unsure about the safety of such investments.

The term **securities** refers to bonds, stocks, and other documents that are sold by corporations and governments to raise large sums of money. These investments are commonly divided into two major categories—debt and equity.

Debt Securities

Sometimes you are in need of money when funds are not available. You might consider borrowing from a relative or friend. Companies and governments also borrow. Bonds and other documents that represent borrowing are called *debt securities*.

Equity Securities

People commonly invest money in companies in hopes of earning more money. One way of investing in a company is to purchase part ownership in the company. Ownership in a company is represented by *equity securities*. For example, a share of stock is an equity security.

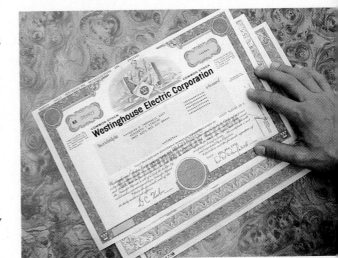

Illus. 30-1
A share of stock is an equity security.

INVESTING IN CORPORATE BONDS

To raise money for operations or future expansion, many corporations sell bonds. To better understand bonds, it is helpful to know the answers to two questions: What is a bond? Why do the values of bonds change?

Buying a Bond Is Making a Loan

A **bond** is a certificate representing a promise to pay a definite amount of money at a stated interest rate on a specified maturity date (due date). Bonds are similar to promissory notes, which were discussed in Chapter 25. When you buy a bond, you are lending money to the organization selling the bond. You become a creditor of the organization. Bonds issued by corporations are called **corporate bonds**.

Each bond has its face value printed on the front of the certificate. The **face value**, also called the *maturity value*, is the amount being borrowed by the seller of the bond. Interest is paid periodically to the investor based on that amount and the stated interest rate. On the bond's maturity date, the face value is repaid to the investor.

Changing Bond Values

Bonds are bought and sold in bond markets. Figure 30-1 gives an explanation of listings for the corporate bond market. Note that the prices are stated in 100s, but the bonds are sold in $1,000 denominations (ten times the listed amount). Therefore, the Mobil

Figure 30-1

Bonds that are traded on the exchanges are listed daily in newspapers.

CORPORATION BONDS
Volume, $37,477,000

Bonds	Cur Yld	Vol	Close		Net Chg
Mobil 8⅜01	7.6	38	109¾	+	⅞
Moran 8¾408f	cv	37	72½	+	½
Motrla zr09	...	8	111	+	½
Motrla zr13	...	25	76	+	½
NJBTI 7¼11	7.4	15	97¾	+	¼
NRUt 9s21	8.2	10	110	+	7½
Nabis 7⅜s03	7.8	10	100	+	⅜
Nabis 8.3s99	7.9	279	105	+	1⅝
Nabis 8s00	7.6	145	105	+	⅜
NMed 9⅝02	9.1	100	106	+	½
Navstr 9s04	9.0	35	99¾	−	¼
NETelTel 7⅜07	7.4	5	99⅝	+	⅛
NYTel 7½09	7.5	6	100	+	⅞
NYTel 7⅜11	7.6	25	97½		
NYTel 7⅞17	7.9	30	100	+	⅞
NYTel 7s25	7.6	10	92¼	+	⅛
Novacr 5½2000	cv	16	85¼	+	1½
OcciP 11¾11	10.8	31	108⅜	+	¼
OcciP 9⅝99	9.3	10	103⅞	+	1⅛

Explanatory Notes: zr – zero coupon

Bonds			Cur Yld	Vol	Close	Net Chg.
Mobil	8⅜	01	7.6	38	109¾	+⅞
(1)	(2)	(3)	(4)	(5)	(6)	(7)

1. Mobil (Mobil Co.) is the corporation that issued the bond.
2. The original rate of interest paid on the face value of the bond; e.g., 8.375%.
3. Year in which the bond matures is 2001.
4. Current yield based on the selling price of the bond. If a cv appears in this column, it refers to a convertible bond, which can be traded for stock in the corporation.
5. Number of bonds traded that day which had a face value of $1,000 each.
6. The final price for a bond that day; e.g., $1,097.50.
7. Change in the closing price compared with the previous day; e.g., $8.75.

bond quoted at 109¾ costs $1,097.50 ($109.75 × 10). These bonds closed up (+) ⅞ from the previous day; that is, the increase of today's price over yesterday's is $8.75 (⅞, or $0.875, × 10).

The price investors are willing to pay for a bond depends upon the bond's stated interest rate. If interest rates on similar bonds are higher than the bond's stated rate, investors will want to buy the bond for less than its face value. On the other hand, if the bond's stated interest rate is higher than interest rates on similar bonds, the seller of the bond will want to receive more than its face value. Bond prices are determined by buyers and sellers in the bond market.

TYPES OF GOVERNMENT BONDS

Like corporations, governments also issue bonds to raise money for funding public services. Local, state, and the federal governments issue a variety of bonds.

Municipal Bonds

A city may want to build a new park or a new school. A state may need funds to build or repair highways and bridges. Bonds issued by local and state governments are called **municipal bonds,** or *munis.*

Municipal bonds have an advantage over corporate bonds. Most often, interest earned on the municipal bonds is exempt from federal and most state income taxes. In order to avoid taxes, people buy municipal bonds even though the interest rate usually is not as high as that offered on corporate bonds. Like corporate bonds, municipal bonds are normally sold in amounts of $1,000 or larger. Municipal bonds are usually considered to be safer investments than corporate bonds.

U.S. Savings Bonds

One of the safest investments, and one desirable for investors with only small amounts to invest, is U.S. government savings bonds. Figure 30-2

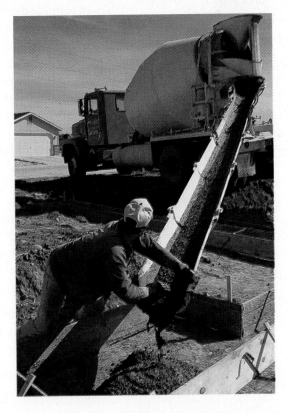

Illus. 30-2

Local governments often fund construction projects through municipal bonds.

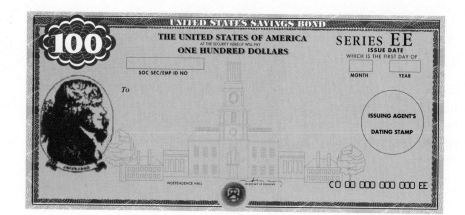

Figure 30-2
A Series EE savings bond with a face value of $100.

shows an example of a Series EE savings bond. Series EE savings bonds, which come in denominations from $50 to $10,000, pay interest through a process called *discounting*.

A Series EE bond is bought at half its face value. A $50 bond costs $25 and, at the end of its full term, pays at least $50. The difference between the purchase price and the redemption (payoff) value is the interest earned. The interest earned is determined by the length of time the bond is held. The time it takes for a savings bond to mature will vary depending on the current interest rate being paid.

The convenience of buying U.S. government EE bonds is an attractive feature to some investors. Amounts can be deducted, for instance, from a person's paycheck and accumulated until a bond can be purchased in the employee's name. A weekly deduction of $10 would result in a $100 EE bond being acquired after five weeks. This approach is an easy way for someone to get started on an investment program.

The U.S. government also sells Series HH savings bonds. These bonds are available to investors in face values from $500 to $10,000, are not discounted, and pay a fixed rate of interest through a check mailed to the investor. Series HH bonds are different from EE bonds in three important ways:

1. EE bonds pay interest only when the bond is cashed, while HH bonds pay interest semiannually directly to the bondholder.

2. EE bonds can be purchased at financial institutions throughout the United States and through

The stocks of new and smaller companies are bought and sold through the over-the-counter (OTC) market. The OTC is a network of stockbrokers connected through a system of computers, teletype machines, fax machines, and telephones.

payroll deduction plans, while HH bonds are available only in exchange for eligible EE bonds or savings notes called Freedom Shares.

3. There is an annual purchase limit of $30,000 (face value) on EE bonds, but there is no such limit on HH bonds.

Other Federal Securities

The federal government also borrows using Treasury bills, notes, and bonds. The difference among these debt securities is the length of time to maturity. Treasury bills (T-bills) involve short-term borrowing, with maturities from 91 days to 1 year. Treasury notes (T-notes) are intermediate-length borrowing with maturities from 1 to 10 years. Treasury bonds (T-bonds) range from 10 to 30 years and are considered long-term borrowing.

INVESTING IN STOCKS

Investing in stocks is quite different from investing in bonds. When you invest in bonds, you lend money. When you invest in stock, you become a part owner of a business. As you learned in Chapter 6, you become a stockholder when you buy one or more shares in a corporation. Ownership is shown by a printed form known as a *stock certificate*. If a business is profitable, part of the profits may be paid to the stockholders in the form of *dividends*.

The opportunity to earn a high rate of return attracts people to invest in stocks. However, the risk of losing your money is usually greater with stocks than with bonds. A corporation must pay bondholders the rate of interest promised before it can pay any dividends to stockholders. If there is not enough money left to pay dividends or if the corporation decides to use the money earned for business expansion, stockholders receive no dividends. If a corporation goes out of business, a stockholder may get little or nothing back from the investment. Bondholders, on the other hand, may get back all or part of the money owed to them.

Stocks have a market value. The **market value** of a stock is the price at which a share of stock can be bought and sold in the stock market. The market value is the best indicator of the current

A stockbroker's job duties include:

- Searching for potential clients using advertising, mailing lists, and personal contacts
- Interviewing clients to determine financial goals and resources
- Selling financial products and services to clients for investment purposes
- Completing computerized forms to process transactions requested by clients.

A zero-coupon bond does not earn regular interest; instead it grows to the maturity value. If you purchase a zero-coupon bond for $600, you will receive $1,000 at maturity.

value of a share of stock. The market value can change rapidly. If the business is doing well, the market value is likely to go up. If the business has a poor record, the market value usually goes down. The market value also may be affected by the state of the economy and the phase of the business cycle we are in, as discussed in Chapter 4.

Preferred Stock

Preferred stock is one of two main classes of stock issued by corporations. **Preferred stock** has priority over common stock in the payment of dividends. A preferred stockholder, for example, is paid first if profits are used to pay any stock dividends.

The dividends paid to preferred stockholders are usually limited to a set rate. Preferred stock usually has priority on the return of the amount invested if the corporation goes out of business. Preferred stock is less risky than common stock. However, preferred stockholders generally have no voting rights within the corporation.

Environmental *Perspective*

Socially Responsible Investments

Can investors make stock selections that help society? Many investors only choose securities of companies that display environmental awareness and have business practices that address other social ills. These investors' dollars buy bonds and stocks of companies that practice energy conservation, waste management, and pollution control.

Another method with which some investors express social concern applies to enterprises that may not serve the best interests of society. Some people avoid investments in organizations that sell alcohol or tobacco or that operate gambling establishments.

A variety of mutual funds have been created to meet the financial goals of socially responsible investors. For example, in recent years, the Calvert Social Investment Fund, the Dreyfus Third Century Fund, and the Parnassus Fund concentrated on companies that made socially responsible business decisions.

How do socially responsible investments perform? Market results are mixed. Some stocks and mutual funds do very well while others are not as profitable for investors. However, many people are satisfied with a fair return while knowing they are helping the environment and improving the quality of life in our society.

Critical Thinking

1 How can investors improve the environment and influence other social concerns?

2 To what extent should social responsibility be a factor when selecting an investment?

Common Stock

Common stock represents general ownership in a corporation and a right to share in its profits. Common stock has no stated dividend rate. As part owners of the corporation, common stockholders are invited to the annual meeting of the corporation and are entitled to one vote per share of common stock owned.

Common stockholders receive dividends only after preferred stockholders are paid their share of any dividends. Yet, if the profits of a company are large, the common stockholders may receive more in dividends than preferred stockholders. For example, suppose that a company has issued $100,000 worth of common stock and $100,000 worth of preferred stock with a stated dividend rate of 6 percent. If the company earns a profit of $20,000 and pays all the profit out as dividends, preferred stockholders would be paid $6,000 in dividends ($100,000 × .06). The remainder, or $14,000 ($20,000 − $6,000), would be available to pay dividends to the common stockholders. The common stockholders would be paid a return of 14 percent.

unicipal bonds do have risk. In recent years, some local governments have defaulted on their bond payments.

SELECTING STOCK INVESTMENTS

Buying a stock that is right for you is an important decision. This could start with a process as shown in Figure 30-3. By viewing various economic and social trends in our country and in the world, you will determine what types of companies would benefit from those trends. For example, as people live longer, increased health care is required. Companies involved in health care products may be a wise investment.

Analyzing Potential Stocks

In selecting a specific stock to buy, you should learn something about the business record of the corporation. There are a number of sources of information that can be used, including *Moody's Handbook of Common Stocks, Value Line*, and *Standard and Poor's Encyclopedia of Stocks*. Publications like these provide information such as the company's net worth, amount of debt, sales revenue, profits, dividend history, and the current outlook for the company's product or service. These publications often are available in public libraries.

Figure 30-3
You can decide whether to buy a stock using a four-step process.

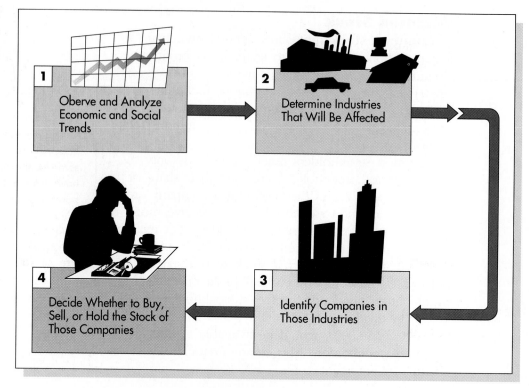

If you are considering investing in a company, you should ask the following questions:

- Has the company been profitable over a period of years?

- Have the company's managers made good business decisions?

- Does the company have growth potential in coming years?

- Does the company have an unusually large amount of debt?

- How does the company compare with others in its industry?

Other information about a company should also be considered. The *yield* of a stock is important if your goal is to earn a good return from your investment. Suppose, for example, that the XYZ Corporation is paying a quarterly dividend of $0.60 a share. The total dividend for the year would be $2.40, and if the stock is selling for $40 a share, the current yield (return) would be calculated as:

$$\text{Dividend Yield} = \frac{\text{Dividend per Share}}{\text{Market Price per Share}}$$

$$= \frac{\$ 2.40}{\$40.00} = .06 \text{ or } 6 \text{ percent}$$

The price of a stock also will be important. Many investors look at the stock's **price-earnings ratio (P/E),** the ratio of a stock's selling price to its earnings per share. The P/E gives you an indication of whether the stock is priced high or low in relation to its earnings per share. For instance, if a company has 100,000 shares of stock and it earns a net profit of $150,000, it has earned $1.50 ($150,000÷100,000) per share. If the stock is selling for $30 per share, its P/E is 20 ($30÷$1.50). The yield, the P/E ratio, and other information about the company are used by investors in deciding whether to buy a stock.

Using a Stockbroker

Stocks normally are bought and sold through stockbrokers. A **stockbroker** is a licensed specialist in the buying and selling of stocks and bonds. Through brokers, stockholders state prices at which they are willing to sell their shares. Interested buyers tell brokers what they would be willing to pay for those shares. The brokers then work out a price that is acceptable to both buyers and sellers.

The prices at which stocks are being bought and sold are available through stock market listings in newspapers. Examine Figure 30-4, which gives an explanation of the stock market listing. The highest, lowest, and closing prices for stocks sold each day are included in the stock market listing. Many newspapers and other publications have special business sections providing financial information.

For their services, brokers charge a fee called a **commission.** Brokers work through **stock exchanges,** which are business organizations that accommodate the buying and selling of securities. The best known stock exchange is the New York Stock Exchange in New York City. The American Stock Exchange is also in New York City. Regional stock exchanges operate in Boston, Chicago, Philadelphia, and San Francisco. Brokers throughout the nation deal directly with these exchanges by telephone and computer.

Two types of brokers are most common: full-service and discount

NET FACTS

In the 1980s, the National Science Foundation (NSF) created the NSFNET. The NSFNET connected several supercomputers from around the country and allowed scientists to access the network from remote locations. Later, the ARPANET was connected to NSFNET.

Illus. 30-3

Stocks are traded on the floor of the New York Stock Exchange.

Quotations as of 5 p.m. Eastern Time
Thursday, June 15, 19--

52 Weeks Hi	Lo	Stock	Sym	Div	Yld %	PE	Vol 100s	Hi	Lo	Close	Net Chg
		-A-A-A-									
15¾	11⅞	AAR	AIR	.48	3.1	26	212	15½	15⅜	15½	...
24⅜	19	ABM Indus	ABM	.60	2.7	13	75	22⅜	21⅛	22⅜	+⅜
11¾	8	ACM Gvt Fd	ACG	.90a	9.7	...	583	9⅜	9¼	9¼	-⅛
8⅝	6⅜	ACM OppFd	AOF	.66	9.1	...	297	7¼	7⅛	7¼	+⅛
10¼	7¼	ACM SecFd	GSF	.90	10.8	...	1056	8⅜	8¼	8⁵⁄₁₆	-⅛
9	5¾	ACM SpctmFd	SI	.75	10.9	...	430	7	6⅞	6⅞	-⅛
12½	7⅝	ACM MgmdInc	ADF	1.26	12.8	...	231	9⅞	9¾	9⅞	...
10	7⅜	ACM MgdIncFd	AMF	1.08a	11.7	...	441	9⅜	9¼	9¼	-⅛
12¼	9⅛	ACM MuniSec	AMU	.90a	7.6	...	149	12⅛	11⅞	11⅞	-⅛
12¼	9⅝	ADT	ADT		...	14	334	11⅜	11¼	11¼	-⅛
44¾	31⅝	AFLAC	AFL	.52f	1.2	14	232	43½	43¼	43¼	-¼
41	24	AGCO Cp	AG	.04	.1	6	2626	39¼	38⅜	38¾	-⅛
24	12⅝	AL Pharma	ALO	.18	1.0	dd	784	18¼	17⅞	17⅞	-½
22⅞	17	AMLI Resdntl	AML	1.72f	8.8	18	173	19¾	19⅛	19⅝	...
43⅝	32⅜	AMP	AMP	.92	2.1	23	9219	45¼	42¾	44¼	+1½
75⅛	48⅛	AMR	AMR			25	13398	75¾	74½	74¾	-¼
51	41¼	ARCO Chm	RCM	2.50	5.4	13	241	46½	46	46	-⅛
53¾	41½	ASA	ASA	2.00	4.5	...	2991	45⅜	44⅜	44¾	+⅜
27¾	19¾	ATT Cap	TCC	.40	1.5	11	125	26⅜	26¼	26½	+¼
57	47¼	AT&T Cp	T	1.32	2.6	17	14140	51⅞	51⅜	51½	...
41	26⅝	AbbotLab	ABT	.84	2.1	21	8338	40¼	39¾	40	...

52 Weeks Hi	Lo	Stocks	Sym	Div	Yld %	PE	Vol 100s	Hi	Lo	Close	Net Chg.
15¾	11⅞	AAR	AIR	.48	3.1	26	212	15½	15⅜	15½	...
(1)	(2)	(3)	(4)	(5)	(6)	(7)	(8)	(9)	(10)	(11)	(12)

1. Highest price paid for AAR common stock during the past 52 weeks.
2. Lowest price paid for AAR common stock during the past 52 weeks.
3. The company name abbreviated. If the stock quoted is preferred, the letters *pf* would be shown.
4. AAR's ticker tape symbol.
5. The current dividend in dollars per share based on the last dividend paid.
6. The dividend yield based on the current selling price per share.
7. The P/E ratio, comparing the price of the stock with the earnings per share.
8. The number of shares traded, expressed in hundreds. An underline below the stock listing indicates that the stock on that day had a large change in the volume of shares traded.
9. Highest price at which shares changed hands during the day.
10. Lowest price at which shares changed hands during the day.
11. Closing price per share for the day.
12. The change in the closing price today compared with the closing price on the previous day. If the price changed more than 5 percent, the entire stock listing appears in bold type.

Figure 30-4

Newspapers provide important information on stocks being traded.

brokers. A *full-service broker* is one who provides you with information about securities you may want to buy. Full-service brokers work for brokerage houses that have large research staffs.

In contrast, a *discount broker* just places orders for you and offers limited research and other services. They charge lower commissions than do full-service brokers. Investors who have a great deal of information available to them and who can do their own research can save money on commissions by using a discount broker.

INVESTING WITH OTHERS

Some investors like to join with others in making investments. Investment clubs and mutual funds are two common ways you can pool your investments.

In recent years, the average P/E ratio for stocks traded on the New York Exchange was about 18.

Investment Clubs

An **investment club** is a small group of people who organize to study stocks and to invest their money. An agreement is drawn up which states how often the club will meet and how much the members will invest each month. At the meetings, members report on stocks they have studied. The group makes decisions on what stocks to buy. The club's earnings are shared in proportion to the members' investments. Brokers often help groups form investment clubs.

One advantage of an investment club is that membership encourages regular saving. Another advantage is that you learn a great deal about how to judge a stock. Members of the club spread their risk because the combined funds of all members are used to buy stocks in a number of corporations. If the club loses money on one investment, the loss may be offset by other investments that do quite well.

More than 40 stock exchanges are in operation around the world, including those in Bombay, Johannesburg, London, Mexico City, Prague, Seoul, Sydney, Tel Aviv, and Toronto.

Mutual Funds

Investment clubs are not available to everyone. You may not be able to take the time needed to study the stock market and make investment decisions. A good understanding of securities, however, is needed to make wise decisions. A mutual fund is another way to join with others in investing and take advantage of their research and knowledge of securities.

Mutual funds are funds set up and managed by investment companies that receive money from many investors and then usually buy and sell a wide variety of stocks or bonds. Mutual fund investors own shares of the mutual fund. A part of the dividends received from the fund's investments is used to pay operating expenses of the fund. The major portion of earnings, however, is distributed to the mutual fund shareholders as dividends or reinvested in the fund.

The U.S. T-bill rate, reported daily in newspapers, is a commonly used indicator of the current level of short-term interest rates.

Many mutual funds are available to investors, and the funds have many different objectives. For instance, some emphasize investing in growth stocks, some emphasize stocks that pay high dividends, and some emphasize international stocks. Selecting a mutual fund in which to invest also requires you to consider your investment objectives before selecting a particular fund.

WHICH INVESTMENT IS BEST FOR YOU?

You must decide carefully whether or not to invest in stocks and bonds. One important guideline in the decision is whether you can afford to lose part or all of your investment. If you have to sell your stock or your mutual fund when an emergency arises, it might sell for much less than the amount that you paid for it. Before investing in securities, you should have adequate savings in a safe place, such as a bank savings account. You also should have sufficient insurance coverage. The money invested in securities should not be needed to meet your basic living expenses.

Ask yourself which of the following factors are most important to your personal investment plan: safety, liquidity, or rate of return? From your answer, an investment plan can be selected. As shown in Figure 30-5, no single investment can give you the highest possible return and still be very liquid and safe.

Figure 30-5

Your investment goals will determine which investments are best for you.

Which Investment?	How Safe?	How Liquid?	How Is Rate of Return?
Savings accounts	Excellent	Excellent	Fair to good
Savings bonds	Excellent	Very good	Good
Other bonds	Very good	Good	Good
Preferred stocks	Fair to good	Good	Very good
Common stocks	Fair	Good	Poor to excellent
Mutual funds	Fair to good	Good	Fair to excellent

Key Ideas

1 A bond represents a debt owed by an organization. Stock is equity and represents ownership.

2 Organizations sell bonds to raise funds to finance current operations or future business expansion.

3 Local and state governments sell municipal bonds. The federal government sells savings bonds, Treasury bills, notes, and bonds.

4 Preferred stockholders receive dividends paid at a set rate. Common stockholders vote to elect the officers of the corporation.

5 When selecting stock investments consider a company's net worth, amount of debt, sales revenue, profits, dividend history, the current outlook for the company's product or service, managerial talents, growth potential, yield, and price-earnings ratio (P/E).

6 Investment clubs and mutual funds allow people to combine their funds to buy a variety of securities, which reduces risk and increases potential returns.

7 Carefully consider investing in stocks and bonds based on your financial needs and goals. Determine the safety, liquidity, and rate of return you require.

End of Chapter Activities

Increasing Your Business Vocabulary

The following terms should become part of your business vocabulary. For each numbered item, find the term that has the same meaning.

bond 4

commission 6

common stock 9

corporate bonds 13

face value 12

investment club 10

market value 8

municipal bonds 2

mutual funds 7

preferred stock 5

price-earnings ratio 14
(P/E)

securities 3

stockbroker 1

stock exchanges 11

1 A licensed specialist who helps investors buy and sell stocks and bonds.

2 Bonds issued by local and state governments.

3 A general term for bonds and stocks that are sold by corporations and governments to raise large sums of money.

4 A certificate representing a promise to pay a definite amount of money at a stated interest rate on a specified maturity date.

5 Stock that has priority over common stock in the payment of dividends.

6 A fee charged by brokers for their services.

7 Funds set up and managed by investment companies that receive money from many investors and then usually buy and sell a wide variety of stocks or bonds.

8 The price at which a share of stock can be bought and sold in the stock market.

9 Stock that represents general ownership in a corporation and a right to share in its profits, but has no stated dividend rate.

10 A small group of people who organize to study stocks and invest money.

11 Business organizations that accommodate the buying and selling of securities.

12 The amount borrowed by the seller of a bond.

13 Debt securities issued by corporations.

14 The ratio of a stock's selling price to its earnings per share.

Reviewing Your Reading

1 How does a debt security differ from an equity security?

2 Why do corporations sell bonds?

3 What is a common benefit of investing in municipal bonds?

4 What makes U.S. government Series EE savings bonds a convenient investment?

5 What are some differences between preferred and common stock?

6 What sources of information about stocks are available to investors?

7 What are some important questions to ask when deciding whether or not to purchase stocks?

8 How do full-service stockbrokers differ from discount brokers?

9 Who selects stocks to be purchased by an investment club?

10 What are some different objectives of mutual funds?

11 Before investing in securities, what two financial safeguards should you have?

Using Your Business Knowledge

1 Why do municipal bonds usually pay a lower rate of interest than corporate bonds?

2 Why does the government pay a higher rate of interest on Series EE bonds held for their full term than on Series EE bonds cashed in early?

3 Give several reasons why people buy stocks even though they are not as safe as some investments.

4 Why would a broker be interested in helping a group of people form an investment club?

5 Susan Haugen bought $5,000 worth of gold mining stocks a few years ago. Last week she received a letter saying that the company went out of business. It could not operate profitably so it closed down. How much of her investment might Susan lose?

Calculating Business Problems

1 Jerome Aili owns five Morgan Enterprises bonds, each with a face value of $2,500. Morgan Enterprises pays 6 percent interest on the bonds it has issued.

　a. How much interest does Jerome receive each year on each bond?

　b. What is the total amount of interest Jerome receives each year?

c. If the interest payments are made semiannually to each bondholder, how much total interest does Jerome receive every six months?

Hint: Refer to Appendix C: Determining Percentage and Interest in Business.

2 Shana Matsumi bought the following Series EE bonds: two $100 bonds and two $5,000 bonds.

   a. How much did she pay for the bonds?
   b. How much will the bonds be worth when the stated time period has passed?
   c. How much interest will she have earned when the stated time period has passed?

---

3 At the stock exchange, the last sale on Tuesday for the Dandy Auto Corporation was $9.50. The next day it closed at $11.00.

   a. How much was the net change from Tuesday to Wednesday?
   b. By what percentage did the stock increase in value between the close of the first day and the close of the second day? Round your answer to the nearest percentage point.
   c. How much would 100 shares have cost on Tuesday at the closing price?

---

4 The P/E is the ratio of a stock's price per share compared with the earnings per share.

   a. For each of the stocks in the table, compute the P/E. Round each answer to the nearest whole number.
   b. If each of the stocks had a P/E of 18, what would be the price per share of each stock?

Stock	Price per Share	Earnings per Share
X	$ 54.63	$0.99
Y	8.77	0.51
Z	156.98	3.14

---

5 Referring to the table, compute the yield for each of the stocks listed. Round your answers to the nearest tenth of a percentage point.

	Price Paid	Annual Dividend
Consolidated Engineering	$40	$2.80
Electro-Jet Company	42	3.50
Federated Industries	25	1.90
Instrumentation, Inc.	25	1.50
Martinez Corporation	32	2.20
Seaboard Steel	54	3.00

Applying Technology

Using the *Introduction to Business* template and your database program software, select problem CH30. After the problem appears on your screen, complete the following activities. Then, after you have completed each step, display or print a report for each activity. If you do not have a printer available, answer the questions before you leave the computer.

1 Select and list the stocks with a closing price of more than $60. How many stocks are listed?

2 Select and list the stocks with a dividend of more than $2.

    a. What is the amount of the highest dividend listed?

    b. What is the company with the highest dividend listed?

3 Sort the database in descending order by price over the last 52 weeks.

    a. Which is the fourth stock listed?

    b. Which is the third-to-last stock listed?

Making Decisions

Wini Cruz understands the need to evaluate security investments based on safety, liquidity, and rate of return. In addition she realizes that the investments she selects must be guided by her personal financial needs and goals.

1 Wini wants to invest in stocks that will be very safe, highly liquid, and earn an excellent return. Is there anything wrong with this investment goal?

2 What advice would you give Wini to help her study the companies from which she is considering buying bonds and stocks?

Chapter Thirty-One

Making Other Types of Investments

Objectives

After studying this chapter and completing the end-of-chapter activities, you will be able to:

1 Identify methods for getting started in real estate.

2 Discuss activities involved in buying a home.

3 Explain the advantages of home ownership.

4 Describe four major costs associated with owning a house.

5 List agricultural and nonagricultural commodities that could be considered for investments.

6 Discuss collectibles as a form of investment.

riving home from their honeymoon, Joshua Moskowitz turned to his bride Carrie. "You know, we have some money that we received as wedding gifts," said Joshua. "We should buy some stocks for our long-term financial future. I have heard of a lot of people who made fortunes with stocks."

"What do you know about stocks? Are you sure we won't lose our money?" asked Carrie.

"Well, it's true, I don't know much about stocks," responded Joshua. "But I do know baseball cards! Let's invest our money in baseball cards."

"That's kind of risky, isn't it?" was Carrie's next question.

"OK . . . OK. Then let's buy gold bars. Gold can be a solid investment," replied Joshua. "You can't go wrong with gold."

"Hold on. We both want what's best for our future, but don't you think that first we better find a place to live?" responded Carrie.

GETTING STARTED IN REAL ESTATE

Real estate—land and anything that is attached to it—is one investment that most people eventually acquire. Getting started with real estate for most people means finding a place in which to live. Joshua and Carrie Moskowitz are newlyweds. They cannot afford to buy a house right away, although buying a house is a long-term goal they set for themselves.

Renting Your Residence

Joshua and Carrie met their housing needs by renting an apartment. As renters, they were freed from much of the work and expense of repairing the property, fixing the plumbing, and other maintenance. Renting also made it easier for them to move if they changed jobs.

As tenants, Joshua and Carrie took care of their rented property, but they were not able to call the apartment their own. They knew that they wanted to own a house and yard that they could maintain and fix up just the way they wanted. To realize their goal, Joshua and Carrie saved as much money as possible for a down payment on a house.

Owning a Mobile Home

Joshua and Carrie did well in their jobs and felt ready to settle down. They had their first child and decided to examine the housing market. Houses were too expensive for them, but they did find a mobile home in a good location that they could afford. They purchased the mobile home and took their first step toward becoming real estate owners.

The biggest advantage of owning a mobile home was having a place they could call their own. Borrowing money to help buy the mobile home was

FYI

ost people will rent a place to live at some time in their lives, usually when first starting on their own or when living alone later in life.

fairly easy. Their monthly payments were about the same as when they were renting. So they were able to continue to save for their house purchase.

After several years, Joshua and Carrie decided they needed more space. They now had two children and wanted to own a house. They sold their mobile home for almost what they had paid for it. Keeping it in good condition paid off. The experience they had in renting an apartment and owning a mobile home helped them know what kind of house they desired.

Obtaining a Mortgage

Unless you have many thousands of dollars available, you will need to borrow to buy a house. A **mortgage** is a legal document giving the lender a claim against the property if the principal, interest, or both are not paid as agreed. Joshua and Carrie had monthly mortgage payments that were much higher than the rent or mobile home loan payments they had been making. They now had to watch their spending more carefully.

Mortgages generally are long-term loans—usually for 15, 20, or 30 years—that require monthly payments. Mortgage payments often include property taxes and property insurance in addition to a percentage of the principal and interest charges. Figure 31-1 shows what monthly payments would be required to cover the principal and interest for mortgages of 15, 20, and 30 years at a 10 percent interest rate.

Interest rates on mortgages are commonly set for long periods of time and do not change during the term of the mortgage. This

Cultural Notes

The United States has been known as a *melting pot* because of the variety of people representing many cultures who have settled in the U.S. People from different cultures have learned to live and work together, keeping valued traditions from their own culture while learning to appreciate the traditions of others.

BUYING A HOME

Figure 31-1

The monthly house payment is usually the family's largest monthly expenditure.

Amount Borrowed	15 Years	20 Years	30 Years
$ 5,000	$ 53.73	$ 48.25	$ 43.88
10,000	107.46	96.50	87.76
20,000	214.92	193.00	175.51
30,000	322.38	289.51	263.27
40,000	429.84	386.01	351.03
50,000	537.30	482.51	438.79

Illus. 31-1
Most people require a mortgage to purchase a home.

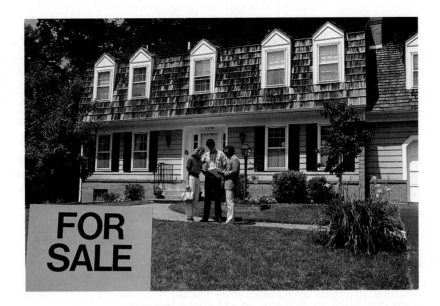

type of mortgage is called a **fixed rate mortgage.** Market interest rates, however, generally increase or decrease quite a bit during the life of a mortgage depending upon economic conditions. Therefore, lenders also offer an **adjustable rate mortgage (ARM).**

The interest rate of an ARM is raised or lowered periodically depending upon the current interest rate being charged by lenders. Monthly payments for ARMs often are lower, especially in the early years of the mortgage, compared with fixed rate mortgages.

Using Real Estate Agents and Lawyers

Buying a house is not a simple matter. Most home buyers use a **real estate agent,** a person trained and licensed to help with the buying and selling of real estate. Someone who wants to buy a house contacts a real estate agent who helps the person decide what is wanted in a house. The agent will usually arrange for the prospective buyer to view homes available for sale.

Sellers of real estate may also require the assistance of a real estate agent. Someone who wants to sell a house contacts an agent who then helps to set the selling price and lists the house for sale.

Legal matters are involved when purchasing real estate. A lawyer, working with the real estate agent, should help you with the transaction. A lawyer will help assure that your property has no claims against it, such as back taxes and liens. You need to have

A lease is a legal agreement between a renter and the landlord. This document presents information such as a description of the rental unit, dates of the rental agreement, the amount of the security deposit, and the amount and due date of the monthly rent.

your own lawyer represent you in the transaction to help avoid future legal problems.

When buying a house, it is also important to have an appraiser report on the value of the house. An **appraiser** is one who is trained to estimate the value of property and who can give an official report on its value. Such things as the quality of construction, the location, and the price of similar houses are taken into account in the appraisal.

Buying a Condominium

In recent years, condominiums, or condos, have become popular. A **condominium** is an individually owned unit in an apartment-like building or complex where maintenance and yard work are normally taken care of for a service fee.

hen mortgage rates decline, homebuyers may *refinance* their mortgages. This means they obtain a new loan at a lower rate.

BENEFITS OF HOME OWNERSHIP

The advantages of home ownership include tax benefits, increased equity, and pride of ownership.

Tax Benefits

Reduced income taxes result when the interest paid on a mortgage is included as a deductible expense. Real estate property taxes are usually also deductible when computing your federal income taxes.

f a person with a $75,000, 30-year, 10 percent mortgage pays an extra $25 a month on the loan balance, that homebuyer would save over $34,000 in interest. In addition, the loan would be paid off in less than 25 years.

Increased Equity

From an investment standpoint, the increase in equity is an important aspect of home ownership. **Equity** is the difference between the price at which you could currently sell your house and property and the amount owed on the mortgage. Equity builds up over the years and increases rapidly in the last few years of a mortgage.

Because of **appreciation,** a general increase in the value of property that occurs over a period of time, homes increase in value. After Joshua and Carrie lived in their home for ten years, its market value had increased to $144,000 and their debt decreased to $65,000; their equity was $79,000.

Pride of Ownership

Ownership is one of the basic rights in a democracy. An overriding advantage of owning real estate is pride of ownership. Having a home to use and decorate as desired is a strong motivation for many home buyers.

COSTS OF HOME OWNERSHIP

While there are some important advantages to owning your own property, disadvantages also exist. Home ownership has costs such as property taxes, interest payments, property insurance, and maintenance.

Technological *Perspective*

On-line Investing Information

A brand-new, completely different resource for investors has recently appeared—on-line investing information! Where is this exciting resource located? It's on the Internet.

This unique resource is dominated by small investors as opposed to large firms of stockbrokers and analysts. Through E-mail, message boards on commercial service providers, and Usenet Newsgroups, investors can rapidly exchange data and intimate knowledge of companies with each other. This information often contrasts with sometimes one-sided, sales-oriented presentations by Wall Street firms.

On-line investing information has positive and negative aspects. The positive aspects relate to the availability of information. Government documents and annual reports can be obtained for free. More and more companies are creating World Wide Web sites that provide background information that may be used to predict changes in their stock prices. Stock, monetary, and economic statistics are available at many WWW and Gopher sites. Most important, however, is that all investors—whether small or large—have equal access to share or obtain all this information.

There are some negatives to on-line investment information. When you read words on a screen, you don't know who is actually writing them. A person who seems to be an expert on stocks may be a brilliant faker. And the wonderful new technology of the Internet is no protection from ancient get-rich-quick scams.

Technology makes it possible to distribute a greater amount of information to a greater number of people. On-line investing information is a good example of technology making more data available. You would benefit by learning to take advantage of the wealth of information that can be found on-line.

Critical Thinking

1 *How will the increasing availability of on-line investing information affect the number of people who invest in financial securities?*

2 *What can you do to protect yourself against on-line scams?*

NET FACTS

When the messages posted to a discussion group are first read and screened, we call the group a moderated group. Messages and flames that do not fit the subjects of the group are deleted by the moderator. Discussion groups without moderators are called unmoderated.

Property Taxes

Property taxes vary greatly from state to state and community to community. Generally real estate taxes range from 2 to 4 percent of the market value of the property. Taxes are based on the **assessed value,** the amount that your local government determines your property to be worth for tax purposes. Assessed values normally are lower than the market value, often only about half.

A home with a market value of $90,000 may be assessed at $45,000. If the tax rate is $60 per $1,000 of assessed value, this would result in annual taxes of $2,700 ($45,000 ÷ $1,000 × $60). This rate is 6 percent of the assessed value but only 3 percent of the market value.

Interest Payments

Interest payments add to the cost of the house. For instance, 12 percent interest for 25 years results in payments that more than triple the amount borrowed. A total of $126,387 is paid on $40,000 borrowed.

Property Insurance

Property insurance is an essential cost. The value of the house, its construction material, its location with respect to other buildings, and the availability of fire protection are among factors affecting the price of homeowners insurance. Typical annual home insurance costs are less than 1 percent of the market value of the house. (See Chapter 34 for more information about homeowners insurance.)

Maintenance

The cost of *upkeep*—maintaining your property in good condition—is important in home ownership. Annual upkeep costs average about 2 percent of the property's value. Postponing repairs or not taking good care of the house and yard through regular maintenance can be very costly in the long run.

Illus. 31-2

Even a new home will soon require maintenance.

INVESTING IN COMMODITIES

Another type of investment considered by experienced investors is commodities. Commodities include grain, livestock, precious metals, currency, and financial instruments. Generally commodity investing is considered to be speculative. A **speculative investment** is one that has an unusually high risk. Commodity investors deal in **futures,** a commodity contract purchased in anticipation of higher market prices for the commodity in the near future.

A futures contract for wheat, corn, or soybeans consists of 5,000 bushels of the particular grain.

Commodity Exchanges

Commodities are bought and sold on exchanges similar to stock exchanges. Buyers and sellers are represented by traders on the exchanges. One of the best known exchanges is the Chicago Board of Trade (CBOT). The CBOT was established in 1848 to provide a central market for agricultural products. It was also designed to help avoid the huge price fluctuations that had been taking place in the market. The CBOT is governed by the Commodity Futures Trading Commission (CFTC) and the National Futures Association (NFA).

Agricultural Commodities

Agricultural products—such as corn, soybeans, and wheat—are examples of commodities traded on the CBOT and other commodity exchanges. Agricultural producers sell their crops in advance of a harvest at what they believe is a good price. Farmers, then, will know in advance how much they will receive for a crop. The buyers assume that the price of the crop will go up when harvested so that they can earn a profit. Many conditions affect the agricultural commodities that are traded, such as weather conditions, international trade agreements, and worldwide demand and supply.

A Eurodollar, which is traded in the futures market, is a U.S. dollar deposited in a bank outside of the United States. These funds are used to make payments among countries for foreign trade.

Gold, Silver, and Other Precious Metals

Precious metals are of major worldwide importance. Gold and silver have been traded on commodity markets for centuries. Gold has the longest history as a monetary commodity, going back to gold coins that were circulated as early as 500 B.C. Gold is also highly prized for both ornamental and industrial reasons. More recently other metals, such as copper and platinum, have been become valuable commodities.

Illus. 31-3
Agricultural products and precious metals are both traded on the commodity exchanges.

Prices of these metals are affected by factors such as general economic conditions as well as supply and demand. For example, in 1879 gold sold for $18.79 per ounce. Since 1979, the price of an ounce of gold has ranged from over $800 to less than $400.

Precious metals are quoted as spot prices per one troy ounce. The **spot price** is the current price quoted for precious metals in the world markets. You can find the spot price for gold in London and New York in *The Wall Street Journal* or the business section of a daily newspaper.

Money invested in precious metals does not earn interest. If you hold gold, silver, or platinum, you might profit by selling them later at a price higher than what you paid. Gold and other precious metals have another advantage—many investors see them as protection against currency becoming worthless. Gold is recognized for its value throughout the world. It could be used for buying goods and services when printed money might not be accepted.

Currency and Financial Instruments

Currency, such as the U.S. dollar and the Japanese yen, and financial instruments, such as Treasury bonds and Treasury bills, also are traded on the Chicago Board of Trade and other futures markets. The price of currency and financial instruments is affected by a country's economic outlook and by current interest rates. Here again, investors buy currency or financial instruments expecting the prices to increase in the future so that they can sell them to others at a profit.

INVESTING IN COLLECTIBLES

Another form of investment that is popular with many people is collectibles. **Collectibles** are items of personal interest to collectors that can increase in value in the future. Examples include stamps, coins, sport trading cards, and antiques.

An advantage of collectibles is the personal pleasure of buying, collecting, storing, arranging, and displaying what is collected. Often organizations of collectors are formed. For example, stamp clubs around the country bring together stamp collectors who buy, sell, trade, display, and discuss their stamps. Baseball card trading takes place at scheduled events in huge arenas as well as over kitchen tables. Antique dealers and collectors gather for major events at which they buy and sell their items.

The possibility of the average buyer of collectibles making a large profit is not great. Only rare stamps, coins, and antiques—which may cost several hundred or thousands of dollars—tend to be those items on which a considerable profit can be made. The wise investor in collectibles studies the market, knows the product well, and analyzes the risk to be taken.

Illus. 31-4
Collectibles such as baseball cards are commonly bought and sold at stores and outdoor markets.

Key Ideas

1 A person can get started in real estate by renting a place to live or by buying a mobile home.

2 When buying a home you may need to obtain a mortgage and use the services of a real estate agent and lawyer.

3 The advantages of home ownership are tax benefits, increased equity, and pride of ownership.

4 The major costs associated with owning a house include property taxes, interest payments, property insurance, and maintenance.

5 Commodities commonly used as investments include corn, soybeans, wheat, gold, silver, copper, platinum, U.S. dollars, Japanese yen, Treasury bonds, and Treasury bills.

6 Collectibles can combine a pleasurable hobby with an investment that may increase in value.

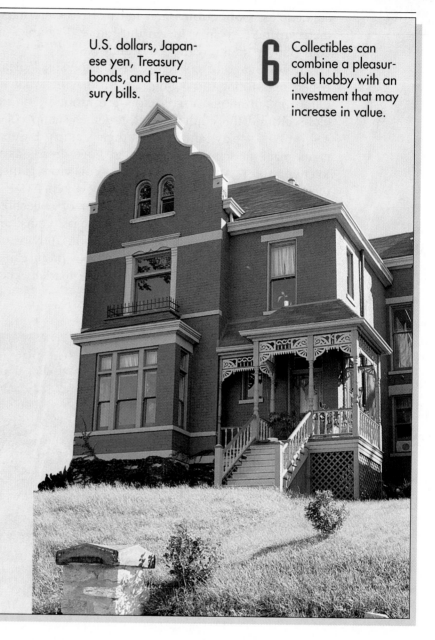

End of Chapter Activities

Increasing Your Business Vocabulary

The following terms should become part of your business vocabulary. For each numbered item, find the term that has the same meaning.

adjustable rate mortgage (ARM)

appraiser

appreciation

assessed value

collectibles

condominium

equity

fixed rate mortgage

futures

mortgage

real estate

real estate agent

speculative investment

spot price

1 Land and anything that is attached to it.

2 Someone who is trained and licensed to help with the buying and selling of real estate.

3 An individually owned unit in an apartment-like building or complex where maintenance and yard work are normally taken care of for a service fee.

4 A general increase in the value of property that occurs over a period of time.

5 One who is trained to estimate the value of property and who can give an official report on its value.

6 The difference between the price at which you could currently sell your house and property and the amount owed on the mortgage.

7 A traditional mortgage with an interest rate that does not change during the life of the mortgage.

8 The amount that your local government determines your property to be worth for tax purposes.

9 A mortgage for which the interest rate is raised or lowered periodically depending upon the current interest rate being charged by lenders.

10 A legal document giving the lender a claim against the property if the principal, interest, or both are not paid as agreed.

11 The current price quoted for precious metals in the world markets.

12 Items of personal interest to collectors purchased in anticipation of an increase in value in the future.

13 An investment that has an unusually high risk.

14 A contract for a commodity purchased in anticipation of higher market prices in the near future.

Reviewing Your Reading

1 Name two advantages of renting an apartment.

2 In what ways can real estate agents, lawyers, and appraisers help with real estate transactions?

3 Name three benefits of home ownership.

4 What costs, in addition to the original investment, are included in the cost of owning a house?

5 What factors help determine the amount charged for insurance on a house?

6 What are some agricultural products that are traded on commodity exchanges?

7 Give examples of precious metals that are used as investments.

8 What can affect the price of currency and financial instruments that are traded as commodities?

9 What makes collectibles attractive to many investors?

10 What is good advice for wise investors who purchase collectibles and other forms of investments?

Using Your Business Knowledge

1 People who buy and sell land and houses commonly say that the three most important factors to consider when buying real estate are "location, location, and location!" Why do you think this is their belief?

2 In what types of economic conditions would a person prefer a fixed rate mortgage? When might an adjustable rate mortgage be preferred?

3 Why is a condominium often desirable to retired people?

4 Blair Vazquez owns a house that has a value of $80,000. For the past three years, the upkeep has averaged less than $500 a year. Can Blair assume that his expenses will be only $500 in future years?

5 Mei-ling Shen has been collecting coins for several years. She estimates that they are worth about $2,000. Someone told her that she could make more money investing in commodities. She is considering selling her collection and going into commodities. What advice would you give Mei-ling?

Calculating Business Problems

1 Don Smith rents an apartment for $500 per month. He has just received a notice that his rent will increase 7 percent. What will be Don's total rental cost for twelve months at the new rate?

2 Bill Fields has been renting an apartment for three years and pays $550 per month for rent. He has an opportunity to buy a house that will require him to pay $820 per month as a mortgage payment.

a. In one year, how much more will he have to pay for house payments than he now pays for rent?

b. During the first year, 90 percent of each payment will be for interest and 10 percent will be for principal repayment. What will be the amount he pays for interest for the year? for principal repayment for the year?

3 The Brocks own a house valued at $65,000 and they have a balance on their mortgage of $40,000. Last year they had expenses as shown in the table.

Interest on mortgage	$4,000
Taxes	1,500
Upkeep	900
Insurance	250

a. What was the total of their expenses for last year?

b. What is the amount of equity the Brocks have in their house?

4 Steve Fujiwara bought 30,000 bushels of corn in the futures market at $2.98 a bushel. The price of corn rose to $3.02 a bushel.

a. What was Steve's total dollar profit on this investment?

b. What was his percentage gain? Round your answer to the nearest tenth of a percentage point.

c. If the price of corn had dropped to $2.90 a bushel, what would have been Steve's loss in total dollars?

d. What would have been his percentage loss? Round your answer to the nearest tenth of a percentage point.

Applying Technology

Using the *Introduction to Business* template and your word processing program software, select problem CH31. After the problem appears on your screen, complete the following activities. Then, print and sign your completed applications. If you do not have a printer available, save the applications on a data disk to give to your teacher.

1 You are applying to rent an apartment. Complete the application with information about yourself plus the following information. You have lived at your current address for 1½ years; at your job you make $7.00 per hour and work 8 hours per day, 21 days per month.

For the information that you enter, use a different type font from the one used on the rest of the application.

2 You are applying to rent a mobile home. Complete the application with information about yourself plus the following information. You have lived at your current address for 4¼ years and at your job you make $24,000 per year. For the information that you enter, use italics and a different font of type from the one used on the rest of the application.

Making Decisions

Robin Greer has decided to purchase a house. As a result of her business classes and work experience at a real estate office, she has decided to take care of all the details herself. Robin does not plan to use the services of a real estate agent, a lawyer, or an appraiser.

1 What activities will Robin need to understand in the home buying process?

2 What problems might arise for Robin as a result of not using the services of these professionals?

People save and invest their money in many ways. A growing need exists for savings and investment workers to guide investors in choosing just the right plan. This results in employment opportunities for those interested in helping others plan their financial futures.

Job Titles

Job titles commonly found in this career area include:

- Brokerage Clerk
- Collection Clerk
- Economic Analyst
- Financial Planner
- Financial Services Sales Representative
- Margin Clerk
- Mortgage Accounting Clerk
- Order Clerk
- Real Estate Appraiser
- Real Estate Agent
- Real Estate Broker
- Real Estate Clerk
- Securities Analyst
- Securities Clerk
- Statistical Clerk
- Stockbroker
- Transfer Clerk

Employment Outlook

- As more individuals become involved in investments, the demand for securities sales workers will increase.
- Clerical and research workers with computer skills and finance knowledge are used in a variety of areas.
- Real estate workers will be needed in areas with strong economic growth.

Education and Training

- Familiarity with legal terminology as well as a knowledge of investment technical terms is valuable
- Sales workers, who generally serve as stockbrokers, must obtain a state license to sell securities.
- Sales workers need training about legal forms and documents related to securities or real estate transactions.
- Real estate agents and brokers must also pass a state test for their licenses.
- Financial planners should have a knowledge of money management, taxes, investments, and retirement planning, and may attain a certified financial planner designation. A college education with business courses is desirable.

Salary Levels (in recent years)

- Brokers and sales agents generally work on a commission basis.
- Beginning securities salespeople average about $1,500 per month; with experience, they eventually can earn $40,000 to $90,000 or more a year.

Critical Thinking

1 How do economic conditions affect the demand for investment jobs?

2 What training and knowledge would be important for success in investment careers?

Investments

Unit Nine

Risk Management

Malpractice is a term used to describe substandard or even irresponsible performance on the part of lawyers, physicians, and other professionals on behalf of their clients. Professionals who perform their duties in an acceptable manner and meet the criteria of their trade do not have to worry actively about malpractice. But in order to protect themselves against economic loss, all professionals should have malpractice insurance in the event that an action beyond their control brings a malpractice suit.

Malpractice and subsequently, malpractice insurance, has been cast as the villain that has contributed significantly to the increased cost of professional services—especially with health care. Because of the added cost of malpractice insurance and the practice of defensive medical care, health costs have skyrocketed.

Physicians practice defensive medical care by sometimes ordering more diagnostic tests than necessary to protect themselves against misdiagnosis. Physicians have reported that they engage in such defensive practices as prescribing the safest possible treatments, telling patients more about treatment risks, and keeping more complete records. It is difficult to distinguish defensive medicine from good care delivered for appropriate reasons.

The American Medical Association has estimated that the total cost of medical malpractice, including insurance premiums and defensive medicine, was about 17 percent of physicians' earnings. Malpractice costs are higher in the United States than in other countries. In the mid-1980s, malpractice claims—and accordingly, insurance premiums—took a sharp, upward swing. There was a great deal of discussion then of a "malpractice crisis." But that crisis now seems to have abated. At the moment, malpractice claims have been on a downswing. The rate of insurance claims has declined steadily since the peak of the last "crisis" in 1985.

Because malpractice claims have decreased, so have malpractice insurance premiums. Recently, doctors' malpractice premiums on average consumed only 3.7 percent of their practice receipts. This savings will hopefully be passed on to the consumer through lower doctor bills.

Critical Thinking

1 How does malpractice add to the cost of the consumer's medical costs?

2 Why do you think malpractice costs are higher in the United States than in other countries?

The Truth About Malpractice

Chapter Thirty-Two

The Fundamentals of Insurance

Key Terms

risk

economic risk

personal risk

property risk

liability risk

insurance

insurance companies

insured or policyholder

policy

premium

claim

deductible

self-insurance

coinsurance

insurance agent

Objectives

After studying this chapter and completing the end-of-chapter activities, you will be able to:

1 Compare and contrast the various types of risk.

2 Explain how economic risks can be avoided.

3 Describe insurance and which losses can be covered.

4 List and explain the factors that affect the cost of insurance to policyholders.

5 Explain how insurance can be purchased.

6 Describe how insurance can provide economic security.

"Tien, did last night's storm do any damage to your parents' home?"

"Yes, Katie, it blew the roof right off the house! But since we were all unharmed, Dad isn't too upset about it because we have insurance to cover the loss. You know how conscientious my parents are about everything.

We even have smoke detectors and a fire extinguisher on every floor of the house! They say that by being safety oriented, they protect us and even save money on insurance premiums each year."

"I wonder what kind of coverage my parents have. We were lucky not to have had any storm damage last night. Maybe I will bring this up with them at dinner tonight."

Tien's parents know that by being careful and conscientious—and being insured—we can protect ourselves against unexpected loss. However, no matter how careful we are, there are certain losses that may occur that are beyond our control.

RISK

Risk can be thought of as the possibility of incurring a loss. Even if you are very careful, you probably will not be able to avoid all losses. **Economic risk** can be related to property liability and one's own personal well being. Economic risks can be placed into three categories: personal risks, property risks, and liability risks. **Personal risks** are risks associated with illness, disability, loss of income, unemployment, old age, and premature death. The risks of damage to or loss of property due to theft, wind, fire, flood, or some other hazard are called **property risks.** While personal and property risks involve economic losses to you, **liability risks** are potential losses to others that occur as a result of injury or damage that you may have caused. You can insure against all of these types of risk.

Illus. 32-1
Most property risks related to a home are insurable.

SHARING ECONOMIC RISK

Large economic losses can be avoided by sharing the loss with other people. Suppose you and nine of your friends have new sets of golf clubs. Each of your sets is worth about $300. You and your friends decide to form an organization called the Golf Club Owners Insurance Association (GCOIA) as shown in Figure 32-1. The purpose of the GCOIA is to protect members from financial loss should one member's clubs get stolen. To provide protection, each member agrees to share the cost of any stolen clubs. Therefore, if your golf clubs are stolen, each member (including yourself) would contribute $30 to buy new ones for you.

Consider the largest deductible you can afford. The higher the deductible, the lower the premium.

Figure 32-1

Providing insurance for most risks is not as simple as it is for the Golf Club Owners Insurance Association.

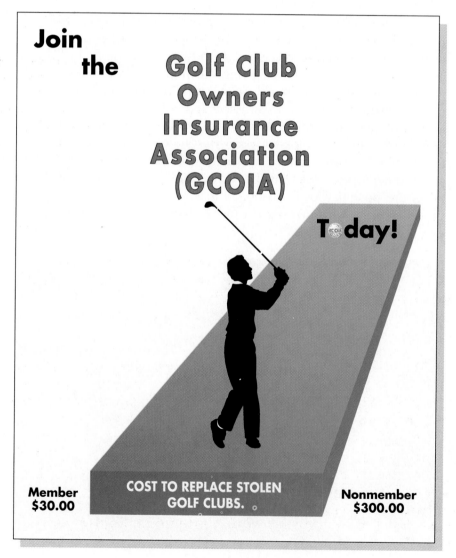

Join the Golf Club Owners Insurance Association (GCOIA) Today!

COST TO REPLACE STOLEN GOLF CLUBS.

Member $30.00

Nonmember $300.00

If you are not a member of the GCOIA and your clubs are stolen, you would have to pay the total cost ($300) of new clubs. As a member, new clubs would only cost you $30. When a member loses golf clubs, each member suffers only a relatively small economic loss. In that way, the members help one another by sharing the risk of economic loss.

Insurance is the planned protection provided by sharing economic losses. You will learn about several kinds of insurance in this unit, but they all have one thing in common. Insurance provides you with the peace of mind that comes from knowing you are protected from economic loss. With insurance, a house fire, car accident, appendectomy, or early death will not cause you or your family economic difficulties.

Insurance companies are businesses that provide planned protection against economic loss. Insurance companies, similar to the GCOIA, agree to assume certain economic risks for you and to pay you if a loss occurs. The person for whom the risk is assumed is known as the **insured** or **policyholder.**

To show that risk has been assumed, the company issues a contract to the policyholder. A contract issued by the insurance company for coverage for the policyholder is called a **policy.** The policy states the conditions to which the insurance company and the policyholder have agreed. For example, a policyholder may agree not to keep gasoline in the house, not to allow an unlicensed person to drive an insured car, or not to go skydiving.

The amount the policyholder must pay for insurance coverage is called a **premium.** The policyholder usually makes payments once a month, once every six months, or once a year. The premiums from all the policyholders make up the funds from which the company pays for claims.

A **claim** is a policyholder's request for payment for a loss that is covered by the insurance policy. A **deductible** is an amount you must pay before the insurance company pays a claim. For example, if your car suffers $2,500 damage in an accident and your deductible amount is $500, you would pay

Career Highlights

A *claim adjuster's* job duties include:
- Determining whether the customer's insurance policy covers a loss
- Determining the amount of loss
- Collecting information from claimants regarding expenses
- Interviewing claimants and witnesses
- Consulting police and hospital records
- Inspecting property damage
- Negotiating with the claimants and settling claims.

FYI

Most insurance policies have a monetary limit on the coverage of items that are lost or stolen.

$500 and the insurance company would pay $2,000 (damages $2,500 − $500 deductible = claim $2,000).

Insured Losses

Both consumers and businesses are able to buy insurance to cover almost any kind of economic loss. Violinists can insure their fingers, professional athletes can insure against injuries, and writers may insure their manuscripts. Businesses are able to insure against the loss of rent from property damaged by fire, injury to consumers caused by a faulty product, or theft by employees. The kinds of insurance protection that will be important to most people, however, are insurance for automobiles and homes, life insurance, health insurance, and insurance for income security. You will learn about vehicle, property, life, and health insurance in the next four chapters. Insurance for income security will be presented as a part of Chapter 39.

In the last 10 years, the cost of health care has risen at a faster pace than all other goods and services.

Large businesses or institutions are sometimes able to insure themselves against certain kinds of losses. A company might, for example, determine that the average cost for damages to its fleet of company cars is $25,000 per year. It then establishes a special self-insurance fund for this purpose each year. In this way, the business can insure itself against the economic losses associated with automobile damage.

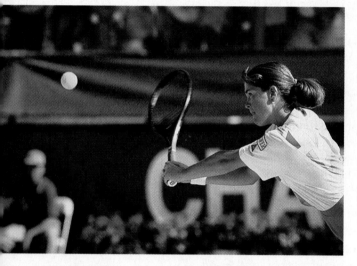

Illus. 32-2 Professional athletes can insure themselves against economic loss due to injuries.

Policyholders should know exactly what protection is provided by the kinds of insurance they have. Some people fail to tell their insurance companies about losses they have suffered because they did not know that their policies covered those losses. Other people have assumed that losses they suffered were covered by their insurance, only to find out by reading their policies that the losses were not covered.

Self-Insurance

Some individuals, families, and businesses have decided that the best way to protect against economic losses is through self-insurance. **Self-insurance** means that the individual, family, or business assumes the total risk of economic loss. For instance, a family might regularly place money in a savings account to cover possible financial losses. Most families, however, would find it almost impossible to self-insure against economic catastrophes such as the cost of an extended illness or the cost of replacing a house that was destroyed by a fire.

Coinsurance

Coinsurance is the sharing of expenses by the policyholder and the insurance company. The policyholder typically pays a deductible, then shares the remaining loss with the insurance company. For example, if the insurance company pays 80 percent of

Environmental *Perspective*

Insuring Against Natural Disasters

Wind damage in the South, earthquake damage in the West, and flooding in the Midwest are common newspaper headlines. These events have brought new attention to perils not usually covered by standard homeowners policies. In addition to the human misery associated with these tragedies, there can be a significant amount of economic loss. Insurance companies have paid billions of dollars in claims to people whose houses were blown down, crumbled, or soaked beyond repair.

Most homeowners policies include insurance for windstorm damage. However, companies may exclude coverage

for the peril if a house is unusually vulnerable to windstorms by virtue of its location. Six coastal states (Alabama, Florida, Louisiana, Mississippi, North Carolina, and Texas) have beach and windstorm plans to pick up where the regular policies leave off.

Most insurance companies offer earthquake coverage as an endorsement on homeowners policies. Premiums can run as high as 50 percent of a home's regular coverage, but rates vary according to the vulnerability of the house. Wood frame homes, which tend to withstand quakes better than brick, cost much less to insure.

The National Flood Insurance Program, administered by the Federal Emergency Man-

agement Agency (FEMA), offers flood insurance through the federal government and approximately 85 private insurers. To qualify, homeowners must live in a designated flood-prone community that has taken specified steps to control flood damage.

Critical Thinking

1 *When buying insurance, should people from all across the United States be asked to share the risk of natural disasters that occur most frequently in predictable areas? Why?*

2 *If you were a resident of Illinois living in a low-lying area near the Mississippi River, how would you deal with the high cost of flood insurance?*

the cost for medical treatment after the deductible is paid, the policyholder will pay the remaining 20 percent. The share, however, is capped or limited to a specific dollar amount stated in the policy. Once the deductible and the coinsurance amounts are satisfied, the insurance company reimburses 100 percent of the cost up to the policy's coverage limits.

Looking at the example in Figure 32-2, assume you have a claim for $5,250 and your deductible is $250. The remaining amount after the deductible is paid is $5,000 (claim $5,250 − deductible $250 = remaining $5,000). Your insurance policy says that once the deductible is subtracted from the total amount of the claim, the policyholder will pay 20 percent of the remaining amount. Therefore, you would pay $1,000 ($5,000 × 20% = $1,000) as the coinsurance portion. The insurance company would pay the remaining $4,000 ($5,000 − $1,000 = $4,000). Your total payment would be the $250 deductible plus the coinsurance of $1,000 for a total of $1,250.

Figure 32-2

Coinsurance helps reduce premiums while still protecting you against huge losses.

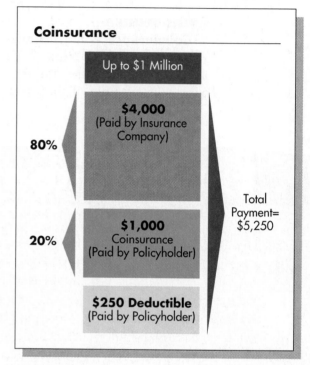

Coinsurance

Up to $1 Million

$4,000
(Paid by Insurance Company)

80%

20%

$1,000
Coinsurance
(Paid by Policyholder)

$250 Deductible
(Paid by Policyholder)

Total Payment= $5,250

COST OF INSURANCE

Insurance companies are always looking for ways to reduce the cost of premiums to policyholders. The premium charged for each type of policy is determined partly by the past experiences of insurance companies in paying for the kinds of losses covered by each policy. For example, insurance companies have found that a 20-year-old driver is a greater risk because he or she is more likely to have an auto accident than a 40-year-old driver. Therefore, car insurance premiums for 20-year-old drivers are higher than they are for older drivers.

Premiums charged a policyholder also are affected by the cost of replacing the insured item. If you insure a luxury car, premiums will be higher than they would be for a less expensive model.

NET FACTS

A *client* is a computer connected to the Internet. Clients contain software needed to exchange data with other computers on the Internet.

The larger the number of claims an insurance company has to pay, the higher the premiums for the policyholder. Therefore, insured people play an important part in determining the cost of insurance. By locking doors and driving defensively, losses associated with thefts and automobile accidents can be reduced. Practicing good health habits will reduce life and health insurance costs.

Everyone benefits if the losses covered by insurance decrease. Assume, for example, that there is a decline in losses caused by fire and that fire insurance premiums are reduced as a result. If your family owns a house and has fire insurance on it, you gain directly because you pay lower premiums. If a business owner pays lower premiums, expenses will be less and prices on goods and services may be less. Anything that you can do to reduce losses covered by insurance helps you and the entire community.

Illus. 32-3
The cost of insurance is partly determined by the insurance company's history of past claims.

PURCHASING INSURANCE

Insurance companies perform educational services by conducting campaigns on safety, health, and accident prevention. They conduct these activities to help reduce both losses and premiums.

Insurance protection can be acquired in several ways. Sometimes an employer will provide insurance for you as part of your compensation. For example, employers may pay all or part of life and/or health insurance premiums for their employees.

However, in other cases, you will buy insurance directly from an **insurance agent.** An important part of an insurance agent's job is to help you select the proper kind of protection from economic loss. There are two basic types of insurance agents. One works for a large insurance company and sells only policies written by that company. The other is an independent agent who may sell many kinds of policies from a number of different companies.

INSURANCE FOR ECONOMIC SECURITY

Insurance is important to everyone because it provides economic security. If you have no insurance, you could probably take care of small losses such as those resulting from minor accidents. However, a large loss from a fire or serious illness could be a real financial hardship. Protection against such major events gives everyone a feeling of security.

Insurance also helps our economy. Insurance makes it possible for many people and businesses to do things they otherwise could not do. Suppose that someday you want to buy a $100,000 home but can make only a $10,000 down payment. You will need to borrow $90,000. It is very doubtful that anyone would lend you that amount at a reasonable rate if the house were not insured. Money to buy a new car cannot be borrowed at a reasonable rate unless the car is insured against risks such as theft and collision.

Premiums collected by insurance companies are invested. Many insurance companies, mainly life insurance companies, also use premium money to make loans. The loans are used to build government and private business projects, which help our economy grow.

FYI

Always review your insurance policies on a regular basis to make sure they are up-to-date and fit your current needs.

Illus. 32-4

Insurance protection against a major accident or illness provides a sense of security.

Key Ideas

1 Personal risks are risks associated with illness, disability, loss of income, unemployment, old age, and premature death. Property risks are risks of damage or loss due to theft, wind, fire, flood, or some other hazard. Liability risks are potential losses to others that occur as a result of injury or damage that you may have caused.

2 Sharing risks with others can help policyholders protect themselves against economic losses.

3 Insurance is the planned protection provided by sharing economic losses. Both consumers and businesses are able to buy insurance to cover almost any kind of economic loss.

4 The cost of insurance is influenced by factors such as the age of the person being insured, the type of property at risk, and the number of claims the insurance company pays over a period of time.

5 Insurance can be purchased from a large company or from an independent agent.

6 Insurance provides economic security by protecting the policyholder from economic loss.

End of Chapter Activities

Increasing Your Business Vocabulary

The following terms should become part of your business vocabulary. For each numbered item, find the term that has the same meaning.

claim

coinsurance

deductible

economic risk

insurance

insurance agent

insurance companies

insured or policy-holder

liability risk

personal risk

policy

premium

property risk

risk

self-insurance

1 The planned protection provided by sharing economic losses.

2 The person for whom risk is assumed by an insurance company.

3 The amount you must pay before the insurance company pays a claim.

4 A contract that states the conditions to which the insurance company and the policyholder have agreed.

5 A person who sells insurance.

6 A policyholder's request for payment for a loss that is covered by the insurance policy.

7 The amount that a policyholder must pay for insurance coverage.

8 When an individual, family, or business assumes the total risk of economic loss.

9 When you and the insurance company share expenses.

10 The possibility of incurring a loss.

11 Risks associated with illness, disability, loss of income, unemployment, old age, and premature death.

12 The possibility of incurring a loss related to property liability and one's own personal well being.

13 The risk of damage to or loss of property due to theft, wind, fire, flood, or some other hazard.

14 Businesses that provide planned protection against economic loss.

15 Potential losses to others that occur as a result of injury or damage that you may have caused.

Reviewing Your Reading

1. List the three types of economic risks.

2. How does insurance protect against economic losses?

3. List several possible economic losses that people face.

4. Name four kinds of insurance protection that are important to most people.

5. Why aren't most people able to use a self-insurance plan?

6. Name one of the factors that determine the cost of insurance premiums.

7. How can policyholders influence the cost of insurance?

8. What are the two basic types of insurance agents?

9. Why is insurance important to everyone?

10. How do insurance companies use the premiums they collect?

Using Your Business Knowledge

1. How would the need for insurance against property risks differ between a family and a business?

2. What factors would you consider when deciding on the level of deductible on a property insurance policy?

3. Some people feel most comfortable when they are insured for almost every loss—large or small. Others believe that most people can handle small losses and favor insuring against only major or catastrophic losses. In which group would you place yourself? Why?

4. The residents of a subdivision with 100 homes decided that they can save money by providing their own fire insurance. Since the houses in the area are of equal value, each owner agrees to contribute $800. The money is to be placed in a savings account in a bank. If a homeowner suffers a fire loss, the loss would be paid out of this account. Do you think this is a wise plan? Why or why not?

5. Develop a list of ways you could reduce the property risks associated with owning a car.

6. Why do you think insurance companies are willing to spend large amounts of money on health and safety education?

Calculating Business Problems

1 Linda Caldwell is a 25-year-old computer technician living in an apartment. She pays the following insurance premiums every year: life insurance, $225; renter's insurance, $165; automobile insurance, $595; and health insurance, $650.

a. What is the total annual cost of Linda's insurance premiums?

b. If she paid her insurance premiums in equal monthly payments, how much would her total monthly insurance cost be?

---

2 A fire and casualty insurance company collected $978,000 in premiums in one year. That same year, the company paid out $821,520 in claims. What percentage of the premiums did the company pay out in claims?

---

3 Erin Michael's auto insurance company believes it can reduce premiums by an average of 10 percent. This reduction is possible because of lowered speed limits with fewer and less costly accident settlements. Erin's last annual premium was $380.

a. How much will she save if the proposed premium reduction is put into effect?

b. What will be the amount of her new premium?

---

4 A fish wholesaling business decided to self-insure itself for damage to the property it owned. The property includes several forklifts, a large warehouse, office equipment, and a great deal of fish-handling equipment. The owners decided to put $47,000 in the self-insurance account the first year. Claims against the account that year are shown in the table at right.

a. What was the total of the property claims for the year?

One burned forklift	$6,500
One computer ruined by an electrical surge	3,200
Hail damage to the warehouse roof	7,400
One fish conveyer damaged by a supplier's truck	3,700

b. Was any money remaining in the account at the end of the year? If so, how much?

c. What percent of the account was paid out in claims?

5 The Lafferty family has coinsurance whereby the insurance company will pay 80 percent of the cost of medical treatment after the deductible of $350 is paid, with a cap of one million dollars. The family filed a claim of $6,000. How much will the Lafferty family actually have to pay out of their pocket assuming the cap of one million dollars has not been reached?

6 Kala Matumba is a professional marathon runner from Mali who insures her future income stream by insuring her ability to run. Her training routine is to run 16 kilometers each of the first six days of the week and rest on Sundays. Six days before each marathon, she increases her daily distances to from 16 kilometers to 20 kilometers per day.

a. During regular training, how many kilometers does she run in a week?

b. How many miles does she run each day during regular training?

c. How many miles does she run each week during regular training?

d. Before each marathon race, how many kilometers does she run in a week?

e. How many miles does she run each day?

f. How many miles does she run each week?

Applying Technology

Using the *Introduction to Business* template and your database program software, select problem CH32. After the problem appears on your screen, complete the following activities. Then, after you have completed each step, display or print a report for each activity. If you do not have a printer available, answer the questions before you leave the computer.

1 Sort the database in ascending order by model of car. Answer the following questions:

a. Which model of car has the highest insurance rate?

b. Which model of car has the lowest insurance rate?

2 Select and list the companies that cover sports cars. How many companies are listed?

3 Sort the companies in descending order by rate. Answer the following questions:

a. Which company is listed second?
b. Which company is listed last?

Optional: Create a bar graph showing the average rate for each company.

Making Decisions

Jane is a rather careless driver. She is a 17-year-old with a late model compact Japanese car that looks sporty and is equipped for speed. Jane loves to drive fast and be seen in her car and has compiled a rather poor traffic record. In only one year, she has had two "fender bender" accidents and received two speeding tickets. Those who care about Jane have suggested that her reckless driving habits are putting her and others at risk.

1 What personal property and liability risks associated with an auto accident do you think Jane is taking?

2 If Jane's driving doesn't improve, what will happen to the auto insurance premium she will be required to pay?

3 What helpful suggestions do you have for Jane in regard to her driving?

Chapter Thirty-Three

Vehicle Insurance

Key Terms

automobile liability insurance

bodily injury liability coverage

medical payments coverage

uninsured motorist coverage

property damage liability coverage

collision coverage

comprehensive coverage

compulsory insurance laws

financial responsibility laws

assigned-risk plan

no-fault insurance laws

Objectives

After studying this chapter and completing the end-of-chapter activities, you will be able to:

1 Describe the economic risks of owning an automobile and how the owner can provide protection through personal injury coverage and property damage coverage.

2 Explain the factors that affect insurance rates, ways to reduce your insurance costs, and how to select an insurance company.

3 List the vehicles, other than automobiles, that carry insurance similar to automobiles.

4 List the four basic vehicle insurance laws.

"Chris! What a great looking car! How did you ever afford it?"

"It's not easy, Roberto, to afford a car and still be in school. Not only do I have to make car payments, but I have to pay for insurance. It's been quite a shock! I did save enough money from a part-time job last summer to buy the car but I forgot about insurance. I'm looking for a job right now so I can afford to keep the car."

Purchasing car insurance can be painfully expensive. In fact, American car owners together spend about $115 billion annually on car insurance premiums.

However, not everyone has to pay high premiums. Those who are seen by their insurance companies as low risks pay significantly less than those in the high risk category. The difference is in the economic risk.

ECONOMIC RISKS OF OWNING A CAR

Owning a vehicle puts you in a position of high economic risk. You might have an accident and injure yourself, your vehicle, other people, or others' property. The vehicle might be stolen or damaged by vandals. You could be sued by someone claiming to suffer damages as a result of an accident involving your vehicle.

The costs of treating injured people and repairing damaged property could easily bring financial ruin to people who do not have insurance and must pay for damages. Court action is costly, and awards to injured people and to owners of damaged property have increased dramatically. Vehicle insurance is designed to provide protection from the financial risks involved in owning and driving a car or another vehicle.

Protection from the economic risks of car ownership is available with an automobile insurance policy. You can buy insurance to

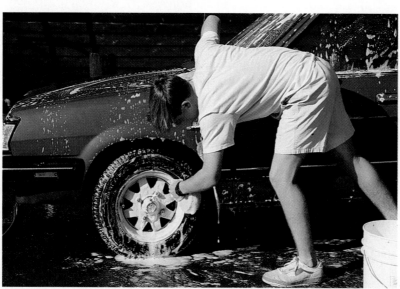

Illus. 33-1
Owning a vehicle puts you in a position of economic risk.

protect yourself from the financial loss caused by almost anything that could happen to your car. You can also buy **automobile liability insurance** to protect yourself against financial loss if you injure someone else or damage someone else's property in an automobile accident.

Sometimes an accident is unavoidable, that is, no one can be directly blamed for it. In most cases, however, someone is at fault. The person who is found to be at fault normally is responsible for damages and financial losses that result from the accident. Although you may think you are completely faultless, you can be sued. If you are insured, your insurance company will provide legal defense for the suit. If the court decides that you are legally liable for injuries and damage to property, your insurance company will pay the costs up to the limits stated in your insurance policy.

Several kinds of protection are available through companies that provide automobile insurance. This coverage is available in different combinations and for different amounts. Although some of the coverage can be bought separately, most car owners buy package policies that include most or all of the necessary coverage. There are two main categories of automobile insurance: personal injury coverage and property damage coverage. Figure 33-1 summarizes the types of automobile insurance coverage.

Figure 33-1
The six types of automobile insurance coverage

A Summary Chart of Automobile Insurance Coverage

Types of Coverage:	Coverage On:	
Personal Injury Coverages	**Policyholder**	**Others**
Bodily injury liability	No	Yes
Medical payments	Yes	Yes
Uninsured motorist protection	Yes	Yes
Property Damage Coverages	**Policyholder's Automobile**	**Property of Others**
Property damage liability	No	Yes
Collision insurance	Yes	No
Comprehensive physical damage	Yes	No

Personal Injury Coverage

Personal injury coverage includes bodily injury liability, medical payments, and uninsured motorist protection. These three types of personal injury coverage are the source of most of the money paid in claims by automobile insurance companies.

Bodily Injury Liability Protection **Bodily injury liability coverage** protects the insured from claims resulting from injuries or deaths for which the insured is found to be at fault. This type of insurance covers people in other cars, passengers riding with the insured, and pedestrians. It does not cover the insured or, in most cases, the insured's immediate family.

Dollar amounts of bodily injury coverage are generally expressed as two numbers divided by a slash. The first number refers to the limit, in thousands of dollars, that the insurance company will pay for injuries to any one person in an accident. For example, if the insured had bodily injury liability coverage of 100/300 and had an accident for which the insured was found to be at fault, the insurance company would pay up to $100,000 if just one person were injured. The second number, in this case 300, refers to the limit, in thousands of dollars, that the insurance company would pay if more than one person were injured. This means that the insurance company would pay a total of $300,000 for all the injuries. Larger amounts of bodily injury protection often are needed and add surprisingly little to the cost of your premium.

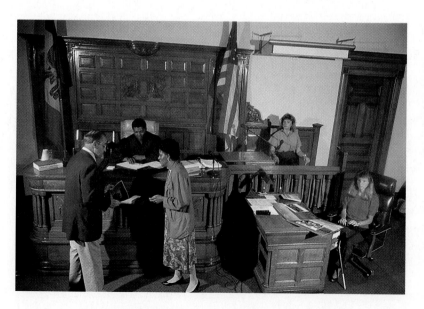

Illus. 33-2
Sometimes as a result of jury awards, the cost of an automobile accident can be very high.

Medical Payments Protection Through **medical payments coverage,** policyholders and their family members are covered if they are injured while riding in their car or in someone else's car. It may cover them if they are walking and are hit by a car. Guests riding in the insured car are also protected.

Medical payments insurance covers the costs of medical, dental, ambulance, hospital, nursing, and funeral services. Payment, up to the limit stated in the policy, is made regardless of who is at fault in the accident. Normally car owners purchase medical payments insurance along with their bodily injury liability coverage.

Approximately 10 percent of the nation's motorists drive illegally without automobile insurance.

Uninsured Motorist Protection In some cases, injuries are caused by hit-and-run drivers or by drivers who have no insurance or money to pay claims. Therefore, insurance companies make available **uninsured motorist coverage** to protect against these drivers. It is available only to those people who carry bodily injury liability coverage. In addition to covering the policyholder and family members, it also covers guests riding in the policyholder's car. Unlike medical payments coverage, which pays regardless of who is at fault in the accident, uninsured motorist protection covers the insured person only if the uninsured motorist is at fault.

Property Damage Coverage

There are three types of automobile insurance designed to protect you from economic loss due to damage to the property of others and to your car. They are property damage liability, collision, and comprehensive damage. While the claims paid in these categories are usually not as large as claims paid under personal injury coverage, it is still important to have these coverages.

Massachusetts was the first state to adopt a no-fault insurance law. The current total of no-fault states is 14.

Property Damage Liability Property damage liability coverage protects the insured against claims if the insured's car damages someone else's property and the insured is at fault. The damaged property is often another car, but it may also be property such as telephone poles, fire hydrants, and buildings. Property damage liability insurance does not cover damage to the insured person's car.

Collision Insurance Collision coverage protects a car owner against financial loss associated with damage resulting from a collision with another car or object or from the car turning over. Collision coverage does not cover injuries to

people or damage to the property of others. Most collision coverage is written with a deductible clause, which is explained in Chapter 32. Deductible amounts are often $200, $500, or more. This means that the insured may agree to pay the first $200 or $500 of damage to the car in any one collision and the insurance company agrees to pay the rest. Larger deductible amounts will reduce the premium paid by the policyholder.

Collision coverage does not provide for payment of damages greater than the car's value. Suppose the insured's car incurs $3,500 in damages in a collision with another vehicle. If the car has a value of only $3,100, the collision coverage would pay $3,100, not $3,500. Collision coverage should not be carried on a car that is of little value because the cost of repairing the car may be more than the car is worth. The car's worth is normally set by a book that reports the value of similar cars that have been sold recently. Collision insurance usually accounts for approximately two-thirds of the total cost of an insurance policy.

Comprehensive Coverage Even if you do not have an accident with another vehicle, your car can still be damaged or destroyed. The car could be stolen, or it could be damaged by fire, tornado, windstorm, vandalism, or falling objects. **Comprehensive coverage** protects the insured against almost all damage losses except those caused from a collision or from the car turning over.

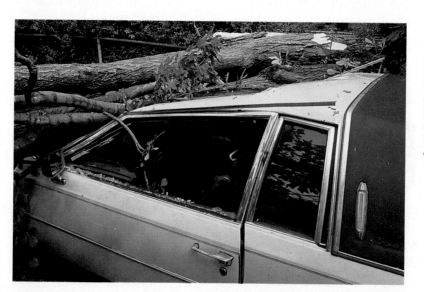

Illus. 33-3
Comprehensive coverage protects your car against damage inflicted by fire, storms, vandalism, or falling objects.

If the insured's car is totally destroyed or stolen, the amount paid is not necessarily equal to the amount paid for the car. Rather, it is equal to the car's estimated value at the time of the loss. Suppose the insured's car costing $15,000 is stolen soon after it is purchased. The insurance company will probably pay almost as much as the car cost, perhaps $14,500. However, if the car is stolen two years after it is purchased, the insurance company may pay only $10,500. The car has grown older and its value has decreased.

Always ask for a good-student discount if your grades are high.

BUYING AUTOMOBILE INSURANCE

People in the United States spend more than $115 billion a year insuring over 143 million vehicles. This expenditure is about 45 percent of all of the money spent on property and casualty insurance. This indicates that a great deal of money is spent insuring cars and other vehicles. That money should be spent wisely and carefully. Therefore, car owners need to understand how to get the most protection for their insurance dollar.

Insurance Rates

Insurance companies use several factors to determine the cost of your automobile insurance. Some of those factors include:

- Your age and other characteristics, such as accident record, marital status, or academic standing.

- The purpose for which you use your car.

- The number of miles you drive your car each year.

- The value and type of your car.

- The community in which you live.

- Types of coverage and deductibles.

Since some drivers are more likely to have accidents than others, they must pay higher premiums. To determine premium rates, drivers are classified according to age, marital status, driving record, and scholastic achievement. The lowest rates are reserved for the best risks, those least likely to have an accident. The cost of insurance is usually higher when one of the drivers in the insured's family is under age 30 than it is if all family drivers are over age 30.

The purpose for which a car is driven and the number of miles it is driven in a year are also important in determining insurance rates. Cars used for business purposes are generally driven more miles in a year than are cars driven for pleasure and are therefore more likely to be involved in an accident.

Legal *Perspective*

No-Fault Automobile Insurance

No-fault automobile insurance was first introduced in the 1970s as a way to control insurance costs. Under no-fault automobile insurance laws, people injured in an automobile accident are required to collect for their financial losses—such as their medical bills, loss of wages, and other related expenses—from their own insurance companies no matter who is at fault.

In the past, victims sometimes had to sue insurance companies or individuals to receive compensation for their injuries. These lawsuits cost the insurance companies large sums of money. In turn, the insurance companies passed these costs down to policyholders through increased premiums.

With no-fault insurance, lawsuits usually are unnecessary because each party collects from their respective insurance company. Money is saved from lawsuits and insurance settlements become more equitable to people who suffer serious injuries. No-fault insurance is one way to keep automobile insurance costs affordable.

In the 14 states with no-fault automobile insurance, policyholders are covered by their own insurers, regardless of who was at fault in an accident. In a state with a no-fault law, the victim may sue the other party in the accident only in limited circumstances, not over relatively minor injuries.

Where no-fault insurance laws are in effect, the benefits to insured automobile owners are significant. In New York, for example, victims can sue only if an accident results in a fracture, dismemberment, significant loss of a body organ, or death. The total premiums paid for automobile insurance in New York are estimated to be 30 percent lower than they would be if the no-fault law did not exist.

A recent study of legal actions in states without no-fault laws suggests that victims with minor injuries are collecting awards that are too large and those with major injuries are not adequately compensated. The study also suggests that no-fault laws in the remainder of the states would reduce these inequities and would save consumers about 12 percent on their premiums.

There are currently 14 states with no-fault insurance laws: Colorado, Connecticut, Florida, Hawaii, Kansas, Kentucky, Massachusetts, Michigan, Minnesota, New Jersey, New York, North Dakota, Pennsylvania, and Utah.

Critical Thinking

1 Who do you think tends to benefit the most from no-fault insurance laws?

2 Why do you think with such influential supporters of strong no-fault laws, only 14 states have adopted them?

The value of your car naturally has an important effect on the cost of insurance. Premiums for collision coverage and comprehensive physical damage coverage must be higher for a car worth $15,500 than for a car worth only $8,000. The insurance company runs the risk of paying out much more to the insured if the $15,500 car is destroyed or stolen. The type of car also affects the rate. If you have a high-performance car, a luxury car, or an expensive sports car, you will have to pay higher rates.

Rates for automobile insurance are not the same everywhere. Rates vary from state to state and even from city to city within a state. Automobile insurance rates are also affected by the population in a particular area and the number of accidents that occur over a certain period of time in the area. Insurance companies gather statistics on the dollar amount of claims paid for in an area and base their insurance rates on this information.

The cost of your automobile insurance will also vary according to the types of coverage you have and the amounts of the deductibles you choose. Naturally, the more coverage you carry, the higher the cost.

Reducing Your Cost

By planning your automobile insurance purchase carefully, you may save a great deal of money. For example, the extra amount charged for young drivers may be decreased if they have completed an approved driver education course. Companies in most states offer young people a good-student discount. The discount may amount to as much as 25 percent of the premium.

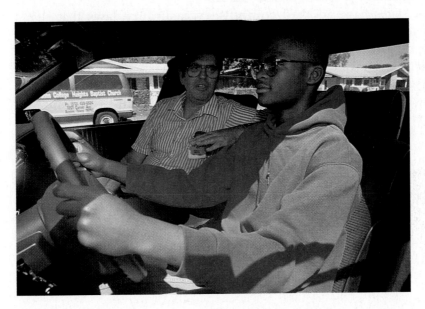

Illus. 33-4
Taking an approved driver education course can reduce the cost of your car insurance.

Selecting a Company

Just as automobile insurance premiums vary with the conditions associated with your car and your driving, they also vary from company to company. It pays to shop around and compare rates.

While it is difficult to find out all of the possible rates from all companies, you should compare a few companies. The cost of the insurance will depend greatly on your choice of coverage.

INSURING OTHER VEHICLES

Insurance on motorcycles, recreational vehicles, and snowmobiles is similar in some respects to automobile insurance. For example, bodily injury liability, property damage liability, collision, and comprehensive physical damage insurance are the most important coverages on these vehicles. The engine size and value of the vehicle are the important factors in determining the cost of insurance. Generally, the larger and more expensive the vehicle, the higher the insurance cost.

Individual states regulate laws relating to vehicle insurance. Most of these laws are advantageous to responsible drivers. All owners of vehicles should know about compulsory insurance laws, financial responsibility laws, assigned-risk plans, and no-fault insurance laws.

Compulsory Insurance Laws

All states have adopted **compulsory insurance laws** that require you to carry certain types of automobile insurance before your car can be licensed. It is compulsory that an automobile owner carry insurance to pay for personal injury and for property damage that he or she causes due to an accident. Compulsory insurance laws state that you may not register a car or obtain a license to drive without presenting proof of having the minimum amounts of insurance coverage required.

Financial Responsibility Laws

All states have some kind of financial responsibility law. **Financial responsibility laws** provide that if you cause an accident and cannot pay for the damages either through insurance, your savings, or the sale of property, your driver's license will be suspended or taken away. Most of these laws make you legally liable (responsible) for any damages you cause to people or their property.

Assigned-Risk Plans

Usually because of bad accident records, some drivers are unable to buy automobile insurance in the normal fashion. Because of this, every state also has an **assigned-risk plan.** Under this plan, every automobile insurance company in the state that sells liability insurance is assigned a certain number of high risk drivers. That number is based on the amount of insurance each company sells. Using this plan, each company has to insure a fair proportion of high risk drivers. The insurance industry calls this their automobile residual insurance market. Drivers in high risk categories must pay much higher premiums than those who are not high risks.

sk your insurance agent about payment plans for your premiums. Some companies will customize payments on various schedules to meet your needs.

No-Fault Insurance Laws

In an effort to speed up the payment of claims and reduce the hardship of long delays, **no-fault insurance laws** have been adopted by some states. Under these laws, people injured in an automobile accident are required to collect for their financial losses—such as their medical bills, loss of wages, and other related expenses—from their own insurance companies no matter who is at fault.

Let's look at an example. Blake Samari, who is insured with Vehicle Insurance Company, and Heather McCarthy, who is insured

ead your insurance policy carefully so that you understand your coverages.

with State Insurance Company, are injured in a serious two-car accident. Under no-fault insurance, Samari would collect from Vehicle Insurance and McCarthy's claims would be paid by State Insurance. It would not be necessary to decide whether Samari or McCarthy caused the accident.

No-fault insurance laws vary in some ways from state to state. Ordinarily the right to sue is retained for the more serious injury cases and for death. In such cases, it is necessary to decide how much each driver was at fault in the accident.

Key Ideas

1 You can protect yourself against risk by purchasing personal injury insurance and property damage liability insurance. Personal injury insurance covers bodily injury liability, medical payments, and uninsured motorist protection. Property damage liability insurance protects you against claims if your car damages someone else's property and you are at fault.

2 Insurance rates are affected by factors such as age, accident record, marital status, academic standing, purpose for which the car is used, number of miles driven each year, and value and type of car. By planning your automobile insurance purchase carefully and comparing rates, you may save a great deal of money.

3 Insurance on motorcycles, recreational vehicles, and snowmobiles is similar in some respects to automobile insurance.

4 There are four insurance laws with which all vehicle owners should be familiar: compulsory insurance, financial responsibility, assigned-risk plans, and no-fault insurance.

End of Chapter Activities

Increasing Your Business Vocabulary

The following terms should become part of your business vocabulary. For each numbered item, find the term that has the same meaning.

assigned-risk plan

automobile liability insurance

bodily injury liability coverage

collision coverage

comprehensive coverage

compulsory insurance laws

financial responsibility laws

medical payments coverage

no-fault insurance laws

property damage liability coverage

uninsured motorist coverage

1 Insurance coverage that provides medical expense protection for the policyholder, immediate family members, and guests while in the insured person's car.

2 Automobile insurance that provides coverage to high risk drivers who are unable to purchase it otherwise.

3 Insurance protection against almost all losses except those caused from a collision or from the car turning over.

4 A plan in which people injured in automobile accidents are required to collect for their financial losses from their own insurance companies no matter who is at fault.

5 Insurance coverage that protects you from claims resulting from injuries or deaths for which you are found to be at fault.

6 Laws whereby your driver's license will be suspended or taken away if you cause an accident and cannot pay for the damages either through insurance, your savings, or the sale of property.

7 The general term used to describe insurance to protect you against financial loss if you injure someone else or damage someone else's property in an automobile accident.

8 Laws that require you to carry certain types of automobile insurance before your car can be licensed.

9 Insurance coverage that protects a car owner against financial loss associated with damage from a collision with another car or object or from the car turning over.

10 Insurance coverage that protects the policyholder and immediate family members against losses from injuries caused by a hit-and-run driver or by a driver who has no insurance and inadequate money to pay claims.

11 Insurance protection against claims if your car damages someone else's property and you are at fault.

Reviewing Your Reading

1. What is the purpose of vehicle insurance?

2. If you are protected by an automobile insurance policy and are sued as the result of an accident, how will the insurance company help you?

3. What are the two categories of automobile insurance?

4. What are the three types of personal injury coverage?

5. What does 100/300 mean in terms of bodily injury liability coverage?

6. What are the three types of automobile insurance designed to protect you against economic loss due to damage to the property of others and to your car?

7. Which type of automobile insurance protects you against damage caused by a hit-and-run driver?

8. Which factors determine the cost of automobile insurance coverage?

9. What other vehicles, other than automobiles, may be covered with insurance similar to automobile insurance?

10. What are four vehicle insurance laws with which all drivers should be familiar?

11. What kind of coverage is required under compulsory insurance laws?

12. Why would someone be required to purchase insurance from an assigned-risk plan?

Using Your Business Knowledge

1. Which type of automobile insurance coverage would Jane Edmunds need in order to be covered in the following situations?

   a. Jane was found to be at fault in an accident in which a pedestrian was injured.
   b. Jane's daughter, who was riding in the back seat, was injured when Jane ran into a parked car.
   c. Jane, in an attempt to avoid hitting a dog in the street, ran into a parked car.
   d. During a storm, a heavy tree branch damaged Jane's car, breaking the windshield and denting the hood.

2. Jim Pikkert was the driver at fault in an accident in which his three passengers were badly hurt. The court awarded two of the injured people $30,000 each, and it awarded the third person $45,000. Pikkert had bodily injury liability coverage in the amount of 50/100. Was this enough insurance to protect him from financial loss? Why or why not?

3. Why is it less important to carry collision coverage on a ten-year-old car than on a three-year-old car? Are there circumstances when

you may still want to have collision coverage on a ten-year-old car?

4 If there were a four-car pileup in foggy conditions on the interstate highway, how would claims be settled in a state with a no-fault insurance law? What would happen in a state without such a law?

Calculating Business Problems

1 Karen Samson carried a $500 deductible collision insurance policy on her automobile. She had an accident that was determined to be her fault. The cost of repairing her car was $1,750. How much of the repair bill would her insurance company pay?

2 The number of automobile accidents in one year was 171,508,491. Of these accidents, 8,945,740 involved drivers under the age of 20. What percentage of the total number of accidents involved drivers under 20? (Round to the nearest whole percent.)

3 When Erik England drove 53 kilometers round-trip to work each day, his automobile insurance premium was $650 a year. Erik changed jobs and now drives 24 kilometers round-trip. His insurance company gives a 10 percent premium discount to policyholders who drive less than 25 kilometers to and from work each day.

a. How much will he save per year?
b. How much is Erik's current premium?

4 Joan Nordland is a college student. She took a driver education course while in high school. She also earned an overall scholastic average of B+ in her college work. These qualify her for a driver education discount of 20 percent of the premium and a good-student discount of 15 percent of the premium for her automobile insurance.

a. If the standard premium for her policy is $850 per year, how much will Joan pay for her automobile insurance this year?
b. How much will she save?

Applying Technology

Using the *Introduction to Business* template and your word processing program software, select problem CH33. After the problem appears on your screen, complete the following activities. Then, print each completed application. If you do not have a printer available, save the applications on a data disk to give to your teacher.

1 You just purchased a used car that is four years old and now you need to apply for vehicle insurance. Fill in the blanks with information about yourself. For the

information that you enter, use boldface and a different type font from the one used on the application.

2 Copy the application and complete it for another vehicle. You just purchased a brand new pickup truck and now you need to apply for vehicle insurance. Fill in the blanks with information about yourself. For the information that you enter, use italics and a different type font from the one used on the application.

Making Decisions

Eighteen-year-old Chris was planning to purchase a car. The car she liked the most was a seven-year-old compact that had been driven 73,000 miles. She expected to pay about $4,500 for the car. As a good student who had completed a driver education course, she was well aware of the costs of operating a car. She also knew that she was

required to have insurance that would be very expensive.

1 Explain to Chris why automobile insurance is required of her.

2 Create a list of suggestions for Chris that will help her reduce the cost of automobile insurance on the car that she buys.

Chapter Thirty-Four

Property Insurance

Key Terms

personal liability coverage

perils

real property

personal property

standard fire policy

extended coverage

homeowners policy

inventory

depreciation

replacement insurance

adjuster

Objectives

After studying this chapter and completing the end-of-chapter activities, you will be able to:

1 List the three types of economic losses covered by home and property insurance.

2 List and describe the three types of special policies that cover property.

3 Explain how to purchase property insurance.

4 Describe the purpose of business insurance.

5 Describe how to make an insurance claim.

"I love our new apartment! We have spent a lot of money getting it ready to move in when school starts. And now I am broke! Are you sure we really need renters insurance?"

"Trust me, Susan, with three college girls sharing an apartment, we need insurance. If something would happen and our property were destroyed in a fire, we would be out a lot of money. I don't know about you, but I couldn't afford to replace any of my personal items if they were destroyed in a fire. And with three of us sharing the insurance expense, it really won't cost us that much money."

"I guess you're right, Ashley. I know I couldn't replace my personal belongings. You've convinced me. Go ahead and call your mom's insurance agent. Even though Sara hasn't arrived in town yet, I am sure she will go along with us to purchase the insurance."

Property insurance is designed to protect you from the financial loss you would experience if some of your property were lost or destroyed as a result of fire, theft, vandalism, floods, windstorms, or other hazards. Property owners also are at risk of being sued by people who are injured on their property. Because the risks of loss in such situations are high, everyone should carry property insurance.

HOME AND PROPERTY INSURANCE

Home and property insurance protect you against three kinds of economic loss:

1. damage to your home or property,

2. additional expenses you must pay to live someplace else if your home is badly damaged, and

3. liability losses related to your property.

Damage to Home or Property

Every 16 seconds, a fire department responds to a fire somewhere in the United States. Fires cause over $12 billion in damage every year. Much of this damage is to homes. The dollar amount of damage goes up almost every year. Homes and other expensive property should be insured for fire damage as well as damage caused by vandalism, unavoidable accidents, and natural disasters such as lightning, earthquake, wind, and flood. If your home or property is damaged and you are insured, the insurance company will pay all or a portion of the cost of repair or replacement.

Additional Living Expenses

If a fire or other disaster strikes your home, one of the first shocks you will experience is that you do not have a place to live. You may have to move into a hotel, motel, or furnished apartment

Accidents related to cooking start more residential fires than any other cause; faulty furnaces, heaters, and fireplaces are the second leading cause of fires.

while your home is being repaired. Property insurance that includes insurance for additional living expenses will help to pay for the expenses you would incur if something happened to your home.

Liability Protection

The third kind of loss, liability loss, is protected by personal liability coverage. **Personal liability coverage** protects you from claims arising from injuries to other people or damage to other people's property caused by you, your family, or even your pets. If a neighbor slips on your icy sidewalk and you are shown to be at fault, personal liability coverage will pay for any medical and legal costs up to a stated limit. If a child damages a car in an adjacent driveway with a tricycle, claims will be paid through the provisions in the policy of the child's family that cover liability for physical damage to the property of others.

These kinds of events may seem remote and rather trivial. But court awards to those who suffer the damage or injury often are neither remote nor trivial. In fact, these awards (and consequently premiums) are increasing so quickly that the insurance industry often refers to it as the insurance liability crisis. Awards to injured people for millions of dollars are not uncommon. Everyone should have some form of liability protection from economic loss.

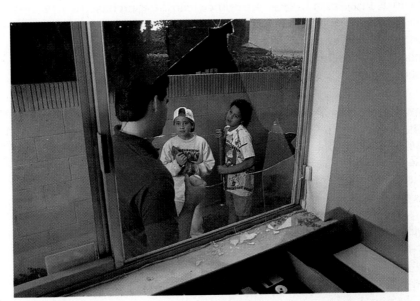

Illus. 34-1
Personal liability coverage will pay for damage you or a member of your family may accidentally inflict on a neighbor's property.

PROPERTY INSURANCE POLICIES

When considering the purchase of property insurance, you must first decide what should be insured and against what perils it should be insured. **Perils** are the causes of loss, such as fire, wind, or theft. Property permanently attached to land, such as a house or garage, is called **real property.** Property not attached to the land, such as furniture or clothing, is known as **personal property.** Real and personal property may be protected by individual policies or by a homeowners policy. If you are a renter like Susan and Ashley, there are also special policies that will cover your property—individual, homeowners and renters.

Illus. 34-2
Real property is attached to the land; personal property is not.

Individual Policies

A property owner can buy separate policies that insure against specific perils. For example, a **standard fire policy** insures against losses caused by fire or lightning. Extended coverage can be included in a standard fire policy. **Extended coverage** broadens the coverage to include damage caused by perils such as wind, hail, smoke, and falling aircraft.

Policies also may be purchased separately for damage caused by flood in a flood-prone area. Insurance can be purchased to protect against economic losses caused by earthquakes. Neither of these two perils is typically covered in other policies. The advantage of purchasing separate policies is that the combination of policies purchased can be fitted to individual needs.

Homeowners Policies

The most common form of home and property insurance policy sold today is a homeowners policy. The **homeowners policy** is a very convenient package-type insurance policy designed to fit the needs of most homeowners wishing to insure their homes and property. A homeowners policy almost always comes in three forms: basic form, broad form, and special form. The number of perils covered by a homeowners policy depends on which form the insured chooses to purchase.

The basic form of a homeowners policy insures property against the first 11 perils listed in Figure 34-1. The broad form is very

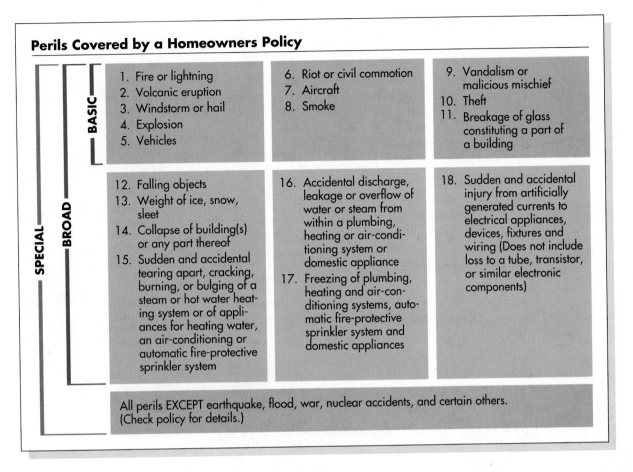

Perils Covered by a Homeowners Policy

BASIC

1. Fire or lightning
2. Volcanic eruption
3. Windstorm or hail
4. Explosion
5. Vehicles

6. Riot or civil commotion
7. Aircraft
8. Smoke

9. Vandalism or malicious mischief
10. Theft
11. Breakage of glass constituting a part of a building

BROAD

12. Falling objects
13. Weight of ice, snow, sleet
14. Collapse of building(s) or any part thereof
15. Sudden and accidental tearing apart, cracking, burning, or bulging of a steam or hot water heating system or of appliances for heating water, an air-conditioning or automatic fire-protective sprinkler system

16. Accidental discharge, leakage or overflow of water or steam from within a plumbing, heating or air-conditioning system or domestic appliance
17. Freezing of plumbing, heating and air-conditioning systems, automatic fire-protective sprinkler system and domestic appliances

18. Sudden and accidental injury from artificially generated currents to electrical appliances, devices, fixtures and wiring (Does not include loss to a tube, transistor, or similar electronic components)

SPECIAL

All perils EXCEPT earthquake, flood, war, nuclear accidents, and certain others. (Check policy for details.)

Figure 34-1

Perils covered by homeowners policies.

widely purchased and covers 18 different risks. This type usually costs about 5 to 10 percent more than the basic form. The special form is even more comprehensive and covers all perils shown in Figure 34-1 and many more. The special form is sometimes referred to as an all-risk policy and costs from 10 to 15 percent more than the basic policy. Actually, such a policy insures against all perils except those excluded by the policy. Personal liability coverage is included with all forms of the homeowners policy.

With a homeowners policy, you are as protected as you would be if you bought several different policies. Yet the cost of a homeowners policy is usually 20 to 30 percent less than if the same amount of coverage were obtained by buying separate policies. It is also more convenient to have one policy and one premium rather than paying two premiums for separate insurance policies.

FYI

About 95 percent of the nation's homeowners carry property insurance to protect themselves against potential financial losses. Only 41 percent of renters buy that same protection.

Renters Policies

Many people in our society rent homes, condominiums, or apartments. They fill these dwellings with their personal property. Renters have many of the same property and liability insurance needs as homeowners. In response to this, the insurance industry has developed a renters policy that is a package property and liability policy appropriate for renters. This policy covers household goods and personal belongings and provides protection against the same kinds of perils covered by homeowners policies. A renters policy may include personal liability coverage, but it doesn't protect the actual dwelling. The dwelling should be covered under the owner's policy. Renters who don't want liability protection may choose a policy that covers only personal property.

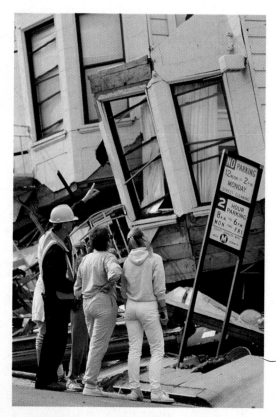

Illus. 34-3
One of the perils not covered by a homeowners policy is damage due to earthquake.

BUYING PROPERTY INSURANCE

As with other large insurance purchases, a wise consumer will work to find the most appropriate property protection at the lowest cost. This process involves making certain that the property is insured for the correct amount and that the factors affecting property insurance costs have all been carefully considered.

The value of a home and furnishings represents the largest investment that many people make. The purchase of a carefully selected insurance plan makes good sense to protect that investment.

Installing deadbolt locks on your doors could save you as much as 5 percent of your homeowners or renters policy premium.

Getting the Correct Coverage

Suppose that Juanita Hernandez built her house in 1988 for $90,000 and she insured it for that amount. If today the cost of building a similar house is $125,000, the current replacement value of the house is $125,000. Yet if Miss Hernandez's house is completely destroyed by fire, the insurance company may pay her only $90,000. Some insurance companies provide for automatic increases in property coverage as the price level increases. Other insurers will pay the current replacement value if the property is insured for at least 80 percent of that replacement value.

Building costs and property values have increased greatly in recent years. Property owners should review the value of their property and insurance coverage every few years. They should determine the cost of replacing their property and make sure that their insurance policies give enough protection.

Special care should be taken to accurately estimate the value of personal property. Since personal property includes many different items, some may be overlooked if a careless estimate of value is made. Most homeowners policies provide personal property coverage at 50 percent of policy value. For example, if your home is insured for $100,000, your personal property is insured for 50 percent of $100,000, or $50,000. The value of personal property that you collect over the years is often surprisingly high. In many cases, a homeowner's personal property is worth considerably more than 50 percent of the coverage on the home. Additional coverage is available for a slightly higher premium.

NET FACTS

FTP stands for File Transfer Protocol. FTP software transfers files of data from one computer to another.

Cultural *Perspective*

Papyrus

If you lived in Egypt around 1600 B.C., your business would have recorded its activities on papyrus. The spongy material inside the plant was cut in strips and pressed into material that resembled a crude form of what we know as paper. This crude form of paper enabled people to write and record information and actually store their records. Up until this time, the early Babylonians used clay tablets. However, the clay tablets were difficult to handle and to write on. With the invention of papyrus, the business world began to change.

Egypt had an elaborate tax system in which taxes were paid in commodities, such as wheat, and sent to local district storehouses. Less perishable items were transferred to a central treasury. All of these transfers were recorded meticulously by the scribes. There was an auditing system in which the records of each scribe were compared and had to match. Scribes were very careful to be accurate because irregularities could be punished by mutilation or death. The papyrus allowed the scribes to work faster and more accurately.

The invention of paper advanced not only record keeping but the artistic and cultural aspects of civilization as well.

Critical Thinking

1 How do you think papyrus would have looked in comparison to paper?

2 In what other ways do you think the invention of paper has contributed to our culture?

Insurance Premiums

Premiums paid for homeowners insurance have grown each year over the last 10 years to over $20 billion annually. The price that you pay for insurance on a home and furnishings is based on a number of factors. The most important factor is the estimated danger of loss based on the insurance company's past experiences. In addition to the loss experiences, an insurance company considers the following factors in determining homeowners insurance premiums:

- The value of the property insured.
- The construction of the building; that is, whether it is made of brick, wood, or concrete; and the construction of the roof.
- The type of policy (basic, broad, or special).
- The number of perils covered.
- The distance to the nearest fire department and water supply.
- The amount of deductible (the higher the deductible, the lower the premium).

You should consider these factors carefully before purchasing or building a home and when shopping for insurance on that home and your property. Also, homeowners insurance discounts are often available for policyholders who are nonsmokers, for installing smoke detectors and burglar alarms, and for buying multiple policies such as life and auto insurance from the same company.

BUSINESS INSURANCE

Like homeowners, businesses insure their personal and real property against economic loss caused by a variety of perils. The same tragedies happen with businesses as with homes. Fires, storms, water damage, burglaries, and liability problems face business owners. Businesses are also threatened by another important economic peril—loss of income. Businesses can use insurance to protect against the loss of income during times when they must be closed due to a tragedy.

MAKING A CLAIM

In the unhappy event that you should have to make a claim to your insurance company for a property loss, you will want to be well prepared. You should keep a list of personal property that you have insured. The list, called an **inventory**, should include:

1. the original cost of each article,

2. when the article was purchased, and

3. how long the article is expected to last.

The age of an insured article of personal property is quite important. As most property becomes older, it gradually wears out and decreases in value. This decrease in value, called **depreciation,** usually affects the amount the insurance company will pay if the property is destroyed. For example, a sofa costing $700 that is expected to last ten years would depreciate $70 each year (cost $700 ÷ 10 years = $70 depreciation per year). Its value after six years would be $280 (depreciation per year $70 × 6 years = total depreciation $420; original cost $700 − total depreciation $420 = $280).

Before purchasing insurance, research the reliability of the insurance company.

However, in recent years, homeowners have purchased replacement insurance. **Replacement insurance** actually replaces an item that has been destroyed. No depreciation is deducted, but instead the item is actually replaced for whatever the current cost may be. A replacement cost policy would pay whatever it cost on the day of the loss to replace your property.

Illus. 34-4

After you file a claim, an adjuster will inspect the property and pay you according to the terms of the policy.

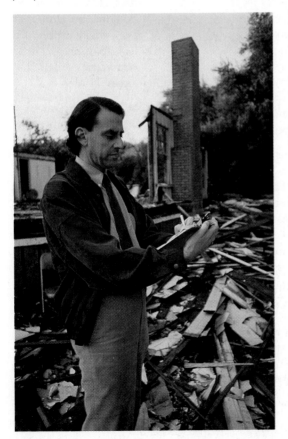

As soon as possible after you discover a loss, you should file a claim with your insurance company. However, before the company will pay, you must provide proof of your loss. This is not a problem with real property. A representative of the insurance company, called an **adjuster,** can look at the damaged property, determine the extent of loss, and pay you according to the terms of the policy. The destroyed contents of a house, however, would pose a problem. In order to prove the amount of personal property loss, you must know the approximate value of each article damaged or destroyed.

In addition to maintaining an up-to-date personal property inventory, some insurance companies suggest keeping receipts from purchases of your possessions and taking photographs or videos of your furniture and other property. These receipts and pictures can be used to support claims. Insurance companies can provide you with inventory forms and information about how to make claims for losses.

Key Ideas

1 Home and property insurance protect against three kinds of economic loss: (1) damage to your home or property, (2) additional expenses you pay to live someplace else if your home is badly damaged, and (3) liability losses related to your property.

2 There are three types of special policies that cover property. Individual policies allow a property owner to buy separate policies that insure against specific perils such as losses caused by fire or lightning. Home-owners insurance is a convenient package-type insurance policy designed to fit the needs of most homeowners wishing to insure their homes and property. Renters insurance is available for those who rent homes, condominiums, or apartments.

3 A wise consumer will work to find the most appropriate property protection at the lowest cost. This process involves making certain that the property is insured for the correct amount and that the factors affecting property insurance costs have all been carefully considered.

4 Businesses insure their personal and real property against economic loss caused by a variety of perils. The same tragedies happen with businesses as with homes, including fires, storms, water damage, burglaries, liability problems, plus an additional peril of loss of income.

5 When making an insurance claim, you will need to give your agent (1) the original cost of the article, (2) when the article was purchased, and (3) how long the article is expected to last so that appropriate action may be taken.

End of Chapter Activities

Increasing Your Business Vocabulary

The following terms should become part of your business vocabulary. For each numbered item, find the term that has the same meaning.

adjuster

depreciation

extended coverage

homeowners policy

inventory

perils

personal liability coverage

personal property

real property

replacement insurance

standard fire policy

1 Property that is permanently attached to land.

2 Additional protection of property that covers damage caused by perils such as wind, hail, smoke, and falling aircraft, among other things.

3 Insurance that protects you from claims arising from injuries to other people or damage to other people's property caused by you, your family, or your pets.

4 A basic type of property insurance that protects against losses caused by fire or lightning.

5 Property that is not attached to the land.

6 A package-type insurance policy designed to fit the needs of most homeowners wishing to insure their homes and property.

7 The decrease in the value of property as it becomes older and wears out.

8 A list of goods showing the original cost of each item, when it was purchased, and how long it is expected to last.

9 The causes of loss, such as fire, wind, or theft.

10 An insurance company representative who determines the extent of loss and pays policyholders according to the terms of the policy.

11 Insurance that actually replaces an item that has been destroyed.

Reviewing Your Reading

1 List the three kinds of economic losses for which home and property insurance provide protection.

2 What kind of loss would you have to suffer in order to take advantage of additional living-expense coverage in your insurance policy?

3 Tell why personal liability coverage is so important today.

4 Name two prominent perils that are not typically covered in most homeowners policies.

5 Which homeowners policy covers more perils, the special or the broad policy?

6 Describe the difference between buying separate policies to cover home and property versus buying a homeowners policy.

7 Why would a person who rents an apartment purchase property insurance? What kind of policy should a renter purchase?

8 Which factors determine a homeowner's insurance premiums?

9 For what amount is property that has been destroyed usually replaced if the owner has cash-value insurance and does not have replacement insurance?

10 What are several ways a property owner can prove the value of items listed in an inventory?

Using Your Business Knowledge

1 In a recent year, several homes in an Iowa valley were destroyed when heavy rains caused the Mississippi River to rise several feet above flood level. Do you think those Iowa residents who had homeowners policies suffered any financial losses? Why or why not?

2 It snowed in Springview one night in February, and Art Shold did not take the time to shovel the snow from his front steps. Two days later a salesperson slipped on Art's snow-covered steps and broke an arm. The salesperson has asked Art to pay the medical expenses associated with the broken arm. Will Art's homeowners policy cover the expenses?

3 Barbara Johnson's property is covered by the basic form of homeowners insurance. Against which of the following losses is she insured? Which of the losses would be covered if she had the broad coverage?

a. A smoldering fire breaks out in a bedroom closet and her clothing is damaged by smoke.
b. Her home is broken into and vandalized, but nothing is stolen.
c. A storm knocks out the electricity for two days in mid-winter and the pipes burst, causing flooding.

4 The Chens had a serious home fire. They had an adequate fire insurance policy in force, but they

had a very difficult time listing for the insurance adjuster all of the possessions they lost in the fire. What advice would you give to others in the Chen's neighborhood who might be in this position someday?

Calculating Business Problems

1 The Popovs were shopping for property insurance policies when they found a basic homeowners policy that would cost them $140 per year. The total of three separate policies that would cover all of the same perils would be $175. What percent of the total of the three separate policies would the Popovs save by buying the homeowners policy?

2 If Ellen Williams owned a home worth $98,000 and wanted to be certain it was insured for at least 80 percent of its value, for how much should it be insured?

3 A thief broke the lock on Ngyen Shan's business and stole the following items:

  15 liters of oak stain, valued at $4.25 a liter
  6 liters of motor oil, valued at $1.45 a liter
  3 kilograms of 2.5 cm finishing nails, valued at 85 cents a kilogram
  68 meters of 2.5 cm × 30.5 cm pine shelving, valued at $4.50 a meter

Since Mr. Shan had recently purchased these items to sell to his customers, for what amount should he make his claim under his business insurance policy?

4 Arlene Arnold lives in an apartment. Her furniture and other personal property are covered under a renters policy. Miss Arnold's apartment was broken into and the following items were stolen:

  A stereo, bought 3 years ago for $350 and estimated to last 10 years
  A camera, bought 4 years ago for $160 and estimated to last 10 years
  A suede jacket, bought 2 years ago for $180 and estimated to last 5 years

If the insurance company pays Miss Arnold the estimated present worth of the lost articles, what amount will she receive?

Applying Technology

Using the *Introduction to Business* template and your database program software, select problem CH34. After the problem appears on your screen, complete the following activities. Then, after you have completed each step, display or print a report for each activity. If you do not have a printer available, answer the questions before you leave the computer.

1 Sort the database in ascending order by purchase cost of item. Answer the following questions:

a. Which household item had the third highest purchase cost?
b. Which household item had the second to lowest purchase cost?

2 Select and list the household items that were purchased in 1996 and that have a purchase cost of at least $100. How many items are listed?

3 Sort the household items in descending order by year when purchased. Answer the following questions:

a. Which household item in the database is the oldest?
b. Which household item in the database is the second oldest?

Making Decisions

Don purchased a very expensive diamond tennis bracelet for his wife. The jeweler suggested that Don insure this bracelet right away because of its cost. Don has two choices of insurance to purchase. One type would provide an actual-cash-value policy, minus depreciation, that would replace the lost item. However, replacement insurance would pay whatever it cost on the day of the loss to replace the bracelet.

1 Why should Don consider buying actual-cash-value insurance?

2 Why should Don consider buying replacement insurance?

Chapter Thirty-Five

Life Insurance

Key Terms

life insurance

term life insurance

beneficiary

renewable policy

level term insurance

decreasing term insurance

permanent insurance

cash value

face value

whole life insurance

ordinary life policy

limited-payment policies

variable life insurance

universal life insurance

insurable interest

group life insurance

Objectives

After studying this chapter and completing the end-of-chapter activities, you will be able to:

1 Describe the reasons why life insurance is important.

2 Compare and contrast the two types of life insurance—term life insurance and permanent life insurance.

3 Explain the procedure for applying for life insurance, designating a beneficiary, and paying premiums.

4 Describe group life insurance.

"Last night I started thinking about college education for my two youngsters. I know they are still in elementary school, but I need to start planning for their future. It seems like I take care of their day-to-day needs, but I have forgotten about their future needs!"

"Rafael, have you considered borrowing on your life insurance policy when the time comes for the children to go to college?"

"Life insurance? You probably won't believe this, Steve, but I don't have any life insurance. I have other kinds of insurance, but I thought I was too young to worry about life insurance."

"Everyone needs life insurance to protect their family against economic loss. And if you buy a permanent policy soon, you may be able to use it to your advantage when your children need cash for college."

While developing a plan for the future welfare of his children, Rafael should certainly include the purchase of life insurance. Rafael will need to decide what kind of life insurance to buy, how much to buy, and where to buy it.

LIFE INSURANCE

Life insurance protects survivors against the financial loss associated with death. Specifically, it is designed to replace a loss of income for family members who are financially dependent upon another person. Life insurance can also be considered a means of saving or investing, but its primary purpose is always protection against financial loss.

Anyone with dependents needs life insurance. A *dependent* is a person who must rely on another for financial support. In the future, you will need to ask the question, "What would happen to the people who are financially dependent on me if I died tomorrow?" If they could not live financially in the manner in which they lived before your death, you probably need life insurance.

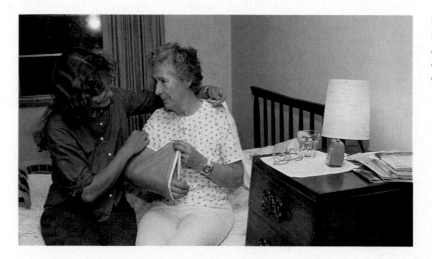

Illus. 35-1
Sometimes an aging parent can become a dependent.

TYPES OF LIFE INSURANCE

Insurance companies offer a variety of life insurance plans that meet the different insurance needs of individuals. The two basic types of life insurance policies are term life and permanent life.

Term Life Insurance

Term life insurance provides financial protection from losses resulting from loss of life during a definite period of time, or term. It is the least expensive form of life insurance. It is also the *only* form of life insurance that is purely life insurance. All other forms of insurance have savings or investment features added to them.

Term policies may run for a period, or term, of from 1 to 20 years or more. If the insured dies during the period for which the insurance was purchased, the amount of the policy is paid to the beneficiary. A **beneficiary** is the person named in the policy to receive the insurance benefits. If the insured does not die during the period for which the policy was purchased, the insurance company is not required to pay anything. Protection ends when the term of years expires.

By paying a slightly higher premium, a person can buy term insurance that is renewable. A **renewable policy** allows the policyholder to continue term insurance for one or more terms without taking a physical examination to determine whether she or he is still a good risk.

Term insurance policies may be level term or decreasing term. With **level term insurance,** the amount of protection and the premiums remain the same while the insurance is in effect. With

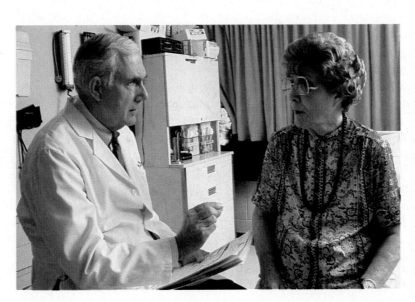

Illus. 35-2

A renewable policy allows the policyholder continued coverage for one or more terms regardless of physical condition.

decreasing term insurance, the amount of protection gradually becomes smaller, but premiums remain the same during the term. This is frequently appropriate because the need for insurance normally declines as children grow up and become independent and other savings and investments grow.

Permanent Life Insurance

The second type of life insurance is called **permanent insurance.** Permanent insurance has cash value and an investment feature as its common characteristics. Part of the premiums you pay for permanent life insurance is used for insurance that provides protection. Another part of the premium, not required for insurance, is invested for you and becomes part of the cash value of your insurance policy. **Cash value** refers to the amount of money received should a policyholder decide to surrender the policy. Cash value builds as a part of the premium that is not required to buy protection. The cash value increases throughout the life of the policy. As long as permanent policies are kept in force, they accumulate cash value in addition to providing life insurance.

The longer you keep your permanent life insurance policy, the higher its cash value will be. If you give up or surrender your policy, you are paid the amount of the cash value. If you need money but do not wish to cancel your policy, you can borrow from the insurance company an amount up to the cash value. If you should die before the loan can be repaid, the unpaid amount will be deducted from the face value of the policy when your survivors are paid. **Face value** is the amount of insurance coverage that was originally purchased and that will be paid upon the death of the insured.

The cash value of permanent life insurance can be seen as a savings plan. The return on your money in the cash value portion of permanent life insurance is often not large. However, permanent insurance plans have a built-in savings feature that encourages people to save for the future. Permanent life insurance comes in the form of whole life, variable life, and universal life policies. Each type accumulates cash value.

Whole Life Insurance Whole life insurance is permanent insurance that extends over the lifetime, or whole life, of the insured.

One type of whole life insurance is called an **ordinary life policy.** Premiums for ordinary life insurance remain the same each year as long as the policyholder lives.

Some whole life insurance policies are intended to be paid in full in a certain number of years and are called **limited-payment policies.** Limited-payment policies may also be designated by the number of years the policyholder agrees to pay on them, such as 20-payment life policies. They are like ordinary life policies, except that premiums are paid for a limited number of years—20 or 30, for example—or until a person reaches a certain age, such as 60 or 65. Limited-payment policies free the insured from paying premiums during retirement when income may be lower.

ife insurance companies collect approximately $210 billion in premiums each year.

Variable Life Insurance **Variable life insurance** is a type of life insurance plan that resembles an investment portfolio. This

GlobalPerspective

Life Insurance for Expatriates

Like other businesses, nothing happens in the life insurance business until somebody sells something. In the case of life insurance, that phrase translates into a constant effort by life insurance marketers to sell insurance to as many people needing life insurance as possible.

One recently discovered rich source of potential life insurance purchasers is U. S. expatriates. An *expatriate* is usually defined as a citizen of the United States who works abroad—often for a multinational company. Even though many services are available to these citizens through the countries in which they work, many prefer certain American services such as life insurance. However, U. S. expatriates, unlike their colleagues in the United States, have little access to life insurance agents from America who are trained to help them with their life insurance needs. Because of foreign selling laws, distance from clients, and unfamiliar territories, insurance agents have not built up a client base in other countries. The insurance industry has now realized this market potential which has created an excellent opportunity for them to increase their business while meeting an important need of our own citizens abroad.

Critical Thinking

1 What types of businesses send U. S. citizens to foreign countries?

2 What methods of communication can the insurance industry use to convey important insurance information to citizens overseas?

plan lets the policyholder choose among a broad range of investments including stocks, bonds, and mutual funds. The death benefits and cash values of variable life policies vary according to the yield on the investments the policyholder selects.

The insurance company first designates an amount of the variable life premiums to cover the cost of insurance. The remaining amount is placed in an investment account. Both the death benefit and the cash value rise and fall with the success of the investment account of your choosing.

A minimum death benefit is guaranteed, but there is no guaranteed cash value. The minimum death benefit, in relation to premiums paid, is well below other types of life insurance. On the positive side, however, a strong rate of return on the investment account can increase the cash value and the death benefit well above the guaranteed level.

Universal Life Insurance   Universal life insurance provides both insurance protection and a substantial savings plan. The premium that you pay for universal life insurance is divided three ways. One portion of it pays for insurance protection. A second portion is taken by the insurance company for its expenses. The third portion is placed in interest-earning investments for the policyholder. The most important feature of universal life insurance is that the savings portion of the policy earns a variable interest rate. This interest rate is usually higher than is paid on other cash value insurance. The yield on the savings portion tends to rise or fall with the Consumer Price Index. Figure 35-1 compares the features of the different types of life insurance.

BUYING LIFE INSURANCE

Virtually everyone needs life insurance as few of us have the financial resources necessary to pay the costs that can overtake us upon the death of someone close to us. Therefore, in order for a life insurance program to be most effective for you, it must be suited to your needs and those of your family.

The answers to the following questions will help to determine the suitability of a life insurance program:

• How much money is required for your dependents' survival?

Figure 35-1
Comparison of alternative life insurance policies.

Alternative Life Insurance Policies

	TERM INSURANCE	PERMANENT INSURANCE			
		Whole Life		**Variable Life**	**Universal Life**
		Ordinary Life	*Limited Life*		
Premium	Begins low but increases gradually	High but usually stays constant	Higher than ordinary life insurance but constant	Fixed and regular	Varies at the discretion of the policyholder
Payment Period	Specified number of years—normally 5,10, or 15 years	Life of the insured	Specified number of years—normally 20 to 30 years	Specified period	Specified period
Cash Value	None	Some cash value	More cash value than ordinary life but less than variable life	Varies with the rise or fall in the value of the investment account	Varies with the interest rate paid on the cash value
Death Benefit	Fixed	Fixed	Fixed	Death benefit always exceeds cash value	Can vary at discretion of policyholder
Purposes	Protection for a specified period of time	Protection for life; some cash value for policy holder	Protection for life; some cash value for policyholder	Life insurance plus an opportunity to select different cash value investment options	Life insurance with a fairly high rate of return on cash value

- How much income will you need when you retire?

- What can you afford to pay for your life insurance needs?

    Answers to these questions will help you purchase the best life insurance program for you.

Applying for Life Insurance

    To buy individual life insurance coverage, one would usually apply for a policy through an insurance agent who represents an insurance company.

Illus. 35-3
The need for retirement income must be considered before you purchase life insurance.

Illus. 35-4
The wife and children of this architect have an insurable interest in him since they benefit from his income.

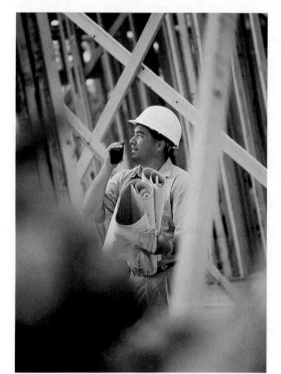

Normally you will be required to take a physical examination so that your health can be assessed. Assuming that you have no serious health problems, you then pay a premium and receive your life insurance policy. If you are in poor health or work in a dangerous occupation, you may be considered a poor risk. For example, if you drive racing cars to earn a living, you are in a dangerous occupation. Even if you are in poor health or work in a dangerous job, you may be able to obtain insurance. However, you will probably pay higher premiums than people who are in good health and are employed in less hazardous occupations.

Designating a Beneficiary

When you buy life insurance, you will be asked to name a beneficiary. This is most often a spouse or one or more children. You may insure not only your own life, but also the life of any other person in whom you have an insurable interest. To have an **insurable interest** in the life of another person, you must receive some kind of financial benefits from that person's continued life. You have, for example, an insurable interest in the lives of your parents. You do not have an insurable interest in a stranger's life. A partner in a business has an insurable interest in the life of his or her partner.

Paying Premiums

In addition to the health and occupation of the insured, the cost or premiums of a life insurance policy depend on the type of life insurance being purchased and the age of the person being insured. In purchasing a whole life policy, for example, the premiums for ordinary life insurance are higher than those for term insurance, but the annual premium stays the same throughout the insured's life. The premiums on limited-payment life insurance are higher than those for ordinary life insurance, but they are payable for only a limited number of years.

NET FACTS

Computer hardware and software that allow different E-mail programs to communicate with each other are called *gateways.* Everyone connects to the Internet through a gateway.

GROUP LIFE INSURANCE

Some individuals are fortunate to have an employer or some other group offer the opportunity to buy group life insurance. An insurance policy that covers a group of people is called **group life insurance.** The group acts as a single unit in buying the insurance. Our U.S. market economy tends to recognize efficiencies and savings that result in selling multiple quantities. You can often buy three pounds of hamburger for a lower per-pound price than buying just one pound. You can sometimes travel 1,000 miles by air for only a few dollars more than 500 miles. So it is, too, with insurance. The cost of group life insurance is less than the cost of a similar amount of protection bought individually because insurance covering many people can be handled economically in one policy.

Most group life insurance contracts are issued on a term basis through employers. Some policies, though, are available through unions, professional associations, and other similar organizations. The amount of protection available to an individual under a group insurance plan is generally limited. Many people, therefore, supplement their group insurance with policies of their own.

There are over 2,000 life insurance companies in the United States today.

Key Ideas

1 Life insurance protects survivors against the financial loss associated with dying. It is designed to replace a loss of income for family members who are financially dependent upon another person.

2 Term life insurance provides financial protection from losses resulting from loss of life during a definite period of time, or term. It is the least expensive form of life insurance. Permanent insurance has cash value and an investment feature as its common characteristics. It is not renewed each term as is term insurance.

3 To buy individual life insurance coverage, one would usually apply for a policy through an insurance agent who represents an insurance company. Normally you will be required to take a physical examination so that your health can be assessed. When you buy life insurance, you will be asked to name a beneficiary. The cost (premiums) of a life insurance policy will depend on the type of life insurance being purchased and the age of the person being insured.

4 An insurance policy that covers a group of people is called group life insurance. The group acts as a single unit in buying the insurance.

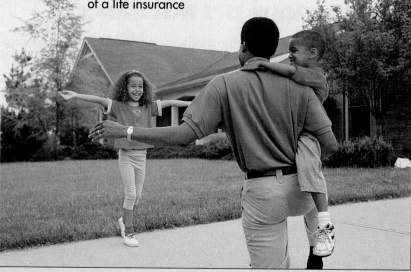

End of Chapter Activities

Increasing Your Business Vocabulary

For each numbered item, find the term that has the same meaning.

beneficiary

cash value

decreasing term
insurance

face value

group life insurance

insurable interest

level term insurance

life insurance

limited-payment
policies

ordinary life policy

permanent insurance

renewable policy

term life insurance

universal life
insurance

variable life
insurance

whole life insurance

1 Life insurance that covers a group of people who are usually employed by the same company or are members of the same organization.

2 A whole life policy intended to be paid up in a certain number of years.

3 The person named in an insurance policy to receive the insurance benefits.

4 The amount of money received should a policyholder decide to give up the protection provided by a policy.

5 A life insurance policy that provides financial protection against loss of life during a definite period of time.

6 Life insurance which provides both insurance protection and a substantial savings plan.

7 A type of whole life insurance for which premiums are the same each year as long as the policyholder lives.

8 A term life insurance policy that allows the policyholder to continue the term insurance for one or more terms without taking a physical examination to determine whether she or he is still a good risk.

9 Insurance designed to protect survivors against the financial loss associated with dying.

10 A financial benefit from the continued life of a person.

11 Term life insurance on which the amount of protection and the premiums remain the same.

12 Permanent insurance extending over the insured's lifetime.

13 Term life insurance on which the amount of protection gradually becomes smaller, but the premiums remain the same during the term.

14 Life insurance that lets the policyholder select from a range of investments.

(Vocabulary continued on the next page)

15 An amount of insurance coverage that was originally purchased and that will be paid upon the insured's death.

16 A type of insurance that has cash value and an investment feature as its common characteristics.

Reviewing Your Reading

1 Why do people need life insurance?

2 What is a dependent?

3 List two basic types of life insurance.

4 What is the only form of life insurance that has no investment or savings feature?

5 How long may a term life insurance policy run?

6 What advantage does cash value life insurance have in comparison to other types of insurance?

7 In what way is a limited-payment policy different from an ordinary life policy?

8 What is the most important feature of universal life insurance?

9 What determines whether you have an insurable interest in someone else's life?

10 Why is the cost of group life insurance less than the cost of insurance that is bought individually?

Using Your Business Knowledge

1 Why would a term policy that is renewable cost more than one that is not?

2 What kind of life insurance policy would you recommend for each of the following people?

   a. Carlos Medina, age 27, wants to buy a policy on which the premiums will be as low as possible for the next ten years.

   b. Julie Van Hovel, age 45, wants to buy a policy that will not require payment of any premiums after she retires.

3 What purpose does a physical examination serve during the process of purchasing a life insurance policy?

4 Do you think the Board of Directors of the Lake Plastics Company has an insurable interest in the company's chief chemist? Why or why not?

5 When a person buys life insurance as a member of a large group, no physical examination is ordinarily required. Why do you think this is so?

Calculating Business Problems

1 The rate of return on the investment portion of Fujio's life insurance policy is 6.47 percent for a given year. If the investment portion (cash value) was $17,643 at the beginning of the year, what will it be worth at the end of the year? Round to the nearest cent.

2 People who have cash value life insurance can borrow up to the cash value of the policy from the insurance company. Frank Hibbard had a $50,000 life insurance policy with a current cash value of $7,000. He decided to borrow $5,000 from that amount to make a down payment on a small house he wanted to buy.

a. If he died before repaying the loan, how much insurance would his beneficiary receive?

b. If Frank repays the loan in one year at 8 percent annual interest, what is the total amount he will pay back?

3 John Larson needed $2,400 for one year's tuition at a technical school. He decided to borrow the money from a bank for four years and pay $600 of the principal each year, plus interest of 12 percent a year on the unpaid balance. To be sure that his debt would be paid if he should die, he purchased a $2,400, four-year decreasing term insurance policy with an annual premium of $22.

a. How much did John pay in premiums and interest each year?

b. What was the total cost of premiums and interest for the four years?

4 Bruce Wright is having the physical examination required for his life insurance policy. His height is 185 centimeters, and his weight is 115 kilograms. The doctor's chart shows that the best weight for someone Bruce's height is 92 kilograms. The insurance company charges 10 percent more than standard rates for overweight people.

a. If the standard annual premium for the insurance that Bruce wants is $1,350, what will his annual premium be?

b. Approximately how many pounds must he lose to qualify for the standard premiums?

Applying Technology

Using the *Introduction to Business* template and your spreadsheet program software, select problem CH35. After the problem appears on your screen, complete the following activities. Then, after you have completed each step, display or print the completed spreadsheet for each activity. If you do not have a printer available, answer the questions before you leave the computer.

1 In the first row of the Premium column, enter a function to calculate the average of the Amount Required for Coverage column. Copy or key the function to each row in the Premium column. What is the average of the Amount Required for Coverage column?

2 In each row of the Change in Cash Value column, enter a formula to calculate the difference between the Premium column and the Amount Required for Coverage column. Answer the following questions:

a. As age increases, does cash value increase or decrease?

b. What is the amount of change in cash value at age 30?

3 Enter formulas to complete the Cumulative Cash Value column. The first two rows have been completed for you. Answer the following questions:

a. What is the cumulative cash value at age 25?

b. What is the cumulative cash value at age 49?

Making Decisions

Mary Larson is 25 years old. She has had the normal childhood afflictions and an occasional cold, but otherwise has never been sick. After graduation from high school, Mary went to work at Steinert Printing, the largest printing company in town. She earns a good salary as a layout design specialist. Her company provides hospitalization, surgical, and major medical insurance. The company does not provide any life insurance benefits. Mary's husband is self-employed, so Mary's health insur-ance covers her, her husband, and her young son and daughter. The Larsons are expecting their third child very soon.

1 What points would an insurance salesperson make to persuade Mary to buy life insurance?

2 Mary's health insurance needs are pretty well taken care of—but not her life insurance needs. What are some options that Mary may have when making a decision to buy life insurance?

Chapter Thirty-Six

Health Insurance

Key Terms

hospital insurance

surgical insurance

regular medical insurance

basic health coverage

major medical insurance

coinsurance clause

comprehensive medical policy

dental insurance

vision care insurance

disability income insurance

health maintenance organizations (HMOs)

preferred provider organization (PPO)

workers' compensation

Medicaid

Medicare

Objectives

After studying this chapter and completing the end-of-chapter activities, you will be able to:

1 List and describe the five types of medical insurance.

2 Describe dental insurance.

3 Discuss the purpose of vision care insurance.

4 State the main purpose of disability income insurance.

5 Name five providers of health insurance.

6 Explain cost containment of insurance.

"Carlota! Welcome back to work! How is your back?"

"Thanks, Martin. My back is doing great. I can't believe I hurt it playing tennis and had to have surgery. But I am one of the lucky ones. The surgery went fine, I am almost feeling normal again, and the insurance company paid all of my bills. Our company really has a great health insurance program for us. You don't realize how important health insurance is until you need it. If I didn't have such great coverage, I would be out over $100,000."

Everyone should be covered by health insurance. Almost no one has enough money to pay the extremely large medical bills associated with a serious illness. Health insurance provides protection against the economic risks associated with paying for medical care and the loss of income that results when an injury or illness prevents you from working. Health insurance is similar to the other forms of insurance. You pay premiums for a policy that guarantees protection. When you are ill and need money to pay medical bills, the insurance company will pay up to specified amounts.

MEDICAL INSURANCE

The insurance industry has created several kinds of health-related insurance coverage. Each of these kinds of health insurance provides for a different kind of coverage. One type of health insurance is medical insurance which can be categorized as (1) hospital, (2) surgical, (3) regular medical, (4) major medical insurance, and (5) comprehensive medical policy. Insurance companies also make a combination policy available.

Hospital Insurance

When an illness or injury requires you to be hospitalized, **hospital insurance** usually pays most or all of the charges for your room, food, and expenses for such items as use of an operating room, anesthesia, X rays, laboratory tests, and medicines. Because of the high cost of hospitalization, more people purchase hospital insurance than any other kind of health insurance. In fact, almost 200 million Americans are covered by hospital insurance.

Hospital insurance can be purchased from insurance companies or from nonprofit corporations. The best known nonprofit organization that offers hospital insurance is Blue Cross. Blue Cross plans usually pay hospitals directly for care provided to their policyholders. If expenses go beyond the amount covered by the Blue Cross contract, the patient must pay the difference.

Surgical Insurance

Surgery is one of the major reasons for hospitalization and is normally very expensive. **Surgical insurance** covers all or part of the surgeon's fees for an operation. The typical surgical policy lists the types of operations that it covers and the amount allowed for each. Some policies allow larger amounts for operations than others. This, of course, requires that a higher premium be paid. Surgical insurance is frequently bought in combination with hospital insurance.

Surgical insurance can be purchased from insurance companies or from nonprofit organizations such as Blue Shield. Blue Shield is linked with Blue Cross; they are often called "the Blues." Blue Shield plans cover mainly medical and surgical treatment rather than hospital care. Most Blue Shield plans list the maximum amounts that will be paid for different types of surgery. They also cover the doctor's charges for care in the hospital and some plans pay the doctor's charges for office or home care. Blue plans are designed to minimize policyholders' expenses. They generally do not provide coverage for pre-existing conditions or illnesses or injuries that are covered by other insurance.

Illus. 36-1
Surgical insurance covers all or part of a surgeon's fees for an operation.

Regular Medical Insurance

Sometimes normal care provided by a physician can be quite expensive. **Regular medical insurance** pays part or all of the fees for nonsurgical care given in the doctor's office, the patient's home, or a hospital. The policy states the amount payable for each visit or call and the maximum number of visits covered. Some plans also provide payments for diagnostic and laboratory expenses. Regular medical insurance is usually combined with hospital and surgical insurance. The protection provided by regular medical, hospital, and surgical coverages is referred to as **basic health coverage.**

NET FACTS

A Home Page contains text, graphics, and links to other Internet resources. The information on a Home Page is related to a particular topic, such as finance or medical care.

Major Medical Insurance

Carlota's problem, presented at the beginning of this chapter, was a good example of why people need major medical insurance. Long illnesses and serious injuries can be very expensive. Bills of $50,000 to $100,000 and higher are not unusual. **Major medical insurance** provides protection against the high costs of serious illnesses or injuries. It complements the other forms of medical insurance. Major medical insurance helps pay for most kinds of health care prescribed by a doctor. It covers the cost of treatment in and out of the hospital, special nursing care, X rays, psychiatric care, medicine, and many other health care needs. Maximum benefits range up to $250,000 and higher.

All major medical policies have a deductible clause similar to the one found in automobile collision insurance, as described in Chapter 33. With this clause, the policyholder agrees to pay the first part, perhaps $500 or more, of the expense resulting from sickness or injury. Major medical policies also usually contain a coinsurance clause. A **coinsurance clause** means that the policyholder will be expected to pay a certain percentage, generally 20 or 25 percent, of the costs over and above the deductible amount.

The deductible clause discourages the filing of minor claims. The coinsurance clause encourages the policyholder to keep medical expenses as reasonable as possible. Thus, both clauses help to make lower premiums possible because they help to reduce payments of insurance claims.

Comprehensive Medical Policy

Insurance providers have developed a **comprehensive medical policy** that combines the features of hospital, surgical, regular, and major medical insurance. A comprehensive medical policy retains the features of each of the separate coverages such as amounts payable limits and the like. It has only one deductible. A combination of coverages is normally less expensive than the total of the separate coverages.

Illus. 36-2
Sometimes the cost of specialized medical treatment such as an organ transplant is greater than a comprehensive policy will pay.

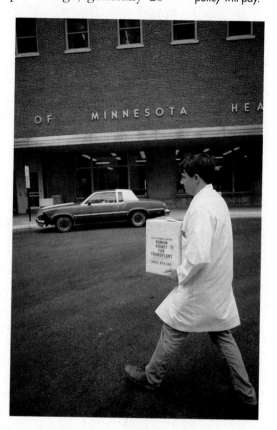

DENTAL INSURANCE

As dental expenses have grown over the years, the public has encouraged insurers to develop policies to help defray the cost of dental care. As a result, insurance companies now offer **dental insurance** which helps pay for normal dental care, often including examinations, X rays, cleaning, fillings, and more complicated types of dental work. It also covers dental injuries resulting from accidents. Some dental plans contain deductible and coinsurance provisions, while others pay for all claims. Dental insurance is offered mainly through group plans and is still growing in popularity. Dental insurance is growing in popularity with annual claims paid for dental expenses now approaching $10 billion.

VISION CARE INSURANCE

In anticipation of eye care expenses, many consumers and groups purchase vision care insurance. **Vision care insurance** covers eye examinations, prescription lenses, frames, and contact lenses. However, vision insurance usually does not cover such things as tinted lenses, coated or plastic lenses, nonprescription lenses, and vision training. The popularity of vision care insurance results from the recognition by many individuals and employers who help pay for group plans that eye care health is very important.

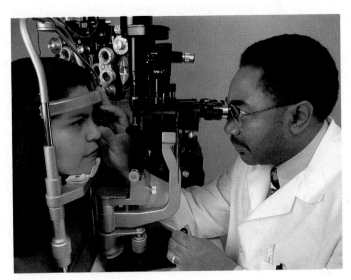

Illus. 36-3
Vision care insurance is provided by many employers.

DISABILITY INCOME INSURANCE

For most people, income from employment is their single most important economic resource. Protecting your income is very important. There is one form of health insurance that provides periodic payments if the policyholder becomes disabled. **Disability income insurance** protects you against the loss of income caused by a long illness or an accident. The insured receives weekly or monthly payments until that person is able to return to work. Disability income policies frequently include a waiting period provision which requires that the policyholder wait a specified length of time after the disability occurs before payment begins.

Hospital insurance is sometimes referred to as basic health insurance.

HEALTH INSURANCE PROVIDERS

Where can you acquire health insurance? Health insurance is available from several sources and in many different forms. You can buy health insurance as an individual or as a member of a group. Some options are group health insurance, individual health insurance, health maintenance organizations, preferred provider organizations, and state government assistance.

Group Health Insurance

The most popular way to buy health insurance is through a group. As with group life insurance, group health insurance policies are made available by employers to their employees and by unions and other organizations to their members. The company, union, or organization receives a master policy. The members who are insured under the plan are given membership cards to indicate their participation in the plan. Companies that sponsor group policies often pay part or all of the premium costs for their employees. This is provided as an employment benefit in addition to salary. The cost of group health insurance is lower per insured than the cost of a comparable individual policy. This is possible because insurance companies can administer group plans more economically, thus lowering costs for each person in the group.

Individual Health Insurance

Some people are not members of a group and are not eligible for group health insurance. They may be self-employed, for example, and have no employer to help buy health insurance for the group. One alternative is to buy individual health insurance. Individual health insurance is available to individuals and is adaptable to individuals' health insurance needs. Individual health insurance policies are usually rather expensive, require a physical examination, and have a waiting period before the policy is in force.

Health Maintenance Organizations

A relatively new type of health care plan has been developed over the past few years as an alternative to health insurance. This plan is called a health maintenance organization. **Health maintenance organizations (HMOs)** normally consist of a staffed medical clinic organized to serve its members. You may join an HMO for a fixed monthly fee. As a member, you are entitled to a wide range of prepaid health care services including hospitalization. HMOs emphasize preventive health care. Early detection and treatment of illnesses help to keep people out of hospitals and keep costs down.

Generally, HMOs do not cover treatment or care that is not authorized by a physician or if the procedure is above the average cost for the area. Cosmetic surgery, if not medically necessary, also often is excluded.

The growth of HMOs has been rapid; membership has increased from less than 2 million in the early 1970s to almost 40 million. There are now approximately 600 HMOs across the United States.

Preferred Provider Organizations

An alternative to the HMO is the **preferred provider organization (PPO).** This health insurance delivery system involves health care providers such as a group of physicians, a clinic, or a hospital contracting with an employer to provide medical services to employees. These providers agree to charge set fees for their services. Employees are

The Franklin Health Assurance Company of Massachusetts in 1890 was the first company to offer health insurance in the United States.

EthicalPerspective

Insurance Fraud

Fraud is the act of intentionally misrepresenting information. Insurance fraud usually means being dishonest when applying for insurance or filing dishonest claims. People applying for health insurance sometimes do not disclose existing medical conditions. Applicants for auto insurance may be dishonest about how many miles they drive their car each year. Policyholders sometimes file insurance claims for injuries that are exaggerated or nonexistent.

Insurance providers and regulators work very hard to monitor and reduce insurance fraud. These organizations engage in public information activities designed to promote honesty in insurance affairs. A group known as the Coalition Against Insurance Fraud works to combat the growing incidence and cost of all forms of insurance fraud, as does each state's Department of Insurance.

However, the efforts by these groups alone are not enough. Insurance fraud is still on the rise. Some people fail to realize that when insurance fraud is committed, it costs the insurance company unnecessary dollars. These unnecessary costs are then trickled down to the policyholder through increased premiums. The solution? Only the insurance consumer can truly help to reduce fraud. Consumers must be honest in all insurance dealings including being truthful when applying for insurance and being truthful when making claims.

Critical Thinking

1 Why do you think some people are not honest on insurance applications?

2 What kinds of costs do you think are incurred when policyholders file fraudulent claims?

encouraged, but not required, to use the PPO's services through financial incentives. The employee is usually able to get medical treatment through the PPO at a significant discount. Employees are free, however, to seek medical treatment elsewhere and may be partially reimbursed for out-of-pocket medical expenses.

State Government Assistance

An important health insurance program established by state governments is workers' compensation. **Workers' compensation** is an insurance plan that provides medical and survivor benefits for people injured, disabled, or killed on the job. Accidents may occur on almost any job. Employees may suffer injuries or develop some illness as a result of their working conditions. To deal with this problem, all states have passed legislation known as workers' compensation laws. These laws provide medical benefits to employees who are injured on the job or become ill as a direct result of their working conditions. Under these laws, most employers are required to provide and pay for insurance for their employees.

The benefits provided through workers' compensation vary from state to state. In some states, all necessary expenses for medical treatment are paid. In others, there is a stated payment limit. Usually there is a waiting period of a few days before a worker is eligible for loss-of-income benefits. If unable to return to the job after this waiting period, the worker is paid a certain proportion of wages as benefits. This usually amounts to about two-thirds of the worker's normal wages. Payments are also made to dependents if the worker is killed in an accident while on the job.

State governments also administer a form of medical aid to low-income families known as **Medicaid.** The federal government shares with states the cost of providing health benefits to financially needy families. A financially needy family is one whose income provides for basic necessities but who could not afford adequate medical care or pay large medical bills.

The services covered by Medicaid include hospital care, doctors' services, X rays, lab tests, nursing home care, diagnosis and treatment of children's illnesses, and home health care services.

Federal Government Assistance

The nation's Social Security laws provide a national program of health insurance known as **Medicare**. It is designed to help people age 65 and older and some disabled people pay the high cost of health care. Medicare has two basic parts: hospital insurance and medical insurance.

The hospital insurance plan includes coverage for hospital care, care in an approved nursing home, and home health care up to a

When an insurance company requests that you obtain a second opinion for proposed non-emergency surgery, be sure to do so or your benefits may be reduced.

certain number of visits. No premium payments are required for the hospital insurance, and almost everyone 65 years old and older may qualify.

The medical insurance portion of Medicare is often called supplementary or voluntary medical insurance. The services covered under this plan include doctors' services, medical services and supplies, and home health services. The medical insurance requires a small monthly premium. The federal government pays an equal amount to help cover the cost of the medical insurance. Some features of the Medicare plan are similar to the deductible and coinsurance provisions in other health policies.

COST CONTAINMENT

No matter who pays the premium, the cost of health insurance, like the cost of health care, is very high. In fact, the cost of health care has been increasing two to three times faster than the rate of inflation. The cost of health insurance is usually determined by at least four factors: extent of the coverage, number of claims filed by policyholders, age of the policyholder, and number of dependents. You have little control over your age and the number of people dependent on you. You can, however, make sure you buy only the kind and amount of insurance you need. You can also take good care of yourself and be careful not to abuse your benefits by using medical services when they are unnecessary.

Insurance companies encourage policyholders to play an active role in "cost containment" or keeping costs down. The most common methods are coinsurance and deductibles.

Some policyholders are covered by their employers and their spouse's insurance. Insurance providers promote the coordination of benefits in order to prevent two or more insurers from making payments on the same health care charges for a policyholder.

The health insurance industry also encourages second medical opinions to assure the necessity of procedures. It is also sometimes necessary to get a second opinion on outpatient surgery, when appropriate, to avoid inpatient costs of overnight hospital stays.

Illus. 36-4
Practicing good health habits, including exercise, may be the best way to control health costs.

Key Ideas

1 The five most common varieties of medical insurance are: hospital insurance (which usually pays most or all of the charges for your room, food, and expenses for such items as use of an operating room, anesthesia, X rays, laboratory tests, and medicines); surgical, which covers all or part of the surgeon's fees for an operation; regular medical, which pays part or all of the fees for nonsurgical care given in the doctor's office, the patient's home, or a hospital; major medical, which provides protection against the high costs of serious illnesses or injuries; and a comprehensive medical policy that combines the features of hospital, surgical, regular, and major medical insurance.

2 Dental insurance helps pay for normal dental care, often including examinations, X rays, cleaning, fillings, and more complicated types of dental work. It also covers dental injuries resulting from accidents.

3 Vision care insurance covers eye examinations, prescription lenses, frames, and contact lenses. However, vision insurance usually does not cover such things as tinted lenses, coated or plastic lenses, nonprescription lenses, and vision training.

4 Disability income insurance protects against loss of income caused by a long illness or an accident. The insured receives weekly or monthly payments until that person is able to return to work.

5 Providers of health insurance include group health insurance, individual health insurance, health maintenance organizations, preferred provider organizations, and state government assistance.

6 Policyholders can play an active role in cost containment through coinsurance and deductibles.

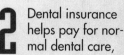

End of Chapter Activities

Increasing Your Business Vocabulary

For each numbered item, find the term that has the same meaning.

basic health coverage

coinsurance clause

comprehensive medical policy

dental insurance

disability income insurance

health maintenance organizations (HMOs)

hospital insurance

major medical insurance

Medicaid

Medicare

preferred provider organization (PPO)

regular medical insurance

surgical insurance

vision care insurance

workers' compensation

1 Insurance that combines hospital, surgical, regular, and major medical insurance into one policy.

2 Insurance that protects a worker against the loss of income because of a long illness or accident.

3 Insurance that pays for nonsurgical care given in the doctor's office, the patient's home, or a hospital.

4 Organizations that provide complete health care to their members for a fixed monthly payment.

5 A combination of hospital, surgical, and regular medical insurance.

6 Insurance that helps pay for normal dental care and covers dental injuries resulting from accidents.

7 Insurance that provides medical and survivor benefits to people injured, disabled, or killed on the job.

8 Insurance that provides benefits to cover part or all of the surgeon's fee for an operation.

9 Medical expense assistance administered by state governments to financially needy families.

10 Insurance that pays most or all of the charges for room, food, and other hospital expenses.

11 Insurance that provides protection against the high costs of serious illnesses or injuries.

12 Health insurance provided by the federal government for people age 65 and older and some disabled people.

13 A provision in which the insured pays a certain percentage of the costs above the deductible amount.

14 Insurance that covers eye examinations, prescription lenses, frames, and contact lenses.

15 A group of physicians, a clinic, or a hospital that contracts to provide medical services to employees.

Reviewing Your Reading

1 What are the five basic types of coverage provided by medical insurance? Explain the kinds of expenses each covers.

2 What well-known nonprofit organization offers surgical insurance?

3 How does a deductible clause in a health insurance policy work?

4 What type of services are covered by vision care insurance?

5 Why is being insured under an individual health insurance policy more expensive than under a group policy?

6 What kind of care is emphasized by HMOs?

7 What three health insurance programs are operated by government agencies?

8 What kind of health insurance covers you if you are injured on the job?

9 What are the two basic parts of the Medicare plan?

10 Which four factors determine the cost of health care?

Using Your Business Knowledge

1 Janice Cordell is studying to be an accountant and has a part-time job to help pay her college expenses. She does not have health insurance because she believes she cannot afford it. She also believes that she does not really need health insurance.

  a. Give several reasons why Janice should protect herself with some type of health insurance.

  b. Where might she find a policy at a reasonable premium?

  c. What can she do to keep the policy premium at a reasonable level?

2 Many major medical policies contain a coinsurance clause. These policies are usually less expensive than a policy without such a clause. What advice would you have for a person or group considering purchasing a major med-ical insurance policy containing a coinsurance clause?

3 The Carney family is trying to determine which kinds of health insurance coverage would best fit their needs. On one hand, they believe that a Blue Cross hospital plan and a Blue Shield surgical plan would be sufficient. On the other hand, a major medical plan might better serve their needs. Mr. and Mrs. Carney are both 48 years old and are employed by the same company. They have two children. There is a history of heart disease in Mr. Carney's family. They have about $30,000 in an investment account. What advice would you offer this family based on their needs?

4 Why do you think a health insurance agent would suggest the addition of major medical coverage to a health insurance policy?

Calculating Business Problems

1 Sally Orland is considering job offers from two different companies. The jobs seem equally desirable to her. The Star Fire Company provides health insurance benefits to their employees that total $140 per month. The Axelrod Company provides no health insurance for its workers. How much money would the Star Fire health insurance benefit be worth to Sally each year?

2 In the table at right is a breakdown of the number of people in a community of 5,000 covered by various types of health insurance.

Hospital	4,600
Surgical	3,200
Regular medical	3,000
Major medical	3,900
Dental	2,000
Vision care	700
Disability income	3,000

a. What percentage of the people in the community are covered by each type of insurance?

b. In one year, 235 people covered by surgical insurance presented claims totaling $176,250. What was the amount of the average claim?

3 Many communities have blood banks that collect blood from donors. They make it available to local hospitals for transfusions for people who are ill or who are accident victims. During a recent blood drive, the Lincoln Blood Bank collected 675 pints of blood from donors.

a. How many liters did they collect?

b. How many milliliters did they collect?

4 Jim Gleason was hospitalized as a result of a skiing accident. His medical expenses were as shown in the table at right.

6 days in hospital	$350	per day
Lab tests and X ray	$585	
Surgeon's fee	$1,375	

Jim is covered by hospital insurance, which pays the cost of his hospital room for up to 120 days for any one illness. Coverage for lab tests, X rays, and other hospital extras is limited to $500. His surgical insurance plan limits benefits to $1,200 for the type of surgery involved.

a. What was the total cost of Jim's medical services?

b. How much of this total cost was paid by his insurance?

c. How much of the medical cost did Jim have to pay?

Applying Technology

Using the *Introduction to Business* template and your spreadsheet program software, select problem CH36. After the problem appears on your screen, complete the following activities. Then, after you have completed each step, display or print the completed spreadsheet for each activity. If you do not have a printer available, answer the questions before you leave the computer.

1 Sort the companies and dental insurance rates into descending order by rate. Answer the following questions:

a. What is the third company listed?

b. What is the second lowest rate listed?

2 At the bottom of the Rate column, enter a function to find the average rate. Format the answer as currency with two decimal places. What is the average rate?

3 In the Difference from Average Rate column, enter formulas to calculate each company's rate minus the average rate. Answer the following questions:

a. Which company has the greatest absolute (positive or negative) difference from the average rate?

b. Which company has the smallest absolute difference from the average rate?

Making Decisions

Laura Anderson is a general insurance agent who sells life, vehicle, property and health insurance. The Riolli family was referred to her as a potential client. After an initial interview, she learned that the Riollis' most pressing insurance need was for health insurance as they had none. She also learned that Salvatore and Maria Riolli were both 27 years old and that they had one child. They were both self-employed—Salvatore as a hairstylist and Maria as a real estate consultant. The Riollis were both in good health with no pre-existing conditions.

1 What additional information about the Riollis would be helpful to Laura?

2 What type of medical insurance policy should Laura suggest as most appropriate to the Riolli's needs?

3 How can the Riollis contain the cost of their health insurance?

Over 1.5 million people work in the insurance industry today. At least one-third of these employees are insurance agents and brokers who have direct contact with the public. In addition to agents and brokers, other career options available in insurance include claims examiner, actuarial clerk, and insurance investigator. The basic task of these employees is to determine and satisfy customers' insurance needs.

Job Titles

Job titles commonly found in this career area include:

- Insurance Agent
- Claims Examiner
- Insurance Investigator
- Claims Clerk
- Sales Representative
- Underwriter
- Statistical Clerk
- Policy Writer
- Policyholder Clerk
- Customer Service Representative
- Benefits Clerk
- Rater
- Claims Supervisor

Employment Outlook (through the year 2005)

- Most job openings will result from the need to replace workers.
- The future demand for insurance workers will depend on the volume of insurance sales, which should increase as more people seek coverage for their homes, cars, valuables, and technology products.
- Most individuals and businesses consider insurance a necessity, regardless of economic conditions. Therefore, insurance workers are not likely to face unemployment because of a recession.

Education and Training

- Insurance companies prefer college graduates—particularly those who have majored in business or economics.
- Some companies hire high-school graduates with potential or proven sales ability or success in other types of work.
- In smaller firms, workers may receive their training through courses offered by the Insurance Institute of America, a nonprofit organization offering educational programs and professional certification to people in the insurance industry.

Salary Levels (in recent years)

- Most earn between $21,000 and $42,000 per year.
- The top 10 percent of sales workers in insurance earn approximately $65,000 per year.
- Most independent agents are paid on a commission-only basis where sales workers are paid either a salary only, salary plus commission, or salary plus bonus.

Critical Thinking

1 Which job title in this career area appeals to you most? Give reasons for your choice.

2 What are some things you will have to do to achieve success in the career selected?

Insurance

Unit Ten

Personal Financial Management

37 Foundations of Money Management
Describes importance of goals and how to manage money wisely.

39 Your Financial Future
Stresses the necessity of financial planning and the importance of planning for the future.

chapter 38 Budgeting Techniques
Discusses the budgeting process and its importance as related to money management.

On-line investment information is becoming one of the most popular ways to keep up-to-date with the investment scene. On-line services provided through the Internet and commercial service providers make investment information readily available at any time of the day.

Information that can be retrieved from on-line services includes full-text copies of corporate filings with the Securities and Exchange Commission; economic, monetary, and stock data from a variety of sources; and electronic versions of useful publications such as *Business Week*. The amount of information available is almost unlimited!

Retrieving investment information is not the only way in which on-line services can be used. Subscribers can also post messages to bulletin boards when in need of particular information or simply to share investment information. Discussion lists are also available whereby subscribers can discuss investment topics and issues with other subscribers.

On-line investment information allows subscribers to be up-to-date at all times without going through a broker or using other financial services. One of the biggest advantages is that this information can be obtained any time of the day.

As for the near future, on-line services promise the opportunity to actually place stock and bond orders, as well as secure other transactions, using a home computer.

To get the most out of on-line investment information, keep in mind the following five-step process:

1. Search for sources of information. Start with an indexing service, and look for listings on investments, the economy, personal finance, and so on.
2. Brainstorm with other investors. Join a Usenet Newsgroup or E-mail discussion list. Watch for advice from experts and people close to various companies. Be careful, however, to avoid get-rich-quick schemes.
3. Collect data. Locate annual reports, documents describing stock offerings, and other financial data. As you focus on specific investments, obtain expert evaluations of the investments as reported in on-line business magazines and financial newsletters.
4. Make your move. Buy or sell bonds, stocks, or shares in funds through a stockbroker or mutual fund company. As security on the Internet improves, you will be able to use an on-line stock brokerage to place your orders.
5. Keep an eye on your money. Use your sources of data and your links with fellow shareholders to regularly monitor your investments. Share your experiences to help others out, and they will be more willing to pass tips and warnings on to you.

Critical Thinking

1 *Why will some investors not wish to use on-line investment information?*

2 *What other types of investment information do you think are available through on-line services?*

Business Brief

On-line Investment Information

Chapter Thirty-Seven

Foundations of Money Management

Objectives

After studying this chapter and completing the end-of-chapter activities, you will be able to:

1 List and describe the four ways to manage your money successfully.

2 Describe two personal financial statements that determine financial status of an individual or family.

3 Explain how you can manage your money wisely.

"My financial situation is just fine—or it is a disaster! It all depends on what day of the week it may be."

"Tell me, what's the problem Yung-su?"

"Mr. Liang, I can't seem to get a grip on my finances. I work 10 hours a week for a telemarketing firm and make just under $10 per hour. That seems like a lot of money for a part-time job while going to school. But I always seem to run out of money before the week is over."

"I suppose that also means you are not saving any money but spending all of your income. My advice is to get some lessons in money management."

The one thing most of us have in common is a desire to use wisely the money we have so that our needs, wants, and goals will be satisfied. While no individual, family, or organization is likely to have every desire met, there are several money management techniques that can help you use wisely the financial resources available to you.

MANAGING YOUR MONEY

Right now $1,000, or maybe $100, seems like a lot of money to you. Once you graduate from high school and/or college and have a full-time job, your thinking about what is a large amount of money will change. You probably will earn well over a million dollars in your lifetime. If you become a college graduate, you can expect to make even more.

While this may seem like a great deal of money, remember that you will be responsible for many living expenses. You will have to pay for food, housing, clothing, and transportation as well as other goods and services you need and want. Upon beginning a career and living on your own, you will face the same problem you face now—having a limited amount of money to pay for all the goods and services you want and need.

This basic economic problem can be resolved by learning to carefully manage your money and live within your income. **Income** is the money you receive from work that you do and from money that you invest. As you know, a person's income will vary based on the type of work he or she does. Your income also will be influenced by the level of education and amount of experience you have.

Money management refers to the day-to-day financial activities associated with using limited income to satisfy your unlimited needs and wants. Money management involves getting the most for your money through careful planning, saving, and spending; it involves creating and using a plan for spending.

Some people have the wrong idea about money management. They think it means pinching pennies, doing without things, and not having any fun. But if you learn to manage your money well, you will be

Your net pay is your net income which is the amount of money you have available to spend.

able to buy the things you really want that you may not have been able to buy before. Planning ahead and deciding what is really important will help you to have money to spend on the things you enjoy. If you set goals, make wise decisions, buy wisely, and live within your income, you will be a successful money manager.

Setting Your Goals

Money management starts with setting attainable financial goals. Goals are those things you want to achieve; they may be short-term or long-term goals. A short-term financial goal, for example, might be to buy some common stock or to purchase a new computer. Long-range goals often involve large amounts of money. A long-range goal for a family might be to buy a house, take a trip to a foreign country, or provide college education for the children. A personal long-range goal might be to open your own business.

Goals are personal. They are not the same for all people or even for everyone within a given age group. Goals are affected by such things as a person's age, family situation, interests, and values. Financial goals, as they relate to developing and implementing a financial plan, will be discussed in greater detail in Chapter 39.

Making Economic Decisions

Money management can be seen as part of a process of making economic decisions. Money, of course, is limited, and individuals and families must decide how to use the money that is available to them. The main decisions we each make involve three areas:

1. *Paying for basic needs.* Needs are things necessary for survival such as food, clothing, and shelter. Everyone's basic needs, however, are not exactly the same. Needs depend on where you live and what lifestyle you follow. If you live in a southern city, for example, you have different transportation and clothing needs from those who live on a large ranch in a northwestern state. For some people, an apartment is ideal; others may need a house. In any case, after you have met these basic needs, you must decide how to use the money that remains.

Always write your financial goals in a place where you see them often. Seeing the goals will sometimes provide the motivation you need to reach them.

2. *Saving for future expenses.* After providing for your basic needs, you should decide how to prepare for large expenses in the future. You do this by developing a savings program. Everyone has special reasons for saving. Maybe you want to buy a car or save for college, or perhaps you want to start a business that requires expensive equipment. Unless you manage your money wisely and plan your savings, you may not be able to do or buy the things you want.

An average family will spend 22 to 24 percent of its income on food and 29 to 32 percent on housing.

3. *Spending discretionary income.* The third decision you must make when managing your money is how to spend any money you have available after you have taken care of your basic needs and future expenses. This money is referred to as **discretionary income.** This is income you spend to buy the things you want for pleasure, satisfaction, and comfort. Discretionary income, for example, is spent on such things as entertainment, travel, compact discs, or hobby supplies. Spending discretionary income is usually more fun than buying basic items or saving money and can be seen as your reward for good money management.

Illus. 37-1

Spending discretionary income is your reward for good money management.

Buying Wisely

Most of us have more needs and wants than we could ever hope to satisfy. We must stretch our limited incomes as far as possible. Wise buying is an important way to stretch your income.

To buy wisely you must gather information carefully before making your purchases. You must plan your purchases so that you buy the right good or service at the right time and at the right price. Unplanned buying often leads to disappointment and wasted money. Planned buying leads to better use of money and greater satisfaction from the things you buy.

Living Within an Income

Do you ever run out of money before the end of the month? Many people have that problem. They have not learned to live within their incomes. Living on the amount that you have available is a central idea in money management. Creating and using a budget to help you live within your income is discussed in the next chapter.

KNOWING YOUR FINANCIAL STATUS

The process of good money management starts with knowing your current financial status. When viewing a baseball or soccer game, most people want to know the score as the game progresses. In the money management game, score is kept with the use of financial statements. Two common financial statements are the balance sheet and cash flow statement.

Preparing a Balance Sheet

"How much money do you have?" may be the first question many people would ask when measuring your financial situation. The answer to that question, however, would not give the entire picture since most people have other items of value besides

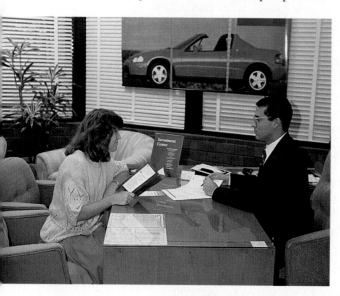

money. A **balance sheet,** which is a type of financial statement, reports what a person or family owns as well as owes.

The main components of a balance sheet are displayed in Figure 37-1 and consist of the following categories:

1. **Assets** are items of value. Assets include such things as money in bank accounts, investments, furniture, clothing, automobiles, jewelry, and rare coins. The current value of all assets of an individual or family is the first thing reported on a balance sheet.

Illus. 37-2

It is important to know your financial status before considering a large purchase.

2. **Liabilities** are amounts owed to others. These debts may include credit card balances, automobile loans, a home mortgage, or personal loans. Total liabilities is the second item on a balance sheet.

3. **Owner's Equity,** or net worth, is the difference between a person's or family's assets and liabilities. This difference represents the amount of money that could be claimed if all assets were sold for cash and all debts were paid off. For example, if a family has $189,000 in assets (including the value of a home and other valuables) and has $87,000 in debts (mainly the home mortgage), the family has a net worth of $102,000.

Knowing how much you own (assets) and how much you owe (liabilities) are keys to good financial management.

Figure 37-1

A personal balance sheet is used to report your current financial position.

A Personal Balance Sheet

Assets			Liabilities	
Checking account	$	450	Home mortgage	$ 45,000
Savings account		2,300	Credit card balance	230
Home		97,000	Education loan	1,800
Automobile		4,600		
Household items and furniture		6,200	Total Liabilities	$ 47,030
Personal computer		1,600		
Jewelry		1,100	**Owner's Equity**	
			Total Assets minus Total Liabilities	$ 66,220
Total Assets		$113,250	Total Liabilities and Owner's Equity	$113,250

A balance sheet is a helpful way to measure financial strength. Every business will prepare a balance sheet either once a month or every three months to determine the financial condition of the business. In the same way, a balance sheet can help an individual or family in measuring its financial condition.

Preparing a Cash Flow Statement

A balance sheet reports assets, liabilities, and owner's equity on a given date. Almost every day, however, business transactions occur that change these balance sheet items. For example, when you make a loan payment, the amount of your liabilities decreases. If you save part of your earnings, your assets and owner's equity increase by the amount of the savings. To examine changes in a person's net worth, another financial statement can be helpful. A **cash flow statement** reports net wages and other income along with spending for a given period of time, such as for a month. Figure 37-2 includes typical items found in a cash flow statement.

The first part of a cash flow statement reports your financial income. This is the money you have available to spend as a result of working or from other income such as interest earned on your savings. When preparing a cash flow statement, you should first report your **net income** or **take-home pay,** which is the amount received after taxes and other deductions have been subtracted from your total earnings. Your take-home pay is recorded on

Net worth is also known as owner's equity.

Figure 37-2

A personal cash flow statement reports your income (cash inflows) and expenses (cash outflows).

Personal Cash Flow Statement

Cash Inflows (Income)

Net Income (take-home pay)	$1,200	
Other Income (interest)	50	
Total Income		$1,250

Cash Outflows (Expenditures)

Food	$ 400	
Clothing	50	
Electricity	100	
Telephone	25	
Transportation	150	
Personal care	30	
Recreation/entertainment	75	
Total Expenditures		830
Net Cash Flow		$ 420

your cash flow statement since this is the amount you actually have available to spend. This amount available to spend is also called *cash inflows*.

The next step necessary for creating a cash flow statement is to maintain records of all spending. The amounts spent for food, clothing, transportation, and other living costs are called **expenditures** or *cash outflows*. Keeping track of how much is spent for various living expenses will help you to plan and control your spending. In the next chapter, you will see how your personal cash flow statement can be used to develop a budget.

The final step in preparing the cash flow statement is to subtract your total expenditures from your total income. If you have spent less than you had in income, the difference represents an increase in your owner's equity. Most likely this amount will be kept in savings for future needs or wants. If you spent more than you had in income, you either had to use some of your savings or had to use credit to pay these additional expenses. As you can see, if you regularly spend more than you have available, you

NET FACTS

An incompatibility occurs when software on your client computer cannot communicate with software on an Internet host. Causes of incompatibilities include different versions of software, mismatched software settings, and different hardware platforms.

will eventually use all of your savings or get into credit difficulty.

MANAGING YOUR MONEY WISELY

While effective money management may seem like a lot of trouble, poor money management practices can result in even more trouble. A poor credit rating, arguments with family members about money, and money shortages are just a few of the problems that can result from poor money management. For wise money management, practice the following behaviors:

- Plan carefully. Setting goals and knowing what you really need and want will help you to avoid financial difficulties while also obtaining enjoyment from the resources you have available.

- Use information. Much is written about budgeting and financial planning. Articles in magazines, such as *Money* and *Kiplinger's*, can help you better understand and take action on your money matters.

When you apply for a large loan for a house, car, or business, the loan officer will want to see copies of your current balance sheet and cash flow statement.

Cultural *Perspective*

The Abacus

Calculators have made completing math and accounting work a snap! But what did people use before the calculator was invented?

Have you ever seen an abacus? An abacus is a calculating device made of wood and metal wires on which moveable beads are strung. The beads are moved from place to place to indicate certain numbers. The abacus was used to add, subtract, multiply, and divide for both business and personal purposes.

The abacus, in various configurations, was developed in several different cultures. The Babylonians in Asia Minor had an early form of the abacus as did the Egyptians in Northern Africa. The earliest abacus was known in China as early as the 6th century B.C. and its use spread to the rest of the Asian world.

Today, some highly skilled people still use the abacus for calculations. These people are so highly skilled that they can sometimes perform calculations faster than a person using an electronic calculator!

Critical Thinking

1 What cultures do you think might still use the abacus?

2 Why do you think that some people can use an abacus and arrive at an answer faster than someone using a calculator?

- Compare products and prices. As discussed in Unit 5, comparison buying—achieved by reading advertisements, using label information, and analyzing different brands—can help you get the most for your money. Being a wise consumer is one of the basic principles of effective money management.

- Make wise decisions. By using the decision-making process discussed in Chapter 1, you will be able to make effective use of your limited resources.

Key Ideas

1 Good money managers start with setting attainable financial goals (short-term or long-term goals); paying for basic needs (those things that are necessary for survival); saving for future expenses, and then spending discretionary income; buying wisely; and living within one's income.

2 Two financial statements are prepared to determine financial status—a balance sheet and a cash flow statement.

3 You can manage your money wisely by planning carefully, using information to help you better understand and take action on your money matters, comparing products and prices, and making wise decisions.

End of Chapter Activities

Increasing Your Business Vocabulary

The following terms should become part of your business vocabulary. For each numbered item, find the term that has the same meaning.

assets

balance sheet

discretionary income

expenditures

income

cash flow statement

liabilities

money management

net income or take-home pay

owner's equity

1 The financial statement that reports what a person or family owns as well as owes.

2 Income available to spend after money has been set aside for basic needs and future expenses.

3 The difference between a person's or family's assets and liabilities.

4 Day-to-day financial activities associated with using limited income to satisfy unlimited needs and wants.

5 The amounts spent for food, clothing, transportation, and other living costs.

6 Amounts owed to others.

7 The financial statement that reports net wages and other income along with spending for a given period of time.

8 The amount received after taxes and other deductions have been subtracted from total earnings.

9 Items of value.

10 The money you receive from work that you do and from money you invest.

Reviewing Your Reading

1. What activities are associated with money management?

2. List factors that affect a person's financial goals.

3. What are the three main decisions associated with money management?

4. List four goods or services for which you might spend discretionary income.

5. What are the three main components of a balance sheet?

6. What is the purpose of a cash flow statement?

7. Why is net income or take-home pay used on a cash flow statement?

8. What must a person or family do if more money is spent than is received in a certain month?

9. Name three wise money management behaviors.

10. How can you practice comparison buying?

Using Your Business Knowledge

1. Describe the difference between short-term and long-term goals. Give two examples of each type.

2. List some items that might be a want for one person but a need for someone else.

3. Identify each of the following items as an asset or a liability:

   a. Money owed to the dentist
   b. An automobile
   c. Clothing
   d. Savings account
   e. Credit card balance
   f. Amount due for a personal loan
   g. 100 shares of stock

4. What two actions could you take if your expenditures were consistently greater than your income?

Calculating Business Problems

1 Beth Hamlin is a computer software marketing representative. She earns a basic salary of $350 per month plus a commission that is 5 percent of her sales. In addition, Beth earns $70 in interest and dividends monthly.

a. In a month with $48,000 in sales, what would Beth's total income be?

b. What percent of her total income comes from each item (basic salary, commission, and interest and dividends)? (Round to the nearest percentage.)

2 Mike Collins has a monthly net income of $1,600. Each month Mike has to make a loan payment of $212 for his car. What percentage of his income is used for the automobile loan payments?

3 The Gage family's assets total $268,400. Their total liabilities are $166,300. What is the amount of their owner's equity?

4 Dorothy Christensen decided to change the oil and filter in her car. She bought five quarts of 10W40 multi-weight oil for $1.35 per quart and an oil filter for $4.29.

a. How much was the total bill for the oil and filter, including 5 percent sales tax?

b. How much did Dorothy save if a service station would have charged her $30 for the oil and filter change?

5 The O'Reilys' house was the largest asset on their balance sheet. Janet O'Reily accepted a job transfer to another city. This required selling their home. A couple from Austria inquired about their home using the Internet as their communication medium. The Austrians wanted to know the metric dimensions and area of each of the home's three bedrooms. The bedrooms were (1) 10' by 12', (2) 12' by 14', and (3) 13' by 16'. Can you help the O'Reilys by giving the dimensions and area of each bedroom in meters and square meters?

Applying Technology

Using the *Introduction to Business* template and your spreadsheet program software, select problem CH37. After the problem appears on your screen, complete the following activities. After you have completed each step, display or print the completed spreadsheet for each activity. If you do not have a printer available, answer the questions before you leave the computer.

1 In the cells containing [F], enter formulas to calculate Net Income, Total Expenditures, and Net Cash Flow. What is the amount of Net Cash Flow?

2 What if your Take-Home Pay increased to $2,500? Copy the Cash Flow Statement to another part of the spreadsheet. Enter the new higher amount of Take-Home Pay. Answer the following questions.

a. What is the new amount of Net Income?

b. What is the new amount of Net Cash Flow?

3 What if your Take-Home Pay decreased to $500? Copy the Cash Flow Statement from Activity 1 to another part of the spreadsheet. Enter the new lower amount of Take-Home Pay. Answer the following questions.

a. What is the new amount of Net Income?

b. What is the new amount of Net Cash Flow?

Optional: Create a pie chart showing the sources of Net Income and a pie chart showing the sources of Total Expenditures. Repeat for each activity.

Making Decisions

Joan Leitzel just graduated from college and got her first job as a speech therapist. Joan wants to make sure she manages her income wisely so that she can be independent and eventually buy a house on her own. She lives with her parents now, so her only expenses are payments on a college loan and an auto loan.

1 What advice would you give Joan if she wants to buy a house in the future?

2 When she eventually goes to the bank for a loan, how should Joan organize her financial information?

Chapter Thirty-Eight

Budgeting Techniques

Key Terms

budget

fixed expenses

variable expenses

allowance

budget variance

Objectives

After studying this chapter and completing the end-of-chapter activities, you will be able to:

1 Describe the main purposes of a budget.

2 Explain the steps in the budgeting process.

3 List the characteristics of a successful budget.

Jing Fang is a Chinese American who has been practicing his Chinese through written communication with his relatives in Hong Kong. He also has taken several business courses in high school. Jing is preparing for an eventual career in international business in the Pacific Rim countries.

"I can't wait to go to Taiwan next summer! But the trip is going to cost me a fortune! The basics of air transportation, housing, food, and passport will cost $4,000. My parents have agreed to pay half. Fortunately for me, I developed a plan for saving money for this trip. I have well over the $4,000 I need to go to Taiwan. It's going to be a great experience. Hey Josh, why don't you go with me?"

"Are you kidding? I am not as disciplined as you! I would never be able to save enough money. You are a pro at managing money. Maybe you can give me a few tips."

A BUDGET

A **budget** allows you to meet your personal goals with a system of saving and wise spending. By developing a specific plan for saving and spending income, you will be able to make wise and satisfying personal economic decisions. The main purposes of a budget are to help you

1. live within your income,
2. achieve your financial goals,
3. buy wisely,
4. avoid credit problems,
5. plan for financial emergencies, and
6. develop good money management skills.

Having a written budget is an important phase of successful money management.

Your budget may be a simple record of how much money you make, how much you plan to spend, and how much you want to save. Or, your budget may be a more detailed record that includes specific amounts to be spent in categories such as food, clothing, and transportation. A good budget should take very little of your time, but it should be specific enough to provide needed information on your spending and savings plans.

Illus. 38-1
A budget allows you to meet personal goals with a system of saving and wise spending.

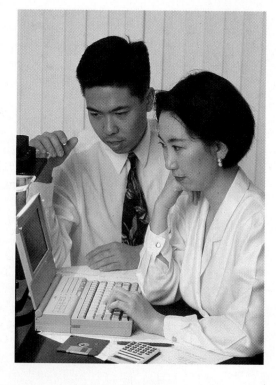

THE BUDGETING PROCESS

The process of creating and using a budget involves

1. setting financial goals,

2. planning budget categories,

3. maintaining financial records, and

4. evaluating your budget.

These steps can be used by any individual, family, or organization to assist them in using available financial resources.

Setting Financial Goals

Establishing financial goals is the first step of any financial strategy. Financial goals help you decide where you would like to be financially and develop your budget accordingly. Writing down your short-term and long-term goals will help assist you in deciding how you want to spend and save your money. If your goals include going to college, your budget will require more for savings. If you are currently working at a job that requires you to spend a large portion of your income for transportation, you are likely to budget more for transportation.

Using the financial statements explained in Chapter 37 can also help you develop financial goals. Your balance sheet presents your current financial position. A cash flow statement reports how you have spent your money over a certain time period, such as a month. By reviewing these documents you can decide where you would like to be financially and develop your budget accordingly.

Planning Budget Categories

Almost all financial advisers recommend that an amount be set aside for savings as the first component of a budget. If savings are not considered first, other expenses may use all of the available income and leave nothing for future goals. After savings, two other types of living expenses must be considered: fixed and variable expenses. **Fixed expenses** are costs that occur regularly and are for the same amount each time. Examples of fixed expenses are rent, mortgage payments, and insurance premiums.

Variable expenses are living costs involving differing amounts each time and are usually more difficult to estimate than fixed costs. These types of expenses include food, clothing, and utilities such as

NET FACTS

Internet hosts use a language called TCP/IP, Transmission Control Protocol/Internet Protocol. TCP keeps track of every part of a transmitted message or file; IP is like an address label that makes sure a message or file reaches the correct user.

Budgeting software is not required for completing a budget on the computer. A simple software spreadsheet can be created to generate a budget.

telephone and electricity. Certain types of variable expenses, such as medical and dental costs, may occur less frequently and may be large when they do occur. Such expenses must be provided for in the budget. If budget categories are not created for these variable expenses, bills for these items could result in using up a large part of your savings.

The amount budgeted for savings and other expenditures is referred to as an **allowance.** This is the amount of money you plan to use for a certain budget category. While the budget categories can vary for different personal and family situations, distribution of savings and expenditures are often classified under eight main divisions:

1. *Savings.* Savings accounts, government bonds, stocks, and other investments.

2. *Food.* Food eaten at home and meals eaten away from home.

3. *Clothing.* Clothing, shoes, dry cleaning, sewing supplies, and repairs.

4. *Household.* Rent, mortgage payments, taxes, insurance, gas, electricity, fuel oil, telephone, water, household furnishings, household supplies, painting, and repairs.

5. *Transportation.* Automobile payments, insurance, automobile upkeep and operating costs, public transportation fares, and auto and drivers' licenses.

6. *Health and personal care.* Medical and dental expenses, medications, eyeglasses, hospital and nursing expenses, accident and health insurance, hair care costs, and children's allowances.

7. *Recreation and education.* Books, magazines, newspapers, theater tickets, concerts, vacations, school expenses, hobbies, radio, television, musical instruments, computer software, and club dues.

8. *Gifts and contributions.* Donations to church, charitable contributions, and personal gifts.

The logical question at this point is, "How much should I set aside for each category?" Planned spending for various budget categories will depend on income, family size, ages of children, the current cost of living in your area, and work-related expenses, as well as personal values, needs, and goals.

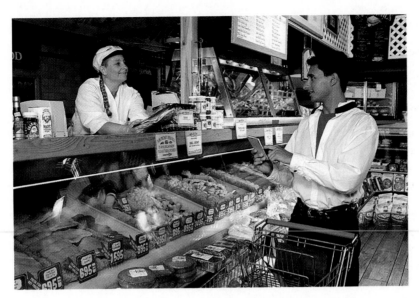

Illus. 38-2
A food allowance is an important budget category.

The cash flow statement discussed in Chapter 37 can help you develop budget categories. This financial statement reports the categories in which your money has been spent and provides a basis for your budget. Other assistance for developing a budget can come from government reports on family spending or from articles in personal finance magazines, such as *Kiplinger's* and *Money*. Your budget should consider estimates for future income and living expenses. The Chung household's budget, as shown in Figure 38-1, is an example of a family budget for one month.

Figure 38-1

This is the Chung household monthly budget.

Chung Household				
Monthly Budget				
January, 19__				
Estimated Inc.			Estimated Exp.	
Manuel's Net Inc.	$2,225		Savings	$1,225
Lydia's Net Inc.	$2,350		Food	$600
			Clothing	$275
			Household	$925
			Transportation	$675
			Health & Personal	$250
			Recreation & Edu.	$400
			Gifts & Contributions	$225
Total Income	$4,575		Total Savings & Exp.	$4,575

Cultural Notes

Cultural and social factors (such as language, education, and customs) affect the way international business is conducted. In some cultures, customs such as handshaking are acceptable behaviors for greeting people, while in other cultures bowing is the acceptable behavior.

Maintaining Financial Records

After planning a budget, individuals and families should set up an income and expenditure record to find out if their plan is working. An example of this type of document is shown in Figure 38-2. The first line of this report shows the monthly income available to the family ($4,575.00) and the budget allowances for each budget category.

The first payment entry of the month was for money put into a savings account. By setting aside that amount first, the Chungs could be sure of saving part of their income. Entries for expenditures were recorded each Saturday and at the end of the month, except for especially large payments which were recorded immediately. Since the family pays most bills by check, a checkbook is an easy reference for the information needed to prepare the income and expenditure record. Incomes were entered on the days they were received, and all columns were totaled at the end of the month.

Technological *Perspective*

Budgeting Software

The ritual of using a pencil, a note pad, and a ruler to develop a budget is almost unnecessary in this computer age. With the introduction of money management and budgeting software, you can put the manual supplies away!

Software is now available that allows you to create your own personal budget. Then, as time progresses, the software actually tracks your income and actual expenses and then compares these figures to what you have budgeted in each income and expense category. Reports can then be developed which show how well you are staying within your budget. Advanced budgeting software may also provide tips from America's leading financial authorities, tools for home inventory management, tax preparing advice, and investment tracking to make the user more efficient in budgeting.

Budgeting software may also provide the capabilities of keeping track of your checking account and actually printing checks. Some software will also allow you to pay your bills by telephone through a bill paying service to which the computer is linked, via a modem.

Budgeting software can make personal record keeping easy for almost any novice!

Critical Thinking

1 What personal advantages could budgeting software provide you?

2 What kinds of reports do you think budgeting software could produce?

Figure 38-2
This is the Chung household income and expenditures record.

Chung Household
Income and Expenditures Record

Date		Explanation	Totals		Distribution of Savings and Expenditures							
			Receipts	Payments	Savings	Food	Clothing	Household	Transpor.	Health/Per.	Rec. & Edu.	Gifts & Con.
		Budget $4,575.00			$1,225.00	$600.00	$275.00	$925.00	$675.00	$250.00	$400.00	$225.00
January	1	Balance	$1,300.00									
	2			$1,225.00	$1,225.00							
	7			$535.00		$110.00	$70.00	$50.00	$55.00	$50.00	$125.00	$75.00
	14	Manuel's Net Inc.	$1,112.50	$455.00		$130.00	$45.00	$50.00	$50.00	$100.00	$45.00	$35.00
	15	Lydia's Net Inc.	$1,175.00									
	16	Mortgage Pay.		$700.00				$700.00				
	17	Car Payment		$425.00					$425.00			
	21			$430.00		$100.00	$80.00	$50.00	$40.00		$80.00	$80.00
	28	Manuel's Net Inc.	$1,112.50	$600.00		$150.00	$80.00	$120.00	$50.00	$105.00	$45.00	$50.00
	29	Lydia's Net Inc.	$1,175.00									
	31	**Totals**	$5,875.00	$4,370.00		$490.00	$275.00	$970.00	$620.00	$255.00	$295.00	$240.00
February	1	**Balance**	$1,505.00		$1,225.00							

*Balance = January 31's Total Receipts 2 Total Payments ($5,875.00—$4,370.00)

Evaluating Your Budget

At the end of the month, it is necessary to compare actual spending with the budgeted amounts. Any difference between these two amounts is called a **budget variance.** If actual spending is greater than planned spending, such as for the Chungs' Household category, it is referred to as a *deficit*. When actual spending is less than the budgeted amount, as with their Food category, a surplus occurs. A category by category comparison allows you to find areas where changes in the budget may be appropriate.

A variance in the actual amount spent and the budgeted amount does not automatically mean a change in your spending plan is necessary. Your budgeted amount may still be appropriate with a slight deficit or surplus occurring every couple of months in certain categories. However, if you expect necessary continued higher or lower spending in a certain category, a change in your budget is probably needed.

CHARACTERISTICS OF A SUCCESSFUL BUDGET

There are several characteristics of a good budget. A successful budget:

1. Must be realistic. It should reflect your current income and planned spending.

2. Should be flexible. When unexpected expenses arise, your spending plan should be able to handle these living costs.

3. Should be evaluated regularly. Every few months, an individual or family should evaluate the budget to determine if it still is appropriate.

4. Must be well planned and clearly communicated to those involved. All members of a family should discuss financial goals, wants and needs, and plans for spending. In addition, the best spending plan should be written so that all affected by it can review its components.

5. Should have a simple format. If it is too detailed and difficult to understand, family members may not be willing to use the spending plan.

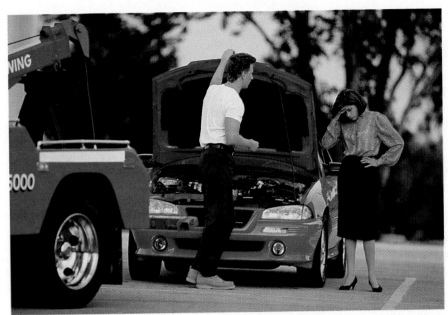

Illus. 38-3
A successful budget should be flexible in allowing for unexpected expenses.

Many software programs have a budgeting feature that allows you to develop a budget, keep track of your accounts, aid in financial planning, and pay your bills. Such software often can be linked to income tax software programs so annual tax forms can be completed in less time than if the tax forms had to be completed by hand.

While handwritten or software-produced budgets are most common, and usually the most appropriate, some people believe a checkbook is an effective budgeting system. However, a checking account does not serve the purpose of planning for spending. Your checks are a record of purchases and paid bills, but you still need a plan for using income. Others say they keep their budgets in their heads rather than on paper. This simple system may work for an individual with limited income and few financial obligations, but a family with a larger income and more living expenses would find it ineffective. A person with a mental budget is also in danger of forgetting how much is to be spent or has been spent on certain items.

Key Ideas

1 The main purposes of a budget are to help you live within your income, achieve your financial goals, buy wisely, avoid credit problems, plan for financial emergencies, and develop good money management skills. Having a written budget is an important phase of successful money management.

2 The process of creating and using a budget involves setting financial goals, planning budget categories, maintaining financial records, and evaluating your budget.

3 A successful budget will be realistic, flexible, evaluated regularly, well planned and clearly communicated to those involved, and in a simple format.

End of Chapter Activities

Increasing Your Business Vocabulary

The following terms should become part of your business vocabulary. For each numbered item, find the term that has the same meaning.

allowance

budget

budget variance

fixed expenses

variable expenses

1 Costs that occur regularly and are for the same amount each time.

2 The amount budgeted for savings and other expenditures.

3 A plan that allows you to meet your personal goals with a system of saving and wise spending.

4 Living costs involving differing amounts each time.

5 A difference between actual spending and planned spending.

Reviewing Your Reading

1 What are the six main purposes of a budget?

2 List the steps involved in the budgeting process.

3 How are financial goals important to budgeting?

4 Name some examples of fixed expenses.

5 Why are variable expenses more difficult to budget for than fixed expenses?

6 What are the eight budget categories that usually appear under Distribution of Savings and Expenditures?

7 What factors influence the amount set aside for various budget categories?

8 Does a budget variance mean that you should change your spending plan?

9 What are the characteristics of a successful budget?

10 Why should a budget be in writing?

Using Your Business Knowledge

1 "If you only spend money on things you really need, you will always have money for the things you really want." Do you agree with this statement? Explain your answer.

2 Some people claim that living by a budget is too structured and restrictive. That is, they do not like to live such a planned and strict economic life. What would you say to those individuals who have that point of view in order to convince them that budgets can be helpful to everyone?

3 Every week Chris Thorson puts any amount he has not spent during the week into a savings account. If he needs more money than he has during a week, he withdraws it from his savings. Is Chris following a good money management plan? Explain.

4 Consider a family of four people: the mother, a supermarket manager; the father, a department store salesperson; and two children, ages 14 and 11.

   a. List four fixed expenses that this family would likely have each month.
   b. What are some variable expenses that they are likely to have?
   c. How are the family's expenses different from those of other families with younger children or no children?

Calculating Business Problems

1 Mary and Fred James budgeted $340 a month for groceries. During the month, they spent $87, $93, $38, $61, and $52 at the supermarket.

   a. What was the total amount spent for food?
   b. Did Mary and Fred have a budget deficit or surplus? What was the amount?

2 You are currently budgeting $750 per year for insurance costs, and you expect the premiums to increase by 7 percent for next year. How much should you budget for insurance next year?

3 A family has $2,600 to spend each month. They plan to spend $625 on food, $250 on clothing, $910 on rent, $300 on transportation, and want to save $200.

   a. What percentage does the family plan to spend on each item?
   b. How much does the family have available to budget for other living expenses?

4 John was considering the purchase of a motorcycle. He had enough money for the purchase price but was concerned about his ability to budget for and pay for operating costs. The advertisement promised the motorcycle could go approxi- mately 35 kilometers on a liter of gasoline. If gasoline cost $1.35 per gallon, how many dollars should John budget for travel 630 miles each week to and from his place of employment?

Applying Technology

Using the *Introduction to Business* template and your spreadsheet program software, select problem CH38. After the problem appears on your screen, complete the following activities. After you have completed each step, display or print the completed spreadsheet for each activity. If you do not have a printer available, answer the questions before you leave the computer.

1 In the Percent column, enter formulas to show each item as a percent of Total Estimated Income. Format the results as percentages with one decimal place. Answer the following questions:

   a. What is the percentage of Total Estimated Income budgeted for savings?
   b. What is the percentage of Total Estimated Income budgeted for recreation?

2 In the Difference column, enter formulas to calculate Actual minus Budget. Format the results as currency with two decimal places. Answer the following questions:

   a. How many expenditures had actual spending greater than budget?
   b. Which expenditure from Question a. has the largest difference?

3 What if your actual Net Income increased to $5,000? Copy the budget from Activity 2 to another part of the spreadsheet. Enter the new amount of actual Net Income. Answer the following questions:

   a. What is the new difference between actual Total Income and budgeted Total Income?
   b. What is the new amount of actual Savings?

Optional: Using the spreadsheet from Activity 2, create a bar chart comparing budgeted expenditures to actual expenditures. Repeat for Activity 3.

Making Decisions

Allison was new to budgeting. She appreciated the concepts and was attempting to employ them in her personal financial life. In fact, she was ready to set up a budget to achieve her vision and goals. She was, however, having difficulty with the idea of fixed and variable expenses. As she explained to her teacher, "Any expense can be variable."

1 What do you think she meant by this statement?

2 How would you explain to Allison the difference between fixed and variable expenses?

Chapter Thirty-Nine

Your Financial Future

Objectives

After studying this chapter and completing the end-of-chapter activities, you will be able to:

1 Name four advantages of financial planning.

2 Explain how to determine financial condition.

3 Describe financial goals.

4 Describe how to create a financial plan.

5 Discuss how to implement a financial plan.

6 Explain why a financial plan should be evaluated and revised.

"**H**ey Gloria, are you going to the Business Speakers Series monthly luncheon on Friday?"

"I really hadn't given it much thought, Maria. Are you?"

"Yes! The speaker is from the local college and is supposed to be very dynamic and informative. The topic is financial planning, and if I am going to go to college, I need some help in planning right now! Why don't you meet me there?"

"Great idea, Maria. I always thought of financial planning as something for people out of college. But it certainly makes sense to start now! I guess if I start planning early, I can get a head start on my future!"

FINANCIAL PLANNING

In order to put into practice all that you have learned about our economy and about earning and saving money, you must have a plan. Successful coaches talk about game plans. Travel agents refer to vacation plans. Builders must have house plans. Successful consumers and businesspeople must have a financial plan. A **financial plan** is a report that summarizes your current financial condition, acknowledges your financial needs, and sets a direction for your future financial activities. **Financial planning** includes evaluating one's financial position, setting financial goals, and guiding activities and resources toward reaching those goals.

Everyone should have a carefully developed financial plan. Your financial plan should encompass all that you have learned about good money management, be developed thoughtfully, and be evaluated and updated frequently. A well-developed financial plan can make your financial life a great deal more satisfying. Ultimately, it will become a blueprint for an improved standard of living. Financial planning will offer you several specific advantages:

- Your financial uncertainties will be reduced.

- You will gain more control of your financial affairs.

- Your family or associates will have a way of knowing more specifically of your financial affairs in case there is a need for them to assume control of your finances.

- Earning, spending, protecting, and saving your resources will be more systematic.

Successful financial planning should follow these steps:

1. Analyze your current financial condition. You should create a balance sheet and cash flow statement as discussed in Chapter 37.

2. Develop financial goals that are responsive to your vision. What short-term and long-term objectives do you have?

The sooner you begin working on your financial plan, the closer you will be to attaining your goals for financial freedom. If at the age of 18 you began saving $50 a month at an interest rate of 9 percent, you will have $444,275 when you reach the age of 65.

3. Next, you must create your financial plan. This activity will take the most time and require the most thought; it may also require additional help from a financial planner.

4. Implement the plan. This may involve buying or selling property or investments, moving bank accounts, acquiring insurance, or any number of financial activities.

5. Finally, as time goes on, you will frequently evaluate and revise your financial plan.

DETERMINING YOUR FINANCIAL CONDITION

The first step in determining your financial condition is usually a careful and honest analysis of where you are by taking a financial inventory. This is then followed by creating a personal filing system to keep track of important records.

Financial Inventory

A financial inventory is a lot like a physician giving you a physical examination. As the doctor's exam requires an assessment of your health, your financial inventory includes a careful appraisal of your finances. A financial inventory is most frequently completed through the use of the personal balance sheet and cash flow statement and should be done at least once each year. It will provide you with a more orderly financial life as well as serve as an important activity in financial planning. You must determine your current financial position in terms of income, savings, investments, property, living expenses, insurance, and money owed. This step is thought by many to be a prerequisite to the development of financial goals.

Culture shock is the reaction a person has when entering a culture that is new or different.

You can purchase tax-free investments. The money earned on tax-free investments can be free from both state and federal income taxes.

Personal Financial Filing System

In order to keep your financial inventory current and to keep all of your records orderly and within easy reach, you will need a personal financial filing system. Well-organized files are valuable to financial planning. These files should contain all of the documents and records associated with such things as contracts, bills, receipts, bank balances, and legal papers. The contents of these files will become an invaluable resource to you as you progress with your financial planning.

SETTING FINANCIAL GOALS

Once you have a clear understanding of your financial condition, you will be able to develop a realistic set of financial goals. Financial goals may be short-term or long-term objectives and are usually stated in dollar amounts. Examples of some short-term financial goals are:

- Saving $1,000 in one year.

- Purchasing a $200 bicycle in June.

- Increasing your annual income by $3,000 by your twentieth birthday.

You will notice that each goal requires that you save or acquire a specific amount of money in a specific period of time. These goals are very simple, straightforward, and relatively short-term. By contrast, long-term financial goals are often more complex and achievable over a long period of time. They might include such objectives as:

- Owning your own home by age 40.

- Taking a trip to Africa in five years.

- Receiving a retirement income equal to 50 percent of your salary at age 64.

In the process of developing and carrying out your financial plan, you will quickly discover that it is often necessary to compromise short-term goals in order to accomplish long-term ones. For example, you may have to forgo a movie to meet the long-term goal of buying a bicycle.

Financial Life Cycle

Most people's lives follow a predictable pattern called a life cycle. Each stage of life is distinguished by unique characteristics, requirements, and expectations. For example, during the teen years, people are exploring career options, developing plans for eventual independence, evaluating future financial needs and resources, and developing an understanding of the financial system. In their twenties, people are training for careers, establishing households, some are marrying, and some are having children.

The thirties and forties evolve into a different phase of life for many people. Some are marrying for the first time and having children for the first time. Some will be paying for children's education, developing retirement plans, investing, and estate

To determine how many years it will take your money to double if you let your investment compound, use the "Rule of 72." To use this rule, divide 72 by the interest rate on your investment. If your investment is earning a 10 percent interest rate, 72 divided by 10 = 7.2. So at a 10 percent interest rate, your money will double every 7.2 years.

planning. Then, in the fifties and sixties, people tend to guard their assets more carefully, work toward financial security, and reevaluate living arrangements.

Each of these life stages has financial matters that need attention. That attention can be provided through the development of a good financial plan. Remember, a good plan is one that is flexible and useful throughout several life cycles.

Illus. 39-1
Each stage in a person's life cycle has different financial requirements.

Retirement and Estate Planning

Although it seems a long time off, retirement is considered by many people to be the heart of financial goal setting. The chances are very good that you will spend many happy and healthy years in retirement. They will be happier and healthier if you have done some financial planning that results in an adequate supply of money to use during those years.

Estate planning involves the accumulation and management of property during one's lifetime and the distribution of one's property at death. It is a part of retirement planning and is an integral part of financial planning. It has two parts. The first part consists of building your estate through savings, investments, and insurance. The second consists of planning for the transfer of your estate, at your death, in the manner that you wish.

CREATING A FINANCIAL PLAN

After you have established your financial goals based on your vision, you can begin to plan for the income you will need to achieve these goals. Some may think that income is not possible to niversities estimate that the cost of a college education will increase 7 percent a year.

plan for or control because it is money received from someone else. To an extent that is correct, but there are aspects of income that can be planned.

You can develop strategies that will help you acquire the amount of income you want when you want it. For example, if you want more income, you might ask for a raise, become qualified for a better paying job, get an additional part-time job, or invest in securities. You can also time your income so that you have money coming in when you want it. This can be done by investing at certain times, seeking increased salary at certain times, or by asking that you be paid on certain days of the month. You should develop and write a plan for generating income that is consistent with your financial goals.

Global *Perspective*

Financial Future

Do you have any money invested for your future? The answer may be *no* right now, but someday, you will more than likely invest money so that your money can work for you. And as an investor, you will have many options from which to choose.

If you decide to invest in stocks and bonds, you may choose to invest in U.S. stock markets such as the New York Stock Exchange or the American Stock Exchange. However, there are also opportunities to make foreign investments. Foreign investments are sometimes appealing to Americans for

several reasons. One reason is the possibility that the currency exchange rate of a particular county is favorable for buying stocks or bonds at a lower price so that Americans get more for their money. Another reason may be that sometimes American investors like to make foreign investments so that they diversify, or spread their investments over many different types of stocks.

Various opportunities are available to make foreign investments. One way is to purchase a specific mutual fund in the United States that invests in international companies' stock. Another way to invest internationally is to purchase an

American Depository Receipt (ADR). ADRs are foreign companies' stock that is traded in U.S. markets. Another way to make a foreign investment is to purchase international stock directly from a specific foreign country's stock exchange. Foreign stock exchanges include London, Paris, Tokyo, Sydney, Toronto, Johannesburg, São Paulo, and Frankfurt.

Critical Thinking

1 How does the currency exchange rate affect investments?

2 How can a person in the United States buy stock directly from another country's stock exchange?

Creating a financial plan is not a simple task. Doing your own financial planning requires a great deal of time, information, and patience. There are professionals called **financial planners** who can help you. A financial planner should have at least two years of training in securities, insurance, taxes, real estate, and estate planning and have passed a rigorous examination.

There are some questions you can ask to help you choose a financial planner. They are:

- What experience and training does the financial planner have?

- Is the financial planner willing to supply you with references?

- Does the financial planner have a good reputation among other financial professionals?

- What are the financial planner's fees?

A financial planner will want to ask you some questions as well. You will need to have some idea of what your financial goals are. You must be prepared to describe your financial inventory. You should be willing to share information about your income, expenditures, and savings. With this information and your cooperation, together you can create a useful financial plan.

IMPLEMENTING A FINANCIAL PLAN

Implementing your plan may involve a wide variety of actions. You may need to move your savings to an account in which you will earn a higher interest rate. You may buy a bond. Maybe you will begin to work more hours on your part-time job to earn more money. As you can see, the list of implementation possibilities is endless. However, for your plan to lead to the satisfaction of your goals, you must carry it out.

Insuring Current Income

There are some safeguards you should take to assure the success of your plan. They involve protecting your income so that it contributes to your goals. Insurance is available that will provide an income to those who fear the two most common causes of loss of income: disability and unemployment.

Disability income insurance helps replace income that is lost when you cannot work because of an illness or injury. Many dif-

NET FACTS

Lurkers are members of newsgroups or E-mail discussion lists who read the postings, but do not post messages of their own. Because you never know all the people who will be reading your messages, always use common sense and etiquette.

ost disability insurance policies provide for payment at the rate of approximately 60 percent or more of monthly earnings. In general, no income taxes are charged on disability insurance payments.

ferent disability income policies are available. The amount of each payment, the length of the waiting period before benefits are paid, and the length of time that payments are made should be chosen on the basis of your needs. Most companies from which you can buy disability income insurance will pay from 40 to 60 percent of your salary while you are disabled. However, before the benefits begin, there is usually a waiting period from 1 week to 90 days after you are disabled. As with other kinds of insurance, the more benefits provided, the higher the price for coverage.

One of the most important forms of income protection comes through the federal government's Social Security system. The Medicare program, which you learned about in Chapter 36, is one part of the Social Security system. The other part is **retirement, survivors, and disability insurance.** This part of the insurance system provides pensions to retired workers and their families, death benefits to dependents of workers who die, and benefits to disabled workers and their families.

Illus. 39-2
The Social Security system helps protect dependents of workers who die or are disabled.

Unemployment is another hazard to a financial plan. To reduce the financial hardship of unemployment, most states have an unemployment insurance program that they operate in cooperation with the federal government. **Unemployment insurance** provides cash payments for a limited time to people who are out of work for a reason other than illness. The local unemployment office will provide guidance to help you find a new job, but if no suitable job is found, you may receive payments to replace part of your lost wages.

Planning for Future Income

The success of any financial plan is largely dependent on a continuing stream of future income. Once people retire, their salaries stop, but they continue to need money to cover living expenses. Workers can insure that they will have an adequate income during their retirement years through Social Security, pensions, individual retirement accounts, and annuities with the help of their employers and the government.

Social Security   During working years, employed people pay **Social Security taxes.** The taxes are deducted from the employees' paychecks. Employers match the amounts paid by their employees. Self-employed people, such as farmers and small-business owners, pay the entire tax themselves. The taxes collected are put into a special trust fund. When a worker retires, becomes disabled, or dies, monthly payments from the trust fund are made. The amount of benefits received depends to a great extent on how long a worker was employed and how much a worker earned while employed.

Those who are covered by Social Security can receive the full amount of the monthly payments to which they are entitled when they reach the appropriate age as shown in Figure 39-1. However, it is possible to retire as early as age 62 and accept lower monthly payments. Workers may be entitled to full benefits if they become

Age to Receive Full Social Security Benefits

Year of Birth	Full Retirement Age
1937 or earlier	65
1938	65 and 2 months
1939	65 and 4 months
1940	65 and 6 months
1941	65 and 8 months
1942	65 and 10 months
1943–54	66
1955	66 and 2 months
1956	66 and 4 months
1957	66 and 6 months
1958	66 and 8 months
1959	66 and 10 months
1960 and later	67

Figure 39-1
Because of longer life expectancies, if you were born after 1960, you will receive full Social Security benefits at age 67.

Source: Social Security Administration

disabled at any age before 65. If an insured worker dies, monthly benefits are also payable to a surviving spouse and/or dependent children.

Pensions A **pension** is a series of regular payments made to a retired worker under an organized plan. Many employers offer plans that provide monthly payments to retired workers. Similar plans are often established by professional and trade associations or unions. To qualify under most pension plans, you must work for the same organization for a minimum number of years. Many employees retire on pensions together with their Social Security benefits.

Individual retirement accounts People can also develop their own retirement income plans. The most popular of these plans is the **individual retirement account (IRA).** An IRA is a tax-sheltered retirement plan in which people can annually invest earnings up to a certain amount. The earnings contributed and the interest earned are tax free until the time of withdrawal at age 59½ or later.

Annuities An amount of money that an insurance company will pay at definite intervals to a person who has previously deposited money with the company is called an **annuity.** An annuity is an investment plan for retirement income that is usually purchased from an insurance company. You pay the insurance company a certain amount of money either in a lump sum or in a series of payments. In return, the company agrees to pay you a regular income beginning at a certain age and continuing for life or for a specified number of years.

EVALUATING AND REVISING A FINANCIAL PLAN

A financial plan must be flexible. It is important to view your financial plan as a fluid, changeable document that will accommodate opportunity. Your plan should be evaluated and adjusted on a regular basis in order to produce the outcomes you have established.

Key Ideas

1 Four advantages of financial planning are that financial uncertainties will be reduced; you will gain more control of your financial affairs; your family or associates will have a way of knowing more specifically of your financial affairs in case there is a need for them to assume control of your finances; and earning, spending, protecting, and saving your resources will be more systematic.

2 To determine your financial condition, you will take a financial inventory and then create a personal filing system to keep track of important records.

3 Financial goals are short-term and/or long-term objectives and are usually stated in dollar amounts.

4 After you have established your financial goals, you can begin to plan for the income you will need to achieve these goals. You should develop and write a plan for generating income that is consistent with your financial goals.

5 Implementing your financial plan may involve moving your savings to an account in which you will earn a higher interest rate, buying a bond, or working more hours to earn more money.

6 A financial plan must be flexible. It is important to view your financial plan as a fluid, changeable document that will accommodate opportunity. If your plan is not producing the expected results, you must make changes.

End of Chapter Activities

Increasing Your Business Vocabulary

The following terms should become part of your business vocabulary. For each numbered item, find the term that has the same meaning.

annuity

estate planning

financial plan

financial planner

financial planning

individual retirement account (IRA)

pension

retirement, survivors, and disability insurance

Social Security tax

unemployment insurance

1 An activity that involves the accumulation and management of property during one's lifetime and the distribution of one's property at death.

2 A report that summarizes your current financial condition, acknowledges your financial needs, and sets a direction for your future financial activities.

3 An activity that includes evaluating one's financial position, setting financial goals, and guiding activities and resources toward reaching those goals.

4 Insurance that provides cash payments for a limited time to people who are out of work for a reason other than illness.

5 A series of regular payments made to a retired worker under an organized plan.

6 An amount of money that an insurance company will pay at definite intervals to a person who has previously deposited money with the company.

7 A tax that is put into a trust fund and provides certain benefits to retirees or beneficiaries.

8 The part of the Social Security system that provides pensions to retired workers and their families, death benefits to dependents of workers who die, and benefits to disabled workers and their families.

9 Professionals who have at least two years of training in securities, insurance, taxes, real estate, and estate planning and have passed a rigorous examination.

10 A tax-sheltered retirement plan in which people can annually invest earnings up to a certain amount. The earnings contributed and the interest earned are tax free until the time of withdrawal at age 59½ or later.

Reviewing Your Reading

1 What four advantages does financial planning offer you?

2 List the five steps in financial planning.

3 What is the purpose of a personal financial filing system?

4 How are financial goals usually stated?

5 What are the two parts of estate planning?

6 State the qualifications of a financial planner.

7 What are the two most common causes of loss of income?

8 What are two forms of income protection?

9 List four ways to plan for future income.

10 Why is flexibility important in revising a financial plan?

Using Your Business Knowledge

1 One financial planner has said, "Doing nothing about financial planning is equivalent to making a decision about financial planning." What do you think she meant by this statement?

2 Tell in your own words how people's financial goals change throughout their life cycle.

3 Why would you want to insure your income?

4 Give examples of activities that might be involved in implementing your financial plan.

Calculating Business Problems

1 If the Coopers invest $31,700 on January 1 in an account that pays 7.34 percent simple annual interest, how much interest will they earn by December 31 of that same year?

2 Your grandparents are both age 64 and are earning $52,000 per year. Their goal is to retire on an income equal to 50 percent of their salary earned at age 64. How much income will they need to have in retirement to achieve that goal?

3 You earn $25,000 per year and receive an automatic annual increase of 5 percent per year. You become disabled after you receive one 5 percent raise. You are protected by disability income insurance that pays 60 percent of your salary. How much would your annual salary be if you were disabled for one year?

4 Shelly Meinke is about to retire. She will collect a pension from a New York gas and electric company where she has been employed, as well as Social Security from the government. She has always planned to spend her retirement years in Florida, but she is worried about missing her children and grandchildren who live in New York. She plans to return to New York twice a year by car for a visit. The distance from New York City where she lives to her new home in Florida is 2,050 kilometers. How many kilometers will she travel the first year, counting the initial trip to Florida from New York?

Applying Technology

Using the *Introduction to Business* template and your database program software, select problem CH39. After the problem appears on your screen, complete the following activities. Then, after you have completed each step, display or print a report for each activity. If you do not have a printer available, answer the questions before you leave the computer.

1 Sort the database in descending order by expected rate of return. Answer the following questions:

   a. Which investment option has the highest expected rate of return?
   b. Which investment option has the lowest expected rate of return?

2 Select and list the investment options that are insured. How many options are listed?

3 Sort the database in ascending order by minimum investment required. Answer the following questions:

   a. How many investment options have a minimum investment required of zero?
   b. What is the minimum investment required for the seventh investment option?

Making Decisions

Paula and John Wilson have been married seven years and have two children—Dennis, age five, and Laura, age three. Paula and John are both employed—Paula as a software programmer and John as a telemarketing supervisor. Together, they earn over $75,000 per year. Each month they have problems paying their bills. It becomes even more difficult when quarterly payments, like their insurance, become due. It seems as if they are always taking money out of their savings account but never putting money in.

1 To what extent do you think John and Paula have engaged in financial planning?

2 What first step would you suggest John and Paula take toward a more predictable and secure financial future?

Almost every firm has one or more financial managers. They prepare financial reports required by the firm to conduct its operations and oversee management of the firm's finances. They also communicate with stockholders and other investors about the finances of the organization.

There are about 700,000 people working in the realm of financial management. Although these financial managers are found in virtually every industry, one-third of them are employed by financial institutions. Nearly another third are employed by service industries.

Job Titles

Job titles commonly found in this career area include:

- Accountant
- Auditor
- Controller
- Financial Planner
- Manager, Credit and Collection
- Manager, Exchange Floor
- Treasurer
- Treasurer, Financial Institution

Employment Outlook (through the year 2005)

- The number of applicants is expected to exceed the number of job openings, resulting in competition for jobs.
- Employment is expected to increase about as fast as the average for all occupations.
- Many financial management positions are filled by promoting experienced, technically skilled professional personnel—for

example, accountants or budget analysts.

Education and Training

- A bachelor's degree in accounting or finance is suitable academic preparation.
- A Master of Business Administration (MBA) degree is increasingly valued by employers.
- Continuing education is becoming vital for financial managers.
- The ability to communicate, both orally and in writing, is increasingly important.

Salary Levels (in recent years)

- The median annual salary is approximately $40,000 per year.
- The lowest 10 percent earned around $20,000; the top 10 percent earned almost $80,000.
- The salary level depends on the manager's experience and the size and location of the organization. The salary is likely to be higher in larger organizations and larger cities.

Critical Thinking

1 Which job title in this career area appeals to you most? Give reasons for your choice.

2 What are some things you will have to do to achieve success in the career you selected?

FocusOnCareers

Financial Managers

Unit Eleven

Small Business Management

Small firms have been the mainstay of the U.S. economy since its beginning. Small businesses are often the first to offer new concepts and new products to the marketplace. Strong small businesses provide the competitive zeal that keeps our free enterprise system effective. They create two-thirds of our GDP today and account for half the work force.

Popular today are home-based businesses. An estimated 25 million Americans operate full-time or part-time businesses from their homes. Many new businesses start as a part-time business in the owner's garage, basement, or spare room. Running a business from home is often a matter of economic necessity. The cost of buying or renting a building may be higher than the owner can afford. Also, since many businesses are indeed part-time and very small, little space is needed. If the business grows, a move to a new facility may be required.

Many business owners plan for and seek out home-based business opportunities. However, many others start a home-based business as the result of some precipitating event. Getting fired or laid off is one of the many experiences that may serve as a catalyst to "taking the plunge" into small-business ownership.

Employees terminated as a result of "downsizing" are often used by large companies as independent contractors. An independent contractor is self-employed and, therefore, can provide similar services to other businesses. For example, a telemarketing salesperson may start a home-based independent sales business as a result of termination. A bookkeeper or a research analyst may work at home providing services for a previous employer. The availability of technology (computers, fax machines, laser printers, and the Internet) make these kinds of business services possible.

Large businesses benefit by reducing the number of regular employees. The lower labor costs resulting from a smaller permanent staff can provide distinct cost savings to a large business. Independent contractors give a company the capability of increasing or decreasing its work force as needed with self-employed people.

An independent contractor loses some of the security of working for someone else and the daily opportunity to interact with colleagues. However, self-confident individuals successfully meet the challenges that confront them. People who leave jobs in large companies frequently speak of the personal satisfaction they experience in their own businesses. The greatest benefits for many are the convenience of working at home and the freedom to operate independently.

Critical Thinking

1 Why are more people considering home office businesses today than ever before?

2 How will the jobs of people working independently be different from the work they were doing previously as an employee of a company?

Home-Based Businesses

641

Chapter Forty

Managing a Small Business

Key Terms

business plan

start-up financing

short-term financing

long-term financing

Objectives

After studying this chapter and completing the end-of-chapter activities, you will be able to:

1 Describe the characteristics of small-business owners.

2 Identify key steps small-business owners follow to start their businesses.

3 Explain the importance of a written business plan for a small business.

4 Define the various types of financing needed for a new business.

uring dinner, Jasmine excitedly told her family what happened in her Introduction to Business class that day. The class had spent the time considering opportunities for owning a small business and Jasmine knew that is what she wanted to do.

After the meal, Jasmine's grandfather sat down with her and said, "Did you know I ran a small business for almost 10 years when I was young?" Jasmine was quite surprised. For as long as she could remember and until he retired, her grandfather had worked for a large hardware store that was a part of a national chain.

"I was as excited as you are about starting a business when I graduated from high school. That was almost 50 years ago. I knew it would be difficult. I went to work for the owner of a small hardware store and hoped that I could save enough money to open my own store. Luckily, after eight years, he decided to retire. We worked out an arrangement where I could buy the store from him over a number of years."

"What happened to the business?" Jasmine asked.

"Being a small business owner is exciting, but it is a difficult life," explained her grandfather. "It took a lot of my time. As the bigger stores moved in, I found it more and more difficult to attract customers. I decided to sell the business but often wonder if I could have kept it going through all those years. I'm excited for you but want you to know that your goals will be a challenge to achieve."

IDENTIFYING THE SMALL-BUSINESS OWNER

Independence; control; the chance to set your own schedule and make your own decisions—it sounds like everyone's dream. But long hours; customer complaints; meeting a payroll; taking responsibility for every problem—most people would want to avoid these job characteristics. As a small-business owner, you have to accept both the good and the bad. You own the business, so it is your responsibility to make it successful.

What It Takes

Small-business ownership is risky. Fewer than half of all new businesses will survive for five years. It takes a unique person to be a successful small-business owner. Some of the requirements are personality-based (such as self-motivation, risk-taking, and persistence). Other requirements are business-related (such as knowledge and skills). The small-business owner will be responsible for most, if not all, of the decisions needed to operate the business. Operating a business requires skill in management, finance, marketing, and other business activities.

One of the most important requirements for a successful small business is effort. Most small-

All successful large businesses today originally started as small businesses.

NET FACTS

Instead of sending and reading written documents as E-mail, in the future you will use the Internet for video and voice mail. If the person you want to reach is not available, you will be able to leave a message for video playback later.

business owners report working much harder than they did when they were employed by someone else. A person starting a business can work 60 to 70 hours each week for the first several years. Small-business owners often are not able to take long vacations and may not even have much free time for hobbies or other interests during those initial years. However, for people who want to own a business, the long hours of work provide a great deal of satisfaction. Small-business owners often spend more hours in the business than are necessary just because they enjoy the work.

Who Owns Small Businesses

No one set of characteristics describes small-business owners. Many years ago, the majority of small-business owners were middle-aged males with less than a college education. Today, small-business owners are more educated, younger, and are more likely to be female or minorities. New business owners who are women are increasing at a rate almost three times that of men. Women now make up over 30 percent of all small businesses.

People of non-white ethnic and racial heritage are another fast growing segment of small-business owners. Minority business ownership has nearly doubled since the early 1980s. The three largest groups of minority business owners are Asian-Americans, Hispanics, and African-Americans. Some minority business owners often face serious limitations in starting a business. These limitations include lack of available financing, limited management experience, and prejudicial treatment by financial institutions, vendors, and other businesses.

Illus. 40-1
Today, small-business owners are more likely to be from a varied ethnic background.

Programs and services have been established by the federal government, and by banks, universities, and some franchisors to assist minorities in their efforts to start and operate their own businesses. Minority-owned small business can be successful when adequate opportunities and resources are available.

Many people think about starting a business but few do. The procedures followed to start a business often determine whether it will be successful. The process begins with an idea and concludes with a careful study of information to determine whether the idea can be successful.

Businesses often fail because they are created in poor economic times. Many people decide to start a business when they lose their jobs.

STARTING THE SMALL BUSINESS

An Idea Plus Experience

Every business begins with an idea. Have you ever thought about opening a business in your community? Business ideas come from many sources. Hobbies, interests, and business experiences often give people ideas for new businesses. Travel to other communities provides opportunities to see businesses that could be successful in another location. Books and magazines suggest new business opportunities including available franchises.

Few people should consider starting a business without working for some time in a small business. Work experience in the same type of business you plan to start is not necessary. However, several years of training in various aspects of business operations will prepare you for the role of owner. Having opportunities to manage people and responsibility for decisions is an important part of that experience.

Right Place and Time

Putting your business idea into action means finding the right location to open the business. Most retail businesses require good customer traffic. If the business is difficult to find, or requires a great deal of travel time, many potential customers will stay away. A wholesaler needs easy access to manufacturers where products are obtained for resale to other businesses. Manufacturers must be located in an area with access to the raw materials used in manufacturing. Transportation systems must also be accessible for distributing finished products.

Timing is another important factor in starting a business. Most successful businesses start during a period when customer demand for certain products or services is high. For example, many retailers make a majority of their sales in the last three months of the year.

One purpose for which bankers use business plans is to see if the prospective business owner is committed to the business.

If a business is not ready to open during the peak retailing season, the business may not be able to survive until the end of the next year.

Team Approach

Many small-business owners are quite independent. Their businesses were started because they do not want to take direction from other people. A business is difficult to start, however, without the help of others. Even the smallest businesses need a few full- or part-time employees. The majority of small businesses have between two and ten employees. The employees must be selected carefully for their ability to work as a team. Choosing the "team" becomes one of the most important initial business decisions. A team gives a new company its general direction.

In addition to employees, small-business owners will require assistance from bankers, lawyers, accountants, and other people with specialized business knowledge. If possible, business professionals who specialize in working with small businesses should be identified.

Preparation and Research

The most important step in starting a business is preparation. Preparation includes having adequate information to make good decisions about the business. Time spent gathering and studying information before the business is started will save time and avoid later problems.

Information is needed about customers, competitors, important operations and activities, government regulations, and many other topics. This information is available through libraries, colleges or universities, and small-business assistance centers. However, occasionally the new business owner will have to do additional research to gather more current data. Information will help to insure that decisions are made objectively.

DEVELOPING A BUSINESS PLAN

When successful businesses are compared with those that failed, one factor stands out as the most important difference. The owners of successful businesses develop and follow a business plan. The owners of businesses that fail often do not have a business plan.

One creative small-business person borrowed over $30,000 on his credit cards to finance the start of his new business.

What Is a Business Plan?

A **business plan** is a written description of the business idea and how it will be carried out, including all major business activities. Key features of a business plan are a general description of the company, the qualifications of the owner(s), a description of the product or service, an analysis of the market (demand, customers, competition), and a financial plan. Most business plans are developed for one year and then updated for the next year. If the business owner needs assistance from others, especially for financing the new business, a business plan will usually be required.

Even if help is not needed, a business plan must be developed. By developing a plan, the owner is forced to think about important activities, the amount of time they will take, and their cost. That process may identify potential problems. The plan also serves as a guide to keep the business on track. Figure 40-1 is an outline of the sections of a business plan.

Description of the Business
- the business idea
- major products and services
- ownership structure
- strengths/weaknesses
- long- and short-term goals

Description of Competition
- characteristics of the industry
- condition of the economy
- strengths and weaknesses of major competitors

Customer Analysis
- description of customers
- location, number, and resources of customers
- sales forecasts

Operations Plan
- organization of the company
- description of major operations
- analysis of resources needed
- human resource plans

Marketing Plan
- description of major marketing activities
- description of resources needed
- schedule of marketing activities

Financial Plans
- start-up costs
- short- and long-term financial needs
- sources of financing
- budgets and financial statements

Figure 40-1

A good business plan provides a detailed operating guide for a new business.

Steps in Developing the Business Plan

The business owner is responsible for developing the business plan. The most popular use of business plans is to persuade lenders and investors to finance the venture. A well developed plan will lay out an idea, require an owner to analyze his or her concept, and make decisions about key business activities such as production, marketing, staffing, and financing.

Some owners hire someone to write the plan. Others get help from a bank or a local office of the Small Business Administration. Even if others are involved in developing the plan, the owner must be familiar with all of the information and make the major decisions for the plan.

Technological *Perspective*

Making Small Businesses Competitive

Small businesses sometimes have difficulty competing with large businesses. The resources of big businesses provide many advantages. Products are produced in greater quantities with attention to quality standards. Research departments provide access to information and new product ideas. Sophisticated computers aid decision making. Transportation systems and warehouses allow quick delivery of products.

Today, technology has leveled the playing field. Inexpensive computer systems provide power to small businesses that once only large businesses could afford. Computer software makes desktop publishing of advertisements and brochures possible that once could only be achieved with skilled graphic designers. A modem and on-line service opens up data to every business at a low cost. Products are transported by express delivery services.

Low-cost technology makes all businesses competitive. Small businesses can compete if they have the technology and can use it. Computer literacy is a requirement for small-business owners. Applying technology to the operation of the business is important for all businesses, but especially for small business. A recent survey showed that small businesses using personal computers, facsimile machines, and cellular telephones were experiencing the highest rate of growth in their markets.

Critical Thinking

1 Most new technology is expensive when first introduced; the technology becomes less expensive later. Should small businesses invest heavily in new technology as soon as it becomes available? Or, should a small business wait until the technology is more affordable? Provide reasons for your answer.

2 What are the important computer skills a small-business owner should have today? How do you believe those skills will change in the next ten years?

The first step in developing the plan is to gather and review information. If possible, the owner should review other business plans and study information on the activities and financial performance of similar businesses, especially potential competitors. Next, the owner should develop the "game plan." Alternative plans for production, marketing, staffing, and financing should be studied and identified. The owner can select the best choices from the alternatives. Finally, each section of the business plan should be written. A plan devotes sections to a general description of the business, including the basic legal form of an organization and major products or services, the competition, potential customers, operations, marketing, and finances. Before the plan is completed, the owner should have other business professionals review the plan and offer their advice about its strengths and weaknesses.

A *job analyst's* duties include:

- Collecting and examining detailed information about job duties to prepare job descriptions.
- Observing and interviewing personnel to determine job requirements.
- Developing written descriptions of the duties, training, and skills for each job in an organization.

FINANCING THE SMALL BUSINESS

A new business with a good product or service idea may run out of money before it can become profitable. Several years of operation usually are required before a new business earns a profit. Obtaining adequate financing is an important step in starting and operating a new business.

Types of Financing

Three types of financing must be considered. **Start-up financing** is the amount of money needed to open the business. It includes the cost of buildings, equipment, *inventory* (goods or raw materials on hand), supplies, licenses, and the like. **Short-term financing** is the money needed to pay for the current operating activities of a business. Short-term financing is obtained for a period of less than a year and often for one or two months. **Long-term financing** is money needed for the important resources of a business (such as land, buildings, and equipment) that will last for many years. These resources usually require large amounts of money and will be paid for over a number of years.

Sources of Financing

Finding the necessary money may be the most difficult part of starting a business. The money needed to start and operate a new

Steven Jobs is an example of an entrepreneur who successfully developed Apple Computer, Inc. Later he left the company because day-to-day management was not as satisfying to him.

business usually comes from a combination of owner-supplied and borrowed funds. The source of owner-supplied money depends on the ownership structure. In a proprietorship, one person will supply the money, while in a partnership, the partners will each be expected to contribute. A corporation is owned and financed by the shareholders. Borrowed funds are obtained through loans from banks and other financial institutions, or through financing provided by other companies. Trade credit, explained in Chapter 25, is an example of credit provided by another company, such as a supplier of equipment or merchandise.

Key Ideas

1 Small-business owners are independent, self-motivated, risk-takers, persistent, hard workers, have technical knowledge and management ability.

2 Small-business ownership begins with an idea. Putting a business idea into action means finding the right location for a business and choosing the right team to help run the business. The most important step in starting a business is preparation—spending time gathering and studying information before the business is started.

3 A written business plan serves as an objective guide to the development of a new business.

4 The three primary types of financing needed by many small businesses are start-up financing, short-term financing, and long-term financing.

End of Chapter Activities

Increasing Your Business Vocabulary

The following terms should become part of your business vocabulary. For each numbered item, find the term that has the same meaning.

business plan

long-term financing

short-term financing

start-up financing

1 The money needed to pay for the current operating activities of a business.

2 A written description of the business idea and how it will be carried out, including all major business operations.

3 The amount of money needed to open the business.

4 Money needed for the important resources of a business (such as land, buildings, and equipment) that will last for many years.

Reviewing Your Reading

1 What are some of the positive and negative aspects of starting a small business?

2 What does it take to be a successful business owner?

3 What are the trends in small-business ownership?

4 What is the first thing from which every business begins?

5 Why is preparation important when starting a business?

6 What are the three steps to follow when developing a business plan?

7 Why might a new business with a good product or service end up in failure?

Using Your Business Knowledge

1 Review the opening scenario about Jasmine and her grandfather. Why do you think Jasmine's grandfather decided to sell his small business instead of competing with larger companies?

2 Michael Andrews worked for a major clothing chain for 10 years then decided to resign so he could open his own clothing store. What possible past experiences could enable Michael to start his own small business?

3 Timing and location are two key factors in starting a small business. Give an example of a particular small business from your community, and tell how either location or timing contributes to its success.

4 A business plan can be described as a "game plan." What features of such a plan justify that label?

5 Start-up financing, short-term financing, and long-term financing are all types of financing that must be considered when starting a new small business. Why should a new business owner be concerned about each of these types of financing?

Calculating Business Problems

1 Jennifer Yukimura, a local high school student, started her own T-shirt business. The business had total sales for the year of $20,000. Jennifer's yearly expenses are shown in the table.

Payroll	$5,000
Rent	$7,000
Inventory	$3,000
Equipment	$2,500

a. What were the total expenses for the T-shirt business?

b. What was the percentage of total expenses for each expense category?

c. What percentage of total sales were the total expenses?

d. How much profit, if any, did Jennifer earn?

2 In a city business directory, 1,500 small businesses were listed. Nationally, the percentage of businesses in several categories is as follows: wholesale businesses, 27 percent; service businesses, 25 percent; construction businesses, 14 percent; retail businesses, 11 percent; manufacturers, 9 percent; and other businesses, 14 percent. Use the national percentages to determine how many of each type of business might be found in the city.

a. Wholesale businesses
b. Service businesses
c. Construction businesses
d. Retail businesses
e. Manufacturers
f. Others

3 Tahisha Bowers received a small-business loan for $110,000 to start a pet grooming business. She also invested $40,000 of her own savings. The amounts of her start-up expenses are shown in the table.

Building	$80,000
Equipment:	
grooming	$ 6,700
office	$ 4,300
Inventory	$ 4,950
Supplies	$ 2,050
Licenses	$ 750

a. What were the total start-up costs for the business?

b. What percentage of the bank loan had to be spent for start-up costs?

c. How much money does Tahisha have available for short-term and long-term expenses?

Applying Technology

Using the *Introduction to Business* template and your spreadsheet program software, select problem CH40. After the problem appears on your screen, complete the following activities. Then, after you have completed each step, display or print the completed spreadsheet. If you do not have a printer available, answer the questions before you leave the computer.

1 Enter formulas to calculate Total Start-up Expenses and Reserves (Total Funds Available − Total Start-up Expenses). Answer the following questions:

a. What is the amount of Total Start-up Expenses?

b. What is the amount of Reserves?

2 Copy all the data to an open part of the spreadsheet. Using absolute references, enter a formula to decrease the amount of the small-business loan by 10 percent. Answer the following questions.

a. What is the new amount of Total Start-up Expenses?

b. What is the new amount of Reserves?

3 Copy the second set of data to an open part of the spreadsheet. Enter formulas to increase each start-up expense by 12 percent. Answer the following questions.

a. What is the new amount of Total Start-up Expenses?

b. What is the new amount of Reserves?

Optional: For each set of data, create a pie chart showing the breakdown of the start-up expenses.

Making Decisions

David Obolski completed a community college program in Small Business Management. He now wanted to own his own florist business. He had worked for Flower-a-Bunda during high school and college. In addition to the work experience, he was able to save almost $20,000 toward starting his own business. However, he knew that he would need more than $20,000 to buy a florist shop. He would need almost double that amount to qualify for the necessary loans to start up the business.

David had studied three ways he might start his business.

a. He could find a partner to provide the additional cash.

b. He could work for the owner of Flower-a-Bunda until she retired in five years and buy the business with his accumulated savings.

c. He could purchase a franchise available for an investment of $20,000. However, David would have to pay a franchise fee of 6 percent of total sales each year to the franchisor.

1 What are the advantages and disadvantages of each route to small-business ownership for David?

2 If you were David, which choice would you make? Why?

Chapter Forty-One

Managing Human Resources

Key Terms

human resources

human resource management

permanent employee

temporary employee

full-time employee

part-time employee

compensation

salary and wages

benefits

time wage

straight salary

commission

piece rate

base plus incentive

profit sharing

Objectives

After studying this chapter and completing the end-of-chapter activities, you will be able to:

1 Explain why human resources are important to the success of small businesses.

2 Name factors to be considered by a small-business owner when assessing human resource needs.

3 Explain types of compensation and typical benefits for employees.

4 Identify several sources of employee training available to small businesses.

Jaqueline Perez had come to the end of a busy week as she locked the door to her bookkeeping service Friday evening. But she knew her work wasn't finished. For the third time this year, she was going to have to replace one of her best employees who had resigned to take a position with a larger competitor. She owned a small company employing 15 full-time and 12 part-time employees. The business had been more successful than she had hoped in its first three years, but the personnel problems were challenging.

Ms. Perez knew that her employees were important to the success of her business. They were responsible for completing the bookkeeping for customers accurately and on time. Because of their importance, Jaqueline had tried to support them with a good work environment. She encouraged them to develop their skills by giving them time off from work to attend training programs and to take college classes. Because of the training, all of her employees had become very skilled at using computer systems for maintaining business records. However, it seemed that just as an employee got to the point where he or she was really doing a good job, the employee would be hired by a larger business paying higher wages or offering better benefits.

Jaqueline knew that as a small-business owner she would not be able to compete with the wages and benefits offered by larger businesses. She had hoped that the small-business work environment and the emphasis on training would help her retain employees. Now it seemed that she was the one paying the training costs for the larger businesses.

IMPORTANCE OF HUMAN RESOURCES

Human resources, the people who work for a business, are important to every business. In small businesses with only a few employees, the impact of one person can be very noticeable. Employees of small businesses are usually responsible for a number of activities. A customer who has a problem with an employee may not have the opportunity to work with another employee of the business.

In a small business, the owner may be the only manager, or in the owner's absence, an experienced employee may be responsible for managing the business. In this case, employees of the small business may be called on to make key decisions and to solve problems as they occur. The employees may be responsible for many of the duties often considered management tasks.

HUMAN RESOURCE NEEDS

Since employees are so important to the success of a small business, the owner must be skilled in human resource management. **Human resource management** ensures that needed employees

Illus. 41-1
Good employees are vital to the success of a small business.

are available, that they are productive, paid, and satisfied with their work. Human resource management begins by an employer analyzing where the business currently is in terms of staffing and where it wants to be.

Categorizing Human Resources

Staffing is a vital part of human resource management. The decision to hire people must be made carefully. Once an employee is hired, the person's salary must be paid whether the company is profitable or not. An employee should be hired when the work of the employee will contribute more to the company's profitability than it will cost. The owner must determine if the person hired will be permanent or temporary.

A **permanent employee** is one to whom the company makes a long-term commitment. It is expected the employee will continue to work for the business as long as the business is profitable and the employee's performance is satisfactory. A **temporary employee** is one hired for a specific time or to complete a specific assignment. Whether permanent or temporary, employees can be hired full-time or part-time. A **full-time employee** regularly works a schedule of 30 hours or more a week. A **part-time employee** works less than a full-time employee by working either fewer hours each day or fewer days each week.

Because permanent employees feel that they are a part of the business, they are often more motivated and productive than temporary employees.

Over 6 million small businesses have fewer than 10 employees. However, they account for less than 15 percent of the total U.S. work force.

Companies that supply temporary employees to other businesses make up one of the fastest growing U.S. industries. Large and small businesses are relying on temporary employees more than ever before.

However, the owner has more control over the company's resources when temporary employees are hired. The employee is paid only until the temporary assignment ends. Temporary employees are usually hired during a particularly busy time for the business or when a special task needs to be completed.

Determining Employee Qualifications

Before beginning the hiring process, the owner should study the work that must be completed in the business and compare the work requirements with the skills of the current employees. The goal is to hire people with skills that benefit the company but are not available from current employees.

There are two parts to the study of work requirements in preparation for hiring new employees. First, the current work of the business should be reviewed. Next, any new activities planned for the business should be considered. The business plan is a good source to identify those new activities. After completing the study, the owner will decide if a new employee is needed and the skills required of that person. At that time, it can be determined if the business's needs can be best met with temporary, permanent, part-time, or full-time employees.

Locating New Employees

Once the specific need and skill requirements are determined, prospective employees meeting the requirements must be located. If not done carefully, a great deal of time and expense may be required to complete the search and an appropriate employee may still not be found.

Young people and older people are frequently hired by small businesses. The first job many people hold in their working lives is in a small business. Also, people who have retired from full-time work and want to continue in part-time employment may be attracted to small businesses. The small business may provide a convenient work location, more flexibility in work schedules, and offer a pleasant place to work.

Another group of prospective employees are skilled people who want more decision-making responsibility, would like greater variety in their work, or prefer to work in a small organization.

Small businesses are considered the best place to prepare for a career in business. Employees learn a greater variety of skillls and are given more independence and responsibility sooner.

They are willing to work for less to obtain the benefits of a small company environment.

There are several good sources of prospective employees that small business owners should consider as identified in Figure 41-1. Sources should be used that will provide an adequate number of candidates for the position who have the skills required for the job and the interest in working for the business.

Hiring a New Employee

The hiring procedure used by new small businesses is often much less formal than that used by larger companies. Even though less time may be spent in the hiring process and the business owner may not be an expert in hiring procedures, care should be taken to gather specific information to determine if the applicant is qualified for the job. Figure 41-2 lists sources of information about the qualifications of job applicants.

NET FACTS

Unwanted Internet messages, particularly messages posted to E-mail mailing lists or USENET groups, are called *spam*. One annoying example of spam is sending unsolicited advertising to as many mailing lists as possible.

Figure 41-1

Business owners should be aware of several good sources to locate potential employees for their businesses.

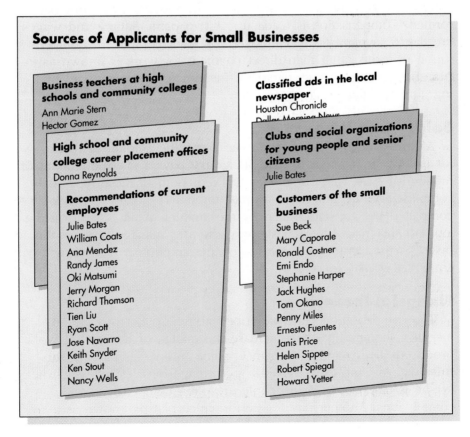

Sources of Applicants for Small Businesses

Business teachers at high schools and community colleges
Ann Marie Stern
Hector Gomez

High school and community college career placement offices
Donna Reynolds

Recommendations of current employees
Julie Bates
William Coats
Ana Mendez
Randy James
Oki Matsumi
Jerry Morgan
Richard Thomson
Tien Liu
Ryan Scott
Jose Navarro
Keith Snyder
Ken Stout
Nancy Wells

Classified ads in the local newspaper
Houston Chronicle
Dallas Morning News

Clubs and social organizations for young people and senior citizens
Julie Bates

Customers of the small business
Sue Beck
Mary Caporale
Ronald Costner
Emi Endo
Stephanie Harper
Jack Hughes
Tom Okano
Penny Miles
Ernesto Fuentes
Janis Price
Helen Sippee
Robert Spiegal
Howard Yetter

Applicant Qualifications	Information Sources
Business and technical knowledge and skills	• Transcripts • Grade reports • Teacher references • Employer references • Work samples
Communications and interpersonal skills	• Personal references • Interview • Role playing • Employer references
Attitude toward work and customers	• Interview • Employer references • Attendance records • Work history from resume
Work experience	• Resume • Employer references

Figure 41-2
Many information sources are available to small-business owners who want to learn more about job applicants.

COMPENSATION AND BENEFITS

One of the reasons people work is to earn money. **Compensation** is the amount of money paid to an employee for work performed. Compensation is made up of two parts. **Salary and wages** are direct payment to an employee for work completed. Compensation in forms other than direct payment for work is known as **benefits.** Examples of benefits are insurance, vacations, paid parking, and the like.

Salary and Wages

A **time wage** pays the employee a specific amount of money for each hour worked. A **straight salary** pays a specific amount of money for each week or month worked. Both of these types of compensation are not based on the amount or quality of work completed but are determined by the amount of time spent on the job. For that reason, it is a simple system to manage because the business just has to keep records on the amount of time each employee works.

Financial Incentives

The compensation plans described above do not provide an incentive for employees to increase the quality or quantity of work produced. To reward performance, some businesses pay a **commission.** An employee is paid a percentage of sales for which he or she is responsible. Salespeople are often compensated with commissions. Another pay for performance plan is known as a

piece rate. An employee receives a specific amount for each unit of work produced. Piece rates are most often used in factories and data processing centers.

Some companies use a base plus incentive compensation system. A **base plus incentive** system combines a wage or salary with an additional amount determined by the employee's performance. A type of base plus incentive plan is profit sharing. With **profit sharing,** employees receive their regular compensation plus a share of the profits earned by a company. This system encourages a commitment to the company, teamwork, and effective customer service so that profits will be high. Profit sharing provides a more direct work incentive in

Cultural Notes

The United States is now recognized as a "tossed salad" instead of a "melting pot." This modern term has surfaced because the United States recognizes and affirms the many cultural heritages in our population.

Ethical *Perspective*

Dishonest Hiring Practices

"Three years of previous experience in the industry required." "Must be energetic and eager." "Requires heavy lifting." Each of these statements is from employment advertisements.

Do the statements reflect important qualifications for a job? Or, are the requirements designed to eliminate certain people as job applicants? Lack of related work experience excludes many high school students and recent graduates. A requirement of energy or stamina might discourage older workers from applying. Women might avoid applying for a position when heavy lifting is a job requirement.

Bias can be eliminated through a careful study of job requirements. Owners must focus on the job and *not* on the type of person best qualified to fill the position. If the owner believes a female is most appropriate for the job, the requirements stated to fill the position will reflect that belief. If the owner considers a person who is physically challenged unsuitable for a job, applicants with handicaps will seldom be hired.

Small-business owners need to hire employees who are both skilled and motivated. An owner should avoid any employment practice that discourages or eliminates applicants who may actually be effective employees.

Critical Thinking

1 Are you familiar with employment advertisements that unfairly restrict the people who will be considered for employment? Why do you believe those requirements were included in the advertisement?

2 Do you believe that small-business owners should develop requirements for new positions that would attract a variety of potential applicants? Why or why not?

small companies than in large companies. The connection between individual performance and company success can be more easily understood.

Fringe Benefits

Fringe benefits can be an expensive addition to the cost of employee compensation. On average for all businesses, an additional 20 to 40 percent of an employee's wages is spent on benefits. If an employee earns $5.00 an hour, 30 percent added for fringe benefits increases the cost to $6.50 per hour. An employee earning $25,000 each year would actually be compensated $32,500.

Some benefits are required by state and federal law. Most new businesses must offer and pay costs of benefits including compensation for hours of overtime worked, Social Security, Medicare, and contributions to funds that pay for injuries to employees and for unemployed workers.

Full-time employees may expect companies to offer insurance plans including health, life, dental, and disability insurance. Many small businesses cannot afford the cost of all of those types of insurance. However, they may assist employees in purchasing insurance at lower rates through a group policy.

Time off for vacations is another popular benefit for employees. Paid vacations are an expensive benefit since employees are being paid for time when they will not be working. However, the time off may result in a more satisfied and productive employee. Many small businesses offer unpaid vacation time to most employees. Paid vacations are reserved as a benefit for those employees who have worked for the business for several years.

Small businesses seldom offer benefits to employees other than those required by law. Instead, small businesses attempt to attract and satisfy employees with non-financial benefits such as flexible schedules and work hours, a supportive work environment, and greater responsibility and involvement in decision making.

TRAINING AND DEVELOPMENT

New employees often receive training within a small business. Training materials and manuals can be purchased or can be developed by experienced employees. Experienced employees can also be given the assignment to work with new employees to help them learn and practice procedures. Many

n average, U.S. employees receive less than two days of training per year. Companies spend less than $100 per year on each employee.

employees enjoy the opportunity to provide training if they are given ample time to do it well. After the initial training is completed, the employee can become a coach for the new employee. Help is provided from time to time until the new employee is comfortable with the job.

When a new piece of equipment or a new procedure is added to a small business, many employees may need to receive training. The owner may hire a trainer and schedule training for a large number of employees at the same time. In this way, training is provided at a low cost for each employee.

Training is available from outside sources. High schools, community colleges, and universities offer short training programs, adult education classes, and advanced courses. The Small Business Administration sponsors seminars and classes and provides a variety of training materials through local offices. Equipment vendors and other businesses that sell products offer training to customers.

Illus. 41-2

Employee training is available from sources such as community colleges and universities.

Key Ideas

1 Employees can make a difference in the success or failure of a business. The impact of one person can be very noticeable in a small business with only a few employees.

2 Small-business owners should carefully determine the category of employee needed, study work requirements in preparation for hiring a new employee, search for people who meet a specific need or skill requirement, and then hire the qualified applicant.

3 Compensation and benefits include a salary or wages, financial incentives, and fringe benefits.

4 Sources of training within a small business include the owner or experienced employees. Other sources include trainers who conduct training sessions at the business site; training programs offered by schools and colleges; seminars, classes, and training materials available through the Small Business Administration; and equipment vendors or other businesses that sell products.

End of Chapter Activities

Increasing Your Business Vocabulary

For each numbered item, find the term that has the same meaning.

base plus incentive

benefits

commission

compensation

full-time employee

human resource management

human resources

part-time employee

permanent employee

piece rate

profit sharing

salary and wages

straight salary

temporary employee

time wage

1 Ensuring that needed employees are available, that they are productive, paid, and satisfied with their work.

2 The people who work for the business.

3 A specific amount of money paid for each week or month worked.

4 An employee who works a schedule of at least 30 hours a week.

5 A system that pays the employee a percentage of the sales for which he or she is responsible.

6 An employee that has a long-term commitment to a company.

7 A system that combines a small wage or salary with an additional amount determined by performance.

8 A compensation plan that pays the employee a specific amount for each unit of work produced.

9 An employee hired for a specific time or to complete a specific assignment.

10 An employee who works less than full-time employees by working either fewer hours each day or fewer days each week.

11 Direct payment to an employee for work completed.

12 Compensation in forms other than direct payment for work.

13 An incentive plan in which employees receive their regular compensation plus a share of the profits earned.

14 The amount of money paid to an employee for work performed.

15 A wage that pays the employee a specific amount of money for each hour worked.

Reviewing Your Reading

1 Of all the resources available to small businesses, which is the most important?

2 How is a permanent employee different from a temporary employee?

3 When are temporary employees generally hired?

4 A small-business owner must be careful to hire the best possible employees. What are some steps that can be taken before a person is hired to be sure the person is right for the job?

5 Why is it important for a small business to develop the right compensation program for employees?

6 What are some examples of benefits?

7 Why do companies implement profit-sharing plans?

8 What is an effective way for small businesses to train employees when a new procedure or a piece of new equipment is added?

9 If a business decides to train its employees outside the company, what sources of training are available?

Using Your Business Knowledge

1 In the opening scenario, Jacqueline Perez faces a problem common to many small businesses. What would you recommend to Ms. Perez that might discourage employees from leaving her business to join larger companies?

2 Lee Chan owns a coffee shop and has problems with poor employee performance. Employees do not appear to be interested in their work. Mr. Chan is worried that if something is not done, his regular customers will begin to leave the business. What are some ways that Mr. Chan can motivate his employees and encourage them to improve their performance?

3 Small-business owners may think they have to choose between hiring part-time and full-time employees. How can a business benefit by employing a combination of full-time and part-time employees?

4 Most small businesses cannot compete with large businesses on the level of salaries and wages paid to their employees. Suggest some types of inexpensive benefits that a small business could offer to attract and retain employees.

5 Training is important to businesses but can be very expensive. What are some ways that small businesses can improve the performance of employees without spending a great deal of money on training?

Calculating Business Problems

1 A small business budgets $95 per year to train each new employee. Last year the business employed 50 people and this year the business hired four additional employees.

  a. What was the total training budget for last year?

  b. How much will the budget increase this year?

  c. The owner of the company decides more training is needed and decides to increase the training budget by $5 per year. What would be the total training budget if the increase is included?

2 A local chamber of commerce research committee surveyed 207 business owners. They asked each of the owners to identify the greatest problem they faced with their employees. The table presents the responses given by the business owners.

Worked is performed slowly	68
Work is completed carelessly	54
Employee dishonesty	37
Poor service is provided to the customer	31
No problems with employees	19

  a. What is the percentage of the total responses represented by each of the categories of employee problems?

  b. What is the difference between the percentage of businesses reporting problems with employees working slowly and the percentage of businesses reporting no problems with employees?

  c. How many more businesses reported employee carelessness as a problem than those who reported they had no problems at all with employees?

3 Nicole Miller works for a store that uses an hourly wage plus commission compensation system. Her base rate is $4.25 an hour, and she earns a commission of 2 percent on all sales if sales are over $500 per day. She worked five days last week. Her hours worked and daily sales are shown in the table.

Monday	6 hrs	$ 735 total sales
Tuesday	4 hrs	$ 320 total sales
Wednesday	5 hrs	$ 570 total sales
Thursday	3 hrs	$ 450 total sales
Friday	0 hrs	
Saturday	8 hrs	$1,050 total sales

  a. How much did Nicole earn in base salary and commission for each of the days she worked?

  b. How much was the total of her base salary for the week?

  c. How much was the total of her commissions for the week?

  d. What were Nicole's total earnings for the week?

Applying Technology

Using the *Introduction to Business* template and your database program software, select problem CH41. After the problem appears on your screen, complete the following activities. Then, after you have completed each step, display or print a report for each activity. If you do not have a printer available, answer the questions before you leave the computer.

1 Select and list the employees that have database skills. How many employees are listed?

2 Select and list the employees that have spreadsheet skills. How many employees are listed?

3 Select and list the employees that have word processing skills. How many employees are listed?

Making Decisions

Serge Vahn was into his fifth year of the successful ownership of an auto parts store. However, the growth in sales and profits had all but ended in the fourth year. Serge was looking for ways to increase both and decided to change his compensation system. All salespeople were currently paid a straight wage ranging from the minimum wage for beginners to $9 an hour for experienced people. Serge wanted to try a commission system. Salespersons' earnings would be directly related to their sales. He believed that the new system would encourage them to increase sales.

When he introduced the idea to the salespeople, most were unhappy. They were worried their earnings would go up and down based on sales. They would never know how much they would make each week. Some also were concerned that salespeople would start pressuring customers to buy in order to earn commissions.

Serge assured them that on average the same amount would be earned. The better salespeople would get more money. If an employee did not make his or her current wages each week from commissions, Serge agreed that for the first six months the company would make up the difference. He assured salespeople that good selling did not require pressuring customers to buy.

1 Do you agree with Mr. Vahn's plan to change to a commission system in order to increase sales and the six-month period to implement the change? Why or why not?

2 What steps can Mr. Vahn take to avoid having salespeople pressure customers into buying?

Chapter Forty-Two

Key Terms

custom manufacturing

mass production

processing

marketing concept

target market

marketing mix

product

distribution

promotion

pricing

Producing and Marketing Goods and Services

Objectives

After studying this chapter and completing the end-of-chapter activities, you will be able to:

1 Describe basic production and manufacturing processes.

2 List common marketing activities and define the marketing concept.

3 Explain the two steps in marketing planning.

4 Explain the advantage of small businesses in providing customer service.

Allan was sitting on the floor listening to music and working on his homework when his mother walked in. "Allan, I know it's your room but you have to find a place for your CDs. They are always all over the room."

Allan knew she was right. He owned nearly 100 CDs in his collection. He had stepped on a few and broken the cases and could never find the CD he wanted. He also liked to listen to CDs in the car but never had the right ones with him.

The next day in his computer design class he decided to develop a solution to the CD storage problem. After a week of hard work, he had developed a model for a collapsible plastic holder for 20 CDs. When unfolded, it formed a pyramid shape that could be placed on a shelf or hung on the wall. When folded, it formed a cube with a carrying handle. He showed the holder to his teacher and several other students. All were excited with the design and encouraged him to develop and sell it. Now Allan had to determine how the CD holder could be produced and marketed.

MANUFACTURING AND PRODUCTION PROCESSES

The businesses that develop products are producers and manufacturers. Producers develop products using natural resources and other materials (such as farming), or obtain raw materials from the environment (such as mining). Manufacturers convert raw materials or partially processed materials into finished products.

Many small businesses are involved in all types of production and manufacturing. Raising animals and crops on farms, tree production, lumbering, fishing, and mining are examples of small-business producers. In addition, small manufacturers design furniture and computers, build houses and office buildings, and print books and magazines.

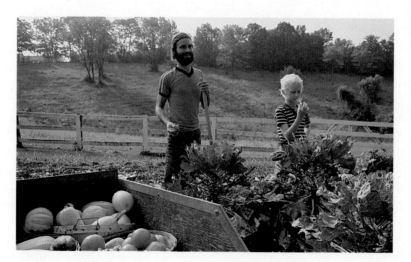

Illus. 42-1
A family farm is one example of small business production.

NET FACTS

Combining your telephone, computer, and television, future supernetworks will expand the power of the Internet and its successors. You will be able to talk to your computer and television, order movies on demand, and play computer and video games with partners across the world.

Types of Manufacturing

Manufacturing businesses can be organized in several ways to produce products. Building a specific and unique product to meet the needs of one customer is done with **custom manufacturing.** Custom home builders work with each buyer to build a unique home. Products ranging from golf courses to dentures are specifically developed to meet particular design standards.

Mass production has been the standard of U.S. manufacturing for almost a century and has spread throughout the world. With **mass production,** a large number of identical products are assembled using a continuous, efficient procedure. Mass production brings to mind automobile assembly lines or large numbers of beverage bottles traveling along a conveyor system to be filled. It's harder to imagine small businesses using mass production. However, small businesses use mass production to produce automobile accessories, clothing, office supplies, and computer parts.

Processing is a third type of manufacturing. **Processing** changes the form of materials so they can be consumed or used to manufacture other products. Crude oil is refined through processing to form gasoline and other petroleum products. Petroleum products are combined to form plastics used by many manufacturers. Grain is processed into flour, cereal, and feed for animals. Film processors convert the film from your camera into pictures.

Product Development

Time and money are needed to set up a manufacturing process. A production facility is needed, materials must be available, equipment purchased, and employees hired and trained. Even when products have been successfully produced, the company will not receive any money until the products are sold. If all products are not sold or if they cost more to produce than customers are willing to pay, the company will lose money.

Whether a new business is being formed to manufacture a product or an older business is deciding to produce a new product, a careful procedure is followed. Figure 42-1 shows the product development steps.

For a new business, product development is different than for a manufacturer that has operated for

Small businesses have an advantage in custom manufacturing because they work with fewer customers and can be more flexible in product design.

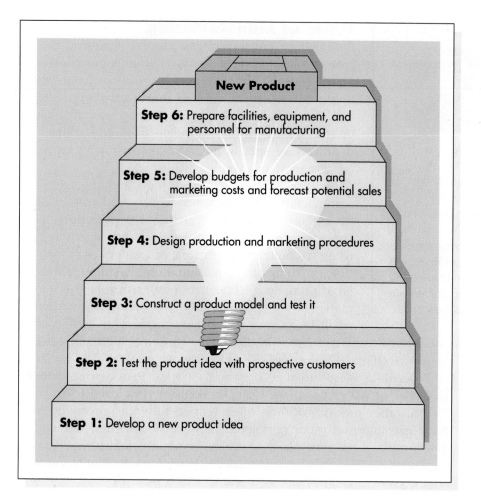

Figure 42-1
Careful planning is needed to develop a successful new product.

New Product

Step 6: Prepare facilities, equipment, and personnel for manufacturing

Step 5: Develop budgets for production and marketing costs and forecast potential sales

Step 4: Design production and marketing procedures

Step 3: Construct a product model and test it

Step 2: Test the product idea with prospective customers

Step 1: Develop a new product idea

several years and is already producing several products. Allan, whom we met in the scenario at the beginning of the chapter, does not have a building or equipment to produce his new CD holder. Even if he determines the product can be produced profitably, it would take some time and a great deal of money to start a manufacturing business. It would be difficult to justify the cost of everything needed to operate the business when there is only one product to produce.

An existing business may already have the resources needed. This business will just need to modify procedures to accommodate a new product. Allan may try to locate an existing manufacturer to produce all of the parts needed for the CD holder.

In a recent survey of customers about quality service in retail stores, the highest rated item was being able to complete shopping in a timely way. Waiting in checkout lines was identified as the greatest time waster.

He can then assemble the parts into the finished product. Or he may decide to have another company complete the entire production process and he will be responsible for marketing activities.

EFFECTIVE MARKETING

Marketing is the most visible business activity in the eyes of consumers yet is often the most misunderstood. As a consumer, you are involved with marketing almost every day. When you use a coupon to reduce the price of a product, decide to pick up a product at a store rather than pay for delivery, or choose to pay with a credit card rather than cash, you have made a marketing decision.

Some people have a negative and narrow view of marketing. When you hear the term *marketing,* do you think of loud advertising or pushy salespeople? That view is held by many consumers but also by some businesspeople who do not understand marketing. Effective marketing includes both a broad set of activities and a philosophy.

Marketing Activities

Marketing includes all of the activities involved in the exchange of products and services between a business and its customers. Figure 42-2 lists the common marketing activities. As you can see,

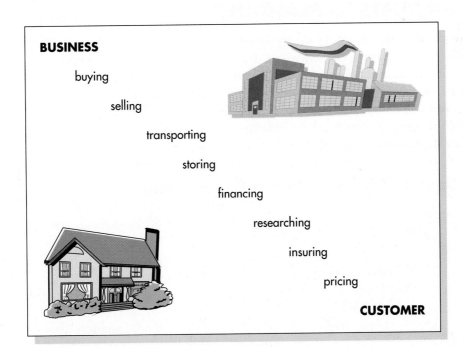

BUSINESS

buying

selling

transporting

storing

financing

researching

insuring

pricing

CUSTOMER

Figure 42-2

Many marketing activities must be completed as products and services move between businesses and their customers.

marketing is much more than advertising and selling. In fact, if the other marketing activities are not completed, advertising and selling will not be successful.

A Marketing Philosophy

For many years, business owners did not consider marketing to be important. Owners believed that if they offered the right products, customers would find and purchase the product. However, when consumers have many choices of products available from a number of sources, a business may have difficulty selling its products.

While manufacturing is a difficult industry to enter, six of the top ten new small businesses in a recent year were manufacturers. Three manufactured computer components, two produced environmental control equipment, and one manufactured bar code labels.

Successful businesses have adopted a philosophy of marketing. This philosophy incorporates the marketing concept. The **marketing concept** directs all marketing activities at profitably satisfying customer needs. Businesses engage in studies to determine what satisfies and dissatisfies customers. Their feelings about competing products are also assessed. Then these businesses try to meet customers' needs with appropriate products and marketing activities.

MARKETING PLANNING

Using marketing to satisfy customers is a two-step process. Before marketing activities can be planned, the business needs to identify the customers to be served. One of the mistakes many businesses make is to assume that everyone will want to buy their products. Not everyone can be satisfied with the same product. Therefore, the first step in effective marketing is to identify a specific group of customers known as a target market.

Target Markets and Marketing Mixes

A **target market** is a group of consumers with very similar needs to whom a company can sell its products. Businesses carefully study consumers, their wants and needs, and their previous experiences with products and services to identify the best target markets. Good target markets have needs that are currently not well satisfied and have the money as well as the authority to make purchase decisions.

After a target market has been identified and information about those consumers has been gathered, the second step in marketing

Illus. 42-2

A target market is a group of consumers with similar needs.

can be completed. Target market information is used to develop a marketing mix. A **marketing mix** is the blending of four marketing elements to satisfy a target market. The four marketing elements are the product, distribution, promotion, and pricing.

Product is anything offered to the target market to satisfy their needs, including physical products and services. It can include the actual product, accessories and options, the brand name, and the product's package.

Distribution includes the locations and methods used to make products and services available to customers. When planning distribution, a business must decide where to locate as well as the layout of the building. In addition, other businesses involved in distributing the products, the methods of distribution, storage, and product handling are determined.

Promotion includes the methods and information communicated to customers to encourage purchases and increase their satisfaction. The common methods of promotion are advertising, selling, sales promotion, product displays, and publicity.

Pricing is the method of increasing the value of the product to customers and the actual amount they pay. Besides setting a product price, pricing includes determining if credit will be accepted, types and amounts of discounts, when to schedule sales, and many other decisions.

On average, companies spend much less than 50 percent of their total marketing budgets on advertising and selling. Even large companies that spend millions of dollars on advertising spend much more on other marketing activities.

Marketing for Small Businesses

Many small-business owners believe that they can never compete with large businesses. Large businesses have many products and services, access to a number of distribution strategies, and can hire the best advertising agencies to plan their promotion. In addition, when faced with competition, it seems like large businesses readily cut their prices to attract customers.

Target marketing provides a tool to small businesses so they can compete with large businesses. You can probably identify some products and services you purchase from large companies and others that you buy from small businesses. You shop the small business when it provides what you need, such as convenience or more personalized service.

Allan must recognize that many other businesses produce and sell CD holders. He may have a unique design that will be attractive to some customers. However, it must be made available at a

Cultural *Perspective*

Native American Enterprise

In Western European cultures, entrepreneurship is based on capitalism. Individual ownership of business and the accumulation of wealth are valued. Resources are used to expand the wealth of the owner.

Native Americans have held a very different view of enterprise. Historically, land for raising crops, hunting territories, and rivers for fishing were collectively owned and used by a village or an extended family. Economic production (hunting, fishing, and agriculture) was not aimed at personal gain.

In contrast to economic production leading to personal gain, the well-being of the village or community guided the work of Native Americans. Wealth was looked upon as a sign of individual greed. Prestige was not granted to the richest people in the community. Social status was gained by demonstrations of generosity.

Today's *consumer cooperatives* reflect the economic principles espoused by Native Americans. Consumer cooperatives are user-owned retail outlets for goods and services. They range from rural electric companies and credit unions to

retail clothing and food stores. These nonprofit cooperatives are organized for the purpose of providing economic services to members who own and control them. Members of cooperatives are often concerned about the well-being of the family and community.

Critical Thinking

1 *What types of today's business organizations reflect the economic roots of Native American culture?*

2 *Can you think of examples of cooperatives in your community?*

competitive (not necessarily the lowest) price. Since it is new, prospective customers must be able to find it. It must have clear instructions so customers will be confident it is easy to assemble and use and will be durable. He will not be able to sell his CD holder to everyone in the market. However, he may be able to identify a target market with unique needs that are not well satisfied with current products.

CUSTOMER SERVICE

A major complaint of consumers today is the quality of service they receive from businesses. Customers expect effective service when they are gathering information about products, while they are buying the product, and after the purchase.

Small businesses have an advantage over many larger businesses when providing customer service. They have fewer customers, so they have the opportunity to know each customer better. Customers usually deal directly with the business and often with the business owner. They do not have to go through several levels of personnel to get answers to their questions. Employees often are very loyal to the business and want it to be successful. They will work very hard to satisfy customers.

Small-business owners need to recognize the importance of service to their customers and identify the services customers expect. Then they must train employees to provide services effectively and pleasantly. The owner needs to be sure that adequate numbers of employees are available to deliver the services when and where customers want them.

A *training and development manager's* duties include:
- Planning, organizing, and directing a wide range of training activities
- Conducting orientation sessions and arranging on-the-job training for new employees
- Conducting surveys to determine training needs
- Preparing training materials and organizing facilities and equipment needed for training
- Evaluating the effectiveness of training.

Key Ideas

1 Producers develop products using natural resources and other materials while manufacturers convert raw materials or partially processed materials into finished products. The three types of manufacturing are custom manufacturing, mass production, and processing.

2 The common marketing activities completed by businesses are buying, selling, transporting, storing, financing, researching, insuring, and pricing. Effective marketing attempts to satisfy customer needs profitably.

3 Marketing planning starts by identifying a target market to serve. Then a marketing mix is developed to determine the best product, distribution, promotion, and price.

4 Small businesses have fewer customers; therefore, the needs of customers are better known and customers have a better opportunity to get answers to their questions directly from the owner.

End of Chapter Activities

Increasing Your Business Vocabulary

The following terms should become part of your business vocabulary. For each numbered item, find the term that has the same meaning.

custom manufacturing

distribution

marketing concept

marketing mix

mass production

pricing

processing

promotion

product

target market

1 The methods and information communicated to customers to encourage purchases and increase their satisfaction.

2 Changing the form of materials so they can be consumed or used to manufacture other products.

3 The locations and methods used to make products and services available to customers.

4 Directing all marketing activities at profitably satisfying customer needs.

5 A group of consumers with very similar needs to whom a company can sell its products.

6 The methods of increasing the value of the product to consumers and the actual amount they pay.

7 Building a specific and unique product to meet the needs of one customer.

8 Anything offered to the target market to satisfy needs including physical products and services.

9 The blending of four marketing elements to satisfy a target market.

10 A large number of identical products are assembled using a continuous, efficient procedure.

Reviewing Your Reading

1 In addition to marketing, what is another important business function?

2 What are the three types of manufacturing used by businesses?

3 Why, for many years, did businesses believe that marketing wasn't an important activity?

4 What are the two steps in using marketing to satisfy the customer?

5 Name the four marketing elements used to satisfy a target market.

6 Why might customers choose to buy the things they need at a small business rather than a large business?

7 Name some reasons small businesses have an advantage over many larger businesses when providing customer service.

Using Your Business Knowledge

1 Examine the opening scenario with Allan and his CD collection. If he decided to create a business with his CD holder idea, would he be considered a retailer, wholesaler, or manufacturer? Justify your answer.

2 Name a small business in your area that uses mass production. Explain how mass production helps this business to be successful.

3 Marketing is important in creating a successful business. Select a familiar business in your commu-

nity. Identify the target market of the business. Also identify the four marketing elements used to satisfy the target market you named.

4 Effective customer service depends on the person providing the service. Janet Diaz owns a local bathroom accessory store and feels that some of her employees are not providing adequate customer service. Name some ways that she can help her employees improve the level of their customer service.

Calculating Business Problems

1 A local business magazine printed a report that examined the most prevalent categories of small businesses in your community. The information in the report (see the table) described the major activity of the 259 businesses in the community and the percentage of each category that are small businesses.

a. Of the total number of businesses in the community, how many are in each category?

	Percent of Total Businesses	Percent that are Small Businesses
Wholesalers	7	35
Retailers	25	68
Manufacturers	18	24
Service providers	46	84
Combination of types	4	5

b. What is the total number of small businesses in the community and how many small businesses are in each category?

2 Teens make up a large potential target market for many businesses because they have very important and unique needs. A local clothing store wanted to see how much of their monthly sales of $65,759 is the result of teen spending. Every time a teen bought some merchandise, the store asked the customer to fill out a brief questionnaire. Of the 376 responses, the figures in the table show how much the teens spent on specific items.

Items	Money Spent
Jeans	$12,820
Shirts	$ 7,870
Shorts	$ 5,250
Pants	$ 3,120
Sweaters	$ 1,090
Socks	$ 890

a. What is the total monthly sales to teenage customers?

b. What percentage of the total monthly sales is due to teens?

c. Create a pie chart that illustrates the percentage of the total sales spent by teens for each of the items.

3 A restaurant distributes comment cards on every table so customers can identify positive and negative experiences with employees. After one month, the owner read all of the cards. Of the total comments, 58 percent were positive and 42 percent were negative. The owner categorized the negative experiences into categories shown in the table and totaled the number of cards for each.

Negative Experience	No. of Comments
Employee did not seem interested in serving me	90
Service took too long	68
Employee was not familiar with the menu	38
Employee couldn't make a decision to solve a problem	30
Employee didn't follow up after a problem was identified	15
No specific reasons given	10

a. What is the percentage of total negative complaints for each category?

b. How many more customers complained about employees' lack of interest than the lack of follow-up after a problem was identified?

c. How many more customers provided comments on positive experiences than on negative experiences in the restaurant?

Applying Technology

Using the *Introduction to Business* template and your database program software, select problem CH42. After the problem appears on your screen, complete the following activities. Then, after you have completed each step, display or print a report for each activity. If you do not have a printer available, answer the questions before you leave the computer.

1 Sort the database in descending order by price. Answer the following questions:

   a. Which item of merchandise has the highest price?

   b. Which item of merchandise has the second to lowest price?

2 Select and list the items of merchandise that have a cost greater than $10. How many items are listed?

3 Sort the database in ascending order by stock number. Answer the following questions:

   a. What is the third item of merchandise listed?

   b. What is the last item of merchandise listed?

Making Decisions

Ariel McKinnsey had always liked woodworking. After completing high school where he spent two years in the construction trades program, he went to work for a local contractor. Over a ten year career, he became an expert cabinet maker. He became well known in the community for high quality, uniquely designed kitchen and bathroom cabinets. He took pride in building the best cabinets possible. When his employer won contracts to install cabinets in new homes, many customers would ask that Ariel be the person assigned to design and help build the cabinets.

Recently, Ariel's boss presented a problem. He indicated the prices of wood products were increasing rapidly and customers were looking for ways to cut costs. Using mass produced cabinets was one solution to the problem. He wanted Ariel to design two styles of cabinets that could then be mass produced by less experienced employees. Mass production of two high quality styles would cut costs. Ariel was not happy with the new idea. He enjoyed the chance to design each set of cabinets for customers. He believed his cabinets were worth the cost of a custom design.

1 Do you agree that mass production can reduce the costs while maintaining the quality of the cabinets? Why or why not?

2 How does the concept of target marketing enter into the decision that needs to be made by the owner?

Chapter Forty-Three

Key Terms

business budget

start-up budget

operating budget

cash budget

financial records

financial statements

income statement

Maintaining Financial Information

Objectives

After studying this chapter and completing the end-of-chapter activities, you will be able to:

1 Identify common sources of financial information for new and established small businesses.

2 Describe the three types of business budgets.

3 Describe the primary financial records needed to manage a small business.

4 Describe the financial statements used by business owners for decision making.

Envision yourself as a small-business owner. One of the constant problems you would face is financing. From the first day that you develop an idea for a business, financing questions must be addressed. The following questions are often asked when you initially plan a business: How much money will it take to start the business? Where will the money come from?

Once a business is open, financing becomes a more immediate concern for you. Few businesses are profitable in the first year. Therefore, you must determine how to obtain enough money to operate the business until it becomes profitable. Several important questions must be answered at this time: How will expenses be paid until the business becomes profitable? What can be done to increase income and reduce expenses?

Even successful small businesses must be concerned about finances. Bills must be paid. Worn out equipment must be replaced. A growing business may need larger facilities, and more employees may need to be hired. As an experienced small-business owner, you will regularly ask these questions: Is the business staying profitable? What expenses must be planned for in order to maintain operations? Will an expansion generate more sales? Will the business be more profitable after a planned expansion?

FINANCIAL PLANNING

In the previous unit, you studied personal financial planning and you learned about budgets. Budgets provide detailed plans for the financial needs of individuals, families, and businesses. A **business budget** has two purposes:

1. to anticipate sources and amounts of income, and

2. to predict the types and amounts of expenses for a specific business activity or the entire business.

If you owned your own small business, the money that you would receive is called *income*. The word *revenue* is often used in place of the word income. The words mean the same. To operate your own business, you will also have expenses. *Expenses* are the costs of operating a business. The business owner must be able to identify and predict the amount of each source of income and each type of expense. In addition, the owner will need to determine when each expense must be paid and when income will be received. To determine financial needs, businesses use the basic financial equation shown in Figure 43-1.

After several years of operation, the task of identifying sources of income and types of expenses will not be difficult. The primary source of that information is the financial records of the business. However, financial planning is difficult for a new business. No financial records exist to serve as a guidepost. Other sources of information must be

New business owners seldom earn a salary during the first year or two. They must rely on savings or a second job until the business earns a profit.

Figure 43-1

In order to make a profit, the revenue of a business must be greater than its expenses. The basic equation is Revenue − Expenses = Profit (or loss).

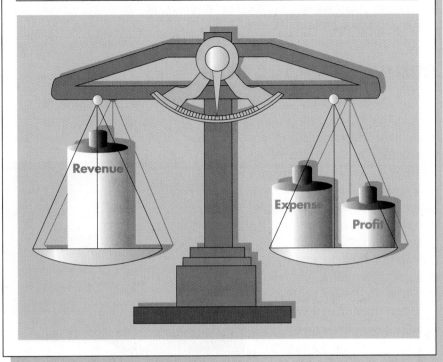

The Basic Financial Equation

used. The Small Business Administration (SBA) provides a number of planning tools for new small businesses. Among those tools are guides to developing a budget, and financial information that will help the new business owner anticipate the amount of revenue and the expenses.

Another source of information is private businesses that collect and publish financial information on similar businesses and industries. Examples of those companies are Dun and Bradstreet, Value Line, and Standard and Poor. Some information is available from business magazines and newspapers including *Fortune, Forbes, Entrepreneur, Black Enterprise*, and *The Wall Street Journal*. Professional associations, such as the National Federation of Independent Business and the National Retail Merchants Association, offer resources to assist with financial planning.

A new franchise will typically receive help with financial planning from the franchisor and may even have a complete beginning budget provided. New

NET FACTS

A Uniform Resource Locator (URL) is an address code for finding hypertext or hypermedia documents on World Wide Web (WWW) servers around the world. URLs can be accessed by WWW Browsers.

businesses working with a bank or other financial institution can obtain information and support there. Franchisors and financial institutions want to see businesses succeed, so they will encourage careful financial planning.

BUDGET PREPARATION

The most important step in financial planning is developing a budget. A budget can be compared to the use of a road map when you are traveling to an unfamiliar location. Without the map, you will have little idea of where you are and where you are going while you travel. If you take a wrong turn, you will have a difficult time knowing your mistake or how to get back to the correct road without the map. In the same way, a budget identifies where a business is going and allows the owner to determine whether the business is making progress toward its financial destination.

Types of Budgets

A large business that has operated for several years may have many specialized budgets. Each manager will be responsible for one or more budgets in his or her area of operations. For a new small business, however, three budgets are essential. They are the start-up budget, the operating budget, and the cash budget.

The **start-up budget** plans income and expenses from the beginning of the business until it becomes profitable. Most new businesses require expenditures of thousands and even hundreds of thousands of dollars in order to open. Buildings and equipment must be purchased or leased. Inventory, supplies, and materials are needed. Employees will be hired who must be paid. Expenses for utilities, licenses, advertising, transportation, and the like, will be incurred before the company begins to sell its products and services.

Money to pay for these expeditures must be contributed by the owner(s) or borrowed from banks or other sources. Financial institutions will want to see a detailed start-up budget before lending money to a new business.

The **operating budget** describes the financial plan for the day-to-day operations of the business. The operating budget is usually planned for six months or a year. This budget follows the basic financial equation. All revenues and expenses are listed and the planned net income (or loss) for the time period is shown.

Every new business needs a cash budget. A **cash budget** is an estimate of the actual money received and paid out for a specific time period. A cash budget anticipates that cash will come into a business and that cash will be paid out during each week or month of operation.

Steps in Budgeting

In a small business, the budgeting goals are much the same as in a household—to determine what the sources of income are and how income will be distributed. The budgeting process involves four fundamental steps. Those steps are listed in Figure 43-2.

Several skills are needed by the person responsible for preparing business budgets. Budgeting requires an understanding of

Figure 43-2

Careful preparation of a budget will result in a good guide for financial decisions.

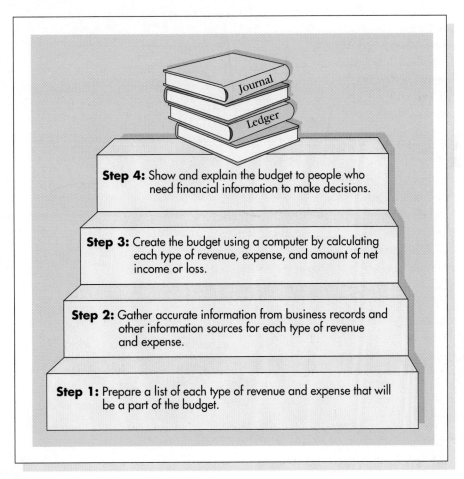

Step 4: Show and explain the budget to people who need financial information to make decisions.

Step 3: Create the budget using a computer by calculating each type of revenue, expense, and amount of net income or loss.

Step 2: Gather accurate information from business records and other information sources for each type of revenue and expense.

Step 1: Prepare a list of each type of revenue and expense that will be a part of the budget.

financial information, computer skills, basic mathematical abilities, and effective communications skills. New small-business owners often seek the help of an accountant or banker when preparing a budget for the first time.

FINANCIAL RECORDS

Budgets identify the financial plans of business. To determine if those plans have been achieved, financial records are needed. **Financial records** are used to record and analyze the financial performance of a business.

All successful businesses maintain accurate financial records. Several types of financial records are maintained by small businesses. Among the records commonly maintained to document the performance of a business are:

Global *Perspective*

Franchising Around the World

Franchising has become a popular form of international business. An estimated 400 U.S. franchisors have international operations. The number of actual franchise locations worldwide is approaching 50,000. The most common international franchises are restaurants. Other successful franchises are automobile rentals, hotels, and retail stores.

The most popular international location for U.S. franchised companies is Canada. Nearly 30 percent of all international franchise outlets are located there. Twenty-six per-

cent are in Japan, followed by the European continent with 14 percent; Australia and the United Kingdom, 9 percent each; and Asian locations, 6 percent. The remaining 7 percent of franchise outlets are located throughout the world.

One of the strengths of franchises in the United States has been a consistent product and image. Customers who shop one franchise location can expect to find the same products and services at any other location of the same franchise they visit. However, international franchisors have learned a valuable lesson. Some of the elements that work in the United States are successful in

other countries. However, changes often need to be made to meet local tastes and expectations. For example, many 7-Elevens in Japan have a barrel from which fresh fish are sold.

Critical Thinking

1 Most small-business owners are reluctant to sell products in other countries. Why are franchisors much more interested in international business operations?

2 How can a franchisor interested in opening outlets in other countries determine whether changes need to be made in the operations of the franchise?

- *Cash records* that list all cash receipts and disbursements.

- *Records of accounts* that identify all credit purchases and sales. (An *accounts payable* record identifies the companies from which credit purchases were made; an *accounts receivable* record identifies customers that made credit purchases.)

- *Inventory records* that identify the type and quantity of products available for sale. (Adequate records are essential to the control and security of inventory items.)

- *Payroll records* that contain information on all employees of the company and their earnings.

- *Asset records* that identify the buildings and equipment owned by the business, their original and current value, and the amount owed if money was borrowed to purchase the assets.

Cultural Notes

Cultural diversity in the United States has played an important role in business development. For example, the number of ethnic restaurants has increased because of the various immigrants that have come to the United States. These restaurants have provided success for the owners and employment for many workers.

In the past, the preparation and maintenance of financial records was both an expensive and time-consuming process. Few new business owners were skilled in record keeping. Usually, a business would hire an accountant to set up a record keeping system and then employ a part-time bookkeeper to maintain the records.

The age of personal computers has made financial record keeping much more efficient and accurate. Complete computerized accounting systems can be purchased at a low cost for small businesses. The systems include all the financial records needed. The computer software will complete the necessary calculations and prepare financial reports. A business owner or employee with understanding of basic accounting concepts and computer skills can now maintain accurate records for the business.

Illus. 43-2

The age of personal computers has made financial record keeping more efficient and accurate.

FINANCIAL STATEMENTS

Financial statements are reports that summarize the financial performance of a business. When used in a business, the *balance sheet* lists the assets, liabilities, and owner's equity (or capital). The balance sheet is normally prepared every six months or once a year. The **income statement** reports the revenues, expenses, and net income or loss from business operations for a specific period of time. *Net income* is derived when income is greater than expenses. A *net loss* occurs when expenses are greater than income. Income statements are often prepared every month in a new business and at least every six

People who have made personal financial planning a part of their lives are often more successful as small business owners.

Figure 43-3
Balance sheets and income statements are used by business owners to analyze financial performance. These financial statements are for a sole proprietorship that is a service business.

Majestic Cleaners
Balance Sheet
December 31, 19--

Assets		Liabilities	
Cash	$22,500	Accounts Payable**	$22,800
Accounts Receivable*	19,050	Note Payable***	18,500
Supplies	12,800	Loan Payable****	16,250
Equipment	26,250	Total Liabilities	$57,550
		Owner's Equity	
		Andre Adams, Capital	$23,050
		Total Liabilities and	
Total Assets	$80,600	Owner's Equity	$80,600

*   Used for charge sales; shows the total amount due from customers.
**   Other businesses owed money for supplies purchased.
*** Money borrowed from a bank to start the business.
****Money borrowed from a bank to purchase equipment.

Majestic Cleaners
Income Statement
For the Period Ended December 31, 19--

Operating Revenue		
Cash Sales	$ 9,854	
Charge Sales	14,781	
Total Operating Revenue		$24,635
Operating Expenses		
Salaries and Wages	$12,600	
Advertising	820	
Rent	4,600	
Utilities	1,640	
Supplies	1,055	
Other	410	
Total Operating Expenses		21,125
Net Income		$ 3,510

months in established businesses. Examples of the two financial statements for a small business are shown in Figure 43-3.

Business owners review financial statements carefully to determine how their businesses are performing. Since the statements summarize financial performance for a specific time, the owner can compare the performance of the current time period with the performance of last month or last year. If net income is increasing, the owner will want to maintain and improve performance if possible. On the other hand, if expenses are increasing but not revenues, the owner will want to determine the reasons for the problem and make changes to improve performance.

In addition to comparing financial performance from one time period to another, the owner will want to make comparisons with similar businesses. A business that is less profitable than similar businesses, or with lower sales or higher expenses, may have difficulty competing.

Key Ideas

1 Common sources of financial information for established businesses are financial records. For businesses with limited or no previous financial information, the SBA provides planning tools. Private businesses also collect and publish financial information on similar businesses. A new franchise gets help from the franchisor.

2 Three types of business budgets are the start-up budget, the operating budget, and the cash budget.

3 Common financial records maintained in small businesses are records of cash, credit accounts, inventory, payroll, and assets.

4 Balance sheets and income statements are used to compare financial performance.

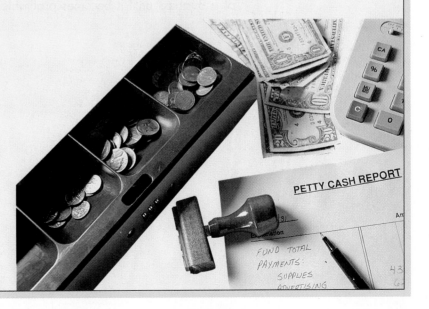

End of Chapter Activities

Increasing Your Business Vocabulary

The following terms should become part of your business vocabulary. For each numbered item, find the term that has the same meaning.

business budget

cash budget

financial records

financial statement

income statement

operating budget

start-up budget

1 An estimate of the actual money received and paid out for a specific time period.

2 A planning tool used to anticipate sources and amounts of income and to predict the types and amounts of expenses for a specific business activity or the entire business.

3 Reports that summarize the financial performance of a business.

4 Used to record and analyze the financial performance of a business.

5 Describes the financial plan for the day-to-day operations of a business.

6 Reports the revenue, expenses, and net income or loss of a business for a specific period of time.

7 Used to plan income and expenses from the beginning of a business until it becomes profitable.

Reviewing Your Reading

1 What four key questions should be asked when deciding how to make effective financial planning decisions?

2 Why do business owners prepare budgets?

3 Why is it hard for new small businesses to do financial planning?

4 What is the most important step in financial planning?

5 Name the three essential budgets for a new business.

6 What skills are needed by the person preparing business budgets?

7 Budgets identify the financial plans of a business. What determines the financial performance of a business?

8 Bookkeeping was once a tedious job that required a business to keep accurate records by hand. What has replaced traditional bookkeeping methods?

9 What are the two most used financial statements?

Using Your Business Knowledge

1 Few businesses are profitable in the first year, so financial planning is very important. How might an owner obtain enough money to operate the business until it becomes profitable?

2 Why is it essential for a business to have a budget, and how will that budget help the business in the years to come?

3 An inventory record is needed to determine the type and quantity of products available for sale. If this type of record is not kept accurately, what can happen to a business?

4 Accurate financial records and budgets must be kept to make good financial decisions. How can a business owner ensure that the records and budgets are accurate?

5 Why are financial statements so important to business owners when they make decisions?

Calculating Business Problems

1   Lee Chan has owned a video business for three years. The first year Mr. Chan barely earned a profit. The next year's profit was more substantial. As shown in the table, he has just received the financial results from the third year and wants to compare them to those of the second year of operations.

	Last Year	This Year
Rent	$28,000	$28,000
Sales	$78,250	$80,725
Inventory (cost of videos)	$15,000	$13,750
Wages and salaries	$17,850	$18,210
Utilities	$10,010	$ 7,075
Supplies and materials	$ 1,020	$ 2,020

a.   How much money did Mr. Chan earn this year? last year?

b.   What was his total cost of doing business this year? last year?

c.   What profit or loss did Mr. Chan earn this year?

d.   What is the difference in profit between this year and last year?

---

2   The basic financial equation is as follows:

Revenue – Expenses = Net Income (or Loss)

For the following problems, calculate the missing amounts based on the financial equation:

a. $27,532 Revenue – $_____ Expenses = $17,820 Profit

b. $_____ Revenue – $28,210 Expenses = $17,023 Loss

c. $20,210 Revenue – $10,132 = $_____ Profit/Loss

d. $23,720 Revenue – $32,017 Expenses = $_____ Profit/Loss

---

3   The list in the table identifies items found on a balance sheet. For each item, decide whether it is an asset or liability. Then figure the total for assets, liabilities, and owner's equity (or capital).

Cash	$12,500
Accounts payable (trade credit)	$27,140
Accounts receivable	$18,750
Loan payable (bank)	$ 7,438
Inventory (goods on hand)	$31,270
Equipment	$ 8,653

Applying Technology

Using the *Introduction to Business* template and your spreadsheet program software, select problem CH43. After the problem appears on your screen, complete the following activities. Then, after you have completed each step, display or print the completed spreadsheet for each activity. If you do not have a printer available, answer the questions before you leave the computer.

1 In the Percent column, enter formulas to show each item as a percentage of Total Estimated Sales. Format the results as percentages with one decimal place. Answer the following questions:

a. What is the percentage of Total Estimated Sales budgeted for Salaries and Wages?

b. What is the percentage of Total Estimated Sales budgeted for Utilities?

2 In the Difference column, enter formulas to calculate Actual minus Budget. Format the results as cur-

rency with two decimal places. Answer the following questions:

a. How many expenditures had actual spending greater than budget?

b. Which expenditure from Question (a) has the largest difference?

3 What if your actual Sales increased to $35,000? Copy the budget from Activity 2 to another part of the spreadsheet. Enter the new amount of actual Sales. Answer the following questions:

a. What is the new difference between actual Total Operating Expenses and budgeted Total Operating Expenses?

b. What is the new amount of actual Net Income?

Optional: Using the spreadsheet from Activity 2, create a bar chart comparing budgeted expenditures to actual expenditures. Repeat for Activity 3.

Making Decisions

Tyrone Anderson turned his hobby into a baseball card business. Tyrone began his business with a small loan from the bank and money saved from working while in college. The business grew steadily each year. By preparing a specific budget at the beginning of each year, Mr. Anderson was able to spend his money wisely on new inventory and improvements to his store.

This year he used the same budgeting process that he had implemented the past four years. He estimated that sales would increase 8 percent, so he planned to increase expenses accordingly. The budget projected another nice profit. The first two months of the year went well. Then the economy suddenly slipped into a recession that continued through the rest of the year. Customers cut back on their spending at his store. Tyrone's sales declined but his expenses continued to increase.

1 Why did Tyrone encounter problems in the fifth year when his planning had been so successful in the past?

2 What financial planning recommendations would you make that might have helped Mr. Anderson avoid the problem that he has experienced?

Human resources as a business function is responsible for identifying, selecting, assigning, training, compensating, and motivating personnel. Human resource specialists must also handle employment problems such as laws, reductions in the number of employees, and employee grievances and terminations.

Job Titles

Job titles in this career area include:

- Directors of Human Resources
- Recruiters
- EEO Representatives (Equal Employment Opportunity)
- Employee Relations Representatives
- Job Analysts
- Compensation Managers
- Employee Benefits Specialists
- Employee Assistance Specialists
- Career Counselors
- Training and Development Managers
- Instructors/Facilitators
- Labor Relations Managers

Employment Outlook (through the year 2005)

- Job growth will be higher than average.
- Demand for specialists will be higher than demand for managers.
- Most jobs will be in the private rather than the public sector.
- Demand for consultants will be particularly high.
- Some companies will expect people to perform human resource tasks on a part-time basis while they do another job in the business.

Education and Training

- Most entry level jobs are filled by college graduates.
- Many colleges offer undergraduate and graduate degrees in human resource management with specializations in areas such as law, finance, and training.
- Special skills are usually required in interpersonal communications, writing, and speaking. Computer skills are more important.
- A master's degree is important for management-level positions; a doctorate is seldom required but may be beneficial for consultants.

Salary Levels (in recent years)

- Average starting salaries in human resources with a bachelor's degree, $22,900; with a master's degree, $30,500.
- Average salaries for all human resources specialists, $32,000; for managers, over $37,000.
- Top salary for the most experienced human resources managers and supervisors, $105,000.

Critical Thinking

1 *What job titles in this career area appeal to you most? Give some reasons for your choice.*

2 *What are some things you will have to do to achieve success in the career selected?*

Human Resource Occupations

Appendix A

Using a Calculator and Computer Keypad

Kinds of Calculators

Many different models of calculators, both desktop and hand held, are available. All calculators have their own features and particular placement of operating keys. Therefore, it is necessary to refer to the operator's manual for specific instructions and locations of the operating keys for the calculator being used. A typical keyboard of a desktop calculator is shown in Figure A-1.

Desktop Calculator Settings

Several operating switches on a desktop calculator must be engaged before the calculator will produce the desired results.

The *decimal selector* sets the appropriate decimal places necessary for the numbers that will be entered. For example, if the decimal selector is set at 2, both the numbers entered and the answer will have two decimal places. If the decimal selector is set at F, the calculator automatically sets the decimal places. The F setting allows the answer to be unrounded and carried out to the maximum number of decimal places possible.

The *decimal rounding selector* rounds the answers. The down arrow position will drop any digits beyond the last digit desired. The up arrow position will drop any digits beyond the last digit desired and round the last digit up. In the 5/4 position, the calculator rounds the last desired digit up only when the following digit is 5 or

Figure A-1

Typical desktop calculator keyboard

Display

483.00

Operating Switches

Non-Add Key

Paper Advance Key

Memory Keys

Total Key

Operation Keys

Number Keys

Decimal Point

Operation Keys

Subtotal Key

greater. If the following digit is less than 5, the last desired digit remains unchanged.

The *GT* or *grand total switch* in the on position accumulates totals.

Kinds of Computer Keyboards

The computer has a keypad on the right side of the keyboard called the *numeric keypad*. Even though there are several styles of keyboards for the IBM® and compatible computers, there are two basic layouts for the numeric keypad. The standard layout and enhanced layout are shown in Figure A-2. On the standard keyboard the directional arrow keys are found on the number keys. To use the numbers, press the key called *Num Lock*. (This key is found above the "7" key.) When the Num Lock is turned on, numbers are entered when the keys on the keypad are pressed. When the Num Lock is off, the arrow, Home, Page Up, Page Down, End, Insert, and Delete keys can be used.

The enhanced keyboards have the arrow keys and the other directional keys mentioned above to the left of the numeric keypad. When using the keypad on an enhanced keyboard, Num Lock can remain on.

The asterisk (*) performs a different function on the computer than the calculator. The asterisk on the calculator is used for the total while the computer uses it for multiplication.

Figure A-2
Standard and enhanced keypads

Multiplication Key
Division Key
Num Lock Key

Standard Keyboard Layout

Enhanced Keyboard Layout

Another difference is the division key. The computer key is the forward slash key (/). The calculator key uses the division key (÷).

Ten-Key Touch System

Striking the numbers 0 to 9 on a calculator or numeric keypad without looking at the keyboard is called the *touch system*. Using the touch system develops both speed and accuracy.

The 4, 5, and 6 keys are called the *home row*. If the right hand is used for the keyboard, the index finger is placed on the 4 key, the middle finger on the 5 key, and the ring finger on the 6 key. If the left hand is used, the ring finger is placed on the 4 key, the middle finger on the 5 key, and the index finger on the 6 key.

Place the fingers on the home row keys. Curve the fingers and keep the wrist straight. These keys may feel slightly concave or the 5 key may have a raised dot. The differences in the home row allow the operator to recognize the home row by touch rather than by sight.

Maintain the position of the fingers on the home row. The finger used to strike the 4 key will also strike the 7 key and the 1 key. Stretch the finger up to reach the 7; then stretch the finger down to reach the 1 key. Visualize the position of these keys.

Again, place the fingers on the home row. Stretch the finger that strikes the 5 key up to reach the 8 key, then down to reach the 2 key. Likewise, stretch the finger that strikes the 6 key up to strike the 9 and down to strike the 3 key. This same finger will stretch down again to hit the decimal point.

If the right hand is used, the thumb will be used to strike the 0 and 00 keys and the little finger to strike the addition key. If the left hand is used, the little finger will be used to strike the 0 and 00 keys and the thumb to strike the addition key.

Hand-Held Calculators

Hand-held calculators are slightly different from desktop calculators, not only in their size and features but also in their operation. Refer to the operator's manual for specific instructions for the calculator being used.

On a hand-held calculator, the numeric keys are usually very close together. In addition, the keys do not respond to touch as easily as on a desktop calculator. Therefore, the touch system is usually not used on a hand-held calculator.

Performing Mathematical Operations on Desktop Calculators

Mathematical operations can be performed on a calculator both quickly and efficiently. The basic operations of addition, subtraction, multiplication, and division are used frequently on a calculator.

Addition

Each number to be added is called an *addend*. The answer to an addition problem is called the *sum*.

Addition is performed by entering an addend and striking the addition key (+). All numbers are entered on a calculator in the exact order they are given. To enter the number 4,455.65, strike the 4, 4, 5, 5, decimal, 6, and 5 keys in that order, and then strike the addition key. Commas are not entered. Continue in this manner until all addends have been entered. To obtain the sum, strike the total key on the calculator.

Subtraction

The top number or first number of a subtraction problem is called the *minuend*. The number to be subtracted from the minuend is called the *subtrahend*. The answer to a subtraction problem is called the *difference*.

Subtraction is performed by first entering the minuend and striking the addition key (+). The subtrahend is then entered, followed by the minus key (−), followed by the total key.

Multiplication

The number to be multiplied is called the *multiplicand*. The number of times the multiplicand will be multiplied is called the *multiplier*. The answer to a multiplication problem is called the *product*.

Multiplication is performed by entering the multiplicand and striking the multiplication key (×). The multiplier is then entered, followed by the equals key (=). The calculator will automatically multiply and give the product.

Division

The number to be divided is called the *dividend*. The number the dividend will be divided by is called the *divisor*. The answer to a division problem is called the *quotient*.

Division is performed by entering the dividend and striking the division key (÷). The divisor is then entered, followed by the equals key (=). The calculator will automatically divide and give the quotient.

Correcting Errors

If an error is made while using a calculator, several methods of correction may be used. If an incorrect number has been entered and the addition key or equals key has not yet been struck, strike the clear entry (CE) key one time. This key will clear only the last number that was entered. However, if the clear entry key is depressed more than one time, the entire problem will be cleared on some calculators. If an incorrect number has been entered and the addition key has been struck, strike the minus key one time only. This will automatically subtract the last number added, thus removing it from the total.

Performing Mathematical Operations on Computers and Hand-Held Calculators

On a computer keypad or a hand-held calculator, addition is performed in much the same way as on a desktop calculator. However, after the + key is depressed, the display usually shows the accumulated total. Therefore, the total key is not found. Some computer programs will not calculate the total until Enter is pressed.

Subtraction is performed differently on many computer keypads and hand-held calculators. The minuend is usually entered, followed by the minus (−) key. Then the subtrahend is entered. Pressing either the + key or the = key will display the difference. Some computer programs will not calculate the difference until Enter is pressed.

Multiplication and division are performed the same way on a computer keypad and hand-held calculator as on a desktop calculator. Keep in mind that computers use the * for multiplication and / for division.

Appendix B

Math Review

This arithmetic review will be helpful to you in solving many of the end-of-chapter problems in this text and the common arithmetic problems you will encounter in business. This review presents several of the kinds of calculations that are the most troublesome to students.

Multiplying Numbers Ending with Zero

When multiplying two numbers, if one or both of the numbers have zeros at the extreme right, place the zeros to the right of an imaginary line, multiply the numbers to the left of the line, and bring down the total number of zeros to the right of the line.

Examples:

$$
\begin{array}{r|l}
36 & \\
\times\ 25 & 00 \\
\hline
180 & \\
72 & \\
\hline
900 & 00
\end{array}
\qquad
\begin{array}{r|l}
36 & 00 \\
\times\ 25 & \\
\hline
180 & \\
72 & \\
\hline
900 & 00
\end{array}
$$

Dividing by Numbers Ending with Zero

When the divisor is 10, 100, 1,000, etc., move the decimal point in the dividend one place to the left for each zero. Moving the decimal point one place to the left divides a number by 10; two places to the left, by 100; three places to the left, by 1,000; etc.

Examples:

$16.8/10 = 1.68$
$246.9/100 = 2.469$
$5,732/1,000 = 5.732$

$$930.9/30 =$$
$$3)\overline{93.09}$$
$$31.03$$

When the divisor is 20, 400, 3,000, etc., drop the zeros in the divisor, move the decimal point in the dividend one place to the left for each zero, and divide by the remaining number 2, 4, 3, etc.

$$65.8/200 =$$
$$2)\overline{.658}$$
$$.329$$

Using Decimals

Following a few simple rules will help improve your calculations using decimals.

1. Adding numbers with decimals—keep decimal points in line.

Examples:

33.65	26.5
72.85	0.4
2.10	385
+ 30.00	+400.329
138.60	812.229

2. Subtracting numbers with decimals—keep decimal points in line.

Example:

$$392.6 \quad \leftarrow \text{fill spaces to the right with zeros} \rightarrow \quad 392.600$$
$$-\ \ 8.794 \qquad\qquad\qquad\qquad\qquad\qquad\qquad -\ \ 8.794$$
$$\qquad\qquad\qquad\qquad\qquad\qquad\qquad\qquad\qquad\qquad 383.806$$

3. Multiplying numbers with decimals.

$$\begin{array}{r} 7.46 \\ \times\ \ 3.2 \\ \hline 1492 \\ 2238 \\ \hline 23.872 \end{array}$$

a. Keep right margin even.
b. Keep figures in line.
c. To position the decimal point in the product, count all digits to the right of the decimal points in the two original figures—in this case three. Count off that number of places from the right in the product, and set the decimal point.

4. Always multiply by the simpler number.

Example: Multiply 3.7 by 327.4. This is the same as multiplying 327.4 by 3.7, which is simpler.

$$\begin{array}{r} 327.4 \\ \times\ \ \ 3.7 \\ \hline 22918 \\ 9822 \\ \hline 1{,}211.38 \end{array}$$

5. Dividing numbers with decimals.

Example: 129.54 (Dividend)/.34 (Divisor) =

$$.34\overline{)129.54}$$

To the right of the decimal point in the dividend, count as many places as are to the right of the decimal point in the divisor. Set the decimal point in the quotient at this point. Keep figures in line.

```
         381. (Quotient)
  .34)129.54
       102
       275
       272
        34
        34
```

Example: 420/75 =

```
       5.6
  75)420.0
     375
     450
     450
```

The decimal point is always at the extreme right of whole numbers although it is not shown. When dividing, a decimal point may be placed at the right of the dividend and zeros added as needed.

Multiplying by Price Figures

Dealers frequently price items for sale at such figures as 49¢, $5.98, $99.95, etc. This is done because a price of $99.95, for example, seems less to the prospective buyer than an even $100.

Example: Let us assume that 27 items are purchased at $0.99 each.

The usual method of multiplication:

```
   $ 0.99
  ×    27
     693
     198
  $26.73
```

```
       27
  ×$ 1.00
    27.00
  −   .27
  $26.73
```

A simpler method: (1) Multiply by the next higher number containing zeros—in this case $1.00. (2) If the price figure ends in 99¢, subtract 1¢ for each item purchased—in this case 27¢.

Example: 32 items at $4.98

$$\begin{array}{r} 32 \\ \times\$\ \ 5.00 \\ \hline \$160.00 \\ -\ \ \ \ .64 \\ \hline \$159.36 \end{array}$$

If the price figure ends in 98¢, subtract 2¢ for each item purchased—in this case 64¢. ($0.02 × 32 = $0.64)

Example: 71 items at $9.97

$$\begin{array}{r} 71 \\ \times\$\ \ 10.00 \\ \hline \$710.00 \\ -\ \ \ \ 2.13 \\ \hline \$707.87 \end{array}$$

If the price figure ends in 97¢, subtract 3¢ for each item purchased—in this case $2.13. ($0.03 × 71 = $2.13)

In some cases, the use of a calculator may make the simpler method of multiplying by price figures unnecessary.

Using Fractional Parts of $1.00 in Multiplying

While goods and services may be priced at any figure, prices are frequently expressed in fractional parts of $1.00, $10.00, $100.00, etc., that can be calculated easily and quickly. For example, 50 cents is ½ of $1.00; 25 cents is ¼ of $1.00; 33⅓ cents is ⅓ of $1.00. Thus:

24 items selling for $1.00 each would cost	$24.00
24 items at 50¢ each would cost ½ of $24 or	$12.00
24 items at 25¢ each would cost ¼ of $24 or	$ 6.00
24 items at 33⅓¢ each would cost ⅓ of $24 or	$ 8.00

Many similar calculations can be made mentally. While there are many fractional parts of $1.00, the ones that follow will be helpful in making arithmetic calculations. This skill will be especially useful when comparing the prices of goods and services.

Fractional Part of $1.00	Halves	Thirds	Fourths	Sixths	Eighths
⅛					$0.12½
⅙				$0.16⅔	
¼			$0.25		
⅓		$0.33⅓			
⅜					$0.37½
½	$0.50				
⅝					$0.62½
⅔		$0.66⅔			

Fractional Part of $1.00	Halves	Thirds	Fourths	Sixths	Eighths
¾			$0.75		
⅚				$0.83⅓	
⅞					$0.87½

Four different types of calculations are involved for determining fractional parts.

First type:

1. Numerator of fractional part is, "1," that is ⅛, ⅙, ¼, etc.
2. There is no remainder; that is, the calculations come to even dollars.

Example: 12 × $0.50 = $6.00

How to calculate:

12 items at $1.00 each would cost $12.00
50¢ is ½ of $1.00; therefore, at 50¢, 12 items will
    cost ½ of $12.00 or .... $ 6.00

Examples:

32 × $0.12½ (32 × ⅛) = $ 4.00
36 × $0.16⅔ (36 × ⅙) = $ 6.00
48 × $0.25   (48 × ¼) = $12.00
39 × $0.33⅓ (39 × ⅓) = $13.00
48 × $0.50   (48 × ½) = $24.00

Second type:

1. Numerator of fractional part is "1."
2. There is a remainder; that is, the calculations will result in dollars and cents.

Example:

33 × $0.25 = $8.25

How to calculate:

33 items at $1.00 each would cost $33.00
25¢ is ¼ of $1.00; therefore, at 25¢ 33 items will cost ¼ of
    $33 or $8¼; ¼ of $1.00 is 25¢ or .... $ 8.25

(*Note:* The fraction of a dollar obtained will always be one of the fractions illustrated in the table on pages 708–709, so that once these fractional parts are mastered there is nothing new to be learned.)

Examples:

39 × $0.16⅔ = $ 6⅖ = $ 6.50 (⅖ = ½ = .50)
37 × $0.25　 = $ 9¼ = $ 9.25
28 × $0.33⅓ = $ 9⅓ = $ 9.33
25 × $0.50　 = $12½ = $12.50

(Note: Since 1¢ is our smallest coin, if the final fraction is ½ or more, the last figure is raised 1 penny; if less than ½, the fraction is dropped. Some retailers convert every fraction to 1¢, even if the fraction is less than ½.)

Third type:

1. Numerator is other than "1."
2. There is no remainder.

Example: 48 × $0.75 = $36.00

How to calculate:

Think of $0.75 as ¾ of $1.00 and solve by cancellation.

$$48 \times \$0.75 \left(\overset{12}{\cancel{48}} \times \frac{3}{\cancel{4}} \right) = \$36.00$$

Examples:

$$24 \times \$0.37\tfrac{1}{2} \left(\overset{3}{\cancel{24}} \times \frac{3}{\cancel{8}} \right) = \$ 9.00$$

$$32 \times \$0.62\tfrac{1}{2} \left(\overset{4}{\cancel{32}} \times \frac{5}{\cancel{8}} \right) = \$20.00$$

$$36 \times \$0.66\tfrac{2}{3} \left(\overset{12}{\cancel{36}} \times \frac{2}{\cancel{3}} \right) = \$24.00$$

Fourth type:

1. Numerator is other than "1."
2. There is a remainder.

Example: 34 × $0.62½ = $21.25

How to calculate:

Think of $0.62½ as ⅝ of $1.00; but since 8 does not divide evenly into 34, first multiply by 5 and then divide by 8.

$$\$34 \times 5 = \$170$$
$$\$170/8 \ = \$21\tfrac{2}{8}$$
$$\$21\tfrac{2}{8} \ \ = \$21.25$$

$$34 \times \$0.62\tfrac{1}{2} \left(\frac{34 \times 5}{8} = \frac{170}{8} \right) = \$21.25$$

Examples:

$$61 \times \$0.37\frac{1}{2} \left(\frac{61 \times 3}{8} = \frac{183}{8} \right) = \$22.88$$

$$43 \times \$0.66\frac{2}{3} \left(\frac{43 \times 2}{3} = \frac{86}{3} \right) = \$28.67$$

$$21 \times \$0.75 \left(\frac{21 \times 3}{4} = \frac{63}{4} \right) = \$15.75$$

$$23 \times \$0.87\frac{1}{2} \left(\frac{23 \times 7}{8} = \frac{161}{8} \right) = \$20.13$$

Note: You will discover that after the number is multiplied by the numerator, the remaining calculation is exactly like that in the second type on page 709.

Fractional parts of other amounts:

To the student who is interested in developing greater skill in calculating fractional parts of other amounts, a few additional examples will demonstrate the large number of applications possible.

Examples:

0.05 is ½ of 0.10	
0.50 is ½ of 1.00	
5.00 is ½ of 10.00	Therefore
50.00 is ½ of 100.00	
500.00 is ½ of 1,000.00	

Therefore
$$\begin{cases} 24 \times & 0.05 = & 1.20 \\ 24 \times & 0.50 = & 12.00 \\ 24 \times & 5.00 = & 120.00 \\ 24 \times & 50.00 = & 1,200.00 \\ 24 \times & 500.00 = & 12,000.00 \end{cases}$$

0.02½ is ¼ of 0.10	
0.25 is ¼ of 1.00	
2.50 is ¼ of 10.00	Therefore
25.00 is ¼ of 100.00	
250.00 is ¼ of 1,000.00	

Therefore
$$\begin{cases} 430 \times & 0.02\frac{1}{2} = & 10.75 \\ 430 \times & 0.25 = & 107.50 \\ 430 \times & 2.50 = & 1,075.00 \\ 430 \times & 25.00 = & 10,750.00 \\ 430 \times & 250.00 = & 107,500.00 \end{cases}$$

Appendix C

Determining Percentages and Interest in Business

Finding percentages and calculating interest are frequent functions in business. Every career in business demands some knowledge of percentages and interest. The well-prepared businessperson is comfortable with percentages and interest.

Finding Percentages

Most business students find that the percent concept is very simple. Percent is derived from two Latin words, "per centum," meaning "by the hundred." You use a fraction whose denominator is always 100. The percent sign is %. Every percent figure can be expressed as either a common fraction or a decimal fraction.

Examples:

Percent		Common Fraction		Decimal Fraction
3%	=	3/100	=	.03
25%	=	25/100	=	.25
57%	=	57/100	=	.57

In fact, you never use the percent figure in calculating percent. You always change the percent figure to either a common fraction or a decimal fraction.

To find:

7% of $300: multiply $300 $\times \dfrac{7}{100}$ = $21.00; or $300 $\times$ .07 = $21.00

12% of $250: multiply $250 $\times \dfrac{12}{100}$ = $30.00; or $250 $\times$ .12 = $30.00

Calculating Interest

Interest is always expressed as a percent; but in calculating interest, both the percent and the length of time are considered.

Examples:

8% interest on $400 for 1 year = $400 $\times$ .08 $\times$ 1 = $ 32.00
15% interest on $550 for 3 years = $550 $\times$ .15 $\times$ 3 = $247.50

One method of calculating interest for less than one year is explained in Chapter 26 of this textbook and is reinforced in the examples that follow.

When you loan or borrow money for less than a year, the amount of interest is calculated on the fractional part of the year. The fraction may be expressed either in months or in days. A month is considered to be one-twelfth of a year regardless of the number of days in the particular month.

Examples:

9% interest on $500 for 3 months = $500 $\times$ .09 $\times \dfrac{3}{12}$ = $11.25

11% interest on $900 for 4 months = $900 $\times$ .11 $\times \dfrac{4}{12}$ = $33.00

When a loan is made for a certain number of days, such as 30, 45, or 85 days, the interest is determined by days. To make the calculating easy, a year is usually considered to be 360 for most business applications.

Examples:

7½% interest on $100 for 15 days = $100 $\times$ .075 $\times \dfrac{15}{360}$ = $0.31

9¼% interest on $2,000 for 85 days = $2,000 $\times$ .0925 $\times \dfrac{85}{360}$ = $43.68

Calculating Interest on Installment Loans

The method of calculating the rate of interest on installment loans presented in Chapter 26 is sufficiently accurate for most purposes. For a more exact calculation of interest, the following method is presented.

Problem:

Evelyn Louis borrowed $120.00 from the small loan department of her bank and signed a note for $126.00. She agreed to pay back the balance in 8 equal monthly installments of $15.75. What annual rate of interest did she pay for the use of the $120.00 that she actually received? Assume that an interest rate of 12% a year, or 1% a month, was charged for the loan.

Solution:

The cost of the loan was $126 − $120 = $6. On this basis, the interest would have been:

$120.00 borrowed for 1 month @ 1% would cost $1.20
− 15.75 1st payment
 104.25 borrowed for 1 month @ 1% would cost 1.04
− 15.75 2d payment
  88.50 borrowed for 1 month @ 1% would cost 0.89
− 15.75 3d payment
  72.75 borrowed for 1 month @ 1% would cost 0.73
− 15.75 4th payment
  57.00 borrowed for 1 month @ 1% would cost 0.57
− 15.75 5th payment
  41.25 borrowed for 1 month @ 1% would cost 0.41
− 15.75 6th payment
  25.50 borrowed for 1 month @ 1% would cost 0.26
− 15.75 7th payment
   9.75 borrowed for 1 month @ 1% would cost 0.10
− 15.75 8th payment

         Interest cost if the money had been borrowed at 1%
           a month, or 12% a year $5.20

Notice that the interest was calculated on the total $120.00 for the first month only, because the borrower had the use of the entire amount only during that month. During the second month, the interest was calculated on $104.25, as $15.75 was repaid at the end of the first month. The amount on which the interest was calculated was decreased in a like manner for each month during the time of the loan.

At 1% a month, or 12% a year, the interest would have been $5.20. The actual cost of the loan was $6.00. How many times greater was this actual cost than $5.20? This may be found by dividing $6.00 by $5.20:

$$\$6/\$5.20 \; = \; 1.1538$$

The amount actually paid was, then, 1.1538 times greater than the amount would be if the rate had been 1% a month, or 12% a year. Since interest rates are stated on a yearly basis, the actual rate was:

$$12\% \; \times \; 1.1538 \; = \; 13.85\%$$

Calculating Interest on Installment Purchases

The method of calculating the rate of interest on installment purchases is similar to the method of calculating the rate of interest on installment loans.

Problem:

William Regier bought a radio on the installment plan from Super Sounds for $102. A down payment of $12 was made at the time of the purchase, and $9 was paid at the end of each of the following 10 months. The radio could have been purchased for $92 in cash. What rate of interest was paid for the privilege of buying on installments?

Solution:

The amount that William paid for the privilege of buying on installments is found by subtracting the cash price of the radio from the installment price of the radio.

$102 the installment price of the radio
− 92 the cash price of the radio
$ 10 the amount paid for the privilege of buying on installments

The radio could have been purchased for $92 in cash. A down payment of $12 was made. The cash price was therefore $80 more than the down payment. William could have bought the radio for cash if he had borrowed $80 from some other source. He was, then, in reality borrowing $80 from the Super Sounds. This may be shown as:

$92 the price that would have been paid if the purchase had been for cash
−12 the down payment at the time of the purchase
$80 the amount borrowed from the dealer

If William had borrowed $80 from some other source at a rate of 1% a month, or 12% a year, the interest would have been found as follows:

$80 borrowed for 1 month @ 1% would cost $0.80
− 9 1st payment
71 borrowed for 1 month @ 1% would cost 0.71
− 9 2d payment
62 borrowed for 1 month @ 1% would cost 0.62
− 9 3d payment
53 borrowed for 1 month @ 1% would cost 0.53
− 9 4th payment
44 borrowed for 1 month @ 1% would cost 0.44
− 9 5th payment
35 borrowed for 1 month @ 1% would cost 0.35
− 9 6th payment
26 borrowed for 1 month @ 1% would cost 0.26
− 9 7th payment
17 borrowed for 1 month @ 1% would cost 0.17
− 9 8th payment
8 borrowed for 1 month @ 1% would cost 0.08
− 9 9th payment
　　Interest cost if the money had been borrowed at 1%　____
　　　　a month, or 12% a year $3.96

Notice that the interest was calculated on $80.00 for the first month only since William had the use of this amount during that month only. During the second month, the interest was calculated on $71.00 because $9.00 was repaid at the end of the first month. The amount on which the interest was calculated was decreased in a like manner for each installment paid.

At 1% a month, or 12% a year, the interest was $3.96. The actual cost for the loan was $10.00 ($102.00 − $92.00 = $10.00). How many times greater was this actual cost than $3.96? This may be found by dividing $10.00 by $3.96:

$$\$10.00/\$3.96 = 2.5252$$

The amount actually paid, then, was 2.5252 times greater than the amount would have been if the rate had been 1% a month, or 12% a year. The actual rate, then, was:

$$12\% \times 2.5252 = 30.30\%$$

Appendix D

Using the Metric Measurement System in Business

The metric system of measure is used in business by most nations in the world. Because of our great amount of trade with other countries, the United States has taken some steps toward conversion to the metric system. Some U.S. businesses and industries have already made the change, and you should become familiar with the metric system.

There are some things about the metric system that may already be familiar to you. For example, if you have been to a track or swimming meet or have seen one on television, you know that distances are sometimes measured in meters, not in feet, yards, or miles. Food is often labeled to show amounts in grams as well as pounds or ounces. Meters, kilometers, and grams are examples of metric units of measurement.

Basic Metric Units

To use the metric system, you will measure weight (or mass), distance, volume, and temperature differently from the way you are accustomed to measuring them. Metric has very few base units, while the U.S. system uses many base units.

The kilogram is the metric base unit of weight. A kilogram is equal to a little over two pounds. The kilogram and units based on the kilogram are used instead of ounces and pounds.

The meter is the metric base unit of distance. A meter is a little longer than a yard. The meter and a few other units based on the meter are used to measure the things we now measure in inches, feet, and miles.

The cubic meter is really the metric base unit of volume. However, for most measurements of volume, you will use the liter. A liter is equal to a little more than a quart. You will use the liter in place of the fluid ounce, the pint, the quart, and the gallon.

The degree Celsius (named after the Swedish astronomer Anders Celsius), once called the centigrade degree, is used instead of the Fahrenheit degree to measure temperature.

Figure D-1 gives you some idea of how these metric units of measure compare with U.S. units.

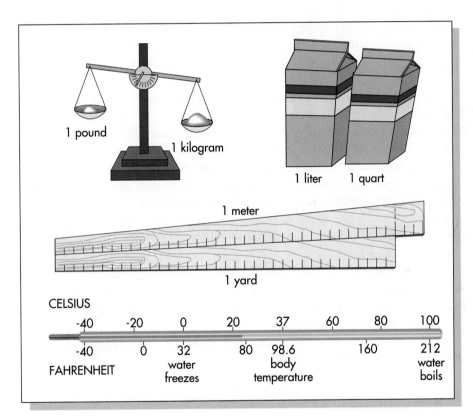

Figure D-1
Some common units of measure in the U.S. and metric systems.

Metric Prefixes

Any measure can be expressed in the base units of the metric system. However, this can be awkward if very large or very small numbers are involved. By using prefixes with the units of the metric system, you can express measurements in a more convenient way. Since the metric system is a decimal system (based on the number 10), the prefixes all mean to multiply or divide the unit by 10, 100, or 1000. There are quite a few metric prefixes, but the ones that are used in this book and in most business applications are:

milli = one one-thousandth or 1/1000 or 0.001
centi = one one-hundredth or 1/100 or 0.01
kilo = one thousand or 1000

Prefixes are added to or taken away from the names of the base units to produce larger or smaller metric units. For example:

1 millimeter = 0.001 meter (about the diameter of a paper clip wire)
1 centimeter = 0.01 meter (about the width of a paper clip)
1 kilometer = 1000 meters (a little over half a mile)
1 gram = 0.001 kilogram (about the weight of a paper clip)

You may wonder why the kilogram, a base unit, has a prefix. Because the gram is extremely small, there was no way to measure it precisely when the standards for metric measurement were being set up. Therefore, the kilogram is considered the base unit.

The metric base units and prefixes are shown with their abbreviations in Figure D-2. Study this illustration until you are familiar with the units, the prefixes, and their abbreviations.

Figure D-2
These units and prefixes are commonly used in the metric system.

Unit	Abbreviation	Use
kilogram	kg	weight
meter	m	distance
liter	L	volume
degree Celsius	°C	temperature

Prefix	Abbreviation	Meaning
milli	m	1/1000
centi	c	1/100
kilo	k	1000

The abbreviations are combined in the same way that metric prefixes and units are combined. For example, millimeter is abbreviated mm; centimeter, cm; kilogram, kg; and kiloliter, kL. The prefixes are never used with degrees Celsius. The degree is the only unit of temperature.

Using Units and Prefixes Correctly

It would not mean much to say that a pill weighs 0.0001 kilogram or that the distance between two towns is 77 058 meters. (In the metric system, a space is used instead of a comma to show thousands when grouping five or more digits.) That would be like telling someone that the distance to the next service station is 10,560 feet instead of 2 miles.

You would not say that your bicycle weighs 12 000 grams, but that it weighs 12 kilograms. The kilogram is ordinarily used wherever we are used to using pounds. The milligram, a very small measure, is used a great deal in the medical and scientific fields. Pills prescribed by doctors are often measured in milligrams.

Meters are used where we are accustomed to using feet or yards, and millimeters usually replace inches for short measurements. Centimeters are used for some measurements such as the dimensions of household objects (towels and sheets) and personal measurements (height).

The liter replaces the fluid ounce, the pint, the quart, and the gallon for small quantities. Gasoline in a car's tank would be measured in liters, but the amount of gasoline in a large storage tank would be measured in kiloliters. The milliliter is used to measure very small quantities such as medicine dosages or amounts of liquid ingredients in recipes.

Changing From One System to the Other

To use the metric system well, you must learn to think in terms of metric units. However, until you get used to doing this, it is sometimes easier to convert the metric units into units you know. Figure D-3 tells you how to convert some commonly used metric units to their U.S. equivalents and some U.S. units to their metric equivalents. The numbers that you are to multiply by have been rounded off to make them easier for you to use and remember.

Take a look at Figure D-3 on the next page, then study these examples.

1. If you buy a 6-ounce bag of candy, what is its weight in grams? (6 ounces × 28 = 168 grams)
2. If you have 9 meters of masking tape, how many yards of tape do you have? (9 meters × 1.1 = 9.9 yards)
3. What is the volume in liters of 5 quarts of oil? (5 quarts × 0.95 = 4.75 liters)
4. If the temperature is 77° F, what is the temperature in degrees Celsius? (77 − 32 = 45; 5/9 × 45 = 25° C)

When You Know:	You Can Find:	If You Multiply By:
DISTANCE		
inches	millimeters (mm)	25.4
inches	centimeters (cm)	2.5
feet	meters (m)	0.3
yards	meters (m)	0.91
miles	kilometers (km)	1.61
millimeters (mm)	inches	0.04
centimeters (cm)	inches	0.4
meters (m)	inches	39.4
meters (m)	feet	3.3
meters (m)	yards	1.1
kilometers (km)	miles	0.6
WEIGHT (MASS)		
ounces	grams (g)	28.0
pounds	kilograms (kg)	0.45
grams (g)	ounces	0.035
kilograms (kg)	pounds	2.2
VOLUME		
pints	liters (L)	0.47
quarts	liters (L)	0.95
gallons	liters (L)	3.8
liters (L)	pints	2.1
liters (L)	quarts	1.06
liters (L)	gallons	0.26
TEMPERATURE		
degrees Fahrenheit	degrees Celsius (°C)	5/9 (after subtracting 32)
degrees Celsius (°C)	degrees Fahrenheit	9/5 (then add 32)

Figure D-3
Approximate conversions from U.S. to metric and metric to U.S.

Photo Credits

Glossary

A

Ability
The quality of being able to perform mental or physical tasks. (p. 224)

Ability test
A test that measures how well a job applicant can perform certain job tasks. (p. 239)

Adjustable rate mortgage (ARM)
A mortgage for which the interest rate is raised or lowered periodically depending upon the current interest rate being charged by lenders. (p. 507)

Adjuster
An insurance company representative who determines the extent of loss and pays policyholders according to the terms of the policy. (pp. 501 and 561)

Allowance
The amount budgeted for savings and other expenditures. (p. 614)

Annual percentage rate (APR)
The percentage cost of credit on a yearly basis. (p. 429)

Annuity
An amount of money that an insurance company will pay at definite intervals to a person who has previously deposited money with the company. (p. 634)

Antitrust laws
Laws designed to promote competition and fairness to prevent monopolies. (p. 143)

Application software
Computer programs that perform specific tasks such as word processing, database management, or accounting. (p. 160)

Appraiser
One who is trained to estimate the value of property and who can give an official report on its value. (p. 508)

Appreciation
A general increase in the value of property that occurs over a period of time. (p. 508)

Artificial intelligence (AI)
Programs that enable computers to reason, learn, and make decisions using logical methods similar to the methods humans use. (p. 188)

Assessed value
The amount that your local government determines your property to be worth for tax purposes. (p. 510)

Assets
Items of value. (p. 602)

Assigned-risk plan
Automobile insurance that provides coverage to high risk drivers who are unable to purchase it otherwise. (p. 547)

Automobile liability insurance
The general term used to describe insurance you buy to protect yourself from financial loss if you injure someone else or damage someone else's property in an automobile accident. (p. 539)

B

Balance of payments
The difference between a country's total imports and total exports of goods. (p. 130)

Balance of trade
The difference between a country's total exports and total imports of goods. (p. 129)

Balance sheet
The financial statement that reports what a person or family owns as well as owes. (p. 602)

Bank reconciliation
A statement showing how the checkbook balance and the bank statement were brought into agreement. (p. 381)

Bankruptcy
A situation in which a business does not have enough money to pay its creditors even after selling its equipment and other capital resources. (p. 255)

Bank statement
A report sent by the bank to a

depositor showing the status of his or her account. (p. 378)

Base plus incentive
A system that combines a small wage or salary with an additional amount determined by the employee's performance. (p. 661)

Base year
The year chosen to compare an item, such as price, to the same item in another year. (p. 54)

Basic economic problem
The problem which faces individuals, businesses, and governments of satisfying unlimited wants with limited resources. (p. 10)

Basic health coverage
A combination of hospital, surgical, and regular medical insurance. (p. 583)

Beneficiary
The person named in an insurance policy to receive the insurance benefits. (p. 569)

Benefits
Compensation in forms other than direct payment for work. (p. 660)

Blank endorsement
An endorsement consisting of only the endorser's name. (p. 346)

Board of directors
A group of people elected by shareholders to guide a corporation. (p. 96)

Bodily injury liability coverage
Insurance coverage that protects you from claims resulting from injuries or deaths for which you are found to be at fault. (p. 540)

Bond
A certificate representing a promise to pay a definite amount of money at a stated interest rate on a specified maturity date. (p. 488)

Brand name
A name given to a product or service by a manufacturer that is intended to distinguish it from other similar and/or competitive products or services. (p. 288)

Budget
A plan that allows you to meet your personal goals with a system of saving and wise spending. (p. 612)

Budget account
A credit plan requiring that payments of a certain fixed amount be made over several months. (p. 409)

Budget variance
A difference between actual spending and planned spending. (p. 618)

Business
An establishment or enterprise that supplies goods and services in exchange for some form of payment. (p. 26)

Business budget
A planning tool used to anticipate sources and amounts of income and to predict the types and amounts of expenses for a specific business activity or the entire business. (p. 684)

Business cycle
The movement of an economy from one condition to another and back again. (p. 57)

Business ethics
Rules about how businesses and their employees ought to behave. (p. 115)

Business plan
A written description of the business idea and how it will be carried out including all major business operations. (p. 647)

Canceled checks
Checks that have been paid by the bank. (p. 379)

Capacity
The factor in credit that refers to a customer's ability to pay a debt when it is due. (p. 398)

Capital
Tools, equipment, and buildings used in producing goods and services. (p. 8) The factor in credit that refers to the value of the borrower's possessions. (p. 398)

Capitalism
An economic system in which most economic resources are privately owned and decisions are largely made by free exchange in the marketplace. (p. 25)

Capital resources
Tools, equipment, and buildings used in producing goods and services. (p. 8)

Career
A goal in life that is fulfilled through a job or series of jobs. (p. 218)

Career information interview
A planned discussion with a worker to find out about the work that person does, the preparation necessary for that career, and the person's feelings about the career. (p. 221)

Career planning
The process of studying careers, assessing yourself in terms of careers, and making decisions about a future career. (p. 218)

Cash budget
An estimate of the actual money received and paid out for a specific time period. (p. 687)

Cash flow statement
The financial statement that reports net wages and other income along with spending for a given period of time. (p. 603)

Cashier's check
A check that a bank draws on its own in-house funds. (p. 363)

Cash value
The amount of money received should a policyholder decide to give up the protection provided by a policy. (p. 570)

CD-ROM
A data storage device that uses laser optics for reading data. (p. 161)

Central processing unit (CPU)
The control center of the computer. (p. 159)

Certificate of deposit (CD)
A long-term deposit that has certain restrictions and pays higher interest rates than a regular savings account. (p. 477)

Certificate of incorporation
A document, generally issued by a state government, giving permission to start a corporation. (p. 89)

Certified check
A personal check for which a bank has guaranteed payment. (p. 363)

Channel of distribution
The path that a product travels from producer to consumer. (p. 75)

Character
The factor in credit that refers to a customer's honesty and willingness to pay a debt when it is due. (p. 397)

Check register
A separate form on which the depositor keeps a record of deposits and checks. (p. 349)

Check stub
A form attached to a check on which a depositor keeps a record of the checks written and any current deposit. (p. 349)

Claim
A policyholder's request for payment for a loss that is covered by the insurance policy. (p. 525)

Clearance sale
A sale in which a price reduction is used to sell items that a store no longer wishes to carry in stock. (p. 287)

Clearing
Returning a check to the drawer's bank to be paid and charged to his or her checking account. (p. 375)

Clearinghouse
A place where member banks exchange checks to clear them. (p. 377)

Closing
A situation in which a business is discontinued with a loss occurring to at least one creditor. (p. 255)

Code of ethics
A statement of values and rules that guides the behavior of employees or members of an organization. (p. 115)

Coinsurance
The sharing of expenses by the policyholder and the insurance company. (p. 527)

Coinsurance clause
A provision in which the insured pays a certain percentage of the costs above the deductible amount. (p. 584)

Collateral
Property that is offered as security for some loan agreements. (p. 416)

Collectibles
Items of personal interest to collectors purchased in anticipation of an increase in value in the future. (p. 513)

Collision coverage
Insurance coverage that protects a car owner against financial loss associated with damage from a collision with another car or object or from the car turning over. (p. 541)

Commercial bank
A bank that offers a full range of financial services. (p. 321)

Commission
A fee charged by brokers for their services. (p. 495) A percentage of sales employees are paid on sales for which they are responsible. (p. 660)

Common stock
Stock that represents general ownership in a corporation and a right to share in its profits, but has no stated dividend rate. (p. 493)

Comparison shopping
Comparing the price, quality, and services of one product with those of another product. (p. 284)

Compensation
The amount of money paid to an employee for work performed. (p. 660)

Competition
The rivalry among businesses to sell their goods and services to buyers. (p. 29)

Compound interest
Interest computed on the amount

saved plus the interest previously earned. (p. 463)

Comprehensive coverage
Insurance protection against almost all losses except those caused from a collision or from the car turning over. (p. 542)

Comprehensive medical policy
Insurance that combines hospital, surgical, regular, and major medical insurance into one policy. (p. 584)

Compulsory insurance laws
Laws that require you to carry certain types of automobile insurance before your car can be licensed. (p. 546)

Computer-assisted design (CAD)
Technological assistance used to create product styles and designs. (p. 189)

Computer-assisted instruction (CAI)
The use of computers to help people learn or improve skills at their own pace. (p. 179)

Computer language
A system of letters, words, numbers, and symbols used to communicate with a computer. (p. 160)

Computer network
Several computers linked into a single system. (p. 157)

Computer system
The combination of an input device, a processing unit, memory and storage facilities, and an output device. (p. 156)

Computer virus
A program code hidden in a system that can later do damage to software or stored data. (p. 194)

Condominium
An individually owned unit in an apartment-like building or complex where maintenance and yard work are normally taken care of for a service fee. (p. 508)

Consumer
A person who buys and uses goods or services (p. 269)

Consumer movement
The fight against unfair business practices by consumers joining together to demand fair treatment from businesses. (p. 300)

Consumer Price Index (CPI)
Shows changes in the average prices of goods and services bought by consumers over a period of time. (p. 292)

Contract
An agreement to exchange goods or services for something of value. (p. 139)

Consumer finance company
A financial institution that specializes in making loans for long-lasting or durable goods and financial emergencies. (p. 323)

Convenience store
A small store that emphasizes the sale of food items, an accessible location, and long operating hours. (p. 290)

Cooperative
A business that is owned by the members it serves and is managed in their interest. (p. 101)

Copyright
Protection of the work of authors, composers, and artists. (p. 140)

Corporate bonds
Debt securities issued by corporations. (p. 488)

Corporation
A business made up of a number of

owners but authorized by law to act as a single person. (p. 89)

Cosigner
Someone who becomes responsible for payment of the note if you do not pay as promised. (p. 416)

Credit
The privilege of using someone else's money for a period of time. (p. 395)

Credit application
A form on which you provide information needed by a lender to make a decision about granting credit or approving a loan. (p. 439)

Credit bureau
A company that gathers information on credit users and sells that information in the form of credit reports to credit grantors. (p. 441)

Credit insurance
Special insurance that repays the balance of the amount owed if the borrower dies or becomes disabled prior to the full settlement of the loan. (p. 430)

Credit memorandum
A written record of the amount subtracted from an account when merchandise has been returned. (p. 444)

Creditor
A person or business that is owed money. (p. 255) One who sells on credit or makes a loan. (p. 395)

Credit rating
A person's reputation for paying debts on time. (p. 400)

Credit record
A report that shows the debts you owe, how often you use credit, and whether you pay your debts on time. (p. 438)

Credit references
Businesses or individuals from whom

you have received credit in the past and/or who can help verify your credit record. (p. 397)

Credit union
A not-for-profit financial institution formed by people who have like occupations or live in the same community. (p. 322)

Creditworthy
Having established a credit record that shows you are a good credit risk. (p. 438)

Custom-based economy
An economy in which goods are produced the way they always have been produced. (p. 24)

Custom manufacturing
Building a specific and unique product to meet the needs of one customer. (p. 671)

Data
Facts in the form of numbers, alphabetic characters, words, or special symbols. (p. 155)

Database
A collection of organized data whose elements are in some way related to one another. (p. 174)

Database software
A computer program that processes an organized collection of information. (p. 174)

Debtor
One who buys on credit or receives a loan. (p. 395)

Debt-repayment plan
An agreement developed cooperatively by a creditor and debtor to reduce payments to a more manageable level and still pay off the debt. (p. 449)

Decreasing term insurance
Term life insurance on which the amount of protection gradually becomes smaller, but the premiums remain the same during the term. (p. 570)

Deductible
The amount you must pay before the insurance company pays a claim. (p. 525)

Deflation
A decrease in the general price level. (p. 60)

Demand
The quantity of a product or service that consumers are willing and able to buy at a particular price. (p. 40)

Dental insurance
Insurance that helps pay for normal dental care and covers dental injuries resulting from accidents. (p. 584)

Deposit slip
A form that accompanies a deposit and lists the items you deposited—currency, coins, or checks. (p. 342)

Depreciation
The decrease in the value of property as it becomes older and wears out. (p. 561)

Depression
A phase marked by high unemployment, weak sales of goods and services, and business failures. (p. 57)

Derived demand
A demand for factors of production affected by consumer demand for a product or service. (p. 208)

Desktop publishing
A process of writing and designing high quality publications with the use of microcomputers. (p. 173)

Direct channel of distribution
The process through which goods are bought by the consumer directly from the producer. (p. 76)

Directed economy
An economy in which the resources are owned and controlled by the government. (p. 24)

Disability income insurance
Insurance that protects a worker against the loss of income because of a long illness or accident. (p. 585)

Discount stores
Large stores that sell large quantities of goods at low prices. (p. 290)

Discretionary income
Income available to spend after money has been set aside for basic needs and future expenses. (p. 601)

Disk drive
A device that is used to store information onto a magnetic disk so that the information can be recalled and used again. (p. 161)

Distribution
The locations and methods used to make products and services available to customers. (p. 675)

Dividend
The part of the profits of a corporation that each shareholder receives. (p. 98)

Down payment
A payment of part of the purchase price that is made as part of a credit agreement. (p. 415)

Downsizing
Planned reduction in the number of employees needed in a firm. (p. 210)

Drawee
The bank or other financial institution in which the account is held. (p. 357)

Drawer
The owner of the account and the

person who signs the check. (p. 357)

E

Economic decision making
The process of choosing which wants, among several wants being considered, will be satisfied. (p. 11)

Economic resources
The means through which goods and services are produced. (p. 7)

Economic risk
The possibility of incurring a loss related to property liability and one's own personal well being. (p. 523)

Economic system
A nation's plan for answering the key economic questions. (p. 23)

Electronic funds transfer (EFT)
A system through which funds are moved electronically from one account to another and from one bank to another. (p. 325)

Electronic mail (E-mail)
The delivery of correspondence through a computer system. (p. 172)

Embargo
Stopping the importing or exporting of a certain product or service. (p. 128)

Endorsement
Written evidence that you received payment or that you transferred your right of receiving payment to someone else. (p. 344)

Entrepreneur
Someone who takes a risk in starting a business to earn a profit. (p. 258)

Entrepreneurship
The process of starting, organizing, managing, and assuming responsibility for a business. (p. 259)

Equal Credit Opportunity Act
An act that prohibits creditors from denying credit because of age, race, sex, or marital status. (p. 446)

Equity
The difference between the price at which you could currently sell your house and property and the amount owed on the mortgage. (p. 508)

Estate planning
An activity that involves the accumulation and management of property during one's lifetime and the distribution of one's property at death. (p. 629)

Ethics
Principles of morality or rules of conduct. (p. 115)

Exchange rate
The value of the money of one country expressed in terms of the money of another country. (p. 125)

Exit interview
An interview in which an employer asks questions about how an employee likes his/her work and inquires about job improvements that might be made. (p. 245)

Expenditures
The amounts spent for food, clothing, transportation, and other living costs. (p. 604)

Expert systems
Programs that assist people in solving technical problems. (p. 188)

Exports
Goods and services sold to another country. (p. 124)

Express warranties
Guarantees made orally or in writing that promise a specific quality of performance. (p. 305)

Extended coverage
Additional protection of property

that covers damage caused by perils such as wind, hail, smoke, and falling aircraft, among other things. (p. 556)

Extractor
A business that grows products or takes raw materials from nature. (p. 73)

F

Face value
The amount borrowed by the seller of a bond. (p. 488) The amount of insurance coverage that was originally purchased and that will be paid upon the death of the insured. (p. 570)

Factors of production
The means through which goods and services are produced. (p. 7)

Factory outlet stores
Stores selling products at low prices that sometimes have minor flaws. (p. 290)

Fair Credit Billing Act
A law that requires prompt correction of billing mistakes when they are brought to the attention of a business in a prescribed manner. (p. 447)

Fair Credit Reporting Act
A law that gives consumers the right to know what specific information credit bureaus are providing to potential creditors, employers, and insurers. (p. 447)

Fax
A system in which a copy of a document is transmitted from one location to another through an electronic device connected to telephone lines. Also called facsimile (p. 180)

Federal Deposit Insurance Corporation (FDIC)
A federal agency that protects

depositors' money in case of the failure of a bank or financial institution that it regulates. (p. 321)

Federal Reserve System (Fed)
A nationwide banking plan set up by our federal government to supervise and regulate member banks. (p. 328)

Finance charge
The additional amount you must pay for using credit. (p. 410)

Financial plan
A report that summarizes your current financial condition, acknowledges your financial needs, and sets a direction for your future financial activities. (p. 626)

Financial planners
Professionals who have at least two years of training in securities, insurance, taxes, real estate, and estate planning and have passed a rigorous examination. (p. 631)

Financial planning
An activity that includes evaluating one's financial position, setting financial goals, and guiding activities and resources toward reaching those goals. (p. 626)

Financial records
Used to record and analyze the financial performance of the business. (p. 688)

Financial responsibility laws
Laws whereby your driver's license will be suspended or taken away if you cause an accident and cannot pay for the damages either through insurance, your savings, or the sale of property. (p. 546)

Financial statements
Reports that summarize the financial performance of a business. (p. 690)

Fixed expenses
Costs that occur regularly and are

for the same amount each time. (p. 613)

Fixed rate mortgage
A traditional mortgage with an interest rate that does not change during the life of the mortgage. (p. 506)

Forgery
The crime of writing another person's signature on the check without his or her authority. (p. 359)

Franchise
A written contract granting permission to sell someone else's product or service in a prescribed manner, over a certain period of time, and in a specified area. (p. 100)

Franchisee
The person or group of people who have received permission from a parent company to sell its products or services. (p. 100)

Franchisor
The parent company that grants permission to a person or group to sell its products or services. (p. 100)

Fraud
When false information is given to a customer in an effort to make a sale. (p. 302)

Free enterprise system
An economic system in which most economic resources are privately owned and decisions are largely made by free exchange in the marketplace. (p. 25)

Full endorsement
An endorsement including the name of the person to whom the check has been transferred. (p. 347)

Full-service store
Stores that offer a wide variety of goods and emphasize customer service. (p. 289)

Full-time employee
An employee who works a schedule of at least 30 hours a week. (p. 657)

Futures
A contract for a commodity purchased in anticipation of higher market prices in the near future. (p. 511)

Goods
Things you can see and touch. (p. 6)

Goods-producing industry
Businesses that manufacture many kinds of products. (p. 206)

Government employment office
A tax-supported agency that helps people find jobs and provides information about careers. (p. 220)

Grade
An indication of the quality or size of a product. (p. 272)

Graphics software
A computer program that prepares charts, graphs, and other visual elements. (p. 173)

Gross domestic product (GDP)
The total value of all final goods and services produced in a country in one year. (p. 53)

Gross domestic product (GDP) per capita
The GDP divided by the total population of a country. (p. 55)

Group life insurance
Life insurance that covers a group of people who are usually employed by the same company or are members of the same organization. (p. 575)

Guarantee
A promise by the manufacturer or dealer, usually in writing, that a

product is of a certain quality.
(p. 305)

Hardware
The components or equipment of a
computer system. (p. 156)

Health maintenance organizations (HMOs)
Organizations that provide complete
health care to their members for a
fixed monthly payment. (p. 586)

Homeowners policy
A package-type insurance policy
designed to fit the needs of most
homeowners wishing to insure their
homes and property. (p. 556)

Hospital insurance
Insurance that pays most or all of the
charges for room, food, and other
hospital expenses that the insured
person incurs. (p. 582)

Human resource management
Ensuring that needed employees are
available, that they are productive,
paid, and satisfied with their work.
(p. 656)

Human resources
People who work to produce goods
and services. (p. 7) People who
work for a business. (p. 656)

Immigrants
People from other countries who
come to live in our country for a
variety of reasons and often become
citizens. (p. 211)

Implied warranties
Guarantees imposed by law that are
not stated orally or in writing and
which require certain standards to
be met. (p. 306)

Imports
Goods and services bought from
another country. (p. 123)

Impulse buying
Buying too rapidly without much
thought. (p. 291)

Income
The money you receive from work
that you do and from money you
invest. (p. 599)

Income statement
Reports the revenue, expenses, and
net income or loss of a business
for a specific period of time.
(p. 690)

Indirect channel of distribution
The process through which goods
move through one or more middle
firms between the producer and the
consumer. (p. 76)

Individual retirement account (IRA)
A tax-sheltered retirement plan in
which people can annually invest
earnings up to $2,000 annually. The
earnings contributed and the interest
earned are tax free until the time of
withdrawal at age 59½ or later.
(pp. 480 and 634)

Inflation
An increase in the general price
level. (p. 59)

Input device
A mechanism used to enter data into
a computer system. (p. 158)

Installment loan
A type of loan in which you agree to
make monthly payments in specific
amounts over a period of time.
(p. 415)

Installment sales credit
A contract issued by the seller that
requires periodic payments to be

made at times specified in the
agreement with finance charges
added to the cost of the purchase.
(p. 414)

Insurable interest
A financial interest in or benefit from
the continued life of a person.
(p. 574)

Insurance
The planned protection provided by
sharing economic losses. (p. 525)

Insurance agent
A person who sells insurance.
(p. 529)

Insurance companies
Businesses that provide planned
protection against economic loss.
(p. 525)

Insured
The person for whom risk is assumed
by an insurance company. (p. 525)

Integrated software
A computer program capable of
performing more than one basic
function. (p. 177)

Interest
An amount paid for the use of
money. (p. 324)

Interest rate
The percentage that is applied to a
debt, expressed as a fraction or
decimal. (p. 425)

International business
The business activities necessary for
creating, shipping, and selling
goods and services across national
borders. (p. 122)

Interstate commerce
Business transactions involving
companies in more than one state.
(p. 138)

Intrastate commerce
Business transactions involving

companies that do business only in one state. (p. 139)

Inventory
A list of goods showing the original cost of each item, when it was purchased, and how long it is expected to last. (p. 561)

Investing
Using your savings to earn more money for you. (p. 462)

Investment club
A small group of people who organize to study stocks and invest money. (p. 497)

Investments
Savings that are put to work to earn more money. (p. 327)

J

Joint account
A bank account that is used by two or more people. (p. 342)

L

Label
A written statement attached to a product giving useful information about its nature or contents. (p. 274)

Labor
People who work to produce goods and services. (p. 7)

Labor productivity
The quantity of a good an average worker produces in one hour. (p. 44)

Letter of application
A sales letter about an applicant written for the purpose of getting a personal interview. (p. 234)

Level term insurance
Term life insurance on which the amount of protection and the premiums remain the same while the insurance is in effect. (p. 569)

Liabilities
Amounts owed to others. (p. 602)

Liability risk
Potential losses to others that occur as a result of injury or damage that you may have caused. (p. 523)

Life insurance
Insurance designed to protect survivors against the financial loss associated with dying. (p. 568)

Limited-payment policies
A whole life policy intended to be paid up in a certain number of years. (p. 571)

Liquidity
The ease with which an investment can be changed into cash quickly without losing any of its value. (p. 467)

Loan credit
Borrowing money to be used later for some special purpose. (p. 396)

Long-term financing
Money needed for the important resources of a business (such as land, buildings, and equipment) that will last for many years. (p. 649)

M

Major medical insurance
Insurance that provides protection against the high costs of serious illnesses or injuries. (p. 583)

Management information system (MIS)
An organized system of processing and reporting information in an organization. (p. 170)

Manufacturer
A business that takes an extractor's products or raw materials and changes them into a form that consumers can use. (p. 73)

Market economy
An economy in which individuals are free to engage in business transactions with buyers who are willing and able to buy and sellers who supply goods and services from which they earn a profit. (p. 24)

Marketer
A business involved with moving goods from producers to consumers. (p. 75)

Marketing concept
Directing all marketing activities at profitably satisfying customer needs. (p. 674)

Marketing mix
The blending of four marketing elements to satisfy a target market. (p. 674)

Marketplace
Any place where buyers and sellers exchange goods and services for some form of money. (p. 25)

Market value
The price at which a share of stock can be bought and sold in the stock market. (p. 491)

Mass production
A large number of identical products are assembled using a continuous, efficient procedure. (p. 671)

Maturity date
The date on which a loan must be repaid. (p. 427)

Medicaid
Medical expense assistance administered by state governments to financially needy families. (p. 588)

Medical payments coverage
Insurance coverage that provides medical expense protection for the policyholder, immediate family members, and guests while in the insured person's car. (p. 541)

Medicare
Health insurance provided by the federal government for people age 65 and older and some disabled people. (p. 588)

Memory
Storage locations for the instructions and data that the computer will use. (p. 160)

Menu
A list of computer functions that appears on the screen. (p. 173)

Mobility
The willingness and ability of a person to move to where jobs are located. (p. 222)

Modem
A device that allows you to communicate with other computers through the use of telephone lines. (p. 180)

Money management
Day-to-day financial activities associated with using limited income to satisfy unlimited needs and wants. (p. 599)

Money market account
A special account that pays a variable interest rate based on rates paid to holders of short-term government debt. (p. 477)

Money market rate
The current cost of money in the marketplace. (p. 341)

Money order
A form of payment that orders the issuing agency to pay the amount printed on the form to another party. (p. 365)

Monopoly
A business that has complete control of the market for a product or service. (p. 143)

Mortgage
A legal document giving the lender a claim against the property if the principal, interest, or both are not paid as agreed. (p. 506)

Multimedia system
A computer system that presents information using a combination of sound, graphics, animation, and video. (p. 156)

Multinational company or corporation (MNC)
An organization that conducts business in several countries and has management prepared to do business worldwide. (p. 130)

Municipal bonds
Bonds issued by local and state governments. (p. 489)

Municipal corporation
An organization that provides services for citizens with revenue from their taxes and does not have earning a profit as a goal. (p. 102)

Mutual funds
Funds set up and managed by investment companies that receive money from many investors and then usually buy and sell a wide variety of stocks or bonds. (p. 497)

Mutual savings bank
A bank owned by depositors that mainly handles savings accounts and makes loans to home buyers. (p. 321)

N

Natural resources
Raw materials supplied by nature. (p. 7)

Needs
Things that are necessary for survival, such as food, clothing, and shelter. (p. 5)

Net income
The amount received after taxes and other deductions have been subtracted from total earnings. (p. 603)

No-fault insurance laws
A plan in which people injured in automobile accidents are required to collect for their financial losses from their own insurance companies no matter who is at fault. (p. 547)

Non-renewable resource
A natural resource, such as gas, coal, copper, and iron ore, that cannot be replaced once used up. (p. 111)

Occupation
A task or series of tasks that are performed to provide a good or service. (p. 218)

On-line computer service
A computer network connection with information, shopping, and entertainment services. (p. 190)

Operating budget
Describes the financial plan for the day-to-day operations of a business. (p. 687)

Operating system software
Software that translates a computer user's commands and allows application programs to interact with the computer's hardware. (p. 160)

Opportunity cost
The value of any alternative that you give up when you buy something else or make another choice. (p. 276)

Ordinary life policy
A type of whole life insurance for which premiums remain the same each year as long as the policyholder lives. (p. 571)

Output devices
Mechanisms used to present data in

a form that can be used or retrieved later or may be communicated immediately. (p. 162)

Outstanding checks
Checks that have not been deducted from the bank-statement balance. (p. 381)

Overdrawing
Writing a check for more money than is in one's account. (p. 360)

Owner's equity
The difference between a person's or family's assets and liabilities. (p. 602)

 P

Partnership
An association of two or more people operating a business as co-owners and sharing profits or losses according to a written agreement. (p. 89)

Part-time employee
An employee who works less than full-time employees by working either fewer hours each day or fewer days each week. (p. 657)

Patent
The exclusive right given to a person to make, use, or sell an invention for a period of 17 years. (p. 140)

Payee
The person to whom the check is written. (p. 357)

Pension
A series of regular payments made to a retired worker under an organized plan. (p. 634)

Perils
The causes of loss, such as fire, wind, or theft. (p. 556)

Permanent employee
An employee that has a long-term commitment to a company. (p. 657)

Permanent insurance
A type of insurance that has cash value and an investment feature as its common characteristics. (p. 570)

Personal data sheet
A summary of job-related information about yourself. (p. 234)

Personal liability coverage
Insurance that protects you from claims arising from injuries to other people or damage to other people's property caused by you, your family, or your pets. (p. 555)

Personal property
Property that is not attached to the land. (p. 556)

Personal references
People who can give a report about your character, education, and work habits. (p. 235)

Personal risk
Risks associated with illness, disability, loss of income, unemployment, old age, and premature death. (p. 523)

Personnel interviewer
Someone who has special training for talking with job applicants and hiring new employees. (p. 240)

Piece rate
A compensation plan that pays the employee a specific amount for each unit of work produced. (p. 661)

Piracy
Stealing or illegally copying software packages or information. (p. 194)

Planned economy
An economy in which the resources are owned and controlled by the government. (p. 24)

Policy
A contract that states the conditions to

which the insurance company and the policyholder have agreed. (p. 525)

Policyholder
The person for whom risk is assumed by an insurance company. (p. 525)

Position application form
A document used by employers that asks for information related to employment. (p. 237)

Position interview
A two-way conversation in which the interviewer learns about you and you learn about the job and the company. (p. 240)

Postdated check
A check dated later than the date on which it is written. (p. 360)

Preferred provider organization (PPO)
A group of physicians, a clinic, or a hospital that contracts with an employer to provide medical services to employees. (p. 587)

Preferred stock
Stock that has priority over common stock in the payment of dividends. (p. 492)

Premium
The amount that a policyholder must pay for insurance coverage. (p. 525)

Price earnings ratio (P/E)
The ratio of a stock's selling price to its earnings per share. (p. 495)

Price index
Series of figures showing how prices have changed over a period of years. (p. 292)

Pricing
The methods of increasing the value of the product to consumers and the actual amount they pay. (p. 675)

Principal
The amount of debt to which the interest is applied. (p. 425)

Private enterprise
The right of the individual to choose whether to own a business, what business to enter, and what to produce with only limited government direction. (p. 26)

Private enterprise system
An economic system in which most economic resources are privately owned and decisions are largely made by free exchange in the marketplace. (p. 25)

Private property
The right to own, use, or dispose of things of value. (p. 26)

Processing
Changing the form of materials so they can be consumed or used to manufacture other products. (p. 671)

Product
Anything offered to the target market to satisfy needs including physical products and services. (p. 675)

Productivity
The quantity of a good an average worker produces in an hour. (p. 44)

Profit
Money left from sales after subtracting the cost of operating the business. (p. 28)

Profit motive
The desire to work hard and be creative to earn a higher profit. (p. 28)

Profit sharing
An incentive plan in which employees receive their regular compensation plus a share of the profits earned by the company. (p. 661)

Program
A series of detailed step-by-step instructions that tell the computer what functions to complete and when to complete them. (p. 159)

Promissory note
A written promise to repay based on the debtor's excellent credit rating. (p. 415)

Promotion
The methods and information communicated to customers to encourage purchases and increase their satisfaction. (p. 675)

Promotional sale
A sale in which items are sold below their regular price to publicize the opening of a new store or location and to build acceptance for new products. (p. 287)

Property damage liability coverage
Insurance protection against claims if your car damages someone else's property and you are at fault. (p. 541)

Property risk
The risks of damage to or loss of property due to theft, wind, fire, flood, or some other hazard. (p. 523)

Prosperity
A phase of the business cycle when most people who want to work are working and businesses produce goods and services in record numbers. (p. 57)

Public goods
Things that are needed and provided by a community and are equally accessible to everyone. (p. 45)

Public utility
A business that supplies a service or product vital to all people; the price charged for the service (or product) is determined by government regulation rather than by competition. (p. 142)

Quota
A limit on the quantity of a product that may be imported and exported within a given period of time. (p. 127)

Real estate
Land and anything that is attached to it. (p. 505)

Real estate agent
Someone who is trained and licensed to help with the buying and selling of real estate. (p. 507)

Real property
Property that is permanently attached to land. (p. 556)

Receipt
A written form that acknowledges payment was made. (p. 445)

Recession
A period where demand begins to decrease, businesses lower production of goods and services, unemployment begins to rise, and GDP growth slows for several quarters. (p. 57)

Recovery
A phase of the business cycle in which unemployment begins to decrease, demand for goods and services increases, and GDP begins to rise again. (p. 58)

Regular account
A credit plan in which the seller or provider expects payment in full at the end of a specified period—usually a month. (p. 409)

Regular medical insurance
Insurance that pays for nonsurgical care given in the doctor's office, the patient's home, or a hospital. (p. 583)

Regular savings account
A savings plan with a low or no minimum balance and the ability to make withdrawals at almost any time. (p. 474)

Renewable policy
A term life insurance policy that allows the policyholder to continue the term insurance for one or more terms without taking a physical examination to determine whether she or he is still a good risk. (p. 569)

Replacement insurance
Insurance that actually replaces an item that has been destroyed. (p. 561)

Restrictive endorsement
An endorsement that limits the use of a check to the purpose given in the endorsement. (p. 347)

Retailer
A business firm that sells directly to the consumer. (p. 76)

Retirement, survivors, and disability insurance
The part of the Social Security system that provides pensions to retired workers and their families, death benefits to dependents of workers who die, and benefits to disabled workers and their families. (p. 632)

Revenue
Business or government income. (pp. 145 and 684)

Revolving account
A credit plan that allows purchases to be charged at any time but requires that at least part of the debt be paid each month. (p. 410)

Risk
The possibility of incurring a loss. (p. 523)

Robots
Mechanical devices programmed to do routine tasks. (p. 188)

S

Safe-deposit boxes
A secured area in a bank vault for storing valuables. (p. 327)

Salary and wages
Direct payment to an employee for work completed. Short-term financing: The money needed to pay for the current operating activities of a business. (p. 660)

Sales credit
Credit offered at the time of sale. (p. 396)

Savings account register
A record in which you record deposits, withdrawals, interest earned, and the balance of your savings account. (p. 474)

Savings and loan association (S&L)
A financial institution that specializes in savings accounts and loans for mortgages. (p. 321)

Savings plan
Putting money aside in a systematic way to help reach an established financial goal. (p. 461)

Scarcity
The problem which faces individuals, businesses, and governments of satisfying unlimited wants with limited resources. (p. 10)

Secured loan
A type of loan in which the lender has the right to sell property used as collateral to get back the amount of the loan in the event the loan is not repaid. (p. 416)

Securities
A general term for bonds and stocks that are sold by corporations and governments to raise large sums of money. (p. 487)

Self-insurance
An individual, family, or business assuming the total risk of economic loss. (p. 526)

Service business
A business that does things for you instead of making products. (p. 76)

Service charge
A fee a bank charges for handling a checking account. (p. 340)

Service Corps of Retired Executives (SCORE)
A group of retired executives who can provide assistance to small-business owners. (p. 256)

Service-producing industry
Businesses that perform services to satisfy the needs of other businesses and consumers. (p. 206)

Services
Things that satisfy our wants through the efforts of other people or equipment. (p. 6)

Sharedrafts
Withdrawals made on a member's shares of ownership (deposits) in a credit union. (p. 341)

Shareholders
People who own stock in a corporation. (p. 89)

Signature card
A card, kept by a bank, that shows the signatures of all individuals authorized to draw checks against the account. (p. 342)

Simple interest
An expression of interest based on a one-year period of time. (p. 425) Interest that is computed only on the amount saved. (p. 462)

Single-payment loan
A type of loan in which you do not pay anything until the end of the loan, possibly 60 or 90 days. (p. 415)

Small business
A business that usually has the owner as manager, is not dominant in its field of operation, employs fewer than 500 people, and usually serves its nearby community. (p. 252)

Small Business Administration (SBA)
A government-funded organization that helps small-business owners borrow money as well as manage their businesses more efficiently. (p. 256)

Small Business Institutes (SBIs)
Programs offered in cooperation with colleges and universities to provide management counseling. (p. 256)

SMART card
A plastic card with a silicon chip for storing information. (p. 190)

Social responsibility
The obligation of a business to contribute to the well-being of a community. (p. 110)

Social Security tax
A tax that is put into a trust fund and provides certain benefits to retirees or beneficiaries. (p. 633)

Software
Instructions that run a computer system. (p. 157)

Sole proprietorship
A business owned by one person. (p. 89)

Special endorsement
An endorsement including the name of the person to whom the check has been transferred. (p. 347)

Specialty stores
Stores that carry a wide variety of products in a narrow line. (p. 290)

Speculative investment
An investment that has an unusually high risk. (p. 511)

Spot price
The current price quoted for precious metals in the world markets. (p. 512)

Spreadsheet software
A computer program that uses a row and column arrangement of data to perform calculations. (p. 174)

Standard fire policy
A basic type of property insurance that protects against losses caused by fire or lightning. (p. 556)

Standard of living
A measure of how well people in a country live; the quality and quantity of wants and needs that are satisfied. (p. 43)

Start-up budget
Used to plan income and expenses from the beginning of a business until it becomes profitable. (p. 686)

Start-up financing
The amount of money needed to open the business. (p. 649)

Statement of account
A record of the transactions that you have completed with a business during a billing period. Also called statement (p. 442)

Stockbroker
A licensed specialist who helps investors buy and sell stocks and bonds. (p. 495)

Stock exchanges
Business organizations that accommodate the buying and selling of securities. (p. 495)

Stop-payment order
The form instructing a bank not to pay a certain check. (p. 362)

Straight salary
A specific amount of money is paid for each week or month worked. (p. 660)

Supermarket
A large, full-service food store that carries a wide variety of national, store, and generic brands at moderate prices. (p. 290)

Supply
The quantity of a product or service that businesses are willing and able to provide at a particular price. (p. 41)

Surgical insurance
Insurance that provides benefits to cover part or all of the surgeon's fee for an operation. (p. 582)

T

Talent
A natural, in-born aptitude to do certain things. (p. 224)

Take-home pay
The amount received after taxes and other deductions have been subtracted from total earnings. (p. 603)

Target market
A group of consumers with very similar needs to whom a company can sell its products. (p. 674)

Tariff
A tax that a government places on certain imported products. (p. 127)

Telecommuting
A term used to describe the activities of a worker using a computer at home to perform a job. (p. 180)

Temporary employee
An employee hired for a specific

time or to complete a specific assignment. (p. 657)

Tentative career decision
A career decision that is subject to change or modification as new information is received. (p. 226)

Term life insurance
A life insurance policy that provides financial protection against loss of life during a definite period of time. (p. 569)

Time factor
The length of time for which interest will be charged. (p. 425)

Time wage
A wage that pays the employee a specific amount of money for each hour worked. (p. 660)

Trade associations
Organizations of businesses engaged in the same type of business. (p. 305)

Trade credit
A business receives goods from a wholesaler and pays for them later at a specified date. (p. 396)

Trademark
A word, letter, or symbol associated with a specific product or company. (p. 140)

Traveler's check
A form designed for the traveler to use in making payments. (p. 364)

Trust
The creditor's belief that the debtor will honor the promise to pay later for goods and services that have already been received and used. (p. 395)

Trust companies
Financial institutions that specialize in managing the money and property of others. (p. 327)

Truth-in-Lending Law
A law that requires that you be told the cost of a credit purchase in writing before you sign a credit agreement. (p. 446)

U

Unemployment insurance
Insurance that provides cash payments for a limited time to people who are out of work for a reason other than illness. (p. 632)

Uninsured motorist coverage
Insurance coverage that protects the policyholder and immediate family members against losses resulting from injuries caused by a hit-and-run driver or by a driver who has no insurance and inadequate money to pay claims. (p. 541)

Unit price
The price per unit of measure of a product. (p. 285)

Universal life insurance
Life insurance which provides both insurance protection and a substantial savings plan. (p. 572)

V

Values
The things that are important to you in life. (p. 222)

Variable expenses
Living costs involving differing amounts each time and are usually more difficult to estimate. (p. 613)

Variable life insurance
Life insurance that lets the policyholder select from a range of investments. (p. 571)

Venture business
A business that has been in operation for less than three years and has no employees other than the owner. (p. 253)

Venture capital
Money used to start up a new small business or help a business expand during a growth period. (p. 256)

Vision care insurance
Insurance that covers eye examinations, prescription lenses, frames, and contact lenses. (p. 585)

Voluntary exchange
Buyers and sellers make their own economic decisions to determine what the price will be for goods and services produced and sold. (p. 25)

W

Wants
Things that are not necessary for survival but that add comfort and pleasure to our lives. (p. 6)

Warehouse market
A no-frills food outlet emphasizing the sale of large quantities of items at reasonable prices. (p. 290)

White-collar crime
An illegal act performed by office or professional workers while at work. (p. 193)

Whole life insurance
Permanent insurance that extends over the lifetime of the insured. (p. 570)

Wholesaler
A middle firm that assists with distribution activities between businesses. (p. 76)

Withdrawal slip
A written request to take money out of your account. (p. 476)

Word processing software
A computer program used to create and revise written documents. (p. 173)

Worker productivity
The quantity of a good an average worker produces in one hour. (p. 44)

Workers' compensation
Insurance that provides medical and survivor benefits to people injured, disabled, or killed on the job. (p. 588)

Work force
All of the people 16 years and older who are employed or are looking for a job. (p. 205)

Yield
The percentage of interest that will be added to your savings over a period of time. (p. 466)

Index

A

Abacus, 605
Ability, 224
Ability test, 239
Aboriginal Australians, 570
Academic achievement, 6
Accounting, 89, 239
Accounts
  budget, 409
  charge, 409–11
  individual retirement (IRAs), 480,
    634
  joint, 342
  regular, 409
  revolving, 410
Accounts payable clerk, 339
Adjustable rate mortgage
  (ARM), 507
Adjuster, 561
Administrative support
  careers, 265
Advanced Research Projects
  Agency Network
  (ARPANET), 466
Advertising, 675–76
Age Discrimination in
  Employment Act, 112
Agent, real estate, 507
Agricultural commodities, 511
Agriculture, 670
Alaska Natives, 190
Allowance, 614
American Bankers
  Association, 343–44
American Depository Receipt
  (ADR), 630

American Express Company,
  411
  Blue Box Values of, 115–16
American Gas Association,
  270
Americans With Disabilities
  Act, 111–12
American Stock Exchange,
  495, 630
America OnLine, 290
Annual compounding, 466
Annual percentage rate
  (APR), 429–30
Annual percentage yield
  (APY), 464
Annual yield, 465
Annuities, 481, 634
Antiques, 513
Antitrust laws, 143
Apple Computer, Inc., 650
Application, letter of, 234
Application form, 237
Applications, computer,
  169–85
Application software, 160
Appraiser, 507
Appreciation, 508
Arab-Americans, 60
Arabic numerals, 42
Articles of partnership, 94
Artificial intelligence (AI), 188
Asia, ethics of doing business
  in, 113
Asia Minor, 344
Asians and Pacific Islanders,
  60
Assessed value, 510

Asset records, 689
Assets, 602
Assigned-risk plan, 547
Association of Home
  Appliance Manufacturers
  (AHAM), 270
ATM. *See* **Automated teller**
  machines
Attitude towards job, 243
Attorney General, Office of,
  304, 308
Auditor, 600
Australia
  credit unions in, 479
  environmental awareness of
    Aborigines in, 570
  wool industry in, 122
Automated clearinghouse
  (ACH), 378
Automated teller machines
  (ATMs)
  bank statement record of
    transactions, 379
  cards, 326
  convenience of, 326
  expanding services at, 327
  failure to record transactions
    from, 381
  fees for, 317
  recording transactions made at,
    361
  savings deposits made at, 476
Automatic pilot, 192
Automobile insurance
  buying, 543–46
  economic risks and, 538–43
  rates for, 543–45